CWNA

Certified Wireless Network Administrator Official Study Guide

(EXAM PW0-100)

FOURTH EDITION

Tom Carpenter

Joel Barrett
Series Editor

McGraw-Hill is an independent entity from Planet3 Wireless and is not affiliated with Planet3 Wireless in any manner. This publication may be used in assisting students to prepare for the CWNA Exam. Neither Planet3 Wireless nor McGraw-Hill warrant that use of this publication will ensure passing any exam. CWNA and CWNP are registered trademarks of Planet3 Wireless in the United States and/or other countries.

New York Chicago San Francisco Lisbon London Madrid
Mexico City Milan New Delhi San Juan Seoul Singapore Sydney Toronto

The McGraw-Hill Companies

Cataloging-in-Publication Data is on file with the Library of Congress

McGraw-Hill books are available at special quantity discounts to use as premiums and sales promotions, or for use in corporate training programs. For more information, please write to the Director of Special Sales, Professional Publishing, McGraw-Hill, Two Penn Plaza, New York, NY 10121-2298. Or contact your local bookstore.

CWNA® Certified Wireless Network Administrator Official Study Guide (Exam PW0-100), Fourth Edition

1 2 3 4 5 6 7 8 9 0 DOC DOC 01987

ISBN: 978-0-07-149490-8
MHID: 0-07-149490-1

Sponsoring Editor
Timothy Green

Editorial Supervisor
Jody McKenzie

Project Manager
Sam RC
(International Typesetting and Composition)

Acquisitions Coordinator
Jennifer Housh

Technical Editor
Criss Hyde

Copy Editor
Robert Campbell

Proofreader
Yumnam Ojen
(International Typesetting and Composition)

Indexer
Valerie Haynes Perry

Production Supervisor
Jean Bodeaux

Composition
International Typesetting and Composition

Illustration
International Typesetting and Composition

I dedicate this book to my God, Jesus Christ, without whom I could not have written a single word, and to my amazing wife, Tracy, and my children, Faith, Rachel, Thomas, and Sarah, who tolerated my odd hours and lack of attention during the writing of this book. Tracy, you are the most amazing and wonderful thing that has ever happened to me and this book exists because of your faith in me—you have my eternal gratitude.

Acknowledgments

I would like to acknowledge the helpful staff at McGraw-Hill for bearing with my delays on this project. Writing two books at the same time is quite a challenge, but we did it together. I want to thank Criss Hyde particularly. His technical knowledge of the IEEE 802.11 standard (among other standards) is amazing, and he is an exceptional technical editor. I also want to thank Joel Barrett, the series editor for this book, who helped to keep me sane during the rough stages. Thanks everyone. The book turned out very well, and it could not have happened without you all.

About the Author

Tom Carpenter is a technical experts' expert. He teaches in-depth courses on Microsoft technologies, wireless networking, and security, and professional development skills such as project management, team leadership, and communication skills for technology professionals. Tom holds a CWNA, CSWP, and Wireless# certification with the CWNP program and is also a Microsoft Certified Partner. The Wireless Networking, Windows Administration, and IT Project Management Bootcamps that Tom offers annually provide the in-depth knowledge IT professionals need to succeed. He lives with his lovely wife, Tracy, and their four children, Faith, Rachel, Thomas, and Sarah, in Ohio. His company, SYSEDCO, provides training and consulting services throughout the United States. For more information about Tom and the services offered by his company, visit www.SYSEDCO.com.

About the Series Editor

Joel Barrett is a senior-level wireless networking expert with Cisco Systems. Joel has attained networking certifications such as Cisco's CCNP and CCDP, Microsoft's MCSE, and Novell's Master CNE. For wireless certifications, he holds Cisco's Wireless Design and Support specializations, as well as the CWNP Program's Wireless#, CWNA, CWSP, CWAP, and CWNE certifications. He is CWNE #6 and a founding member of the CWNE Roundtable, a steering committee for the CWNE certification program. Joel is also certified to instruct Cisco's Unified Wireless and Mesh Networking courses.

Within Cisco, Joel consults primarily with large enterprise customers concerning wireless deployments. He is a senior advisor for Cisco's wireless virtual team. He is also an author and technical editor for books such as *CWNP Dictionary of Terms and Acronyms, CWNP Wireless# Exam Mega Guide, Wireless Networks First-Step, CWSP Official Study Guide, First Edition,* and *Managing and Securing a Cisco Structured Wireless-Aware Network.* He is the series editor for McGraw-Hill's CWNP Official Study Guides.

Joel and his wife, Barbara Kurth, live with their three children, Ashley, Shane, and Paige, in the Atlanta, Georgia, metro area. Joel has two tenets he lives by:

- "Do what you love, the money will come."
- "If it were easy, anyone could do it."

About the Technical Editor

Criss Hyde has thirty years of IT experience beginning with punch cards and Fortran. He holds engineering and law degrees from Pennsylvania State University and George Mason University respectively, and current certifications from Apple, Cisco Systems, The CWNP Program, $(ISC)^2$, Sun Microsystems, and WildPackets. He became an early friend to The CWNP Program, has edited many of its books and exams, and has earned all of its certifications. He has worked 16 years for Raytheon Company and is a member of the IEEE Standards Association and the Virginia Bar Association. Criss is the husband of one wife and the father of eight home-schooled children. He heartily agrees with Vint Cerf that for the good of mankind and the IPv6 Internet, the NAT boxes have to go away.

Contents

Introduction

The wireless networking market is in a continual state of change. There have been more than a dozen amendments to the IEEE 802.11 standard since it was first released, and as I write these words in mid-2007, the IEEE is preparing to release the IEEE 802.11-2007 rollup any day now. For this reason, it is important that a wireless network administrator stay on top of the changes in wireless networking. This book and the CWNA certification is a great place to start.

This *CWNA Certified Wireless Network Administrator Official Study Guide* is intended to help you understand the wireless LAN (WLAN) technology in depth and to help you prepare for the CWNA certification exam (PW0-100). The CWNA certification is an intermediate-level certification that prepares the candidate to implement, troubleshoot, and maintain small, medium, and large wireless networks. The certification covers the following major wireless networking topics:

- Radio Frequency Technologies
- IEEE 802.11 Regulations and Standards
- IEEE 802.11 Protocols and Devices
- IEEE 802.11 Network Implementation
- IEEE 802.11 Network Security
- IEEE 802.11 RF Site Surveying

If you are new to wireless networking, or to networking in general, this book is a great place to start. When you accomplish the level of expertise needed for the CWNA exam and certification, you'll find it much easier to move on to more advanced certifications such as the CWSP (Certified Wireless Security Professional), and CWNE (Certified Wireless Network Engineer). You'll also find it much easier to understand the material and concepts included in vendor-specific wireless certifications.

Who This Book Is For

This book focuses on the objectives for the CWNA exam, but it's also a useful learning tool for anyone wanting to master the many domains of wireless. You'll learn about wireless technology basics such as radio frequency–based communications, and you'll learn about specific standards and protocols that make it all work. In addition, using step-by-step procedures, you will learn how to install, secure, and troubleshoot Wi-Fi or 802.11-based networks effectively. You'll even learn to use wireless LAN analysis tools that reveal the way your wireless network works and help you troubleshoot network problems. The glossary provides you with a quick reference for definitions and basic knowledge of the many topics covered in this book.

As you prepare for the CWNA certification, as with most other certifications, you need some hands-on experience with the technology to seal the information in your mind. In particular, be sure you have experience configuring access points and client devices. Linksys access points will provide all the features with which you should be familiar, and you can connect to them with most any client device. However, you'll get the best experience if you have access to small and medium business–class wireless LAN switches as well. Make sure you learn to use a wireless LAN protocol analyzer as Chapter 11 teaches. This makes for good testing and experience, but any vendor's access point should suffice as long as it provides most of the common features provided by autonomous access points. The main goal is to get your hands on some equipment and work through the configuration steps.

The CWNP web site (www.cwnp.com) lists official CWNA training courses available in your area. These courses provide you with access to a certified instructor who can help answer any questions you may have related to the certification. You will also see demonstrations of equipment that may be more difficult to acquire on your own. I always recommend attending the official courses when time and the budget allow.

Wireless Experts

Though the Wireless CWNA exam is not as advanced as the CWNE exam, many wireless experts might decide to gain this valuable certification because of the essential wireless topics that it covers. You will also earn a valuable credential in the CWNA certification. In addition to the enhanced credentials, the process of studying these wireless LAN technologies makes you think differently about wireless technology and may bring greater value to your employer or customers. I work as an independent consultant and have been enriched greatly by going through the process of understanding these standard uses of radio frequency–based technologies. My clients have benefited as well.

Wireless Beginners

If you're new to the world of wireless networking or have just acquired your Wireless# certification, the CWNA certification is for you too.

There is no other vendor-neutral certification that does a better job of proving you understand how wireless really works.

What's New in the Fourth Edition

In order to keep up with the changes in wireless networking, the Fourth Edition diminishes the coverage of older technologies such as Frequency Hopping Spread Spectrum and unused technologies such as the Point Coordination Function. Basic coverage of IEEE 802.11n has been included, but the coverage is not in-depth as the standard has not yet been ratified at publication time. More in-depth information is provided on the topics of protocol and spectrum analyzers as well as site survey processes and utilities. In addition, different perspectives and depth of coverage can be found in the foundational chapters that focus on radio frequency and its behavior and functionality. The book is a complete rewrite from the ground up and readers of previous editions should find many new thoughts and practical applications to assist with exam preparation and wireless network administration.

How This Book Is Organized

The *CWNA Certified Wireless Network Administrator Official Study Guide* is organized so that you can start at the beginning and work your way through, or if you have mastered the information in the first few chapters, you can jump right to the chapter most relevant to your current needs. Each chapter begins with a list of exam objectives covered in that chapter and ends with review questions and answers to help you retain the important information covered. There are notes throughout the book that highlight interesting nuggets of information or warn you of common mistakes made with wireless technology.

Exam Objectives

The CWNA certification exam certifies that successful candidates understand the following topics and concepts related to wireless LANs:

- Radio Frequency Technologies
- IEEE 802.11 Regulations and Standards
- IEEE 802.11 Protocols and Devices
- IEEE 802.11 Network Implementation

- IEEE 802.11 Network Security
- IEEE 802.11 RF Site Surveying

The exam lasts 90 minutes and consists of 60 questions. You must answer 70 percent of the questions correctly to achieve a passing score (80 percent if you hope to become a CWNT – Certified Wireless Networking Trainer). Practice exams are available at the CWNP web site, and the objectives listed next might change, so you should consult the web site frequently for the most current objectives. The following table breaks down the weight of each section of objectives on the exam.

Subject Area	Approximate Percent of Exam
Radio Frequency Technologies	21 percent
IEEE 802.11 Regulations and Standards	12 percent
IEEE 802.11 Protocols and Devices	14 percent
IEEE 802.11 Network Implementation	21 percent
IEEE 802.11 Network Security	16 percent
IEEE 802.11 RF Site Surveying	16 percent

Radio Frequency (RF) Technologies – 21%

1.1. RF Fundamentals

1.1.1. Define and explain the basic concepts of RF behavior

- Gain
- Loss
- Reflection
- Refraction
- Diffraction
- Scattering
- VSWR
- Return Loss
- Amplification
- Attenuation
- Absorption
- Wave Propagation
- Free Space Path Loss
- Delay Spread

1.2. RF Mathematics

1.2.1. Understand and apply the basic components of RF mathematics

- Watt
- Milliwatt

- Decibel (dB)
- dBm
- dBi
- dBd
- SNR
- RSSI
- System Operating Margin (SOM)
- Fade Margin
- Link Budget
- Intentional Radiator
- Equivalent Isotropically Radiated Power (EIRP)

1.3. RF Signal and Antenna Concepts

1.3.1. Identify RF signal characteristics, the applications of basic RF antenna concepts, and the implementation of solutions that require RF antennas

- Visual LOS
- RF LOS
- The Fresnel Zone
- Beamwidths
- Azimuth and Elevation
- Passive Gain
- Isotropic Radiator
- Polarization
- Antenna Diversity
- Wavelength
- Frequency
- Amplitude
- Phase

1.3.2. Explain the applications of basic RF antenna and antenna system types and identify their basic attributes, purpose, and function

- Omnidirectional / Dipole Antennas
- Semidirectional Antennas
- Highly Direction Antennas
- Sectorized Antennas
- Multiple Input, Multiple Output (MIMO)

1.3.3. Describe the proper locations and methods for installing RF antennas

- Pole/Mast Mount
- Ceiling Mount
- Wall Mount

1.4. RF Antenna Accessories

1.4.1. Identify the use of the following WLAN accessories and explain how to select and install them for optimal performance and regulatory domain compliance

- Amplifiers
- Attenuators
- Lightning Arrestors
- Mounting Systems
- Grounding Rods/Wires
- Towers, Safety Equipment, and Concerns
- RF Cables
- RF Connectors
- RF Signal Splitters

IEEE 802.11 Regulations and Standards – 12%

2.1. Spread Spectrum Technologies

2.1.1. Identify some of the uses for spread spectrum technologies

- Wireless LANs
- Wireless MANs
- Wireless PANs
- Wireless WANs

2.1.2. Comprehend the differences between, and explain the different types of spread spectrum technologies and how they relate to the IEEE 802.11 standard's PHY clauses

- FHSS
- ERP
- DSSS
- OFDM
- HR-DSSS

2.1.3. Identify the underlying concepts of how spread spectrum technology works

- Modulation
- Coding

2.1.4. Identify and apply the concepts which make up the functionality of spread spectrum technology

- Colocation
- Channel Centers and Widths
- Carrier Frequencies

- Dwell Time and Hop Time
- Throughput Versus Data Rate
- Bandwidth
- Communication Resilience

2.2. IEEE 802.11 Standard (as amended)

2.2.1. Identify, explain, and apply the frame and frame exchange sequences covered by the IEEE 802.11 standard (as amended).

2.2.2. Identify and apply regulatory domain requirements

2.2.3. IEEE 802.11 CSMA/CA

2.3. IEEE 802.11 Industry Organizations and Their Roles

2.3.1. Define the roles of the following organizations in providing direction, cohesion, and accountability within the WLAN industry

- Regulatory Domain Governing Bodies
- IEEE
- Wi-Fi Alliance

IEEE 802.11 Protocols and Devices – 14%

3.1. IEEE 802.11 Protocol Architecture

3.1.1. Summarize the processes involved in authentication and association

- The IEEE 802.11 State Machine
- Open System Authentication, Shared Key Authentication, and Deauthentication
- Association, Reassociation, and Disassociation

3.1.2. Define, describe, and apply the following concepts associated with WLAN service sets

- Stations and BSSs
- Starting and Joining a BSS
- BSSID and SSID
- Ad Hoc Mode and IBSS
- Infrastructure Mode and ESS

- Distribution System (DS)
- Distribution System Media
- Layer 2 and Layer 3 Roaming

3.1.3. Explain and apply the following power management features of WLANs

- Active Mode
- Power Save Mode
- WMM Power Save (U-APSD)
- TIM/DTIM/ATIM

3.2. IEEE 802.11 MAC & PHY Layer Technologies

3.2.1. Describe and apply the following concepts surrounding WLAN frames

- IEEE 802.11 Frame Format Versus IEEE 802.3 Frame Format
- Layer 3 Protocol Support by IEEE 802.11 Frames
- Terminology Review: Frames, Packets, and Datagrams
- Terminology Review: Bits, Bytes, and Octets
- Terminology: MAC & PHY
  - MSDU
  - MPDU
  - PSDU
  - PPDU
- Jumbo Frame Support (Layer 2)
- MTU Discovery and Functionality (Layer 3)

3.2.2. Identify methods described in the IEEE 802.11 standard for locating, joining, and maintaining connectivity with an IEEE 802.11 WLAN

- Active Scanning (Probes)
- Passive Scanning (Beacons)
- Dynamic Rate Switching

3.2.3. Define, describe, and apply IEEE 802.11 coordination functions and channel access methods and features available for optimizing data flow across the RF medium

- DCF and HCF Coordination Functions
- EDCA Channel Access Method
- RTS/CTS and CTS-to-Self Protocols
- Fragmentation

3.3. WLAN Infrastructure and Client Devices

3.3.1. Identify the purpose of the following WLAN infrastructure devices and describe how to install, configure, secure, and manage them

- Autonomous Access Points
- Lightweight Access Points
- Enterprise WLAN Switches/Controllers
- Remote Office WLAN Switches/Controllers
- PoE Injectors and PoE-Enabled Ethernet Switches
- WLAN Bridges
- Residential WLAN Gateways
- Enterprise Encryption Gateways
- WLAN Mesh Routers

3.3.2. Describe the purpose of the following WLAN client devices and explain how to install, configure, secure, and manage them

- PC Cards (ExpressCard, CardBus, and PCMCIA)
- USB, CF, and SD Devices
- PCI and Mini-PCI Cards

IEEE 802.11 Network Implementation – 21%

4.1. IEEE 802.11 Network Design, Implementation, and Management

4.1.1. Identify technology roles for which WLAN technology is appropriate and describe implementation of WLAN technology in those roles

- Corporate Data Access and End-User Mobility
- Network Extension to Remote Areas
- Building-to-Building Connectivity - Bridging
- Last-Mile Data Delivery – Wireless ISP
- Small Office / Home Office (SOHO) Use
- Mobile Office Networking
- Educational / Classroom Use
- Industrial – Warehousing and Manufacturing
- Healthcare – Hospitals and Offices
- Hotspots – Public Network Access

- Power over Ethernet (PoE) (IEEE 802.3-2005, Clause 33)
    - Formerly Known as IEEE 802.3af

4.2. IEEE 802.11 Network Troubleshooting

4.2.1. Identify and explain how to solve the following WLAN implementation challenges using features available in enterprise-class WLAN equipment

- System Throughput
- Co-Channel and Adjacent-Channel Interference
- RF Noise and Noise Floor
- Narrowband and Wideband RF Interference
- Multipath
- Hidden Nodes
- Near/Far
- Weather

IEEE 802.11 Network Security – 16%

5.1. IEEE 802.11 Network Security Architecture

5.1.1. Identify and describe the strengths, weaknesses, appropriate uses, and appropriate implementation of the following IEEE 802.11 security-related items:

- Pre-RSNA Security
    - WEP-40 and RC4
    - WEP-104 and RC4
    - Open System Authentication
    - Shared Key Authentication
- RSNA Security
    - IEEE 802.11, Clause 8
    - TKIP and RC4
    - CCMP and AES
    - IEEE 802.1X Authentication and Key Management (AKM)
    - Preshared Key (PSK) / Passphrase Authentication
    - Certificates and PACs
    - The Four-Way Handshake

    - Key Hierarchies
    - Transition Security Network (TSN)
- AAA Security Components
- EAP types
- RADIUS
- LDAP Compliant/Compatible
- Local Authentication Database

5.1.2. Describe the following types of WLAN security attacks, and explain how to identify and prevent them where possible

- Eavesdropping
- Denial of Service (Physical and Data Link Attacks)
- Man-in-the-Middle
- Management Interface Exploits
- Encryption Cracking
- Authentication Cracking
- Hijacking

5.1.3. Describe, explain, and illustrate the appropriate applications for the following client-related wireless security solutions

- Role-Based Access Control
- IPsec VPN
- Profile-Based Firewalls
- Captive Portals / Web Authentication
- Network Access Control (NAC)

5.1.4. Describe, explain, and illustrate the appropriate applications for the following WLAN system security and management features

- Rogue AP and Client Detection and/or Containment
- SNMPv3 / HTTPS / SSH2

5.2. IEEE 802.11 Network Security Analysis and Troubleshooting

5.2.1. Identify the purpose and features of the following wireless analysis systems and explain how to install, configure, integrate, and manage them as applicable

- Handheld and Laptop Protocol Analyzers
- RF Spectrum Analyzers

- Distributed Wireless Intrusion Prevention Systems (WIPS)
- Distributed RF Spectrum Analyzers

5.3. IEEE 802.11 Network Security Policy Basics

5.3.1. Describe the following General Security Policy elements

- Risk Assessment
- Security Auditing
- Impact Analysis

5.3.2. Describe the following Functional Security Policy elements

- Baseline Practices
- Design and Implementation Practices
- Physical Security
- Social Engineering
- Monitoring, Response, and Reporting

IEEE 802.11 RF Site Surveying – 16%

6.1. IEEE 802.11 Network Site Survey Fundamentals

6.1.1. Explain the importance and processes involved in conducting a complete manual RF site survey

6.1.2. Explain the importance of and the processes involved in documenting manual RF site surveys

- Gathering Business Requirements
- Interviewing Managers and Users
- Defining Security Requirements
- Gathering Site-Specific Documentation
- Documenting Existing Network Characteristics
- Gathering Permits and Zoning Requirements
- Indoor- or Outdoor-Specific Information
- Outdoor WLANs Versus Mesh Networks

6.1.3. Explain the technical aspects and information collection procedures involved in manual and virtual RF site surveys

- Interference Sources
- Infrastructure Connectivity and Power Requirements
- RF Coverage Requirements

- Data Capacity Requirements
- Voice Considerations
- Client Connectivity Requirements

6.1.4. Describe site survey reporting procedures for manual and virtual RF site surveys

- Customer Reporting Requirements
- Reporting Methodology
- Graphical Documentation
- Hardware Recommendations and Bills of Material

6.2. IEEE 802.11 Network Site Survey Systems and Devices

6.2.1. Identify the equipment, applications, and system features involved in performing virtual site surveys

- Predictive Analysis / Simulation Applications (Also Called RF Planning Tools)
- Integrated Virtual Site Survey Features of WLAN Switches/ Controllers
- Site Survey Verification Tools and/or Applications
- Indoor Site Surveys Versus Outdoor Site Surveys

6.2.2. Identify the equipment and applications involved in performing manual site surveys

- Site Survey Hardware Kits
- Active Site Survey Tools and/or Applications
- Passive Site Survey Tools and/or Applications

Tips for Succeeding on the CWNA Exam

Here are some general tips that will help you become a successful CWNA examinee:

- Take advantage of the CWNA practice tests available through the CWNP web site at www.cwnp.com.
- Arrive a few minutes before your exam is scheduled to start. This gives you time to review your notes and relax before entering the exam center.

- Read each question carefully to be sure you understand it. (I always read each question at least twice even if I'm "sure" I know the answer.)
- Do not leave any unanswered questions, as these count against your score.
- Do not rely on this study guide as your only learning resource. This book is not intended to provide you with direct answers to every CWNA exam question, but it is intended, when used in conjunction with hands-on experience, to provide you with the knowledge and skills you need to determine the proper answers to the questions.

You are provided with instant notification of passing in the Examination Score Report. These scores are also sent to Planet3 Wireless, Inc., within ten working days. After you pass the exam, you receive a CWNA Certificate and a welcome e-mail with your CWNP ID number within three weeks.

Feel free to e-mail me with any questions you have about the technologies covered in this book. My e-mail address is carpenter@sysedco.com, and I love helping people learn technology and success skills, so don't hesitate to ask your questions. Happy studying and good luck on your certification journey!

Understanding Wireless Technologies

PART

I

In This Part

CHAPTER

1

Wireless Standards, Organizations, and Applications

CWNA Exam Objectives Covered:

- Define the roles of the following organizations
  - Regulatory Domain Governing Bodies
  - IEEE
  - Wi-Fi Alliance
- Identify some of the uses for spread spectrum technologies
  - Wireless LANs, PANs, MANs, and WANs
- Identify technology roles for WLAN technologies

In This Chapter

Wireless local area networks (WLANs) are being used very heavily in government and private sector networks today. The technology needs no introduction from the perspective of awareness, but there is still much to do in the areas of understanding and effective utilization. Various branches of government have come to see WLAN technology as a value-added solution instead of a threat that is to be avoided. However, they have also seen the need to implement security, which has led to both good and bad security policies, as reflected in government regulations and memos. The good policies are born from a proper understanding of the functionality of WLANs, and the bad policies have evolved from errors in the understanding of foundational principles of wireless networks. The goal of this chapter—and this book—is to take you on a journey that will lead you to a solid foundational knowledge of WLANs. My hope is that fewer mistakes will be made in the areas of security and technology investment as more engineers and administrators are trained and certified in WLAN technology.

When you extend the analysis to health care, private sector organizations, and home environments, the impact of wireless networking technologies greatly increases. There are very few homes remaining in the United States that do not have at least one wireless device—even if it is a cordless telephone. There are even fewer businesses that are not taking advantage of the benefits of wireless equipment. In business, this equipment list includes the following items, as well as others that are not listed:

- Cordless phones
- Wireless Voice over IP phones
- Wireless print servers
- Wireless access points, routers, and bridges
- Radio Frequency Identification devices
- Wireless presentation gateways
- Wireless conferencing systems
- Laptop computers, PDAs, and other mobile wireless client devices

Since this list is only partial and represents some of the more common devices implemented, you can see that wireless technology is being used in many beneficial ways. In this chapter, you will learn about the organizations that guide the WLAN industry and also briefly consider the standards that are used within WLANs. Next, the four main uses of wireless spread spectrum technology are discussed, leading to an understanding of the applications available. Finally, you investigate many of the specific ways in which wireless technology is being implemented today.

Roles Organizations Play Within the WLAN Industry

There are three primary categories of organizations that guide the wireless industry. These categories include regulation, standardization, and compatibility. The *Federal Communications Commission (FCC)* and the European Telecommunications Standards Institute (ETSI) are examples of regulatory bodies. The *Institute of Electrical and Electronics Engineers (IEEE)* is an example of a standards development organization, and the *Wi-Fi Alliance* is a compatibility testing and certification group.

It is important to understand what these organizations do, but it is equally important to understand how they work together. As an example, consider the interdependency between the FCC and the IEEE or the relationship between the Wi-Fi Alliance and the IEEE. The FCC sets the boundaries within which the IEEE may develop standards. The Wi-Fi Alliance tests equipment to certify it as being reasonably interoperable. These three organizations provide regulation, standardization, and compatibility services for WLAN technologies within the United States.

The benefits to the consumer are clear. When there are regulations in place, such as power output limits, it is easier to implement localized wireless networks with less interference from surrounding networks. When there are standards in place, such as the IEEE 802.11 standard, it is easier to purchase devices from different vendors that are interoperable. When there are certifications in place that validate interoperability, consumers can buy products with confidence that those similarly certified devices should be interoperable at some level and fewer man-hours are required for compatibility testing.

In the ideal world, we would get all these benefits with exact perfection. In the real world, interference is reduced, but not eliminated; hardware is interoperable, but not necessarily fully compatible; testing time is reduced, but not completely eliminated. If you are installing a wireless network in an office, which shares space with other offices, you may still encounter interference—even with the lower output power. If you are working with devices from different vendors, you may encounter specific compatibility issues outside the standards upon which the devices are based. If you are implementing hardware that has been certified by the Wi-Fi Alliance, you should still test it with your hardware to ensure there are no compatibility issues. Even with these realities, the benefits that the regulatory, standards, and compatibility organizations have brought to the wireless industry are immeasurable.

Regulatory Domain Governing Bodies

A *regulatory domain* can be defined as a bounded area that is controlled by a set of laws or policies. Currently, there are governing bodies at the city, county, state, and country levels within the United States. In other countries, governments exist with similar hierarchies or with a single level of authority at the top level of the country. In many cases, these governments have assigned the responsibility of managing communications to a specific organization that is responsible to the government. In the United States, this organization is the FCC. In the UK, it is the Office of Communications (OfCom). In Australia, it is the Australian Communications and Media Authority. The following sections outline just four of these governing bodies and the roles they play in the wireless networking industry of their respective regulatory domains.

FCC

The Federal Communications Commission (FCC) was born out of the Communications Act of 1934. Charged with the regulation of interstate and international communications by radio, television, cable, satellite, and wire, the FCC has a large body of responsibility. The regulatory domain covered by the FCC includes all 50 states of the United States as well as the District of Columbia and other U.S. possessions like the Virgin Islands and Guam.

Because WLAN devices use radio wave communications, they fall under the regulatory control of the FCC. The factors regulated by the FCC include

- Radio frequencies available
- Output power levels
- Indoor and outdoor usage

Radio Frequencies Available You will learn more about radio frequencies in Chapters 2 and 3. For now, it is enough to know that a radio frequency is measured in hertz (Hz). *Hertz* is the measurement of wave cycles per second; therefore, a radio frequency of 2.412 gigahertz (GHz) cycles 2,412,000 times per second. The FCC regulates which frequencies may be used within the regulatory domain it manages. For example, the FCC provides two types of license-free bands for radio communications: the Industrial Scientific Medical (ISM) bands and the Unlicensed National Information Infrastructure (U-NII—usually pronounced *you-knee*) bands. Currently, there are 11 ISM bands in various frequencies throughout the radio frequency spectrum, but only the one starting at 2.4 GHz is used by IEEE 802.11, and it is the frequency band most familiar to WLAN users. The four U-NII bands exist in the 5 GHz frequency range, and are all used by IEEE 802.11. Table 1.1 provides a summary of the ISM and U-NII license-free bands used by IEEE 802.11.

These license-free bands provide both a benefit and a disadvantage. The benefit comes from the fact that you are not required to obtain a license to communicate within these license-free bands. This means that you can buy FCC authorized equipment and install it in your environment without any required permits or fees. However, the disadvantage of using license-free bands is that others can also use them. This means you will have to deal with contention and interference issues and ensure that you have the bandwidth available for your intended purpose in the environment where you will be implementing the WLAN.

It would be nice if we could even say that the use of the license-free bands is on a "first-come, first-serve" basis, but it is not. You may have a WLAN installed for years only to have a nearby organization install a WLAN on the same frequencies you've been using, which can cause major contention on your network. The reality is that, as long as this neighboring

TABLE 1.1 Unlicensed (License-Free) Bands Used by IEEE 802.11

Frequency Band	Total Bandwidth	License-Free Band
2400–2500 MHz	100 MHz	ISM
5.15–5.25 GHz	100 MHz	U-NII
5.25–5.35 GHz	100 MHz	U-NII
5.470–5.725 GHz	255 MHz	U-NII
5.725–5.825 GHz	100 MHz	U-NII

TABLE 1.2 FCC Power Output Limits—U-NII Bands

Band	Power Output Limits	Area Usage
U-NII 5.15–5.25 GHz	40 mW	Restricted to indoor operations
U-NII 5.25–5.35 GHz	200 mW	Indoor/outdoor
U-NII 5.470–5.725 GHz	200 mW	Indoor/outdoor
U-NII 5.725–5.825 GHz	800 mW	Higher output power assumes outdoor operations

network is within FCC regulations, there is very little that can be done aside from some careful negotiations on wireless device placement and channel usage. I will provide more information about this in Chapter 6.

Output Power Levels The FCC also regulates the output power levels of radio frequency devices within these license-free bands. Table 1.2 gives a brief summary of the output power limits imposed by the FCC. There are more complex scenarios that apply to the use of the ISM band that will be covered in Chapter 2.

Indoor and Outdoor Usage Finally, the FCC limits the 5.15–5.25 U-NII band to indoor-only usage. The other U-NII bands can be used indoors or outdoors; however, the 5.725–5.825 band is especially well suited for outdoor operations. The area usage of the U-NII bands is summarized in Table 1.2.

The 2.4 GHz ISM band may be used indoors or outdoors, and the output power at the intentional radiator cannot exceed 1 watt. For indoor devices, the output power is usually well under 1 watt and generally resides in a range from 30 to 300 milliwatts.

I'll cover output power concepts and regulations in more detail in Chapter 2. For now, you will want to remember that in the United States, the FCC regulates the frequencies used, the output power levels, and the indoor/outdoor usage limitations.

OfCom and ETSI

The Office of Communications (OfCom) is charged with ensuring optimal use of the electromagnetic spectrum, for radio communications, within the UK. OfCom provides documentation of and forums for discussion of valid frequency usage in radio communications. The regulations put forth by the OfCom are based on standards developed by the European

Telecommunications Standards Institute (ETSI). These two organizations work together in much the same way the FCC and IEEE do in the United States.

MIC and ARIB

In Japan, the Ministry of Internal Affairs and Communications (MIC) is the governing body over radio communications. However, the Association of Radio Industries and Businesses (ARIB) was appointed to manage the efficient utilization of the radio spectrum by the MIC. In the end, ARIB is responsible for regulating which frequencies can be used and such factors as power output levels.

ACMA

The Australian Communications and Media Authority (ACMA) replaced the Australian Communications Authority in July 2005 as the governing body over the regulatory domain of Australia for radio communications management. Like the FCC in the United States, the ACMA is charged with managing the electromagnetic spectrum in order to minimize interference. This is done by limiting output power in license-free frequencies and by requiring licenses in some frequencies.

ITU-R

The International Telecommunications Union Radiocommunication Sector (ITU-R) is a sector of the International Telecommunications Union (ITU). The ITU, after an evolving history, was designated as a United Nations specialized agency on October 15, 1947. The constitution of the ITU declares its purposes as

- To maintain and extend international cooperation between all its Member States for the improvement and rational use of telecommunications of all kinds
- To promote and enhance participation of entities and organizations in the activities of the Union, and to foster fruitful cooperation and partnership between them and Member States for the fulfillment of the overall objectives embodied in the purposes of the Union
- To promote and offer technical assistance to developing countries in the field of telecommunications, and also to promote the mobilization of the material, human, and financial resources needed to improve access to telecommunications services in such countries

- To promote the development of technical facilities and their most efficient operation, with a view to improving the efficiency of telecommunication services, increasing their usefulness and making them, so far as possible, generally available to the public
- To promote the extension of the benefits of new telecommunication technologies to all the world's inhabitants
- To promote the use of telecommunication services with the objective of facilitating peaceful relations
- To harmonize the actions of Member States and promote fruitful and constructive cooperation and partnership between Member States and Sector Members in the attainment of those ends
- To promote, at the international level, the adoption of a broader approach to the issues of telecommunications in the global information economy and society, by cooperating with other world and regional intergovernmental organizations and those nongovernmental organizations concerned with telecommunications.

The ITU-R, specifically, maintains a database of the frequency assignments worldwide and helps coordinate electromagnetic spectrum management through five administrative regions. These five regions are

- Region A: The Americas
- Region B: Western Europe
- Region C: Eastern Europe
- Region D: Africa
- Region E: Asia and Australia

Each region has one or more local regulatory groups such as the FCC in Region A for the United States or the ACMA in Region E for Australia. Ultimately, the ITU-R provides the service of maintaining the Master International Frequency Register of 1,265,000 terrestrial frequency assignments.

IEEE

The Institute of Electrical and Electronics Engineers (IEEE) states their mission as being the world's leading professional association for the advancement of technology. This means, of course, that they provide standards and technical guidance for more than just the wireless industry. In this section, I focus on the specific standards developed by the IEEE that impact and benefit wireless networking. These standards include wireless-specific standards as well as standards that have been implemented in the wired networking domain, which are now being utilized in the wireless networking domain. First, I provide you with a more detailed overview of the IEEE organization.

Overview of the IEEE Organization

The IEEE is a global professional society with more than 350,000 members. The constitution of the IEEE defines the purpose of the organization as scientific and educational, directed toward the advancement of the theory and practice of electrical, electronics, communications, and computer engineering, as well as computer science, the allied branches of engineering, and the related arts and sciences. Their mission is stated as promoting "the engineering process of creating, developing, integrating, sharing, and applying knowledge about electronics and information technologies and sciences for the benefit of humanity and the profession." Ultimately, the IEEE created many standards for many niche disciplines within electronics and communications. In this book, the focus is on computer data networks and specifically wireless computer data networks. In this area, the IEEE has given us the 802 project and, specific to wireless, the IEEE 802.11 standard.

Overview of IEEE WLAN Standards

IEEE projects, such as the IEEE 802 project, are divided into working groups. The Ethernet standard comes from the IEEE 802.3 working group, and the WLAN standard comes from the IEEE 802.11 working group. The IEEE 802.11 working group was the eleventh group formed under the IEEE 802 project.

Other working groups of interest to wireless professionals include the IEEE 802.16 working group, which focuses on broadband wireless access, commonly known as WiMAX, and the IEEE 802.20 working group, which focuses on mobile broadband wireless access. It is interesting to note that the majority of the newly developed working groups, since IEEE 802.11, are wireless specific. This is evidence of the importance of wireless technology in the digital future.

The original IEEE 802.11 standard was ratified in 1997 and is embodied in a document called IEEE 802.11-1997. The standard was amended in 1999; the base document was altered slightly and replaced by a new base document called IEEE 802.11-1999, and several amendment documents were ratified. This base document was reaffirmed in 2003 when yet another amendment document was ratified, and renamed IEEE 802.11-1999 Edition (R2003). Several more amendment documents have been ratified since.

In addition to the IEEE 802.11-1999 Edition (R2003) document, it is expected that a new base document will be released in the year 2007. This document is likely to be called IEEE 802.11-2007, but at the time of this writing, this document is not yet finalized.

The original IEEE 802.11-1997 standard specified three ways of implementing a physical communication layer (PHY). Frequency-hopping spread spectrum (FHSS) and direct-sequence spread spectrum (DSSS) both use the 2.4 GHz ISM band. The third PHY used infrared but never saw the light of day and is not covered by the CWNA certification for this reason. Each of these PHYs operates at a mandatory nominal data rate of 1 megabit per second (Mbps) and optionally at 2 Mbps. You will learn more about the detailed specifications of the IEEE 802.11 standards in Chapter 3.

It is interesting to note the massive growth in wireless LAN technology since the release of the IEEE 802.11 standard. Before that time, wireless LAN devices used proprietary technologies for communications, and this meant that one vendor's hardware could not communicate with another vendor's hardware. With the introduction of the IEEE 802.11 standard, a communications structure was defined that vendors could adopt and that would allow for interoperability between the various vendors' hardware solutions. The next step was the release of the high-rate DSSS (HR/DSSS) PHY, which provided data rates up to 11 Mbps. Once we passed this milestone, the wireless LAN market exploded with growth, revealing a tremendous benefit of standardization: compatibility.

As Joel Barrett, series editor for this book, pointed out to me, we may have indeed learned some lessons from the past. The telephone industry was locked up in a monopolistic structure based around large organizations that developed the standards and owned the backbone. Eventually, an act of Congress put a stop to this and opened up the telephone industry to real competition. The IEEE stepped in and developed these standards before wireless networking became as popular as it is today, giving us a wonderful variety of vendors while still providing compatibility.

In addition to the working groups, the standards they create are often updated by task groups, and these updates are released as amendments. Amendments can be either ratified or in draft. When in draft mode, the amendment may still be modified and hardware or software development against the draft amendment is not usually recommended. When the amendment is ratified, it has been stabilized and development of hardware and software is usually forthcoming. However, in the real world, many vendors do leap onto amendments that are in the draft mode, as we have seen with IEEE P802.11n—the newer multiple-input, multiple-output (MIMO)-based amendment to IEEE 802.11—in the months leading up to the first quarter of 2007. Additionally, task groups may be active on a task with no draft yet provided. Table 1.3 provides a brief description of the amendments to the IEEE 802.11 standard.

TABLE 1.3 IEEE 802.11 Amendments and Descriptions

IEEE 802.11 Amendment (status as of January 2007)	Description
IEEE 802.11a-1999	Uses Orthogonal Frequency Division Multiplexing (OFDM) instead of DSSS. Provides data rates up to 54 Mbps. Uses the 5 GHz U-NII bands. Not compatible with PHYs that use the 2.4 GHz ISM band such as DSSS and HR/DSSS.
IEEE 802.11b-1999 (amended slightly in 2001)	Uses high-rate direct-sequence spread spectrum (HR/DSSS) instead of the original DSSS. Provides data rates up to 11 Mbps. Uses the 2.4 GHz ISM band. Backward compatible with DSSS.
IEEE 802.11c-1998 (incorporated into the IEEE 802.1D-2004 standard, section 6.5.4)	Updates the IEEE 802.1D bridging standard for 802.11 operations.
IEEE 802.11d-2001	Provides specifications for the use of IEEE 802.11 in more regulatory domains (countries) than were originally specified.
IEEE 802.11e-2005	Defines the layer 2 MAC controls used to meet the Quality of Service (QoS) requirements of multimedia and voice applications over IEEE 802.11 networks.
IEEE 802.11F-2003 Recommended Practice, withdrawn on Feb 3, 2006	An attempt at standardizing how reassociation should occur from access point to access point in a WLAN. Recommended the use of the Inter-Access Point Protocol (IAPP).

TABLE 1.3 IEEE 802.11 Amendments and Descriptions (*cont.*)

IEEE 802.11 Amendment (status as of January 2007)	Description
IEEE 802.11g-2003	Supports DSSS and HR/DSSS and adapts OFDM modulation to 2.4 GHz band. Provides data rates up to 54 Mbps. Not compatible with the 5 GHz OFDM PHY due to the use of the 2.4 GHz band.
IEEE 802.11h-2003	Enhances the IEEE 802.11 MAC and OFDM PHY with network management and control. Provides Dynamic Frequency Selection (DFS) and Transmit Power Control (TPC) mechanisms.
IEEE 802.11i-2004	One of the most important enhancements to the IEEE 802.11 standard. Specifies the use of Counter Mode with Cipher Block Chaining Message Authentication Code Protocol (CCMP), which is reliant on the Advanced Encryption Standard (AES) and allows for the use of the Temporal Key Integrity Protocol (TKIP). Requires the use of either IEEE 802.1X or preshared key (PSK) for authentication.
IEEE 802.11j-2004	Extends the 802.11 MAC and OFDM PHY to operate in the newly available 4.9–5 GHz band in Japan (and the United States).
IEEE P802.11k (ratification is expected in 2007)	Specifies the use of TPC in frequencies other than 5 GHz band, reporting of client statistics such as signal-to-noise ratio and frame transmissions, and channel statistics of channel management. General purpose is to provide radio resource measurements.
IEEE P802.11n (ratification is expected in 2008)	Defines modifications to the IEEE 802.11 physical and media access control layers that will allow for much higher throughputs and a maximum throughput of at least 100 Mbps. This is currently being accomplished with the use of MIMO (multiple-input-multiple-output) technology in conjunction with OFDM technology.
IEEE P802.11p (ratification is expected in 2009)	Specifies support for the licensed Intelligent Transportation Systems (ITS) band of 5.9 GHz and other 5 GHz bands, specifically 5.850 GHz to 5.925 GHz in North America, for data exchanges between high-speed vehicles. Data communications occur at speeds up to 200 km/h and distances up to 1000 meters.

TABLE 1.3 IEEE 802.11 Amendments and Descriptions (*cont.*)

IEEE 802.11 Amendment (status as of January 2007)	Description
IEEE P802.11r (ratification is expected in 2008)	Enhancements to the IEEE 802.11 MAC to improve basic service set transitions within extended service sets (ESSs). Sometimes called the fast roaming amendment.
IEEE P802.11s (ratification is expected in 2008)	Specifies the interoperable formation and operation of an ESS Mesh network.
IEEE P802.11T (recommended practice—ratification is expected in 2009)	Provides a set of performance metrics, measurement methodologies, and test conditions to enable measuring and predicting performance of 802.11 WLAN devices and networks as a recommended practice.
IEEE P802.11u (ratification is expected in 2009)	Provides amendments to the IEEE 802.11 PHY and MAC layers that enable interworking with other networks. May provide for handoffs between WiMAX and WLANs or between WLANs and cellular networks.
IEEE P802.11v (ratification is expected in 2009)	Enhancements to provide wireless network management to the IEEE 802.11 MAC, and PHY, to extend prior work in radio measurement that results in a complete and coherent upper-layer interface for managing 802.11 devices in wireless networks. Defines SNMP Management Information Bases that will allow for the configuration of a WLAN client device from a WLAN infrastructure device.
IEEE P802.11w (ratification is expected in 2008)	Improves security of IEEE 802.11 management frames like deauthentication and deassociation frames. Provides data integrity, nonrepudiation, confidentiality, and replay protection to these management frames.
IEEE P802.11-REVma (ratification is expected in early 2007)	A rollup project intended to roll the 802.11-1999 (R2003) base document and all its ratified amendments into a new expanded IEEE 802.11 standard base document. Also to be included are some specific definitions of behavior only hinted at in the original standard. Expected to be called IEEE 802.11-2007.

IEEE Standards Impacting WLANs

Other than the specific IEEE 802.11 standard and amendments, there are at least two other project 802 standards that have a tremendous impact on IEEE 802.11. These are IEEE 802.1X and IEEE 802.3-2005, Clause 33. Additional IEEE standards of note are the IEEE 802.1D and 802.1Q standards.

IEEE 802.1X As Table 1.3 reveals, IEEE 802.1X is a mentioned portion of the IEEE 802.11i amendment. IEEE 802.1X provides port-based authentication and control for your wireless networks in a similar way that it provides the same to wired networks. I will cover IEEE 802.1X in more detail in Chapter 10, and it is covered in even more completely in the *CWSP: Certified Wireless Security Professional Official Study Guide, Second Edition* by Tom Carpenter, Grant Moerschel, and Richard Dreger, also published by McGraw-Hill (2006).

IEEE 802.3-2005, Clause 33 Formerly known as the IEEE 802.3af amendment, this is the standard that defines PoE (Power over Ethernet). Many wireless access points and bridges have support for PoE so that you can install them in locations where Ethernet cables exist but power connections do not. This is particularly useful in closets, on towers, and on rooftops. PoE is covered in more detail in Chapter 7.

IEEE 802.1D and IEEE 802.1Q IEEE 802.1D is a standard that defines bridging and priority handling, whereas IEEE 802.1Q focuses on priority tagging and virtual LAN (VLAN) handling for Quality of Service (QoS). IEEE 802.1D includes specifications for bridging, a spanning tree protocol, and specifications for handling IEEE 802.11 MACs in the bridging process (Section 6.5.4). The IEEE 802.1Q standard specifies the operation of bridges that support VLANs.

IETF

The Internet Engineering Task Force (IETF) is another standards development organization that has impacted the wireless networking industry. You can learn more about the IETF as an organization by visiting their web site at http://ietf.org. The primary IETF standards impacting WLANs directly include request for comments (RFC) 3748 and RFC 2865.

IETF RFC 3748

The IETF RFC 3748 details the functionality of the Extensible Authentication Protocol (EAP). EAP is used when IEEE 802.1X port-based authentication is implemented and is, therefore, an integral part of WLAN security. EAP will be discussed more in Chapter 10.

IETF RFC 2865

While EAP provides the authentication flow and specifications, RADIUS provides the highway on which EAP passes. In most implementations of IEEE 802.1X, EAP messages are passed to a RADIUS server where authentication is either approved or rejected. RADIUS will also be covered briefly in Chapter 10.

Wi-Fi Alliance

The Wi-Fi Alliance is a certification organization that provides testing and interoperability analysis for the wireless industry. While the FCC makes the rules and the IEEE determines how to live within those rules, the Wi-Fi Alliance ensures that devices are compatible with the IEEE's way of implementing WLAN technology.

Originally, the Wi-Fi Alliance was known as the Wireless Ethernet Compatibility Alliance (WECA). In October 2002, the organization was rebranded as the Wi-Fi Alliance. This was done as a measure to improve brand awareness and make the name a more memorable and associative one (a fancy way of saying: to make the name more marketable).

Only products of Alliance members that have been tested successfully by the Wi-Fi Alliance are actually allowed to claim that they are Wi-Fi Certified. This is a subtle distinction as many vendors say their equipment is Wi-Fi equipment and this equipment may or may not be Wi-Fi Certified. The result has been confusion for some consumers. Ultimately, consumers should look for logos like the ones in Figure 1.1. If a logo like this is on the packaging, the product has been certified by the Wi-Fi Alliance.

FIGURE 1.1 The Wi-Fi Certified logo

Spread Spectrum Technology Uses

Spread spectrum technology is used in multiple ways within modern organizations; however, these different ways can be organized within four primary categories: wireless LANs, *wireless PANs (WPANs)*, *wireless MANs (WMANs)* and *wireless WANs*. Table 1.4 summarizes these uses and the following sections provide more detailed information.

Wireless LANs

Wireless LANs (local area networks) are the primary focus of the CWNA certification. The most popular WLAN technology employed today is the IEEE 802.11 standard as amended. These wireless LANs provide mobility, nomadic ability, and unwired fixed connectivity. Mobility is provided because the user can move around within the coverage area of the access point or even multiple access points, while still maintaining connectivity. Nomadic ability—the ability to move from place to place and use the network although you may not be using it while moving—is provided because you can power on a wireless client device from any location within a coverage area and use it for a temporary period of time as a fixed location device. Of course, unwired fixed connectivity must exist if nomadic ability is provided.

There are three primary roles that wireless LANs play in today's enterprise organizations:

- Access role
- Distribution role
- Core role

In the *access role*, the wireless network is used to provide wireless clients with access to wired resources. The access point remains fixed

TABLE 1.4 Spread Spectrum Uses and Examples

Use	Examples	Range	Speeds
WLAN/Backhaul	IEEE 802.11	112 meters/375 feet to several miles	2 Mbps and higher
WPAN	Bluetooth	1–3 meters	723 Kbps to 3 Mbps
WMAN/Backhaul	WiMAX and EDGE	10 kilometers	40 Mbps estimated
Wireless WAN/ Backhaul	AT&T microwave, Free Space Optics	Variable	75–135 Kbps estimated

while the clients may move. The access point is usually connected to an Ethernet network where other resources, such as file servers, printers, and remote network connections, reside. In this role, the access point provides access to the wireless medium first and then, when necessary, provides bridging to the wired medium or other wireless networks (such as in a mesh network implementation).

In the *distribution role*, wireless bridges provide a backhaul connection between disconnected wired networks. In this case, each network is connected to the Ethernet port of a wireless bridge and the wireless bridges communicate with each other using the IEEE 802.11 standard and amendments. Once these connections are made, network traffic can be passed across the bridge link so that the two previously disconnected networks may act as one.

The final role is the *core role.* In the core role, the wireless LAN is the network. This may be suitable for small networks built on-the-fly, such as those built at construction sites or in disaster areas; however, the limited data throughput will prohibit the wireless LAN from being the core of the network in a large enterprise installation. Future technologies may change this, but for now, wireless LAN technologies play the access and distribution roles most often.

Wireless PANs

A wireless PAN (personal area network) provides hands-free connectivity and communications within a confined range and limited throughput capacity. Small-scale mesh-type wireless networks like those implemented with Zigbee technology are also classed as PANs. In addition, RFID systems are frequently categorized as wireless PAN technologies, since they have a short communications range. Bluetooth is also a perfect example of a wireless PAN technology that is both beneficial and in widespread use. Everything from Bluetooth mice to headsets are being used on a daily basis throughout the world. I travel frequently, and the proliferation of Bluetooth headsets in just the past year or two has been really amazing.

My moment of opportunity has arrived. How about a new courtesy rule: When you're talking on your Bluetooth headset, you're not allowed to look anyone in the eyes within your physical space. This way, the light waves being reflected off your face and into my retina do not cause my brain to interpret your sound waves as being intended for my enjoyment. In other words, please don't make me think you're talking to me. My moment has ended.

Operating in the 2.4 GHz ISM band, Bluetooth technologies can cause interference with wireless LAN technologies like DSSS, HR/DSSS, and ERP. However, the newer adaptive frequency hopping technology helps to reduce this interference if not completely remove it. Adaptive frequency hopping is a new feature found in Bluetooth 1.2 devices and higher.

Wireless MANs

Wireless MANs (metropolitan area networks) differ from wireless LANs and wireless PANs in that they are not usually implemented by the organization that wishes to use the network. Instead, they are generally implemented by a service provider, and then access to the network is leased by each subscribing organization. However, unlike with wireless WANs, this does not have to be the case. For example, 802.16-compliant hardware could be purchased and frequency licenses could be acquired in order to implement a private wireless MAN, but the expense is usually prohibitive.

WiMAX is the most commonly referenced wireless MAN technology. Now, in 2007, WiMAX solutions are just beginning to see production and installation. In fact, the first WiMAX Professional Certification training class was held in Hawaii, in January and February 2007. WiMAX is based on the IEEE 802.16 standard and provides expected throughput of approximately 40 Mbps for fixed, line of sight connections and approximately 15 Mbps for mobile, non–line of sight connections. In addition to the throughput speeds, WiMAX incorporates QoS mechanisms that help to provide greater throughput for all users and important applications using the network.

WiMAX is covered in more detail in the CWNP Wireless# certification. This certification is an entry-level wireless certification covering such technologies as Bluetooth, RFID, IrDA, Zigbee, WiMAX, and WLANs. See my previous entry-level book, *Wireless# Certification Official Study Guide* (McGraw-Hill, 2006).

Wireless WANs

Wide area networks (WANs) are usually used to connect LANs together. If the LANs are separated by a large distance, WAN technologies may be employed to connect them. These technologies include Frame Relay, analog dial-up lines, Digital Subscriber Line (DSL), ISDN, and others.

What they have traditionally had in common is a physical wire connected to something that is connected to something that is eventually connected to the remote LAN. The wireless WAN is completely different because no wire is needed from your local LAN to the backbone network or from the backbone network to your remote LAN. Wireless connections are made from each of your LANs to the backbone network.

Examples of wireless WAN technologies include Free Space Optics, Licensed and Unlicensed Radio, and hybrids of the two. For WAN links that span hundreds of miles, you may need a service provider such as AT&T microwave, but for shorter links of a few miles, you may be able to license frequency bands or use unlicensed technology to create the links. The key differentiator of wireless WAN technologies from WLAN, WPAN, and WMAN is that the wireless WAN link aggregates multiple communications channels together (multiplexing) and passes them across the single WAN link.

Wireless LAN Technology Roles

The roles played by wireless technology include data networking, voice communications, and video transfer, among others. In addition to the three primary roles discussed earlier in this chapter, there are dozens of specific uses of wireless LAN technologies. This last chapter section will provide an overview of these varied uses as well as a few case studies along the way.

Corporate Data Access and End-User Mobility

In enterprise environments, there has traditionally been a lot of walking. I remember, when I was employed as a Systems Analyst in a large organization, how I would walk from one building to the next to meet with users who were in need of my assistance. Of course, I could only access my e-mail from my desk, in those days, so I had to go back to my office periodically to find out if something urgent had come into my inbox.

The first technology that came along and helped solve the problem was the Internet and Intranets. Once web-based e-mail became available, I could access my e-mail from any computer that had a connection to the Intranet. However, web-based e-mail came along long after I left that large organization, and by the time IEEE 802.11 wireless networks arrived, I had been gone for even longer.

Consider the technical world we live in today. You can check your web-based e-mail while you walk down the hall on your HR/DSSS-compliant PDA. I was in a meeting with a client recently, and the network administrator was also attending the meeting. She received an e-mail on her Pocket PC from the network-monitoring software she was running on a centralized server during the meeting. The e-mail informed her that a network device was not responding. She immediately launched an SSH session that allowed her to cycle that device and test to verify that it was back online. All this took about 3 minutes to transpire. The Pocket PC, she later told me, was using IEEE 802.11b to log on to her e-mail account periodically to see if there were any e-mails from the centralized monitoring server. If there were any such e-mails, it would alert her with a special tone and she could take action. As you can see, there is a great benefit to information technology (IT) professionals as well as our end users. We look better because we can respond to outages faster, and our end users truly receive superior service.

Decision support is a critical IT system in today's corporate environments. Many times a few seconds lost can cost the organization thousands or even millions of dollars. Using wireless LANs in conjunction with newer database technologies like Microsoft's Notification Services in SQL Server 2005 can provide exceptional value to management and other decision makers. Scaled-down database systems can also be installed on portable devices so that these decision makers can take the data with them even when they leave the corporate wireless LAN, and these systems can often be configured to automatically replicate new data down to the portable device as soon as a connection is made to the wireless LAN again. After years of supporting Microsoft servers, including SQL Server, I am finally able to give them what they've needed: portable on-demand access to the data that helps them make the decisions that can thrust their organizations into the next level of competition.

In 2006, I consulted with a company that was implementing Microsoft SQL Server 2005, and they happened to be implementing HR/DSSS-compliant (formerly known as 802.11b-compliant or Clause 18-compliant) PDAs at the same time for their salespeople. These PDAs were all running the same version of Pocket Windows, which supports SQL Server 2005 Mobile Edition. They were only planning to have the salespeople use the PDAs as calendaring tools. After a few discussions, we were able to create a simple application on the PDAs that would replicate data from the SQL Server anytime the employees entered into the wireless LAN coverage area.

The CWNP Program (an inclusive title for all CWNP certifications such as Wireless#, CWNA, CWSP, CWNT, and CWNE) is moving away from referencing IEEE Physical layer technologies by their document name. Instead, Physical layers are referenced by their given name within the IEEE standards. For example, IEEE 802.11b was an amendment to the IEEE 802.11 standard that specified the functionality of the HR/DSSS Physical layer. This amendment will be incorporated into a new base document likely to be named something like IEEE 802.11-2007. The HR/DSSS Physical layer will simply be Clause 18 of this new document.

In the industry, some have taken to referencing the Physical layers by their clause numbers, and others have chosen to continue referencing them by the original document number. The one thing that is consistent, while clauses and documents could change, is the name of the Physical layer. This is the reason the CWNP Program has chosen to use the Physical layer names as a reference point.

The ability to download their newest personalized customer and product information automatically was priceless. In fact, the salespeople had always come into the office every morning and printed off pages and pages of information about the clients they were going to visit that day. Now, all they have to do is walk into the office, say good morning to the receptionist, fill up their coffee cups, and walk back out to begin their day of selling. In that brief time, their PDAs have connected to the wireless LAN, uploaded their information from the previous day, and downloaded any relevant new information. Now that's corporate data access and end-user mobility for the new millennium!

Network Extension to Remote Areas

Rick looked perplexed and unsure of himself as he started the meeting. He had to communicate the bad news to the group that it would cost more than $37,000 to extend the network into the old part of the school building, which was about twice what was allocated from the school funds. This was a small public school district in southern Michigan (also known as the LP or lower peninsula), and funding was always a problem. Thankfully, I was in the next room that day working on an ailing server, and I overheard what he had told the group. After the meeting was over and the teachers left thinking they were not going to get Internet access into those classrooms for a long time, I stepped into his office to ask him if the vendors had suggested using wireless LAN technologies.

I'll never forget the look on his face. It was a mixture of angst and awareness. The words that came out of his mouth were simple, "Of course!" The reality is that it just hadn't crossed his mind because they weren't using wireless LAN technology anywhere else in the building. We sat down and drew up a plan for installing wireless access points in the right places so that the Internet could reach inside the walls of a 70-year-old school house.

This case study illustrates the reality of network extension: it can be very expensive. However, if you can avoid running cables and installing expensive infrastructure hardware, you can often extend your network to remote areas at a fraction of the cost. These reduced costs even hold true when you use enterprise-class access points and other wireless devices from vendors like Cisco and Colubris. The reduction in cost comes from eliminating the cable costs, time costs, and other labor costs involved in running the cables.

Building-to-Building Connectivity: Bridging

There are many ways to connect another building to your network. You can dig a trench and bury a line that you own. You can place poles and hang a line that you own. You can lease a line from the telephone company. However, the first two have a high initial cost in both money and time, and the last one has an ongoing cost of monthly service fees. Another problem with running your own line is the common scenario where the remote building is actually on the other side of someone else's property. Very few people are kind enough to let you dig a ditch across their property; however, you could run an invisible line—an IEEE 802.11–based connection.

By installing a wireless bridge at each building, you overcome these problems. At first, it may seem that a license-free link is unlikely, since so many people use IEEE 802.11–based wireless hardware. With a little thought and a lot of planning, however, you can usually get the job done. Remember that you can use ERP (formerly known as IEEE 802.11g or Clause 19) devices on both ends, and there are multiple channels from which you can choose. You can also use OFDM (formerly known as IEEE 802.11a or Clause 17) devices, and there are even more channels from which you can choose. I'll cover all the channels that are available to you in Chapter 3, but for now, just remember that you have many channels from which you can choose. It is actually very likely that you can find one, for a short-distance building-to-building link, that is available.

When creating building-to-building links, you can create point-to-point (PtP) and point-to-multipoint (PtMP) links. PtP links are created when one wireless bridge talks to another wireless bridge and both use directional antennas. PtMP links are created when one wireless bridge acts as the center or hub of communications for multiple other wireless bridges. Due to the large amounts of traffic that can flow through the center bridge in a PtMP configuration, you must be careful when configuring these types of building-to-building links. If the throughput is insufficient for business demands, you might consider creating multiple PtP links instead.

Last-Mile Data Delivery: Wireless ISP

A wireless Internet service provider (WISP) is an Internet service provider (ISP) that is accessed using wireless technologies. WISPs often fulfill the need at the last mile. *Last mile* refers to the last section that must be spanned to reach remote customers. It can be very expensive and, without wireless, sometimes impractical. Sometimes these WISPs will also lease bandwidth to businesses that require Internet access but are too far from DSL stations and have no other options.

WISPs may use IEEE 802.11 technologies for the entire delivery, or they may use other wireless technologies, like WiMAX (IEEE 802.16), from the operations center to the delivery area and then use IEEE 802.11 technologies within the delivery area. Some WISPs will use WiMAX all the way to the end destination, and it will be up to the subscriber whether to use IEEE 802.11 technologies within their house or business. Since WiMAX and IEEE 802.11 use different frequencies (if the 802.11 devices use the 2.4 GHz spectrum), there should be no conflicts or interference.

To help you understand last-mile delivery, consider the home where I grew up in West Virginia. We lived on a very old country road. It was not paved; it was a gravel road. We lived in the last house on the road, which was approximately 2.5 miles from the nearest paved road. I remember that my father had to pay a large fee just to get electricity to the house, when I was 12 years old. The electric company required that he pay the fee, since there were no other houses close to ours. This is an example of the problems related to last-mile delivery. It's no different for the Internet today than it was for electricity then. Wireless technologies provide an excellent solution to the problem of last-mile delivery of Internet access.

Small Office/Home Office (SOHO) Use

In Small Office/Home Office (SOHO) environments, it is very common to have fewer than 25 or even fewer than 10 computers in the entire company. In these scenarios, a wireless LAN can often be your core network. I've installed many wireless LAN routers—sometimes called residential gateways—in these scenarios. From small dentists' offices to small lawyers' offices and the office in the basement, a simple wireless LAN router may be all that is needed.

A SOHO installation can also take advantage of wireless LAN technology at the same time that it utilizes wired technology. For example, using the uplink port found in many switches, you could connect a larger switch to a basic Linksys WRT54G router (or one similar to this from another vendor such as D-Link, Buffalo Technologies, or Netgear). The wireless LAN router can provide both wireless access to the network and routing out to the Internet all in one device. The ISP may be using dial-up, DSL, or Cable TV modems to provide the Internet connectivity. Today, Cable TV modems regularly provide between 1 and 6 Mbps, as does DSL. Of course, dial-up Internet is still much slower; however, dial-up is also still commonly used in rural areas. Thankfully, many brave entrepreneurs have been installing last-mile service in these rural areas using licensed and unlicensed wireless solutions.

Mobile Office Networking

Similar to the SOHO installation is the mobile office installation. Mobile offices are used during construction, in disaster zones, on hunting trips (Am I the only one?), and in other such scenarios where you need to have network access with little installation time or complexity. Interesting devices are coming on the market that can assist in these mobile office installations. One example is the SonicWALL TZ190 (see Figure 1.2), which supports wireless WAN PC cards so that you can route a local network out to the wireless WAN Internet connection. The card protruding from the left side of the device in Figure 1.2 is the wireless WAN card.

FIGURE 1.2 SonicWALL TZ190 firewall with wireless WAN support—front view

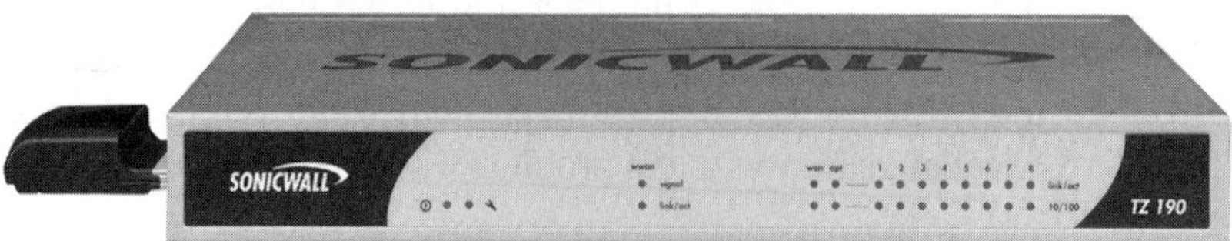

FIGURE 1.3 SonicWall TZ190—back view

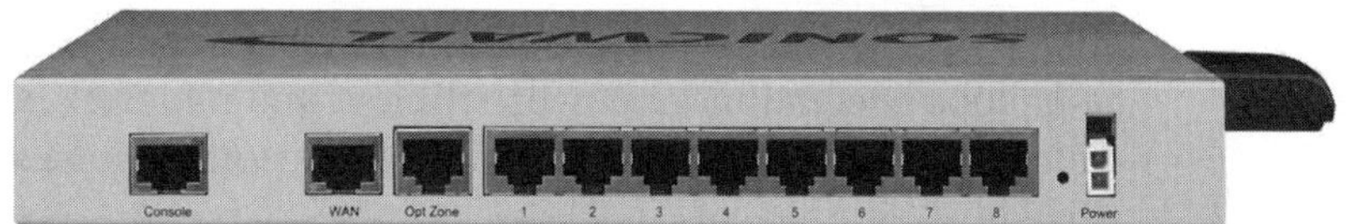

Using a device like the SonicWall TZ190 as the gateway to a wireless WAN ISP means that you can set up a LAN that has access to the Internet in very short time windows. Additionally, you could connect a wireless access point to the LAN port on the SonicWall TZ190 and have wireless on both sides: a wireless LAN routed to a wireless WAN installed in minutes. As you can see, in Figure 1.3, this device actually comes equipped with a built-in eight-port switch, so you can actually install a wireless LAN, install a wired LAN, and have both routed to the wireless WAN ISP in less than 10 minutes—assuming you've preconfigured the SonicWall TZ190. This device is just one example of the newer devices that are making mobile office setup much faster and easier.

Educational/Classroom Use

Educational organizations were among the first to begin WLAN implementations. By having a WLAN, schools can allow their teachers to work from anywhere and not be locked to their desks. Laptops can be taken to auditoriums where Internet demonstrations can occur on large projected screens without the need for Ethernet cabling. Students can access both the Internet and Intranet sites in order to do research or submit assignments.

I remember teaching classes in the 1990s (it seems so long ago) and having to provide presentation slides and handouts to attendees either in printed form or using previously developed CD-ROMs. Today, when I teach a class, I can just share my presentation folder on the ad hoc WLAN that I've created with my students. The students take whatever slides or documents they desire and then display them on their laptops. The future looks even brighter with the newer batteries and lower-power–consuming laptops giving us 4–6 hours of battery life. It won't be long until you can attend a training class that lasts 2–3 days and use your laptop every day without ever plugging it in to recharge the batteries.

I can do that now, but it requires carrying along a few extra batteries. (The really exciting moment will occur when computer projectors are able to run for hours from small battery-based power supplies.) Of course, as laptops become more power efficient and batteries become more enduring, it means that we can use wireless technologies for even longer periods of time.

On college campuses, WLANs have become an expected benefit. Most colleges publish maps that show the coverage areas of the WLAN so that students and faculty can be sure they plan to have a meeting or personal time in a covered area. Many schools now require students to have a laptop with an HR/DSSS or ERP network card, while others only require it for students taking computer-related or computer-dependent classes.

The difficulty in college and university environments is controlling the rogue WLANs. Many students are entering college today with an advanced knowledge of computers, and they often have the ability to install and configure SOHO-class wireless routers like the popular Linksys WRT54G. When the students install these routers, the routers can cause interference problems with the school's authorized WLAN. Of course, these wireless routers don't really benefit the students if there is no wired Internet connection to which the router can be connected. For this reason, many schools are implementing strict rules in relation to the enabling of Ethernet ports in dorm rooms. The Ethernet ports are often left in a disabled state until the student requests for them to be enabled. Many students never request that one be enabled, since they have access to the authorized WLAN. Those who request it may be asked to sign agreements that they will not install certain type of devices, such as wireless routers, and that they will be subject to dismissal if they breach the agreement. This can be successful in deterring many would-be rogue WLANs. Enterprise-class rogue detection systems can also be used when the budget provides for them.

Industrial: Warehousing and Manufacturing

Warehouses and manufacturing environments are excellent applications of wireless LAN solutions. These environments have often existed for many years and lack the proper cabling to reach even the speeds that wireless LANs can currently provide. At the same time, motors and equipment used in these environments can cause interference problems, so an effective site survey is essential. Storage racks and other materials in and around these types of environments can also be problematic.

Health Care: Hospitals and Offices

Hospitals can benefit from wireless LAN technology in order to have roaming access to patient records as well as pharmacy information. Medical prescriptions can be sent to the hospital pharmacy directly from the patient's rooms, and nurses can give instant digital feedback using PDAs as they make their rounds throughout the hospital. Of course, security will be a top priority in health care installations, so newer equipment supporting the more recent security provisions will be a requirement.

Hotspots: Public Network Access

A Wi-Fi *hotspot* provides wireless Internet access in public areas. Some hotspots are free and wide open, while others are free and secured. Yet other hotspots are subscription -based, pay-as-you-go, or a mixture of these. PDAs and laptops are usually the devices used to connect to hotspots. These hotspots are found everywhere, from coffee shops to libraries to public parks. It is important to remember that a hotspot is defined as a wireless network that is *intended to give* wireless Internet access either free or for a fee. There are many locations where you can connect to a wireless network, but many, if not most, of these are *inadvertently giving* wireless Internet access. Examples of these inadvertent networks include homes, businesses, and even government installations that are not properly secured.

Specialty devices have been created that can print receipts, authenticate users, and even disconnect users after time limits expire. These devices are often called hotspot gateways. There are many business models associated with the implementation of a hotspot. Following are a few examples:

- **Paid Access** This model profits from the fees for access to the Internet. This is very common today in airports, though I'm happy to say that my local Columbus, Ohio, airport is providing free wireless Internet access—for now, anyway.
- **Traffic Generation** This model profits from the sales of items like coffee, books, music, and other items to the individual who come to the hotspot location for Internet access.

- **Mixed** This model profits from both the fee for access and the sale of items in the area where access is provided. In the United States, Starbucks is probably the most well-known enterprise using this model.
- **Walled Garden Model** This is currently being implemented by many hotels and retail outlets. The concept is to allow connected devices to browse a select group of Internet sites. These sites will pay a fee in order to be in the walled garden. The fees are distributed among the participating hotspots according to the amount of traffic the various hotspots generate.
- **Philanthropist Model** This model assumes that people will love you for giving them free Internet access and that love is reward enough. I know I love this model when I encounter it in my travels. NOTE: I am not referring to stealing network access. I am actually referring to those providers (libraries, municipalities, airports, etc.) that really intend to provide you with network access. If you access a network that is open but not intended for your use, you may be breaching local or regional laws, and you should, therefore, be very cautious and ethical.

Summary

In this chapter, you learned about the different wireless organizations that exist. You learned that there are three primary types of organizations: regulatory, standardization, and compatibility. The FCC falls into the first category, the IEEE into the second, and the Wi-Fi Alliance into the third.

You also learned about the IEEE 802.11 standard that has been developed and the amendments that have been made to it since 1997. Finally, you considered some of the many possible uses of wireless LAN, MAN, PAN, and WAN technologies. Next, review the key terms present here and be sure you can define them all. Then, go through the review questions and answers to be sure that you've grasped the key elements from this chapter.

Key Terms

- ☐ **access role**
- ☐ **core role**
- ☐ **distribution role**
- ☐ **FCC**
- ☐ **IEEE**
- ☐ **hotspots**
- ☐ **last mile**
- ☐ **Wi-Fi Alliance**
- ☐ **Wireless WAN**
- ☐ **WLAN**
- ☐ **WMAN**
- ☐ **WPAN**

Review Questions

1. Which of the following organizations is responsible for compatibility testing of 802.11 hardware?

   A. IEEE

   B. ETSI

   C. Wi-Fi Alliance

   D. FCC

2. You want to read the 802.11 standard so that you can better understand the details of the MAC and PHY layer functionality in wireless LANs. Which organization's web site should you visit?

   A. IEEE

   B. ETSI

   C. Wi-Fi Alliance

   D. FCC

3. ABC company has contracted with you to install a wireless LAN in their facilities. They inform you that there is a warehouse approximately 400 feet from the main building and that there are no Ethernet wires run to that building. Which of the following technologies will you most likely use to provide wireless network access in the remote warehouse?

   A. Wireless PAN

   B. Wireless LAN

   C. Wireless MAN

   D. Wireless WAN

4. What are the two types of wireless bridge links that can be created? (Choose two.)

   A. Point-to-point

   B. Building-to-building

   C. Point-to-multipoint

   D. Remote-to-local

5. Which of the following technologies are not wireless WAN solutions? (Choose all that apply.)

   A. Zigbee

   B. Free Space Optics

   C. Wi-Fi Access Points

   D. Bluetooth

Review Answers

1. **C.** The correct answer is the Wi-Fi Alliance. The IEEE creates standards based on FCC regulations. The ETSI is a European standards body.

2. **A.** The correct answer is IEEE. The IEEE web site, at www.ieee.org, will contain the full text of the IEEE 802.11 standard documents 6 months after each new document is published. In fact, it can be found at this URL: http://standards.ieee.org/getieee802/802.11.html.

3. **B.** The correct answer is wireless LAN. Since the building is 400 feet away, it is certainly too far for wireless PAN technologies and too close for wireless MAN technologies. Wireless WAN technologies would not likely be used, as you would have to route data from the warehouse to the Internet and then to the main facility and vice versa. In the end, wireless LAN technologies are the only logical solution.

4. **A, C.** The correct answers are point-to-point and point-to-multipoint. Building-to-building is a common phrase used, but it is not the technical term for these wireless bridge links. Remote-to-local is unused terminology.

5. **A, C, D.** The correct answers are Zigbee, Wi-Fi Access Points, and Bluetooth. Free Space Optics (FSO) is the only wireless WAN solution in this list. Zigbee and Bluetooth are wireless PAN solutions, and Wi-Fi Access Points are WLAN solutions.

CHAPTER

2

Radio Frequency and Antenna Fundamentals

In This Chapter

CWNA Exam Objectives Covered:

- Define and explain the basic concepts of RF behavior
  - Gain and Loss
  - Reflection, Refraction, Diffraction, Scattering, and Absorption
  - VSWR
  - Return Loss
  - Amplification and Attenuation
  - Wave Propagation, Free Space Path Loss, and Delay Spread
- Understand and apply the basic components of RF mathematics
  - Watts and Milliwatts
  - Decibel (dB), dBm, dBi, and dBd
  - SNR and RSSI
  - System Operating Margin (SOM), Fade Margin, and Link Budget
  - Intentional Radiators and EIRP

CWNA Exam Objectives Covered:

- ❖ Identify RF signal characteristics, the applications of basic RF antenna concepts, and the implementation of solutions that require RF antennas
  - Visual and RF LOS
  - The Fresnel Zone
  - Beamwidth, Azimuth, and Elevation
  - Passive Gain
  - Isotropic Radiators
  - Polarization and Antenna Diversity
  - Wavelength, Frequency, Amplitude, and Phase
- ❖ Explain the applications of basic RF antenna and antenna system types and identify their basic attributes, purpose, and function
  - Omnidirectional, Semidirectional, Highly Directional, and Sectorized Antennas
  - Multiple-Input, Multiple-Output (MIMO) Antenna Systems

Wireless communications must utilize one of two primary media: sound waves or electromagnetic (EM) waves. When one human speaks to another human, the sound waves travel through the air and are interpreted by the receiving human's ears. These sound waves form the most ancient kind of wireless communications. However, sound waves do not provide an effective form of wireless communications over great distances because of the tremendous interference in the sound wave spectrums (frequency ranges) and the massive amounts of power required to send a sound wave over those great distances. Electromagnetic waves, on the other hand, offer a very effective means of wireless communications due to the very structured way the frequencies can be divided and the low amounts of power required to communicate across a vast expanse.

In this chapter, you will first learn about electromagnetic waves and how they can be used for wireless communications. You will then move on to the specific electromagnetic waves that are used within IEEE 802.11–based networks, specifically radio frequency (RF) waves. Next, you will discover the calculations that you can make against RF waves using RF math, and finally, you'll learn about antennas, including both the types of antennas and their functionality.

Electromagnetic Waves: A Quick Tour

Simply defined, an *electromagnetic wave* is a fluctuation of energy consisting of electric and magnetic fields. The electric and magnetic fields oscillate or move back and forth at right angles to each other, and the wave moves out from the propagating antenna in a direction related to the shape of the antenna, which you will learn about later. Electromagnetic waves and their uses have been discovered over a lengthy period of time and have required the joint efforts of many dedicated researchers, engineers, and scientists.

History of Electromagnetic Waves

The focus of this book is not on the detailed physics of electromagnetism but is aimed at a higher level of understanding. That higher level is a specific use of electromagnetism: radio waves. There are many good resources that detail the history of wireless communications using electromagnetic waves, including *History of Wireless* by Tapan K. Sarkar et al. (IEEE Press, 2006) and *Energy, Force, and Matter* by P.M. Harman (Cambridge University Press, 2005). However, a quick reminder of how

FIGURE 2.1 Electromagnetic spectrum with wavelengths and example uses

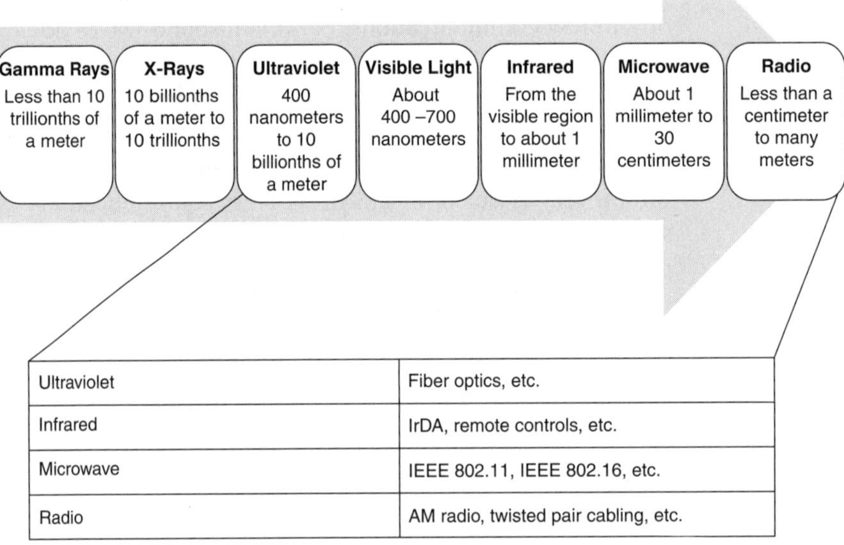

electromagnetic waves have been used will be beneficial and is covered in the next section. Figure 2.1 shows the electromagnetic spectrum and where radio and microwave electromagnetic waves fall.

Early Radio Technologies

Electromagnetic wave–based communications have been utilized for many decades. In fact, radio and television both depend on these electromagnetic waves. Additionally, these electromagnetic waves—or *radio waves*—have been used for purposes such as wireless voice conversations (today, we call these cell phones) and data communications. The military has used wireless communications for many decades, and expensive proprietary equipment has also been available.

You could say that wireless communications over great distance all started with the letter *S*. It was this letter that Guglielmo Marconi transmitted, received, and printed with the Morse inker across the Atlantic in the first decade of the twentieth century. Though Marconi was not the first to communicate over a distance without wires, this event started a greater stirring through the government and business communities that resulted in the many uses of wireless technology we see today.

By the 1920s, radio waves were being used for telecommunications. In fact, the first transatlantic telephone service became available in 1927 from New York to London. Twenty-one years earlier, in 1906, Reginald Fessenden successfully communicated from land to sea over a distance of 11 miles using radio waves to carry voice communications. Bell Laboratories had created a mobile two-way voice-carrying radio wave device by 1924, but mobile voice technology was not really perfected and used widely until the 1940s.

If you are familiar with modems, you are aware that computer data can be transferred over land-based telephone lines using these devices. A modem modulates the binary data into analog signals and demodulates the analog signals into binary data. This allows two computers to talk to each other across these land lines. As you can imagine, the leap to communicating digital data across wireless connections is not a large leap. From the early use of radio technology for broadcasting (radio and television) and voice communications to today's massive data transfer over wireless links, radio wave communications have evolved rapidly.

One of the greatest problems with these early technologies was the proprietary nature of the devices. Just like humans, in order for two devices to communicate with each other, they must share a language. Without standards, each company would create devices that communicated either in ways they thought were best or simply in the only ways their engineers knew how to implement. This resulted in incompatibilities among the different devices. Organizations such as the IEEE, IETF, and ANSI have developed many standards that have helped overcome this hurdle. When it comes to wireless data communications in local area networks (LANs), the IEEE 802.11 standard is the one that started it all.

Fundamentals of Electromagnetic Waves

You will not have to know a great deal about the physics behind electromagnetic waves to pass the CWNA exam or to implement enterprise-class wireless networks. I do, however, hope this overview gives you a desire to learn more. This summary of the fundamentals will also help you to better understand the section "RF Behavior" later in this chapter.

For more information on electromagnetic waves, I suggest the books *How Radio Signals Work* by Jim Sinclair and *Physics Demystified* by Stan Gibilisco. Both books are published by McGraw-Hill (1998 and 2002, respectively).

Waves

The first thing I want to define is a wave. A *wave,* in the realm of physics, can be defined as a motion through matter. Notice I did not say that the wave is a movement of matter, but it is a motion—such as oscillation—through matter or space. Think of the waves in the ocean bobbing up and down. Now imagine a ball placed on top of the waves. The waves pass by and the ball bobs up and down as they pass by, but the ball does not travel with the waves. If you were to investigate even more closely, you would see that the water does not travel with the waves either, but the waves pass through the matter (water).

An electromagnetic wave is an oscillation traveling through space. In the early days of electromagnetic wave study, some thought an invisible medium existed through which the waves traveled. This invisible medium was called the ether. You may recognize this term as it is used today in the word Ethernet, paying homage to this earlier thinking. In fact, electromagnetic waves can travel in a vacuum where all matter has been removed, and because of this, we theorize that they need no material medium to travel. How then do they propagate through space? It is through an interesting relationship, though not fully understood, between electric and magnetic fields.

Electric Fields

An *electric field* is the distribution in space of the strength and direction of forces that would be exerted on an electric charge at any point in that space, according to the *American Heritage Science Dictionary.* In other words, the electric field is the space within which an electrically charged object will feel a pull or a push, depending on whether the charge on the object is unlike (pull) or like (push) that of the pulling or pushing source. Positively charged objects attract negatively charged objects, and negatively charged objects attract positively charged objects. The measurable strength of this attraction is greater when the objects are closer together and lesser when they are farther apart. The electric field represents the space within which this attraction can be detected, although theoretically, the attraction extends infinitely, though it cannot be measured.

Electric fields result from other electric charges or from changing magnetic fields. *Electric field strength* is a measurement of the strength of an electric field at a given point in space and is equal to the force induced on a unit of electric charge at that point.

Magnetic Fields

A *magnetic field* is a force produced by a moving electric charge that exists around a magnet or in free space. Magnetic fields extend out from the attracting center, and the space in which it can affect objects is considered the extent of the magnetic field. A changing magnetic field generates an electric field.

Electromagnetic Waves

Now that you have definitions of electric fields and magnetic fields, you are ready to investigate electromagnetic waves. An electromagnetic wave is a propagating combination of electric and magnetic fields. Remember that a magnetic field can generate an electric field and an electric field can generate a magnetic field. While the analogy is not perfect, consider that a chicken creates an egg that creates a chicken that creates an egg ad infinitum. The alternating current (AC) in the antenna generates a magnetic field around the antenna that generates an electric field that generates a magnetic field ad infinitum.

The electric and magnetic fields are oscillating perpendicular to each other, and they are both perpendicular to the direction of propagation, as is shown in Figure 2.2. You can see that the electric field is parallel to the generating wire (antenna) and the magnetic field is perpendicular to the generating wire. The wave is traveling out from the generating wire.

A very specific form (wavelength and frequency) of these electromagnetic waves is used to communicate wirelessly in IEEE 802.11 networks. This form of wave is a radio frequency wave, often shortened to RF wave. An RF-based system, then, is a system that relies on the phenomenon of electromagnetic wave theory to provide data and voice communications wirelessly.

FIGURE 2.2 Electromagnetic wave propagation direction

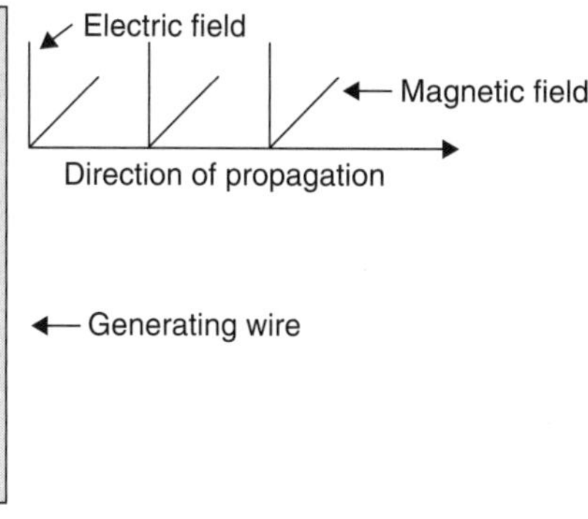

RF Characteristics

All RF waves have characteristics that vary to define the wave. Some of these properties can be modified to modulate information onto the wave. These properties are *wavelength, frequency, amplitude,* and *phase.*

Wavelength

The *wavelength* of an RF wave is calculated as the distance between two adjacent identical points on the wave. For example, Figure 2.3 shows a standard sine wave. Point A and Point B mark two identical points on the wave, and the distance between them is defined as the wavelength. The wavelength is frequently measured as the distance from one crest of the wave to the next.

The wavelength is an important measure of which you should be aware. The wavelength dictates the optimum size of the receiving antenna, and it determines how the RF wave will interact with its environment. For example, an RF wave will react differently when it strikes an object that is large in comparison to the wavelength from when it strikes an object that is small in comparison to the wavelength.

You will learn about frequency next, but it is important you understand that the wavelength and the frequency are interrelated. In fact for a given medium, if you know the wavelength, you can calculate the frequency and if you know the frequency, you can calculate the wavelength.

One of the great discoveries in the history of electromagnetism is that electromagnetic waves travel at the speed of light. Since we know the speed of light to be 299,792,458 meters per second, we also know that this

FIGURE 2.3 Wavelength measurement

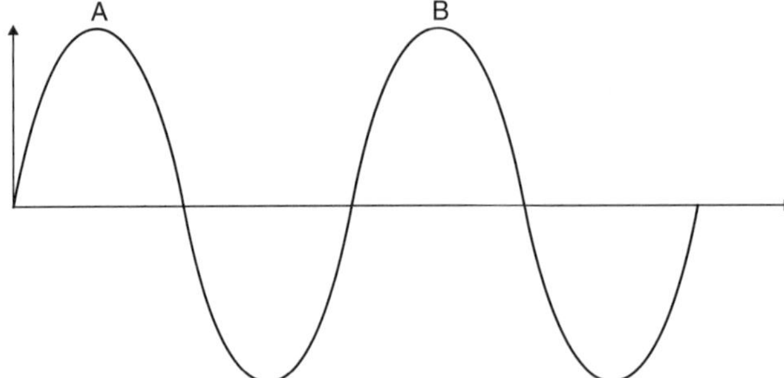

is the speed at which electromagnetic waves travel in a vacuum. This was theorized by James Clerk Maxwell and proved through experimentation by Heinrich Hertz.

You are probably familiar with measurements like 100 megahertz and 3.6 gigahertz. These measurements refer to the number of cycles per second. When we say that the access point is using the 2.45 gigahertz spectrum, we say it is using the spectrum that uses a wave cycle rate of 2,450,000,000 times per second. This measurement is named after Heinrich Hertz and his research in electricity and magnetism. A kilohertz is 1000 hertz or cycles per second. A megahertz is 1,000,000 hertz, and a gigahertz is 1,000,000,000 hertz. A terahertz is one trillion hertz, but these frequencies are not commonly found in today's wireless communications.

Since we know that RF waves travel at the speed of light, we can calculate the frequency when we know the wavelength or the wavelength when we know the frequency. The following formula can be used to calculate the wavelength in meters when the frequency is known:

$$w = 299{,}792{,}458/f$$

Here, w is the wavelength in meters and f is the frequency in *hertz* and the medium is a vacuum. Therefore, the 2.45 GHz spectrum would have a wavelength that is calculated with the following formula:

$$w = 299{,}792{,}458/2{,}450{,}000{,}000$$

The result is 0.123 meters or approximately 12.3 centimeters. This translates to about 4.8 inches. To calculate inches from centimeters, just multiply the number of centimeters by 0.3937. The formal character used to represent a wavelength is the Greek lambda (λ), and the symbol for the speed of light is c. Therefore, the formal representation of the previous formula would be

$$\lambda = c/f$$

The calculation for frequency is just the opposite. You will divide the speed of light by the wavelength in meters to discover the frequency. Keep in mind that the numbers we've been using have been rounded and that impacts the results of the following formula; however, the results are close enough to recognize that a wavelength of 0.123 meters would indicate an RF wave in the 2.45 GHz spectrum:

$$f = 299{,}792{,}458/.123$$

$$f = 2437337056.91$$

Due to the complex number that is the speed of light, this number is often rounded to 300 billion meters per second. While this will change formula results, the findings are close enough for understanding the behavior of RF waves; however, engineers developing RF systems must use more precise measurements. Additionally, formulas like the following simplify matters:

$$\text{Wavelength in inches } (\lambda) = 11.811/f \text{ (in GHz)}$$

$$\text{Wavelength in centimeters } (\lambda) = 20/f \text{ (in GHz)}$$

Because wireless networks use such high frequency ranges, formulas like this make the calculations easier.

While I provide formulas like this, for your reference and use as a WLAN administrator, you will not see these formulas on the CWNA exam. However, my goal is to help you fully understand wireless networking as you journey toward your CWNA certification. For this reason, I will frequently go deeper than the exam requires. I will also point these areas out to you so that you will not have to spend time memorizing facts that you can always reference in this book as you go about your administration tasks.

Frequency

Frequency refers to the number of wave cycles that occur in a given window of time. Usually measured in second intervals, a frequency of 1 kilohertz (KHz) would represent 1000 cycles of the wave in 1 second. To remember this, just keep in mind that a wave cycles frequently and just how frequently it cycles determines its frequency.

Since all electromagnetic waves, including radio waves, move at the speed of light, the frequency is related to the wavelength. In other words, we observe that wavelength, frequency, and medium are interdependent. Higher frequencies have shorter wavelengths, and lower frequencies have longer wavelengths.

The concept of frequency is used in sound engineering as well as RF engineering. Figure 2.4 shows a piano keyboard and the sound frequencies to which the keys are traditionally tuned. Knowing this can help establish your understanding of frequencies in RF communications; however, you must be clear in your thinking about the differences between sound waves and electromagnetic waves. The two wave types are not the same phenomenon, but they share similar characteristics. Since most people are already somewhat familiar with the behavior of sound waves through life experience, they make a good analogy as a starting point for your understanding of electromagnetic waves.

Remember that an analogy is nothing more than a comparison of the similarities of two different things or concepts. For this reason, you must hold in mind the fact that sound waves are not exactly the same as electromagnetic waves, but that they have similarities that can be used for progressive learning.

With sound waves, the right string that is tightened to the right tension will emit a sound of the appropriate frequency. Sound waves travel much more slowly than electromagnetic waves, at a rate of approximately 344 meters per second or 1100 feet per second through the air. In other words, if you are standing 100 feet (30.5 meters) from the source of the sound, it will take that sound approximately 1/10 of a second to reach you, but that sound's wavelength and frequency cannot be known from this alone.

Looking again at the piano keyboard in Figure 2.4, you can see that Middle C has a frequency of 261 Hz. From this, the wavelength can be calculated by dividing 344 meters by 261 Hz for a wavelength of 1.32 meters or 4.33 feet. In effect, we are saying that there are 261 waves generated in a second and, in any given second, each existing wave travels 344 meters. Now, it is important to note that the lower frequencies still travel at a rate of 344 meters per second; however, there are fewer—though longer—waves in each second. Just like RF waves, lower-frequency sound waves can be

FIGURE 2.4 Sound frequencies on a piano keyboard

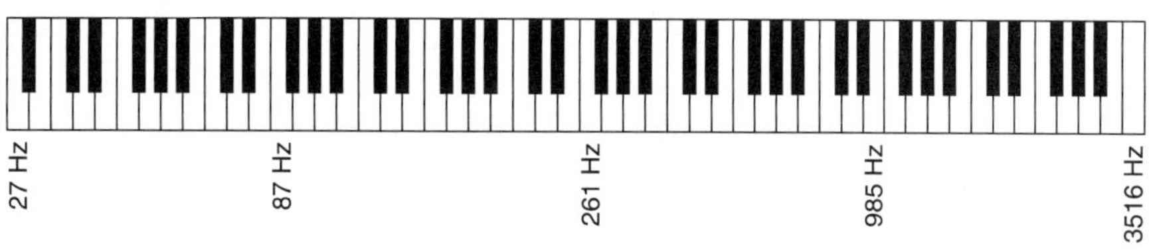

perceived at a greater distance due to the mechanism known as the human ear. To show that the other sound waves still exist at the greater distance, you can use an amplifier like that commonly seen along the sidelines at American football games. This device has a larger "receive" space than the human ear, so it is able to "pick up" sound waves that would otherwise be missed.

The impact of frequency usage on wireless local area networks (WLANs) is tremendous. By using different frequencies, you can enable distinct connections or RF links in a given coverage area or cell. For example, an IEEE 802.11g network using channel 1 can exist in the same cell as an IEEE 802.11g network using channel 11. This is because these channels use different frequencies that do not cancel or interfere with each other.

Think of it like a beautiful orchestra. There are many instruments playing on many different frequencies, but together they make wonderful music. Now, consider the sound you get when you walk up to a piano and press the palm of your hand down on six or seven keys simultaneously. Few people call that pleasant music. The sound frequencies are so close together that they just sound like noise. In a similar way, overlapping RF waves will be very difficult, if not impossible, to distinguish from one another. However, consider the melodious sound of the C major chord or the D minor chord. In the same way, multiple IEEE 802.11g networks can work side by side when they are configured to channels 1, 6, and 11 in a cell.

Amplitude

Given the explanation in the preceding section, you might be tempted to think that the volume of sound waves is dependent on the frequency, since lower-frequency waves are heard at a greater distance; however, there is actually another characteristic of waves that impacts the volume. Remember, at greater distances, shorter-wavelength waves are more difficult to detect as the waveform spreads ever wider (though this may be more a factor of the antenna used than of the waveform itself). The characteristic that defines the volume is known as *amplitude.* In sound wave engineering, an increase in amplitude is equivalent to an increase in volume; hence, an amplifier adds to the volume, or makes the sound louder. While the frequency affects the distance a sound wave can travel, the amplitude affects the ability to detect (hear) the sound wave at that distance. RF waves are similar.

An RF wave with greater amplitude is easier to detect than an RF wave with lesser amplitude, assuming all other factors are equal. In other words, in a vacuum, an RF wave will be said to have better quality at a distance if it has greater amplitude. Realize that RF waves travel, theoretically, forever. This being the case, the detectability of the wave is greater at certain distances when the wave starts with a greater amplitude. A wave with a lesser amplitude may not be detectable due to the noise floor. The *noise floor* can be defined as a measure of the level of background noise. In other words, there is a point in space where an RF wave still exists, but it cannot be distinguished from the electromagnetic noise in the environment.

In effect, both the high-amplitude and low-amplitude waves exist at that point, but only the high-amplitude wave can be detected. This means that both waves have traveled the distance, but only the high-amplitude wave is useful. For this reason, in common usage, engineers often say that an increase in amplitude will extend the range of the RF wave. What is meant by this is that the RF wave's useful range has been extended. Figure 2.5 shows an RF signal with original, increased, and decreased amplitudes.

FIGURE 2.5 RF waves at different amplitudes

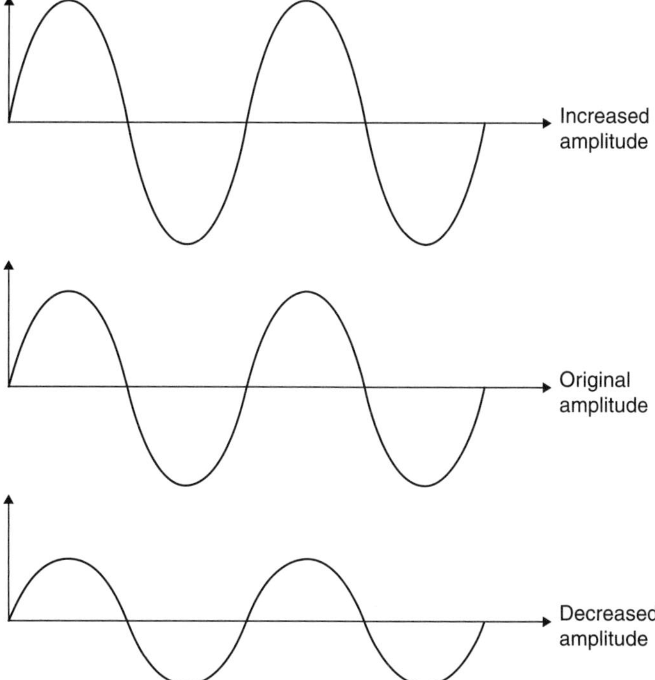

Phase

Unlike wavelength, frequency, and amplitude, *phase* is not a characteristic of a single RF wave but is instead a comparison between two RF waves. If two copies of the same RF wave arrive at a receiving antenna at the same time, their phase state will impact how the composite wave is able to be used. When the waves are in phase, they strengthen each other, and when the waves are out of phase, they sometimes strengthen and sometimes cancel each other. In specific out-of-phase cases, they only cancel each other.

Phase is measured in degrees, though real-world analysis usually benefits only from the knowledge of whether the waves are in phase or out of phase. Two waves that are completely out of phase would be 180 degrees out of phase, while two waves that are completely in phase would be 0 degrees out of phase. Figure 2.6 shows a main wave signal, another in-phase signal, and an out-of-phase signal.

Phase is used for many modern RF modulation algorithms, as you will learn in Chapter 3. When troubleshooting wireless networks, the phase of duplicate RF signals is mostly an implication of reflection or scattering in an area that may cause dead zones due to the out-of-phase signals.

FIGURE 2.6 RF wave phases

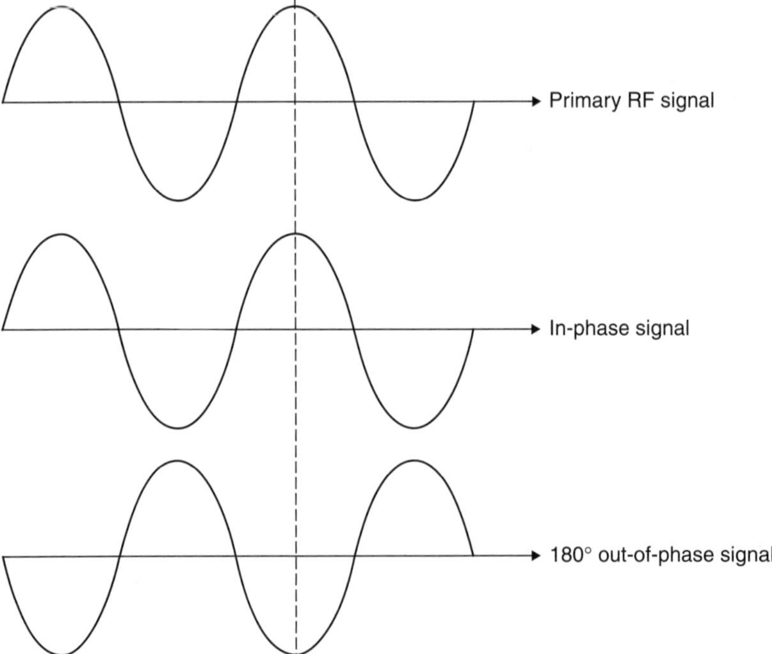

RF Behavior

RF waves that have been modulated to contain information are called *RF signals.* These RF signals have behaviors that can be predicted and detected. They become stronger, and they become weaker. They react to different materials differently, and they can interfere with other signals. The following sections introduce you to the major RF signal behaviors and their implications, including

- Gain
- Loss
- Reflection
- Refraction
- Diffraction
- Scattering
- Absorption
- VSWR
- Return Loss
- Amplification and Attenuation
- Wave Propagation
- Free Space Path Loss
- Delay Spread

Gain

Gain is defined as *the positive relative amplitude difference between two RF wave signals* (hereinafter known as only RF signals). *Amplification* is an active process used to increase an RF signal's amplitude and, therefore, results in gain. There are two basic types of gain: *active* and *passive.* Both types can be intentional, and passive gain can also be unintentional. Figure 2.7 shows an example of a signal that demonstrates both gain and loss.

Active Gain

Active gain is achieved by placing an amplifier in-line between the RF signal generator (such as an access point) and the propagating antenna. These amplifiers, covered in more detail in Chapter 7, usually measure

FIGURE 2.7 RF signal amplitude gain and loss

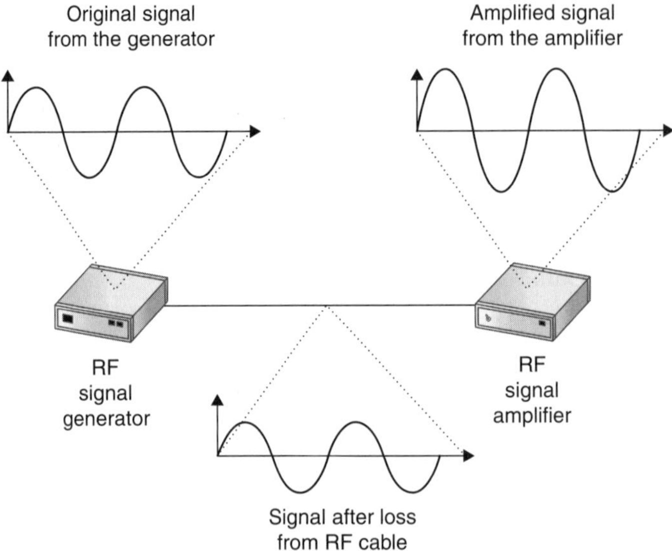

the gain they provide in decibel (dB). For example, an amplifier may provide 6 dB of gain to the incoming RF signal. To determine the actual power of the signal after passing through the amplifier, you will have to know the original power of the signal from the RF generator and then perform the appropriate RF math as discussed in the "Basic RF Math" section later in this chapter.

When using any type of intentional gain, you must be careful not to exceed the legal output constraints within your regulatory domain. For example, the FCC in the United States limits the output power at the intentional radiator to 1 watt and at the antenna to 4 watts for point-to-multipoint (PtMP) applications in the unlicensed 2.4 GHz ISM band.

While the concept of the intentional radiator is covered in greater depth later in this chapter, it is mentioned periodically throughout the chapter. For now, consider the following definition: The intentional radiator is the point in the radio system where the system is connected to the antenna. In other words, there are restrictions on the output power at the point where the system connects to the antenna, and then there are restrictions on the output power of the antenna after passive gain.

Passive Gain

Passive gain is not an actual increase in the amplitude of the signal delivered to the intentional radiator, but it is an increase in the amplitude of the signal, in a favored direction, by focusing or directing the output power. Passive gain can be either intentional or unintentional.

Intentional Passive Gain Intentional passive gain is like cupping your hands around your mouth as you yell to someone at a distance. You are directing the sound waves, intentionally, toward that targeted location. You are not increasing your ability to yell louder. If you yell at your loudest without cupped hands, it will not be as detectable at a greater distance as it would with cupped hands. This is intentional passive gain. To experience this, read this paragraph out loud. As you are reading, cup your hands around your mouth and notice how the sound changes (becomes muffled and seems to change tonality). This is because more of the sound waves are traveling out from you and your ears detect the difference. Of course, anyone else in the room with you can tell a difference as well, and they might even think you're a little strange—so be sure you are alone when you perform this test.

Antennas are used to provide intentional passive gain in wireless networks using RF signals. The antenna propagates more of the RF signal's energy in a desired direction than in other directions. The RF signal is said to have gain in that direction. You'll understand this more fully once you've read the section "Isotropic Radiator" later in this chapter.

Unintentional Passive Gain Unintentional passive gain happens because of reflection and scattering in a coverage area. When the RF signal leaves the transmitting antenna, the primary signal travels out from the antenna according to the propagation patterns for which the antenna is designed. However, this signal may encounter objects that cause reflection and scattering, resulting in multiple copies of the same signal arriving at the receiving antenna. If these signals arrive in phase, they can cause the signal strength to actually increase and this would be a form of unintentional passive gain; however, some RF engineers doubt that RF energy, once scattered, is ever joined with other signal paths to produce passive gain of any measurable value.

Loss

Loss is defined as *the negative relative amplitude difference between two RF signals.* Like gain, loss can be either intentional or unintentional (referenced as natural in this section).

Intentional

Due to FCC regulations and the regulations of other regulatory domains, you will have to ensure that the output powers of your wireless devices are within specified constraints. Depending on the radios, amplifiers, cables, and antennas you are using, you may have to intentionally cause loss in the RF signal. This means that you are reducing the RF signal's amplitude, and this is accomplished with an attenuator. Attenuation, the process that causes loss, is discussed in greater detail in the later section "Attenuation."

Natural

In addition to the intentional loss that is imposed on an RF signal to comply with regulatory demands, natural or unintentional losses can occur. This kind of loss happens because of the natural process of RF propagation, which involves spreading, reflection, refraction, scattering, diffraction, and absorption.

Reflection

When an RF signal bounces off of a smooth, nonabsorptive surface, changing the direction of the signal, it is said to *reflect* and the process is known as *reflection.* This is probably the easiest RF behavior to understand simply because we see it frequently in our daily lives. You can shine a light on a mirror at an angle and see that it reflects off that mirror. In fact, when you look in the mirror, you are experiencing the concept of electromagnetic reflection, which is the same as RF reflection.

Figure 2.8 illustrates this concept. As you can see, the light waves, which are electromagnetic waves similar to RF signals, first reflect off the object and travel toward the mirror. Next, the light waves reflect off the mirror and travel toward your eye. Finally, your eye acts as a focusing device and brings the light waves together at the back of the eye, giving you the sense of sight. However, the important thing to note is that what you are "seeing" is the light reflected off the object into the mirror and off the mirror into your eyes.

RF signals also reflect off objects that are smooth and larger than the waves that carry the signals. Earlier it was noted that the wavelength impacts the behavior of the RF wave as it propagates through space. This is the first example of the relationship of the wavelength and the space through which the wave travels. If the space were empty, there would be no reflection, but since all space we operate in (Earth and its atmosphere)

FIGURE 2.8 Illustrating reflection with a mirror

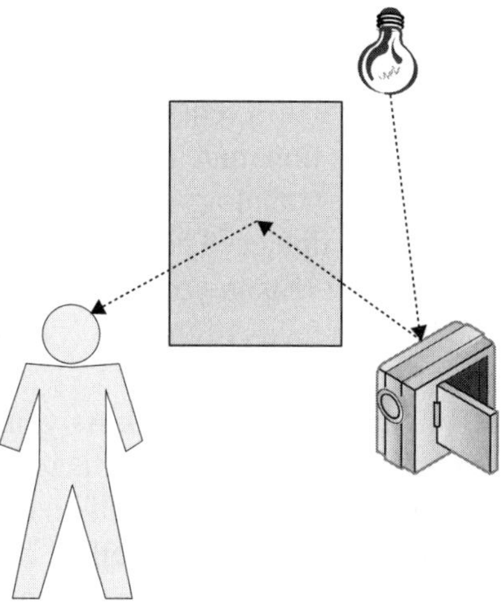

contains some elements of matter, reflection, refraction, scattering, diffraction, and absorption are expected.

Since the object that causes reflection will normally be smooth and larger than the wavelength and since waves used by IEEE 802.11–compliant radios are between 5 and 13 centimeters, it follows that the objects will be greater than 5 centimeters in size (for 5 GHz U-NII bands) or 13 centimeters in size (for the 2.4 GHz ISM band) and smooth. Such objects include metal roofs, metal or aluminum wall coverings, elevators, and other larger smooth objects. Figure 2.9 shows the traditional diagram of RF signal reflection. It is important to remember that reflected signals are usually weaker after reflection. This is because some of the RF energy is usually absorbed by the reflecting material.

FIGURE 2.9 RF signal reflection

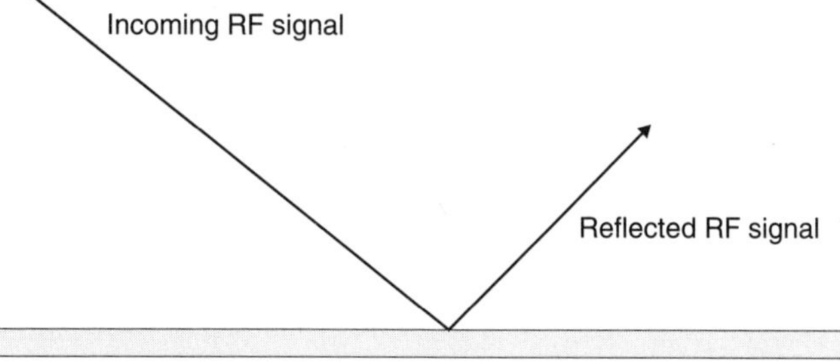

Refraction

Refraction occurs when an RF signal changes speed and is bent while moving between media of different densities. Different mediums, such as drywall, wood, or plastic, will have different *refraction indexes*. The refraction index helps in determining how much refraction will occur.

Let's go back to the light reflection analogy for a moment. If you wear glasses, you are wearing a refraction device. The lens refracts, or bends, the light to make up for the imperfect lens in your eye. This allows you to see clearly again because the lacking focus of the eye is corrected by the refraction caused on the lens of the glasses.

Figure 2.10 shows an RF signal being refracted. As you can see, when refraction occurs with RF signals, some of the signal is reflected and some is refracted as it passes through the medium. Of course, as with all mediums, some of the signal will be absorbed as well.

RF signal refraction is usually the result of a change in atmospheric conditions. For this reason, refraction is not usually an issue within a building, but it may introduce problems in wireless site-to-site links outdoors. Common causes of refraction include changes in temperature, changes in air pressure, or the existence of water vapor.

The issue here is simple: if the RF signal changes from the intended direction as it's traveling from the transmitter to the receiver, the receiver may not be able to detect and process the signal. This can result in a broken connection or in increased error rates if the refraction is temporary or sporadic due to fluctuations in the weather around the area of the link.

FIGURE 2.10 RF signal refraction

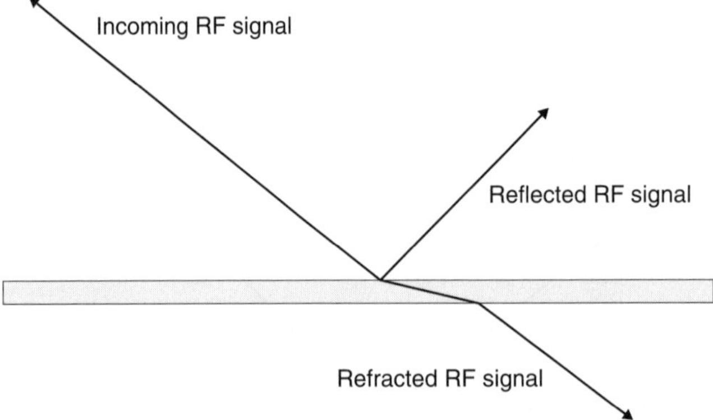

An excellent experiment can be performed easily that demonstrates the concept of refraction. Take a large clear bowl and fill it with water. Now place a large butter knife into the water at an angle and look through the clear side of the bowl at the knife. What does the knife do? Well, nothing other than enter the water; but what does it appear to do? It appears to bend. This is because the light waves are traveling slower in the water medium and this causes refraction of the light waves. It's not the knife that's bending—because it's not the knife you actually see. It's the light that's bending—because it's the light that you actually see.

Diffraction

Diffraction is defined as a change in the direction and/or intensity of a wave as it passes by the edge of an obstacle. As seen in Figure 2.11, this can cause the signal's direction to change, and it can also result in areas of RF shadow. Instead of bending as it passes into or out of an obstacle, as in the case of refraction, light is diffracted as it travels around the obstacle.

FIGURE 2.11 RF signal diffraction

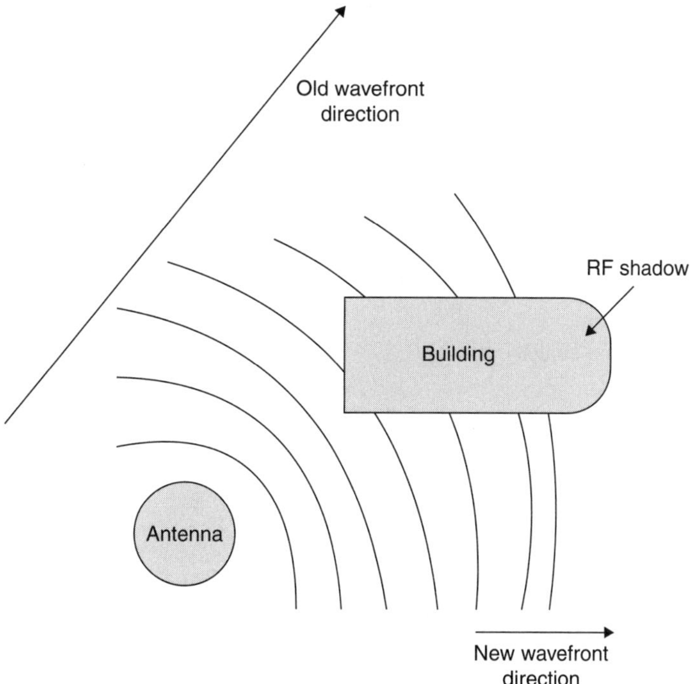

Diffraction occurs because the RF signal slows down as it encounters the obstacle and this causes the wave front to change directions. Consider the analogy of a rock dropped into a pool and the ripples it creates. Think of the ripples as analogous to RF signals. Now, imagine there is a stick being held upright in the water. When the ripples encounter the stick, they will bend around it, since they cannot pass through it. A larger stick has a greater visible impact on the ripples, and a smaller stick has a lesser impact. Diffraction is often caused by buildings, small hills, and other larger objects in the path of the propagating RF signal.

Scattering

Scattering happens when an RF signal strikes an uneven surface (a surface with inhomogeneities) causing the signal to be scattered instead of absorbed so that the resulting signals are less significant than the original signal. Another way to define scattering is to say that it is multiple reflections. Figure 2.12 illustrates this.

Scattering can happen in a minor, almost undetectable way, when an RF signal passes through a medium that contains small particles. These small particles can cause scattering. Smog is an example of such a medium. The more common and more impactful occurrence is that caused when RF signals encounter things like rocky terrain, leafy trees, or chain link fencing. Rain and dust can cause scattering as well.

Absorption

Absorption is the conversion of the RF signal energy into heat. This happens because the molecules in the medium through which the RF signal is passing cannot move fast enough to "keep up" with the RF waves.

FIGURE 2.12 RF signal scattering

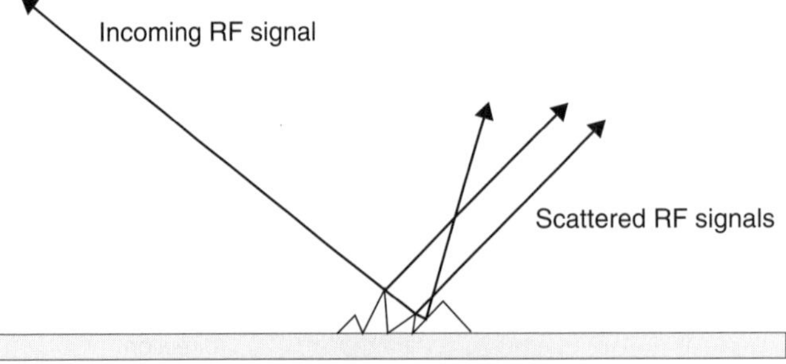

FIGURE 2.13 RF signal absorption

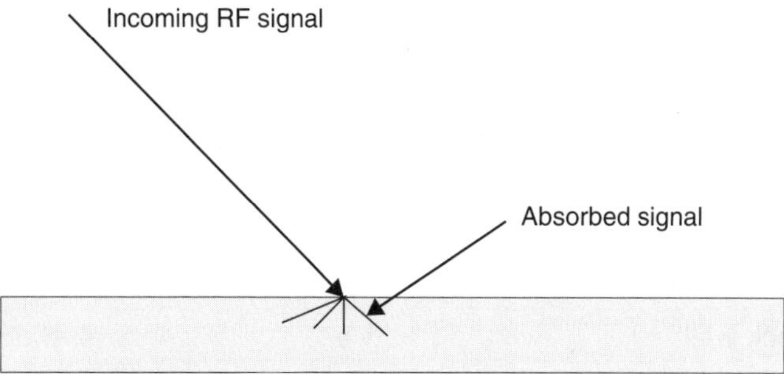

Many materials absorb RF signals in the 2.4 GHz ISM spectrum. These include water, drywall, wood, and even humans. Figure 2.13 shows RF signal absorption.

Microwave ovens use the 2.45 GHz frequency range to heat food. While your WLAN devices have output power levels from 30 milliwatts to 4 watts, microwave ovens usually have an output power between 700 and 1400 watts. What does this have to do with WLAN engineering? Well, the microwave oven works because RF waves are absorbed well by materials that have moisture (molecular electric dipoles) in them. This absorption converts the RF wave energy into heat energy and therefore heats your food.

If you've ever set up a wireless network in a large auditorium, only to notice that the coverage was less acceptable after the room was filled with hundreds or thousands of people, you've experienced the phenomenon of absorption at first hand. Before the people were in the room, most of the items were reflecting, refracting, scattering, or diffracting the RF signals. People tend to absorb the RF signals instead of reflecting them, causing a reduction in the available signal strength within the coverage area.

Different materials have different absorption rates. Table 2.1 provides a breakdown of some of the more common types of materials and the absorption rates associated with them. When performing a site survey or troubleshooting a communications problem, you should certainly consider the effects of these types of materials.

TABLE 2.1 RF Absorption Rates by Common Materials

Material	Absorption Rate
Plasterboard/drywall	3–5 dB
Glass wall and metal frame	6 dB
Metal door	6–10 dB
Window	3 dB
Concrete wall	6–15 dB
Block wall	4–6 dB

Earlier, I suggested that you cup your hands in front of your mouth to see the impact this has on sound waves, and I used this as an analogy of intentional passive gain. This total output power was not increased, but it was focused in a specific direction. Let's do another experiment. Begin reading this text aloud. As you continue to read, place your hand over your mouth so that your hand completely covers it and continue reading. If you are reading this with your hand over your mouth, you're experiencing the results of absorption in relation to sound waves. The sound disturbance has great difficulty passing through your hand, and so the sound is muffled. RF signals can be absorbed by materials in a similar manner.

VSWR

Before the RF signal is radiated through space by the antenna, it exists as an alternating current (AC) within the transmission system. Within this hardware, RF signal degradation occurs. All cables, connectors, and devices have some level of inherent loss. In a properly designed system, this loss by attenuation is unavoidable. However, the situation can be even worse if all the cables and connectors do not share the same *impedance* level.

If all cables, connectors, and devices in the chain from the RF signal generator to the antenna do not have the same impedance rating, there is said to be an impedance mismatch. For example, you would not want to use cables rated at 50 ohms with connectors rated at 75 ohms. This would cause an impedance mismatch. Maximum power output and transfer can only be achieved when the impedance of all devices is exactly the same.

TABLE 2.2 VSWR Ratings

VSWR	Definition
1.0:1	One to one. Exact match. An ideal that cannot be accomplished with current technology.
1.5:1	One point five to one. Good match. Only 4 percent loss in power.
2.0:1	Two to one. Acceptable match. Approximately 11 percent loss in power.
6.0:1	Six to one. Poor match. Approximately 50 percent loss in power.
10:1	Ten to one. Unacceptable match. Most of the power is lost.
∞:1	Infinity to one. Useless to measure, as the mismatch is so great.

Voltage standing wave ratio (VSWR) is a measurement of mismatched impedance in an RF system and is stated as an X:1 (read as "X to one") ratio. Table 2.2 provides a reference for different common VSWR ratings and their meanings.

In a VSWR rating, a lower first number means a better impedance match. Therefore, 1.5:1 is better than 2.0:1. To help with your understanding, think of a series of pipes connected to a water pump as depicted in Figure 2.14. The water pump is analogous to the RF transmitter, and the pipes are analogous to the cables and connectors leading up to the antenna.

Assuming the water pump can pump water at a rate and force equal to pipe A, pipe B will cause a mismatch in impedance because it is a smaller pipe. In other words, pipe B cannot handle the amount of water at the level of pressure that pipe A and the pump can handle. This results in a buildup of pressure in pipe A and within the pump. At this point, two things can happen: the water flowing out of the end of pipe B will be less than the original potential of the water pump or the pipe A and the water

FIGURE 2.14 VSWR analogy using a water pump and pipes

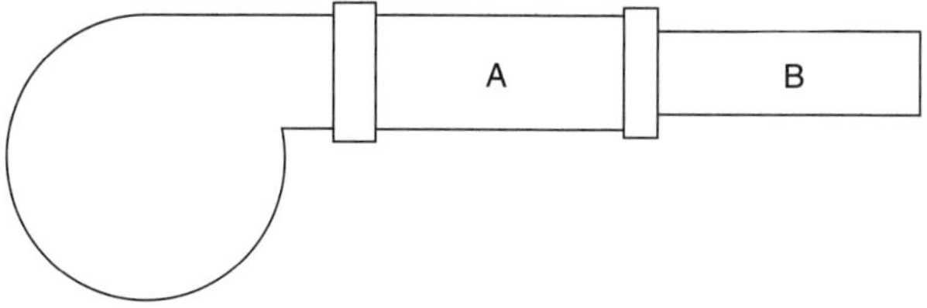

pump may be destroyed in some way. Pipe A could burst, or the seals around the connectors between the water pump and pipe A and between pipe A and pipe B could leak. The water pump itself could begin leaking internally or even overheat and malfunction. As you can see, the least impacting result would be that the water flow is less than what the pump and pip A are capable of. RF systems have similar potentials as you will see in the next section on return loss.

Return Loss

When there is VSWR greater than 1.0:1 (and there always will be), there is some level of power loss due to backward reflection of the RF signal within the system. This energy that is reflected back toward the RF generator or transmitter results in *return loss*. Return loss is a measurement, usually expressed in decibels, of the ratio between the forward current (incident wave) and the reflected current (reflected wave). The results of this return loss will be similar to those in the water pump analogy presented previously. The RF transmitter may be destroyed, as may other components in the RF system, but this would be a worst-case scenario. It is most commonly seen that the output power at the intentional radiator is less than the original potential generated by the RF transmitter.

To minimize VSWR and return loss, you must avoid impedance mismatches. This means you will want to use all equipment (RF transmitters, cables, and connectors) with the same ohm rating. This rating is usually 50 ohms when considering RF systems. If you purchase an entire RF system as a unit from a manufacturer, all the components should have the same ohm rating already. If you build an RF system from scratch, you will have to take the responsibility of ensuring there is no impedance mismatch.

When discussing VSWR, there are two extreme scenarios that create the ∞:1 value listed in Table 2.2: perfect open and perfect short. A perfect open would mean that someone forgot to connect the end of the cabling to an antenna, and a perfect short would occur if someone shorted out a perfect open with something like a paper clip (though that might hurt). In these cases most of the RF energy is reflected and the VSWR leans toward ∞:1. This, of course, should be avoided if you value your RF equipment.

Amplification

Amplification is an increase of the amplitude of an RF signal. Passive gain, as discussed earlier, is not an amplification of an RF signal up to the intentional radiator. Passive gain is a focusing or directing of an RF signal. Amplification is achieved through active gain and is accomplished with an amplifier.

Many access points contain variable power output settings, and while this capability is not technically an amplifier, these settings will impact the amplitude of the RF signal that is generated. Therefore, the changing of this setting to a higher setting results in a stronger RF signal from the access point.

Earlier in this chapter, I mentioned that two identical signals arriving at the receiving antenna in phase increases the signal's strength. These two signals would have started as one, but due to reflection, refraction, scattering, and diffraction, they have arrived at the antenna as separate signals. The received signal is stronger than the received signal would have been, had the two signals not combined.

Attenuation

Attenuation is the process of reducing an RF signal's amplitude. This is occasionally done intentionally with attenuators to reduce a signal's strength to fall within a regulatory domain's imposed constraints. Loss is the result of attenuation, and gain is the result of amplification. RF cables, connectors, and devices may have some level of imposed attenuation, and this attenuation is usually stated in decibels and is often stated as loss in decibels per foot—this is also known as insertion loss. Insertion loss is the loss incurred by simply inserting the object (cable, connector, etc.) into the path of the RF signal between the source and the intentional radiator.

Wave Propagation

The way RF waves move through an environment is known as *wave propagation*. Attenuation occurs as RF signals propagate through an environment. When the RF signal leaves the transmitting antenna, it will begin propagation through the local environment and continue on, theoretically, forever. The signal cannot be detected after a certain distance, and this becomes the usable range of the signal. Since the signal could theoretically propagate forever, why is there a point at which it can no longer be detected? This is because attenuation occurs as the signal propagates through the environment. Some of the signal strength is lost through absorption by materials encountered by the RF signal; however, even without any materials in the path of the signal, the amplitude will be lessened. This is due to a phenomenon known as free space path loss.

Free Space Path Loss

Free space path loss, sometimes called free space loss (FSL) or just path loss, is a weakening of the RF signal due to a broadening of the wave front. This broadening of the wave front is known as signal dispersion. Consider the concentric circles in Figure 2.15 as representing an RF signal propagating out from an omnidirectional antenna. Notice how the wave front becomes larger as the wave moves out from the antenna. This broadening of the wave front causes a loss in amplitude of the signal at a specified point in space.

In other words, if you place a receiving antenna at point B in Figure 2.15, you will detect a weaker signal than if you place a receiving antenna at point A. This broadening of the wave is also called beam divergence. Beam divergence can be calculated by subtracting the beam diameter (D_1) at a greater distance from the beam diameter (D_2) closer to the antenna and then dividing by the distance between these two points (L). The following formula illustrates this:

$$\text{Divergence} = (D_1 - D_2)/L$$

Free space path loss can be understood by thinking of the results you get when blowing bubbles with bubble gum. Either imagine you are blowing a bubble or actually do it. Either way, you will notice that

FIGURE 2.15 Free space path loss demonstrated

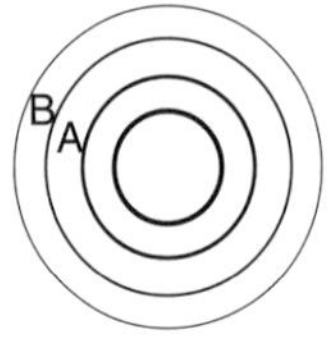

the outer shell that forms the bubble boundary becomes thinner as the bubble grows larger. Similarly, RF signals grow weaker as the cell grows larger or the distance becomes greater. The reduction in signal strength is logarithmic rather than linear. For example, a 2.4 GHz signal, such as that used by many IEEE devices, will attenuate by approximately 80 dB in the first 100 meters and then by another 6 dB in the second 100 meters. As you can see, the attenuation becomes much less in the second 100 meters than in the first, and this is due to logarithmic attenuation.

The following formulas are used to calculate free space path loss in dB:

$$LP = 36.6 + (20 \times \log_{10}(F)) + (20 \times \log_{10}(D))$$

where *LP* is the free space path loss, *F* is the frequency in MHz, and *D* is the path length in miles. The result is based on a distance measurement in miles. To get the results based on a distance measurement in kilometers (for example, *D* is the path length in kilometers), change 36.6 to 32.4, giving you the following formula:

$$LP = 32.4 + (20 \times \log_{10}(F)) + (20 \times \log_{10}(D))$$

For example, assuming you are using the 2.4 GHz ISM spectrum (we'll say 2450 MHz), and the distance you want to evaluate is 2.5 miles, the following equation will result in the free space path loss:

$$36.6 + (20 \times \log_{10}(2450)) + (20 \times \log_{10}(2.5))$$

or

$$36.6 + 67.78 + 8 = 112.38$$

The result is a loss of roughly 112 dB at 2.5 miles. I rounded the numbers in this case. More accurate numbers can be found in Table 2.3, which provides a breakdown of free space path loss attenuation in dB for different distances with both the 2.4 GHz spectrum and the 5 GHz spectrum. The next major section in this chapter, "Basic RF Math," will give you the knowledge you need to calculate an estimate of signal strength in dB after the signal travels this 2.5 miles through free space. There is an element not considered in the free space path loss calculations that will be added at that time: output power. When you know the free space path loss calculation formula and you know the output power, you can estimate the signal power, in dBm, at any point in space. This will be an ideal estimate because weather and other factors can worsen the signal strength in reality.

TABLE 2.3 Free Space Path Loss in dB for 2.4 and 5 GHz Spectrums

Distance (miles)	2.4 GHz	5 GHz
0.5	98.36	104.56
5	104.38	110.58
1.5	107.91	114.10
2	110.40	116.60
2.5	112.34	118.54
3	113.93	120.12
4	116.42	122.62
5	118.36	124.56
10	124.38	130.58

Another method that is simpler to use is the *6 dB rule.* This is an estimation method that is less accurate than the free space path loss formula we've covered, but it provides a quick calculation that is very close to the results that would be provided by the formula. If you look at the 2.4 GHz column in Table 2.3, you will see a pattern that may not stand out at first. Paying close attention to the 1, 2, and 4 mile distances, you can see that there is an increase in dB loss of approximately 6 dB at each of these intervals. You'll also notice that each of these intervals represents a doubling of the distance. Therein lies the 6 dB rule: for every doubling of distance, there is an amplitude loss of approximately 6 dB. Even in the 5 GHz column, you can see that this is true. Though the 5 GHz frequencies attenuate more quickly in the first mile, they follow the 6 dB rule thereafter.

While the general understanding of free space path loss is usually stated as seen here, it is equally valid to consider a different perspective. This alternate perspective states that the RF signal still travels the farther distance, but that the higher frequencies have shorter wavelengths and therefore shorter optimum antenna sizes. The result is that the smaller antenna has a greater difficulty gathering–sufficient RF energy because of its smaller receiving surface. Think of it like the small receiving surface of the human ear compared to the listening devices used on American football sidelines mentioned earlier. In other words, the argument is that the RF signal may not be attenuating any "faster" but that it attenuated the same and the receiver is the actual locus of the problem rather than the attenuated signal strength.

Multipath and Delay Spread

When signals bounce around in an environment through reflection, refraction, diffraction, and scattering, they create an effect known as multipath. *Multipath* occurs when multiple paths of the signal, understood as multiple signals, arrive at the receiving antenna at the same time or within a small fraction of a second (nanoseconds) of each other. Multipath can also occur outdoors when signals reflect off of large objects in the RF link path, as is shown in Figure 2.16.

Multipath occurs very frequently indoors and is so common an occurrence that many access point vendors include multiple antennas for dealing with this phenomenon. Figure 2.16 suggests the potential for multipath indoors. As you can see, file cabinets, walls, desks, and doors—among other things—can cause RF propagation patterns that result in multiple paths arriving at the receiving antenna. In an indoor environment, there is often no direct signal path between the transmitter and the receiver (or the access point and the client station). This means that all signals reaching the client station will have arrived via the RF propagation patterns similar to those in Figure 2.16. Therefore, multipath can become an issue.

The difference in time between the first and second signals arriving at the receiver in a multipath occurrence is known as the *delay spread.* Earlier in this chapter, you learned that signals can be in phase or out of phase. These signals arriving at the receiver with a delay spread of nearly 0 will complement each other and cause signal upfade. In other

FIGURE 2.16 Outdoor multipath

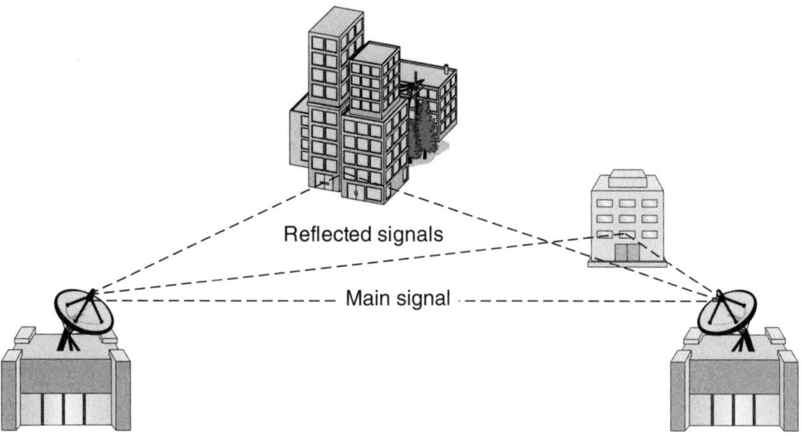

words, the received signal will be stronger at the receiver than it would have been without the multipath occurrence. When the delay spread is greater, so that the signals arrive out of phase, the signal will either be downfaded, corrupted, or nullified. This will be discussed more in Chapter 12.

Basic RF Math

You might be wondering why you have to learn math to implement a network. After all, you've been able to implement wired networks for years with very little math other than counting the number of Ethernet ports needed for your users. Wireless is different. Because the wireless network uses an RF signal, you must understand the basics of RF math in order to determine if the output power of an RF transmitter is strong enough to get a detectable and usable signal to the RF receiver. You had to deal with similar issues with cabling in that you could only use a CAT 5 cable of a particular maximum length, but you didn't really have to calculate anything most of the time. You simply knew you could not span a greater distance than that which was supported by the cabling type.

In order to understand and perform RF math, there are a few basic things you will need to know. First, you'll need to understand the units of power that are measured in RF systems. Second, you'll need to understand how to measure power gains and losses. Third, and finally, you'll need to understand how to determine the output power you will need at a transmitter in order to get an acceptable signal to a receiver. This is true if you are creating a point-to-point connection using wireless bridges or if you are installing an access point in an access role. In both cases, a sufficient signal must reach the receiver listening on the other end of the connection.

Watt

The *watt* (W) is a basic unit of power equal to one joule per second. It is named after James Watt, an eighteenth-century Scottish inventor who also improved the steam engine, among other endeavors. This single watt is equal to one ampere of current flowing at one volt. Think of a water hose with a spray nozzle attached. You can adjust the spray nozzle to allow for different rates of flow. This flow rate is like the amperes in an electrical system. Now, the water hose also has a certain level of water pressure—regardless of the amount that is actually being allowed to flow through the nozzle. This pressure is like the voltage in an electrical system. If you apply more pressure or you allow more flow with the same pressure, either way, you will end up with more water flowing out of the nozzle. In the same way, increased voltages or increased amperes will result in increased wattage, since the watt is the combination of the amperes and volts.

Milliwatt

WLANs do not need a tremendous amount of power to transmit a signal over an acceptable distance. For example, you can see a 7-watt light bulb from more than 50 miles (83 kilometers) away on a clear night with line of sight. Remember, visible light is another portion of the same electromagnetic spectrum, and so this gives you an idea of just how far an electromagnetic signal can be detected. This is why many WLAN devices use a measurement of power that is 1/1000 of a watt. This unit of power is known as a *milliwatt*. 1 W, then, would be 1000 milliwatts (mW).

Enterprise-class devices will often have output power levels of 1–100 mW, while SOHO wireless devices may only offer up to 30 mW of output power. Some wireless devices may support up to 300 mW of output power, but these are the exception to the rule. Ubiquiti Networks develops some devices, such as their 300 mW CardBus wireless adapter and the 600 mW AP-ONE wireless hotspot solution, which is basically an access point with hotspot features and functionality.

For indoor use, it is generally recommended that you transmit at power levels of no more than 100 mW. In most cases, the minimum gain that will be provided by any connected antennas is a 2 dBi gain, which you will read about later. This means that the output power would actually be approximately 160 mW in the propagation direction of this antenna. This usually provides sufficient coverage for indoor WLANs. However, outdoor WLANs may use more power if they are providing site-to-site links or are providing coverage to a large outdoor area as either a public or private hotspot. The FCC limits the total output power from the antenna to 4 W for point-to-multipoint applications in the 2.4 GHz ISM band, and this must be considered when implementing WLAN solutions.

Decibel (dB)

The *decibel* is a comparative measurement value. In other words, it is a measurement of the difference between two power levels. For example, it is common to say that a certain power level is 6 dB stronger than another power level or that it is 3 dB weaker. These statements mean that there has been 6 dB of gain and 3 dB of loss, respectively.

Because a wireless receiver can detect and process very weak signals, it is easier to refer to the received signal strength in dBm rather than in mW. For example, a signal that is transmitted at 4 W of output power (4000 mW or 36 dBm) and experiences –63 dB of loss has a signal strength of 0.002 mW (–27 dBm). Rather than saying that the signal strength is 0.002 mW, we say that the signal strength is –27 dBm.

A decibel is 1/10 of a *bel.* You could equally say that a bel is 10 decibels. The point is that the decibel is based on the bel, which was developed by Bell Laboratories in order to calculate the power losses in telephone communications as ratios. In other words, 1 bel is a ratio of 10:1 between two power levels. Therefore, a power ratio of 200:20 is 1 bel (10:1) and 200:40 is .5 bels (5:1) and 200:10 is 2 bels (20:1). In the end, the decibel is a measurement of power that is used very frequently in RF mathematics.

You may have been asked the same question that I was asked as a child: Would you rather have $1,000,000 at the end of a month or one cent doubled in value every day for a month? Of course, the latter option is worth more than $5,000,000 by the end of the month. This is the power of exponential growth. RF signals experience exponential decay rather than growth as they travel through space. This is also called *logarithmic decay.* The result is a quickly weakening signal. This power loss is measured with decibels.

The decibel is relative where the milliwatt is absolute. The decibel is logarithmic where the milliwatt is linear. To understand this, you'll need to understand the basics of a logarithm or you'll at least need a good tool to calculate logarithms for you, such as a spreadsheet like Microsoft Excel.

A logarithm is the exponent to which the base number must be raised to reach some given value. The most common base number evaluated is the number 10, and you will often see this referenced in formulas as *log10.* For example, the logarithm or log of 100 is 2 with a base of 10. This would be written

$$\log_{10}(100) = 2$$

This is a fancy way of saying $10^2 = 100$, which is a shorthand way of saying $10 \times 10 = 100$. However, knowing the logarithm concept is very important in many RF-based math calculations, though you will not be tested on the complex formulas on the CWNA exam. You will, however, need to be able to calculate simple power level problems. So how will you deal with these problems? Using the rules of 10s and 3s. This system will usually allow you to calculate RF signal power levels without ever having to resort to logarithmic math. Here are the basic rules:

1. A gain of 3 dB magnifies the output power by two.
2. A loss of 3 dB equals one half of the output power.
3. A gain of 10 dB magnifies the output power by 10.
4. A loss of 10 dB equals one-tenth of the output power.
5. dB gains and losses are cumulative.

Now, let's evaluate what these five rules mean and the impact they have on your RF math calculations. First, 3 dB of gain doubles the output power. This means that 100 mW plus 3 dB of gain equals 200 mW of power or 30 mW plus 3 dB of gain equals 60 mW of power. The power level is always doubled for each 3 dB of gain that is added. Rule 5 states that these gains and losses are cumulative. This means that 6 dB of gain is the same as 3 dB of gain applied twice. Therefore, 100 mW of power plus 6 dB of gain equals 400 mW of power. The following examples illustrate this:

$$40 \text{ mW} + 3 \text{ dB} + 3 \text{ dB} + 3 \text{ dB} = 320 \text{ mW}$$

$$40 \text{ mW} \times 2 \times 2 \times 2 = 320 \text{ mW}$$

Both of these formulas are saying the same thing. Now consider the impact of 3 dB of loss. This halves the output power. Look at the impact on the following formula:

$$40 \text{ mW} + 3 \text{ dB} + 3 \text{ dB} - 3 \text{ dB} = 80 \text{ mW}$$

$$40 \text{ mW} \times 2 \times 2/2 = 80 \text{ mW}$$

Again, both of these formulas are saying the same thing. You can see, from this last example, how the accumulation of gains and losses are calculated. Now, rules 3 and 4 say that a gain or loss of 10 results in a gain of 10 times or a loss of 10 times. Consider the following example, which illustrates rules 3, 4, and 5:

$$40 \text{ mW} + 10 \text{ dB} + 10 \text{ dB} = 4000 \text{ mW}$$

$$40 \text{ mW} \times 10 \times 10 = 4000 \text{ mW}$$

As you can see, adding 10 dB of gain twice causes a 40 mW signal to become a 4000 mW signal, which could also be stated as a 4 W signal.

Losses would be subtracted in the same way as the 3 dB losses were; however, instead of dividing by 2 we would now divide by 10 such as in the following example:

$$40 \text{ mW} - 10 \text{ dB} = 4 \text{ mW}$$

$$40 \text{ mW}/10 = 4 \text{ mW}$$

You should be beginning to understand the five rules of 10s and 3s. However, it is also important to know that the 10s and 3s can be used together to calculate the power levels after any integer gain or loss of dB. This is done with creative combinations of 10s and 3s. For example, imagine you want to know what the power level of a 12 mW signal with 16 dB of gain would be. Here is the math:

$$12 \text{ mW} + 16 \text{ dB} = 480 \text{ mW}$$

But how did I calculate this? The answer is very simple: I added 10 dB and then I added 3 dB twice. Here it is in longhand:

$$12 \text{ mW} + 10 \text{ dB} + 3 \text{ dB} + 3 \text{ dB} = 480 \text{ mW}$$

$$12 \text{ mW} \times 10 \times 2 \times 2 = 480 \text{ mW}$$

Sometimes you are dealing with both gains and losses of unusual amounts. While the following numbers are completely fabricated, consider the assumed difficulty they present to calculating a final RF signal power level:

$$30 \text{ mW} + 7 \text{ dB} - 5 \text{ dB} + 12 \text{ dB} - 6 \text{ dB} = \text{power level}$$

At first glance, this sequence of numbers may seem impossible to calculate with the rules of 10s and 3s; however, remember that the dB gains and losses are cumulative, and this includes both the positive gains and the negative losses. Let's take the first two gains and losses: 7 dB of gain and 5 dB of loss. You could write the first part of the previous formula like this:

$$30 \text{ mW} + 7 \text{ dB} + (-5 \text{ dB}) = 30 \text{ mW} + 2 \text{ dB}$$

Why is this? Because +7 plus –5 equals +2. Carrying this out for the rest of our formula, we could say the following:

$$30 \text{ mW} + 7 \text{ dB} + (-5 \text{ dB}) + 12 \text{ dB} + (-6 \text{ dB}) = 30 \text{ mW} + 2 \text{ dB} + 6 \text{ dB}$$

or

$$30 \text{ mW} + 8 \text{ dB} = \text{power level}$$

The only question that is left is this: How do we calculate a gain of 8 dB? Well, remember the rules of 10s and 3s. We have to find a combination of positive and negative 10s and 3s that add up to 8 dB. Here's a possibility:

$$+10 + 10 - 3 - 3 - 3 - 3 = 8$$

If we use these numbers to perform RF dB-based math, we come up with the following formula:

$$30 \text{ mW} + 10 \text{ dB} + 10 \text{ dB} - 3 \text{ dB} - 3 \text{ dB} - 3 \text{ dB} - 3 \text{ dB} = 187.5 \text{ mW}$$

$$30 \text{ mW} \times 10 \times 10/2/2/2/2 = 187.5 \text{ mW}$$

To help you visualize the math, consider the following step-by-step breakdown:

$$30 \text{ mW} \times 10 = 300 \text{ mW}$$

$$300 \text{ mW} \times 10 = 3000 \text{ mW}$$

$$3000 \text{ mW}/2 = 1500 \text{ mW}$$

$$1500 \text{ mW}/2 = 750 \text{ mW}$$

$$750 \text{ mW}/2 = 375 \text{ mW}$$

$$375 \text{ mW}/2 = 187.5 \text{ mW}$$

In the end, nearly any integer dB-based power gain or loss sequence can be estimated using the rule of 10s and 3s. Table 2.4 provides a breakdown of dB gains from 1 to 10 with the expressions as 10s and 3s for your reference. From this table, you should be able to determine the

TABLE 2.4 Expressions of 10s and 3s

Gain in dB	Expression in 10s and 3s
1	+ 10 – 3 – 3 – 3
2	+ 3 + 3 + 3 + 3 – 10
3	+ 3
4	+ 10 – 3 – 3
5	+ 3 + 3 + 3 + 3 + 3 – 10
6	+ 3 + 3
7	+ 10 – 3
8	+ 10 + 10 – 3 – 3 – 3 – 3
9	+ 3 + 3 + 3
10	+ 10

combinations of 10s and 3s you would need to calculate the power gain or loss from any provided dB value. *Always remember that, while plus 10 is actually times 10, plus 3 is only times 2.* The same is true in reverse in that *minus 10 is actually divided by 10 and minus 3 is divided by 2.*

dBm

The abbreviation *dBm* represents an absolute measurement of power where the *m* stands for *milliwatts.* Effectively, dBm references decibels relative to 1 milliwatt such that 0 dBm equals 1 milliwatt. Once you establish that 0 dBm equals 1 milliwatt, you can reference any power strength in dBm. The formula to get dBm from milliwatts is

$$\text{dBm} = 10 \times \log 10(\text{Power}_{\text{mW}})$$

For example, if the known milliwatt power is 30 mW, the following formula would be accurate:

$$10 \times \log 10(30) = 14.77 \text{ dBm}$$

This result would often be rounded to 15 dBm for simplicity; however, you must be very cautious about rounding if you are calculating a link budget because your end numbers can be drastically incorrect if you've done a lot of rounding along the way. Table 2.5 provides a list of common milliwatt power levels and their dBm values.

TABLE 2.5 mW to dBM Conversion Table (Rounded to Two Precision Levels)

mW	dBm
1	0.00
10	10.00
20	13.01
30	14.77
40	16.02
50	16.99
100	20.00
1000	30.00
4000	36.02

One of the benefits of working with dBm values instead of milliwatts is the ability to easily add and subtract simple decibels instead of multiplying and dividing often huge and tiny numbers. For example, consider that 14.77 dBm is 30 mW as you can see in Table 2.5. Now, assume that you have a transmitter that transmits at that 14.77 dBm and you are passing its signal through an amplifier that adds 6 dB of gain. You can quickly calculate that the 14.77 dBm of original output power becomes 20.77 dBm of power after passing through the amplifier. Now, remember that 14.77 dBm was 30 mW. With the 10s and 3s of RF math, which you learned about earlier, you can calculate that 30 mW plus 6 dB is equal to 120 mW. The interesting thing to note is that 20.77 dBm is equal to 119.4 mW. As you can see, the numbers are very close indeed. While I've been using a lot of more exact figures in this section, you'll find that rounded values are often used in vendor literature and documentation. Figure 2.17 shows a set of power level charts that can be used for simple mW to dBm and dBm to mW conversion.

FIGURE 2.17 dBm to mW conversion

dBm	Watts	dBm	Watts	dBm	Watts
0	1.0 mW	16	40 mW	32	1.6 W
1	1.3 mW	17	50 mW	33	2.0 W
2	1.6 mW	18	63 mW	34	2.5 W
3	2.0 mW	19	79 mW	35	3 W
4	2.5 mW	20	100 mW	36	4 W
5	3.2 mW	21	126 mW	37	5 W
6	4 mW	22	158 mW	38	6 W
7	5 mW	23	200 mW	39	8 W
8	6 mW	24	250 mW	40	10 W
9	8 mW	25	316 mW	41	13 W
10	10 mW	26	398 mW	42	16 W
11	13 mW	27	500 mW	43	20 W
12	16 mW	28	630 mW	44	25 W
13	20 mW	29	800 mW	45	32 W
14	25 mW	30	1.0 W	46	40 W
15	32 mW	31	1.3 W	47	50 W

dBi

The abbreviation *dBi* (the *i* stands for isotropic) represents a measurement of power gain used for RF antennas. It is a comparison of the gain of the antenna and the output of a theoretical isotropic radiator. An *isotropic radiator* is an ideal antenna that we cannot create with any known technology. This is an antenna that radiates power equally in all directions. In order to do this, the power source would have to be at the center of the radiating element and be infinitesimally small. Since this technology does not exist, we call the isotropic radiator the ideal against which other antennas are measured. I'll provide more details about dBi in the later section titled "Isotropic Radiator." For now, just remember that dBi is a measurement of directional gain in power and is not a power reference. In other words, the dBi value must be calculated against the input power provided to the antenna to determine the actual output power in the direction in which the antenna propagates RF signals.

dBd

Antenna manufacturers use both dBi, mentioned previously, and *dBd* to calculate the directional gain of antennas. Where dBi is a calculation of directional gain compared to an isotropic radiator, dBd is a calculation of directional gain compared to a dipole antenna. Therefore, the last *d* in dBd stands for *dipole*. Like dBi, dBd is a value calculated against the input power to determine the directional output power of the antenna.

What is the difference between dBi and dBd, then? The difference is that a dBd value is compared with a dipole antenna, which itself has a gain of 2.14 over an isotropic radiator. Therefore, an antenna with a gain of 7 dBd has a gain of 9.14 dBi. In other words, to convert from dBd to dBi, just add 2.14. To convert from dBi to dBd, just subtract 2.14. To remember this, just remember the formula 0 dBd = 2.14 dBi.

SNR

Background RF noise, which can be caused by all the various systems and natural phenomena that generate energy in the electromagnetic spectrum, is known as the *noise floor*. The power level of the RF signal relative to the power level of the noise floor is known as the *signal-to-noise ratio* or *SNR*.

Think of it like this: Imagine you are in a large conference room. Further, imagine that there are hundreds of people having conversations at normal conversation sound levels. Now, imagine that you want to say something so that everyone will hear you; therefore, you cup your hands around your mouth and yell loudly. You could say that the conversations of everyone else in the conference room constitute a noise floor and that your yelling is the important signal or information. Furthermore, you could say that the loudness of your yelling relative to the loudness of all other discussions is the SNR for your communication.

In WLAN networks, the SNR becomes a very important measurement. If the noise floor power levels are too close to the received signal strength, the signal may be corrupted or may not even be detected. It's almost as if the received signal strength is weaker than it actually is when there is more electromagnetic noise in the environment. You may have noticed that when you yell in a room full of people yelling, your volume doesn't seem so great; however, if you yell in a room full of people whispering, your volume seems to be magnified. In fact, your volume is not greater, but the noise floor is less. RF signals are impacted in a similar way.

RSSI

The *received signal strength indicator (RSSI)* is an arbitrary measurement of received signal strength defined in the IEEE 802.11 standards. There is no absolute rule as to how this signal strength rating must be implemented in order to comply with the IEEE standard other than that it is optional (though I've not encountered a vendor that has not implemented it in client devices), that it should report the rating to the device's driver, and that it should use one byte for the rating, providing a potential range of 0–255.

In reality, no vendors have chosen to use the entire range. For example, Cisco uses a range of 0–100 (101 total values) in their devices, and most Atheros-based chipsets use a range of 0–60 (61 total values). The IEEE does specify an RSSI_MAX parameter, which would be 100 for Cisco and 60 for Atheros. This allows software applications to determine the range implemented by the vendors and then convert the rating value into a percentage. It would not be very beneficial if the client software reported the actual rating to the user. This is because the different ranges used by the different vendors would result in unusual matches. By this I mean that an RSSI rating of 75 in a Cisco client is the same relative rating as an RSSI rating of 45 in an Atheros chipset (assuming they are using similar linear stepping algorithms internally). Therefore, most applications use percentages.

For example, if an Atheros-based client card reported an RSSI of 47, the software application could process the following formula to determine the signal strength in percentage:

$$47/60 \times 100 = 78.3\% \text{ signal strength}$$

How does the software know to use the maximum value of 60? From the RSSI_MAX parameter that is required by the IEEE standard. Symbol, a WLAN hardware manufacturer, for example, uses an RSSI_MAX of 31. This means there is a total of 32 potential values, with 31 of the values actually representing some level of usable signal strength. Most vendors have chosen to use an RSSI of 0 to represent a signal strength less than the receive sensitivity of the device and, therefore, a signal strength that is not usable. In the end, an RSSI of 16 with a Symbol client would be 50 percent signal strength. An RSSI of 50 with a Cisco client would be 50 percent signal strength and an RSSI of 30 with an Atheros client would be 50 percent signal strength. This is why most client software packages report the signal strength in percentage instead of RSSI.

Now, let's make this even more complex. Earlier I said that a Cisco rating of 75 is the same as an Atheros rating of 45, assuming the use of the same linear stepping algorithm. By linear stepping algorithm, I'm talking about the connection between dBm and RSSI rating. For example, one might assume that a dBm of –12 gets an RSSI rating of 100 for Cisco and that a dBm of –12 gets an RSSI rating of 60 for Atheros. In other words, it would make sense to assume that the RSSI_MAX parameter is equal to the same actual dBm signal strength with all vendors; however, since the IEEE leaves it up to the vendors to determine the details of RSSI implementation (mostly because it is an optional parameter anyway), the different vendors often use different dBm signal strengths for their RSSI_MAX parameter. What is the result of this complexity? You may show a 100 percent signal strength for one client device and show a lesser signal strength for another client device from the exact same location. Your assumption may be that the client device with the lesser signal strength is actually providing inferior performance when in fact they are identical.

How can this be? Consider a situation where two vendors use an RSSI_MAX value of 100. However, one vendor (vendor A) equates the RSSI rating of 100 to –12 dBm and the other vendor (vendor B) equates the RSSI rating of 100 to –15 dBm. Now assume that both vendors use a linear stepping scale for their ratings where a decrease in dBm of .7 causes the RSSI rating to drop by 1. This means that, at –15 dBm, vendor B will report 100 percent signal strength, but vendor A will have dropped the RSSI rating 4 times to a value of 96 and report a 96 percent signal strength. You can see how one might assume that vendor B's client is performing better because it has a higher percentage signal strength when, in fact, the two clients simply use a different implementation of the RSSI feature.

Due to these incompatibility issues, RSSI values should only be compared with the values from other computers using the same vendor's devices.

The RSSI rating is also arbitrarily used to determine when to reassociate (roam) and when to transmit. In other words, vendors will decide what the lowest RSSI rating should be before attempting to reassociate to a basic service set (BSS) with a stronger beacon signal. Additionally, vendors must determine when to transmit. To do this, they must determine a clear channel threshold. This is an RSSI value at which it can be assumed that there is no arriving signal and therefore the device may transmit.

Link Budget and System Operating Margin (SOM)

The term *budget* can be defined as a plan for controlling a resource. In a wireless network, the resource is RF energy and you must ensure that you have enough of it to meet your communication needs. This is done by calculating a *link budget* that results in a *system operating margin (SOM)*. Link budget is an accounting of all components of power, gain, loss, receiver sensitivity, and fade margin. This includes the cables and connectors leading up the antenna, as well as the antennas themselves. It also includes the factor of free space path loss. In other words, the many concepts we've been talking about so far in this chapter are about to come together in a way that will help you make effective decisions when building wireless links. You will take the knowledge you've gained of RF propagation and free space path loss and the information related to RF math and use that to perform link budget calculations that result in a SOM.

When creating a financial budget, money management coaches often suggest to their clients that they should monitor how they are currently spending their money. Then they suggest that these individuals create a budget that documents this spending of money. The alternative would be to go ahead and create a financial budget without any consideration for what your expenses actually are. I'm sure you can see that the latter simply will not work. First, you have to know how much money you need to live, and then you design your budget around that knowledge.

Similarly, in WLAN links, you will need to first determine the signal strength that is required at the receiving device and then figure out how you will accomplish this with your link budget. The first calculation you should perform in your link budget is to determine the minimum signal strength needed at the receiver, and this is called the *receive sensitivity.* The receive sensitivity is not a single dBm rating; it is a series of dBm ratings required to communicate at varying data rates. For example, Table 2.6 shows the receive sensitivity scale for a Cisco Aironet 802.11a/b/g CardBus adapter.

There are actually two ways to think of the receive sensitivity: the absolute weakest signal the wireless radio can reliably receive and the weakest signal the wireless radio can reliably receive at a specific data rate. The lowest number in dBm, which is –94 dBm in Table 2.6, is the weakest signal the radio can tolerate. This number is sometimes referenced as the receive sensitivity or the *absolute receive sensitivity.* In more accurate terminology, the receive sensitivity of a card is the complete series or system of sensitivity levels supported by the card.

The receive sensitivity ratings are determined by the vendors. They will place the radio in a specially constructed shielded room and transmit RF signals of decreasing strength. As the RF signal strength decreases, the bit error rate in the receiving radio increases. Once this bit error rate

TABLE 2.6 Cisco Aironet 802.11 a/b/g CardBus Adapter

dBm Power Level	Data Rate
–94 dBm	1 Mbps
–93 dBm	2 Mbps
–92 dBm	5.5 Mbps
–86 dBm	6 Mbps
–86 dBm	9 Mbps
–90 dBm	11 Mbps
–86 dBm	12 Mbps
–86 dBm	18 Mbps
–84 dBm	24 Mbps
–80 dBm	36 Mbps
–75 dBm	48 Mbps
–71 dBm	54 Mbps

reaches a vendor-defined rate, the power level in dBm is noted and the radio is configured to switch down to the next standard data rate. This process continues until the lowest standard data rate for that 802.11-based device (1 or 6 Mbps) can no longer be achieved and this dBm becomes the lowest receive sensitivity rating. In the end, a lower receive sensitivity rating is better because it indicates that the client device can process a weaker signal.

The reason you need to know the receive sensitivity rating is that it is the first of your link budget calculations. The SOM is the amount of received signal strength relative to the client device's receive sensitivity. In other words, if you have a client device with a receive sensitivity of –94 dBm and the card is picking up the wireless signal at –65 dBm, the SOM is the difference between –94 and –65 dBm. Therefore, you would use the following formula to calculate the link budget:

$$\text{SOM} = RS - S$$

where S is the signal strength (the second link budget calculation used to determine the SOM) at the wireless client device and RS is the receive sensitivity of the client device. Plugging in our numbers looks like this:

$$\text{SOM} = (-94) - (-65)$$

The resulting SOM is 29 dBm. This means that the signal strength can be weakened by 29 dBm, in theory, and the link can be maintained. There are many factors at play when RF signals are being transmitted, but this number, 29 dBm, will act as a good estimate. You may be able to maintain the link with a loss of 32 dBm, and you may lose the link with a loss of 25 dBm. The link budget is a good estimate but should not be taken as a guarantee for connectivity.

It is rare to calculate the link budget or SOM for indoor connections. This is because most indoor connections are not direct line-of-sight type connections, but instead they reflect and scatter all throughout the indoor environment. In fact, someone can move a filing cabinet and cause your signal strength to change. It can really be that fickle.

Outdoor links are the most common type of links where you will need to create a link budget and determine the SOM. A detailed link budget can be much more complex than what has been discussed here. For example, it may include consideration for Earth bulge, the type of terrain, and the local weather patterns. For this reason, some vendors provide link budget calculation utilities.

FIGURE 2.18 Link budget calculation

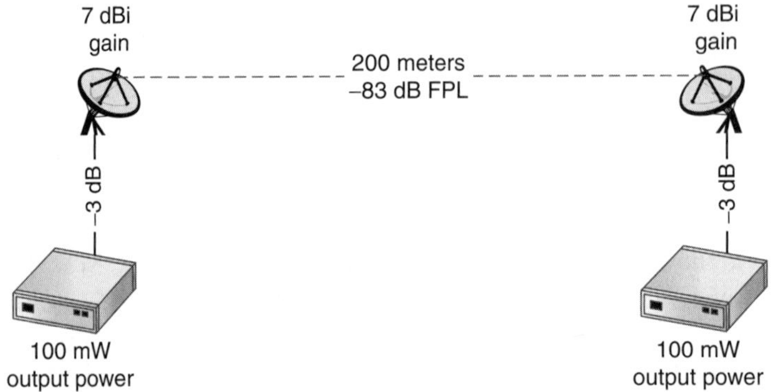

Let's consider an actual example of a link budget calculation. Figure 2.18 shows a site-to-site link being created across a distance of 200 meters with IEEE 802.11 bridges. Based on the output power of the bridge, the attenuation of the cables, the gain of the antennas, and the free space path loss, we can calculate the link budget, since the receive sensitivity of both bridges is –94 dBm. The calculations are as follows:

Link budget calculation 1: 100 mW = 20 dBm

Link budget calculation 2: 20 dBm – 3 dB + 7 dBi – 83 dB = –59 dBm

Link budget calculation 3: (–94 dBm) – (–59 dBm) = 35 dBm

SOM = 35 dBm

Fade Margin

Because of the variableness of wireless links, it is not uncommon to "pad the budget" much as a project manager may do for "risk factors" in a project. This padding of the budget is needed because the weather does change and trees grow and buildings are built. These factors, and others, can cause the signal to degrade over time. By including a few extra dB of strength in the required link budget, you can provide a link that will endure longer. This extra signal strength actually has a name, and it is *fade margin.* You do not add to the link budget/SOM dBm value, but instead you take away from the receive sensitivity. For example, you may decide to work off of an absolute receive sensitivity of –80 dBm instead of the –94 dBm supported by the Cisco Aironet card mentioned earlier. This would provide a fade margin of 14 dBm. It would also change our calculations, based on Figure 2.18, to a SOM of 21 dBm.

Intentional Radiator

The *intentional radiator*, in a WLAN transmission system, is the point at which the antenna is connected. The signal originates at a transmitter and may pass through connectors, amplifiers, attenuators, and cables before reaching the antenna. These components amplify or attenuate the signal, resulting in the output power at the intentional radiator before entering the antenna. The FCC sets the rules regarding the power that can be delivered to the antenna and radiated by the antenna. These are two different allowances. The first is for the intentional radiator, and the second is for the antenna element. For example, the FCC allows 1 watt of output power from the intentional radiator and 4 watts of antenna output power in a point-to-multipoint link in the 2.4 GHz ISM band. To understand this, you'll need to understand something called EIRP.

Equivalent Isotropically Radiated Power (EIRP)

The *equivalent isotropically radiated power (EIRP)* is the hypothetical power that is delivered by an intentional radiator to an imaginary isotropic antenna that would produce an even distribution of RF power with the same amplitude actually experienced in the preferred direction of the actual antenna. In other words, it is the output power from the intentional radiator (output power from the transmitter plus any gains or losses leading up to the connection point of the antenna) plus the directional gain provided by the antenna. Therefore, the FCC allows 1 watt of output power from the intentional radiator and then 6 dBi of gain at the antenna to equal 4 watts of total output power in a point-to-multipoint link in the 2.4 GHz ISM band.

FCC Rules for Output Power

The FCC has specified different rules for different link types at different frequencies or bands. Specifically, there are rules for 2.4 GHz point-to-multipoint links in the ISM band and point-to-point links in the same band. Additionally, there are rules for both link types in the 5 GHz U-NII bands. I'll cover both in this section. Sector and phased-array antenna output power levels must also be considered.

The reality of output power rules is actually more complex than most network administrators realize. The general concept that most administrators hold is that you can output 4 watts of power in an outdoor link. The reality is that you can have more than 4 watts of directional power when creating certain link scenarios. Basically, in a point-to-point link, the more focused your antennas are, the more output power you can have.

Point-to-Multipoint (PtMP): 2.4 GHz ISM

In a PtMP 2.4 GHz ISM configuration, the FCC allows a maximum of 4 watts of EIRP output power and no more. This is due to the nature of a PtMP setup. To have a PtMP setup, you must have at least one antenna that radiates its energy in a fairly wide area. Otherwise, it would be difficult to have multiple points communicating back with that single point. If you are using an omnidirectional antenna, the FCC considers it a PtMP link even if only one other device is communicating with it, and the link must abide by the 4-watt rule.

If things were as simple as this, we would be finished. However, the scenario gets a little more complicated. In the simplest situation, you have 1 watt of output power from the intentional radiator (the maximum allowed) and 6 dB of passive gain at the antenna for 4 watts of total output power. If you have less power at the intentional radiator, you can provide more passive gain at the antenna. To calculate your allowances, use the one-to-one rule (also written 1:1). The 1:1 rule states that you must reduce the output power at the intentional radiator by 3 dB for every 3 dB of passive gain at the antenna. The result is a breakdown like that seen in Table 2.7.

TABLE 2.7 PtMP Power Limit Table for 2.4 GHz ISM

Intentional Radiator Power (dBm)	Antenna Gain (dBi)	EIRP (dBm)	EIRP (watts)
30	6	36	4
27	9	36	4
24	12	36	4
21	15	36	4
18	18	36	4
15	21	36	4
12	24	36	4

Point-to-Point (PtP): 2.4 GHz ISM

A PtP link created in the 2.4 GHz ISM band differs from a PtMP link. This is a logical variation, since the PtP link will focus the RF energy in a more narrow pattern, reducing the amount of interference that would be caused even at higher power levels. The maximum output power at the intentional radiator is still 1 watt or 30 dBm, but with lower intentional radiator output powers, you can have higher-gain antennas that give an EIRP of up to 158 watts or 52 dBm. Table 2.8 gives this breakdown.

The governing rule that causes the breakdown seen in Table 2.8 is called the three-to-one rule or the 3:1 rule. This is because every 3 dBi of antenna gain above the initial 6 dBi requires a reduction of 1 dB in the output power of the intentional radiator. This 1 dB reduction is based on a 30 dBm (1 watt) starting point.

Point-to-Multipoint (PtMP): 5 GHz U-NII

A PtMP link in the four U-NII bands (formerly three bands colloquially known as lower, middle, and upper) has varying power limits depending on the band used. The limits are 40, 200, 200, and 800 mW of intentional radiator output power in the four bands, respectively. The maximum antenna gain allowed is 6 dBi across all four bands. When an antenna with a gain greater than 6 dBi is used, the 1:1 rule will apply and the intentional

TABLE 2.8 PtP Power Limit Table for 2.4 GHz ISM

Intentional Radiator Power (dBm)	Antenna Gain (dBi)	EIRP (dBm)	EIRP (watts)
30	6	36	4
29	9	38	6.4
28	12	40	10
27	15	42	16
26	18	44	25
25	21	46	39.8
24	24	48	63
23	27	50	100
22	30	52	158

TABLE 2.9 Power Output Limits for the UNII Bands in PtMP Links

Band	Intentional Radiator Power (dBm)	Antenna Gain (dBi)	EIRP (dBm)	EIRP (mW)
U-NII 5.150–250 GHz	16 (40 mW)	6	22	160
U-NII 5.250–350 GHz U-NII 5.470–725 GHz	23 (200 mW)	6	29	800
U-NII 5.725–825 GHz	29 (800 mW)	6	35	3200

radiator must reduce the output power by 1 dB for every dBi of antenna gain above 6 dBi. Table 2.9 provides a resulting list of maximum output power levels after the 6 dBi of antenna gain is added.

Point-to-Point (PtP): 5.8 GHz U-NII

The first three U-NII bands follow the exact same guidelines as those specified earlier for PtMP links in the same U-NII bands. There is a separate rule specified by the FCC for devices using the fourth U-NII band in a PtP link. The allowance is for antennas with directional gain up to 23 dBi without any reduction in output power at the intentional radiator. This means that you can have output power of 800 mW at the intentional radiator (or 29 dBm) and provide 23 dBi of gain at the antenna for a total output power of 160 watts or 52 dBm. If you use an antenna with gains greater than 23 dBi, you must apply the 1:1 rule and reduce the intentional radiator's power by 1 dB for every dBi gain over 23.

The limits of 40, 200, and 800 mW were chosen by IEEE 802.11 to implement maximum FCC power levels set out by the FCC in a formulaic way that appears to allow 50, 250, and 1000 mW limits respectively.

Sector and Phased-Array Antennas

A phased-array antenna is an arrangement of a group of antennas connected to a signal processor. Through the adjustment of the relative strength of each antenna's signal and by adjusting the phase of those signals relative to each other, a phased array can actually create individual beams of signal. Each of these beams can focus in a different direction.

Sector antennas are high-gain antennas that are semidirectional in nature. They create a cone-shaped coverage pattern and are usually placed back to back with other sector antennas to cover an entire area effectively.

FCC Report and Order 04-165, released on July 12, 2004 (and adopted on July 8), set new guidelines that impact phased-array and sectorized antennas. Revisions to Part 15, Section 9, read this way:

> *In addition, the Commission proposed to allow* ***sectorized*** *and* ***phased*** *array systems to operate at the* ***same power levels*** *permitted for* ***point-to-point directional antennas*** *by limiting the total power that may be applied to each individual beam to the level specified in Section 15.247(b), i.e.,* ***0.125 watt or 1 watt, depending upon the type of modulation used****. This change implies that when operating along multiple paths, the aggregate power in all beams could exceed the output power permitted for a single point-to-point system. We proposed, therefore, to* ***limit the aggregate power transmitted simultaneously on all beams to 8 dB above the limit for an individual beam****. This added restriction will allow a maximum of six individual beams to operate simultaneously at the maximum permitted power. If more than six individual beams are used, then the aggregate power must be adjusted to fall within the 8 dB limit. Finally, the Commission proposed that* ***the transmitter output power be reduced by 1 dB for each 3 dB that the directional antenna gain of the complete system exceeds 6 dBi****. This requirement is similar to the present rules for point-to-point operation in the 2.4 GHz band* [emphasis added].

This allows for each beam in the antenna array to be treated as a single PtP link; however, the total aggregate power of all antennas transmitting simultaneously cannot be more than 8 dB above the limit for an individual beam. You'll also notice that the 3:1 rule applies for every 3 dB above 6 dBi.

RF Signal and Antenna Concepts

At this point, you should have a good understanding of RF behavior and RF power management and math. The next topic you'll need to master is that of antennas. You'll learn about how antennas "see" each other and the technical ways in which they communicate in this section. The next major section, titled "Antennas and Antenna Systems," will cover the various antenna types. For information on other intentional radiator components, such as cables and connectors, see Chapter 7.

The antenna is the radiating element in an RF system. In other words, it is the device that actually causes RF waves to be propagated through space. Different antennas have different coverage capabilities and different characteristics, which you will learn about in this and the next section.

Visual LOS

If you stand on top of some tall building, you can see for a very great distance. You may even be able to see for many miles on a very clear day. If you can physically see something, it is said to be in your *visual line of sight (visual LOS)* or just your LOS for simplicity. This LOS is actually the transmission path of the light waves from the object you are viewing (transmitter) to your eyes (receiver). This is an apparently straight line from your perspective, but light waves are subject to similar behavior to RF waves like refraction and reflection, and therefore the line may not actually be straight. Consider an object you are viewing in a mirror. The object is not directly in front of you, yet it appears to be.

RF LOS

Since RF is part of the same electromagnetic phenomenon as visible light, there are similar behaviors. However, RF LOS is more sensitive than visible LOS to interference near the path between the transmitter and the receiver. You might say that more space is needed for the RF waves to be seen by each end of the connection. This extra space can actually be calculated and has a name: the *Fresnel zone.*

The Fresnel Zone

The Fresnel zones (pronounced *frah-nell*), named after the French physicist Augustin-Jean Fresnel, are a theoretically infinite number of ellipsoidal areas around the LOS in an RF link. Many WLAN administrators refer to the Fresnel zone when it is more proper to refer to the first Fresnel zone, according to the science of physics. While it may be the intention of most WLAN administrators to reference the first Fresnel zone when they speak of only the Fresnel zone, it is important that you understand the difference. The first Fresnel zone is the zone with the greatest impact on a WLAN link in most scenarios. The Fresnel zones have been referenced as an ellipsoid-shaped area, an American football–shaped area, and even a Zeppelin-shaped area. Figure 2.19 shows the intention of these analogies.

FIGURE 2.19 A first Fresnel zone representation

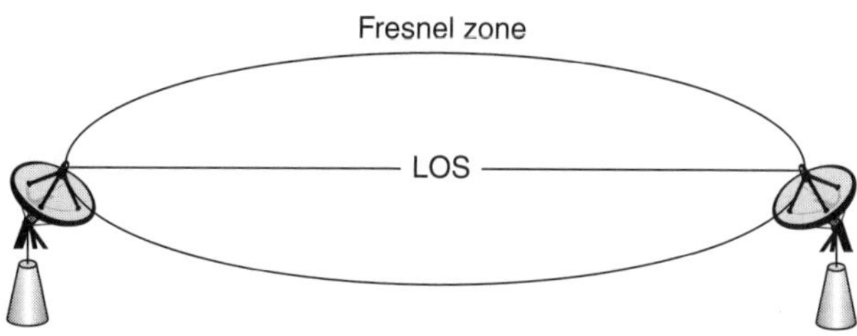

In this text, I will call Fresnel zone 1 *1FZ* from this point forward for simplification. Since 1FZ is an area surrounding the LOS and this area cannot be largely blocked and still provide a functional link, it is important that you know how to calculate the size of 1FZ for your links. You'll also need to consider the impact of Earth bulge on the link and 1FZ.

You will not need to memorize the formulas provided here for the CWNA examination; however, they will prove a useful reference for you when you need to create PtP or PtMP links in the future.

Fresnel Calculations

To calculate the radius of the 1FZ, use the following formula:

$$Radius = \sqrt{}\ 72.2 \times (D / (4 \times F))$$

where D is the distance of the link in miles and F is the frequency used for transmission in GHz and *radius* is reported in feet. For example, if you are creating a link that will span 1.5 miles and you are using 2.4 GHz radios, the formula would be used as follows:

$$72.2 \times \sqrt{(1.5 / (4 \times 2.4))} = 28.54 \text{ feet}$$

This formula provides you with the radius of the 1FZ and, of course, doubling the result would give you the diameter, if you needed it to be calculated. However, it is important to realize that a blockage of the 1FZ of more than 40 percent can cause the link to become nonfunctional. To calculate the 60 percent radius, so that you can ensure it remains clear, use the following formula:

$$Clearance\ radius = 43.3 \times \sqrt{(D / (4 \times F))}$$

where *D* is the distance of the link in miles and *F* is the frequency used for transmission in GHz and *radius* is reported in feet. Using the same example we used to calculate the radius of the entire 1FZ, you will now see that the 60 percent clearance radius is only 17.12 feet. However, this leaves no room for error or change. For example, trees often grow into the 1FZ and cause greater blockage than they did at the time of link creation. For this reason, some WLAN engineers choose to use a 20 percent blockage or 80 percent clearance guideline, and this is the recommended minimum clearance of the CWNP program as well. So how would you calculate this? Use the following formula:

$$\textit{Recommended radius} = 57.8 \times \sqrt{(D/(4 \times F))}$$

Once you've processed this formula, you will see that the recommended minimum of 80 percent clearance (recommended maximum of 20 percent blockage) results in a 1FZ radius of 22.8 feet.

Since it is always better to be safe than sorry when creating WLAN links, you will probably want to make it a habit to round your Fresnel zone calculations upward. For example, I would round the *recommended radius* to 23 feet in our example.

You might be wondering why we calculate the radius instead of the diameter. The reason is simple: we can determine where the visual LOS resides and then measure outward in all directions around that point to determine where the 1FZ actually resides. Remember the 1FZ does not reside in a downward direction only. It might seem that way, since we are usually dealing with trees and other objects protruding up from the ground as sources of interference and blockage. However, it is entirely possible that something could be hanging down from a very high position—such as a bridge—and encroach on the 1FZ from above the visual LOS. Additionally, buildings and other objects can cause blockages from the sides.

Earth Bulge and the Fresnel Zone

Another factor that should be considered in 1FZ blockage is the Earth itself. As you know, the Earth—it turns out—is round. This means that the farther apart you and I are (or any two objects for that matter), the greater will be the likelihood that the Earth is between us. This is demonstrated in Figure 2.20.

FIGURE 2.20 Earth bulge simply demonstrated

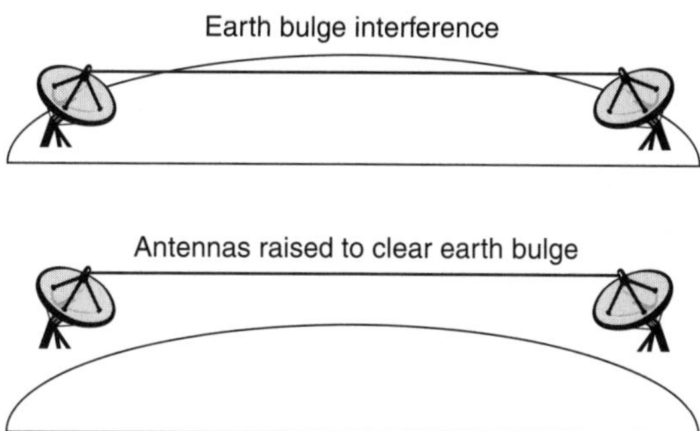

If you are creating wireless links over distances greater than 7 miles using WLAN technologies, you will need to account for Earth bulge in your antenna-positioning formulas. Again, you will not need to memorize this formula for the CWNA examination, but you will need to know that Earth bulge is a potential problem in outdoor wireless links over greater distances. The formula to calculate the extra height your antennas will need to compensate for Earth bulge is

$$\text{Height} = D^2/8$$

where *height* is the height of Earth bulge in feet and *D* is the distance between antennas in miles. Therefore, if you are creating an 8-mile link, you would process the following formula:

$$11^2/8 = 15.12 \text{ feet}$$

Using our guideline of rounding up, I would raise the antenna height by 15.5–16 feet to accommodate Earth bulge.

Solving 1FZ Obstructions

To bring all the discussion of Fresnel zones together, it is important that you learn to deal with 1FZ obstructions. If the obstructions are coming up from the ground into the 1FZ and there are no obstructions anywhere above it, you can often solve the problem by simply raising the antennas involved in the communication link. For example, if there is a forest with maximum tree height of 23 feet that is between the two antennas and there is a distance of 11 miles that must be spanned, we can calculate the needed height for the antennas, including Earth bulge, with the following formula:

$$\text{Minimum antenna height} = (57.8 \times \sqrt{(11/(4 \times 2.4))}) + (11^2/8)$$

This might seem complex, at first, but it is a simple combination of the recommended 1FZ clearance formula and the Earth bulge formula. The result is 77 feet. This means you will need very high towers and you will also need to monitor the forest, though it is unlikely that the trees would grow that much more into the 1FZ in a few years.

If the obstructions are coming into the 1FZ from the sides—if, for instance, buildings are intruding into the pathways—you will have to calculate the 1FZ for a different frequency to see if you can get the clearance, or else you will have to raise the antennas above the buildings. You may also be able to create a multihop link to "shoot" around the buildings if you can gain access rights to a third location that can be seen (RF LOS—including 1FZ) by both of your locations.

Notice that it was an option to calculate the 1FZ with a different frequency. This is because the Fresnel zones are a factor of wavelengths (hence frequencies) and not a factor of antenna gain or beamwidth, which is very important to differentiate. For example, the 77-foot antenna height to allow us to communicate over the top of the forest across 11 miles can be lowered to only 55 feet if you are using IEEE 802.11 devices in the 5 GHz range. However, the trade-off is in a distance. In other words, 2.4 GHz signals are detected more easily than 5 GHz signals at a distance due to the receiving area of the antenna element, but 5 GHz signals have a narrower 1FZ.

An example of this is a link that travels only about a city block (0.1 miles). In the 2.4 GHz spectrum the 1FZ radius would be approximately 6 feet. In the 5 GHz spectrum the 1FZ would only be about 4 feet. Remember this means 6 or 4 feet out from the center point in all directions. Therefore, a 5 GHz link traveling between two buildings would require a space between the buildings of about 8–9 feet, while the 2.4 GHz link would need a space between the buildings of about 12–13 feet. These factors are important considerations.

Beamwidths

Different antennas have different beamwidths, and this *beamwidth* is the measurement of how broad or narrow the focus of the RF energy is as it propagates from the antenna along the main lobe. The *main lobe* is the primary RF energy coming from the antenna. Beamwidth is measured both vertically and horizontally, so don't let the term *width* confuse you into thinking it is a one-dimensional measurement. Specifically, the beamwidth is a measurement taken from the center of the RF signal to the points on the vertical and horizontal axes where the signal decreases by

FIGURE 2.21 Beamwidth concept and measurement

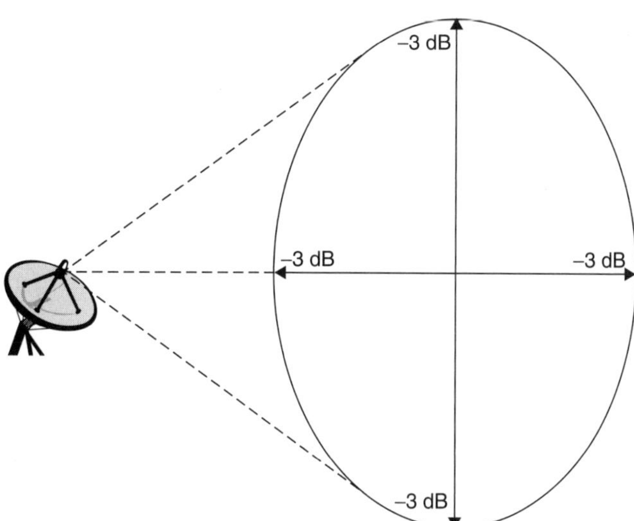

3 dB or half power. In the end, there are vertical and horizontal beamwidth measurements that are stated in degrees. Figure 2.21 shows both the concept of the beamwidth and how it is measured, and Table 2.10 provides a table of common beamwidths for various antenna types (these antenna types are each covered in detail later in this chapter).

Some example antennas are listed in Table 2.11 with their horizontal and vertical beamwidths.

While beamwidth measurements give us an idea of the propagation pattern of an antenna, they are less than perfect in illustrating the actual areas that are covered by the antenna. For more useful visual representations, you will want to reference Azimuth and Elevation charts.

TABLE 2.10 Various Beamwidths for Antenna Types

Antenna Type	Horizontal Beamwidth	Vertical Beamwidth
Omnidirectional	360 degrees	7–80 degrees
Patch/panel	30–180 degrees	6–90 degrees
Yagi	30–78 degrees	14–64 degrees
Sector	60–180 degrees	7–17 degrees
Parabolic dish	4–25 degrees	4–21 degrees

TABLE 2.11 Beamwidths for Specific Antennas

Antenna Model	Horizontal Beamwidth	Vertical Beamwidth
Cisco 9.5 dBi sector antenna	60 degrees	60 degrees
Cisco 2.2 dBi dipole antenna	360 degrees	55 degrees
Cisco Multiband wall-mount (patch/panel) antenna	68 degrees	66 degrees
Hyperlink Technologies 2.4 GHz die-cast grid antenna	8 degrees	8 degrees

Azimuth and Elevation

Where the beamwidth calculations provide a measurement of an antenna's directional power, Azimuth and Elevation charts, which are typically presented together, provide a visualization of the antenna's propagation patterns. Figure 2.22 shows an example of an Azimuth chart, and Figure 2.23 shows an example of an Elevation chart.

FIGURE 2.22 Azimuth chart

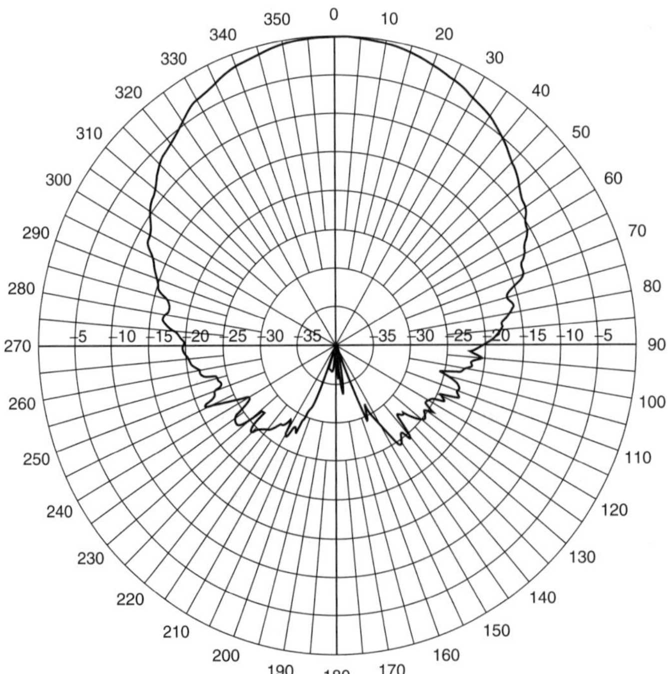

FIGURE 2.23 Elevation chart

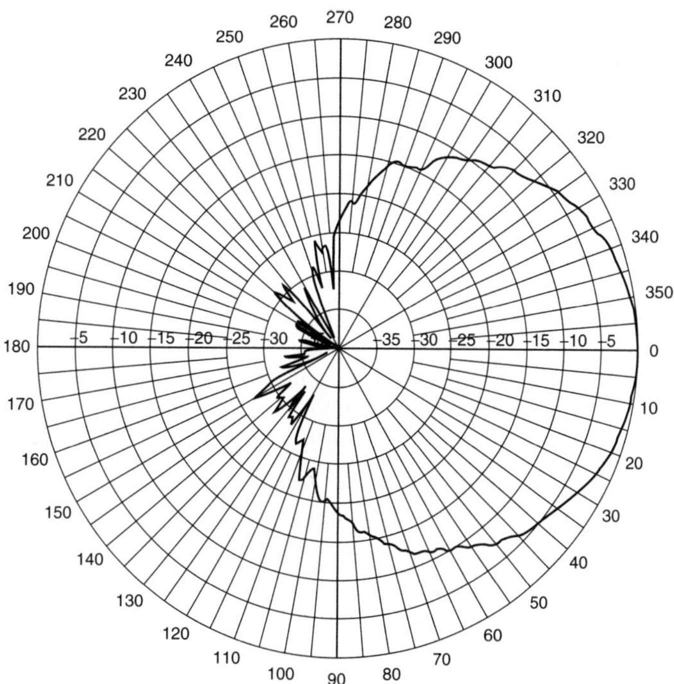

The difference between an Azimuth chart and an Elevation chart is simple: the Azimuth chart shows a top-down view of the propagation path (to the left, in front, to the right, and behind the antenna), and the Elevation chart shows a side view of the propagation path (above, in front, below, and behind the antenna). Think of these charts in terms of a dipole antenna that is positioned vertically upright. If you are standing directly above it and looking down on it, you are seeing the perspective of an Azimuth chart. If you are beside it looking at it from a horizontally level position, you are seeing the perspective of an Elevation chart.

The Azimuth chart in Figure 2.22 is a chart of the Cisco 9.5 dBi sector antenna referenced in Table 2.11. As with most Azimuth charts, the direction of propagation is represented in the upward direction; however, the actual direction will depend on how you position the antenna—more on that in the later section titled "Polarization." The chart is reporting the different signal strength you can expect at different degrees from the antenna. For example, at 90 and 270 degrees (to the immediate left and right of the antenna's intended propagation direction), you will see a loss of approximately 20 dB. Directly behind the antenna, at 180 degrees, you will see a loss of approximately 35–50 dB. This is a sector antenna and is intended to propagate its energy in one direction, but in a fairly wide path.

The Elevation chart in Figure 2.23 is for the same Cisco antenna. You will notice that the pattern of propagation is very similar to the Azimuth pattern. Like most Elevation charts, it is shown with the primary radiation direction to the right. Remember this is intended to represent you looking at the antenna's propagation pattern from the side view. You can see that this antenna has very similar levels of loss along the same degree levels as the Azimuth chart.

Isotropic Radiator

The *isotropic radiator* is a fictional device or concept that cannot be developed using today's technology. Many say that it is not only impossible now, but because of the constraints of physics, it will always be impossible. While the future may be debatable, we know that you cannot currently create an antenna that propagates RF energy equally in all directions. This is due to the fact that the antenna must have some length (it must exist) and it must receive power from some source (it must be connected to something). These two constraints alone make it impossible to create an isotropic radiator at this time.

Even though we cannot create such a device, it is a useful theoretical concept in that we can use it as a basis for measurements. In fact, dBi—as was stated earlier in this chapter—is a measurement of the gain of an antenna in a particular direction over the power level that would exist in that direction if the RF energy were propagated by an isotropic radiator. In other words, dBi is a measurement of the difference between the power levels at a point in space generated by a real antenna versus the theoretical isotropic radiator. Since we can all agree on the behavior of an isotropic radiator, we can all use it as a basis for such power level measurements. Figure 2.24 illustrates the concept of the theoretical isotropic radiator.

The Sun is often used as an analogy of an isotropic radiator. While this is an acceptable analogy, certain theories in physics—such as the hairy ball theorem—would even exclude the Sun from being a true and complete isotropic radiator. However, it is one of the objects we've found to be closest to an isotropic radiator in that light certainly propagates from it in all directions. If we could analyze that light at the molecular level—or even the individual wave level—it is questionable as to whether the rays are truly radiated "equally" in all directions.

FIGURE 2.24 The theoretical isotropic radiator

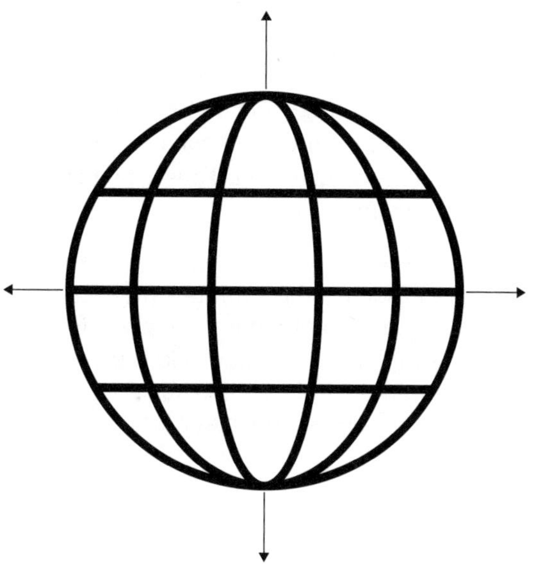

Polarization

A factor that greatly impacts the performance of RF antennas is the polarization of the antennas. *Antenna polarization* refers to the physical orientation of the antenna in a horizontal or vertical position. You'll remember from previous discussions in this chapter that the electromagnetic wave is made up of electric and magnetic fields. The electric field forms what is known as the *E*-plane, and the magnetic field forms what is known as the *H*-plane. The *E*-plane is parallel to the radiating antenna element, and the *H*-plane is perpendicular to it. The *E*-plane, or electric field, determines the polarization of the antenna, since it is parallel to the antenna. Therefore, if the antenna is in a vertical position, it is said to be vertically polarized. If the antenna is in a horizontal position, it is said to be horizontally polarized.

The impact of polarization is seen when antennas are not polarized in the same way. For example, if you have an access point with the antennas positioned vertically (vertical polarization) and you have a USB client adapter with the antenna down (horizontal polarization), your connectivity will be less stable and, at greater distances, may even be lost. However, in most cases, due to indoor reflections, the polarization of antennas does not have as great an impact as it does with outdoor links. In outdoor links, the proper polarization of the antennas can make or break the connection.

Remember this: vertical polarization means that most of the signal is being propagated horizontally, and horizontal polarization means that most of the signal is being propagated vertically. Therefore, the most popular polarization is vertical polarization. However, you might place two antennas on the side of a building—one at the top and one at the bottom—and use them to form a WLAN link between two floors. In this case, you would need to establish horizontal polarization so that the signals would travel up and down vertically.

If you are to configure a link like this, the best practice would be to place the antennas approximately 2 feet out from the wall to prevent the wall from creating 1FZ interference. The link would likely work anyway, but communications can be improved with this consideration. The spacing of 2 feet should keep the 1FZ 80 percent clear for up to 60–70 feet.

Antenna Diversity

Antenna diversity is a feature offered by many WLAN access points and routers that allows the device to receive signals using two antennas and one receiver. In an antenna diversity implementation, only one antenna is used at a time, so this should not be confused with multiple-input, multiple-output (MIMO) configurations.

Remember that the wavelengths of RF signals are very short in the 2.4 and 5.8 GHz frequencies used by WLAN equipment. In fact, they are only about 5 inches long for 802.11 equipment operating at 2.4 GHz and 2 inches long for 802.11 equipment operating at 5 GHz. This means that the antennas used in antenna diversity can actually be within just a few inches of each other and still receive very different signals. As you can imagine, based on what you've read in this chapter so far, RF signals are bouncing all around inside of a building that houses a WLAN. This means that a device can transmit a signal and it may arrive at a receiving device from multiple angles with multiple signal strengths.

The device supporting antenna diversity will look at the signal that comes into each antenna during the frame preamble of a single frame and choose the signal that is best on a frame-by-frame basis. If you're unfamiliar with frames, they will be covered in Chapter 4 in detail. The best frame preamble will determine which antenna is used to receive the rest of the current frame. Again, remember that there is only one receiver that has two connections and two antennas.

I've heard of WLAN administrators adding extension cables and placing the antennas farther apart when using antenna diversity. Through testing, you will find that this usually produces inferior results. The intention is not to provide coverage in a greater area because you have multiple antennas, but rather to provide better coverage in the same area by overcoming some of the problems introduced by multipath.

Antennas and Antenna Systems

In this final section of Chapter 2, I will cover the basic types of antennas that are available to you, including their RF propagation patterns and their intended use. In Chapter 7, you'll learn about the proper installation and configuration of these devices.

There are three major types of antenna systems in use today:

- Omnidirectional
- Semidirectional
- Highly directional

In addition, there are variations on the implementation and management of these antenna types which results in the sectorized and phased-array antennas. These will also be covered in this section. Finally, we'll look very briefly at the forthcoming MIMO antenna systems that are currently being standardized by the IEEE and implemented in prestandardized ways by many vendors.

Omnidirectional/Dipole Antennas

Omnidirectional antennas, the most popular type being the *dipole* antenna, are antennas with a 360-degree horizontal propagation pattern. In other words, they propagate most of their energy outward in a 360-degree pattern shaped much like a doughnut—though a very thick one. The omnidirectional antenna provides coverage at an angle upward and directly out horizontally as is shown in the Elevation chart in Figure 2.25.

Inspecting the Elevation chart in Figure 2.25 reveals that an omnidirectional antenna propagates most of its energy to the right and left of the antenna (from a side view) and very little energy directly above the antenna. At the same time, the Azimuth chart shows a fairly even distribution

FIGURE 2.25 Omnidirectional antenna Elevation chart

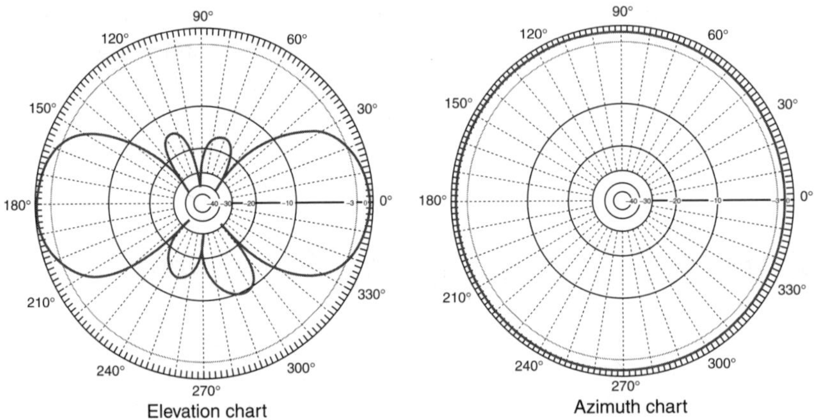

around the antenna (from a top-down view). This is the common propagation characteristic of omnidirectional antennas. Figure 2.26 shows a number of actual omnidirectional antennas.

FIGURE 2.26 Omnidirectional antenna

Omnidirectional Antenna Usage

The omnidirectional antenna is most commonly used indoors to provide coverage throughout an entire space; however, they have become more and more popular in outdoor usage for either hotspots or central antennas in PtMP configurations. Omnidirectional antennas may be mounted on poles, masts, towers, ceilings, or desktops and floors. They provide coverage on a horizontal plane with some coverage vertically and outward from the antenna. This means they may provide some coverage to floors above and below where they are mounted in some indoor installations.

Because all antennas use passive gain—they focus the RF energy—it is important to consider the impact of this passive gain on any antenna that you implement. In the case of omnidirectional antennas, the result is that devices directly above or below the omnidirectional antenna may have a very weak signal or even be unable to detect the signal. This is due to the primary signal being focused outwardly on a horizontal plane.

You can use antennas that have higher dBi gain, such as 12 or 15 dBi omni antennas; however, you must keep the impact of these higher-gain antennas in mind. As an example, consider the two Elevation charts side-by-side in Figure 2.27. The one on the left is from a 4 dBi omni antenna, and the one on the right is from a 15 dBi omni antenna. You can clearly see the flattening of the signal. It is very plausible that a higher-gain antenna, such the one on the right, could cause users on the floors above and below the antenna to lose their connection. Ultimately, when sticking with omni antennas, choosing between a higher gain and a lower gain is

FIGURE 2.27 4 dBi versus 15 dBi Elevation charts

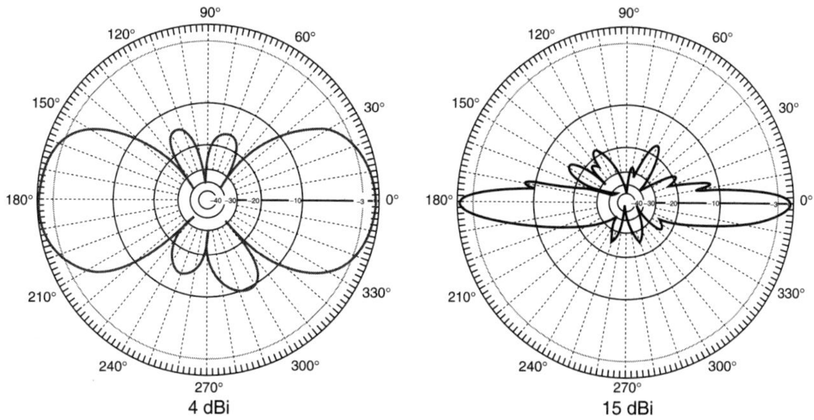

choosing between reaching people farther away horizontally (higher gain) or reaching people farther up or down vertically (lower gain). In many situations, you'll just have to place separate antennas on each floor of a multifloor installation to get the coverage you need.

Semidirectional Antennas

Semidirectional antennas are antennas that focus most of their energy in a particular direction. Examples include patch, panel, and Yagi antennas. (Yagi is pronounced *yah-gee.*) Patch and panel antennas come in flat enclosures and can be easily mounted on walls and Yagi antennas look a lot like TV antennas—a long rod with tines sticking out; however, the Yagi antennas are usually enclosed in a plastic casing that hides this appearance. Patch and panel antennas usually focus their energy in a horizontal arc of 180 degrees or less, whereas Yagi antennas usually have a coverage pattern of 90 degrees or less. Figure 2.28 shows examples of patch, panel, and Yagi antennas.

The Azimuth and Elevation charts for Yagi antennas often look the same. In other words, they often have the same coverage pattern from the top-down view (horizontal coverage) as they do from the side view (vertical coverage). Figure 2.29 shows an example coverage pattern of a 9 dBi Yagi antenna. Panel antennas usually have a similar pattern to Yagi antennas, except the "fish-like design" appears quite a bit fatter.

Semidirectional antennas are most useful for providing RF coverage down long hallways or corridors when using Yagi-style antennas and providing RF coverage in "one" direction when using patch or panel antennas. The patch and panel antennas will have some level of energy propagated behind their intended direction. (This energy is known as the *rear lobe.*) However, most of the energy will be directed inward. For this reason, patch and panel antennas are usually mounted on outside walls facing inward when they are intended to provide coverage inside an area only.

FIGURE 2.28 Examples of semidirectional antennas

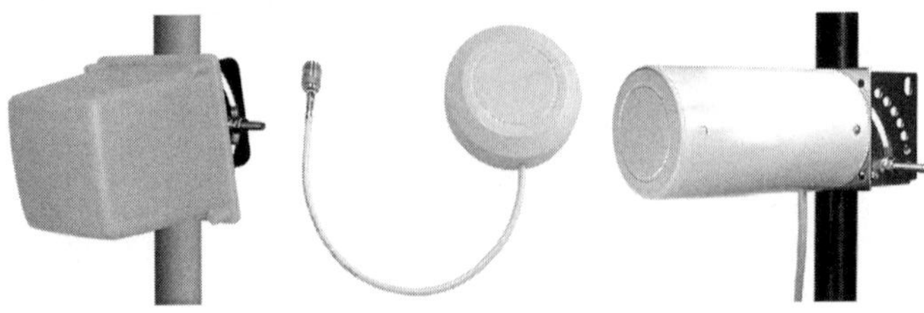

FIGURE 2.29 9 dBi Yagi coverage pattern

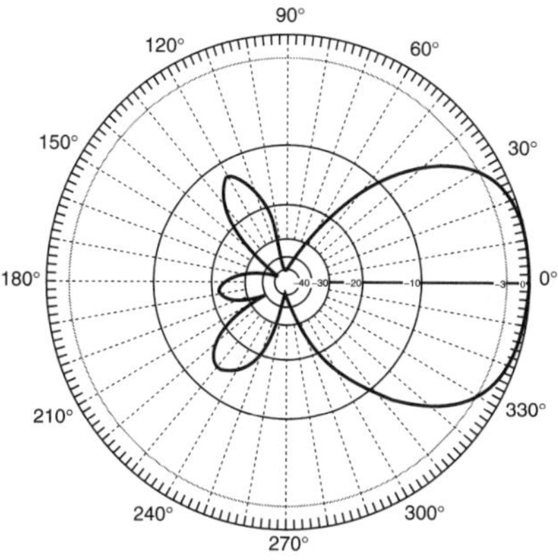

Additionally, they can be used on the outside of a building to create an "external-only" hotspot that is open to the public or possibly less secure than the internal network.

Creatively using Yagi, patch, and panel antennas can prevent the use of large numbers of omni antennas for many situations. For example, a single patch antenna placed on a wall facing inward may provide all the coverage needed when two omni antennas would otherwise be needed. This is because the energy coming from the patch antenna is forced directionally inward instead of being forced in all horizontal directions. The RF energy is going where it is needed instead of losing 1/3 to 1/2 of it outside the walls of your facility.

A common misconception that enters at this point is the fear that using a Yagi, patch, or panel antenna will get the signal to the client, but that it will not get the signal from the client to the access point (or the Yagi, patch, or panel antenna). Stated another way, it is often assumed that you must use semidirectional antennas at the client if you use a semidirectional antenna at the access point; however, this is not the case.

I usually explain this by saying this, "When you place the megaphone over the antenna's mouth, it is smart enough to move it over its ear to listen." What I mean by this statement is simple: the very quality of the antenna that increases its gain in a particular direction also allows it to "hear" better (have receive gain) from that same direction. Therefore, as Joseph Bardwell says, "If you can hear me, then I can hear you." For more information, see the web site http://www.connect802.com/wcu/2005/newsletter_051001.htm.

Highly Directional Antennas

Highly directional antennas are antennas that transmit with a very narrow beam. These types of antennas often look like the satellite dish that is so popular in rural areas, such as where I grew up in West Virginia. They are generally called *parabolic dish* or *grid* antennas. The parabolic dish is the one that looks like a satellite dish, and the grid antenna looks like an antenna with a curved grill grate behind it. My explanations are somewhat simplified, but Figure 2.30 shows examples of each.

Due to the high directionality of these antennas, they are mostly used for PtP or PtMP links (PtMP links will usually use an omni or semidirectional antenna at the center and multiple highly directional or semidirectional antennas at the remote sites). They can transmit at distances of 35 miles or more and usually require detailed aiming procedures that include a lot of trial and error. By positioning one antenna according to visual LOS and then making small movements at the other antenna, accurate alignment can usually be achieved.

The grid antenna provides the added benefit of allowing air to pass through the back panels so that the antenna does not shift as much as the parabolic dish in high-wind scenarios.

Sectorized and Phased-Array Antennas

A *sectorized* antenna (or *sector* antenna) is a high-gain antenna that works back-to-back with other sectorized antennas. They are often mounted around a pole or mast and can provide coverage in indoor environments, such as warehouses, or outdoor environments, such as university campuses or hotspots. Figure 2.31 shows an example of sectorized antennas mounted on a pole.

FIGURE 2.30 Parabolic dish and grid antennas

FIGURE 2.31 Sectorized antennas

A *phased-array* antenna is a special antenna system that is actually composed of multiple antennas connected to a single processor. The antennas are used to transmit different phases that result in a directed beam of RF energy aimed at client devices. Because phased-array antennas are specialized and expensive, they are not commonly used in the WLAN market.

Multiple-Input, Multiple-Output (MIMO) Antenna Systems

The final type of antenna system must be considered carefully at the time of this writing. The IEEE 802.11n amendment when ratified will use MIMO (pronounced my-moe) technology, but the exact implementation is still open for debate. However, certain vendors are releasing what they are calling "pre-n" equipment, and some of them are promising that their devices will be upgradable to the ratified IEEE 802.11n amendment through firmware. Depending on the processing power and memory requirements of the final IEEE 802.11n amendment, this may or may not be possible. Key factors will include the minimum number of antennas and the way those antennas are used in the final standard. For this reason, any device that states its data rate capabilities as greater than 54 Mbps, as of early 2007, may or may not be able to be upgraded to comply with the IEEE 80211n amendment.

MIMO, in its simplest description, is just the use of more than one antenna at the same time. This is different from antenna diversity as discussed earlier in this chapter because multiple antennas are actually used at the same time. With creative use of the antennas and changes in the underlying MAC layer of the IEEE 802.11 standard, bandwidth rates as high as 600 Mbps have been touted. Because the antennas used by MIMO devices are still standard antenna types connected to modern processing systems, MIMO will actually be addressed more in Chapters 3 and 4 where applicable.

Summary

In this chapter, you learned about many fundamental concepts related to WLANs. This is reflected by the length of the key terms list at the end of this chapter. You should be able to describe and define all the terms in that list, if you want to be prepared for the CWNA examination.

As you read through this chapter, you learned about the basics of RF signal behavior and then moved on to the factors related to antenna usage and antenna selection. You also learned how to calculate RF signal powers and how to determine the signal strength you would need to make a particular link function. Finally, you also learned how to read common charts and diagrams such as Azimuth and Elevation charts.

Key Terms

- ☐ **absorption**
- ☐ **amplification**
- ☐ **amplitude**
- ☐ **attenuation**
- ☐ **dBd**
- ☐ **dBi**
- ☐ **dBm**
- ☐ **decibel (dB)**
- ☐ **delay spread**
- ☐ **diffraction**
- ☐ **EIRP**
- ☐ **fade margin**
- ☐ **free space path loss**
- ☐ **Fresnel zones**
- ☐ **frequency**
- ☐ **gain**
- ☐ **highly directional antennas**
- ☐ **impedance**
- ☐ **intentional radiator**
- ☐ **isotropic radiator**
- ☐ **link budget**
- ☐ **LOS**
- ☐ **loss**

- ☐ **milliwatt**
- ☐ **multipath**
- ☐ **noise floor**
- ☐ **omnidirectional antennas**
- ☐ **phase**
- ☐ **radio wave**
- ☐ **receive sensitivity**
- ☐ **reflection**
- ☐ **refraction**
- ☐ **RF signal**
- ☐ **return loss**
- ☐ **RSSI**
- ☐ **scattering**
- ☐ **SNR**
- ☐ **SOM**
- ☐ **VSWR**
- ☐ **wave**
- ☐ **wavelength**

Review Questions

1. You are working as a WLAN engineer and have been asked to modify the link budget so that there will be more room for fluctuations in the link's signal strength without losing the signal. What are you being asked to add?

   A. Gain

   B. Fade margin

   C. Free space path loss

   D. Amplitude

2. Which of the following are absolute measurements of RF signal power? (Choose all that apply.)

   A. Milliwatts

   B. Amperes

   C. dB

   D. dBi

3. Which of the following terms can be defined as an RF signal being reflected in many directions?

   A. Reflection

   B. Diffraction

   C. Refraction

   D. Scattering

4. Which of the following terms is used to define the behavior exhibited when an RF wave bends around an obstacle in its path?

   A. Reflection

   B. Diffraction

   C. Refraction

   D. Scattering

5. When absorption occurs, what happens to the RF signal?

   A. It is bent as it passes through a medium.

   B. It is scattered as it passes through a medium.

   C. It is converted into heat and absorbed into the medium.

   D. It is bent around a medium.

6. You have to convert dBd to dBi. How do you do this?

   A. Add 2.14 to the dBd value.

   B. Subtract 2.14 from the dBd value.

   C. Multiply the dBd value by 2.14.

   D. Use the rules of 10s and 3s.

7. Which of the following is defined as the point at which the antenna is connected to a wireless transmission system?

   A. Intentional radiator

   B. EIRP

   C. Isotropic radiator

   D. Fresnel zone

8. What term defines the strength of an RF signal?

   A. Gain

   B. Amplitude

   C. Frequency

   D. Phase

9. Which of the following are important considerations to factor in when evaluating how an RF signal will travel through space from one antenna to another in a PtP link?

   A. Fresnel zones

   B. Free space path loss

   C. Impedance

   D. Link budget

10. You have an RF system with the following specifications: 100 mW of output power at the access point, passing through a cable with a loss of 3 dB and then transmitting with an antenna with 7 dBi of gain. What is the final output power in mW?

    A. 250 mW

    B. 1500 mW

    C. 100 mW

    D. 50 mW

11. You have an RF system with the following specifications: 30 mW of output power at the access point, passing through a cable with a loss of 3 dB and then through an amplifier with a gain of 5 dB and then through a cable with a loss of 3 dB. Finally, the signal is transmitted through an antenna with 23 dBi of gain. Is this signal power legal, according to FCC regulations for a PtMP link?

    A. Yes

    B. No

Review Answers

1. **B.** The correct answer is fade margin. The fade margin is extra dB that is taken off the receive sensitivity rating in order to allow for greater room for the fluctuations in signal strength that occur in the real world over time. Another way to define fade margin is to say that it is an amount of dB that is removed from the SOM after it is calculated. Either way, the result is the same: you are providing some padding for real-world fluctuations in signal strength.
2. **A.** The correct answer is milliwatts. Only milliwatts, in this list, are absolute measurements of power. dB and dBi are both relative measurements of gain, and an ampere is a portion of the watt power measurement.
3. **D.** The correct answer is scattering. Scattering occurs when an RF signal encounters objects with varying surfaces such as foliage or chain link fences. It is often defined as multiple reflections.
4. **B.** The correct answer is diffraction. Diffraction defines the behavior that occurs when an RF signal bends around an obstacle in its path.
5. **C.** The correct answer is that absorption occurs when a signal is absorbed into a material. The signal is converted into heat, and this is known as absorption.
6. **A.** The correct answer is to add 2.14 to the dBd value. To convert from dBd to dBi, add 2.14 to the dBd value. To convert from dBi to dBd, subtract 2.14 from the dBi value. dBd is a measurement of an antenna's directional gain when compared to a dipole antenna. dBi is a measurement of an antenna's directional gain when compared to an isotropic radiator.
7. **A.** The correct answer is intentional radiator. The intentional radiator is the point at which the antenna connects to the wireless system. The output power at this point is regulated by local regulatory organizations such as the FCC in the United States. The output power at the intentional radiator will be a factor of the original output power from the wireless transmitter and all cables, connectors, and devices up to the intentional radiator.

8. **B.** The correct answer is amplitude. Gain is a measurement of an increase in a signal's strength and may be an increase in amplitude (active gain) or a focusing of the signal (passive gain). Amplitude is the height of the signal or the actual signal strength. Frequency is the number of times the wave cycles per second, and phase is the comparison of two signals to determine if they are in synch or not.

9. **A, B, D.** Fresnel zones, free space path loss, and link budgets should all be considered when creating a PtP link. Impedance is only a factor within the intentional radiator and is not a factor once the RF signal is in space.

10. **A.** The correct answer is 250 mW: 100 mW – 3 dB + 10 dB – 3 dB = 250 mW.

11. **B.** The correct answer is no. The final output power is 4.8 watts, and this is 800 mW over the FCC allowance for a PtMP link.

CHAPTER

3

Spread Spectrum Technologies

CWNA Exam Objectives Covered:

- Comprehend the differences between, and explain the different types of spread spectrum technologies and how they relate to the IEEE 802.11 standard's PHY clauses
  - FHSS, DSSS, HR/DSSS, ERP, and OFDM
- Identify the underlying concepts of how spread spectrum technology works
  - Modulation and Coding
- Identify and apply the concepts which make up the functionality of spread spectrum technology
  - Colocation
  - Channel Centers and Widths
  - Carrier Frequencies
  - Dwell Time and Hop Time
  - Throughput Versus Data Rate
  - Bandwidth
  - Communication Resilience

In This Chapter

This chapter introduces the concepts of spread spectrum radio communication and the way it is implemented in the IEEE 802.11 standards. A comparison is made to narrowband communications for contrasting purposes. From here the chapter moves on to the specific ways spread spectrum technology is used in IEEE 802.11, including frequency hopping spread spectrum, direct sequence spread spectrum, and orthogonal frequency division multiplexing, though the latter is not technically a spread spectrum technology. Next, spread spectrum concepts such as modulation and coding are covered. Finally, the various spread spectrum factors you need to understand so that you can implement and administer a WLAN are addressed, including colocation, channels, throughput, and data rates.

The OSI Model

This chapter and the following two chapters will offer in-depth information related to Layers 1 and 2 of the OSI model. In case you are unfamiliar with this model, this section provides a brief overview.

Introducing the OSI Model

The International Organization for Standardization, known as the ISO, is a global organization focused on developing standards for business, government, and society. The OSI was developed by the ISO. While it might be tempting to think that there is some connection between the acronym OSI and ISO, the truth is that ISO is not an acronym at all. The short name for the International Organization for Standardization, ISO, is derived from the Greek work *isos,* which means *equal.* Being an international organization, it made more sense for them to use a short name for the organization rather than an acronym, given the variety of interpretations of acronyms around the world.

OSI is an acronym; it stands for *Open Systems Interconnection.* It is a model for networking communications. OSI is referenced as the *OSI reference model* or just the *OSI model* in short. The OSI is actually divided into two major portions: the abstract reference model and the specific set of protocols. The more impactful of the two has been the abstract reference model, which is sometimes called the seven-layer model, because of its use of seven layers of communications, and is the portion of OSI referenced by terms like *OSI model* or *OSI reference model.* The OSI model has been of tremendous benefit to the information technology industry as both a model for network design and a language for communicating network technology.

The OSI Model Briefly Explained

The OSI model is broken down into seven layers. Each layer is defined by a descriptive term that helps in understanding the actions that transpire and the technology that is used within that layer. The seven layers are as follows:

- **Layer 7** Application
- **Layer 6** Presentation
- **Layer 5** Session
- **Layer 4** Transport
- **Layer 3** Network
- **Layer 2** Data Link
- **Layer 1** Physical

In this case, I have listed the seven layers from the top down. They can also be listed from the bottom up. When an application communicates across the network—wired or wireless—it is said to send the network communication down from Layer 7 through Layer 1 and then the receiving application will retrieve the data as it passes up from Layer 1 through Layer 7. Additionally, connections are often referenced by their layer. For example, a Layer 4 connection or a Layer 5 connection may refer to the TCP protocol. The phrase "Layer 7 connection" may refer to the connection between an FTP client and an FTP server, and so on.

For the purposes of this book, it is enough to know the basic functionality of each layer and some examples of technologies used at each layer. This information is provided in Table 3.1. If you are completely new to the OSI model, you should consider reviewing a more in-depth study of the concept. An excellent reference, in this regard, is Scott Mueller's *Upgrading and Repairing Networks, 5th Edition* (Que, 2006).

TABLE 3.1 OSI Layers with Functionality Descriptions and Examples

OSI Layer	Layer Name	Functionality	Technology Examples
Layer 7	Application	Defines the provision of services to applications, such as checking for resource availability and authenticating users.	Most firewalls, FTP, POP3, HTTP, etc.
Layer 6	Presentation	The Presentation layer has the primary responsibility of interpreting and presenting data to or from the Application layer.	Many encryption technologies, compression technologies, protocol conversion, etc.
Layer 5	Session	The responsibility for managing sessions (connections) between two networked Application layers rests on the Session layer.	Remote Procedure Call, TCP also resides here (the TCP/IP stack does not match perfectly to the OSI model), etc.
Layer 4	Transport	The Transport layer is the area where packet delivery confirmation and packet rebuilding occur.	TCP, UDP, etc.
Layer 3	Network	The Network layer is responsible for management of routing, relaying, and terminating connections between network nodes.	Internet Protocol (IP), routers, stateless inspection firewalls or packet filters, etc.
Layer 2	Data Link	The Data Link layer is responsible for detecting and correcting errors in the Physical layer and for transmitting data from one place to another. The Data Link layer may be divided into the Logical Link Control (LLC) and Medium Access Control (MAC) sublayers.	Bridges, switches, MAC addresses, IEEE 802.11 framing, etc.
Layer 1	Physical	The Physical layer includes the standards that control the transmission of the data streams on the specific medium.	Frequency-hopping spread spectrum, direct-sequence spread spectrum, OFDM, Ethernet hubs, etc.

The remaining sections of this chapter will present Physical layer technologies used in WLANs. The next chapter will present information related to both the Physical and Data Link layers. Most of what you need to know about IEEE 802.11 operations will be found in these bottom two layers of the OSI model. There are some security technologies residing in other layers used on top of WLANs that will be discussed in this book, but these are actually security technologies that can be used with wired or wireless networks and are not specifically limited to the WLAN world.

Spread Spectrum Technologies and IEEE 802.11 Standards

The original IEEE 802.11-1997 standard specified three Physical layer technologies to be used for WLANs. These three technologies are the Clause 14 frequency-hopping spread spectrum (FHSS) PHY, the Clause 15 direct-sequence spread spectrum (DSSS) PHY, and the Clause 16 infrared PHY (IR). The FHSS and DSSS PHYs use the 2.4 GHz Industrial, Scientific, and Medical (ISM) band for communications. The IR PHY never came to market and will not be covered further here.

The following sections introduce you to the FHSS and DSSS PHYs. This introduction will afford a high-level understanding of how these two spread spectrum technologies work and what capabilities they provide. Additionally, you will learn about the orthogonal frequency division PHY (OFDM) that was originally released as the IEEE 802.11a amendment, the high-rate DSSS (HR/DSSS) PHY that was originally released as the IEEE 802.11b amendment, and the enhanced-rate PHY (ERP) that was originally released as the IEEE 802.11g amendment. These latter three PHYs have been added to the standard since 1997.You will also learn about the much-anticipated high-throughput (HT) PHY to be released as the IEEE 802.11n amendment. Near the end of the chapter, Table 3.9 provides a single point of reference to the different features and capabilities of the IEEE 802.11 PHYs.

Before I explain these Physical layer technologies used by IEEE 802.11 as amended, I will review both spread spectrum and narrowband RF technology in general.

Spread Spectrum Versus Narrowband Technology

To understand the benefits of spread spectrum technology, you must first understand the differences between narrowband and spread spectrum

RF solutions. *Narrowband* wireless communications can be defined as wireless communications using a single frequency center with no redundancy to communicate information at high power levels chosen to overpower interference in that frequency band. *Spread spectrum* wireless communications can be defined as wireless communications using a range of frequencies to communicate information at low power levels. More specifically, spread spectrum and OFDM use multiple frequency centers over a relatively large frequency band to send multiple copies of information (as in DSSS) or error-correcting codes (as in OFDM) so that the information makes it through despite some RF symbols being unrecoverable. Spread spectrum has also been defined as a wireless communications technology that uses more bandwidth than is required to deliver information. Spread spectrum also uses low power and can do so because all interference does not need to be overcome, due to the redundancy and/or error correction.

The differences between these two technologies are important, and these differences have been the driving force behind the varied usages of both technologies. Narrowband wireless communications, for example, are used by the radio stations you listen to in your car or on your home radio. You have learned, through experience, that these stations use a specific frequency for broadcasting. For example, you may tune your radio to 103.9 on the FM band or 880 on the AM band. You do not tune the radio to between 103.1 and 103.7 or some other range of frequencies. You may have also heard things like "50,000 watts of broadcasting power." This is certainly more output power than you would find in even an enterprise-class WLAN device at 100 mW or even 4 W at the antenna. The high output power is both a factor of narrowband transmission and, possibly more important, the need for the signal to travel far. Table 3.2 provides a comparison of narrowband and spread spectrum characteristics as implemented under the constraints of FCC regulations.

One of the most important problems that has been reduced, though not eliminated, by using spread spectrum technology is the issue of interference. For example, radio stations using the same narrowband frequency must be many miles apart; however, WLANs using the same spread spectrum channel (range of frequencies) can easily exist on the same block and, with the right antennas and output power settings, even in the same building with very little problem from interference. This is a factor more of the low-power characteristic of spread spectrum technologies and OFDM in the IEEE standards than it is of spread spectrum technology itself. If I implemented an illegal access point (AP) connected to an antenna with a total output power

TABLE 3.2 Narrowband Versus Spread Spectrum Technology

Narrowband	Spread Spectrum and OFDM
Uses high power levels concentrated close to the carrier frequency	Uses a range or “spread” of frequencies
Characterized by higher output power levels	Characterized by lower output levels
Bandwidth of the radiated signal is very close to the information bandwidth	Bandwidth of the radiated signal is greater than the information bandwidth
More prone to interference	Less prone to interference
Causes tremendous interference with other devices communicating on the same or close frequencies	Causes less interference due to the low power levels of the communications
Generally requires a license from the local regulatory agency	Requires no license when using unlicensed WLAN technology

of 50,000 watts, it would drown out my neighbor’s WLANs for many miles. It would also get me into very big trouble with the FCC.

If the WLAN equipment we are implementing today were based on narrowband technology, we would be in continual disputes over the frequency space. One single device communicating on the same frequency a mile away would cause enough interference to bring our WLAN nearly to a halt. As long as power regulations are followed, this will not be a problem with spread spectrum technology at any point in the future. Currently, spread spectrum and spread spectrum–like technologies are being improved to offer more data throughput, but these improvements are being made with a focus on maintaining the ability to implement the wireless devices in a license-free manner with as little unintentional interference as possible.

An additional wireless communications problem, multipath, is also partly overcome by the use of spread spectrum technology. Spread spectrum systems spread the communications across multiple frequencies. Each frequency has a different RF wavelength, and these varying wavelengths will react differently to the environment through which they propagate, due to the size differences between the various wavelengths compared to the objects they encounter in the environment. This phenomenon results in a lesser multipath impact on some wavelengths and a greater multipath impact on other wavelengths. The end result is that enough of the frequencies will often "get through" to the receiving antenna without being substantially impacted by multipath. This, in conjunction with the redundant data used in DSSS systems, allows for greater resilience in spread spectrum networks.

The multipath problem that is reduced by the utilization of spread spectrum technology is known as *intersymbol interference (ISI)*. ISI occurs when the main signal and the reflected signal paths arrive at the receiving antenna with a time variation between them *(delay spread)* great enough to cause bits to overlap. Wireless technologies have varying delay spread tolerance, and this tolerance can be summarized by the following guideline:

Higher data rates have lower delay spread tolerance, and lower data rates have higher delay spread tolerance.

This guideline is one of the reasons for reducing the data rate; the other major reason is a simple factor of signal strength. Balancing data rate with ISI and other signal quality factors is an important element in achieving stable communications on WLANs.

Due to the benefits of spread spectrum technologies, they have dominated the WLAN market. Spread spectrum is used in wireless personal area networks (WPANs), wireless metropolitan area networks (WMANs), and other proprietary technologies. The ability to have multiple networks or devices communicating on different channels or frequencies in the same unlicensed RF space has been a big part of this growth. Due to the low–output power constraints imposed by the FCC and other regulatory agencies on spread spectrum technologies implemented in the IEEE 802.11 standard (as amended), you can implement multiple WLANs in a single building on the same channels—assuming there is enough distance between them. For example, I planned and installed a WLAN for a school facility where we used channel 1 at one end of the building, channel 11 in the middle of the building, and channel 1 again at the other end. Using a protocol analyzer and a spectrum analyzer, I could see that there was minimal "bleed" from the service area at one end on channel 1 into the service area at the other end, and vice versa. This is the result of low output power. If the access point at one end of the building had an output power setting of 100 watts (which would be an FCC violation), I would not be able to install the second access point at the other end effectively.

You wouldn't want to try implementing a WLAN using a single access point with very high output power anyway, because all the clients would have to share the same access point, and this would greatly reduce overall throughput.

FHSS

FHSS is the first IEEE 802.11 PHY that I will cover. FHSS, as implemented in the IEEE standards, provides a 1 or 2 Mbps data rate using the 2.4 GHz ISM band. Within North America, FHSS uses seventy-nine 1 MHz channels centered on every 1 MHz from 2.400 GHz to 2.4835 GHz. The IEEE 802.11 standards specify channel centers and the distance between them that fit within this range.

The *frequency-hopping* portion of this spread spectrum technology is revealing as to its functionality. FHSS systems use a small frequency bandwidth, which I will simply call a frequency, within the 79 MHz allocated, to communicate and then hop to another frequency and then another until a hopping pattern known as a *hopping sequence* has been completed. When the hopping sequence is completed, it is then repeated, and this process continues until the information being communicated has been transferred. Additionally, a *dwell time* is specified, which determines how long each frequency will be utilized before hopping to the next position in the hopping sequence. I will cover hopping sequences, dwell time, and other features of FHSS in more detail in the section "Spread Spectrum Fundamental Concepts" later in this chapter.

FHSS provides for resistance to interference through the use of small frequency bandwidths and transfer algorithms that accommodate for errors in transmissions. For example, if data is communicated on a particular frequency and interference is encountered, that data will simply be retransmitted once the radios move on to the next frequency in the hopping sequence. Of course, this will reduce the actual data throughput of the system, but this resilience provides for reasonably stable communications.

In modern networks, the reality is that speed is very important. This is where FHSS falls short. While it may provide for resilience in the face of interference, it does not provide for speeds greater than 2 Mbps and, therefore, is not widely implemented today. The exception to this is the Bluetooth devices that are very popular. Bluetooth does use FHSS. Since Bluetooth devices do not usually need high data rates for typical uses (wireless headsets, wireless mice, wireless keyboards, etc.) in one-to-one link scenarios, the limited speeds of FHSS are not as problematic.

It is important to know that Bluetooth devices, since they use the 2.4 GHz ISM band, can cause some level of interference to Wi-Fi equipment. However, the newer Bluetooth standards provide a feature known as *adaptive frequency hopping (AFH)* that can help to prevent this interference problem. AFH actually works on the Bluetooth devices, and a simplification of how it works follows. When a Bluetooth device, using version 1.2 or higher of the Bluetooth standards, detects interference on a frequency being used in the hopping sequence, it removes that frequency from the hopping sequence. Since data is sent and received on the same frequency during a hop, the communicating devices can determine that the data transfer failed because of interference on that frequency (assuming all other frequencies in the hopping sequence have been working fine). In these situations, the Bluetooth devices do not know what caused the interference, which is acceptable, since we only need them to stop using the frequency, regardless of the interference source. This makes Bluetooth devices more compatible with Wi-Fi equipment so that the benefit is twofold: both the Bluetooth devices and the Wi-Fi equipment can coexist without interference, since one set of them (the Bluetooth devices) is looking both ways before crossing the street—or in this case, after crossing the street.

DSSS

DSSS, the second IEEE 802.11 PHY covered here, supports speeds of 1 or 2 Mbps just like FHSS systems. Later amendments to the IEEE 802.11 standard provided for higher data rates and accomplished this through a different implementation of DSSS, which you will read about shortly.

The IEEE specifies that DSSS should operate in the 2.4 GHz ISM band and that it should use frequencies ranging from 2.401 to 2.473 GHz in North America. The IEEE further specifies that the DSSS supported by IEEE 802.11 devices should implement differential binary phase shift keying (DBPSK) at 1 Mbps and differential quadrature phase shift keying (DQPSK) at 2 Mbps. DBPSK and DQPSK are modulation techniques that use phase-based modulation. The IEEE standards divide the DSSS Physical layer into two components: the Physical layer convergence procedure (PLCP) and the physical medium dependent (PMD). The PMD defines that actual method used to transmit data between two wireless devices, and the PLCP acts as an abstraction layer between the PMD and the Medium Access Control (MAC) services.

DSSS systems are also resistant to narrowband interference like FHSS systems. This is because of the use of spread spectrum technologies; however, because DSSS systems use narrow bandwidths and do not hop from one frequency to another, they may be more susceptible to interference than FHSS systems. If a narrowband signal is broadcast on the same frequency as the center channel frequency you've chosen for your DSSS WLAN, it will cause continual interference. If a similar situation should occur with a FHSS system, it would only cause interference when the system hopped to that frequency. In most cases, however, the narrowband interference will be benign, since it only takes out a few copies of the bits (DSSS transmits redundant copies of the data). As long as one copy gets through, it is as though the interference does not exist because there is no loss of information.

HR/DSSS

High-rate DSSS (HR/DSSS) is the PHY defined in the IEEE 802.11b-1999 amendment. Due to the fact that this amendment document specifies the details of HR/DSSS functionality, many refer to HR/DSSS devices as 802.11b devices. HR/DSSS PHY is backward compatible with IEEE 802.11 DSSS equipment, but it is not compatible with IEEE 802.11 FHSS equipment. This is because of the use of different modulation schemes (frequency hopping versus direct sequence).

The primary objective of TGb (task group b) was to provide higher data rates within the 2.4 GHZ ISM band and compatibility with modulations used by DSSS PHY. This was accomplished using the same frequency range as used by DSSS, specifically, from 2.4000 to 2.4835 GHz. Using *complementary code keying (CCK),* TGb was able to achieve data rates of 5.5 and 11 Mpbs. This resulted in a collection of data rates, 1, 2, 5.5, and 11 Mbps.

OFDM and ERP-OFDM

Orthogonal frequency division multiplexing, or *OFDM*, is not a spread spectrum technology, though it is often called such, but is sometimes said to be spread spectrum–like because of its similar resilience against interference. A special implementation of OFDM is used in IEEE 802.11g, and it has been widely implemented in IEEE 802.11a technology as well.

OFDM offers high data rates and exceptional resistance to interference and corruption. OFDM is actually a digital modulation method that splits the signal into multiple narrowband subcarriers at different frequencies. Another way of saying this is to say that OFDM splits a high-speed information signal into multiple lower-speed information signals and then transmits these lower-speed signals in parallel. Due to the interference problems you would encounter if the single high-speed or high-bandwidth signal were transmitted, the use of multiple lower-speed or lower-bandwidth subcarriers actually results in higher data rates.

Whether OFDM is a spread spectrum technology or not has been debated among WLAN engineers, but the FCC has specified that, though OFDM may not be spread spectrum, it is similar enough in features to be used in the unlicensed bands. OFDM is now used in both the 5 GHz U-NII bands (IEEE 802.11a) and the 2.4 GHz ISM band (IEEE 802.11g), though it was first introduced to WLANs through the IEEE 802.11a standard.

The benefits of OFDM include spectral efficiency (meaning that the use of the electromagnetic spectrum is more efficient than with other technologies), resistance to RF interference, and lowered multipath distortion. The spectral efficiency is achieved by effectively transmitting multiple modulated signals as closely together as possible in relation to the frequencies used. The goal is to keep these modulated signals orthogonal so that they do not cause large amounts of interference with each other. RF interference is less of a problem for the same basic reasons that it is a lesser problem in spread spectrum systems. The signal is spread across a wider frequency bandwidth than it needs, though OFDM spreads the signal differently. Multipath distortion is also reduced for this reason. OFDM systems implement error correcting so that any subcarriers experiencing interference are "balanced out" by the other subcarriers through a sort of parity algorithm similar to that used in fault-tolerant hard drive systems.

OFDM is not only used in WLAN technology, but is also used in asymmetric digital subscriber lines (ADSL) and in IEEE 802.16—also known as WiMAX. OFDM is similar to its namesake FDM (frequency division multiplexing), but OFDM is more focused on reducing interference between subcarriers than on perfecting the signal quality of each subcarrier. OFDM reduces crosstalk between subcarriers even though the sub carriers overlap in the spectrum used. Crosstalk is a negative impact of one frequency or channel's signal on another frequency or channel's signal. The crosstalk is reduced through the orthogonality of the OFDM communication channels.

In the IEEE 802.11a amendment, OFDM is referenced as simply OFDM. However, in order to use OFDM in the 2.4 GHz ISM band, some changes had to be made throughout the PHY originally specified in IEEE 802.11. This newer PHY standard is known as an *extended-rate PHY* or *ERP*. For this reason, the OFDM used in IEEE 802.11g, which uses the 2.4 GHz ISM band, is called ERP-OFDM.

IEEE 802.11n

Like OFDM today, IEEE 802.11n is not planned to use spread spectrum technology as its primary communications mechanism. Instead, it is expected to use a modified version of OFDM that is currently referenced as High Throughput–OFDM (HT-OFDM). The current draft for IEEE 802.11n, which defines the HT-OFDM PHY, will be based on the current OFDM PHY specified in Clause 17 of the IEEE 802.11a amendment. The draft calls for up to four spatial streams using 20 MHz of bandwidth each or up to four spatial streams using 40 MHz of bandwidth each. The latter would result in data rates of up to 600 Mbps.

The draft also states that the IEEE 802.11n PHY will operate in one of three modes: non-HT mode, HT mixed mode, and Greenfield mode. *Non-HT mode* calls for wireless communications using either OFDM or ERP-OFDM, depending on whether the 5 or 2.4 GHz spectrum is used, respectively. The *HT mixed mode* allows for communications that are compatible with non-HT devices (OFDM or ERP-OFDM). Both non-HT and HT mixed modes are required. *Greenfield mode* is optional and can be thought of as HT-only. This would be much like placing today's IEEE 802.11g devices in "g-only" mode.

The access points developed to support HT-OFDM must support both non-HT and 20 MHz HT to be considered IEEE 802.11n compliant in the current draft. This means that the access point will have to support backward compatibility with IEEE 802.11g and IEEE 802.11a as well as one to four spatial streams 20 MHz wide using HT-OFDM. With this constraint, down-level stations such as IEEE 802.11g–compatible laptops will be able to communicate with the IEEE 802.11n access points.

A station claiming to be IEEE 802.11n compliant will have to be able to support non-HT mode and 20 MHz HT mode with one spatial stream. This, again, means the station will be able to communicate with older IEEE 802.11a or IEEE 802.11g equipment as well as newer IEEE 802.11n equipment.

You will not currently be tested on the specifics of IEEE 802.11n when taking your CWNA exam. However, during the life of this book, the standard will likely be ratified and the technical functionality will be solidified. For more up-to-date information about the proposed IEEE 802.11n amendment, be sure to visit the CWNP forums at www.CWNP.com and the IEEE web site at www.IEEE.org.

How Spread Spectrum Technology Works

In order to more fully understand the functionality of spread spectrum technology, you will need to learn about two important concepts: modulation and coding.

Modulation

Modulation is defined as the process of manipulating a carrier signal so that it can represent intelligent information. There are multiple kinds of modulation, but they fall into two general categories: digital modulation and analog modulation. WLAN technologies use digital modulation only, and that is the modulation type that will be covered here.

An RF signal can be modulated by manipulating the frequency, phase, or amplitude. Amplitude modulation is not sufficient alone for WLAN technologies, since the amplitude is often affected by interference. This leaves frequency and phase modulation, and newer WLAN technologies use different kinds of phase modulation to achieve communications. Frequency modulation is also used, though it is less common today.

Keep in mind that all computer processing is the manipulation of binary 1s and 0s. You can think of them as positive or negative, on or off, or true or false; but they are usually referred to as bits, and we call combinations of these bits binary numbers. For example, the computer byte is eight bits, and these eight bits are said to form an eight-bit binary number. The binary number 01101101 is one byte and can represent anything that a coding system specifies. If it is used to represent whether eight different lights are off or on and a 0 means the light is off while a 1 means the light is on, we know that three of the lights are off and five of the lights are on in this case. The point is simple: once you define what the 0s and 1s mean, you can use them to communicate massive amounts of information.

How does this relate to modulation? RF signals are modulated so that they can represent these 0s and 1s. As long as a 0 or 1 can be represented, any computer information can be transferred on the signal.

Consider the following very simple example. Assume that two devices are configured to read signals at 1-millisecond intervals and that a change in phase would indicate a change in bit representation. In other words, every time the phase changes, we toggle the bit. If there is no phase change, the devices assume the bit should stay the same as it was during the last 1-millisecond interval. Therefore, once communications are established and a starting bit (let's say 0) is defined, any sequence of bits can be transmitted going forward. Let's further say that when actual data communications are about to begin, there is always a flip from 0 to 1 to 0 so that the receiving device knows to begin processing the next phase changes as information. Figure 3.1 illustrates this fictitious simple communications system.

In this example, as depicted in Figure 3.1, the sending alert—which you could refer to as a preamble—is sent first as 180-degree phase shifts from 0 to 1 and then back to 0. Next, two 0s are sent, so there is no phase shift, and these two 0s are followed by four 1s, indicated by a phase shift at millisecond 6. Finally, another phase shift at millisecond 10 indicates that the transmission should now represent a 0, and the two 0s end the eight-bit binary number that was transmitted.

FIGURE 3.1 Fictional simplified modulation system

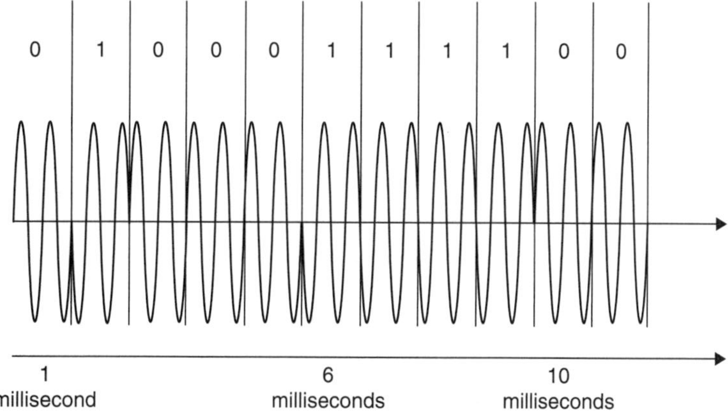

While this is not an actual "in-use" modulation, it simplifies the modulation concept and helps you to begin understanding how phase-based modulation can function. Even this simple modulation example is dependent on the devices knowing the modulation scheme, which includes both the phase shifting algorithm and the time window within which to accept a single bit. This phase shifting algorithm is often called the *keying* mechanism of the modulation, and the time window is called the *symbol* or *symbol period.* Technically, the symbol is the smallest unit of data transmitted at one time. For example, BPSK modulation transmits one bit at a time, whereas 16 quadrature amplitude modulation (16-QAM) transfers four bits at a time.

The most common type of modulation used in WLANs is one of many varieties of phase shift keying. *Phase shift keying* works similar to the fictional example represented in Figure 3.1. While the example used milliseconds as a measurement, most phase shift keying modulation schemes define the symbol time in hertz. For example, a modulation scheme may define that a symbol time is 3 hertz long. This means that three complete cycles of the RF wave form a single symbol period. With phase shift keying, if there is a 3-hertz symbol period and an advance of 0 degrees in the phase (no phase change), the value might be said to be equal to 0; if there is an advance of 180 degrees in the phase (a phase change is present), the value might be said to be equal to 1.

Keep in mind that an advance of 180 degrees followed by another advance of 180 degrees is equal to the original phase before any advance. Phase, unlike frequency, can be "advanced" until it is eventually back to the starting phase. If you advance a frequency, the frequency will get higher and each new advance will go higher still.

The following sections provide a high-level overview of the modulation schemes used for the FHSS, DSSS, HR/DSSS, and OFDM systems. The high-level overview is sufficient, since you do not have to understand the technical details of the modulation schemes in order to implement WLAN hardware or even to analyze WLAN communications, because most WLAN analyses happen at the MAC layer and higher. For the most part, only those programming chips and designing IEEE 802.11–compliant hardware will need to understand the technical details behind these modulation schemes.

FHSS Modulation

FHSS systems, which meet the specifications of the IEEE 802.11 standard, use a form of modulation known as *Gaussian frequency shift keying (GFSK).* Both two-level and four-level GFSK (2GFSK and 4GFSK) are supported by the standard for 1 and 2 Mbps data rates, respectively. Do not confuse the modulation scheme with the hopping sequence. I'll review hopping sequences later, in a section titled "Dwell Time and Hop Time." When the FHSS device hops to a frequency, it will use GFSK modulation to communicate on that frequency. When it hops to the next frequency, it will use the same modulation. The modulation scheme and the hopping sequence are two different concepts, though they are often confused because of the use of the word frequency in the modulation scheme title.

Frequency shift keying (FSK) has been used as a modulation technique for many years. Early modems used on standard telephone landlines used a form of FSK. As you can infer from the modulation name, this modulation technique does use the frequency as the manipulated characteristic of the RF signal to impress data on the wave. GFSK, as it is implemented in IEEE 802.11, uses either two frequencies (2GFSK—sometimes called binary or 2-ary GFSK) or four frequencies (4GFSK—sometimes called 4-ary GFSK) to encode the information onto the signal. Because most interference causes a reduction in amplitude and not a change in frequency, FSK is resistant, though not immune, to interference-based corruption. GFSK is a modulation technique where the data is first passed through a Gaussian filter in the base band and then modulated with frequency modulation.

DSSS Modulation

DSSS systems use differential phase shift keying (DPSK) to modulate information onto carrier signals. The actual phase of the waveform (RF wave used for signaling) does not matter because it is a phase shift or change in phase that encodes information. Like FSK, phase-shifting modulation schemes are resistant to interference because the phase is not usually impacted by interference.

This first kind of DPSK used in DSSS systems, called *differential binary phase shift keying (DBPSK),* provides a data rate of 1 Mbps. DBPSK uses the term *binary* because a single entity (a phase shift) is used to encode information onto the signal. For example, if there is no phase shift, the information is a 0 bit, and if there is a 180-degree phase shift, the information is a 1 bit. Keep in mind that this works according to symbols or frequency

TABLE 3.3 DQPSK Phase Shifts and Values

Phase Shift in Degrees	Value
0	00
90	01
180	11
270	10

spans that are considered an analysis time period. When an analysis time period—a symbol—ends, the radio knows to look for a phase shift when entering the new analysis time period. The information is determined by whether or not there is a phase shift in the new analysis time period.

The second kind of modulation used in DSSS systems is *differential quadrature phase shift keying (DQPSK)*. As you can probably guess from the name, this phase-shifting technique uses four different shifts to represent four different values. Table 3.3 provides a reference for the phase shifts and the value represented by those shifts.

Using a four-shift modulation scheme allows for faster data rates, and this is why DQPSK is used when communicating at 2 Mbps; however, DQPSK is more sensitive to multipath interference than DBPSK. For this reason, IEEE 802.11 equipment may have to be throttled back to 1 Mbps in high-multipath environments.

HR/DSSS Modulation

HR/DSSS uses a combination of DQPSK and complementary code keying (CCK) for modulation. Either four or eight bits are encoded in each symbol period. Four bits are used for 5.5 Mbps communications, and eight bits are used for 11 Mbps. In either case, two bits are always modulated using DQPSK, and the remaining bits are modulated using CCK. Since CCK is more of an encoding or coding mechanism, you'll learn more about it in the later section "Coding."

OFDM Modulation

OFDM systems, such as IEEE 802.11a and 802.11g, use different modulation techniques depending on the data rate. Modulations include DBPSK, DQPSK, 16-QAM, and 64-QAM. Table 3.4 provides a summary of the modulations used at the different data rates. You will not be tested on the information in Table 3.4, but it is useful for reference purposes.

TABLE 3.4 OFDM Modulation Schemes and Data Rates

Modulation Scheme	Data Rate (Mbps)
DBPSK	6
DBPSK	9
DQPSK	12
DQPSK	18
16-QAM	24
16-QAM	36
64-QAM	48
64-QAM	54

You will notice that Table 3.4 does not list the data rates of 1, 2, 5.5, and 11 Mbps. If you are wondering why they are not listed even though they are supported by IEEE 802.11g devices, it is because the devices use IEEE 802.11b modulation (HR/DSSS) or IEEE 802.11 modulation (DSSS) when communicating at these data rates.

When describing QAM modulation, the number before the modulation type represents the number of possible phase shifts that the modulation supports. For example, 16-QAM supports 16 possible phase shifts, whereas 64-QAM supports 64 possible phase shifts.

Coding

Before information is modulated onto RF carrier signals, it is encoded with different coding schemes. These coding schemes provide resilience to the communications process in that they spread the data using pseudorandom numbers (PN) that allow for error correction on the receiving end.

FHSS Coding

The only *coding* employed in FHSS systems is the hopping sequence, which will be covered later. In the past, many considered this to be an element of security, since devices communicating on the FHSS network would have to know the hopping sequence; however, due to standardization, this feature of FHSS systems can no longer be considered a security feature. For this reason, it is not commonly considered a coding mechanism either, and hopping sequences will be covered in the later section "Dwell Time and Hop Time."

DSSS Coding

Unlike FHSS systems, DSSS systems do encode the information to be transferred. Redundant information is added to the information to be transferred through a process known as *processing gain.* Each data bit is processed mathematically against a fixed-length binary number known as a pseudorandom number, or PN. The mathematical operation performed, called XOR'ing, results in a much larger amount of data than the original bit. The IEEE requires a processing gain of 11 for DSSS systems, which results in an 11 bit chunk of information for every single bit of actual data. The resulting 11 bit chunk is called a *chip.* This chip is still just a binary number, but it is important that you understand the terminology so that you can understand various documents and reference materials such as the IEEE standards themselves.

The specific code that is used as a PN code is known as the *Barker sequence* or the *chipping code.* This code is equal to 10110111000 and is referenced as +1 –1 +1 +1 –1 +1 +1 +1 –1 –1 –1 in the IEEE standards. This means that the bit value of 0 is transmitted as 01001000111 and the bit value of 1 is transmitted as 10110111000. This encoding occurs before the data is modulated, and in the end, the actual data is never modulated onto the carrier signal. Instead, the result of XOR'ing each signal bit against the Barker sequence is modulated. This result (11 chips) is also known as the *Barker code.*

By transferring this calculated information (the chips) instead of the original bits, the standards make it possible to recover from interference problems. For example, if the receiver is missing some of the information due to corruption, it can still determine the value of the original bit. Imagine that the receiver has received 0???1000?11. The receiver will be able to infer the actual bit that was intended. How can it do this? Because only a 0 bit would have a chipping code that starts with a 0, then three values, then a 1000, then some value, and then an 11.

HR/DSSS Coding

CCK is used in HR/DSSS implementations such as IEEE 802.11b and is much more complicated than the processing gain used in IEEE 802.11 systems. You will not be required to understand the complex processes of CCK for the CWNA exam, but I will provide a brief overview of how it differs from Barker sequences and the reasons it provides faster data rates.

First, CCK uses a PN code that results in a processing gain of 8 instead of 11. This 8-chip sequence results in 1.375 million codes per second instead of the 1 million codes per second in DSSS systems. Eleven million chips per second are processed by both DSSS and HR/DSSS, but HR/DSSS uses the shorter 8-chip PN code, and this provides the higher rate of total codes per second. Of course, with a higher rate of codes per second, you reduce the amount of resilience against interference. This is why you can only maintain 11 Mbps when the two communicating devices are closer together, and that's why they fall back to lower data rates as they get farther apart. Increasing the chipping code size increases the resilience against interference.

The second difference between CCK and Barker sequencing is that CCK uses different PN codes for different bit sequences. Whereas the Barker sequence is always 10110111000, the CCK 8-chip sequence is calculated according to the data being encoded. The data being encoded is encoded in 8-bit chunks at 11 Mbps and 4-bit chunks at 5.5 Mbps. There is a one-to-one relationship (complementary) that exists between every possible 8 bits of actual data and the 8-chip sequence that is calculated to represent that data. The same is true for the 4-bit data when it is encoded. Once the data is encoded with CCK, it is modulated onto the carrier signals, using DQPSK.

OFDM Coding

OFDM systems support a type of coding known as *convolution coding.* Convolution coding is not actually part of OFDM but is an IEEE 802.11a/g–supported forward error correction mechanism that provides error correction to OFDM communications. Convolution coding adds extra information to the transmitted data that is comparable to the parity data used to provide fault tolerance in storage systems. If an OFDM subcarrier is experiencing interference, the receiving device can regenerate the original data using the parity-type information that has been added to the data before transmission.

To understand how convolution coding operates, consider the following situation. Imagine you want to store and send two numbers: the number 13 and the number 47. You would send the number 60 (47 + 13) along with these two numbers. Now, assume the receiver is only able to receive the number 13 and the number 60 with a flag that informs the receiver that the number 60 is the recovery code. If the receiver knows the proper algorithm (recovery code – number received = number missing), it can regenerate the number 47 even though it did not properly receive that transmission.

This is an oversimplification, but it should help you understand how convolution coding works, particularly if you are not familiar with parity bits and storage-based fault tolerance.

As stated earlier, DSSS systems use a technique known as processing gain; the higher the processing gain, the lower the data rate, but the higher the interference resistance. In convolution coding systems, higher convolution coding ratios (compared to the actual information) equal lower data rates and lower convolution coding ratios equal higher data rates.

Spread Spectrum Fundamental Concepts

So far in this chapter, you've been introduced to the general concept of spread spectrum and the specific spread spectrum and other modulation techniques that are specified within the IEEE 802.11 standards and amendments. In this final section of the chapter, I will cover these technologies in greater detail in the areas of greatest important to WLAN administrators. These areas include

- Dwell Time and Hop Time for FHSS Systems
- Carrier Frequencies, Channel Centers, and Widths
- Colocation
- Throughput Versus Data Rate
- Bandwidth
- Communication Resilience

Dwell Time and Hop Time

FHSS systems include characteristics that are not included in any of the other modulation and communication technologies used within the IEEE 802.11 standard or the amendments. These characteristics include dwell time, hopping sequences, and hop time. These characteristics come together to make up how the FHSS system will function and the actual data throughput that will be available.

Dwell Time

The amount of time spent on a specific frequency in an FHSS hopping sequence is known as the *dwell time*. These channels, 1 MHz of bandwidth each, provide 79 optional frequencies on which to dwell for the specified length of the dwell time.

Hopping Sequence

The *hopping sequence* is the list of frequencies through which the FHSS system will hop according to the specified dwell time. This hopping sequence is also known as a hopping pattern or hopping set. The IEEE 802.11 standard, section 14.6.5, states that 1 MHz channels should be used. These channels exist between 2.402 and 2.480 GHz in the United States and most of Europe. Every station in a Basic Service Set must use the same hopping sequence. Every station must also store a table of all the hopping sequences that are used within the system. These hopping sequences must have a minimum hop size of 6 MHz in frequency. In other words, if the device is currently communicating on the 2.402 GHz frequency, it must hop to 2.408 GHz at the next hop at a minimum.

Hop Time

The completion of any action-oriented task, whether performed by a computer or a human, requires some duration of time. Since hopping from one frequency to another is an action, it takes some duration of time. The duration of time required to hop from one frequency in the hopping sequence to the next is called the *hop time.* Hop times are measured in microseconds (μs) and are commonly rated at 200–300 μs. Even though these durations are drastically short, they can add up to an impacting amount of time, given enough hops over a long enough duration of time; however, many consider these small measures of time inconsequential.

The reality is that no station can transmit during the hop time; therefore, the hop time must be considered as overhead. This is where dwell times and hop times begin to impact one another. A longer dwell time means fewer hops and therefore less overhead. This would lead you to think that an infinite dwell time would be best, since it would involve no hop time overhead; however, an infinite dwell time is effectively narrowband communications. To prevent this, the FCC specifies that a maximum dwell time of 400 ms per carrier frequency in any 30-second window must be enforced.

If you do the math, you will quickly see that you will need at least 75 hops in a hopping sequence to make the math work. For example, 100 ms dwell times multiplied by 75 hops equals 7500 ms, or 7.5 seconds. If you multiply 7.5 times 4 (to achieve a total of 400 ms), you end up with just over 30 seconds due to the inclusion of hop time overhead. This would be in compliance with FCC regulations. Table 3.5 provides a reference for some common combinations of dwell times and the results that come out to a maximum of 400 ms on any single frequency within the hopping sequence.

TABLE 3.5 FHSS Dwell Times and Hopping Sequence Cycles

Dwell Time	Time for One Pass	Number of Passes	Milliseconds on a Hop
50 ms	3,750 ms	8	400
100 ms	7,500 ms	4	400
200 ms	15,000 ms	2	400
400 ms	30,000 ms	1	400

Carrier Frequencies, Channel Centers, and Widths

In this section, I will provide information on the channels available in the various IEEE-specified systems. I will give the frequency ranges available to the different modulation techniques and then provide tables that break down the frequency ranges into the separate channels as specified by the IEEE standards. FHSS, DSSS, and OFDM will all be covered.

FHSS

FHSS systems use the frequency range from 2.402 to 2.480 GHz, providing 79 MHz of frequency space in the 2.4 GHz ISM band. Another way of saying this is to say that 79 MHz of bandwidth is specified for use in the 2.4 GHz ISM band for FHSS systems. While 79 MHz of frequency is provided, it is not uncommon to use only 75 MHz of the bandwidth due to the minimum requirement of 75 hops to meet FCC regulations. However, because of the regulations imposed by the FCC, 75 MHz is also the least amount of bandwidth that can be utilized. Unlike DSSS systems, FHSS systems do not use channels continually. The FHSS systems use hopping sequences across multiple carrier frequencies, and these carrier frequencies are also sometimes called channels. The carrier frequencies are 1 MHz wide in FHSSS systems. This means that every carrier frequency is centered on a channel from 2.402 to 2.480 GHz; therefore, 2.402 and 2.403 GHz would be two different carrier frequencies.

The IEEE standard also calls for at least 6 MHz of carrier frequency separation between hops. This means that a hopping sequence of 2.402, 2.404, and 2.406 would not be compliant with the IEEE specifications. However, a hopping sequence of 2.402, 2.408, and 2.414 would be. It is important that you do not misunderstand the hopping sequence concept.

Hopping sequences do not have to be sequential across the bandwidth. This means that a hopping sequence of 2.402, 2.418, 2.404, 2.420, and 2.406 would be valid.

The FCC regulations changed in 2000 (8/31/2000 specifically) to allow for greater flexibility in the implementation of FHSS systems. Before the year 2000, FCC regulations required at least 75 of the 79 carrier frequencies to be used in a hopping sequence. After the year 2000, FHSS systems are allowed to perform only 15 hops in a sequence with a width of 5 MHz for each channel; however, when implemented with 5 MHz channels, the output power is throttled back from the original 1 W at the intentional radiator to 125 mW.

Possibly because newer FHSS WLAN systems are rarely being developed today, the IEEE did not update the 802.11 standard to reflect the changes allowed by the FCC. This means that any equipment taking advantage of the new rules will be proprietary and may not be compatible with standards-based equipment. However, these new rules do allow for higher data rates with FHSS systems of 10 Mbps.

The actual FCC regulations as of 8/31/2000 require that a hopping sequence span 75 MHz of the 79 MHz of available bandwidth. The result is that you can perform any number of hops in a hopping sequence as long as the hop–to–channel bandwidth ratio works out somewhere between 75 and 79 MHz. For example, you could use 25 hops with 3 MHz of bandwidth for each channel. You could also theoretically use 20 hops with 3.75 MHz of bandwidth.

DSSS

The IEEE 802.11 standard calls for use of the 2.4 GHz ISM band ranging from 2.400 to 2.497 GHz. In the United States and Europe, the range from 2.4000 to 2.4835 GHz is specified as the total frequency space available. The DSSS channels are 22 MHz wide, and the center of each channel is spaced 5 MHz from the closest channels. Table 3.6 provides a breakdown of the DSSS channels used in IEEE 802.11 and the regulatory domains where they may be utilized.

The benefit of using channel numbers as a reference point becomes clear when you begin to have discussions about network configuration and colocation issues. It is much easier to say that you are going to use channels 1, 6, and 11 to provide wireless coverage in a conference facility than to say you are going to tune your radio to 2.412 GHz on the first device,

TABLE 3.6 DSSS IEEE 802.11 and HR/DSSS IEEE 802.11b Channels

Channel	Center Frequency (GHz)	North America	Europe	Spain	France	Japan
1	2.412	X	X			X
2	2.417	X	X			X
3	2.422	X	X			X
4	2.427	X	X			X
5	2.432	X	X			X
6	2.437	X	X			X
7	2.442	X	X			X
8	2.447	X	X			X
9	2.452	X	X			X
10	2.457	X	X	X	X	X
11	2.462	X	X	X	X	X
12	2.467		X		X	X
13	2.472		X		X	X
14	2.484					X

2.437 GHz on the second device, and 2.462 GHz on the third device. HR/DSSS uses the same channel structure as DSSS.

OFDM

IEEE 802.11a and IEEE 802.11g both use OFDM modulation. The 5 GHz U-NII bands are used with IEEE 802.11a, and the 2.4 GHz ISM band is used with IEEE 802.11g.

OFDM—IEEE 802.11a The frequency bands specified in the IEEE 802.11a standard are

- 5.150–5.250 GHz—Lower U-NII Band
- 5.250–5.350 GHz—Middle U-NII Band
- 5.725–5.825 GHz—Upper U-NII Band

These bands are each divided into four nonoverlapping channels for a total of 12 nonoverlapping channels available to IEEE 802.11a devices.

Most consumer and SOHO devices use the lower and middle bands, which provide a total of eight channels in these devices. Remember that OFDM uses subcarriers, so each of these channels will have 52 subcarriers that actually transmit the data. The channel numbers do not start at 1 like the channel numbers used in DSSS systems. Table 3.7 provides a breakdown of the channels available in IEEE 802.11a systems.

A brief investigation of Table 3.7 reveals that the IEEE 802.11a OFDM technology uses 20 MHz of spacing between each channel. You would also know that the channels are 20 MHz wide. This means that channel 157 would span the frequencies from 5.775 to 5.795 GHz, since the center of the channel is 5.785 GHz. Additionally, the 52 subcarriers are 300 kHz each.

OFDM—IEEE 802.11g Since the IEEE 802.11g standard calls for the use of the 2.4 GHz ISM band, the frequencies used for OFDM channels are different from those used in IEEE 802.11a. In fact, the OFDM (ERP-OFDM) implemented in IEEE 802.11g uses the same channels as HR/DSSS and DSSS implemented in IEEE 802.11b and IEEE 802.11, respectively. This is why an IEEE 802.11g–compliant access point or wireless router has the same channels available in the configuration screens as the older IEEE 802.11 and 802.11b devices. Table 3.6 can be used as a reference for the channels used by IEEE 802.11g.

TABLE 3.7 IEEE 802.11a Channels

Channel	Center Frequency (GHz)	U-NII Band
36 40 44 48	5.180 5.200 5.220 5.240	Lower (5.15–5.25 GHz)
52 56 60 64	5.260 5.280 5.300 5.320	Middle (5.25–5.35 GHz)
11 OFDM channels	Unassigned by IEEE	"Extended" UNII (5.470–5.725 GHz)
149 153 157 161 165	5.745 5.765 5.785 5.805 ISM (5.825)	Upper (5.725–5.850 GHz)

Colocation

Once you understand the channels used by the different IEEE 802.11–based technologies, you can begin to consider the colocation abilities of these systems. *Colocation* refers to the ability to place multiple devices in an environment so that they will cause little or no interference to each other. While the recommendations put forth in the IEEE standards for colocation do still result in some low levels of interference, they provide a functional guideline for implementing WLAN technology.

FHSS

FHSS systems can be colocated by using hopping sequences that result in infrequent simultaneous channel usage. In other words, the hopping sequences will be arranged in such a way that there are very few times, if any, where two different service sets are trying to dwell on the same channel. When they do land on the same channel, the interference will only last the length of one dwell time.

The IEEE standard defines hopping sequences that will allow for multiple service sets to exist in a service area. These hopping sequences use patterns that are based on mathematical algorithms that you do not need to be familiar with, in order to understand colocation of FHSS systems. Since there are 79 channels, it is theoretically possible to synchronize 79 service sets in one service area without ever having any two of them dwelling on the same channel. However, due to costs involved with this synchronization, most environments will max out at 12 colocated systems. With 12 colocated systems, you have a total speed of 12 × 2 Mbps, or 24 Mbps, in a service area. Even if you were to employ synchronization techniques for the use of 79 colocated FHSS service sets, you would still have a top end speed of 158 Mbps. This latter implementation is not practical in the real world because the technology simply does not exist to manage the number of access points that would be required to accomplish this. The main reason this technology does not exist is not that it is impossible, but that it is much easier to accomplish this level of bandwidth with OFDM-based technologies.

DSSS

The maximum number of nonoverlapping service sets that can be created using DSSS technology is three. The center channel frequencies must be spaced by 25 MHz in order to be considered nonoverlapping by the IEEE standards. The reality is that there is still some level of overlap, but the interference is so minimal that it is not considered in most installations. In North America and most of Europe, the three nonoverlapping channels that can be used in the same service area simultaneously are 1, 6, and 11.

You might have noticed that the nonoverlapping channels are spaced by five channels. This results in the ability to have any two channels, spaced apart by five channel numbers, function in the same service area without detrimental interference. For example, you could use channel 3 and channel 8, or you could use channel 2 and channel 7. Of course, a channel spread of more than five will also provide nonoverlapping channels. In fact, it would provide the lowest real levels of interference. If you need only two channels and they are available, channels 1 and 11 would be ideal.

From the information provided here, you can perform the math and realize that, with 11 Mbps data rates in IEEE 802.11b (HR/DSSS) and three nonoverlapping channels, three service sets will provide 33 Mbps of total speed to a service area. If you are using older DSSS technologies at 2 Mbps, you can only provide 6 Mbps of total speed in a service area.

OFDM

Thanks to the higher data rates in OFDM, you can provide much more total speed. IEEE 802.11g (ERP-OFDM) can use the same three nonoverlapping channels as DSSS systems and can provide a total of 163 Mbps. IEEE 802.11a can use all eight nonoverlapping channels in the lower and middle U-NII bands for an aggregate speed of 432 Mbps in a service area.

Colocation Technologies Compared

Ultimately, the technology you choose to implement will impact the throughput available to networking applications. However, the decision is never as simple as choosing the technology with the highest data rate and highest number of colocated service sets. This is because some technologies will lower their data rates before others. For example, IEEE 802.11a devices will throttle back to a lower data rate at a shorter distance than IEEE 802.11g devices. This is because the receiving device cannot detect the signal as easily at a greater distance. IEEE 802.11a devices use shorter antennas and are able to "pick up" less of the RF signal at the same point in space as an IEEE 802.11g device. The result is that, at 150 feet from the access point, you may have more bandwidth available to your network applications with three IEEE 802.11g devices than you would with five to eight IEEE 802.11a devices.

In most modern network installations, the choice will be between IEEE 802.11a (OFDM) and IEEE 802.11g (ERP) devices; however, this will change in the next few years as the IEEE 802.11n standard is ratified and those devices begin to infiltrate the market. It is important, however, that you still understand the basic functionality of FHSS and DSSS systems and HR/DSSS systems. The FHSS and DSSS systems are disappearing quickly in the WLAN market, but the HR/DSSS systems are still very widely deployed.

Throughput Versus Data Rate

It is very important to distinguish between throughput and data rate. The data rate of a WLAN system is a component of the entire bandwidth that is available for communications between WLAN devices. Much of this bandwidth and the time usage of the same is consumed by WLAN management data and redundant data in the WLAN signals. Because of this, the throughput of the system is always lower than the data rate. Defined, *data rate* is the measurement of the total amount of data that can be transferred through the system, including intentionally transferred data and overhead data. *Throughput* is defined as the amount of useful information that can be intentionally transferred through the system.

To make it simple, if you transfer a 50KB Microsoft Word document from one computer to another across a WLAN, much more than 50KB of network traffic will be generated. While the data rate may be 54 Mbps, you may find that throughput is as low as 20 to 28 Mbps.

Table 3.8 compares the various data rates of the different PHY technologies covered in this chapter. You will notice that FHSS and DSSS have the lowest data rates and OFDM provides the highest that is available at this writing. I've included some estimates of data rates for IEEE 802.11n technology, based on the draft amendment available in early 2007.

TABLE 3.8 Data Rates and Throughput Estimates

PHY	Standards Introducing the PHY	Data Rate	Estimate of Throughput
FHSS	IEEE 802.11-1997	1–2 Mbps	0.7–1 Mbps
DSSS	IEEE 802.11-1997	1–2 Mbps	0.7–1 Mbps
HR/DSSS	IEEE 802.11b-1999	1, 2, 5.5, and 11 Mbps	3–6 Mbps

PHY	Standards Introducing the PHY	Data Rate	Estimate of Throughput
ERP	IEEE 802.11g-2003	1, 2, 5.5, 11, 6, 9, 12, 18, 24, 36, 48, 54 Mbps	3–29 Mbps
OFDM	IEEE 802.11a-1999	6, 9, 12, 18, 24, 36, 48, 54 Mbps	3–29 Mbps
HT	IEEE 802.11n-2009	1–600 Mbps (with 4 spatial streams)	Untested

Bandwidth

In the wireless world, *bandwidth* refers to the frequency space made available to the networking devices. For example, an IEEE 802.11g channel is 22 MHz wide, so it has 22 MHz of bandwidth. However, it is not uncommon to hear the word "bandwidth" used to refer to the amount of "space" available for data transfer. For example, it is common for many networking professionals to say they have 10 Mbps of bandwidth available on their network. This seems to have evolved over the years from an understanding that if you have more bandwidth (more frequency space), you can transfer more information. This is true, in general; however, it is often better to refer to bandwidth in its most absolute sense, and that is the width of the frequency band that you are using, and then refer to data rates and throughput for the rest.

Communication Resilience

When it comes to communication resilience, FHSS and OFDM systems currently provide the best resistance to interference. All of the technologies covered in this chapter provide some level of resilience, but the higher data rates and colocation abilities tend to make OFDM—whether in IEEE 802.11a or IEEE 802.11g—more appealing at this time. FHSS is the most resilient but has the lowest data rates, being equal to the original DSSS. OFDM has the second highest level of resilience and the highest data rates while we wait for HT-OFDM in IEEE 802.11n.

Summary

Table 3.9 provides a summary of the knowledge you've gained in this chapter. This table and this chapter will provide a solid foundation for you as you move ahead in this book. The next chapter will dive deeper into the IEEE 802.11 PHY but will also introduce you to the MAC layer and how it is addressed in IEEE 802.11.

TABLE 3.9 Summary of IEEE Technologies and Features

PHY	Data Rates	Frequency Band	IEEE Standards Introducing the Technology	Maximum Colocated WLANs	Max Total Data Rate in a Service Area
FHSS	1 or 2 Mbps	2.4 GHz ISM	IEEE 802.11-1997	79 max, 12 practical	158 Mbps max, 24 Mbps practical
DSSS	1 or 2 Mbps	2.4 GHz ISM	IEEE 802.11-1997	2 or 3	6 Mbps
HR/ DSSS	1, 2, 5.5, or 11 Mbps	2.4 GHz ISM	IEEE 802.11b-1999	3	33 Mbps
ERP	1, 2, 5.5, 11, 6, 9, 12, 18, 24, 36, 48, or 54 Mbps	2.4 GHz ISM	IEEE 802.11g-2003	3	162 Mbps
OFDM	6, 9, 12, 18, 24, 36, 48, or 54 Mbps	5 GHz U-NII	IEEE 802.11a-1999	19 in consumer or SOHO, 23 total	648 Mbps

Key Terms

- ☐ **bandwidth**
- ☐ **coding**
- ☐ **colocation**
- ☐ **data rate**
- ☐ **DSSS**
- ☐ **ERP**
- ☐ **FHSS**
- ☐ **HR/DSSS**
- ☐ **modulation**
- ☐ **OFDM**
- ☐ **throughput**

Review Questions

1. In order to implement multiple WLANs in the same location using HR/DSSS systems, how many channels must separate the WLANs?

   A. 1

   B. 5

   C. 6

   D. 11

2. OFDM modulation techniques are applied at what layer of the OSI model?

   A. Layer 4

   B. Layer 2

   C. Layer 6

   D. Layer 1

3. If you were to install five OFDM WLANs in the same location, what aggregate data rate would be available to the service area, assuming the highest data rate could be achieved in each WLAN?

   A. 55 Mbps

   B. 10 Mbps

   C. 270 Mbps

   D. 128 Mbps

4. Which modulation technique is used by DSSS systems communicating at 2 Mbps?

   A. DQPSK

   B. DBPSK

C. 16-QAM

D. 64-QAM

5. How many channels are specified for use with DSSS?

A. 14

B. 12

C. 11

D. 8

6. How many channels are specified for use by the IEEE in the lowest two U-NII bands for OFDM technologies?

A. 4

B. 8

C. 11

D. 14

7. FHSS systems use what frequency range within the 2.4 GHz ISM band?

A. 2.400–2.4835 GHz

B. 2.400–2.485 GHz

C. 2.401–2.480 GHz

D. 4.435–2.485 GHz

8. If an IEEE HR/DSSS device is used, what are the supported data rates? (Choose all that apply.)

A. 54 Mbps

B. 11 Mbps

C. 2 Mbps

D. 36 Mbps

9. How many subcarriers are used in each OFDM channel to transmit data?

   A. 14

   B. 12

   C. 52

   D. 54

Review Answers

1. **C.** Six channels of separation are required for HR/DSSS systems, and 5 channels are required for DSSS systems.
2. **D.** The correct answer is Layer 1. The Physical layer is where wireless modulation takes place, and therefore, this is where OFDM modulation occurs.
3. **C.** The correct answer is 270 Mbps. Since there are five service sets communicating at 54 Mbps each, the aggregate would be 270 Mbps for the data rate.
4. **A.** The correct answer is DQPSK. DBPSK is used for 1 Mbps DSSS communications, and 16-QAM/64-QAM is used with OFDM technologies.
5. **A.** The correct answer is 14. While only 11 channels are used in North America, due to FCC regulations, 14 channels are specified in the standard.
6. **B.** The correct answer is 8. There are 12 total channels specified for IEEE 802.11a technologies. Four channels are specified in each of the three bands: lower, middle, and upper. There is also a fourth band, but the IEEE standards do not yet utilize it. This results in eight channels being available in the lower and middle bands.
7. **A.** The correct answer is 2.400–2.4835 GHz. FHSS systems use 1 MHz of bandwidth for each of 79 channels, starting with the first channel at 2.402 GHz and moving up sequentially to 2.480 GHz, but they exist within the boundaries of 2.400–2.4835 GHz.

8. **B, C.** The correct answers are 11 Mbps and 2 Mbps. IEEE 802.11b supports data rates of 11, 5.5, 2, and 1 Mbps. The data rates of 36 and 54 Mbps are supported by IEEE 802.11g and IEEE 802.11a technologies.

9. **C.** The correct answer is 52. Fifty-two subcarriers are used within each of the 12 OFDM channels used by IEEE 802.11a in the U-NII bands. Fifty-two subcarriers are also used within each of the 11 OFDM channels used by IEEE 802.11g in the ISM band. Only 48 of the 52 carry actual data.

CHAPTER

4

IEEE 802.11 In Depth

CWNA Exam Objectives Covered:

- Describe and apply the following concepts surrounding WLAN frames
  - Terminology Review: Frames, Packets, and Datagrams
  - Terminology Review: Bits, Bytes, and Octets
  - Terminology: MAC and PHY
- Understand IEEE 802.11 CSMA/CA
- Understand and compare frame types and formats
  - IEEE 802.11 Frame Format Versus IEEE 802.3 Frame Format
  - Layer 3 Protocol Support by IEEE 802.11 Frames
  - Jumbo Frame Support (Layer 2)
  - MTU Discovery and Functionality (Layer 3)
- Identify, explain, and apply the frame and frame exchange sequences covered by the IEEE 802.11 standard (as amended)
  - Active (Probes) and Passive (Beacons) Scanning
  - Dynamic Rate Switching

In This Chapter

CWNA Exam Objectives Covered:

- ❖ Summarize the processes involved in authentication and association
  - The IEEE 802.11 State Machine
  - Open System Authentication, Shared Key Authentication, and Deauthentication
  - Association, Reassociation, and Disassociation
- ❖ Identify and apply regulatory domain requirements
- ❖ Define, describe, and apply IEEE 802.11 coordination functions and channel access methods and features available for optimizing data flow across the RF medium
  - DCF and HCF Coordination Functions
  - EDCA Channel Access Method
  - RTS/CTS and CTS-to-Self Protocols
  - Fragmentation

In the preceding chapter, you discovered the basics of modulation and coding at the Physical layer. This chapter will reveal more information related to the Physical layer of IEEE 802.11 communications, but it will also begin the process of revealing the Medium Access Control (MAC) layer functionality. You will learn about the terms related to IEEE 802.11 networks and then move on to understanding the collision domain management technologies as well as the framing techniques used. Finally, you'll learn about authentication and association as well as data flow optimization.

Terminology Review

Understanding any technology requires the use of a shared language. This means that not only the grammar of that language, but the definitions must be agreed upon, if you are to have meaningful dialog. This section provides an encyclopedic overview of many terms that will be used throughout this chapter and the remaining chapters of this book. Rather than simply provide a definition, I will provide a detailed description of the functionality of these terms and an explanation of how they are related to each other.

Frames, Packets, and Datagrams

The first terms I will cover relate to the conceptualization of data before it is transmitted onto the wire or RF medium. These terms are *frames, packets,* and *datagrams.* Figure 4.1 illustrates the OSI layers associated with these terms. As you can see, packets and datagrams reside at Layer 3 of the OSI model and these objects are framed at Layer 2.

FIGURE 4.1 Frames, packets, and datagrams

Network layer – Layer 3 | Packets or datagrams

Data Link layer – Layer 2 | Frames

Physical layer – Layer 1 | Bits and bytes

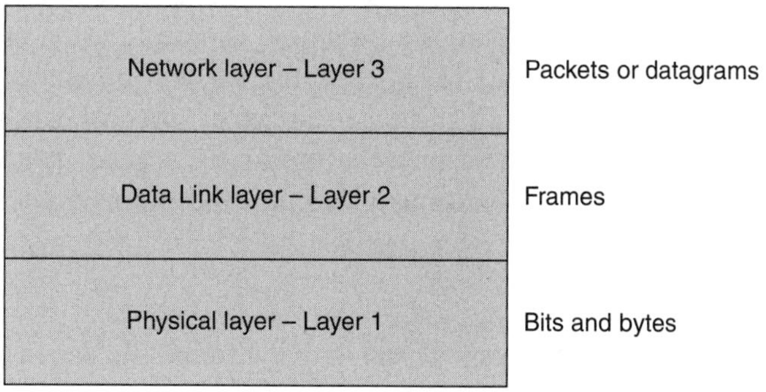

What is the difference between a packet and a datagram? In many cases, they are used interchangeably; however, the technical difference is that the term *packet* is usually used for connection-oriented communications (TCP) and the term *datagram* is usually used for connectionless communications (UDP). I'll speak only of packets to keep things simple.

Whatever data is communicated, Layer 4—the Transport layer—usually breaks the data into TCP segments. These segments are sent to Layer 3 and become the packets. At this time, the destination IP address is attached to the data and it is ready to be placed on the wire or RF medium using the Layer 2 and Layer 1 technologies implemented. When these packets are passed on to Layer 2, they become frames.

What is a frame? Technically, a frame is the exact same thing as a packet or a TCP segment: a series of 1s and 0s. However, we usually think about frames at a higher level, and here *frames* are collections of data and management information needed to carry the data from one place to another on the network. Different networking technologies use different frame formats, but all IEEE 802–based networks use framing concepts.

One way to conceptualize this is to think about the original data, which is actually the intentional information being sent across the network. Imagine this data is a Microsoft Excel spreadsheet. In order for the data to be transmitted across the network, it must be broken into manageable chunks known as packets. This has happened by the time the Excel spreadsheet has reached Layer 3 of the OSI model. While the original spreadsheet was actually millions of 1s and 0s, it has now been broken down into chunks that are just a few thousand 1s and 0s. The 1s and 0s that make up the data have been prefixed and suffixed with more information that is used to manage the transfer of the data. This information includes the destination IP address, error checking information, and more. The final step, at Layer 2, is to add the frame information, which includes a preamble and destination and source MAC addresses. At this point, an entire frame exists. Remember this frame is a series of 1s and 0s that started as an Excel spreadsheet, but it is now a chunk of an Excel spreadsheet (assuming the spreadsheet is larger than 1500 bytes) with network management information added.

Bits, Bytes, and Octets

In the preceding paragraph, I stated that a frame is a series of 1s and 0s. We looked at the process of breaking a large piece of data into smaller, more manageable pieces of data for network transmission. Ultimately, the smallest element that can be transmitted on any network is a *bit.* A bit is a single value equal to 1 or 0. When you group these bits together, they form *bytes*. An 8-bit byte is the most commonly referenced byte and is the basis of most networking measurements; it is specifically called an *octet* in most standards even though the vendors and networking professionals have leaned more toward the term byte. For example, 1 kilobyte is 1024 bytes, and 1 megabyte is 1,048,576 bytes. You will often see these numbers rounded to say that 1000 bytes is a kilobyte or 1,000,000 bytes is a megabyte. The term octet could also be used in these statements; for example, 1 kilobyte is 1024 octets.

You might be wondering how a simple bit, or even a byte, can represent anything. This is an important concept to understand; otherwise, you may have difficulty truly understanding how a network works. Let's consider just an 8-bit byte. If you have one bit, it can represent any two pieces of information. The 1 can represent one piece of information, and the 0 can represent another. When you have two bits, you can represent four pieces of information. You have the values 00, 01, 10, and 11 available to use as representative elements. When you have three bits, you can represent eight pieces of information, and for every bit you add, you double the amount of information that can be represented. This means that an 8-bit byte can represent 2^8 pieces of information, or 256 elements.

There are standard mapping systems that map a numeric value to a piece of information. For example, the ASCII system maps numbers to characters. Since I can represent up to 256 elements with an 8-bit byte, I can represent 256 ASCII codes as well. A quick Internet search for ASCII codes will reveal a number of sites that provide tables of ASCII codes. For example, the ASCII codes for 802.11 are 56, 48, 50, 46, 49, and 49 in decimal form. Since I can represent any number from 0 to 255 with an 8-bit byte, I can represent these numbers as well. Table 4.1 shows a mapping of characters to ASCII decimal codes to 8-bit bytes.

TABLE 4.1 Representing Characters with Bytes

Character	ASCII Decimal Codes	8-Bit Byte
8	56	00111000
0	48	00110000
2	50	00110010
.	46	00101110
1	49	00110001
1	49	00110001

TABLE 4.2 Converting Bytes to Decimal Values

Bit Position	8	7	6	5	4	3	2	1
Represented Decimal Number	128	64	32	16	8	4	2	1
Example Binary Number	0	0	1	1	0	0	0	1
Translated	0	0	32	16	0	0	0	1

In order for all this to work, both the sender and the receiver of the bytes must agree on how the bytes will be translated. In other words, for information to be meaningful, both parties must agree to the meaning. This is the same in human languages. If I speak a language that has meaning to me, but you do not understand that language, it is meaningless to you and communication has not occurred. When a computer receives information that it cannot interpret to be anything meaningful, it sees it as either noise or corrupted data.

To understand how the binary bits, in an octet, translated to the ASCII decimal codes, consider Table 4.2. Here you can see that the first bit (the rightmost bit) represents the number 1, the second bit represents the number 2, the third bit represents the number 4, and so on. The example, in the table, is 00110001. Where there is a 0, the bit is off. Where there is a 1, the bit is on. We add up the total values in the translated row, based on the represented number for each bit, and find the result of 49 because we count only the values where the bit is equal to 1. This is how the binary octet of 00110001 represents the ASCII decimal code of 49, which represents the number 1 in the ASCII tables.

MAC and PHY

Two other terms that are used heavily in the networking knowledge domain are *MAC* and *PHY. MAC* is an acronym for *medium access control.* Within the Data Link layer (Layer 2) of the OSI model, there are two sublayers known as the Logical Link Control (LLC) sublayer and the MAC sublayer. The LLC sublayer is a shared sublayer, also known as IEEE 802.2, among all IEEE 802 standards such as IEEE 802.3 (Ethernet) and IEEE 802.11 (wireless).

PHY is an abbreviation for the Physical layer of the OSI model or a specific networking implementation. Phrases such as “IEEE 802.11 PHY” or “that takes place at the PHY” refer to Layer 1 and the processes that occur at this layer. In order to provide for different physical technologies (Infrared, DSSS, FHSS, etc.) in IEEE 802.11, the PHY is divided into two sublayers called the Physical Medium Dependant (PMD) and the Physical Layer Convergence Protocol (PLCP).

PMD and PLCP

The *Physical Medium Dependent (PMD)* sublayer is the portion of the IEEE 802.11 PHY that is responsible for actually transmitting the information using some form of modulation such as GPSK, DBPSK, or DQPSK. The *Physical Layer Convergence Protocol (PLCP)* is responsible for abstracting the PMD from the Data Link layer protocols and abstracting the Data Link layer protocols from the PMD. You might say that it acts as a translator or coordinator between the real physical medium (PMD) and the MAC processes.

The details of how GPSK, DBPSK, and DQPSK work are beyond the scope of this CWNA study guide. It is enough for you to know that there are different modulations used at different data rates and with different PHYs.

The IEEE 802.11 standard and amendments that specify a PHY each provide different PMDs. The modulation techniques you learned about in Chapter 3 make up these different PMDs in large part. For example, there is one PMD for FHSS (using GPSK) and another for DSSS (using either DBPSK or DQPSK). The PMDs may add additional functions such as the scrambling of the data units before transmission. The MAC layer is mostly the same for all of the current IEEE 802.11 PHYs in production, but there are features peculiar to the PHY, such as ERP protection mechanisms for the ERP PHY, that will vary. Additionally, the WLAN MAC standard offers optional features that are not likely to be found with older PHY implementations or hardware, such as Quality of Service (QoS).

Data Link Layer and Logical Link Control (LLC) Sublayer

The Data Link layer of the OSI model, like the Physical layer, is divided into two sublayers. These sublayers, in IEEE 802.11 systems, are the IEEE 802.2 Logical Link Control (LLC) sublayer, which is the same for all 802-based networks, and the Media Access Control (MAC) sublayer, which is the same for all current IEEE 802.11–based technologies. Figure 4.2

FIGURE 4.2 Layer 1 and Layer 2 sublayers

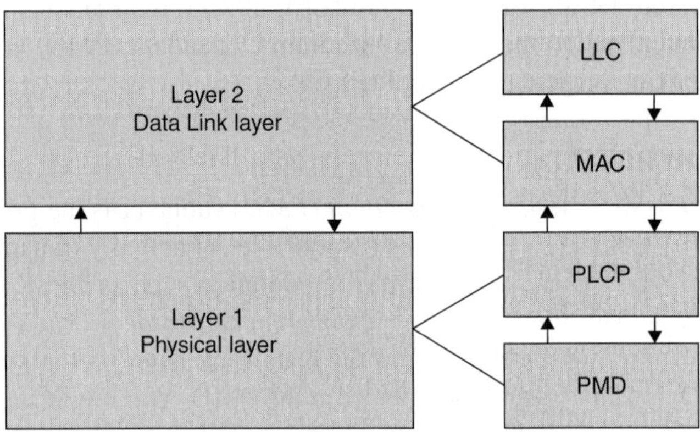

provides a visual representation of both the Physical and Data Link layers and how they are separated into sublayers. While IEEE 802 defines LLC for all its LAN types, including Ethernet, Ethernet is allowed to skip the LLC, and IP over Ethernet almost never uses LLC.

MSDU

The data units, or frames, that are passed down through the layers have specific names. These names are used to distinguish the frame at one layer from the frame at another layer and to distinguish the preserviced frame from the serviced frame at each layer. These names are MSDU, MPDU, PSDU, and PPDU.

The first, MSDU, stands for *MAC service data unit.* The MSDU is what is received from the upper layers (OSI layers 7–3 via the LLC sublayer) to be managed and transmitted by the lower layers (OSI layers 2–1). It is the data accepted by the MAC layer to be transmitted to the MAC layer of another station on the network. MSDUs are included in all wireless frames that carry upper-layer data; however, IEEE 802.11 management frames do not contain MSDUs, since there is no upper-layer data to transfer.

MPDU

The MPDU, *MAC protocol data unit,* is what is delivered to the PLCP so that it can ultimately be converted into a PPDU and transmitted.

The MSDU is what is received by the Data Link layer, and the MPDU is what comes out of the Data Link layer and is delivered to the Physical layer; specifically, it is delivered to the PLCP. Another way of saying this is to say that the MSDU is received by the MAC from upper layers and the MPDU is provided by the MAC to the lower layer.

PSDU

The PSDU is the *PLCP service data unit.* The PSDU is what the PLCP receives from the MAC sublayer. While the MAC sublayer calls it the MPDU, the Physical layer references the exact same objects as the PSDU. The PLCP adds information to the PSDU and provides the result to the PMD as a PPDU.

PPDU

The PPDU, *PLCP protocol data unit,* is what is actually transmitted on the RF medium. The PPDU is what the PMD receives from the PLCP. Ultimately, the PPDU is the culmination of all that has happened to the data from the time it left the application starting at Layer 7 of the OSI model to the time it is actually transmitted on the RF medium by the PMD at Layer 1.

Understanding Data Units at Layer 1 and Layer 2

The concept of the data units and their relationships to Layer 1 and Layer 2 can become difficult to grasp, so I will explain them in sequence. First, I'll explain it from the upper layers (the LLC component of Layer 2 and Layers 3–7) down to the physical medium and then from the physical medium to the upper layers.

The life of a data unit begins as a TCP segment in most TCP/IP communications. This information is either passed directly to the MAC layer from the IP protocol or passed to the MAC layer through the LLC layer. Either way, when the information is passed to the MAC layer, it is called an MSDU. The MSDU is always 2304 bytes or smaller, and this size limit is a constraint of the IEEE 802.11 MAC specifications, which limit the upper-layer frame payload to 2304 bytes in Clause 6. The MAC layer adds a header and a trailer and expands the frame for encryption overhead. At this point, the MAC layer has created an MPDU. The MPDU is the MSDU with the extra information added by the MAC layer.

Next, the MAC layer hands off the MPDU to the PLCP component at the Physical layer. The PLCP component receives the MPDU and considers it a PSDU. The PSDU is the same thing as the MPDU; however, from the perspective of the PLCP, it must be serviced in some way. The PLCP and PMD sublayers work together to create a PLCP preamble, a PLCP header, and an altered PSDU; in so doing, they create a PPDU out of the PSDU. This PPDU is transmitted as bits on the physical medium or RF by the PMD.

In reverse, the bits are received from the physical medium or RF and the PMD sends a PPDU up to the PLCP. The PLCP strips its header from the PPDU and passes the resulting PSDU up to the MAC layer. The MAC receives the PPDU and processes it as an MPDU by stripping away its header, trailer, and encryption frame expansion and passes the result to the upper layers as an MSDU.

In large part, the difference between an MPDU and a PSDU is a factor of perception. When looking at it from the perspective of the MAC layer, it is an MPDU. When looking at it from the perspective of the PLCP layer, it is a PSDU. However, there is a very important reason for the different naming schemes. The *s* in MSDU and PSDU stands for *service.* The indication is that the frame needs to be serviced by the specified layer. This is why the MPDU is a PSDU when it is received by the PLCP. The frame must be serviced before sending it on to the PMD. The service offered is to exchange an SDU with a peer entity in a source or destination system. This is usually accomplished by encapsulation and availing the service of a lower layer; however, encapsulation is not the service offered.

IEEE 802.11 CSMA/CA

Ethernet networks (IEEE 802.3) use a form of collision management known as collision detection (CD). Wireless networks use a different form of collision management known as collision avoidance (CA). The full name of the physical media access management used in wireless networks is carrier sense multiple access/collision avoidance or CSMA/CA. We'll investigate CSMA/CD—the MAC method used in Ethernet networks—and then we'll look at CSMA/CA.

The essence of CSMA/CA is that collisions can happen many places on the medium, at any time during a transmission, and likely cannot be detected by the transmitter at its location. Listening for evidence of a collision while transmitting is thus worthless and not a part of the protocol.

This is because transmissions cannot be aborted early. Collisions are only inferred as one possible explanation for failure to receive an immediate acknowledgment (ACK) after transmitting a frame in its entirety. The frame must be retransmitted completely. Under these circumstances there is much value in collision avoidance, and there is much of it in the IEEE 802.11 protocols.

If you've ever had a conversation with another person on the telephone, you've probably experienced a communications collision. When you both started speaking at the same time, neither of you could hear the other effectively. Usually, you will both stop speaking for some amount of time and then one of you start will speaking again. Since the time that both of you choose to wait is slightly different, there is a good chance that one of you will be able to communicate the next time. This would be similar to CD. The *carrier sense* in CSMA means that the devices will attempt to sense whether the physical medium is available before communicating. The *multiple access* indicates that multiple devices will be accessing the physical medium. In a CD implementation of CSMA, when a collision is detected, both devices go silent for a pseudo-random period of time. Since the time period is different for each device, they are not likely to try communicating at the same time again. This process helps recover from collisions and avoid another collision. In a CSMA/CD implementation, collisions occur because devices can begin communicating at the same time even though they both listened for "silence" on the physical medium. There was indeed silence, but both devices broke the silence at the same moment.

CSMA/CA is used in wireless networks and it was also used in early Apple LocalTalk networks, which were wired networks that were common to Apple devices. Collision avoidance is achieved by signaling to the other devices that one device is about to communicate. This would be like saying "Listen, for the next few minutes, because I will be talking" in a telephone conversation. You are avoiding the collision by announcing that you are going to be communicating for some time interval. CSMA/CA is not perfect due to hidden node problems, which will be covered in detail in Chapter 12, but it provides a more efficient usage of a medium like RF medium than would CSMA/CD.

Carrier Sense

Carrier sense is the process of checking to see if the medium is in use or busy. If you have multiple telephones in your house and a single line that is shared by all of these telephones, you use a manual form of carrier sense every time you use one of the phones to make a call. When you pick up the phone, you listen to see if someone else is already using the phone. If they are, you may choose to hang up the phone and wait until it becomes available. If you've ever been on the phone when someone else begins dialing without first checking to see if anyone is using the line, you've experienced a form of collision as the tones penetrated your ears and overcame your conversation with noise.

In IEEE 802.11 WLANs, there are two kinds of carrier sense that are performed: virtual carrier sense and physical carrier sense.

Physical carrier sense uses *clear channel assessment (CCA)* to determine if the physical medium is in use. CCA is accomplished by monitoring the medium to determine if the amount of RF energy detected exceeds a particular threshold. Due to the nature of WLAN architectures, there is no requirement for all stations to be able to hear all other stations existing in the same basic service set (BSS). This is because the wireless access point forms a kind of hub for the BSS. A station may be able to hear the access point and the access point may be able to hear the other station, but the two stations may not be able to hear each other. This results in what is commonly known as the *hidden node problem.* For this reason, wireless networks must use other forms of carrier sense to deal with medium access control.

The other form of carrier is virtual carrier sense, which uses a network allocation vector (NAV). The NAV is a timer in each station that is used to determine if the station can utilize the medium. If the NAV has a value of 0, the station may contend for the medium. If the NAV has a value greater than 0, the station must wait until the timer counts down to 0 to contend for the medium. Stations configure their NAV timers according to Duration fields in other frames using the medium. For example, if a station detects a frame with a specific duration set in the Duration field, it will set the NAV timer to this duration and will then wait until that time has expired before contending for access.

To be clear, both the physical carrier sense and the virtual carrier sense must show that the medium is available before the station can contend for access. In other words, if the NAV timer reaches 0 and the station uses CCA to detect activity on the medium only to find there is such activity, the station still cannot transmit. In this case, another frame may be pulled from the medium and used to set a new NAV timer value for countdown. While it may seem that this would prevent a station from ever communicating, the rate of frame transfer is so high that all of these actions usually take place in far less than 1 second.

An additional form of carrier sense that is not often written about is what you might call phantom frame sensing. In this scenario, the PHY reads an incoming PLCP header length value and loses the incoming signal completely. However, since the header length was read, the device can still defer to the rest of the phantom frame.

Interframe Spacing

After the station has determined that the medium is available, using carrier sensing techniques, it must observe *interframe spacing (IFS)* policies. IFS is a time interval in which frames cannot be transmitted by stations within a BSS. This space between frames ensures that frames do not overlap each other. The time interval differs, depending on the frame type and the applicable IFS type for that frame.

While the IFS implementation in IEEE 802.11 systems can result in the appearance of QoS, it should not be confused with *IEEE 802.11e* or any Layer 3 or higher QoS solution. IFS is an 802.11 feature that allows for dependent frames to be processed in a timely manner. For example, a standard 802.11 data frame is transmitted using the distributed IFS (DIFS) interval and the ACK to this data frame is sent back using the short IFS (SIFS) interval. Because the ACK uses a SIFS interval, the ACK frame will take priority over any other data frames that are waiting to be transmitted. This way, the original station that transmitted the data frame will receive the ACK frame and not attempt to resend the data frame. In other words, the frame-to-IFS interval relationships that are specified in the IEEE 802.11 standard ensure that frames will be processed in their proper sequence.

I've mentioned some of the IFS types defined by the IEEE 802.11 standard already. These IFS types include the following types, which will now be covered in more detail:

- SIFS
- PIFS
- DIFS
- EIFS

SIFS

Short interframe spacing (SIFS) is the shortest of the available IFS parameters. Frames that are specified to use SIFS will take priority over frames that are specified to use PIFS, DIFS, or extended IFS (EIFS).

This priority function is simply a result of the IFS length. Since the SIFS is the shortest IFS, stations that are waiting to send a frame that is specified to use a SIFS interval will have a shorter wait time and will therefore have access to the wireless medium (WM) before other stations with frames specified for other IFS types.

SIFS is used for many different frames, including:

- ACK frames immediately following the receipt of a data frame
- Clear to Send (CTS) frames sent as a response to Request to Send (RTS) frames
- Data frames that immediately follow CTS frames
- With the exception of first exchange and error conditions, all frame exchanges made in Point Coordination Function (PCF) mode
- With the exception of the first fragment, all fragment frames that are part of a fragment burst

As technically defined by the IEEE 802.11 standard as amended, the SIFS time interval is the time from the end of the last symbol of the previous frame to the beginning of the first symbol of the preamble of the subsequent frame as seen at the air interface. The accuracy level required is ±10% of the slot time for the PHY in use. For example, the actual SIFS time interval must be within 2 μs of the specified time interval for the DSSS PHY. Slot times for the various PHYs are listed in the later section of this chapter "Random Backoff Times." The SIFS times for the various PHYs are listed here:

- FHSS—28 μs
- DSSS—10 μs
- OFDM—16 μs
- HR/DSSS—10 μs
- ERP—10 μs

PIFS

Point (coordination function) interframe spacing (PIFS) is neither the shortest nor longest interval; it results in a priority greater than DIFS, but less than SIFS. When an access point needs to switch the network from *Distributed Coordination Function (DCF)* mode to PCF mode, it will use PIFS frames. PCF is an optional part of IEEE 802.11 and has not been implemented in any market devices. The PIFS duration interval is equal to the SIFS interval for the PHY and one slot time duration for the PHY. For example, DSSS has a 20 μs slot time and a 10 μs SIFS interval. Therefore the PIFS interval in a DSSS PHY will be 30 μs. For another example, the OFDM PHY has a 9 μs slot time and a 16 μs SIFS interval. Therefore the PIFS interval in an OFDM PHY is 25 μs.

DIFS

Distributed (coordination function) interframe spacing (DIFS) is the longest of the three IFS types covered so far. It is used by standard data frames. The greater delay interval ensures that frames specified for SIFS and PIFS intervals are able to transmit before DIFS data frames. The DIFS interval is calculated as the PHY's SIFS interval plus two times the PHY's slot time. Based on the same numbers used in the previous paragraphs for the PIFS interval calculations and this new algorithm for calculating the DIFS interval, the DSSS PHY has a DIFS interval of 50 μs and the OFDM PHY has a DIFS interval of 34 μs.

EIFS

Extended interframe spacing (EIFS) is used when a frame reception begins but the received frame is incomplete or is corrupted based on the Frame Check Sequence (FCS) value. When the last frame of the station received was corrupted, the station uses EIFS for the next frame that it transmits. The EIFS interval is the longest of the IFS intervals and is calculated based on the following more complex algorithm:

$$\text{EIFS} = \text{SIFS} + (8 \text{ X ACKsize}) + \text{Preamble Length} \\ + \text{PLCP Header Length} + \text{DIFS}$$

where the time calculation is the amount of time in microseconds that it takes to transfer the 8 ACKs, preamble, and PLCP header. As you can see, the EIFS is more than the DIFS and SIFS combined.

Contention Window

The IFS delay interval is not the end of the wait for devices that are seeking time on the WM. After the IFS delay interval has passed, the device must then initiate a random backoff algorithm and then contend for the WM if the Distributed Coordination Function is in effect. This random backoff algorithm is processed and applied using the *contention window.*

The phrase *contention window* has caused much confusion, but it is the phrase in use in the IEEE 802.11 standard. This "window" is actually a range of integers from which one is chosen at random to become the backoff timer for the immediate frame queued for transmission. Think of it like a contention range instead of a contention window and it will be a little easier for you.

Random Backoff Times

All stations having a frame to transmit choose a random time period within the range specified as the contention window. Next, the predefined algorithm multiplies the randomly chosen integer by a *slot time*. The slot time is a fixed-length time interval that is defined for each PHY, such as DSSS, FHSS, or OFDM. For example, FHSS uses a slot time of 50 µs, and DSSS uses a slot time of 20 µs. The slot times for each of the currently ratified PHYs are listed here:

- FHSS—50 µs
- DSSS—20 µs
- OFDM—9 µs
- HR/DSSS—20 µs
- ERP—Long Slot Time—20 µs
- ERP—Short Slot Time (802.11b compatible)—9 µs

As you can see, there are definite variations among the different PHYs supported in the IEEE 802.11 standard as amended. Though the IEEE 802.11n amendment is still in the draft stage at this writing, it is expected to use the standard 9 µs slot time used in existing PHYs that support OFDM. You are not required to understand all the specific details about how the random backoff time is generated and utilized in order to become a CWNA; however, the following section provides a high-level overview of how the IFS and backoff time come together to provide WM contention management.

Contention Explanation

Now that you have most of the pieces to the media contention puzzle, you can begin to put them together in order to understand how a wireless station decides when it should try to communicate on the WM. In order to understand this, imagine that a station has a data frame that it needs to transmit on the WM. This data frame will be required to use the DIFS, since it is a standard data frame. Furthermore, imagine that the station uses carrier sense to determine that a frame is currently being transmitted. For discussion's sake, let's assume that the station detected that the frame being transmitted had a Duration/ID field value of 20 μs. The station sets its NAV to count down the 20 μs and waits. The NAV reaches 0, and the station uses carrier sense and detects that the WM is silent. At this time, the station must wait for the DIFS interval to expire, and since the station is using the DSSS PHY, it waits for 50 μs. Next, the station waits for the random backoff time period to expire, and when it does, the station uses carrier sense and detects that the WM is silent. The station begins transmitting the data frame. All of this assumes the network is using the Distributed Coordination Function, which is the only contention management functionality that has been widely implemented in hardware at this time.

Collision Avoidance

Ultimately, the carrier sense, IFS, and random backoff times are used in order to decrease the likelihood that any two stations will try to transmit at the same time on the WM. The IFS parameters are also used in order to provide priority to the more time-sensitive frames such as ACK frames and CTS frames. The CCA (PHY and MAC), IFS, variable contention window, and random backoff times, together, form the core of the Distributed Coordination Function.

Even with all of these efforts, a collision can still occur. In order to deal with these scenarios, *acknowledgment,* or *ACK,* frames are used. An ACK frame is a short frame that uses the SIFS to let the sending device know that the receiving device has indeed received the frame. If the sending device does not receive an ACK frame, it will attempt to retransmit the frame. Since the retransmitted frame will be transmitted using the rules and guidelines we've talked about so far, chances are that the next frame—or one of the next few—will make it through.

Frame Types and Formats Compared

While there are similarities between IEEE 802.3 and 802.11 frames, there are also differences. In this section, you will learn about the basic differences between these frame types. Then you will learn about the different frame types supported by the 802.11 standard, and after that you will discover the way 802.11 WLANs support Layer 2 and Layer 3 functionality.

IEEE 802.11 Frame Format Versus IEEE 802.3 Frame Format

Project 802 frames all have similar structures. (Project 802 is the IEEE project that is inclusive of all 802 standards.) They are all defined as fields that are made up of bits, which together form octets and ultimately frames. This similarity in frame structure makes for easier conversion from 802.3 networks to 802.11 networks and vice versa. For example, a frame originating from a wired client and destined for a wireless client will first be transmitted on the wire as an 802.3 frame, and then the access point will strip off the 802.3 headers and reframe the data unit as an 802.11 frame for transmission to the wireless client.

The first difference between IEEE 802.3 and 802.11 frames is the frame size. IEEE 802.3 frames support a maximum MSDU payload size of 1500 bytes or octets. IEEE 802.11 frames support a maximum MSDU payload size of 2304 bytes. At first, it may seem that extra processing will have to occur in order for 802.3 and 802.11 networks to coexist. In other words, you might think that a lot of frame fragmentation will have to occur to convert 802.11 frames to 802.3 frames. However, since TCP/IP is the most commonly used protocol and since IP packets are usually no larger than 1500 bytes, the vast majority of data units passed to the IEEE 802.11 MAC layer will be 1500 bytes or smaller, allowing for easy conversion to the 802.3 format.

Most network engineers are familiar with the IP maximum transfer unit (MTU) of 1500 bytes that exists because of Ethernet networks. WLAN standards were designed to easily bridge with Ethernet. For this reason, the IP MTU on a WLAN is held to 1500 bytes even though it could be as high as 2304 minus 8 for the LLC SNAP header. A 1500-byte IP PDU becomes a 1508-byte LLC PDU with the LLC SNAP header, and this, in turn, becomes the WLAN MSDU. The LLC 8-byte header is often ignored, and this results in the varied and confusing byte or octet size values you read and hear about.

The second difference between the 802.3 and 802.11 frames is the MAC address fields. Both frame types use the same standard for MAC address structuring based on Clause 5.2 of the IEEE 802-1990 standard; however, 802.3 frames have only two MAC address fields, whereas 802.11

frames have one, two, three, or four. Figure 4.3 shows these fields as Address 1, Address 2, Address 3, and Address 4. These four MAC address fields can contain four of the following five MAC address types, and the contents will be dependent on the frame subtype:

- Basic Service Set Identifier (BSSID)
- Destination Address (DA)
- Source Address (SA)
- Receiver Address (RA)
- Transmitter Address (TA)

Frame Types

Clause 7 of the IEEE 802.11 standard documents the frame types supported by the IEEE 802.11 MAC. According to this clause, three frame types are supported in IEEE 802.11 networks: management frames, control frames, and data frames. The *Type* subfield in the *Frame Control (FC)* field of a general IEEE 802.11 frame may be 00 (management), 01 (control), or 10 (data). The *Subtype* subfield determines the subtype of frame, within the frame types specified, that is being transmitted. For example, a *Type* subfield value of 00 with a *Subtype* value of 0000 is an association request frame; however, a *Type* value of 10 with a *Subtype* value of 0000 is a standard data frame. Figure 4.3 shows the relationship of the general IEEE 802.11 frame format to the format of the FC field's subfields. Understanding all of the details about the frame structures and formats is not required of a CWNA; however, it would be of great benefit to you to review Clause 7 of the IEEE 802.11 standard, which defines each frame and each frame field with diagrams similar to the one in Figure 4.3.

FIGURE 4.3 General IEEE 802.11 frame with FC field extracted

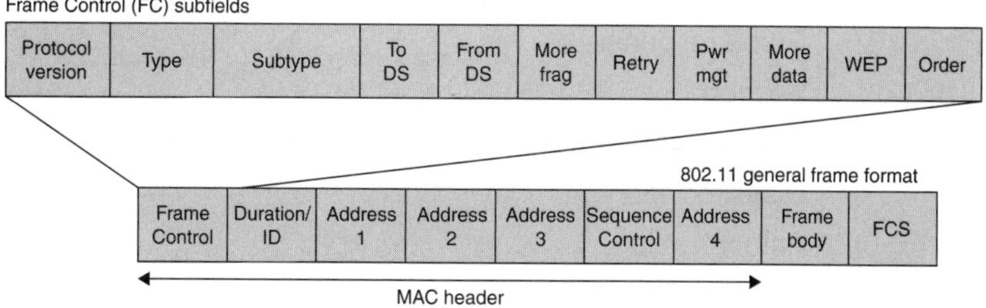

While Figure 4.3 represents the general frame format in the IEEE 802.11-1999 standard and even the IEEE 802.11-1999 (R2003) standard, the standard as amended by IEEE 802.11i calls for a change in the FC subfields format. The WEP subfield is now called the Protected Frame subfield. There are other changes in the usage of the subfields and their values that have been introduced in both IEEE 802.11i and IEEE 802.11e. Though you will not be tested to this level of depth on the CWNA exam, you should be aware of these changes and realize that they constitute IEEE 802.11 as amended. In other words, all ratified amendments have become part of IEEE 802.11 such that when we speak of the IEEE 802.11 standard, we must incorporate these amendments into our conceptualization of the standard. Otherwise, it is important to state that you are referring to IEEE 802.11-1999 and not IEEE 802.11 as amended. Today, if we speak of the IEEE 802.11 standard, this is inclusive of the IEEE 802.11-1999 (R2003) document and all ratified amendments.

Management Frames

Management frames are used to manage access to wireless networks and to move associations from one access point to another within an extended service set (ESS). Of the original frames specified in IEEE 802.11-1999, management frames make up the majority. Table 4.3 lists the IEEE 802.11 management frames as amended and their associated *Subtype* field values.

TABLE 4.3 Management Frame Types and Subtype Field Values

Frame Subtype	Subtype Field Value
Association request	0000
Association response	0001
Reassociation request	0010
Reassociation response	0011
Probe request	0100
Probe response	0101
Beacon	1000
Announcement Traffic Indication Message (ATIM)	1001
Disassociation	1010
Authentication	1011
Deauthentication	1100
Action (added with 802.11i amendment)	1101

TABLE 4.4 Control Frame Subtypes and Subtype Field Values

Frame Subtype	Subtype Field Value
Block ACK Request (added with 802.11i amendment)	1000
Block ACK (added with 802.11i amendment)	1001
Power Save Poll (PS-Poll)	1010
Request to Send (RTS)	1011
Clear to Send (CTS)	1100
Acknowledgment (ACK)	1101
Contention-Free (CF)-End	1110
CF-End + CF-ACK	1111

Control Frames

Control frames are used to assist with the delivery of data frames and must be able to be interpreted by all stations participating in a BSS. This means that they must be transmitted using a modulation technique and at a data rate compatible with all hardware participating in the BSS. Control frames and their associated *Subtype* field values are listed in Table 4.4.

Data Frames

Data frames, the third frame type in our discussion, are the actual carriers of application-level data. These frames can be either standard data frames or Quality of Service (QoS) data frames for devices supporting the IEEE 802.11e amendment. Table 4.5 lists the various data frame subtypes and their *Subtype* field values. Those beginning with *QoS* were added with the introduction of the IEEE 802.11e amendment.

Layer 3 Protocol Support by IEEE 802.11 Frames

Layer 3 protocols include the IP protocol, and wireless networks introduce new problems to the IP protocol that did not exist with wired networks. The primary new problem is also one of the main benefits of wireless networking: mobility. Users can walk around your facility with their HR/DSSS PocketPC or their laptop using some other IEEE WLAN technology, and as they walk, they may move beyond the range of the original access point to which they connected. When this happens, their device may find

TABLE 4.5 Data Frame Subtypes and Subtype Field Values

Frame Subtype	Subtype Field Value
Data	0000
Data + CF-ACK (PCF mode only)	0001
Data + CF-Poll (PCF mode only)	0010
Data + CF-ACK + CF-Poll (PCF mode only)	0011
Null (no data)	0100
CF-ACK (no data) (PCF mode only)	0101
CF-Poll (no data) (PCF mode only)	0110
CF-ACK + CF-Poll (no data) (PCF mode only)	0111
QoS data	1000
QoS data + CF-ACK (PCF mode only)	1001
QoS data + CF-Poll (PCF mode only)	1010
QoS data + CF-ACK + CF-Poll (PCF mode only)	1011
QoS Null (no data)	1100
QoS CF-Poll (no data) (PCF mode only)	1110
QoS CF-ACK + CF-Poll (no data) (PCF mode only)	1111

a new access point with a stronger signal. This new access point may actually exist on a different LAN segment with different IP configurations. The result is that the user loses his or her existing IP address and gets a new one from the DHCP service on the new segment.

Since many IP-based applications rely on the TCP protocol and since the TCP protocol is a connection-oriented protocol, this release and reassignment of IP addresses can result in the loss of connection in the higher layers of the OSI model. For example, if the user was engaged in a Voice over IP (VoIP) or an FTP session, she will need to reconnect and restart that session. This is not only frustrating for the users, but can lead to corrupted or lost data.

There are both standard and proprietary solutions to this problem. Mobile IP is a standard that is not covered on the CWNA exam, but that can help solve this problem. Another solution, though proprietary, is the Cisco Unified Wireless Network solution, which provides roaming at Layer 2 and Layer 3 and even VPN services that allow clients to maintain VPN connections while roaming.

Jumbo Frame Support (Layer 2)

As you've learned earlier in this chapter, the frame payload for an IEEE 802.11 frame (the MSDU) has a maximum size limit of 2304 bytes. However, both IP at Layer 3 and IEEE 802.3 at Layer 2 support a default data unit of 1500 bytes. This limit is also known as the MTU (maximum transfer unit). In certain scenarios, this limit of 1500 bytes can be prohibitive to network performance. For this reason, *jumbo frames* have been introduced into the hardware of many vendors. Jumbo frames are technically any frames allowing an MTU of greater than 1500. *Baby giant frames,* in Cisco terminology, are frames that support an MTU of up to 1552 bytes with a total frame size of 1600 bytes after headers and trailers are added. Most vendors max out jumbo frames at around 9000 bytes. For example, the Cisco Catalyst 4000s and 6000s support a jumbo frame MTU of 9198 bytes and 9216 bytes, respectively. After headers and trailers are added, the maximum frame size is 9216 bytes for the Catalyst 4000s and 9234 bytes for the Catalyst 6000s. These are examples of jumbo frames, and you will not be tested on the specifics of what a certain vendor's hardware supports; however, you should know that jumbo frames are frames with an MTU larger than 1500 bytes and many vendors support sizes of more than 9000 bytes.

When using lightweight access points, which are covered in more detail in Chapter 7, with wireless controllers, you have what is known as a *split MAC architecture.* This means that some of the MAC services are handled by the controller and some of the services are handled by the access point. For example, it is common to handle authentication, association, reassociation, and frame translation at the controller, while beacon frame transmission, sending ACKs and CTS frames, buffered frames for power save modes, and other time-sensitive or physically dependent functions are performed at the access point. In order to provide for greater performance in such a split MAC architecture, many wireless controllers support jumbo frames between the controller and the access points. For example, a frame that is fragmented between the client station and the access point station can be transmitted to the wireless controller as a single jumbo frame instead of transmitting multiple frame fragments. Likewise, an IEEE 802.11 frame that carries a payload larger than the normal IP over Ethernet 1500 MTU size can be sent to the wireless controller as a single jumbo frame, but this is only true if all intervening Ethernet switches support Ethernet jumbo frames.

For the most part, only Gigabit Ethernet devices support jumbo frames, and then they only support them on the Gigabit ports that they provide. For example, Cisco's LWAPP protocol does support a mechanism to determine if the path from the access point to the wireless controller supports jumbo frames; it uses the standard 1500 MTU size if it does not.

MTU Discovery and Functionality (Layer 3)

As was stated in the preceding section, the maximum MSDU for an IEEE 802.11 frame is 2304 octets (bytes) while the maximum MSDU for an Ethernet IEEE 802.3 frame is 1500 octets. It was also stated, however, that most IP packets are 1500 bytes due to the default setting for the IP MTU size. Going up one more layer to Layer 4, TCP uses an MSS (maximum segment size) of 1460 bytes, which is the amount of space left for higher-layer information when you strip the IP headers (40 bytes) from the IP packets or datagrams. Therefore, a 1460-byte TCP segment becomes a 1500-byte IP packet, which becomes a 1518-byte frame, when transmitted on IEEE 802.3 Ethernet networks (excluding the Ethernet preamble and start of frame delimiter). This same 1500-byte IP packet might become a 1534-byte IEEE 802.11 MPDU.

The size of the MTU impacts the final size of the data frames that are transmitted onto the WM. Larger MTU sizes can result in larger data frames, and smaller MTU sizes can result in smaller data frames. Realize that the MTU size is the maximum size that a transmit unit can be and that the transmit unit does not have to be that large.

IEEE 802.11 Frames and Frame Exchange Sequences

While you will not be required to understand every detail of the frames and frame exchanges that occur on a WLAN in order to become a CWNA, you will need to understand the basics of frame exchange sequences and the flow of creating a WLAN, accessing a WLAN, and disconnecting from a WLAN. In this section you will learn about the beacon management frame, which is used to announce information about an available WLAN. You will also learn about the methods used by client stations to find these WLANs. Finally, you'll learn how *dynamic rate switching* works so that a balance of data rate and efficient WM utilization is reached. First, you will learn about many of the functions or services provided by the IEEE 802.11 MAC.

MAC Functions

The IEEE 802.11 MAC provides the following functions:

- **Scanning** Before a station can participate in a BSS, it must be able to find the access points that provide access to that service set. Scanning is the process used to discover BSSs or to discover access points within a known BSS.
- **Synchronization** Some IEEE 802.11 features require all stations to have the same time. Stations can update their clocks based on the time stamp value in beacon frames.
- **Frame Transmission** Stations must abide by the frame transmission rules of the BSS to which they are associated. These rules are the Distributed Coordination Function in all known systems at this time.
- **Authentication** Authentication is performed before a station can be associated with a BSS. This will be covered in more detail in the later section of this chapter "Authentication and Association Processes."
- **Association** Once authentication is complete, the station can become associated with the BSS. This includes discovery of capability information in both directions—from the station to the access point and from the access point to the station. Association is covered in more detail in the later section of this chapter "Authentication and Association Processes."
- **Reassociation** When a user roams throughout a service area, that user may reach a point where one access point within an ESS will provide a stronger signal than the currently associated access point. When this occurs, the station will reassociate with the new access point.
- **Data Protection** Data encryption may be employed to assist in preventing crackers from accessing the data that is transmitted on the WM.
- **Power Management** Since the transmitters/receivers (transceivers) in wireless client devices consume a noteworthy amount of power, power management feature are provided that assist in extending battery life by causing the transceiver to sleep for specified intervals.

- **Fragmentation** In certain scenarios, it is beneficial to fragment frames before they are transmitted onto the WM. This type of scenario most often occurs as a result of intermittent interference. Fragmentation is covered in more detail later in this chapter.
- **RTS/CTS** Request to Send/Clear to Send is a feature of IEEE 802.11 that will help prevent hidden node problems and allow for more centralized control of access to the WM. RTS/CTS is covered in more detail later in this chapter.

Beacon Management Frame

The *beacon management frame* is a special type of frame used in IEEE 802.11 networks. This frame is often referred to as the beacon, since this is the frame subtype specified in IEEE 802.11 as amended. Table 4.6 lists the information provided in the beacon frame body common to all IEEE 802.11 PHYs.

TABLE 4.6 Beacon Frame Body Information

Information	Description
Time stamp	Used for synchronization.
Beacon interval	Used to specify the amount of time between beacon transmissions.
Capability information	Used to communicate capability information such as WEP requirements, PCF support, whether the service set is an ESS or an IBSS, and other capabilities as specified in the IEEE 802.11 standard as amended.
SSID	The ID or name of the network identified by the beacon.
FH parameter set	Element is present within beacon frames generated by stations using FH PHYs. Provides information for hop patterns, dwell time, and other parameters needed for FH PHYs.
DS parameter set	Element is present within beacon frames generated by stations using DS PHYs. Provides information for channel specification.

TABLE 4.6 Beacon Frame Body Information (*cont.*)

Information	Description
CF parameter set	Element is only present within beacon frames generated by access points supporting Point Coordination Function (PCF). Parameters provided are used to manage PCF.
IBSS parameter set	Element is only present within beacon frames generated by stations in an IBSS (ad hoc network). Contains the ATIM Window information for power save operations in an ad hoc wireless network (IBSS).
TIM	Element is only present within beacon frames generated by access points. This is the Traffic Indication Map. Used by stations employing power save modes.
Supported rates	Specifies up to eight data rates.
Extended supported rates	Specifies any other data rates not specified in supported rates.
ERP information	Contains information that allows Clause 19 (ERP PHY) devices to coexist with Clause 15 (DSSS PHY) or Clause 18 (HR/DSSS PHY) devices.

In an ad hoc wireless network (IBSS), all the stations take turns broadcasting the beacon frame. This is because there is no access point in an independent basic service set (IBSS).

Beacon frames can be used by client stations seeking wireless network to join, or these client stations may use other frames known as *probe request* and *probe response* frames. Both methods will be covered in the following sections, "Active Scanning" and "Passive Scanning."

Active Scanning (Probes)

Active scanning uses probe request and probe response frames instead of the beacon frame to find a WLAN to join. A client station can use either of two general methods to find the WLAN. The first is to specify the SSID of the network being sought, and the second is to seek for any BSS that may be able to hear and respond to the probe request.

If the SSID is specified in the probe request frame transmitted by the requesting station, all access points that are configured with a matching SSID should respond, assuming they receive the probe request frame. It is certainly possible that a set of access points using the same SSID could cover an area large enough that all of the access points will not receive the probe request transmitted from a specific location in that area. The response from the access points that hear the probe request is a probe response frame. The probe response frame contains the same basic information that the beacon frame contains with the exception of the Traffic Indication Map.

In an ad hoc wireless network, which is a network without an access point, the station that last transmitted the beacon frame will respond to probe requests. There are also times when no station will respond to a probe request. This happens when vendors provide a feature to disable probe responses even though the IEEE 802.11 standard requires that all access points respond with a probe response when a probe request is received matching the access point's configured SSID or when the probe request contains a wildcard SSID (an SSID of zero length, formerly called the broadcast SSID). The vendors often allow their access points to be configured so that they ignore wildcard SSIDs. While this is a nonstandard configuration, as long as the WLAN administrator has configured all valid clients to specify the SSID, it should not cause problems within the WLAN for these clients.

This is sometimes thought to provide a more secure environment; however, it is important to remember that the beacon frames have the SSID in them by default. Unless this SSID broadcasting is turned off, those wishing to penetrate your network can easily discover the SSID with WLAN analysis software and then configure their clients with the appropriate settings. Even if you disable both the response to wildcard SSID probe requests and the broadcasting of your SSID in the beacon frames, the intruders can patiently wait until a frame is transmitted onto the WM that contains the SSID and then use this information to configure their client stations. Ultimately, the SSID should not be considered a factor in security management unless you are only concerned with casual Wi-Fi war drivers who lack any WLAN technical skills.

You are not likely to take your wireless security so lightly in any business setting, and I don't recommend you take it that lightly in a home setting either.

If a probe request is transmitted onto the WM having a wildcard SSID (a null value for the SSID), all access points that receive the probe request will respond with a probe response containing their SSIDs. This is the standard behavior. Any devices that do not respond in this way are operating in a nonstandard way as mentioned previously. Figure 4.4 illustrates the process of active scanning. The top half illustrates the probe request being transmitted, and the bottom half illustrates the probe response coming from the access points.

FIGURE 4.4 Active scanning process

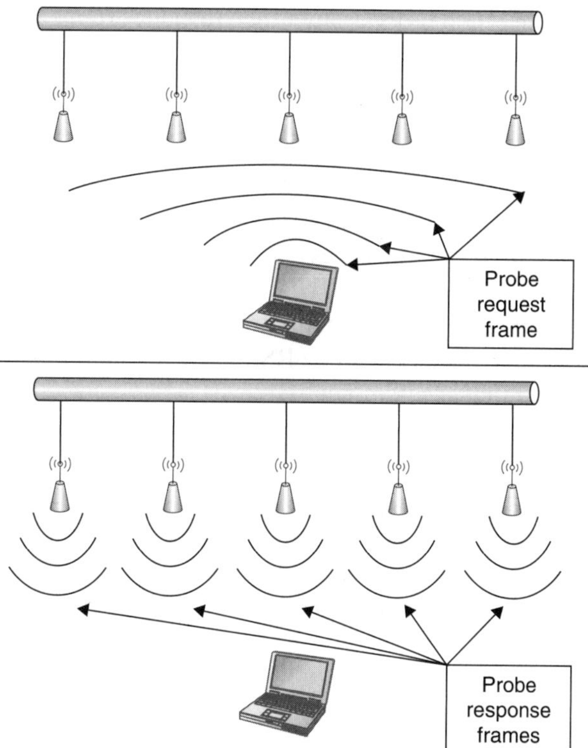

The exact details of the active scanning process are a bit more complex than the simple overview presented up to now. In fact, active scanning involves channel switching and scanning each channel in a station's channel list. The basic process is outlined here:

1. Switch to a channel.
2. Wait for an incoming frame or for the ProbeDelay timer to expire.
3. If the ProbeDelay timer expires, use DCF for access to the WM and send a probe request frame.
4. Wait for the MinChannelTime to pass.
    a. If the WM was never busy, there is no WLAN on this channel. Move to the next channel.
    b. If the WM was busy, wait until MaxChannelTime has expired and then process any probe response frames.

Passive Scanning (Beacons)

The *passive scanning* process is a much different process. Instead of transmitting to find the access points, the client station listens (receives) in order to find the access points. This is done by receiving beacon frames and using them to find the access point for the BSS to be joined. When multiple access points transmit beacon frames that are received by the passive scanning station, the station will determine the access point with the best signal (as determined by RSSI) and attempt to authenticate and associate with that access point.

A popular WLAN finder application is the freeware tool NetStumbler. When you click the Scan button, in NetStumbler, you are telling the application to initiate active scanning. This results in the generation and transmission of probe request frames on each supported channel for the client adapter that is configured for use with NetStumbler.

Authentication and Association Processes

Once a station has located the WLAN to which it seeks to connect, which is the first stage of station connectivity, it must go through the *authentication* and *association* processes, which are the second and third stages of connectivity. This involves being authenticated by the access point or WLAN controller and then determining the PHY, data rate, and other parameters within which the association must operate. The first step is authentication and the second is association, and each step is covered in sequence in this section. First, we'll look at the IEEE concept of the *state machine.*

The IEEE 802.11 State Machine

The *state machine* of the IEEE 802.11 standard can be in one of three states:

- Unauthenticated/Unassociated
- Authenticated/Unassociated
- Authenticated/Associated

Unauthenticated/Unassociated

In the initial state, a client station is completely disconnected from the WLAN. It cannot pass frames of any type through the access points to other stations on the WLAN or the wired infrastructure. Authentication frames can be sent to the access points. These frames are not sent through the access points, with the exception of a split MAC implementation where a WLAN controller performs the authentication, but are sent to the access point. The distinction is important. Frames must be transmitted to the access point in order to eventually reach the authenticated and associated stage; however, until the final stage is reached, only authentication and association request frames will be processed by the access point.

Access points, or WLAN controllers, keep a list known as the association table. Vendors report the stage of the station's state machine differently. Some vendors may report that a client that has not completed the authentication process is unauthenticated and other vendors may simply not show the client in the association table view.

Authenticated/Unassociated

The second state of the state machine is to authenticate an unassociated state. To move from the first state to the second, the client station must perform some kind of valid authentication. This is accomplished with authentication frames. Once this second state is reached, the client station can issue association request frames to be processed by the access point; however, other IEEE 802.11 frame types are not allowed. In most access points, the association table will now show "authenticated" for the client station. Since the interval between reaching the authenticated and unassociated stage and moving on to the authenticated and associated stage is very small (usually a matter of milliseconds), you will not see client stations in the state very often. In most cases, you will either see "unauthenticated" or nothing for the first state and associated for the third state.

The only exception to this is what is sometimes called "preauthentication." A station can authenticate with any number of access points, but it can only be associated with one access point at a time. The access point to which the station is associated must be a single entity in order for other devices on the network to be able to reach that station. In some systems, the station is capable of authenticating with multiple access points so that it can roam more quickly when the need arises.

Authenticated/Associated

The third and final state is the authenticated and associated state. In order for a station to be in this state, it must have first been authenticated and then associated. The process of moving from state 2 (authenticated and unassociated) to this state is a simple four-frame transaction. The client station first sends an association request frame to an access point to which it has been authenticated. Second, the access point responds with an acknowledgment frame. Next, the access point sends an association response frame either allowing or disallowing the association. The client sends an acknowledgment frame as the fourth and final step. If the third step resulted in an approval of the association request, the client station has now reached the authenticated and associated state and may communicate on the WLAN or through the WLAN to the wired network if encryption keys match and 802.1X is not enabled.

The association response frame includes a status code element. If the status code is equal to 0, the association request is approved or successful. There are three other status codes that may apply: 12, 17, and 18. A status code of 12 indicates that the association was rejected for some reason outside of the scope of the IEEE 802.11 standard. A status code of 17 indicates that the access point is already serving the maximum number of client stations that it can support. Finally, a status code of 18 indicates that the client station does not support all of the basic data rates required to join the BSS.

This last constraint is imposed to ensure that all stations will be able to receive certain frame types that are communicated at the basic data rates. If they cannot receive these frame types, they cannot participate in the BSS lest they cause interference by not understanding such frames as CTS or by not having the ability to interpret frames at all. The result would be that the station not supporting the basic data rates would cause interference due to an internal misconception that the WM was clear. This is a simplification of a complex technical constraint, but it is sufficient for a WLAN administrator to know that a station cannot associate with a BSS if it does not support the basic data rates required. Thankfully, these data rates are specified by administrators, and assuming the station is standards-based and compatible with the PHY being used, this shouldn't be a problem with proper configuration settings.

The key point is to realize that you cannot transmit data frames for processing until you've been associated and you cannot transmit association frames for processing until you've been authenticated. Now that you understand the three states in which a station can reside, let's explore the details of how the station can become authenticated and then associated.

Authentication

Based on the three states of a wireless station, you know that the second step to joining a WLAN, after discovery through scanning, is authentication. The IEEE 802.11-1999 (R2003) standard specifies two methods of authentication: *Open System authentication* and *Shared Key authentication.* The first seems it would be used in less secure environments, while the second seems it would be used in more secure environments; however, you will soon learn why the opposite is true.

Open System Authentication

Open System authentication is essentially a null algorithm. In other words, no true authentication (verification of identity) occurs. Additionally, Open System authentication is specified as the default authentication mechanism in Clause 8 of the IEEE 802.11 standard. Table 4.7 provides a step-by-step sequence of events that transpire in the Open System authentication process.

TABLE 4.7 Open System Authentication Process

Step	Station Acting	Action Taken	Results
1	Client	Transmits an authentication frame with the code indicating that Open System authentication should be used.	Authentication frame transmitted
2	Access point	Receives the authentication frame and responds with an ACK frame.	Authentication frame received
3	Access point	Transmits an authentication frame to the client indicating a positive authentication.	Authentication approved
4	Client	Receives the positive authentication frame and response with an ACK frame to the access point.	Approved authentication acknowledged

You will notice that the four steps in Table 4.7 do not include any actual authentication of identity. Access points configured to use Open System authentication will always respond with a positive authentication to any authentication request.

Be careful not to confuse authentication with confidentiality. Data privacy or confidentiality is about protecting transmitted data from interception. Authentication is about verifying identities of senders and receivers on the network. The point is that WEP is used in authentication (Shared Key) and it can also be used for confidentiality (data encryption). You can use WEP with both Open System authentication and Shared Key authentication for data confidentiality. Just as the next section points out the weaknesses of WEP as an authentication tool, you should consider it weak as a confidentiality tool.

Before you move away from Open System authentication with an assumption that it provides no use, keep the following realities in mind:

- Open System authentication is preferred at hotspots where you want to provide unauthenticated access to the Internet.
- More secure authentication technologies, such as 802.1X, rely on Open System authentication. In other words, Open System authentication leaves the access point open to other layers of security beyond the pre–IEEE 802.11i authentication standards.

Shared Key Authentication

Shared Key authentication utilizes the *wired equivalent privacy (WEP)* key for authentication. WEP can also provide encryption of the MSDU, but Clause 8 defines this algorithm as providing protection from *casual eavesdropping* and should be understood as not providing protection from structured attacks. Due to the weaknesses discovered in the WEP algorithm, very few networks should implement and use Shared Key authentication or WEP encryption today. Certainly, the networks that do utilize these algorithms are insecure and should be upgraded as soon as possible.

When Shared Key authentication is used, the client station and the access point must both use the same WEP key. Access points can store multiple WEP keys so that some stations can communicate using one WEP key and other stations can communicate using another. The fact that both stations (the client and the access point) share the same key gives rise to the name Shared Key. The Shared Key authentication process is documented in Table 4.8 as a sequence of steps with descriptions of the activities that occur in each step.

TABLE 4.8 Shared Key Authentication Process

Step	Station Acting	Action Taken	Results
1	Client	Transmits an authentication frame with the code indicating that Shared Key authentication should be used.	Authentication frame transmitted
2	Access point	Receives the authentication frame and transmits an ACK frame to the client.	Authentication frame received
3	Access point	Generates challenge text (randomly generated plain text) and transmits it to the client station in an authentication frame.	Authentication challenge transmitted

TABLE 4.8 Shared Key Authentication Process (*cont.*)

Step	Station Acting	Action Taken	Results
4	Client	Receives the authentication challenge frame and transmits an ACK frame to the access point.	Authentication challenge received
5	Client	Places the challenge text in another frame while encrypting it with the WEP key and transmits the challenge response to the access point in another authentication frame.	Authentication challenge response transmitted
6	Access point	Receives the challenge response authentication frame from the client and transmits an ACK frame to the client.	Authentication challenge response received
7	Access point	Decrypts the encrypted text in the authentication challenge response frame and, if it matches the original text, authenticates the client by transmitting a positive authentication frame to the client. If it does not match the original text, a negative authentication frame is sent to the client.	Authentication challenge response processed
8	Client	Client station received the results and transmits an ACK frame to the access point.	Authentication process complete

Do not allow the greater complexity of the authentication process in Table 4.8 to mislead you. Even though Shared Key authentication performs real authentication, it is not more secure than using Open System authentication followed by EAP, WPA, or WPA2. These more secure technologies will be discussed in Chapter 10.

Deauthentication

Deauthentication frames are known as advisory frames. This is because they advise the network of something and the network cannot prevent that thing from occurring. In other words, a standard IEEE 802.11–based access point cannot deny a deauthentication frame. This frame would be transmitted to the access point (or other members of the IBSS in an ad hoc network) and the receiving device would simply acknowledge the deauthentication. This would also result in a lowering of the state machine's state in the access point's association table.

A deauthentication frame will include the address of the station being deauthenticated and the address of the station with which the deauthenticating station is currently authenticated. The deauthentication frame will have a reason code of 3, which indicates that the deauthenticating station is either leaving or has left the BSS or ESS. Remember that authentication must happen before association can take place; for this reason, a deauthentication frame effectively disassociates and deauthenticates the transmitting client station from the access point.

Association, Reassociation, and Disassociation

After authentication comes association. As was stated earlier, a station can be authenticated with multiple access points, but it can be associated with only one. There are three frames related to association: association frames, reassociation frames, and disassociation frames.

Association

The process of association is very simple. Four frames are transmitted between the client station and the access point station. The first frame is an association request frame, which is followed by an acknowledgment frame from the access point. The third frame is an association response frame, which is followed by an acknowledgment frame from the client station. It is extremely rare for a client station to successfully authenticate and then fail to associate. This is because the client station can usually determine if it is compatible with the BSS by inspecting the beacon frames or probe response frames sent from the access points.

Reassociation

Reassociation occurs when a client station roams from one access point to another within an ESS. Because reassociation is part of the roaming process, it will be covered in more detail in the next chapter. An immobile station may also reassociate with its access point in order to change its Robust Security Network Association (RSNA).

Disassociation

Like the deauthentication frame, a *disassociation* frame is an advisory frame in that the access point cannot deny the disassociation. The disassociation service is the component of the MAC layer that is responsible for processing a disassociation. This is one of the 13 architectural services of the IEEE 802.11 MAC layer. The full list of services is provided in Table 4.9 with link to the station type that contains the service.

All stations, in Table 4.9, is inclusive of access points, client devices, and any other station that communicates on the IEEE 802.11 WM. The *Distribution System Service (DSS)* is provided by the *Distribution System (DS)* and may be in an access point or may be fully or partially contained in a WLAN controller device when using a split MAC architecture.

TABLE 4.9 MAC Sublayer Services and Associated Station Types

Service	Station Type
Authentication	All stations
Deauthentication	All stations
Association	Distribution System Service
Disassociation	Distribution System Service
Reassociation	Distribution System Service
Distribution	Distribution System Service
Integration	Distribution System Service
MSDU delivery	All stations
Data confidentiality	All stations
DFS	All stations
TPC	All stations
Higher-layer timer synchronization	All stations
QoS traffic scheduling (optional)	All stations and DSS

Besides managing station association and message forwarding within an infrastructure BSS, the DS is used to interconnect a set of BSSs to form an ESS.

Regulatory Domain Requirements

Amendments *d, h,* and *j* define a Country element for the IEEE 802.11 standard. This code must be present in any beacon frame where the dot11MultiDomainCapabilityEnabled attribute is equal to TRUE. In other words, if the access point supports operation in multiple regulatory domains and is IEEE 802.11 compliant, it must include a Country code in order for connecting stations to configure their available channels, minimum output power, and maximum output power settings.

This is an example of a situation where you must learn to combine the amendments with the IEEE 802.11-1999 (R2003) standard documents. Without investigating the 802.11d, 802.11h, and 802.11j amendments, you would miss this Country code element. It is through the implementation of the Country element that a BSS or ESS can identify the local regulatory domain and automatically configure itself to adhere to the regulations of the local regulatory domain.

Data Flow Optimization Across the RF Medium

Because the RF medium is not a physical medium that can implement limited access by disallowing physical connections, some method must be used to control access to the medium. Two methods are defined in the IEEE 802.11-1999 (R2003) standard, and more specifications are defined in IEEE 802.11e, which is an amendment that details QoS in wireless networks. The two methods that have been described since the earliest IEEE 802.11 standard was released are DCF and PCF.

DCF

The Distributed Coordination Function (DCF) is the WM access method that was described earlier in this chapter as CSMA/CA. At least, DCF is the IEEE 802.11 implementation of CSMA/CA. This means that DCF is inclusive of the carrier sensing mechanisms, interframe spacing, and backoff timers discussed earlier. DCF is said to be a *distributed* coordination function because the coordination of access to the WM is distributed among the wireless stations. Using the various methods covered in this chapter, all the stations work together to provide cooperative access to the WM without the need for a centralized medium access controller. However, DCF is not the only RF MAC method. PCF and HCF are both valid access methods as well.

PCF

The *Point Coordination Function* has not been covered in this chapter. In this section, I will provide a very brief overview. Though PCF is defined in the IEEE 802.11 standard, it has not been implemented in any widely used devices. There are also no known plans for its implementation at this time. Many wireless vendors speak of PCF in their literature and then state that it is not implemented due to lack of industry support or because of extra overhead incurred by implementing it.

Many books have been written on IEEE 802.11 wireless technology. Quite a few of these books state that PCF may be implemented in the future as if there were some limitation that is keeping it from being implemented today. Today's hardware is powerful enough to implement PCF. In fact, PCF was implemented in a few devices and firmware versions that simply never caught on. Unless the industry finds a practical demand for PCF, it is not likely to be implemented at any point. Though PCF might improve the handling of hidden node issues, it appears that, in the real world, DCF is working out fine with a little help from humans, and support for pervasive QoS is mounting.

Unlike DCF, PCF centralizes access to the WM. There is one *point* (station) in the WLAN that is responsible for controlling access to the WM. This point is the access point. In order to implement PCF, you will need both an access point and a client station that support the PCF specifications within IEEE 802.11. Thorough searches of eBay and Internet stores reveal no such devices, and I wouldn't expect to ever see any.

When an access point is configured to use PCF, it will actually use both DCF and PCF. This will be accomplished by alternating between a *contention period (CP)* and a *contention-free period (CFP)*. The CP is the window of time when DCF (CSMA/CA) is used to control access to the WM, and the CFP is the window of time when both DCF and PCF are used. Technically, there is more involved than just switching between CFP and

CP windows. The access point goes through a CFP *repetition interval* process that involves the following cycle:

1. The access point waits for the duration of a PIFS.
2. The access point sends a beacon frame announcing the CFP is about to begin.
3. The CFP window begins and the access point polls each station that indicated a desire to participate in the CFP.
4. The CP window begins and the stations contend for access to the WM using normal DCF rules.

This process begins again at step 1 and continues to repeat itself. The interesting thing to note is that PCF provides an apparent benefit that, up to this time, has not really been needed. The reason is that, though DCF uses random backoff timers that have a probability of giving one station more access to the WM than another during a given window of time, there seems to be a good balance among the stations that access the WM using DCF. It is actually very logical to assume that, if one station had less access to the WM in one interval of time, it will not have less access during the next interval of time. In other words, DCF seems to work well at balancing access to the WM for larger intervals (more than 2–4 seconds) of time.

There is a new use of WLANs that has shown some real problems with DCF, and it is unknown whether PCF could help solve these problems, since it is not available. (PCF could even help with the hidden node problem if it were available.) The new use is Voice over WLAN or VoWLAN. As a solution to this problem and others, many vendors are beginning to turn to IEEE 802.11e as a potential solution; however, they are not turning to PCF, so I would consider it dead.

IEEE 802.11e and WMM

Many networking technologies require very low latency. In fact, latency issues have even been a problem in some wired networks. The holy grail of networking today is convergence: voice and data on the same medium. One way to provide lower latency is to dedicate a medium to a single pair of devices; however, this is cost prohibitive. The alternative is to somehow identify the higher-priority information and make sure that information gets preferential access to the medium. This is the heart of QoS.

PCF was an early contender as a solution to the QoS puzzle in WLANs. However, there was one great limitation: PCF can only prioritize a given device (or MAC address) and not different applications coming from that device. Even with this limitation, there are no PCF access points that could be installed today anyway. Since the IEEE has released a solution to the QoS problem in the form of the IEEE 802.11e amendment, it is unlikely that PCF will be implemented in its older form in the future.

IEEE 802.11e specifies the use of EDCA and HCF. IEEE 802.11e was ratified on September 22, 2005, and is a 211-page document describing the QoS mechanisms that have become the standard for QoS in IEEE 802.11. The purpose of the document is stated as defining MAC procedures to support LAN applications with QoS requirements like voice, audio, and video.

Two new station types are introduced by IEEE 802.11e: QoS access points (QoS AP) and QoS stations (QoS STA). A QoS AP is an access point that can support the QoS facility. A QoS STA is a station that supports the QoS facility and can act as a standard station when associated with a non-QoS AP. The QoS facility is inclusive of the following components that distinguish a QoS STA from a non-QoS STA:

- QoS functions
- Channel access rules
- Frame formats and frame exchanges
- Managed objects

EDCA

EDCA is the IEEE 802.11e enhancement of DCF. Eight traffic categories, or priority levels, are defined by EDCA. The traffic having the higher priority level will gain access to the WM before traffic having a lower priority level. Ultimately, EDCA does not provide a guarantee of access to the WM; however, it does increase the probability over DCF that a higher-priority frame will be transmitted before a lower-priority frame.

These eight traffic categories are defined by the User Priority (UP) value. This value can be from 0 to 7. The UP values are identical to those used in 802.1D. Clause 6 of the IEEE 802.11e amendment further explains these UP values and their interpretation.

HCF

HCF provides a preemptive capability to the QAP (QoS AP) that was not available to an access point with PCF. A PCF access point, if it were available, would have the ability to preempt other stations in the BSS during the contention-free period; however, it could not preempt other stations during the contention period. HCF adds this capability. This preemption should not be thought of as interrupting a station's frame transmittal, but rather ensuring that the QAP will be able to transmit on the WM next.

Wireless Multimedia (WMM)

While IEEE 802.11e was being developed, the Wi-Fi Alliance released their Wireless Multimedia (WMM) extensions certification. This certification is based on the draft IEEE 802.11e standard and was released to provide QoS for Voice over WLAN. The WMM certification will continue to be updated and redefined to mean the latest interoperable QoS features available from multiple chip vendors.

RTS/CTS and CTS-to-Self Protocols

DCF provides a CSMA/CA implementation for WLANs using distributed coordination. PCF could have provided CSMA/CA through centralized or point coordination. Sometimes, you need something different from what is offered by either DCF or PCF. Instead of the access point polling the stations to see which station needs to communicate, the stations can tell the access point they need to communicate and then wait for the access point to give them the go-ahead. This method is called *Request to Send/Clear to Send (RTS/CTS)*.

When you are traveling on business or holiday, you have two basic ways of determining where you will sleep at night, assuming you plan to stay in a hotel. You can call ahead and make reservations, or you can just stop at a hotel when you get tired and ask if they have a vacancy. I remember going on trips with my father that followed the latter pattern. We would stop at hotel after hotel only to be rejected many times before finally finding one with a vacancy. However, there was also the chance that the first hotel would indeed have a vacancy. If it did have a vacancy, this would take less time than calling ahead to make the reservation (remember, we didn't have cell phones back then, so calling to make the reservation would have taken extra time).

A similar scenario can happen on a WLAN when the hidden node problem occurs. In this situation, there are two or more clients that can hear the access point and be heard by the access point, but they can't hear each other. Therefore, when a frame is sent from one of the client stations (STA1) to the access point, the other client station (STA2) might not be able to sense that it is transmitting using physical sensing. This results in STA2 transmitting a frame at the same time, causing corruption or cancellation of the other station's frame. It's as if the frames reached the access point and were told, "No vacancy."

RTS/CTS is like calling ahead and making reservations. Like calling ahead to make reservations, it requires extra overhead every time. If you stop at a hotel and check for a vacancy and find that 99 percent of the time, or more, there is one, calling ahead to make a reservation wouldn't pay off in the end. However, it you find that a large percentage of the time there are no vacancies, calling ahead would pay off quickly. RTS/CTS is like this too. If you are having problems like hidden nodes, enabling RTS/CTS can help resolve them. If you are not, then "calling ahead" will only add unnecessary overhead to your WLAN.

RTS/CTS works according to the following process:

1. A station wishing to transmit using RTS/CTS sends a *Request to Send frame* to the access point.
2. When the access point receives the RTS request, it sends a *Clear to Send frame* to the WLAN as a broadcast.
3. The stations in the vicinity all hear the duration in either the Request to Send frame or the Clear to Send frame and know to stay silent.
4. The original requesting station transmits its frame and receives an acknowledgment during this quiet window.

RTS/CTS can function in an infrastructure BSS or an independent basic service set (IBSS). In the BSS, the RTS/CTS exchange is between the client stations that wish to send or receive data and the access point, and either may initiate the exchange. In the IBSS, the RTS/CTS exchange is between the two communicating client stations. The noninvolved stations hear the exchange and set their NAV timers to cooperate with the RTS/CTS process.

An additional implementation of Clear to Send is found in the IEEE 802.11g amendment for the ERP PHY. This implementation provides for a CTS-to-self. Essentially, the station using the ERP PHY can communicate using OFDM and faster data rates than older stations such as those using the HR/DSSS PHY. In order for these stations to coexist, the station with the ERP PHY will transmit a CTS frame that was not preceded by an RTS frame. This frame will be transmitted using modulation that can be understood by the stations with the non-ERP PHYs. Those stations will go silent as they honor the duration value in the CTS frame. During this silent period, the ERP-based station will transmit its OFDM-modulated signal without further concern for the non-ERP PHYs.

Fragmentation

As you read earlier in this chapter, IEEE 802.11 frames can support an MSDU of 2304 bytes. However, because TCP/IP uses an MTU of 1500 bytes as a default and most data is transmitted using TCP/IP, most WLAN frames are considerably smaller than the maximum potential frame size. There are situations where these frames of roughly 1500 bytes (1508 after the LLC) may still be too large. The IEEE 802.11 MAC layer has the functionality to fragment the data even more. This is done through a process known as *fragmentation.*

You can configure a setting in your wireless client software called the *fragmentation threshold.* This is a setting, in bytes, that determines when the MAC layer will fragment the frames into smaller frames. A higher fragmentation threshold usually means less fragmentation protocol overhead but less resilience against interference. A lower fragmentation threshold usually means more fragmentation protocol overheads but more resilience against interference. If at any moment there is no interference to cause retransmission, the additional fragmentation protocol overhead reduces data throughput. If at the next moment there is interference causing retransmission, the additional fragmentation protocol overheads increases data throughput above what it would have been without the fragmentation. Your job, as a WLAN administrator, will require you to find the optimum threshold for a given connection. In the real world, default fragmentation thresholds are normally left as is (no fragmentation) and they are only changed when there is a communications problem. This is due to the fact that a wireless client may perform better with a lower fragmentation threshold in one area and a higher fragmentation threshold in another area. You will learn more about fragmentation threshold settings and their usefulness in the troubleshooting process in Chapter 12.

Dynamic Rate Switching

Dynamic rate selection, dynamic rate switching, automatic rate shifting, and dynamic rate shifting all refer to IEEE 802.11 Section 9.6 Multirate support, but whatever you call it, it is the process of reducing or increasing the data rate to the next supported data rate as the quality of the RF signal changes.

Remember that signal strength attenuates over distance. This results in a weaker signal at a longer distance than is available at a shorter distance. Other factors, such as absorption into materials in the service area, can also result in a weaker signal at a point equidistant from the access point as another point with a stronger signal. Whatever the reason for reduced signal quality, the data rate is lowered to provide more effective use of the WM.

Consider that modulation schemes used in the DSSS PHY, for example, change fewer attributes of the RF signal fewer times in order to modulate data onto the signal than do the modulation schemes used in the OFDM or ERP PHYs. As the quality of the signal degrades, it becomes more and more difficult to demodulate the more complex modulation schemes. By slowing down the data rate, either with a different or the same modulation, it becomes easier to demodulate the data.

A standards-based device will only change the data rate to a supported data rate of the standard. For example, a HR/DSSS PHY will shift from 11 to 5.5 Mbps, but will not shift from 11 to 6 Mbps because 6 Mbps is not supported by the HR/DSSS PHY. In the same way, an ERP PHY will shift from 48 to 54 Mbps, but it will never shift from 48 to 51 Mbps, since 51 Mbps is not a supported data rate.

Summary

This chapter provided an overview of terms related to the IEEE 802.11 MAC and PHY and then presented the MAC layer services in detail. You learned about frames and frame exchanges as well as the process used to go from MSDU to PPDU for transmission on the WM. Finally, you learned about the different methods used to control access to the WM, including DCF, PCF, and RTS/CTS.

Key Terms

- ☐ **active scanning**
- ☐ **association**
- ☐ **authentication**
- ☐ **bits**
- ☐ **bytes**
- ☐ **contention window**
- ☐ **dynamic rate switching**
- ☐ **DCF**
- ☐ **EDCA**
- ☐ **fragmentation**
- ☐ **frames**
- ☐ **HCF**
- ☐ **IEEE 802.11e**
- ☐ **interframe spacing**
- ☐ **MPDU**
- ☐ **MSDU**
- ☐ **octets**
- ☐ **passive scanning**
- ☐ **PCF**
- ☐ **PPDU**
- ☐ **PSDU**
- ☐ **RTS/CTS**

Review Questions

1. The IEEE 802.11 state machine supports three states. These three states are different combinations of which two functions?

   A. Authentication

   B. Accounting

   C. Association

   D. Interframe spacing

2. The time interval that a station must wait before beginning a random backoff time, when using DCF, is called what?

   A. Data rate

   B. Interframe spacing

   C. Country code

   D. Gap window

3. When there is interference in an area, which of the following settings may improve performance if it is modified?

   A. Fragmentation threshold

   B. DIFS

   C. Carrier sense

   D. Contention window

4. The unit of data being manipulated is the PSDU. It is being converted into a PPDU. In which layer of the OSI model is this data unit currently?

   A. Data Link layer

   B. Application layer

C. Physical layer

D. Transport layer

5. What is the name of the sublayer that is actually responsible for modulating data onto the WM?

 A. PLCP

 B. MAC

 C. LLC

 D. PMD

6. Which of the following amendments introduce Country elements into the IEEE 802.11 standard? (Choose all that apply.)

 A. 802.11e

 B. 802.11d

 C. 802.11j

 D. 802.11i

Review Answers

1. **A, C.** The correct answers are authentication and association. The three states are unauthenticated and unassociated, authenticated and unassociated, and authenticated and associated.
2. **B.** The correct answer is interframe spacing (IFS). There are multiple IFS intervals, including SIFS (shortest), PIFS (neither shortest nor longest), and DIFS (longer than PIFS).
3. **A.** The correct answer is fragmentation threshold. By decreasing the fragmentation threshold, you reduce the amount of time it takes to transfer a frame and, therefore, increase the likelihood that the frame will be transmitted before interference occurs.
4. **C.** The correct answer is Physical layer. The Physical layer is where the PSDU becomes a PPDU for transmission on the WM.

5. **D.** The correct answer is PMD. The PLCP is the communications layer between the MAC and the PMD that allows for the use of a similar MAC layer with all of the PHYs in IEEE 802.11 as amended. The MAC layer is where the upper-layer data units are converted into IEEE 802.11 frames.

6. **B, C.** The correct answers are 802.11d and 802.11j. In addition to these two, 802.11h introduces a Country entity as well.

PART

Deploying Wireless LANs

In This Part

CHAPTER

5

Wireless Design Models, Topologies, and Infrastructure

CWNA Exam Objectives Covered:

- Define, describe, and apply the following concepts associated with WLAN service sets
  - Stations and BSSs
  - Starting and Joining a BSS
  - BSSID and SSID
  - Ad Hoc Mode and IBSS
  - Infrastructure Mode and ESS
  - Distribution System (DS) and DS Media
  - Layer 2 and Layer 3 Roaming
- WLAN design models
- Explain and apply the following power management features of WLANs
  - Active Mode, Power Save Mode, and WMM Power Save (U-APSD)
  - TIM/DTIM/ATIM

In This Chapter

WLAN Service Sets

WLAN Design Models

WLAN Power Management Features

Chapters 2 through 4 primarily focused on WLAN technology and standards from the bottom up. This chapter investigates WLANs from a top-down perspective in that it covers the logical entities that exist within WLANs and the different design models that are commonly implemented. Additionally, power management operations are covered because it is important to understand how a station can exist as part of a WLAN network when the transceiver is not actually powered on at all times.

WLAN Service Sets

The concept of a service set, to which previous chapters allude, has not been fully defined up to this point. The service set is the basic logical entity that exists in IEEE 802.11 WLANs. Service sets and stations are both defined and explained in this section. Additionally, the distribution system is explored in order to understand how a WLAN is spread throughout a service area using both wired and wireless technologies. Finally, this section provides an overview of roaming within IEEE 802.11 WLANs.

Stations, BSSs, and BSAs

The IEEE 802.11 standard defines an entity known as a *station* and uses the term *STA* to refer to this entity. The STA is defined as any device that has an IEEE 802.11–compliant MAC and PHY interface to the WM. This means that the following devices, among others, would all be considered valid STAs, assuming they use IEEE 802.11–compliant radios and drivers:

- Access points (APs)
- Laptops, desktops, and servers with wireless NICs
- PDAs with IEEE 802.11b radios
- Residential gateways (mostly known as wireless routers)
- Wireless print servers
- Wireless presentation gateways
- Wireless bridges
- Wireless gaming adapters (mostly just wireless bridges)
- Wireless VoIP (Voice over IP) phones

This list is just a partial list. Many devices use IEEE 802.11–compliant radios and drivers and are capable of acting as an IEEE 802.11 STA.

However, it is also possible to use IEEE 802.11 devices in ways that are not defined within the IEEE standards and in ways that are not compatible with IEEE-based WLANs. These implementations usually have alternate MAC or PHY layers that change the functionality of the IEEE 802.11–compliant device in such a way that it is no longer considered a valid IEEE 802.11 STA. In other words, the device is capable of operating in an 802.11-compliant manner, but the drivers or software cause it to function in a noncompliant manner. This can be done because an IEEE 802.11 device uses a radio that has the capability of behaving in ways that are not in compliance with the standard. Keep in mind that the standards are used to ensure interoperability between devices and that nonstandard devices should be avoided in common WLAN implementations.

It might seem odd to you to think of an AP as a station if you are used to wired networks where you use the term client station to mean an end user's computer; however, even in wired networks, any computer or device using the IEEE 802.3 Ethernet standard is technically a *node* on the network, where node is the generic term for any Ethernet device, and station is the generic term for any IEEE 802.11 device. If the device can communicate on an IEEE 802.11 conformant WLAN, it has a set of STA services and is able to participate in a basic service set (BSS).

This brings us to the phrase *basic service set.* The BSS is defined as a set of stations that have successfully synchronized after one station has executed the START primitive. In the previous chapter, you learned about DCF. The stations that are all cooperating together in the same DCF group form a BSS. There are more than one type of BSS. There is a BSS that is more dynamic (independent) and another that is more static (infrastructure). You can also combine more than one BSS together to form a logical group through which a STA may pass without network interruption. The following sections describe the components of a BSS, the BSS types, and the process of starting and joining a BSS.

The BSA is the *basic service area.* This is the conceptual area within which BSS members may communicate. Another way of saying this is to say that the BSA is the physical space within which the STAs that are participating in the BSS may communicate with each other. In some BSS implementations, the client STAs communicate directly with each other, and in other BSS implementations, the client STAs communicate with each other through the AP STA. In either case, the BSA is the physical space boundary within which these STAs may communicate with each other. The BSA will vary or change slightly over time in most environments and can vary greatly in some environments. This is due to changes in the physical space such as atmospheric changes, physical item placement, the number of people present, and so forth. This is why a particular signal strength can be seen at a location at one time and a very different signal strength can be seen at the exact same location at another time. Though the AP has not moved, environmental conditions change, and this results in a varying BSA.

Ad Hoc Mode and IBSS

The dynamic topology offered by the IEEE 802.11 standard is the *independent BSS (IBSS)*. This is sometimes called an *ad hoc* wireless network. An IBSS is a collection of STAs that are communicating with each other directly without the use of an AP. In order for a STA to be able to communicate with another STA, they must be within RF range of each other. There is no relaying of signals from one STA to another through the various STAs in the IBSS. For this reason, an IBSS is constrained to a fairly small BSA.

As an example, consider Figure 5.1. In this figure, the STAs on the right and the left can communicate with each other at an acceptable rate. All the STAs in between the extreme right and left STAs can also communicate with STAs A through E effectively. However, signals from STA F, represented in the lower portion of Figure 5.1, cannot reach the other STAs in the IBSS and the other STAs' signals cannot reach it. STA F is outside the BSA of the IBSS.

FIGURE 5.1 IBSS BSA

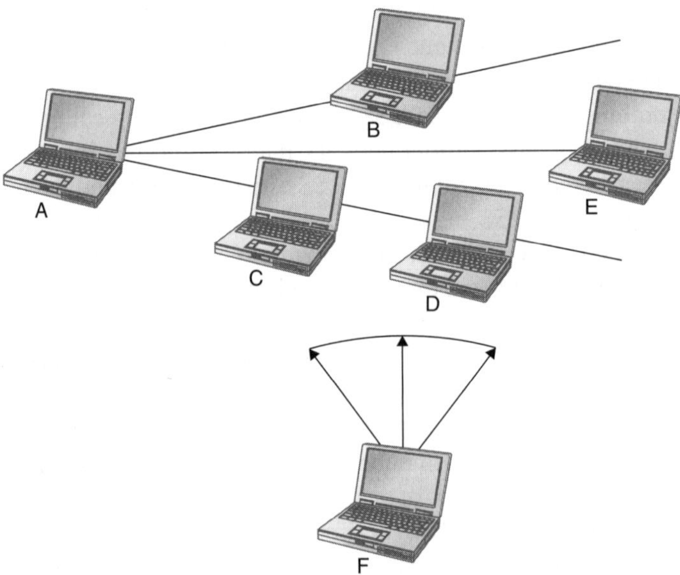

Infrastructure Mode and ESS

When a wireless AP station is used, an *infrastructure BSS* (simply called a BSS) is implemented. At the same time, an *extended service set (ESS)* is made possible. An ESS, as defined in IEEE 802.11-1999 (R2003), is a collection of one or more BSSs sharing the same service set identifier (SSID) (defined in the next section). The following is the definition of an ESS pulled directly from the standard:

> *A set of one or more interconnected basic service sets (BSSs) that appears as a single BSS to the logical link control (LLC) layer at any station associated with one of those BSSs.*

The definition in the standard reveals that a single BSS can indeed form an ESS. The phrase, "A set of one… BSSs," reveals such. This is also seen in the definition of the extended service area (ESA), which is the ESS equivalent of the BSA. The ESA is defined as being larger than or equal to a BSA. You may be wondering why I am taking the time to explain the technical reality that an ESS exists as soon as an infrastructure BSS exists. Allow me to explain.

The vast majority of WLAN literature indicates that you *create* an ESS when you group more than one BSS together using the same SSID. This is an incorrect understanding and it leads to a misunderstanding of what an ESS really is. An ESS is more like a Windows Workgroup than a Windows Domain, for those familiar with Windows environments. In other words, there is no real "central" controller of the ESS or requirement for more than one BSS to have an ESS. The ESS exists logically the moment the first AP comes online and forms a BSS—just as a Windows Workgroup exists as soon as a computer comes online using the Workgroup name. The first computer cannot prevent other computers from using the same Workgroup name or control their access to the Workgroup. An ESS is the same in that the first AP that comes online starts the ESS and additional APs can join the ESS by using the same SSID (they may even become a virtual enlarged ESS even though they have different SSIDs), and this is not controlled by the initial AP. Though some WLAN switches or controllers may be able to control entry to an ESS, this is not part of the IEEE 802.11 standard.

To get clarity on this subject, you can read the *IEEE 802.11F* recommendation for the management of STA handoff between APs in an ESS. This recommendation states that *the initialization of the first AP via the MLME-START.request(BSSType=Infrastructure) establishes the formation of an ESS.* It goes on to say that *subsequent APs that are interconnected by a common DS* (distribution system) *and that are started with the same SSID extend the ESS* ***created by the first*** [emphasis added]. While the IEEE 802.11F recommendation is just that, a recommendation, and it has been withdrawn as of February 3, 2006, it states the reality of ESS creation more clearly than the IEEE 802.11 standard itself.

Another angle of approach would be to say that the SSID is actually the ID of the ESS and not the BSS. In fact, as stated earlier, the BSS has an ID, which is the BSSID. The ESS has an ID too, which is the SSID. This understanding clears up the confusion that results in common questions like:

- What is the difference between the SSID and the BSSID?
- Where is the ESSID set?
- How do you "create" an ESS?

The answer to the first question is that every service set has a machine-friendly name (the BSSID) and a people-friendly name (the SSID). The answer to the second question is nowhere. There is no such thing as an ESSID and where it is referenced in the IEEE 802.11 Annex, it should read SSID. The answer to the third question is that you create an ESS when the first AP comes online and executes a START primitive as an infrastructure BSS. The IEEE has not determined how to make multiple ESSs into one ESS but has suggested that this is something that needs to be addressed in the future.

Ultimately, you might consider that there are two perspectives to the creation of an ESS. The first is that the ESS is logically created when the first AP comes online, as it is now available for other APs to join. By this, I mean that there is only one BSS and most people think of an ESS as "more than one BSS," but the ESS exists the moment the first AP comes online. The second is that the ESS is created physically or in reality when the second AP is brought online and configured to use the same SSID or when it uses some other method of joining the ESS on the shared distribution system.

Though an ESS is often said to have an ESSID, in fact, the IEEE 802.11 standard does not identify such an element as an ESSID. The ID of an ESS is effectively the SSID that is shared among the infrastructure BSSs that are participating in the ESS. The BSSID of each infrastructure BSS is used by the APs in order to track which STA is associated in which BSS so that data can be transferred from one BSS to another within the ESS. If you had a hard time following all those acronyms, make sure you read this note more than once.

Effectively, an ESS exists when the first AP comes online and defines the SSID. As each new AP, which is connected to the same distribution system, comes online with the same SSID as the first, it joins the existing ESS. This reveals that the ESS is really using the SSID to determine which APs should participate in the ESS. This is the default behavior that is most frequently implemented. The exceptions to this basic functionality would include when roaming specifications are implemented and configured to use RADIUS to control the APs that are allowed in the ESS or when some other proprietary protocol is used to constrain the APs that can participate in the ESS.

It is also important to note that there is no requirement that STAs be able to roam between BSSs within an ESS without losing their upper-layer connections such as IP addresses and MAC-layer connections. In other words, BSSs that form an ESS may overlap to allow for such roaming, or they may not overlap at all and allow for nomadic type connections. This will be covered more in the later section "Layer 2 and Layer 3 Roaming."

BSSID and SSID

The SSID, or service set identifier, is used to indicate the identity of an ESS or IBSS, depending on the implemented topology. The SSID can be from 2 to 32 characters in length and is normally sent in the beacon frames. A STA seeking to join a WLAN may send probe request frames including the SSID of the desired WLAN. If an AP "hears" the probe request frame and it uses the same SSID, it will respond with a probe response frame. The STA that transmitted the original probe request frame may now authenticate and, if successful, associate with the BSS.

The *basic service set identifier (BSSID)* should not be confused with the SSID. The BSSID is a 48-bit identifier that is used to uniquely identify each service set. The BSSID is usually the MAC address of the STA within the AP in an infrastructure BSS.

In an IBSS, the BSSID will be an ID generated according to the rules for locally administered addresses specified in Clause 5.2 of the IEEE 802-1990 standard. This means that the first bit (the individual/group bit) will be 0 to indicate an individual and the second bit (the universal/local bit) will be 1 to indicate that the address is a locally administered address. The remaining 46 bits of the BSSID will be generated using an algorithm that minimizes the likelihood of other STAs generating the same BSSID.

Where the SSID identifies the service set, which may extend across multiple BSSs, the BSSID is unique to each BSS in an ESS or to each independent BSS. In order to help you better understand this, the following sections will provide details of the different types of service sets.

Distribution System (DS)

The *distribution system (DS)* is defined as a system used to interconnect a set of BSSs and an integrated LAN to form an ESS. Additionally, the DS is used for the transfer of communications between the APs in the ESS. The communication that occurs between APs may be proprietary to the AP vendor, it may be according to a non-IEEE specification, or it may be in accordance with the IEEE 802.11F recommendation—even though this recommendation was withdrawn. Every AP has a DS within it, regardless of whether it is connected to other APs across some other shared system such as Ethernet. The DS is composed of two parts: the Distribution System Medium and the Distribution System Services.

You may note that the *f* in IEEE 802.11F is capitalized. This is because it is a stand-alone specification and is not an amendment to a standard. The *g*, for example, in the IEEE 802.11g amendment is in lowercase because it is not a stand-alone specification. You will not be tested on lowercase versus uppercase nomenclature on the CWNA exam, but it is good to know the whys behind the whats. While the IEEE 802.11F recommendation has been withdrawn, it is still an example of this notation.

Distribution System Medium (DSM)

The *Distribution System Medium (DSM)* is the medium or set of media used for communications among APs in the ESS. The most popular medium in use today is certainly Ethernet, but the IEEE standard allows for the use of other media such as Token Ring or even another form of wireless.

Distribution System Services (DSS)

The *Distribution System Services (DSS)* are composed of the services that provide the delivery of frame payloads between stations that are in communication with each other over a shared instance of WM and in the same infrastructure BSS. In other words, the DSS provide communications between stations in the same BSS. At this point, the IEEE 802.11 standard does not specify the full delivery path from a STA in a BSS to a station in another BSS or from a STA in a BSS to a network node outside the BSS. Usually, each AP drops the frames out the connected portal (usually Ethernet) and hopes the Ethernet infrastructure (routers, switches, etc.) knows how to reach the destination.

Starting and Joining a BSS

The process of starting a BSS differs depending on whether it is an IBSS or an ESS (infrastructure BSS). In the case of an IBSS, the first station coming online starts the IBSS. In the case of an ESS, the AP starts the BSS when it comes online. The following sections provide more details on the start-up of an IBSS or an ESS. Joining a BSS was covered in Chapter 4 in the topics "Active Scanning" and "Passive Scanning."

Starting an IBSS

An IBSS is started when the first station comes online. Specifically, the station processes an MLME-START.request primitive with the parameter BSSType set to independent. This station sets the SSID to use in the IBSS, and all other stations that wish to join the same IBSS must use the same SSID. Additionally, this first station will set the BSSID according to the guidelines specified in the IEEE 802.11 standard. A station may scan before attempting to start the IBSS, or the station may start the IBSS without performing a scan first.

Starting an ESS

An infrastructure BSS (ESS) is started when the AP is started. The AP will process an MLME-START.request primitive with the parameter BSSType set to infrastructure. The AP sets the SSID to use in the ESS. The BSSID

TABLE 5.1 ESS Start-Up Parameters

BSS Parameter	Description
SSID	The SSID to use for the ESS.
PHY parameter set	The parameter set used by the PHY that is being implemented. For example, OFDM, DSSS, etc.
Beacon period	The Beacon Period to be used in the ESS.
Data rates	Information such as supported data rates.

will likely be the MAC address of the AP. At this starting point, the AP will specify the parameters to be used within the ESS. These parameters are presented in Table 5.1. Other parameters are also configured, and Table 5.1 is intended only to provide an understanding of the basic start-up process for an ESS.

Layer 2 and Layer 3 Roaming

When a station associates with an AP in a BSS, it is joining a potentially larger network (the ESS). If the station moves out of the range of the initial AP, it may disassociate and reassociate with another AP that is participating in the same ESS. This process of reassociation is known as *roaming*. Roaming provides mobility, but there are different types of mobility. This section will present the different types of mobility and then covers the basics of roaming.

Mobility Types

There are three basic types of mobility that can occur in an IEEE 802.11 WLAN.

- **No-Transition** Static or local movement.
- **BSS-Transition** Moving around to different BSSs within an ESS.
- **ESS-Transition** Moving from a BSS in one ESS to a BSS in another. The IEEE states that upper-layer connections are not guaranteed and are likely to be lost.

FIGURE 5.2 No-transition mobility

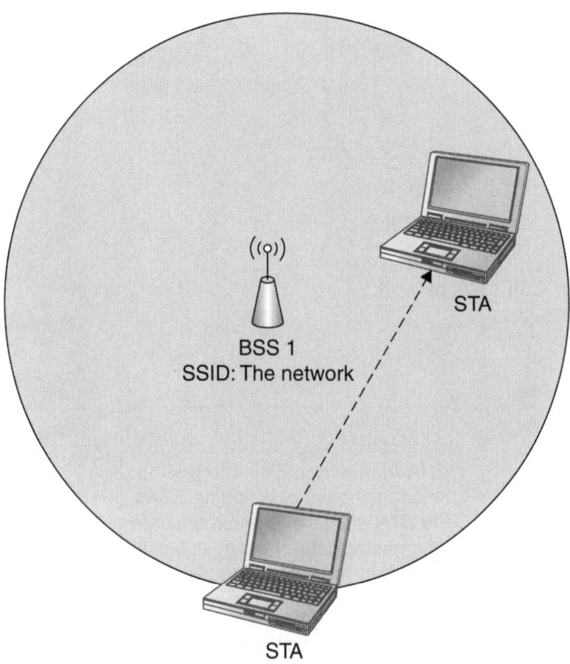

STA moves around within range of its BSS. No roaming occurs and the connection is not lost. This is no-transition mobility.

The first, no-transition, indicates that the station will not transition from one BSS to another while attempting to maintain upper-layer connections. In other words, it stays in range of its BSS. Figure 5.2 illustrates nonoverlapping BSSs and a no-transition type of mobility.

The second type is what is most commonly referenced as roaming. The BSS-transition mobility model is one that does allow for the maintenance of upper-layer connections while moving from one BSS to another within the same ESS. Also called seamless roaming, this is represented in Figure 5.3.

The third type occurs when a station moves from a BSS in one ESS to a BSS in a different ESS. Since an ESS can be thought of as a "virtual" LAN even though it may spread across massive areas, it is logical that you can maintain upper-layer connections while roaming within an ESS (BSS-transition). However, separate ESSs can be thought of as separate "virtual" LANs and it is also logical that you will lose upper-layer connections while roaming from one ESS to another (ESS-transition).

FIGURE 5.3 Seamless roaming (BSS-transition mobility)

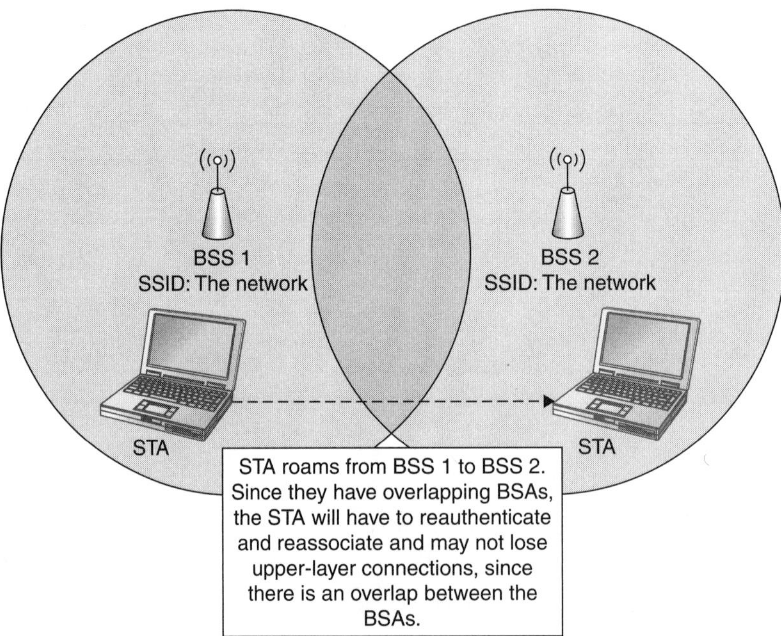
BSS 1
SSID: The network
BSS 2
SSID: The network
STA
STA
STA roams from BSS 1 to BSS 2. Since they have overlapping BSAs, the STA will have to reauthenticate and reassociate and may not lose upper-layer connections, since there is an overlap between the BSAs.

There are technologies which allow for roaming between ESSs while still maintaining upper-layer connections. IEEE 802.11 does not specify such a technology, but proprietary solutions do exist.

General Roaming Overview

In general you could say that there are two types of roaming: seamless and reconnecting. Seamless roaming would be roaming that allows a station to move its association from one BSS to another without losing upper-layer connections. Think of it as like being able to start a large FTP download while associated with one BSS and then walking to another area where you are reassociated with another BSS within the ESS. Seamless roaming allows the FTP download to continue and not fail. Seamless roaming is usually an implementation of BSS-transition mobility.

Reconnecting roaming would require a new connection to the FTP server and, unless the server supported failure resume, a restart of the download. BSS-transition mobility may fall into this category if there is no association handoff operation that can be performed between the two BSSs even though they are in the same ESS.

Because the IEEE 802.11 standard does not specify the details of how roaming should occur, it is possible to implement a WLAN using APs from different vendors (or even different model APs from the same vendor) that cannot communicate with each other and will not allow for seamless roaming. If you want to purchase differing hardware and still allow for seamless roaming, you will have to either purchase and test the hardware to ensure that the APs can interoperate or ensure that both vendors provide support for the same roaming procedures.

At the time of this writing, IEEE 802.11r is being developed. IEEE 802.11r is targeted at providing fast roaming and may provide a future solution to the current nonstandard roaming procedures.

You will not have to understand the complete frame exchange process and functionality of IEEE 802.11F for the CWNA exam; however, you will need to understand the basic concepts of IEEE 802.11F and how it solves the roaming association handoff problem in WLANs. To understand the IEEE 802.11F specification, we'll explore the two protocol sequences implemented in IEEE 802.11F APs: IAPP-ADD and IAPP-MOVE. The optional IAPP-CACHE will not be explored. Each of these protocol sequences triggers specific actions and these actions are presented here.

IAPP-ADD An AP will receive an IAPP-ADD request whenever a station associates with the AP. Upon receipt of this request, the AP should do the following:

- Send an IAPP-ADD-notify packet.
- Send a Layer 2 update frame.

The IAPP-ADD-notify packet is an IP packet that is sent using a multicast address and will only be processed by other nodes utilizing IAPP. This packet informs the other APs of the MAC address of the station that is now associated with the IAPP station that is transmitting the IAPP-ADD-notify packet. The ADD-notify packet also includes the Sequence Number from the Association request sent by the STA. All APs that receive the ADD-notify packet should update their association tables accordingly; if the STA is listed in their association tables, it should be removed. The Layer 2 update frame is used to update the learning table in other APs and other Layer 2 devices.

IAPP-MOVE The IAPP-MOVE request will be processed whenever a STA sends a reassociation request to an AP. The AP that is processing the reassociation, which is the AP to which the STA wishes to roam, should send an IAPP-MOVE-notify packet to the old AP. This will be an IP packet. The IP address of the old AP will either be discovered using a RADIUS server for mapping purposes or by using a proprietary internal mapping engine within the AP. The IEEE 802.11F standard specifies the use of RADIUS or an unspecified internal IP address to AP mapping function. The old AP should respond with an IAPP-MOVE response to inform the new AP that the STA's association has been removed from the old AP.

You will not be tested on the intricacies of the IEEE 802.11F standard on the CWNA exams any longer. This is largely due to the fact that as quickly as the recommendation came, it went—it is no longer in play.

WLAN Design Models

With an understanding of the basic logical entities that exist in a WLAN and the roles played by various station types, you can begin to explore the different WLAN design models. Many WLAN design models exist; the one you choose to implement will depend on the needs discovered during a site survey and customer interviews. This section provides an overview of these WLAN design models.

In this book, the term *customer* is used to reference the end user of the WLAN and is not intended to reference an external purchaser of services only. In this way, the term customer can refer to both internal and external customers of the Information Systems (IS) or information Technology (IT) group.

Site-to-Site Connections

When using WLAN technology to form site-to-site links, you will either create *point-to-point (PtP)* or *point-to-multipoint (PtMP)* links. This section describes both.

Point-to-Point (PtP)

A PtP WLAN connection is a dedicated connection between two wireless devices. These two devices are usually bridges that allow for the bridging of two otherwise disconnected LANs. These wireless connections allow for the creation of large-scale campus networks and may even be used to create metropolitan networks that span cities. They provide the benefit of connecting disconnected LANs over some distance without the need for leased lines or running cable when the connection is created within a large campus or otherwise owned area. Figure 5.4 shows a PtP connection and a PtMP connection.

These PtP connections will use semidirectional or highly directional antennas to form the connection. These antennas, unlike the more common indoor omnidirectional antennas that are seldom aimed at anything but rely on reflections to get the job done, do focus the signal mostly in a desired direction so that more amplitude is available in that desired direction.

FIGURE 5.4 PtP and PtMP wireless connections

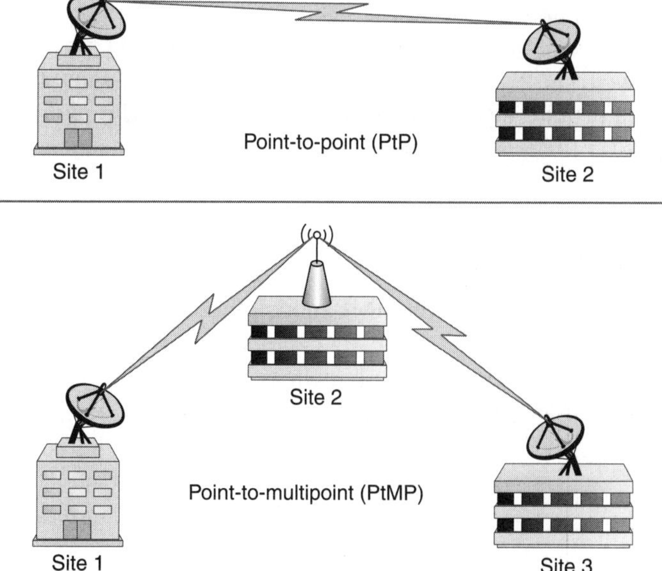

Point-to-Multipoint (PtMP)

A PtMP wireless link is created when more than one link is made into a central link location like that represented in Figure 5.4 in the lower half of the image. An omni- or semidirectional antenna is usually used at the central location, and semidirectional or highly directional antennas are used at the other locations. This is a kind of hub-and-spoke configuration.

When creating outdoor or indoor bridge links, you will have to decide between these two topologies. When only one connection is needed, you will usually choose the PtP model, and when there is a need for multiple locations to link back to a central location, you will usually choose the PtMP model. However, there are times when multiple PtP links may be justified instead of using the PtMP model. Specifically, this may be needed when you cannot accept the throughput constraints imposed by having a single antenna positioned centrally that is accessed by all remote locations.

While PtP and PtMP links are mostly considered when creating bridge links, the truth is that an AP is a bridging device accessed by laptops and desktops in a typical WLAN installation. The common WLAN implementation of multiple stations accessing a single AP is a PtMP model. If each station had its own AP, this would be a PtP model. I've seen this PtP implementation scheme used in situations where shared access to an AP would not provide the needed throughput, though this is both costly and extremely rare.

It is important to note, however, that "real" IEEE 802.11 bridge devices implement a full or nearly full IEEE 802.1D feature set between 802.11 and 802.3. Doing the full IEEE 802.1D processes does require significantly more RAM and CPU power, hence the greater price of dedicated WLAN bridges.

WLAN Models

In the common WLAN PtMP model, there are two primary implementation methodologies: the *single MAC model* and *the split MAC model*. The single MAC model is also known as an *edge* or *intelligent edge* model, and the split MAC model is also known as a *centralized* model.

Single MAC Model (Edge, Autonomous, or Stand-Alone)

When a single MAC model is used, it means that the APs contain all of the logic within them to perform MAC-layer operations. In other words, all IEEE 802.11 services reside within the AP, with the possible exception of security services when IEEE 802.11i is implemented. The single MAC model is the oldest and is still very popular in small- and medium-sized WLANs. There are both costs and benefits of the single MAC model.

Single MAC model costs:

- Decentralized administration may require more ongoing support effort.
- APs may be more expensive, since they have more powerful hardware.
- Each AP may be able to handle fewer client stations.

Single MAC model benefits:

- No single point of failure. If one AP goes down, the others continue to function.
- Less wired network traffic is required to manage the wireless stations.
- More features are available within the APs themselves.

Split MAC Model (Centralized)

The split MAC model is called such because portions of the MAC-layer operations are offset to centralized controllers and other portions remain in the AP. These types of APs are often called thin APs because they do not perform as many functions as the traditional APs (fat APs). The split MAC model is very popular in large networks today and is becoming more popular in smaller networks as well. There are costs and benefits associated with the split MAC model, too.

Split MAC model costs:

- A possible single point of failure occurs at the WLAN controller.
- Increased wired network traffic is required to manage the wireless stations.
- There are fewer features within the APs themselves when using truly thin APs.

Split MAC model benefits:

- Centralized administration may reduce ongoing support efforts.
- APs may (or may not) be less expensive, since they can have less memory and processing power.
- Each AP may be able to handle more client stations, since the AP doesn't have to handle management processing overhead.

You may have noticed that, in a large way, the benefits of the split MAC model are the costs of the single MAC model and the benefits of the single MAC model are the costs of the split MAC model. While there are certainly more details involved than this, it is important to understand that you will be giving up something regardless of the model you choose. The key is to determine what is best for the organizational and technical needs of the organization in which you are implementing the WLAN. You will learn more about this in Chapter 6 when you learn about site surveys and WLAN network planning.

Wireless Mesh Networks

Another wireless networking model that is now more than a theory is the wireless mesh networking model. Earlier you learned about the PtP and PtMP models. In the database world, you have a one-to-one relationship model, and this is like the PtP model in WLANs. You also have a one-to-many relationship model, and this is like the PtMP model in WLANs. However, database theory also presents a many-to-many relationship model, and this is much like the mesh networking model in WLANs. Therefore, you could say that mesh networking is like a multipoint-to-multipoint (MPtMP) model.

In a mesh network, all APs can connect to all other stations that are turned on and within the range of each other. Additionally, data travels through each node so that each node is both a router/repeater and an end node at the same time. The benefits of a mesh networking model include

- Communications within areas that would normally have many LOS obstructions
- Data routing redundancy

The first benefit is seen because mesh nodes are placed close enough to each other that a path will always be available around obstructions that would normally prevent wireless links. Figure 5.5 illustrates this benefit. Notice that data can travel from node A to node B and then to node C and finally to node D. If this were not a mesh network, there would be no clear path from node A to node D.

The second benefit is also seen in Figure 5.5. If the route mentioned previously (A to B to C to D) was to become unavailable, there is data routing redundancy in that the route from A to F to E to D could be utilized.

The IEEE 802.11s amendment is currently in development and will specify a standard for wireless mesh networking. Earlier in this chapter, you learned that the normal DS for a WLAN is an Ethernet LAN. However, the IEEE standard leaves the specification open so that a wireless distribution system (WDS) could also be used. The IEEE 802.11s amendment is aimed at detailing just such a WDS. This means that our future could see networks that are entirely wireless without a single Ethernet cable (or other wired standard) anywhere. Right now, it seems that the more wireless we implement, the more wires we install; but this could change with evolving modulation schemes, frequency distribution, and powerful processors at lower prices. This will be aided by both the IEEE 802.11n amendment for a MIMO PHY and the 802.11s amendment for a mesh-based WDS, but there is still plenty of work

FIGURE 5.5 Solving LOS issues with mesh networking

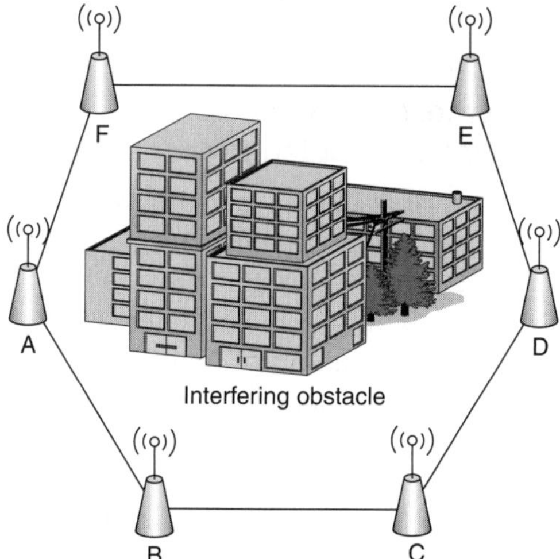

to do and plenty of uses for those wires. While we are years and more likely decades from an entirely wireless infrastructure (and some suggest it will never come), the potential is exciting.

Evolution of WLAN Models

To put the pieces together, this section will present the WLAN models that have evolved over time. I will start with the first model that was implemented using IEEE 802.11 technology and then progress through the evolutionary stages of WLAN design models. While the models did not necessarily evolve in a precisely sequential order as presented here, the adoption of the differing models does seem to have followed a path much like this.

Intelligent Edge (Distributed)

The first devices to be released to the market were the standard fat APs that are still used heavily today. This kind of AP contains the entire logic system needed to implement, manage, and secure (according to the original IEEE 802.11 specification) a WLAN. The benefit of this type of WLAN is that implementation is very quick when you are implementing only one AP. The drawback to this type of WLAN is that implementation is very slow when you are implementing dozens or hundreds of APs. There are many networks around the world that have more than 1000 APs. You can imagine the time involved if you have to set up each AP individually. At stage one, intelligent edge, this was your only choice. The APs implemented in this model are also known as autonomous APs.

WLAN Network Management Systems (Centralized Management/Distributed Processing)

When we arrive at stage two in the evolution of WLAN management, we encounter centralized configuration management with distributed intelligence. The devices and software that provide this functionality are known as a WLAN Network Management System (WNMS). This stage provided much faster implementations of traditional fat APs and worked using SNMP or other proprietary communication protocols to configure the APs across the network. The WNMSs usually supported the rollout of firmware so that the APs could be updated without having to visit each one individually. This model provided scalability, but did not reduce the cost of the APs and did not offset any processing from the APs so that they could handle more stations at each AP. In this model, autonomous APs are still used.

Centralized WLAN Architecture (Split MAC)

That brings us to stage three: Centralized WLAN Architecture. This networking model utilizes lightweight or thin APs and depends on a wired network connection to the WLAN switches. The WLAN switch contains all the logic for processing and managing the WLAN. This allows the APs to handle more client stations and provides for simple implementation. For example, most of these systems allow you to simply connect the lightweight AP (sometimes called an access port to differentiate them from an access point) to the switch that is connected to the WLAN controller, and the AP and controller will automatically synchronize without any intervention from the engineer. Of course, there is still the requirement of initial setup and configuration of the controller, but moving forward, it can be automatic. The things that are automatically configured may include the channel used by the AP, the encryption methods used, the SSID, and more.

Distributed Data Forwarding (DDF) WLAN Architecture

The DDF WLAN architecture uses a WLAN controller like the centralized architecture and represents stage four. The difference is that DDF APs are used instead of lightweight APs. A DDF AP is an AP that can perform some or all of the functions needed within a BSS and can also allow for some or all of these functions to be managed by the central controller.

Unified WLAN Architecture

The stage is now set for another evolutionary move where the wireless controlling functions are simply integrated into the standard wired switches used within our network cores. This would mean that the switches that provide wired network functionality to wired clients will also have the capability to serve the needs of wireless APs so that specialty wireless switches/controllers are no longer needed as separate devices. Today's centralized and hybrid solutions usually depend on a connection from the wireless controller to a wired switch that actually has connections to the APs. The future may see more development of multiport switches that have wireless controller functionality built in, reducing the need for an extra wired switch.

The devices used to create all of these WLAN networking models will be discussed in detail in Chapter 7. At that point, more details of the capabilities, costs, and benefits of the different models will also be explained.

WLAN Power Management Features

The stations that participate in a WLAN and provide mobility to the end users will likely be battery powered. For this reason, the IEEE has defined a set of power save operations that are implemented in 802.11 WLAN devices in order to provide for longer battery life. These operations are explained in this section.

Active Mode

When a station is in *active mode*, it does not utilize any power management features. Instead, the radio is left on at all times and frames that are destined for the station do not have to be cached at the AP. This mode is usually used by desktop computers that are using wireless connections and may be used by laptop computers as well. It is not uncommon for a laptop user to disable power save features when connected to power so that network communications are more efficient. By disabling power save mode on static devices that are always plugged into power outlets, you may also improve the performance of your WLAN overall. This is because the APs will no longer have to cache frames for any stations in the WLAN that have the power save features disabled. Figure 5.6 shows the device driver interface where power management settings can be configured on a Windows XP client station.

Power Save Mode

When a station is configured to use *power save mode*, it alternates between two states: dozing and awake. In the dozing state, much of the wireless NIC is disabled or powered down in order to save battery life. The dozing state lasts a specific interval, and then the station switches to awake so that it can check for cached frames at the AP that are intended for it. The actual activity that takes place when a station is configured in power save mode is covered in the section "TIM/DTIM/ATIM" later in this chapter.

FIGURE 5.6 Power Management Wireless Configuration screen

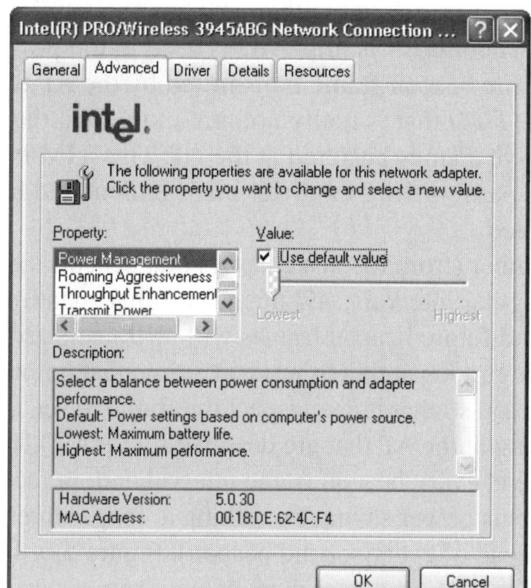

WMM Power Save (U-APSD)

The WMM certification includes a power management function known as *unscheduled automatic power-save delivery (U-APSD)*. Devices supporting U-APSD will support both legacy power management (as described in the section "TIM/DTIM/ATIM") and triggered U-APSD. In order to implement U-APSD, QAPs (QoS APs) must be used. These are APs supporting IEEE 802.11e. The intention of the WMM Power Save procedures is to provide longer battery life in QoS-demanding devices such as VoIP phones. Both unscheduled and scheduled APSD are documented in the IEEE 802.11e-2005 amendment.

TIM/DTIM/ATIM

When an IEEE 802.11 station uses power management, it uses information known as the Traffic Indication Map, the Delivery Traffic Indication Message or the Ad Hoc Traffic Indication Message window. The following sections describe these concepts.

Traffic Indication Map (TIM)

Every station that is associated with an AP has an association identifier (AID). In infrastructure BSSs, this AID is used in the power management process. Within the beacon frame transmitted by the AP is a *Traffic Indication Map (TIM)* that is really nothing more than the list of AIDs that currently have frames buffered at the AP. This TIM is used by all stations that are participating in power management and have their power save mode enabled.

You'll remember (from the last chapter) that beacon frames are transmitted at regular intervals, and this means that a station can predict when the next and future beacon frames will be transmitted. The station can go into dozing mode and then wake at a time just before a beacon frame is transmitted so that it can inspect the frame to see if any cached frames are waiting at the AP that are destined for its AID. The station is not required to wake at every beacon frame interval and, in fact, can balance performance versus power saving by waking at longer intervals (say, every third beacon instead of every second beacon). Figure 5.6 shows a slider that can be used to balance power management versus performance.

Delivery Traffic Indication Message (DTIM)

Some frames are intended to go to multiple specific stations (multicast) or all stations (broadcast). IEEE 802.11 specified the *DTIM* for managing these frame types. All stations must be awake when the DTIM is transmitted. The AP indicates the DTIM interval to the stations so that they can be awake for every DTIM. The DTIM includes the same information that the TIM contains and additionally contains information about broadcast or multicast frames.

While every beacon contains a TIM, only every *n*th beacon contains a DTIM. This may be every third or some other interval. If the DTIM interval were every third beacon, then all stations would be required to wake for every third beacon.

Ad Hoc Traffic Indication Message (ATIM)

As you'll remember, ad hoc WLANs or IBSS WLANs do not have APs. Since this is the case, something other than the TIM and DTIM must be used to facilitate power management. The ATIM is used in the IBSS WLAN. The *ATIM* is a window of time (known also as the ATIM window) when all stations are required to be awake. Any station in the IBSS having frames buffered for any other station sends a unicast ATIM frame to the station for which the frames are destined. The recipient of the ATIM frame will acknowledge the frame and remain awake so that it can receive the buffered frames. Stations not receiving an ATIM frame within the ATIM window will go back to dozing after the ATIM window expires.

When considering power management within a WLAN, it is important to strike a balance between performance and endurance. While you may be able to greatly extend battery life by configuring your WLAN stations to wait for longer periods before waking, this will also degrade the performance of the WLAN. Equally, when you have the stations wake more frequently, you lessen the length of time in which the stations can operate on battery power. The balance is usually found by considering the use of the stations and then setting the power management capabilities accordingly. For example, if you are using a laptop for VoIP communications, you may want to lean more toward performance and further away from battery conservation. On the other hand, if you are using a laptop strictly for e-mail and web browsing, you will likely lean in the opposite direction.

Summary

This chapter provided you with an overview of the WLAN topologies and architectures that are available to today's WLAN engineer. Additionally, you learned about the power management and roaming capabilities of wireless stations in IEEE 802.11 WLAN. You learned that a BSS is the fundamental building block of a WLAN and that there are two types of BSSs: infrastructure and independent. You also learned that multiple BSSs can be joined together to form an ESS in order to provide coverage to larger or more areas.

Key Terms

- ☐ **active mode**
- ☐ **ATIM**
- ☐ **BSSID**
- ☐ **DTIM**
- ☐ **extended service set (ESS)**
- ☐ **IEEE 802.11F**
- ☐ **independent basic service set (IBSS)**
- ☐ **infrastructure basic service set (BSS)**
- ☐ **point-to-point**
- ☐ **point-to-multipoint**
- ☐ **power save mode**
- ☐ **roaming**
- ☐ **single MAC model**
- ☐ **split MAC model**
- ☐ **TIM**

Review Questions

1. There are two types of basic service sets specified in the IEEE 802.11 standard. What are these two types?

   A. Independent basic service set

   B. Extended service set

   C. Infrastructure basic service set

   D. Integrated basic service set

2. A station roams from BSS A to BSS C. These BSSs are managed by APs from different vendors. Both APs support the IAPP, and the BSSs do overlap their BSAs. Finally, they both share the same SSID and function on the same LAN. Should the client station lose its IP address after roaming from BSS A to BSS B and why?

   A. Yes, because the APs do not support IEEE 802.11F

   B. Yes, because the DHCP server is on BSS A

   C. No, because all conditions are met for seamless roaming

   D. No, because any ESS provides seamless roaming regardless of these various specified details

3. You want to implement 34 thin APs with as little time invested as possible. You have also determined that you must support seamless roaming for all wireless stations. Which model are you likely to implement? (Choose one.)

   A. Split MAC

   B. Single MAC

   C. Active mode

   D. Power save mode

4. You are operating a station in power save mode. The station is participating in an IBSS. What is the window called within which the station must be awake?

   A. DTIM

   B. TIM

   C. MSDU

   D. ATIM

5. What is the ID of an ESS?

   A. BSSID

   B. SSID

   C. ESSID

   D. It doesn't exist

6. You are implementing a WLAN based on the intelligent edge architecture. What kind of APs are you installing?

   A. Thin APs

   B. Hybrid APs

   C. Lightweight APs

   D. Autonomous APs

7. What kind of APs are used with a centralized architecture?

   A. Autonomous

   B. Cisco

   C. Lightweight

   D. None

8. Which part of the beacon frame sent from the AP is the list of STAs that have data buffered at the AP when they awake?

A. Traffic Indication Map

B. Header Frame

C. Footer Frame

D. Contention Window

Review Answers

1. **A, C.** The correct answers are infrastructure basic service set and independent basic service set. An extended service set is a collection of one or more basic service sets sharing the same SSID. There is no such thing as an integrated basic service set in the IEEE 802.11 standards.
2. **C.** The correct answer is no. The station should not lose its IP address since IEEE 802.11F, or IAPP, is in use and a true ESS with overlapping BSAs among the BSSs does exist.
3. **A.** The correct answer is the split MAC model. The split MAC model will allow you to implement a large number of APs with less effort than the single MAC model in most scenarios. The roaming is a factor that is not addressed by any of the models presented and therefore does not factor into the decision.
4. **D.** The correct answer is ATIM. The Ad Hoc Traffic Indication Message window must be acknowledged by all stations participating in the IBSS, in that they must all be awake during this window of time.
5. **D.** The correct answer is it doesn't exist. Many books reference an ESSID, but this is improper terminology, as no such entity exists in the IEEE 802.11 standards.
6. **D.** The correct answer is autonomous APs. The autonomous or fat AP is the AP with all the intelligence needed to manage the BSS, with the possible exception of security capabilities when implementing IEEE 802.11i.
7. **C.** Lightweight APs are used with a centralized architecture.
8. **A.** The Traffice Indication Map (TIM) includes a list of all the STAs with frames waiting in the AP's buffer.

CHAPTER

6

Site Surveys and Network Planning

CWNA Exam Objectives Covered:

- ❖ Explain the importance of and processes involved in preparing for a complete manual RF site survey
- ❖ Explain the importance of and the processes involved in documenting manual RF site surveys
  - Gathering Business Requirements
  - Interviewing Managers and Users
  - Defining Security Requirements
  - Gathering Site-Specific Documentation
  - Documenting Existing Network Characteristics
  - Gathering Permits and Zoning Requirements
  - Indoor- or Outdoor-Specific information
  - Outdoor WLANs Versus Mesh Networks
- ❖ Explain the technical aspects and information collection procedures involved in manual and virtual RF site surveys
  - Interference Sources
  - Infrastructure Connectivity and Power Requirements
  - RF Coverage Requirements
  - Data Capacity Requirements
  - Voice Considerations
  - Client Connectivity Requirements
  - Advanced Topics
  - Describe Site Survey Reporting Procedures for RF Site Surveys

In This Chapter

CWNA Exam Objectives Covered:

- Identify the equipment, applications, and system features involved in performing virtual site surveys
  - Predictive Analysis/Simulation Applications
  - Integrated Virtual Site Survey Features of WLAN Switches/Controllers
  - Site Survey Verification Tools and/or Applications
  - Indoor Site Surveys Versus Outdoor Site Surveys
- Identify the equipment and applications involved in performing manual site surveys for indoor and outdoor deployments
  - Site Survey Hardware Kits
  - Active Site Survey Tools and/or Applications
  - Passive Site Survey Tools and/or Applications
  - Manufacturer's Client Utilities

When implementing a new WLAN, the site survey is one of the most important tasks. Interestingly, some have suggested that site surveys are no longer needed with the use of modern WLAN equipment that is self-configuring and autonegotiating. However, the reality is that you must perform a site survey to determine that these automatic systems will work effectively, or you must at least perform postimplementation analysis to ensure that the recommendations of these automatic systems have been effective. Even if you are implementing a small WLAN with one access point (AP), you still perform a site survey. In these scenarios, the survey is less complex and less detailed.

For example, you may determine that there will be four client stations in a doctor's office that will access the Internet through a SOHO wireless gateway like a Linksys WRT54G wireless router. You will then turn on your laptop and use the built-in Windows wireless client to see the networks in the immediate area and the channels they are using. Next, you turn on the Linksys WRT54G router and configure it to use an available channel. While this is a very simple example, a site survey was performed and it consisted of two phases:

- Determine the organization's needs.
- Discover how the environment can support a WLAN to meet these needs.

This chapter is about breaking these two phases into the component parts so that you can understand how to perform a site survey from start to finish. You may not perform every task mentioned in this chapter on every site survey; however, you should know about all of the tasks and technologies covered in this chapter. This will help you prepare for the CWNA exam and increase your effectiveness as a WLAN administrator.

Physical and RF Site Surveys

There are two major categories of site surveys. The first is the physical site survey, and the second is the RF site survey; both will be addressed in detail in this chapter. Some resources differentiate between the physical site survey and the RF site survey; however, there are many overlaps between these two types. For example, does the physical site survey or the RF site survey discover physical objects that interfere with RF transmissions? I would suggest that this is part of the RF site survey, but it can certainly be debated. Because of this potential overlap, this chapter will quickly define the intention of a physical site survey and an RF site survey. After this, the remaining sections will merge the two and use the phrases *RF site survey* and *site survey* to indicate all aspects of the site survey—both physical and RF.

Physical Site Surveys

The *physical site survey* is an examination of the physical environment in which the WLAN or wireless links will operate. This is inclusive of the physical premises owned by the organization operating the WLAN and possibly physical locations leased for antenna placement or cable runs. It may also include an analysis of the physical space between two wireless bridges in a point-to-point (PtP) or point-to-multipoint (PtMP) link implementation. The primary objective of a physical site survey is to ensure that the location can accommodate a WLAN. Questions answered by a physical site survey include

- Can you place wireless equipment where it is needed in order to provide RF coverage in the intended service area?
- What is the best location for placement of antennas, APs, bridges, and other WLAN devices?
- For external links that are PtP or PtMP, does the proper RF LOS exist?
- Is power located at the placement locations for WLAN devices, or is Power over Ethernet (PoE) required?
- Can Ethernet cables be run to the desired AP locations?
- Can you protect outdoor antennas and devices from the weather through strategic placement on or under existing structures, or will you need to plan for device enclosures that are weather resistant?

There are more questions to be addressed, but as you can see, the physical site survey really is about analyzing the physical space within which the WLAN will operate. One of the greatest areas of overlap between physical and RF site surveys is in the dependencies they have on one another. For example, the RF site survey will tell you how RF waves behave in the environment and this will dictate where you should place antennas; however, the physical site survey may restrict the placement of antennas so that you cannot place them in ideal locations. The result is a combination of the two types of site surveys that causes you to dynamically change your plans so that you can implement a WLAN that meets the demands of the physical space while providing the needed RF coverage. This is why this chapter treats the two site surveys as one—because it is so difficult to perform them independently and achieve success.

RF Site Surveys

The *RF site survey* is the process of examining the current RF activity in the physical space where the WLAN must operate. Additionally, it involves evaluating how your WLAN will function within that physical space. In other words, the RF site survey should answer the following four key questions:

- Is the current RF utilization low enough to allow for the implementation of my new WLAN?
- How must I implement the WLAN in order to provide the needed RF coverage within the designated service areas?
- Will I need to negotiate with neighboring WLAN administrators for such demands as reduction in output power on their WLANs or even channel adjustments on the WLANs?
- Should I implement OFDM (5 GHz) or ERP (2.4 GHz) for my WLAN?

While it may seem simple to think of having to answer only four questions, there are many other questions that we must answer in order to fully answer these four high-level questions. For example, the current RF frequency utilization is both a factor of frequency or channel usage and the signal strength of the frequency usage within the area. You might be able to detect a WLAN on channel 6, for example, but is it strong enough to prevent you from implementing a WLAN on that same channel? Additionally, you might discover that channels 1 and 11 are utilized by networks near you that are showing strong signals; however, you could implement a WLAN on channel 6 and not be seriously impacted by the neighboring WLANs. You may still have to negotiate a reduction in output power on the neighboring WLANs. These issues and more will be discussed throughout the remaining sections of this chapter.

Manual RF Site Survey Preparation

As I stated earlier, you can divide the site survey process into two major phases: determine the organization's needs and determine how to implement a WLAN that meets those needs. However, these two phases can be broken down further into multiple subphases or subtasks. Consider the following breakdown:

- Determine the Organization's Needs and Objectives
  - Determine Requirements
    - User Requirements
    - Business Requirements
    - Functional Requirements
  - Discover Constraints
    - Budgetary Constraints
    - Technical Constraints
    - Regulatory Constraints
  - Define Objectives
    - Business Objectives
    - Technical Objectives
- Determine How to Implement a WLAN That Meets the Objectives
  - Perform an RF Site Survey
  - Document the Site Survey
  - Create an Implementation Plan

Now that you've seen the basic breakdown of the site survey process, I'll cover the basics of these components so that you can understand how all the remaining sections of this chapter fit together.

Determine the Organization's Needs and Objectives

It is more important that you implement a WLAN that meets the organization's needs than that you implement a WLAN. In other words, it's very possible to implement a WLAN that does not provide needed capabilities such as seamless roaming or QoS for Voice over WLAN (VoWLAN) solutions and so on. An improperly implemented WLAN or a WLAN that is not capable of meeting business demands is as much a failure as if no WLAN were implemented at all. For this reason, the site survey must begin by determining what problems the organization is trying to solve or what advantages the organization is trying to create. Once this is known, a proper WLAN implementation plan can be formulated.

The first step in determining the organization's needs is to perform requirements analysis. Once you've determined the organization's requirements, you'll move on to investigate the potential constraints that may exist within the environment or organizational structure. With these two important pieces of information, you are ready to establish objectives that can be agreed upon by management and the solution provider, whether the solution provider is an internal department or an external service firm.

Sometimes you are fortunate enough to walk into a site survey where the organization has already clearly defined their requirements, constraints, and objectives. However, this is rare and I encourage you to gather this information before attempting to perform an RF site survey. Performing an RF site survey without understanding the organization's objectives is like performing heart surgery without understanding human anatomy. It really is that bad.

Determine Requirements

Requirements analysis is a complex topic in itself, which could occupy hundreds of pages. In this book, I'll define requirements analysis and the requirements themselves. For more information on requirements analysis, consider reading Susan Snedaker's book *How to Cheat at IT Project Management* (Syngress Press, 2005).

Requirements analysis can be defined as the process of discovering a project's requirements. A *requirement* is anything, physical or logical, that must be provided by the product of the project in order for the project to be considered successful. In other words, the requirements are the things that you must achieve at the completion of the implementation of your WLAN. The product of a project is defined as the result or outcome of the project. It is what the project gives you. The requirements, then, are those things that the product must provide in order for the project to be deemed successful. I'll focus on three key requirement types next.

User Requirements User requirements include the goals or tasks that users must perform when using the WLAN. For example, users may need to roam throughout the organization's facilities while using a VoWLAN phone. They may need to transfer files that are rather large without requiring an unacceptable amount of time. This last one is a perfect example of the kinds of "requirements" you often get during user interviews that require you to dig deeper into the intentions of the user. In this situation, you might ask, "How much time would an unacceptable amount of time be?" and "What size are the large files you will be transferring?" You will be more likely to meet the requirements of the users if you gather specific user requirements instead of vague user requirements.

The point is this: when a user or group of users informs you of a requirement that is stated in nonspecific terminology, always ask for clarification. The example in the preceding paragraph is very illustrative. Users or managers will often use the term unacceptable without defining what they mean. For example, if the users must be able to transfer large files without requiring an unacceptable amount of time, you must get the answers to three questions:

- What is a typical size for these large files?
- How long would be unacceptable?
- To or from where are the files being transferred?

The first question clarifies the size of the referenced files. The second question could also be stated in the positive as "How long would be acceptable?" Either way, you will gain a more specific number for your analysis. The third question is of utmost importance in this scenario. If the users are transferring files to or from an FTP server on the Internet that is out of your control, you will have a limited amount of impact on the performance the users perceive. You can only control the performance from the users' client stations to the Internet connection. The speed of the Internet, the remote network, and the remote FTP server may be completely out of your control. In cases such as this, you must be sure to communicate what you can and cannot promise.

Imagine the users tell you that they are transferring files that are typically 5 megabytes in size and that they are transferring them to and from an internal FTP server. Furthermore, they tell you that the files should be transferred in less than 1 minute to be seen as acceptable. You also determine that there could be as many as three users transferring these files at a given time. This results in the following equation:

$$5 \times 3 = 15 \text{ megabytes per minute}$$

You now know that you must provide a WLAN that will allow the users to transfer 15 megabytes per minute. Assuming you also determine that there will be 1 megabyte of normal network traffic per minute, you actually need to be able to transfer 16 megabytes per minute. Since you are implementing an enterprise-class access point with approximately 18–24 Mbps of actual data throughput (resulting in 2.25–3 MBps), you are confident that the WLAN will be able to maintain the demands of the users.

There has been much confusion over the difference between megabits per second and megabytes per second. A bit is a value equal to 0 or 1, and a byte (in most computer systems) is a collection of 8 bits. Therefore, you can convert megabits per second (Mbps) to megabytes per second (MBps) by dividing the Mbps by 8. A 54 Mbps WLAN device is a 6.75 MBps device. Since a 54 Mbps WLAN only provides for half or less than half the data rate as actual data throughput, you end up with the 18–24 Mbps referenced in the preceding paragraph (sometimes even less). This is a very important differentiation when you are attempting to calculate and ensure proper available throughput for your WLAN.

Business Requirements Business requirements could be said to be a superset of user requirements. In other words, the user requirements should be things that help the users act in such a way as to achieve business or organizational requirements. Business requirements come from two primary sources: internal business requirements and external business requirements. Internal requirements will be based on organizational objectives and policies such as security policies, employment policies, and so on. External requirements will be based on regulations from local regulatory bodies such as federal and local governments and their agencies.

An example of a business requirement would be to say that the WLAN must allow the users to perform at the same level they have been able to perform on the wired LAN. Ultimately, this business requirement is born out of the objective to improve performance or at least maintain it while also providing mobility. In other words, the organization wants to move forward in the area of mobility, but not backward in the area of performance (data throughput). Modern applications have grown far more throughput-intensive, and it is usually unacceptable to reduce data throughput with any modern network implementation.

Functional Requirements Finally, functional requirements are those technical capabilities that, when implemented, allow your WLAN to meet the requirements of users and the business. For example, Fast/Secure Roaming (FSR) more recently known as Fast BSS Transition (FT) may be required to support the user requirement of roaming from a BSS in one building to a BSS in another without losing voice connections. FSR implements robust security network features such as CCMP and fast authentication methods like preauthentication to allow for fast and secure roaming by only requiring the 4-way handshake at the time of actual roaming (the 4-way handshake is introduced in Chapter 10). Additionally, specific QoS devices may be required. The point is that multiple functional requirements may be needed in order to meet one user or business requirement.

Table 6.1 provides a reference of these different requirement types, their definitions, and examples of their application.

Discover Constraints

Constraints are restrictions that will impact the decisions you make related to your WLAN design and implementation. Some constraints cannot be discovered before the site survey is performed and other constraints will be discovered during user or management interviews. There are three key constraints that you must deal with as a WLAN administrator or engineer: budget, technical, and regulatory constraints.

TABLE 6.1 Requirement Types

Requirement Type	Definition	Example
User	User goals or tasks that users must perform using the WLAN	Walk around while maintaining connectivity to a web server
Business	Business goals or objectives that must be met by the WLAN	Compliance with corporate security policy
Functional	The technical capabilities of the WLAN that allow for or support user and business requirements	WLAN FSR support or IEEE 802.11i support

Budgetary Constraints There are many projects that begin with the words, "Can you get this done for X amount of dollars?" In other words, the budget is already set before the plan has even been created. To make it less painful, this kind of budget is often called a top-down budget. Of course, the opposite is a bottom-up budget, where you are asked to determine what it would cost to implement a WLAN that meets all requirements. Either way, you will likely run into budget limitations, as there is simply a practical limit on how much money is available. This may impact decisions such as the wireless equipment you purchase or the saturation of wireless devices you can afford. In turn, this can impact available throughput in a coverage area. The point is simple: what you can implement is directly linked to the demands of the users and the available resources.

Technical Constraints The second type of constraint is the technical constraint. This is a limit of capability in the currently available hardware and software in the marketplace. Unless you want to completely engineer a solution from scratch, which is usually prohibited by the budgetary constraints, you will have to live within the boundaries of the current technology. For example, as I write this, the IEEE is still working on the final IEEE 802.11n amendment. This means that most enterprise-class networks cannot even consider the WLAN technology that promises greater throughput and greater range of coverage. If they do implement the pre-N devices that are currently in the marketplace, they risk potential incompatibility with final IEEE 802.11n devices after the amendment is ratified (this is because the current pre-N devices are based on the draft standard and that standard could still change drastically). This is a perfect example of the technical constraints that will be imposed on your WLAN design and implementation.

Regulatory Constraints The final type of constraint is the regulatory constraint. These can be constraints imposed by regulations such as Sarbanes-Oxley or HIPAA, among others. They can also be constraints imposed by parent companies in many situations. Whatever the source, they force specific implementations to be utilized. As an example, any U.S. government or nongovernment agency currently connected to the DOD-GIG (Department of Defense—Global Information Grid) must comply with policy DODD 8100.2 and amendment DODD 8100.2p in regard to the wireless devices that are attached to the networks as defined in the policy and amendment. This type of regulatory constraint will often answer the question of whether you can implement a WLAN or not. If you cannot implement a WLAN that meets the regulatory constraints (due to budget constraints), you cannot implement a WLAN at all.

Define Objectives

Once you have defined the requirements and constraints, you can set forth objectives to be achieved through the implementation of a WLAN. These objectives can be written from two perspectives: the business perspective and the technical perspective.

Business Objectives From the business perspective, the objectives should be written in the language of business outcomes. For example, all organizations, whether for profit, not for profit, or governmental, have the following objectives at practically all times:

- Quality improvement
- Efficiency improvement
- Cost reduction
- Increased production
- Organizational continuity

The first four are commonly known as *better, faster, cheaper,* and *more*, respectively. The last one simply indicates that the organization wishes to remain and not cease to exist. Many regulatory constraints cause us to implement projects for the sole purpose of organizational continuity. Sarbanes-Oxley, for many organizations, is a perfect example of something we implement for organizational continuity; however, with a little analysis, you can often discover ways to improve quality, efficiency, cost management, or productivity while implementing an imposed solution.

Most organizations desire to improve quality at all times. This means doing what you do better. Sales representatives may be able to respond to customer inquiries more quickly if they have a wireless PDA connected to a WLAN. Inventory management employees may be able to keep the inventory data more current if they have a tablet PC with WLAN connectivity that they carry with them while checking stock. These are both examples of improving the quality of your process outputs: the customer response and the inventory data.

WLANs have been very helpful in the area of performance improvement. Performance improvement is about doing what you do faster. WLANs help by providing connectivity and mobility. Users can respond to e-mails more quickly, enter data from any covered location, and receive alerts shortly after they are issued. The ability to be notified of an alert (a price change, a network intrusion, a factory accident, etc.) quickly is very important. In the past, we've often used pagers and cell phones to accommodate the speedy delivery of alerts. Today, we can accomplish this with WLANs and mobile-connected devices as well.

Of course, reducing costs and increasing production are always foremost in mind for managers and executives. WLANs help you reduce costs by removing costly delays and saving business deals that would be lost if not for the timely response provided by instant communications across a WLAN. They can increase productivity as well. I assisted in the implementation of a WMS (warehouse management system) recently that utilized the benefits of a WLAN. The warehouse workers used handheld devices based on Pocket PCs to enter information about inventory and process barcodes. In the past, the workers were required to peel stickers off boxes as they were received and then take those stickers to a central (and shared) PC that had a barcode scanner attached. The process of adding new inventory was very time consuming. Now, the WLAN-connected scanners transfer the information back to a central database immediately. This also provides notification to the sales staff. The sales staff is aware of new inventory immediately and can begin selling this inventory to waiting clients.

From this information, you can see how a business objective might look like any of the following:

- Increase user mobility and therefore ready access to information.
- Reduce delays in digital information delivery.
- Implement a secure wireless network that also meets the performance demands of the organization.

Technical Objectives Technical objectives are usually written in a language that can only be understood by the WLAN administrators and engineers. These objectives specify the major technologies that will be implemented, and they are aligned with the business objectives discussed previously. Table 6.2 provides the previous list of business objectives

TABLE 6.2 Business to Technical Objective Mapping

Business Objective	Technical Objective
Increase user mobility and therefore ready access to information.	Implement multiple BSSs within one large ESS that provides seamless roaming capabilities.
Reduce delays in digital information delivery.	Implement wireless access in all conference rooms so that users can receive urgent e-mail messages and VoWLAN pages while in meetings.
Reduce delays in digital information delivery.	Provide sufficient service area AP saturation so that throughput is high and urgent information is delivered in a timely fashion.
Implement a secure wireless network that also meets the performance demands of the organization.	Install WLAN controllers to offset the processing of security techniques such as authentication from the AP so that the APs can better serve already-connected stations.

and maps them to the technical objectives that make them possible. Notice that the objectives are high level, whereas the requirements usually become very specific.

To be sure you understand the relationship of objectives to requirements and constraints, consider that objectives are high-level statements of what you will achieve by balancing your requirements with the constraints.

Determine How to Implement a WLAN That Meets the Objectives

After you've completed phase one, you are ready to perform the manual work of an RF site survey. This work may be a manual site survey, an automated site survey, an assisted site survey, or a theoretical site survey. Regardless of the type of site survey you are performing, it will ultimately lead to documentation that is specific to the organization and its physical locations. This documentation will be used heavily during the process of developing a WLAN implementation plan.

Perform an RF Site Survey

There are four primary types of RF site surveys that can be performed. The list includes manual, automated, assisted, and theoretical. Their pros, cons, and applications are summarized in Table 6.3.

Manual Site Surveys The traditional site survey is the *manual site survey.* In this type of survey, the WLAN engineer enters the physical area that is to be provided with WLAN coverage with an RF site survey kit. The engineer will place one or more APs at strategic locations and walk throughout the intended service area to test signal strengths and coverage. The APs may then be moved to another location, or multiple sets of APs

TABLE 6.3 Site Survey Types: Pros, Cons, and Applications

Site Survey Type	Pros	Cons	Applications
Manual	Very accurate; real readings in a real environment.	Time consuming; high level of RF knowledge required.	Small and medium WLANs; large WLANs requiring exacting measurements.
Automated	Dynamic reconfiguration when the environment changes; automatic power and channel management for frequency bandwidth usage.	Less accurate in relation to hardware required; may require some overengineering.	Predictable environments (national chain shops and stores); open outdoor environments (city parks, open outdoor areas like corporate gardens and picnic areas).
Assisted	Less overengineering than the fully automated site survey.	More physical activity than the automated site survey.	Any scenario that demands a balance between the pros and cons offered by the manual and assisted site surveys.
Virtual	No physical activity required; RF map generated automatically.	Costly; may require large amounts of time for data entry.	Fabricated buildings; large-scale installs that warrant the data entry time; consulting firms that repeat similar site surveys.

may be used. The use of more than one AP will allow the engineer to discover more exact roaming points and determine the best cooperative placement for the APs that results in the most effective coverage of the service area.

Manual site surveys are the most accurate, assuming the engineer understands the process and results. Because the engineer is making decisions based on actual RF information in the intended coverage area, guesswork and theorized analysis is mostly removed. However, the manual site survey takes much more time when the service area being covered requires the use of hundreds or even dozens of APs.

Manual site surveys are covered specifically in the later section "Performing Manual and Automated Site Surveys" of this chapter.

Automated Site Surveys *Automated site surveys* rely on intelligent communications between the APs and a centralized controller that adjusts the APs' output power and channel selection in order to automatically configure the WLAN environment. In order for the controller to properly configure the WLAN without large amounts of engineer intervention, automated site surveys often require what some vendors call overengineering. *Overengineering* is a term commonly used to describe placing more APs in a coverage area than are actually needed to cover that area. This overengineering allows the controller to dynamically adjust the APs to achieve the desired coverage and throughput in the serviced area. Other vendors suggest that overengineering is not needed if the right APs are utilized. Either way, the automated site survey ends up requiring more knowledge and action on the part of the WLAN engineer than is anticipated. The knowledge would be required to select the right APs that do not need overengineering, and the action would be required to place those APs in the right locations so that the controller can configure them appropriately.

It certainly seems that, whether you perform a manual site survey or an automated site survey, you will need the knowledge of a WLAN engineer. Organizations that have implemented controllers or WLAN switches that have the ability to automatically reconfigure APs have found that much of the benefit actually comes after the installation and not during the initial site survey. This is because the controller is able to adjust the AP settings over time to accommodate changes in the environment.

Automated site surveys are covered specifically in the later section "Performing Manual and Automated Site Surveys" of this chapter.

Assisted Site Surveys The *assisted site survey* is a combination of the manual and automated site surveys. Some manual work is still required, but the software performs many calculations and makes recommendations for the WLAN installation. In an assisted site survey, the engineer may perform some measurements and then input this data into the site survey software, or the site survey software may make general recommendations for the facility type (including building materials, ceiling heights, etc.) that the engineer will then test in the actual service area. After this, the site survey software or hardware will analyze the WLAN, once installed, and make appropriate adjustments to provide the coverage and throughput needed.

Theoretical or Virtual Site Surveys The *theoretical* or *virtual site survey* (also known as a *predictive site survey*) is a completely hands-off site survey method. This method usually requires the import of a blueprint, an aerial photo, or some other form of area map. Some tools will also provide a drawing component of their own. Next the materials of the building or the area are described and the type of WLAN desired is specified. With this input, the virtual site survey tool will predict placement of APs and the configuration settings for those APs. Most applications will even generate an RF map showing the coverage patterns the suggested network will provide.

The downside of such tools is that they are usually very expensive and they require a tremendous investment of time in order to learn the application and input all the data related to materials, coverage area, and WLAN specifications. For this reason, a small or medium WLAN will often be serviced better by a manual, automated, or assisted site survey. This is because it will often take less time to perform a manual site survey than it will take to enter all the information needed by the virtual site survey software. However, many vendors that sell theoretical or virtual site survey software also offer a site survey service. You will send them the blueprints of your facility and information about the materials and contents of the facility, and they will input the data into the application and generate a report for you. Since you are not required to learn the application, this offers a good trade-off. This service is sometimes offered for less than $1000 per 50,000 square feet (at the time of this writing).

At the same time, many facilities are built using common architectures and materials. These buildings may be able to be blueprinted, materialed, and virtually site-surveyed in a few hours. In these scenarios, only the cost of the application is a hindrance, and that may not be a barrier for WLAN consultants who will be performing many WLAN site surveys.

Virtual site surveys are covered specifically in the section "Performing Virtual Site Surveys" later in this chapter.

Document the Site Survey

Once you've completed the work of the site survey, regardless of type, you must document your findings. Automated and virtual site survey software will usually generate a set of site survey diagrams and documents. Manual site surveys will require that you generate all of the documents yourself. Regardless of the type of site survey, there will always be some level of manual documentation required. For example, even virtual site survey software may require that you document the details of the business objectives or security requirements outside the context of the site survey application.

At a minimum, you will need to document the business objectives, requirements (user, business, and functional), and constraints. In addition, you may have to manually document the facility (blueprints or floor plans) or coverage area (location maps, etc.) if your site survey software does not do this for you. More information on the step-by-step details for gathering information and documenting your findings is provided in the section "Documenting Manual RF Site Surveys: Before and After" later in this chapter.

Create an Implementation Plan

The final step, after performing the actual site survey, is to create an implementation plan. Will you implement a small pilot network first, or will you simply implement the infrastructure services and then layer the WLAN over them (for example, implement a RADIUS server and then install the wireless APs)? I provide detailed instructions for creating an implementation plan in the subsection "Creating an Implementation Plan" later in this chapter.

Documenting Manual RF Site Surveys: Before and After

There are really two stages at which you may document an RF site survey. The first is before you perform the survey; at this point, you are documenting the existing environment and the needs or objectives of the organization. The second is after you perform the survey; at this point, you are documenting the findings of the survey and possibly the recommendations for the WLAN implementation. In both stages, there is work to do that will impact the quality of your site survey. This section details the work that must be done in order to gather the information needed for your site survey documentation.

Gathering Business Requirements

Many methods have been proposed and utilized to gather business requirements. Among these are brainstorming, interviews, focus groups, and systems analysis. In addition to these methods, I'll also cover the security requirements that must be considered in order to properly plan and implement a WLAN.

Brainstorming

The most common method for defining requirements seems to be brainstorming. This method can be very useful as long as those involved in the brainstorming process understand the intended uses of the WLAN, WLAN technologies and their capabilities, and the constraints imposed on the particular WLAN implementation. Many brainstorming techniques have been developed over the years, including the following:

- Brain dumps
- Free association
- Clustering

Probably the most common, brain dumps seem to come natural to most people. This process involves the simple task of listing everything you can think of that you will need from the WLAN. It is the process of answering the question *What do I need the WLAN to provide and do?* again and again. This is a useful technique as an individual, but it may result in more confusion and debate than a more organized method when performed in a group.

The free-association method involves bouncing ideas off of one or more people. You may bring focus to the discussion by asking a question, like *What uses of the WLAN will impact the throughput needed?* Of course, those involved must understand what you mean by throughput and what a *use* is. The point of this method is to provide focus to the human process of idea or concept association. It is called *free* association because each individual is free to think of the *uses* that are most relevant to him or her in relation to the question presented.

The final method, clustering, involves a specific tool sometimes called a mind map. This tool looks similar to that seen in Figure 6.1. The cluster shown represents the answer to the question, *What uses of the WLAN will impact the throughput needed?* This tool can be drawn on paper, flip charts, PostIt notes, or whiteboards. Regardless of the method used, many creativity experts suggest that this is the most effective brainstorming tool available. The cluster represented in Figure 6.1 was created with Microsoft Office Visio 2007, but other tools such as Mind Manager and Mind Mapper were created specifically for this purpose.

Interviewing Managers and Users

It is important to meet with key managers and users when determining how a WLAN will be utilized. If you're not careful, you can assume too much and end up making bad decisions. To avoid this, meet with the users and observe them performing their day-to-day operations. This will give you a picture of how they currently use the network and how they perceive themselves using the network. These are often two different realities.

I often perform an experiment in my training classes where I ask an IT professional to tell me the steps he or she takes to go to work in the morning on a typical day. The IT professional usually says something like this: "I walk out the door and get in my car. I back out of the driveway

FIGURE 6.1 A WLAN cluster or mind map of uses

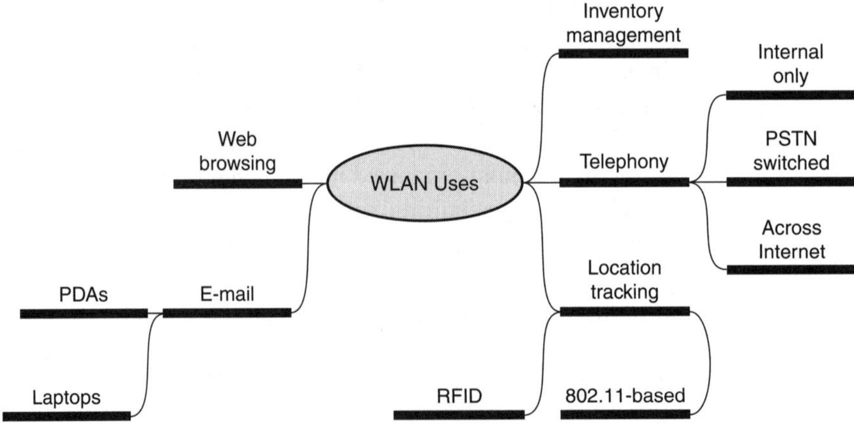

and drive south on my street. I turn right on…" At this point, I usually stop him or her and ask these two questions:

- Do you always leave the door to your house open?
- Do you always leave your car running so that you don't have to start it after you get in?

The purpose of this exercise is to point out the fact that we all leave out information when we describe our routines. Only observation can truly shed light on the actual steps a user takes in his or her daily work routines. A user may indicate that she downloads a file and then places it on her SD memory stick. She then places the memory stick in a computer in the lab and reads the data in the downloaded file. Next she destroys the data on the memory stick. However, when you actually observe her actions, you see that she downloads two files from two different FTP servers (one internal and one external) and then aggregates them together. She then runs a parsing script against the aggregated file to remove redundant information. Then she places the parsed file on an SD memory stick and removes the memory stick from her computer. She takes the memory stick to the lab and puts it in a lab computer. Finally, she reads the data from the memory stick using a special analysis program and prints the results before destroying the data on the memory stick.

Do you see how different the user's behavior is from her stated routine? For example, you have learned that she uses internal and external FTP servers. This may be valuable information if you are planning to implement a WLAN that allows her to accomplish the task in question without the use of the SD memory stick. I always try to observe the users instead of assuming I understand their work routines. This leads to better project scope documents and better-resulting systems.

Managers should also be interviewed in order to determine their perspective on the organizational needs of the WLAN and the benefits they expect to receive from it. This means you will need to gain an understanding for their short- and long-term expectations of the WLAN. Many WLANs that utilize the HR/DSSS Physical layer (also called 802.11b devices) were implemented in the early part of this decade (between 2000 and 2003), and these networks are greatly limited in their available throughput due to the 11 Mbps data rate of this PHY. These WLANs are already experiencing growth pains as is witnessed by frequent business travelers attempting to share a hotel's WLAN with dozens of other users at the same time. Regardless of what the managers project for the future, you will be limited by available technology. For this reason, you will need to clearly communicate the constraints of the current technologies, and you may need to provide a tentative migration plan to future wireless technologies that will increase the data rate, such as the HT PHY used in the future IEEE 802.11n devices.

Users should also be interviewed in order to discover how they use the existing network and how they expect to use the WLAN. If they are moved onto a WLAN with no wired access, they will expect the WLAN to perform as well as the wired LAN has in the past. This may not be possible, but when it is, it should be done. Additionally, the users may know of realities in their environments of which the managers are not aware. For example, I've seen inventory workers, who are thought to perform all their duties within the warehouse, walking more than 100 feet outside of the warehouse and expecting their PDA to maintain a WLAN connection. These users may be aware of constraints that require them to access the network from outside the warehouse—such as meeting delivery trucks and authorizing them to access a restricted area—of which the managers are unaware. The simplest way to discover these issues is to meet with the people that actually do the work and to observe their behaviors.

Focus Groups

When the supported group of users is very large, you may consider meeting with a select few of these users. This subgroup is sometimes called a *focus group* and the group can help you discover issues like those mentioned in the preceding paragraphs, without having to meet with every user. Be careful to select a group that represents the entire body of users instead of a small subsection. I was involved in a project in 2006 where a focus group was used to determine the needs of the system, but the focus group was handpicked by a manager with an agenda that did not serve the best interests of the users or the organization. Needless to say, the feedback from this focus group was less valuable than what could be acquired from a more random cross section of employees.

Systems Analysis

The more technical method available is called a *systems analysis*. This involves evaluating the existing systems (network applications and their use) in order to determine how and if they will function in a WLAN environment. This means looking at the network as it exists today, but it also means considering future growth.

Current Network Usage When considering the current network usage, look at the applications that are running on the network and be sure to answer the following questions about them:

- How many users use the application on the network at the same time?
- What is the average size of a data transmission resulting from the usage of this application?
- On average, how many of these transmissions are made in a given minute?
- What is the maximum transmission size?
- What is the maximum transmission found in a given minute?
- Is the application WLAN aware in that it can modify its network usage patterns to work more effectively on a WLAN?
- Does the application involve bursts of large data transfers, moderate data transfers sustained over time, or both?

There are certainly application-specific questions you should ask as well, but this list may be used to begin your analysis of any application. With the answers to these questions, you can determine the maximum throughput needed at peak times, the average throughput needed over time, and any specific Quality of Service (QoS) requirements that the WLAN may need to accommodate.

Future Network Usage The rate of change in technology appears to be higher today than it has ever been, and computer networks are no exception. It is a rare environment that does not have a planned change in the network at any given time. For this reason, you should be sure to consult the network administrator or IT manager to see if there are any future projects that are expected to increase the throughput needed on your WLAN.

Additionally, many WLANs are implemented so that the organization can begin using a new technology such as wireless inventory management systems, health care management systems, or even VoWLAN. Many of the users will expect to gain the advantage of the new technology and will also expect to continue performing the work they used to do on the wired LAN using the WLAN. This will demand more throughput than what was previously required and should be a part of the site survey and WLAN implementation plan documentation.

Defining Security Requirements

Chapter 10 will provide information on the basics of security in a WLAN; however, as part of the site survey and WLAN implementation plan, you must consider the security requirements. These security requirements should cover three areas at a minimum: authentication, confidentiality, and auditing. You will need to determine whether an EAP-based authentication mechanism is required or if WPA-Personal or WPA2-Personal will be sufficient. You must decide if you will need to use certificates for authentication at the client and the server, only at the server, or neither. These decisions, and more, will become part of your WLAN implementation plan and may not be considered in detail during the actual site survey. This is because the site survey is mostly aimed at providing the needed coverage and throughput; however, it is very important to consider the extra encryption and authentication overhead and how it will impact the resulting throughput that your WLAN achieves. The moral of the story is that the security solutions you implement will—at least—impact the throughput on your WLAN and may even impact the coverage area in some situations. Figure 6.2 illustrates the fact that authentication and encryption have an impact on throughput and that the throughput demand imposes constraints on authentication and encryption.

Authentication *Authentication* is defined as the process of verifying a person's or object's identity. Many networks will have an authentication infrastructure already in place, based on Novell servers, Unix/Linux

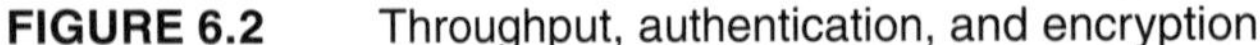

FIGURE 6.2 Throughput, authentication, and encryption

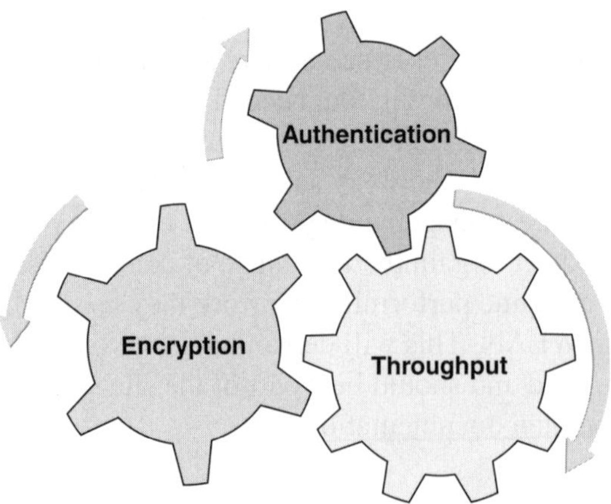

servers, Windows servers, or other solutions. When an authentication infrastructure exists, you can incorporate it into your plans as long as it provides support for WLAN client authentication. If there is no existing infrastructure, you may have to implement RADIUS servers or some other method of authentication that is compatible with IEEE 802.11 networks. You will learn more about authentication solutions in Chapter 10.

Confidentiality *Confidentiality* is a state of confidence in the privacy of data being transmitted across a network. The method used to provide confidentiality is encryption, and WLANs support many different encryption algorithms and key lengths. While this is covered in more detail in Chapter 10, for now, it is enough to realize that you must ensure that an encryption method is provided to prevent both casual and skilled eavesdropping. In many environments, a quick evaluation of the documented network security policy will provide all the details you need to make a decision related to the required encryption for your WLAN implementation.

Auditing Finally, it is essential that network activities are logged in order to provide historical documentation of the events that have transpired on or against your WLAN. You certainly want to be able to determine if a particular account has been involved in failed log-ons, and you may even want to know when successful log-ons occur. Either way, auditing—also known as accounting—is an essential process that should be implemented as part of your WLAN or provided to your WLAN by an existing wired LAN service or device. *Auditing* or *accounting* is the process of documenting selected activities that transpire on your network, usually for the purpose of ensuring compliance with network security policies.

Gathering Site-Specific Documentation

Documentation is frequently available that can assist you in becoming familiar with a site before you actually visit on location. This documentation can also help you utilize predictive and virtual site survey software. In particular, there are documents related to the physical buildings and area landscaping that may be useful. Network diagrams—particularly those linked to building blueprints or drawings—can also be very helpful.

Physical Building/Area Characteristics

Among the documents that you should gather related to the physical building are

- Floor plans/blueprints/site maps
- Building inventories
- Building construction plans
- Office layout/people densities

While many of the benefits of these documents are quickly evident, some of the beneficial uses are not quite as obvious. In the following sections, I will describe how you can use these documents to prepare for and perform a site survey.

Floor Plans Whether they are called floor plans, blueprints, or site maps, drawings like the one in Figure 6.3 are priceless to the RF site surveyor. They reveal the location of internal walls, external walls, closets,

FIGURE 6.3 Sample hotel floor plan

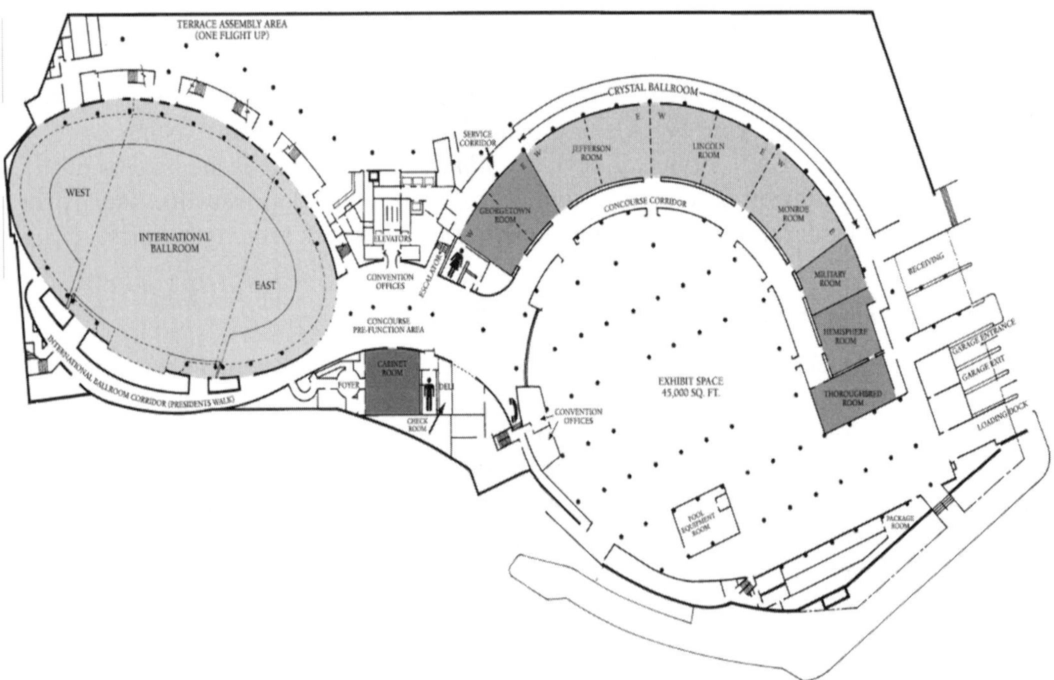

elevators, and more. If they are scaled and show that scale, you can even estimate how far you can go from an AP before the detectability of the signal is so degraded that you will lose acceptable performance.

These floor plans can be strategically used in your documentation of the site survey to show where you will place access points and the expected coverage patterns of those APs, given your survey findings. For example, Figure 6.4 shows the same sample hotel floor plan as Figure 6.3, faded and modified to show how the International Ballroom will be covered by the WLAN.

Building Inventories If you know the building materials used to construct the facility in which you are installing a WLAN, you will have an advantage in that you can estimate the impact these materials will have on RF propagation. An area that is commonly overlooked is the actual items that are in the building. Everything from a filing cabinet to storage shelves and furniture can have an impact on the RF coverage within the facility. For this reason, it is useful to inventory the contents of the area. While you

FIGURE 6.4 Sample hotel floor plan with APs

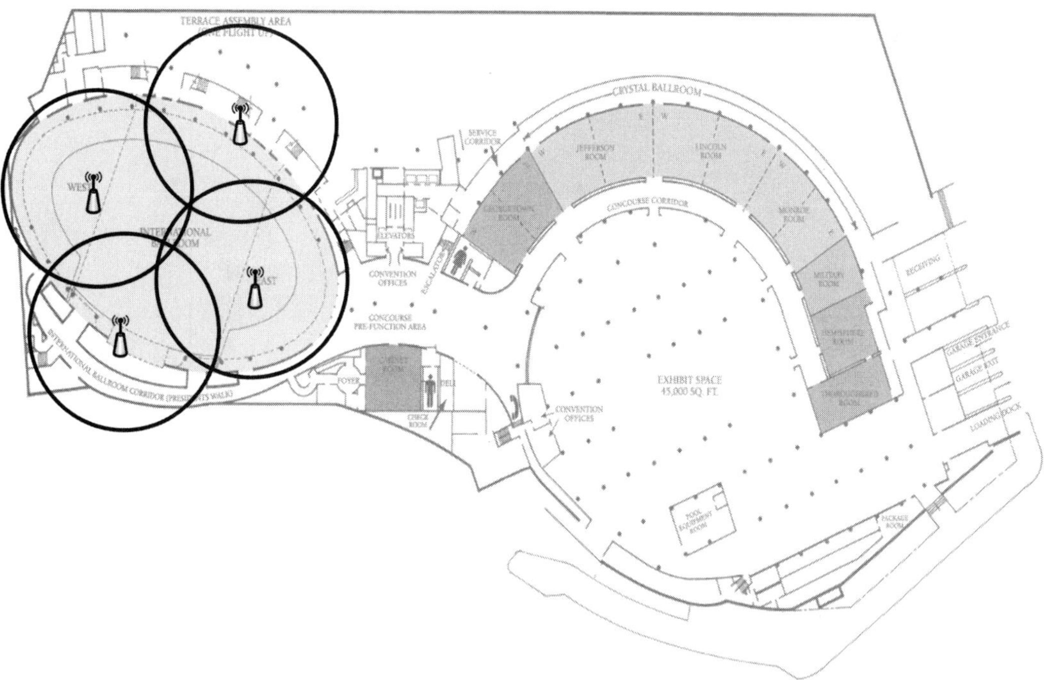

may not take the time to consider every piece of furniture, you should at least consider items like metal storage racks, metal filing cabinets, microwave ovens, and walls lined with metal filing cabinets. These items can impact the RF signal's ability to reach certain areas.

As an example, consider the floor plan segment represented in Figure 6.5. Here you see meeting rooms that are behind a row of wall-to-wall and ceiling-to-floor metal filing cabinets. Due to the placement of the access point and the barrier presented by the filing cabinets, there are sure to be dead spots (areas without RF coverage) within the meeting rooms and particularly within Meeting Room A. Of course, a simple relocation of the access point may resolve the issue, but depending on placement, it could introduce other problems like hidden node issues, which are discussed in Chapter 12.

Building Construction Plans Because buildings are constructed from different material types in different parts of the world, it is important to gain an understanding of the materials used in construction. For that matter, different building materials are used in buildings within the same city or even the same city block. If construction plans are available, they can reveal the materials used. Are the walls concrete or wood framed? Are they

FIGURE 6.5 Impact of inventoried items on RF coverage

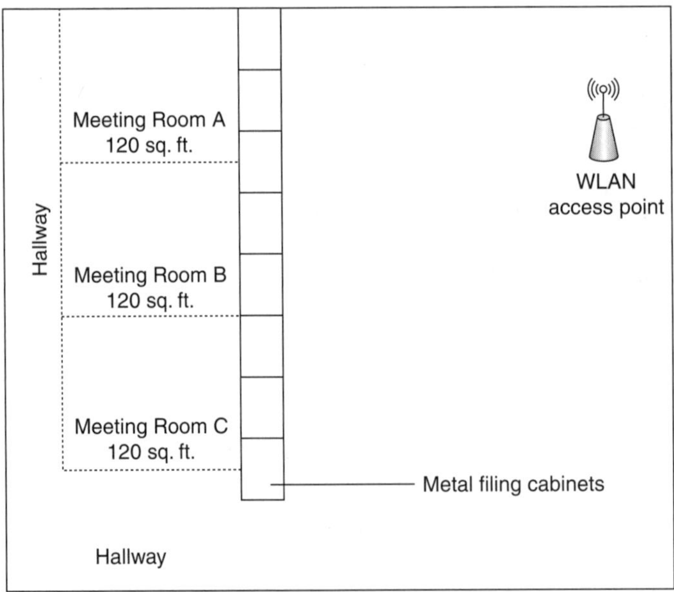

metal framed? Do they contain insulation, and if so, what type? Are there different materials, as is likely, in the internal walls from those used in the external walls?

Some multifloor buildings have concrete floors that are reinforced with rebar and other metal materials that, while they cause attenuation of the RF signal, will likely allow the signal to pass through floors. Other multifloor buildings have a steel or metal sheet or pan on which the concrete floor is poured. In these cases, the metal pan—after the concrete attenuation—will often cause enough reflection that the RF signal cannot pass through cleanly. It should be noted that different building code standards require different amounts of rebar or steel to be used in concrete reinforcement. Depending on the amount of rebar or steel used, the attenuation of the RF signal, as it passes through the concrete, can be so great that it is very difficult to detect the signal on the other side.

Internal walls can pose similar problems. They may be constructed with wood or steel frames that are covered with drywall. In these cases, the RF signal will likely pass through with no problem or with only minimal attenuation. It is not uncommon for first floor (or higher floor) walls to be poured concrete or prefabricated concrete. The same issues exist in that the amount of supporting rebar or steel used will impact the attenuation caused by the walls. In certain scenarios, reflection of the RF signal throughout the internal space may allow for coverage on both sides of a highly reinforced wall, but this must be tested for accuracy—usually by doing a physical site survey.

Additionally, some walls are intentionally shielded to prevent the exit of electromagnetic energy. An example of this would be in a hospital X-ray room. These walls are usually shielded to prevent the electromagnetic energy of the X-ray machine from escaping the room; however, the design also prevents RF energy from entering the room. It is also possible, though uncommon, that a building once used for testing wireless equipment may later be used for other purposes. The design of the testing rooms will probably be such that electromagnetic waves are trapped in the testing rooms. This could cause the same problems as in the hospital X-ray room when implementing a WLAN.

The point is this: you never know what you're going to encounter unless you are building a building from scratch. Even then, you may be surprised at the twists and turns that happen during building projects. My father worked in the construction industry, and I've heard the tales of woe from building projects where the ordered materials were no longer available and substitute materials had to be used. In the end, you need to know what materials *are* in the building and not what materials were planned for use.

Office Layouts A final topic of importance is the layout of offices and work areas within the facility. You can only determine proper placement of access points for effective coverage when you know where the users needed wireless access are to be located. It would be convenient if you could verify that the RF signal was detectable at an acceptable data rate in a given location and then move on; however, reality dictates that you divide this coverage among multiple users. These users will have minimum throughput demands that vary with the usage of VoIP solutions, applications in use, and more. This minimum throughput will dictate that you install more access points in a coverage area than are actually needed to provide "just coverage" in that area. The end result may be that you install two or three access points in small cells (lower–output power settings) on different channels (1, 6, and 11 is common) and then limit the number of users on each access point to ensure each user is able to have his or her minimum throughput provided.

In addition to throughput, you must consider latency issues. Certain applications, such as VoIP, require faster response times than others. If an access point is serving too many users, the DCF routines may cause the response time to grow to a point where the application either fails or provides less than acceptable quality. In these cases, QoS mechanisms may be used and multiple access points may also be implemented. As you can see, there is more to planning a WLAN than simply installing a sufficient number of access points to provide RF signal coverage throughout the service area.

Existing Network Characteristics

For some reason, there seems to be a tendency, in the discussions of WLAN site surveys, to assume that site surveys are only performed where there is no existing WLAN. The reality is that many site surveys are performed after a WLAN is implemented because the implemented WLAN is not performing well or because it needs to be upgraded to support modern uses of wireless such as VoWLAN, streaming video, and broadband Internet access. The point is that you must discover both existing networks that are managed by the requesting organization and WLANs that are not managed by the requesting organization. If you can detect a WLAN from the requesting organization's facilities, it must be considered when creating your WLAN implementation plan. I'll discuss this further in the later section of this chapter "Interference Sources."

Among the things you should document are the current wired LAN connections. Where are they? What speed do they provide (10 Mbps, 100 Mbps, gigabit)? Are they all in use? Is there power at the port locations if you need to connect more switches or routers? What applications are running on the LANs and WLANs, and will they continue to be used in the new WLAN?

If you can acquire network diagrams showing the switching and routing infrastructure along with the locations of authentication, authorization, and accounting servers as well as service servers (e-mail, web, file, print, etc.), this will be very helpful. From these diagrams, you can determine where traffic flows on the network and strategically place WLAN access points so that they can have unobstructed (or less-obstructed) access to mission-critical servers like Call Manager servers in Cisco VoWLAN implementations.

Gathering Permits and Zoning Requirements

Depending on the scenario, government permits may be required. For example, the FCC requires that you notify the FAA any time a tower will be more than 200 feet or 60.96 meters above ground level. Additionally, structures placed on top of existing buildings that cause the total height to exceed 200 feet will require the notification of the FAA. The proper forms and where they should be sent can be found in the Code of Federal Regulations, title 47, part 17. Simply search the web for "47 CFR Part 17" and you will find it.

The exception to this rule is when a tower or building plus tower that is more than 200 feet is shielded by other existing structures. For example, if you were to place a tower right next to the Empire State Building in New York City, it would not require the notification of the FAA, though I'm sure other city regulators would be involved. This exception is granted to reflect the logical reality that your new tower is not likely to cause a problem for aircraft, given that it is shielded from aircraft by the other buildings or structures of equal height or greater.

Additional algorithmic calculations are required to determine the maximum height of a tower or structure when it is closer to an actual airport. These special calculations need to be made only if the structure is being placed within 20,000 feet of an airport. The measurements are different at 20,000 feet from they are at 10,000 feet, and they are different at 10,000 feet from they are at 5000 feet. You can read the details in 47 CFR Part 17.7.

Special painting and lighting rules may also apply to towers that exceed 200 feet in height. These rules vary according to FAA advisory circulars, and at times you may be required to paint or light the tower in a different way from that stated in the circulars. This is usually due to unique issues in the construction area that demand unique lighting or painting in order to provide for safe flight passage by or near the tower.

In addition to tower issues, some cases may demand building permits when building outside enclosures to house wireless equipment. Since these enclosures are usually small, they may pose no problem; however, electrical and other inspections may be required.

Indoor- or Outdoor-Specific Information

Indoor-specific information was covered in the sections "Building Inventories," "Building Construction Plans," and "Office Layout" earlier. In this section, I'll focus on outdoor-specific information that you will need to gather for wireless bridge links or outdoor service areas.

Wireless Bridge Links

When creating outdoor wireless bridge links, you will be implementing one of two primary types: point-to-point and point-to-multipoint. In a point-to-point implementation, two wireless bridges are configured to communicate with each other and provide the link across which network traffic is routed, as seen in Figure 6.6.

When creating a point-to-multipoint bridge link, you will configure one bridge to act as the centralized bridge and the other bridges to act as remote bridges. The remote bridges will communicate with each other through the centralized bridge, and users from all LANs may be allowed to

FIGURE 6.6 Point-to-point bridge link

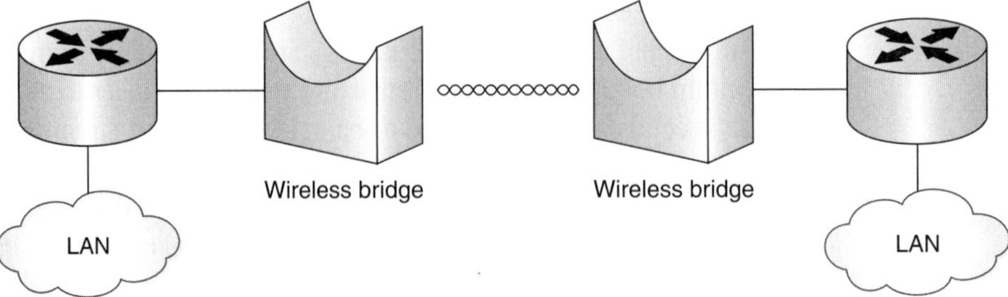

communicate with all other LANs through some link pathway. Figure 6.7 shows a point-to-multipoint bridge link.

When creating these bridge links, you must ensure that proper LOS exists and that the first Fresnel zone is acceptably clear. This may mean gathering terrain maps from online and local government sources. It may also require that you photograph the surrounding areas to document buildings, trees, and other structures that may factor into your link configuration. You may also benefit from local weather information that can be used to predict the amount of fog, smog, and other weather factors common to the area in which the link is expected to operate.

With this information gathered, you can begin to plan the links. You will need to determine the optimal height and directionality, in order to overcome obstacles that were discovered in the information gathering phase. You may need to obtain permits for towers of greater than 200 feet in the United States, as was noted earlier. Check with your local flight regulatory agency to determine the constraints imposed on towers and tall construction projects in your regulatory domain.

Outdoor WLANs Versus Mesh Networks

Not all outdoor WLAN implementations are intended to act as bridge links. In fact, many outdoor WLANs are being implemented today that are intended to provide direct client connectivity for network access. There are

FIGURE 6.7 Point-to-multipoint bridge link

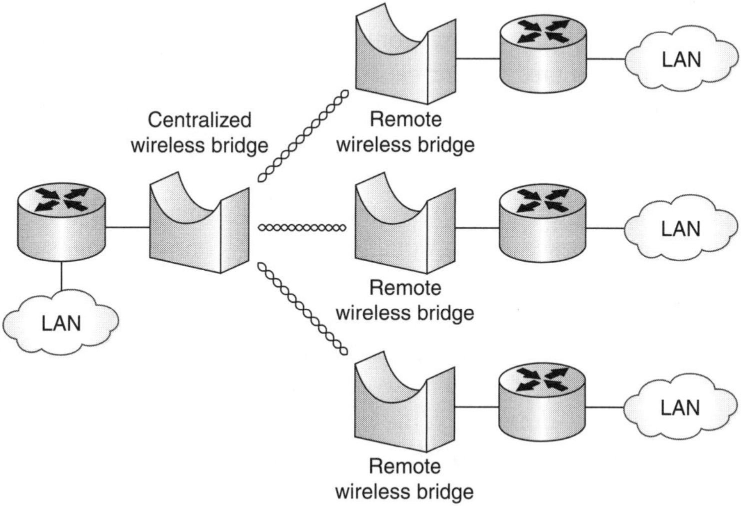

two primary implementation models that use IEEE 802.11 technologies: hotspot-type WLANs and mesh networks.

Hotspot WLANs Outdoor WLANs that implement standards-based IEEE 802.11 equipment are sometimes called hotspots as well. Most people think of a hotspot as a location that provides wireless network access to the Internet for the public. These hotspots may provide Internet access for free or for a charge. The term hotspot has more recently been used to mean a location where authorized users can gain access to a private network as well. In this case, the WLAN is simply taken outdoors and it provides client–access point connectivity.

In most outdoor WLAN implementations, a wire is run to the location where the access point is placed. The access point acts as a bridge between the wireless clients and the wired network, and the wired network may or may not provide a gateway to the Internet. Some outdoor WLANs may use a wireless bridge to connect back to the private network and then connect one or more access points to this wireless bridge via a small switch. Electrical power is all that is required at the location to implement such an outdoor WLAN. This type of implementation, which could still utilize all IEEE 802.11–compliant hardware, is represented in Figure 6.8.

Mesh Networks Mesh networks are newer wireless networks that are sometimes called self-healing and self-forming. Both infrastructure and client meshing may be supported. Infrastructure mesh networks usually consist of wireless links between remote sites with built-in redundancy provided by the mesh infrastructure. They may not allow clients to connect but may, in these cases, only provide a series of links across which data may be routed. Client mesh networks may consist of wireless client and infrastructure devices, and some devices may be both. These devices may be self-configuring in that they automatically determine whether they are acting as a client or an infrastructure device, and the network is self-healing in that new routes can be determined when a device that was involved in routing becomes unavailable. This self-configuration is called automatic topology learning, and the self-healing is called dynamic path selection in the IEEE 802.11s draft amendment.

Security may be a concern in mesh networks. Due to the somewhat open nature of mesh networks, they are not always configured with the best security. Additionally, the mesh network devices are not currently standards based, though the IEEE is working in an amendment to the IEEE 802.11 standard as task group *s*. Table 6.4 compares mesh networks to outdoor WLAN networks.

FIGURE 6.8 Outdoor WLAN with a wireless bridge

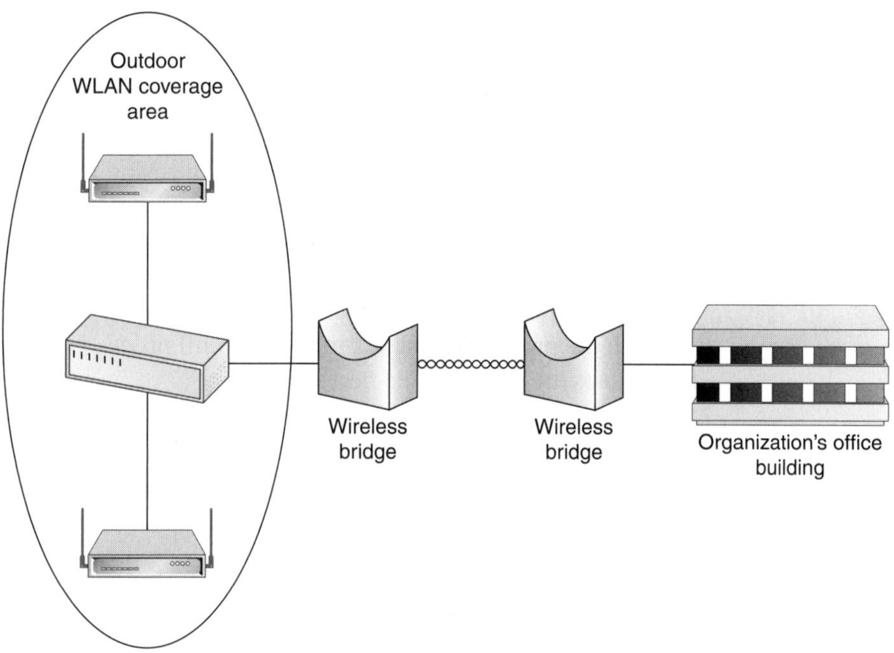

TABLE 6.4 Outdoor WLANs Versus Mesh Networks

Outdoor WLANs	Mesh Networks
Less tolerant to failures.	More tolerant to failures.
Usually completely standards based.	Standards based with implementations outside the standards until IEEE 802.11s (Clause 11A) is ratified.
May require wired line or dedicated bridge links.	Does not require wired line or dedicated bridge links throughout the mesh network, but will be connected to a wired network at one or more points.
No standard for self-configuration, though it is implemented by many vendors' WLAN controllers and management software.	No standard for self-configuration at this time, though vendors have implemented proprietary protocols for this. IEEE 802.11s (Clause 11A) does specify procedures for neighbor discovery and automatic configuration.

Performing Manual and Automated Site Surveys

The actual process of performing a site survey involves many steps. Assuming you've gathered the various documents referenced in the first portion of this chapter, your job will be much easier. In addition to these documents, you should also be sure to have a contract—in writing—if you are performing the site survey as an outside vendor. This document can be used to prove authorization to be on site, and in some of the strange places, you'll find yourself as you perform the site survey.

With the proper documents in hand, you'll proceed to the next steps. These steps are summarized here:

1. Gather the appropriate site survey kit.
2. Utilize site survey tools to analyze the RF behavior at the intended location.
3. Document your findings as you go.
4. Create the final site survey results documentation.

Steps 1 and 2 are the focus of the remaining content in this section. After this section is complete, we'll investigate virtual site surveys and then look at some more situation-specific factors that must be considered in a site survey. Finally, we'll end this chapter with a summary of the documentation that should come out of the site survey and the contents that should be in an implementation plan, along with a tour of common site survey tools. Ultimately, I will provide you with a list of inputs, the processes to be performed, and a list of outputs from the site survey. Armed with this information, you'll be able to perform a site survey effectively and avoid missing commonly missed factors.

Site Survey Hardware Kits

We will evaluate two sets of site survey kits: indoor and outdoor kits. The outdoor kit will generally include everything in the indoor kit plus a few extra items. This will become clear as you read through the following pages. You can also purchase preorganized site survey kits, and they will be covered here as well.

Indoor Site Survey Tools

When performing an indoor site survey, Fresnel zones and LOS are less important (unless, of course, you are creating a bridge link across a massive auditorium or warehouse). In these settings, you really need to be able to verify that an acceptable signal is available where that signal is needed for client connectivity. This means that you will use the floor plans retrieved earlier to determine where coverage must exist and at what data rates that coverage must exist. The tools you will need include the following:

- Spectrum analyzer
- Protocol analysis software
- Laptop with PC Card and utilities
- Access point
- Antennas
- Batteries
- Binoculars
- Communication devices
- Camera
- Measuring devices
- Mounting tools and devices
- Marking tape
- Rolling carts

Spectrum Analyzer There are many types of spectrum analyzers, but they fall into two main categories: software and hardware. Software spectrum analyzers scan the 2.4 GHz range (assuming that is the spectrum supported by the network interface card (NIC) in the computer running the spectrum analyzer software) and provide a graphical view of the activity in that spectrum. Hardware spectrum analyzers are devices, which may be based on PDAs, that can cost thousands of dollars, depending on their features. Spectrum analyzers, whether software or hardware, are used to view the activity in the spectrum in which you plan to deploy a WLAN. If you can ensure that the WLAN devices of any users in the area are turned off, you can discover noise that may impact the WLAN as well as other WLANs in the area. Figure 6.9 shows a hardware spectrum analyzer.

FIGURE 6.9 Rohde & Schwarz FSH6 (Model .26)

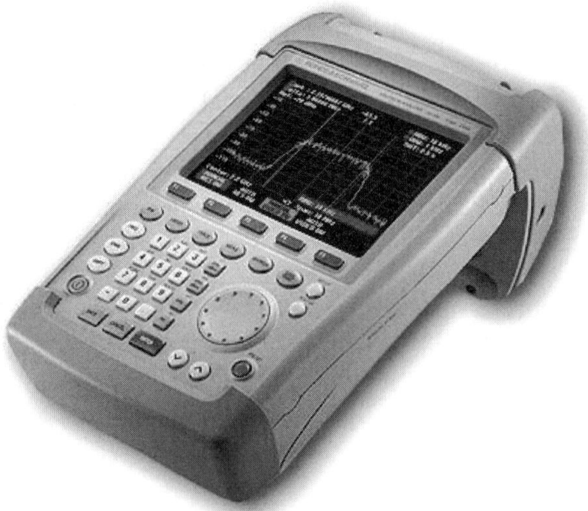

Protocol Analysis Software Whereas a *spectrum analyzer* shows the usage of the spectrum in your intended service area, a *protocol analyzer* can reveal for what that spectrum is being used. The protocol analyzer captures frames that are traversing the service area in which you are running the software. These frames can be analyzed to see if security is being used, the data rate of the communications, the type of data being transmitted, and more. Figure 6.10 shows the AiroPeek NX wireless protocol analyzer.

Laptop with PC Card and Utilities A lightweight laptop is invaluable when performing a site survey. You can work with site survey documentation in digital format and even begin the process of creating your site survey documentation on the fly while you perform the work. Many of these newer laptops have batteries that allow them to operate for 3–4 hours. However, the heavy use of the WLAN device during the site survey will reduce the battery life significantly. For this reason, you should consider purchasing one or two extra batteries if you are going into another organization to perform the site survey. If you are performing the site survey outside your own organization and your office is within the same facilities structure, you may be able to pause for battery recharges between uses. The reality is that, if you are an employee of the organization

FIGURE 6.10 Wireless protocol analyzer

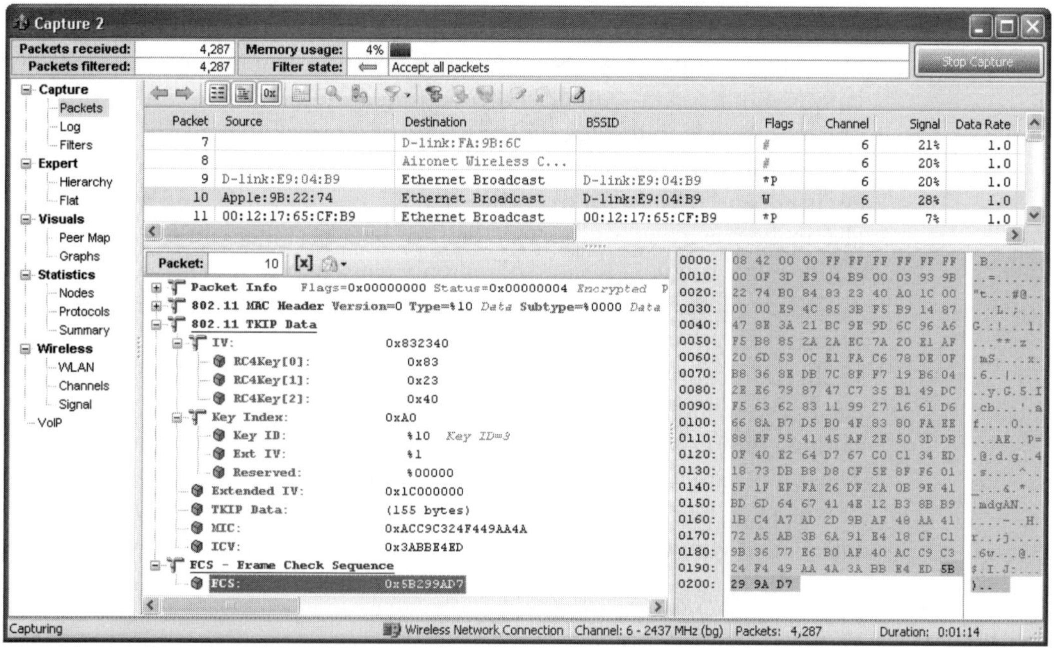

for which the site survey is being performed, you probably do not have the luxury of doing nothing but the site survey for an entire day or more.

The most important feature of the laptop that you will be using for the site survey is the ability to install various WLAN cards. You may want to test with HR/DSSS cards (formerly known as 802.11b) as well as ERP (802.11g) and OFDM (802.11a). By swapping cards in and out of the PC Card slot, you can test with all of these various PHYs using one laptop at one location. Some engineers, however, find that it is much easier to have a different laptop for each of the PHYs so that the testing at each location is faster. If you have three laptops, one with each of the common PHYs mentioned, placed on a rolling cart and open and powered on at all times, you can even monitor all three as you are moving throughout the service area.

Many WLAN NICs come with site survey utilities that report signals detected, signal strength, channel, noise level, signal-to-noise ratio (SNR), and the MAC address of the AP. These utilities can be utilized to perform many of the same analysis steps performed with spectrum and protocol analyzers.

Some WLAN NICs will even allow you to change the output power of the device. This can allow you to easily test for the near/far-type scenarios that are covered in more detail in Chapter 12. You could place one laptop with a high–output power setting closer to the AP and then place another laptop with a lower–output power setting at the same location or at a greater distance to test for the existence of a near/far scenario. While you would never intentionally implement such a scenario in a production environment, it is useful to experience the phenomenon, and it will also make you a better troubleshooter for later problems. In production settings, this problem is more commonly caused by using different WLAN NICs from different vendors that have different power output settings. Figure 6.11 shows such a variable–output power client utility.

In addition to the client utilities that come with WLAN NICs, you can use freeware tools like NetStumbler, Kismet, and KisMAC to discover the settings such as signal strength, noise floor, SNR, and MAC addresses. These tools are useful either when you do not have good NIC client utilities or when you want to have a similar interface regardless of the NIC that is installed in your laptop.

FIGURE 6.11 Wireless NIC client utility with variable output power

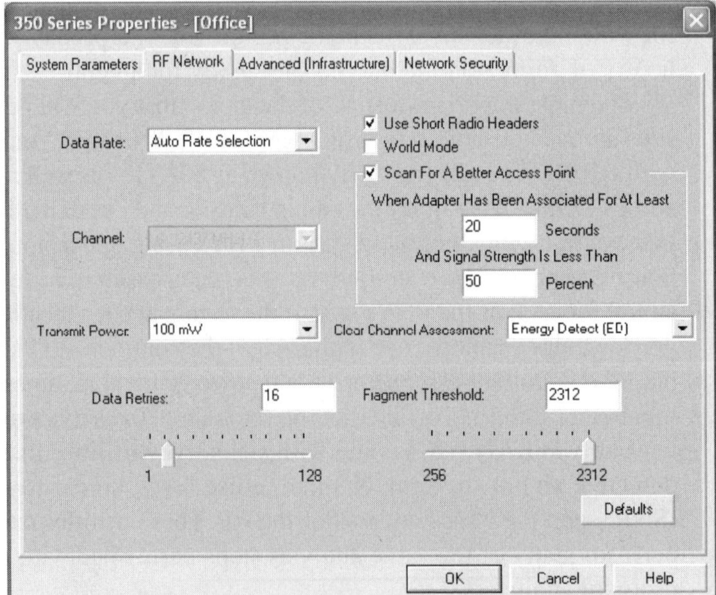

A more recent and more useful tool than even NetStumbler is the Wi-Fi Hopper application. Wi-Fi Hopper can display details such as SSID, network mode, encryption type, RSSI, frequency, and channel among other parameters for a complete picture of the environment. You can also filter out networks by using the network filters. With a combination of other features such as signal graphing, Wi-Fi Hopper can also be used for additional tasks like detecting channel congestion. Overall, this tool is far more powerful than NetStumbler; however, this tool is not freeware and the price must be considered. At less than $40 (U.S.) at the time of this writing, this application is a real bargain. Figure 6.12 shows Wi-Fi Hopper scanning for WLANs.

Figure 6.13 shows the details provided by Wi-Fi Hopper about a connection. As you can see, this utility provides many valuable statistics related to the connection. This data includes the RSSI values, SNR, and even the PHYs that are supported by name. However, the application appears not to differentiate between ERP-OFDM and the OFDM used in the IEEE 802.11a amendment in the output dialog. It certainly can tell the

FIGURE 6.12 Wi-Fi Hopper scanning for WLANs

WiFi Hopper: Trial version, 15 days remaining

File View Mode Network Device System GPS Help

14:48:28 Active networking device has been changed.

Stop Scanning | Broadcom 802.11b/g WLAN (Microsoft's Packet Scheduler) - Wireless LAN | Register Now!

Ssid	Type	MAC Address	Signal	Mode	Encryption	Status	Hits	Score	Frequency	PHY	Vendor
	802.11g	00:40:f4:e7:a5:94	-43 dBm	Infrastructure	WPA	Not Connected	327	0%	2.437 Ghz (6)	OFDM	CAMEO COMMU...
	802.11g	00:20:a6:50:92:f2	-64 dBm	Infrastructure	WEP	Not Connected	327	0%	2.412 Ghz (1)	OFDM	PROXIM, INC.
	802.11g	00:02:04:06:0b:0a	-52 dBm	Infrastructure	None	Not Detected	0	0%	2.462 Ghz (11)	OFDM	Bodmann Indust...
	802.11g	02:13:ce:51:93:45	-71 dBm	Ad Hoc	None	Not Detected	0	0%	2.462 Ghz (11)	OFDM	Fake (Ad Hoc)
	802.11g	00:0f:66:0d:24:f7	-76 dBm	Infrastructure	WEP	Not Detected	0	0%	2.462 Ghz (11)	OFDM	Cisco-Linksys
	802.11g	00:0c:41:f5:d0:21	-77 dBm	Infrastructure	WPA	Not Detected	0	0%	2.462 Ghz (11)	OFDM	The Linksys Grou...
	802.11g	00:11:24:a8:5d:9f	-78 dBm	Infrastructure	WEP	Not Detected	0	0%	2.462 Ghz (11)	OFDM	Apple Computer
	802.11g	00:12:17:1a:4a:f1	-78 dBm	Infrastructure	None	Not Detected	0	0%	2.462 Ghz (11)	OFDM	Cisco-Linksys, LLC
	802.11g	00:02:72:4d:54:7b	-79 dBm	Infrastructure	WPA	Not Detected	0	0%	2.462 Ghz (11)	OFDM	CC&C Technolog...
	802.11g	00:11:50:21:31:9c	-79 dBm	Infrastructure	WEP	Not Detected	0	0%	2.462 Ghz (11)	OFDM	Belkin Corporation
	802.11g	00:09:5b:87:58:00	-80 dBm	Infrastructure	None	Not Detected	0	0%	2.462 Ghz (11)	OFDM	Netgear, Inc.
	802.11g	00:0f:66:91:46:52	-81 dBm	Infrastructure	WEP	Not Detected	0	0%	2.462 Ghz (11)	OFDM	Cisco-Linksys
	802.11g	00:13:a3:5d:7d:ee	-82 dBm	Infrastructure	WEP	Not Detected	0	0%	2.462 Ghz (11)	OFDM	Siemens Com CP...
	802.11g	00:0f:3d:39:1d:04	-83 dBm	Infrastructure	WEP	Not Detected	0	0%	2.462 Ghz (11)	OFDM	D-Link Corporation
	802.11g	00:13:a3:1d:7a:2d	-83 dBm	Infrastructure	WEP	Not Detected	0	0%	2.462 Ghz (11)	OFDM	Siemens Com CP...
	802.11g	00:90:96:9f:1d:0f	-83 dBm	Infrastructure	WEP	Not Detected	0	0%	2.462 Ghz (11)	OFDM	ASKEY COMPUT...
	802.11g	00:11:50:99:23:98	-84 dBm	Infrastructure	WEP	Not Detected	0	0%	2.462 Ghz (11)	OFDM	Belkin Corporation
	802.11g	00:12:17:b5:2e:f4	-84 dBm	Infrastructure	None	Not Detected	0	0%	2.462 Ghz (11)	OFDM	Cisco-Linksys, LLC
	802.11g	00:13:10:b9:dd:86	-84 dBm	Infrastructure	WPA2	Not Detected	0	0%	2.462 Ghz (11)	OFDM	Cisco-Linksys, LLC
	802.11g	00:0f:3d:35:f6:29	-85 dBm	Infrastructure	WEP	Not Detected	0	0%	2.462 Ghz (11)	OFDM	D-Link Corporation
	802.11g	00:13:a3:04:68:ec	-85 dBm	Infrastructure	WEP	Not Detected	0	0%	2.462 Ghz (11)	OFDM	Siemens Com CP...
	802.11g	00:13:a3:1d:87:0b	-86 dBm	Infrastructure	WEP	Not Detected	0	0%	2.462 Ghz (11)	OFDM	Siemens Com CP...
	802.11g	00:13:a3:37:ea:cb	-86 dBm	Infrastructure	WEP	Not Detected	0	0%	2.462 Ghz (11)	OFDM	Siemens Com CP...
	802.11g	00:c0:49:fb:9b:fd	-86 dBm	Infrastructure	WPA2	Not Detected	0	0%	2.462 Ghz (11)	OFDM	U.S. ROBOTICS,...
	802.11g	00:09:5b:6c:ca:a0	-87 dBm	Infrastructure	WEP	Not Detected	0	0%	2.462 Ghz (11)	OFDM	Netgear, Inc.
	802.11g	00:11:50:2f:1f:e6	-87 dBm	Infrastructure	WEP	Not Detected	0	0%	2.462 Ghz (11)	OFDM	Belkin Corporation
	802.11g	00:14:6c:67:95:42	-87 dBm	Infrastructure	WEP	Not Detected	0	0%	2.462 Ghz (11)	OFDM	Netgear Inc.
	802.11g	00:13:a3:37:28:0d	-88 dBm	Infrastructure	WEP	Not Detected	0	0%	2.462 Ghz (11)	OFDM	Siemens Com CP...
	802.11g	00:90:96:cf:c7:d5	-88 dBm	Infrastructure	WEP	Not Detected	0	0%	2.462 Ghz (11)	OFDM	ASKEY COMPUT...
	802.11g	00:11:95:4d:43:3d	-89 dBm	Infrastructure	WEP	Not Detected	0	0%	2.462 Ghz (11)	OFDM	D-Link Corporation

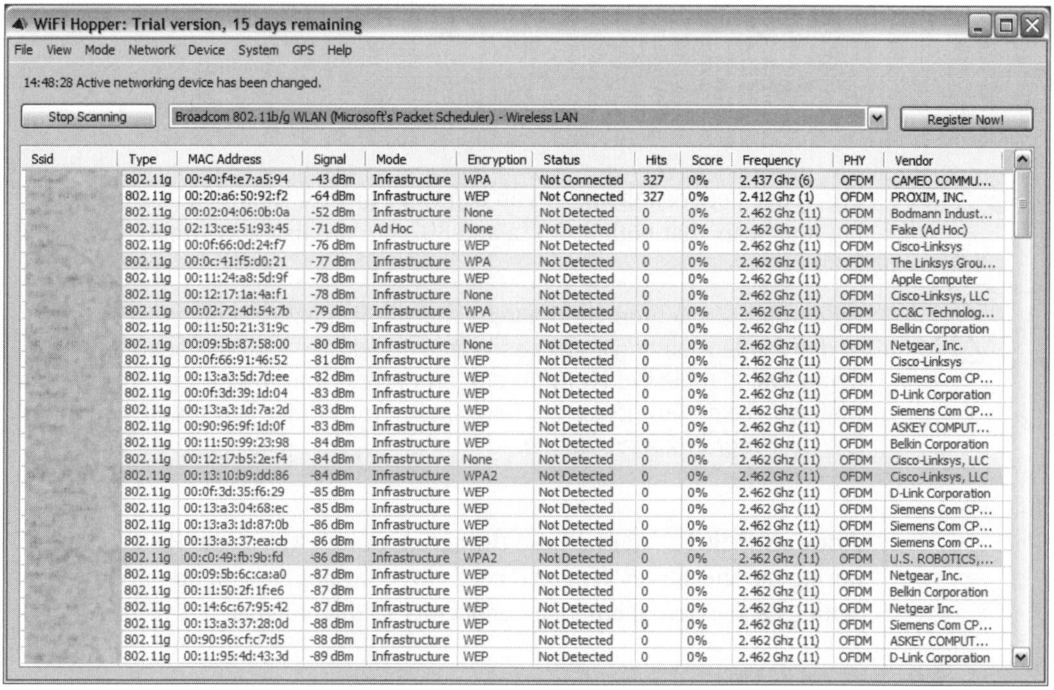

FIGURE 6.13 Wi-Fi Hopper showing connection details

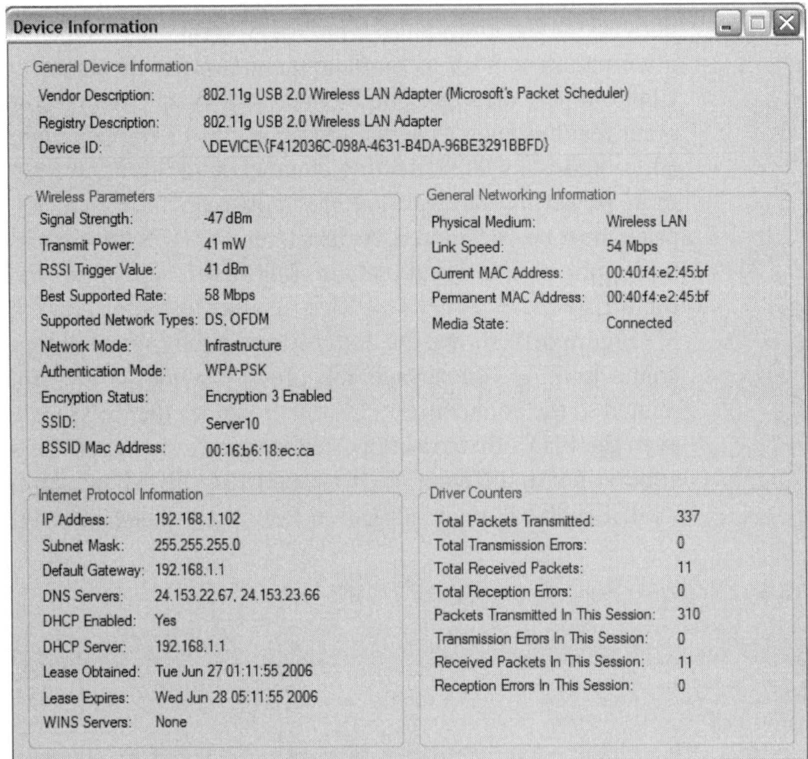

difference between them, as you can filter to view only 802.11a networks, but it appears that both 802.11a and 802.11g are listed as simply OFDM.

Be careful. Many areas of the world have now passed legislation or have had precedent-setting court cases that categorize wireless scanning as a crime. Using tools like NetStumbler and Wi-Fi Hopper to scan for networks that you are not authorized to use is not a recommended practice of the CWNP Program or this author.

Access Point You will use the access point (AP) as the RF generator during the site survey. This AP needs to be equipped with output power settings and external antenna connectors so that you can test different power levels with different antennas to achieve the desired coverage. The variable output power will also allow you to reduce and enlarge service area cell sizes without changing antennas. For example, you will achieve a very different coverage pattern with an output power of 50 mW and a 7 dBi omni antenna from that you will with an output power of 100 mW and a 7 dBi omni antenna. Additionally, you may be able to adjust the output power from your testing client laptop and then restart the AP without having to physically go to the location of the AP. This can save you time during the survey.

Antennas You will want to include at least two of the three primary antenna types, including

- Omnidirectional
- Semidirectional
- Highly directional

The two to include, at a minimum, are omni- and semidirectional antennas. Highly directional antennas are more likely to be needed for outdoor site surveys, but you may wish to include this antenna type in any site survey kit, just to be certain you are prepared. Including multiple omnidirectional antennas with different levels of gain may also be beneficial. For example, you could include a standard omni, which is usually around 2.2 dBi, along with 7 and 12 dbi gain antennas.

By providing different antenna types, you can test AP installation with patch or panel antennas against omni antennas. This can help you provide the right coverage in the right place instead of simply allowing RF energy to be leaked into unneeded areas and, therefore, be wasted.

Batteries Any device that uses electrical power must have a power source. Laptops and handheld protocol or spectrum analyzers may already have a battery; however, APs do not come with batteries, so you may need to provide power to them. You can use a charged uninterruptible power supply (UPS) unit to power the AP. A UPS that is able to power a standard desktop-class server or computer for 5–10 minutes can often power an AP for hours. Since UPS units are often very heavy, this is one of the components that you will likely place on your rolling cart as you move around within the facility.

As you are beginning to see, the equipment that you use in a site survey may appear ominous to onlookers. This is why you need that contract clearly stating your purpose for being there. You also need to ensure you have all the proper clearance, and to avoid time-wasting interruptions, you may even ask for a security escort if the organization has on-site security staff.

Binoculars It might seem odd to think that binoculars should be in an indoor site survey kit, but large auditoriums can be very difficult to see across. The binoculars can help you see if your assistant is placing the AP antennas as desired without having to make the journey across the open space yourself. I know my eyes are not as finely tuned to distant objects as they once were and binoculars help me quite a lot—even indoors.

Communication Devices If you are using an assistant, you may not always be in her visual LOS and you cannot signal her to indicate that she has placed an object where you want it and you cannot get any other visual feedback from her. In these scenarios, some other form of communication is necessary. You could use cell phones or walkie-talkies, but something will be needed.

Camera As you determine the proper locations for APs, Power over Ethernet injectors, power plugs, switches, and more, it is important to document these locations. With the help of a digital camera, you can remove all doubt from your documentation. If you will not be the person implementing the WLAN, digital photos of the recommended locations can be very helpful. You can actually open the photos in graphics editing applications, such as Paint Shop Pro or PhotoShop, and add comments and markups to the images. These images can then be inserted directly into your implementation plan documents so that the install techs can use them as a reference.

Measuring Devices A tape measure is a very important part of your site survey kit, but you should also include a measuring wheel. The tape measure can be used to determine smaller distances such as ensuring enough clearance in a storage closet for a switch or other devices. The measuring wheel allows for fast measurements of distances across large room floors or outdoor spaces. Laser-based measuring devices can also be useful for estimating large distances. These devices, such as the one in Figure 6.14, can often measure tilt as well as distance.

FIGURE 6.14 Laser-based measuring device (Leica – Disto A8)

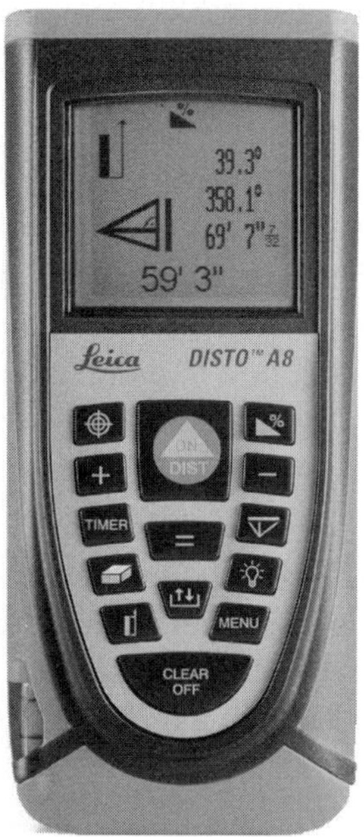

Mounting Tools and Devices Every site survey kit should include a long-lasting rechargeable drill with screwdriver bit sets as well as manual screwdrivers. You will also want a rubber mallet hammer and possibly a standard hammer as well as pliers and vice grips. These tools will help you access areas you could not otherwise access (though I don't encourage crushing your way through with a hammer—the hammer can be very useful for loosening old entry panels that haven't been removed in a while).

Additionally, you should include fastening ties, ropes, and duct tapes in your kit. These items can be used to temporarily position APs and other devices at nearly any location.

Marking Tape Multicolor marking tape is also very useful. These tapes (electrical or bag tape will usually do) can be used for color-coded marking. For example, red tape could indicate the location of one type of AP, while green tape could indicate that another type should be placed there. Alternatively, you could say that red tape indicates that the output power of the AP should be at 100 mW and green tape could indicate that it should be at 50 mW. You get the picture. The point is that color-coded tape can help you mark the areas and ease the actual implementation of the WLAN.

Rolling Carts With all this equipment, and the fact that you have to move around within the facility while performing the site survey, it becomes clear that you are going to need some method for easily moving the items. A standard rolling cart or multimedia cart will usually serve the need. One such cart is shown in Figure 6.15. The cart in Figure 6.15 is a good example of the way site survey equipment can actually change the environment. While a metal cart like this should not have a major impact, bear in mind that due to the high reflectivity of the metal and the mesh-type structure of the base, you should be careful to keep a cart like this out of the general testing area. It is probably best to use a cart made of plastic materials instead.

Outdoor Site Survey Tools

Many of the following tools are unique to outdoor site surveys; however, it is important to consider that some of the tools are only more commonly used in site surveys and they may have uses in indoor site surveys as well. The variable-loss attenuator is a good example of this. Outdoor site survey kits may include the following:

- Topography maps
- Link analysis software and calculators
- Agricultural data
- Variable-loss attenuator
- Inclinometer

FIGURE 6.15 Lightweight rolling cart

- GPS
- More antennas

Topography Maps Since you are working outdoors and likely creating longer-distance links, topography maps with link endpoints marked can be helpful. You should be able to see the elevation levels at each endpoint and determine if there are increases in elevation between them. This information can be used to ensure that your antennas are mounted high enough to overcome any terrain variance issues. These topography maps may or may not show information about the vegetation (trees, shrubs, etc.) between the two endpoints, so you may have to use binoculars or telescopes to view the LOS path and look for such infringements. Sometimes, it is enough to look at the topography of the area and know the greatest height of the tallest tree type that grows in a given region. With this information, you can estimate the needed height for antenna mounting and, therefore, the needed height for towers or building mount points.

Link Analysis Software and Calculators Link analysis software and calculators are used to predict the needed output power, elevation, and other values for bridge links. These applications are known as predictive modeling software because they are not reporting *actual* RF signal information but are predicting how the RF signal will behave, given your input. Figure 6.16 shows an Excel spreadsheet calculator from Cisco for calculating bridge link information related to their WLAN bridging products. You can see a similar tool at the following web site: http://support.tranzeo.com/calcs/wireless.html.

Agricultural Data Regional data such as tree growth information can also aid you in your future projections. Unless a tree has reached a certain level of maturity, it will continue to grow upward as well as outward. For this reason, you will need to know if a park located between your bridge endpoints has been newly planted or if the trees have been there for many decades. If it was newly planted, the trees are likely to encroach on the first Fresnel zone and this is sure to cause link problems. Check with the local Department of Agriculture (or the regional agency that deals with such issues) branch to learn more about tree growth and tree types in your areas.

Variable-Loss Attenuator A variable-loss attenuator gives you the ability to impose signal loss on the signal before it is transmitted by the antenna. Such devices can be used to simulate using different cable lengths

FIGURE 6.16 Cisco predictive link calculation spreadsheet

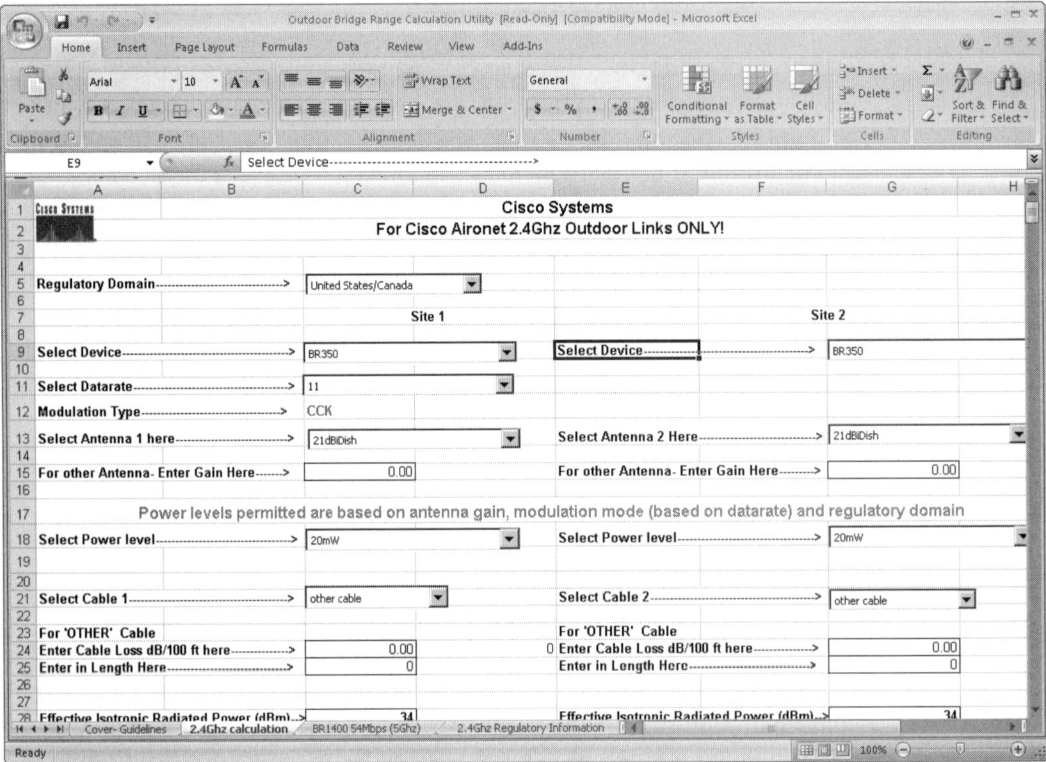

or types when testing outdoor bridge links. They can also be useful for indoor site surveys. For example, you may have the AP connected directly to the antenna during the indoor site survey; however, you may plan to mount the antenna in one place and the AP in another when you actually set up the WLAN. In this scenario, you can install a variable-loss attenuator between the antenna and the AP in order to simulate more closely the behavior you should expect after actual implementation. Figure 6.17 shows an example of a variable-loss attenuator in a schematic view. When purchasing these devices, be sure to select one supporting the frequency with which you are working.

GPS Global Positioning System (GPS) units can be very handy when performing either outdoor site surveys for bridge links or site surveys for outdoor WLANs. The GPS unit can be used to document fairly exact

FIGURE 6.17 Variable-loss attenuator

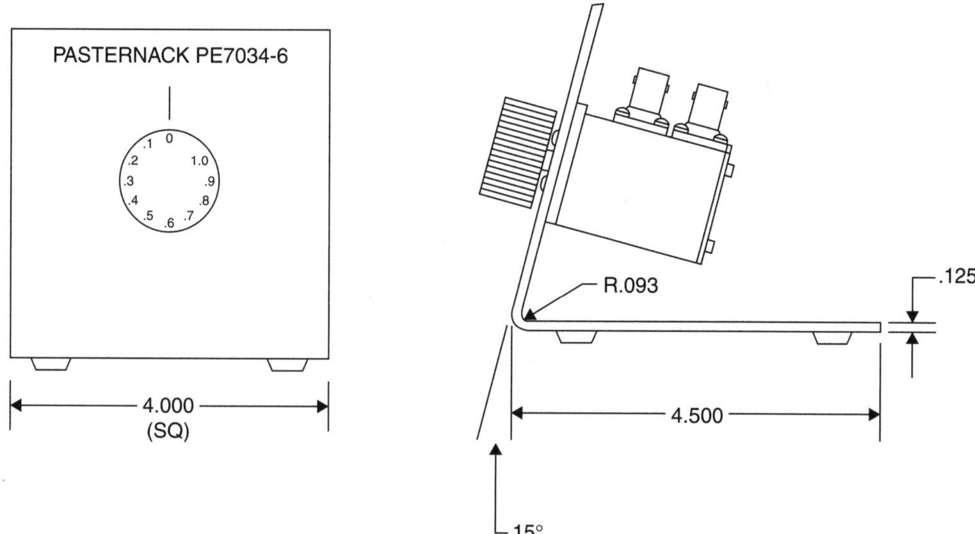

locations for device placement or signal strength measurements. Some PDAs can support both a GPS device and protocol or spectrum analysis. However, most such devices would need to be swapped in and out of the PDA, and because of this, it may be easier to use separate devices. The exception to this is with a laptop. Many laptops can support a GPS unit and a WLAN NIC at the same time.

More Antennas Since you are now performing an outdoor site survey, more antenna types should be included in your site survey kit. Specifically, highly directional antennas are now likely to be needed. While semidirectional antennas are sometimes used to create links of a few meters to a few kilometers, highly directional antennas will be needed for links of many miles.

Preorganized Site Survey Kits

This third type of site survey kit is aimed at making your life as simple as possible. These kits often come with everything you need, and they are usually shipped to you in a rolling case ready to go on-site. An example of such a kit is available from TerraWave at www.TerraWave.com. TerraWave develops kits specifically for Cisco products, and they also include more generic kits for general Wi-Fi site surveys. Their Essentials Kit includes the following:

- 1 – 802.11A/G NON-MODULAR IOS AP; RP-TNC
- 1 – 802.11A/B/G CARDBUS ADAPTER
- 1 – INDOOR 2 DBI OMNI DIVERSITY ANTENNA
- 1 – OUTDOOR 5 DBI OMNI ANTENNA
- 2 – PATCH 6.5 DBI DIVERSITY ANTENNA
- 2 – PATCH 8.5 DBI ANTENNA
- 1 – SITE SURVEY BATTERY PACK/RJ-45 POE PORT
- 1 – ATTENUATOR—SINGLE ROTARY STEP
- 1 – LMR195 CABLE WITH RPTNCJ-RPTNCP
- 1 – TWS-195 50 OHM BRAIDED CABLE
- 1 – 195 SERIES TNC STYLE CONNECTOR
- 1 – PIGTAIL CONNECTOR (ATTENUATOR)
- 1 – CUSTOM FOAM INSERT AND CASE
- 3 – HI-LITER PENS
- 2 – FLAGGING TAPE ROLLS
- 1 – DUCT TAPE ROLL
- 1 – VELCRO STRIP (QTY 1 = 1 FOOT)
- 2 – ZIP TIES – BUNDLE – SMALL (QTY 100)
- 1 – ZIP TIES – BUNDLE – MEDIUM (QTY 100)
- 2 – BUNGEE CORD
- 1 – SITE SURVEY MEASURING WHEEL – US OR METRIC
- 2 – 2 DBI/3 DBI DUAL BAND RUBBER DUCK ANTENNAS
- 1 – 5 GHZ 4.5 DBI DIVERSITY OMNI W/RPTNC
- 1 – 5 GHZ 6 DBI OMNI ANTENNA W/RPTNC
- 1 – AIRMAGNET SURVEY PRO
- 1 – 2.4 GHZ 13.5 DBI YAGI ANTENNA

At the time of this writing, this kit retails for a little over $5000. However, as you can see, nearly everything is included in the kit, so your work of tool collection is mostly done. Figure 6.18 shows this Essentials Kit.

FIGURE 6.18 TerraWave site survey kit

Active Site Survey Tools and/or Applications

Client utilities fall into two categories: active and passive. Active client utilities, covered in this section, actually transmit information to the AP during the site survey tests. Because active utilities actually transmit packets between the client and the AP, they are considered more representative of actual applications that might be used on the WLAN. The Cisco Aironet Client Utility (ACU), though usable only with HR/DSSS Cisco cards, is very useful in this way. The ACU shows the signal strength in dBm as well as the noise level and the SNR. Having these values in dBm instead of just a graphical meter or percentage value allows you to more accurately determine the performance of the WLAN. Figure 6.19 shows the ACU revealing signal strength, noise level, SNR, and AP information.

When a utility, such as the Cisco ACU, supports active mode site surveying, the utility generally allows you to configure the number of packets to transmit, the size of the packet, and other settings such as those shown in Figure 6.20.

Once configured, the utility will show you screens similar to those in Figure 6.21, showing that the data is being transmitted and the statistics are

FIGURE 6.19 ACU passive monitoring screen

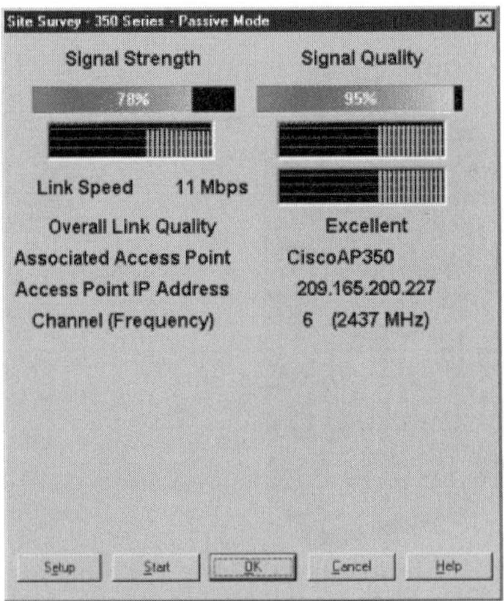

FIGURE 6.20 Configuring active site surveying

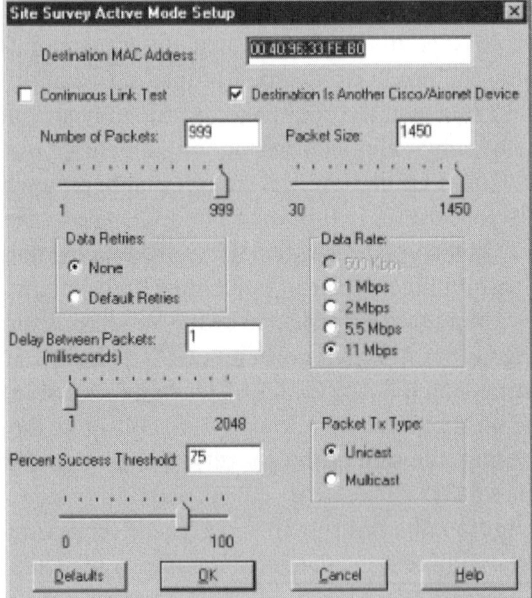

FIGURE 6.21 Active site survey script in progress

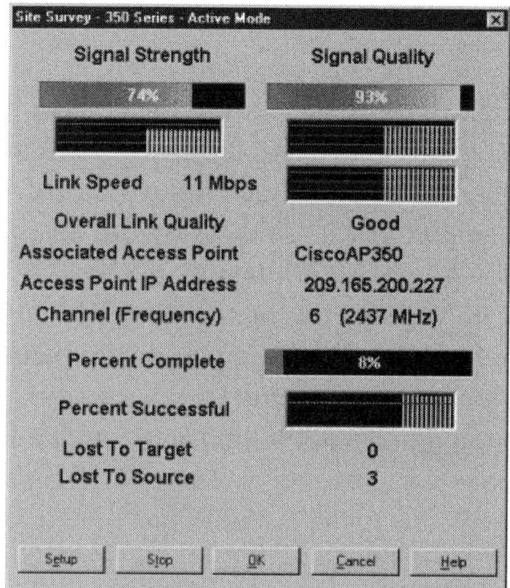

being gathered. As you can see in Figure 6.21, packet loss as well as the overall link quality is being counted. You can rerun your site survey script, configured in Figure 6.20, again and again at different locations while performing the site survey.

Passive Site Survey Tools and/or Applications

Most client utilities provide only passive site survey functionality. In these cases, the tool is simply monitoring the signal strength, noise level, and SNR (usually these three are the minimum supported monitoring values) and reporting this information to you. The utilities may automatically refresh, or you may have to refresh them manually. The Windows wireless client software can be used to monitor similar settings, but most WLAN engineers prefer to use manufacturer client tools or third-party monitoring tools such as those provided by Cognio or AirMagnet.

In addition to standard NIC vendor client utilities, many laptop vendors are now including their own tools or rebranded tools for monitoring and configuring WLAN connections. These tools may be able to be used for WLAN site surveys as well, but they are usually less powerful than the vendor tools.

Manufacturer's Client Utilities

The client utilities, as mentioned before, from many vendors provide useful tools for site surveys. To acquire the older tools, such as the Cisco ACU mentioned earlier, you may have to look for used equipment at sites like eBay, but having these tools is well worth the effort. Look for the Cisco Aironet 350 802.11b PC Card NIC and the Orinoco line of wireless NICs to find some useful manufacturer client tools. As I write this, a Cisco Aironet 350 11 Mbps card is selling on eBay for less than $20 (U.S.). It is important to note that these cards are very useful for site surveys, but you are unlikely to use these cards in deployment. This is in part due to their availability on the used market only and in part due to the fact that most laptops (the most common wireless client on today's networks) come with a WLAN NIC built in. Most IT shops choose to use this built-in WLAN card rather than implementing a redundant card in the laptop. This, of course, assumes the built-in card can support the security requirements of the organization.

Advanced Site Survey Tools

The tools mentioned so far are useful for small-scaled site surveys such as those done for homes, small offices, and possibly even medium-sized facilities. If you will be placing between 1 and 20 APs, you will likely use these simpler tools. When you are placing dozens or hundreds of APs, these simple tools just won't give you the acceptable time cost balance you need. Larger WLAN site surveys demand more advanced tools such as Cisco's WCS Planning Tool, AirMagnet Surveyor, Aruba RF Plan, and RingMaster from Trapeze Networks.

The RingMaster planning tool, from Trapeze Networks, can be used to perform virtual site surveys, and these types of surveys are discussed more in the later section of this chapter "Performing Virtual Site Surveys." However, the RingMaster application set can also be used to create a WLAN network design that can then be implemented manually, so this tool can be used in a manual site survey process as well.

The Aruba RF Plan tool is an offline site planning tool that allows you to add campuses, buildings, and floors and then map out the WLAN within these facilities. You can import floor plans into Aruba RF and then place APs where desired within these plans. You can adjust the output power for the APs and impact the coverage provided. Figure 6.22 shows the Aruba RF Plan tool with APs initialized.

While AirMagnet has produced tools similar to the protocol analyzers mentioned earlier, they have also developed an excellent toolset for site

FIGURE 6.22 Aruba RF Plan tool

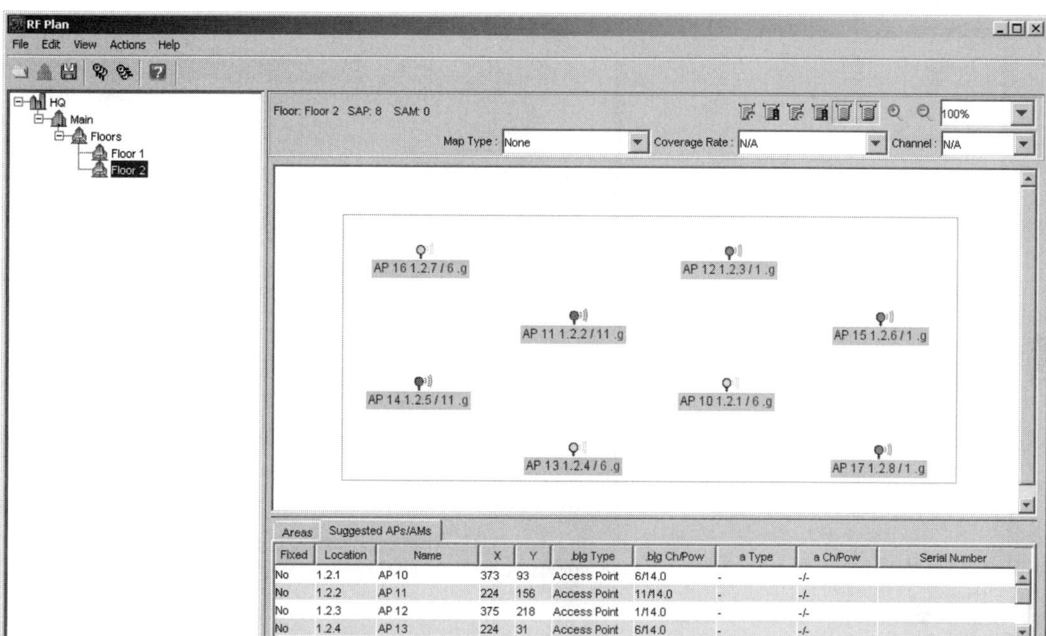

surveying known as the AirMagnet Surveyor. AirMagnet Surveyor allows you to import graphics of floor plans and then perform site surveys on both active and passive modes. Figure 6.23 shows the opening screen of the Airmagnet Surveyor tool.

Once you've set up your floor plans, you are ready to begin a walkabout within the facility. AirMagnet Surveyor will track your movements and provide a survey path showing the areas where you've walked and allow you to review signal information at these locations. The tool can display the information gathered during the survey in different manners, including gradient-based displays of signal quality. At the time of this writing, the software was not available for Windows Vista.

Automated Site Surveys

Automated site surveys fall into two basic categories: assisted and completely automatic. The assisted survey is a mix between the manual and automated surveys, giving you the benefits of both. The manual survey

FIGURE 6.23 AirMagnet Surveyor

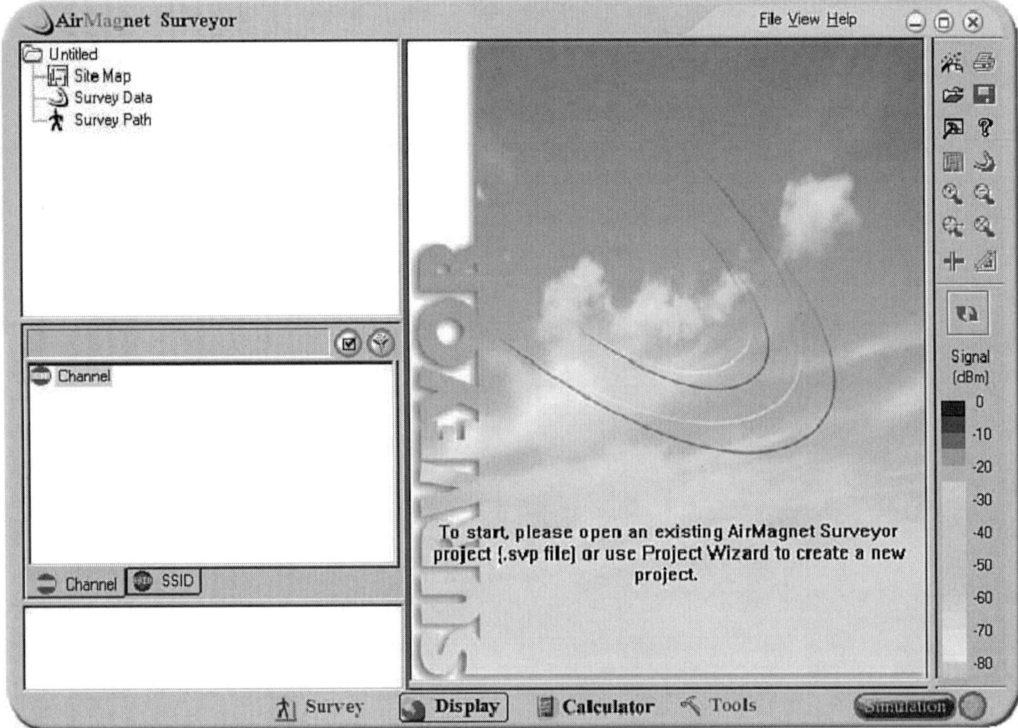

provides accurate predictions of the number of APs needed and their locations, while the automated survey provides faster results. By mixing them together, you get a little less overengineering—as is seen quite frequently in automated surveys—and yet it is faster than a completely manual survey. This section will evaluate common features of automated site survey systems and the pros and cons of using such a system.

Common Features

Automated site surveys usually take advantage of features sometimes known as self-configuration. This is a capability of the wireless switch or controller to configure thin or fat APs remotely. These APs can have their output power levels adjusted as well as their communication channels, allowing for automatic configuration of the RF environment. This capability is also known as Radio Frequency Spectrum Management (RFSM). The Cisco Assisted Site Survey, a component of Cisco's Wireless

LAN Solution Engine (WLSE), provides such spectrum management, though the WLSE is for use with older (or newer) autonomous APs. The newer Cisco WLAN controllers employ Auto RF and support lightweight APs. The Aruba Networks Mobility Management System is another example of a system that provides spectrum management.

These systems usually work in terms of an engineer installing APs in locations where coverage is needed and installing enough APs in these areas to provide the needed throughput for the number of localized users. The system is then informed that all is ready for automatic configuration, and the automatic site survey begins. The result is a configured and operational WLAN, but experience has shown that—if this simplistic approach is taken—the results are not always optimal. For this reason, many RFSM systems now support the addition step of a client walkthrough within the coverage areas. As the client passes through the facility, it transmits information about RSSI, SNR, and more back to the centralized management system. The system takes this information into account when automatically configuring the WLAN, and the results are usually more accurate. This latter method is what I'm referring to as an assisted site survey. The centralized system does the configuration, but it depends on the input from the client, which must be moved throughout the coverage area by a person.

Pros and Cons

Of course, the pros of an automated site survey include the automatic configuration of dozens or even hundreds of APs. Additionally, the software can usually reconfigure the APs when something changes within the environment either at regular intervals or when a failure is detected in one or more devices. The cons include overengineering (installing more APs than may be strictly needed) and the removal of static configurations. When devices are configured on a more static basis, traditionally they are thought to be easier to manage; however, this thinking is dependent on a reality where humans are managing the devices on an ongoing basis. In a self-configured system, this is not the case, so it is arguable whether the lack of static configurations is an issue or not.

Performing Virtual Site Surveys

In the preceding section, I introduced you to the concept of automated site surveys. In many cases, automated site surveys cross over into the category of virtual site surveys because the software/hardware includes predictive modeling capabilities. Technically, to qualify as a virtual site survey tool, the software or hardware would have to be able to simulate RF behavior on the basis of materials and other input criteria provided to the application. These virtual site survey tools fall into two general categories: independent tools and integrated tools.

Independent Tools

Independent tools are sold separately from vendor hardware and can work with simulations of different vendors' hardware. These tools are sometimes called predictive analysis tools, simulation applications, or RF planning tools. The following list, while not exhaustive, does cover the most common such tools:

- AirDefense Architect
- AirTight SpectraGuard Planner
- AirWave Wireless Site Plan
- Aruba RF Plan
- Bluesocket LANPlanner
- Cisco Airespace WLAN Controllers and Wireless Control System (WCS)
- Colubris RF Planner
- Trapeze RingMaster

Most of these tools share the ability to import a floor plan and then have APs positioned in terms of coverage and/or capacity automatically. Some of them also support the incorporation of extra data such as building materials, area inventories, and human densities. Some, such as LANPlanner, come with detailed specification for their own hardware and leave it up to you to add the details for other vendor's hardware. Figure 6.24 shows an example application performing a predictive survey.

Some of these tools, such as AirWave Wireless Site Plan, pictured in Figure 6.24, allow for estimation-based virtual site surveys. In other words, you can specify the type of environment (dense office, normal, open space, etc.) and the application will not require that you provide specific information about the materials within the environment. While this will not result in as accurate a site survey, it allows you to complete the survey much more quickly. Like many areas of project management, WLAN implementation projects can use rough order of magnitude (ROM) estimates early on and get more detailed as the project moves forward.

FIGURE 6.24 AirWave Wireless Site Plan

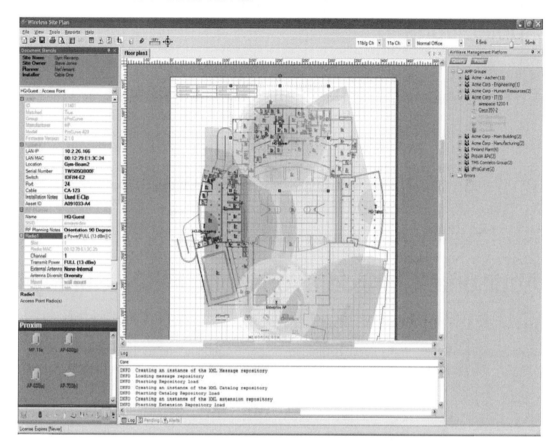

One additional feature of note provided by many of these independent applications is both a 2-D and 3-D view of your WLAN. This allows you to see the top-down and side views of your network. In other words, you can see how the RF signal propagates out from the APs in a horizontal fashion, and you can also see how the RF signal propagates upward and downward to above and below the APs. This provides you with a better understanding of multifloor coverage scenarios.

Integrated Tools

Integrated predictive tools include the features of wireless switches and controllers that are used for autoconfiguration. These tools were covered in the earlier section "Automated Site Surveys" and will not be covered in more detail here.

Site Survey Verification Tools and/or Applications

Whether you perform a site survey manually, with assistance, or virtually, you will need to use tools after the installation to verify that the site survey predictions were accurate and that your WLAN is performing as needed and expected. These tools are usually the same tools used during the site survey. The centralized autoconfiguration software can be used to inspect the actual settings in place on your network and compare these with the expected setting from the manual or predictive site surveys. You can use PC Card client utility software, NetStumbler, Wi-Fi Hopper, and WLAN protocol analyzers to evaluate the performance of your network. Since these tools and their use are covered in detail in Chapters 11 and 12, I will not cover them in any greater detail here.

Additional Considerations for RF Site Surveys

Up to this point, I've covered the presurvey actions needed, such as interviewing users and gathering documents. I've also covered the different types of site surveys that can be performed and the tools used in these site surveys. In this section, I will explain some additional considerations that have been given only a passing mention or have not been mentioned at all up to this point. These important areas of consideration include

- Interference sources
- Infrastructure connectivity and power requirements
- RF coverage requirements
- Data capacity requirements
- Voice over WLAN considerations
- Client connectivity requirements
- Reporting procedures

Interference Sources

An essential part of any site survey and one that cannot be performed remotely with a virtual site survey application (meaning a theoretical application that does not use sensors in the physical environment) is the inspection of current activity in the actual environment where the WLAN will be deployed. This is one of the strongest arguments against completely virtual site surveys. If the WLAN will be implemented in a multitenant facility, there is a good chance that another WLAN already exists and, in one way or another, much of the RF spectrum may already be consumed. As a WLAN site surveyor, you may be called upon to negotiate for frequency bandwidth for your WLAN. This can include requesting that the other networks lower their output power or even change their channel assignments. Remember, the frequencies used by IEEE 802.11 are unlicensed frequencies and you will often have to negotiate for a frequency without any assistance from a governing organization.

Existing WLANs are not the only sources of interference. Additional sources include

- Microwave ovens
- Elevators and other high-powered motors
- Bluetooth and other RF devices in the 2.4 and 5 GHz spectrums

Detecting this interference is the purpose of using a spectrum analyzer. Once you've determined that portions of the unlicensed spectrum are being utilized, you can use a protocol analyzer to discover network names and other network information. You can also use the spectrum analyzer as you move slowly. As you continue slowly moving, you will pay close attention to the readings and ensure that you continue moving in a direction that causes the signal strength to increase. This will lead you closer and closer to the source of the RF transmission, and you can then deal with it appropriately.

You will not likely negotiate with surrounding WLANs during the site survey, but you will document the detection of these WLANs. In order to keep the process moving, you will most likely choose to continue performing the site survey's various steps. However, if you are not certain that you will be able to negotiate for the needed bandwidth, you should consider approaching a higher authority (such as the organization's CEO or President) so that they can use their positional power to get the needed bandwidth.

Infrastructure Connectivity and Power Requirements

Since WLANs are most frequently deployed in an access role, it is essential that the APs are able to connect to the wired infrastructure. One exception to this would be the implementation of a mesh networking device that uses HR/DSSS to provide client access and OFDM to provide backhaul access (this is intended only to be an example of an exception and should not be taken to indicate that it is the only exception). Needing a connection to the wired infrastructure means, for the vast majority of cases, needing an Ethernet switch port for connectivity. The port may be very near to the AP, or it may be some distance away. If it is near the AP (within 100 meters), a simple cable run will usually suffice. If it is farther from the AP (more than 100 meters), the installation of one or more repeaters may be necessary. These needs should be documented to ensure that all needed hardware items (repeaters, switches, cables, and connectors) are available during implementation.

In addition to Ethernet connectivity, you will need to provide power to the APs. Look for nearby power outlets; if there aren't any, you may choose to implement Power over Ethernet (PoE) devices. This may require the purchase of special switches or individual PoE injectors. These devices are covered in Chapter 7.

RF Coverage and Data Capacity Requirements

Before you even begin the site survey work, you should have determined the coverage requirements for the WLAN. What areas need coverage? Within those areas, what capacity (number of users × demanded throughput) is required? You may find that you have to use smaller coverage areas (cell sized) per AP in order to provide the appropriate capacity. Remember, *coverage* and *capacity* are two different things. If you confuse the two, you may not have enough throughput for the applications being used on the WLAN.

To calculate capacity, calculate the number of users in an area. Now, calculate the throughput needed (in Mbps) by each user. For example, assume there are 25 users in an area that could be covered by 1 AP. Now, assume that each user needs approximately 2 Mbps of throughput. One ERP (802.11g) AP could provide a data rate of 54 Mbps, but the throughput would be roughly half that. Since this is the case, you will need to implement 3 ERP APs in the coverage area, which will provide approximately 80 Mbps of throughput. With 25 users at 2 Mbps each, this will provide you with some space for growth or—more likely—unexpected overhead.

Voice Considerations

While the intricate details of Voice over IP (VoIP) and its use in WLANs is beyond the scope of this book, it is important that you understand the impact a VoIP system running on a WLAN will have. VoIP, when implemented in WLANs, is often called Voice over WLAN or VoWLAN. It is also being called Wi-Fi Telephony, VoFi, VoWi-Fi, and wVoIP. At a minimum, you should know the following:

- VoIP data transfer issues
- Impact of WLANs on VoIP

VoIP Data Transfer Issues

Voice and video communications are much more sensitive to latency issues and data loss issues than standard data transfer. For example, if you are attempting to open a document from a file server and some of the packets are lost, the network layers in your system will simply request that the packets be resent and—though the total transfer time will be slightly greater—you'll hardly notice that any problem occurred. With voice and video, this data loss could cause reduced quality in the audio or video, and it could be reduced below acceptable levels. For this reason, it is important that Quality of Service (QoS) factors be considered if VoIP or video conferencing will occur over the WLAN. This will impact the saturation of APs within coverage areas and will even impact the APs that you decide to implement (you will want APs and/or controllers that support QoS).

An additional consideration with VoIP is the issue of lost connections. If you are using a stationary VoIP phone or desktop computer VoIP application while connected to a wired Ethernet, you are not as likely to be concerned with losing the connection (assuming you have sufficient throughput levels). However, if you are moving around and changing from one WLAN to another, dropped connections can mean dropped calls.

The Impact of WLANs on VoIP

Given the issues briefly introduced here, you must consider roaming capabilities within the wireless hardware that you purchase. Many organizations find that it is best to go with a single vendor who can provide the entire WLAN infrastructure (switches and controllers), WLAN edge (APs), and client devices (wireless NICs, VoWLAN IP phones, etc.) to ensure that they are compatible with each other and that seamless roaming can occur. These VoWLAN issues can be considered during the site survey and should be part of the implementation plan, but this is one area where postimplementation testing is crucial. Very few users will use the VoWLAN system if call quality is poor or if their calls are dropped on a regular basis.

Client Connectivity Requirements

Before we wrap up this chapter, with a few pages covering the process of documenting all that we've covered so far together, there is one last issue to address: connectivity requirements. Connectivity issues include not only the ability to connect, but also the ability to connect from where the user needs the connection and with the security demanded by the sensitivity of the information being accessed or transmitted.

The first element is determining from where users need to connect. Do they need to connect from within the building only or also from the outside of the facility? Are you going to allow them to connect in the same way from both locations? Do you need different connectivity options in different places within the facility?

For example, some organizations implement both a private company WLAN and a public guest WLAN. The guest WLAN allows visitors to traverse a public network that may provide local printers and even file services as well as an Internet browser. This guest WLAN, however, is completely separated from the organization's private WLAN and LAN.

The second factor is determining what security requirements will exist. Does the organization have a policy that demands using IEEE 802.11i security solutions like those discussed in Chapter 10, or is the WLAN going to be open, with authentication and authorization handled in a layer beyond the scope of the WLAN? In the latter case, the organization should probably be informed that the WLAN communications will be insecure in that the data will not be encrypted.

The final factor related to client connectivity is ensuring that the WLAN standards supported by the clients are available on the WLAN. For example, the organization in question may already have dozens or hundreds of laptops with IEEE 802.11g cards that support both ERP and HR/DSSS. If you implement OFDM APs that only support IEEE 802.11a, you will have to install additional NICs in all of these laptops either as PC Cards, PCMCIA Cards, or USB devices. This is obviously a tremendous cost factor and may be one (most likely will be one) the organization wishes to avoid.

Documenting the Site Survey Findings

At this point, you have the basic parts and pieces that you need to perform a WLAN site survey. You know about the information you need to gather, the tools you can use, and the things to watch out for during the survey. In this section, I'm going to give you a bird's eye view of the inputs, processes, and outputs of a site survey and then provide you with some more information on how you should consider structuring and presenting your findings to the organization for which the site survey was performed. Figure 6.25 gives you a visual representation of this bird's eye view.

As you can see in Figure 6.25, the inputs are really made up of the information you gather during user interviews and the documentation that pre-exists the site survey. The processes include manual, automated, and virtual site surveys, and you may use one or a combination of these processes. The processes will result in new information, and you will combine this information with the inputs received at the beginning of the site survey to form a set of site survey results documents. From these documents, you will create a WLAN implementation plan. Later in this chapter, in the section "Creating an Implementation Plan," I give a very short overview of this task. You will need the knowledge of the available infrastructure and client hardware documented in Chapters 7 and 8 to create this plan.

Site Survey Reporting Procedures

The site survey documentation will depend on a number of factors. The following information should be considered:

- Customer reporting requirements
- Graphical documentation
- Hardware recommendations

FIGURE 6.25 The inputs, processes, and outputs of a site survey

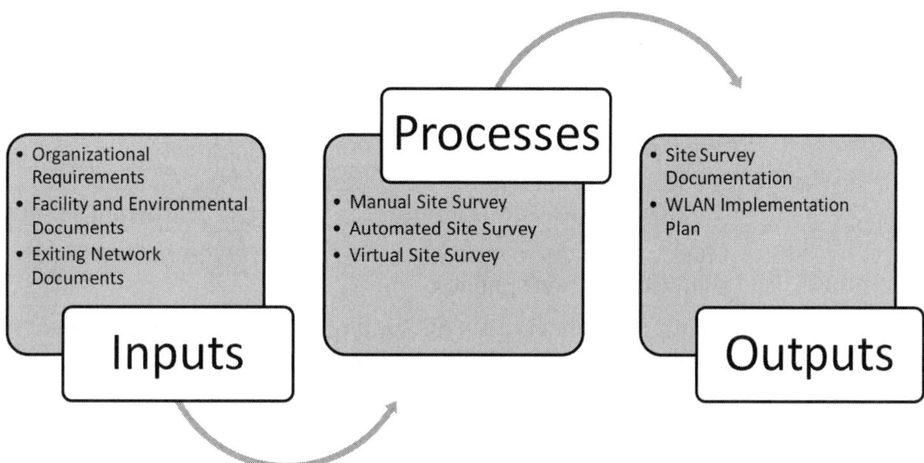

Customer Reporting Requirements

What are the requirements of the customer? The customer may be the organization in which you are employed, or it may be an outside organization if you work for a consulting firm. In either case, the organization may impose constraints on the reporting methods and people involved. For example, the organization may request that you turn in the site survey results to an internal IT staff, or they may expect you to convert the technical knowledge so that the business professionals can understand the results. In this latter case, you may be asked to give a presentation to management so that they can understand the intended WLAN and its benefits.

Graphical Documentation

At a minimum, floor plans with AP location indicators should be provided. If you have the tools available, print out documentation that shows the different expected data rates at different locations as well as the projected throughput at those locations, based on the signal strength and the user densities. You can also provide photos of the intended locations of APs along with documentation specifying power sources and Ethernet connectivity where applicable.

Hardware Recommendations

This portion of the documentation is very important because the organization will be relying on your expertise to choose the appropriate hardware that meets their business requirements. Be sure to link the hardware to these requirements by documenting the technical feature of the hardware that matches to a business requirement. For example, you may include a table similar to that in Table 6.5, but enlarged to include all the business requirements and how they are met by the proposed hardware.

TABLE 6.5 Business Requirements Mapped to Proposed Hardware

Business Requirement	Hardware Feature
Must provide clear voice quality with wireless VoIP phones.	DiffServe-enabled router
Must provide security in the form of authentication and confidentiality.	IEEE 802.11i–compliant AP and wireless switch
Must provide effective throughput for business applications.	IEEE 802.11e–compatible APs and ERP and OFDM PHYs

Do not forget that it is up to you to help many decision makers understand the benefits of the right column in Table 6.5. Simply saying that the AP and switch understand 802.11i will not help them see how security is provided. They do not need to understand all the details of how 802.11i provides a more secure environment, but some simple graphical representations in a slide presentation can go a long way with a knowledgeable person like yourself explaining just enough of the details.

Creating an Implementation Plan

It is important to understand that the resulting documents from a site survey are not, themselves, an implementation plan. The implementation plan document(s) will usually include some of the information from the site survey, but they do not have to have all of the whys behind the whats. In other words, the implementation plan can simply state that a certain device should be installed in a certain location with specific settings without stating why it is being installed there and in that way. Think of it like this: you do not have to know why blood pressure medicine works to put the pill in your mouth and swallow. You'll get the benefit of the medicine even without knowing why you're getting that benefit.

Many organizations lack the on-site IT expertise to understand and implement a WLAN. However, if you tell them how to best implement the WLAN, they can indeed take the steps and they may even be able to troubleshoot failed hardware and software. The point is that you will be the RF expert and they will be the software and hardware implementers. This is perfectly acceptable, though I would encourage anyone working with WLAN equipment to acquire the knowledge given to one seeking the CWNA certification at a minimum.

A WLAN implementation plan can pull from the documents and data retrieved during the site survey. You can use the floor plans to show the physical location of APs and even attach the digital photos of the physical locations to make things as clear as possible. In some instances, you will choose to install the WLAN switches or controllers first and then install the APs. In other cases, it really doesn't matter, so you can install the APs while someone else is installing the switches and controllers or even before they are installed. Of course, self-configuring WLAN technology will have to have the APs installed before they can be automatically configured, but the physical placement of each (the controller and the APs) can actually happen in any order.

Touring Site Survey Tools

In this brief section, I will provide you with some exposure to the interfaces of two popular WLAN management tools that provide site survey functionality. The first is the Aruba Mobility Management System, and the second is RingMaster. Both solutions can provide virtual site survey–type functionality as well as assisted site survey functionality. While my primary intention is to show you the beneficial features they have for site surveys, I will also take this opportunity to show you some of their management and troubleshooting features.

Aruba Mobility Management System

The Aruba Mobility Management System is a complete set of tools used for WLAN planning, configuration, and management. The system is used in conjunction with Aruba APs and WLAN controllers. The focus of the Mobility Management System is user-centric control. This allows administrators to view and manage network objects in relation to specific users instead of network devices. Figure 6.26 shows the Mobility Management System dashboard, which is the first thing you see when you open your Mobility Management System (MMS). The squares represent a certain number of resources, the X axis is time (8 hours in this view), and the Y axis is a percentage moving up a scale, such as 0–100 percent. You can click any of the squares to see a list of resources that are represented. At the bottom is a list of alerts for the administrator's attention.

In addition to the general network summary is a security summary screen (see Figure 6.27). This view displays the summary of security events over the last 8 hours and is the same data represented on the Mobility Controller screen (an Aruba device's independent management interface that's used when this centralized MMS application is not) aggregated for the entire network.

FIGURE 6.26 MMS dashboard

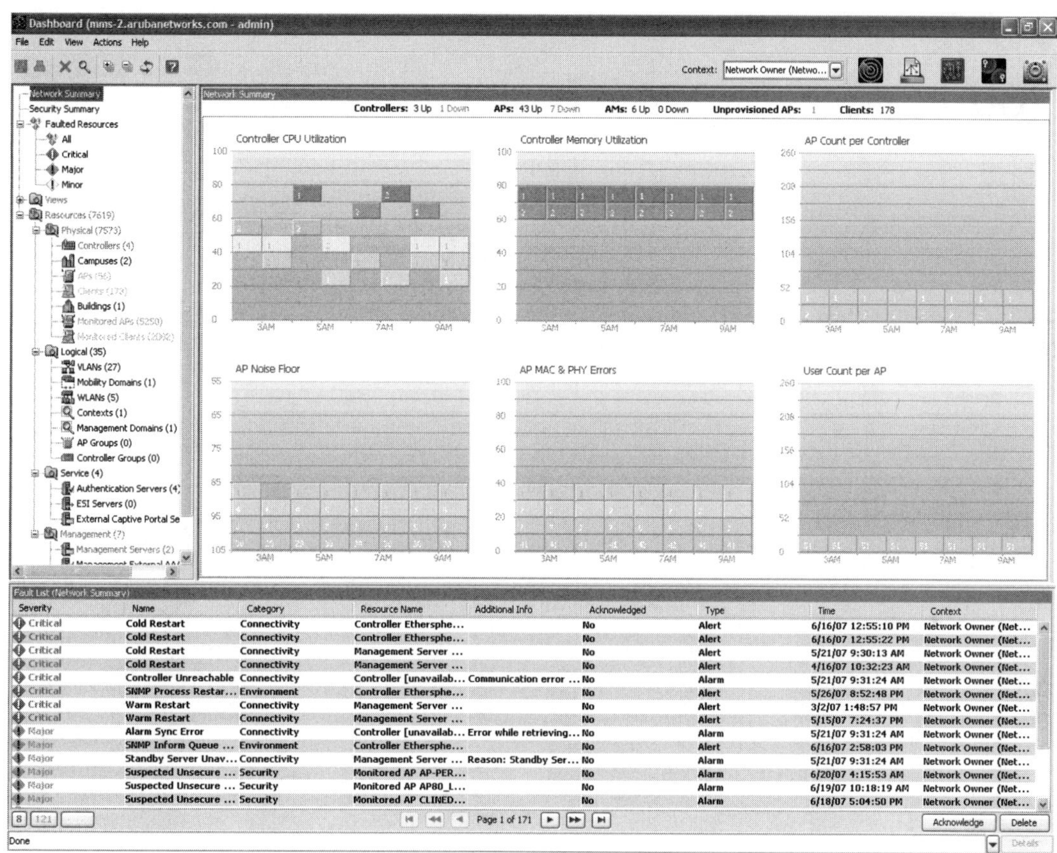

Another valuable feature is the reporting views. Figure 6.28 shows such a view. Notice the dramatic decrease in client association starting at around 5 P.M. and the incline that begins around 8 A.M. The scope is the entire network in this screen capture, but you can narrow that scope down to a controller or another specified boundary if you like. This is the kind of

FIGURE 6.27 MMS security summary

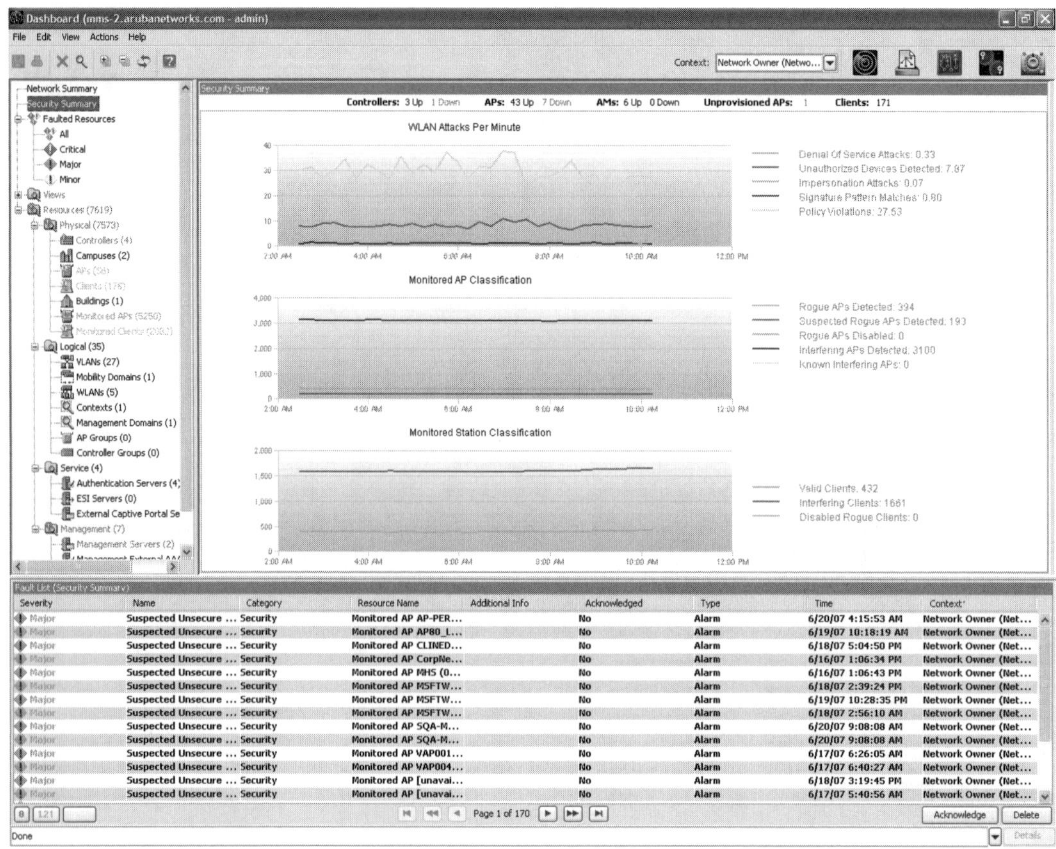

valuable information a centralized WLAN tool like this can provide to you in a simple and easy manner.

Now, we begin to look at the site survey and planning capabilities of Aruba's MMS. Figures 6.29 and 6.30 show the same thing, one with all the channels displayed in different colors (shades in this book) and one with them all combined. The darker the ring, the faster the connection available. If you hover over the rings, the application will display the speed represented. This is the same tool used to plan the WLAN (the virtual or

FIGURE 6.28 MMS reporting tool

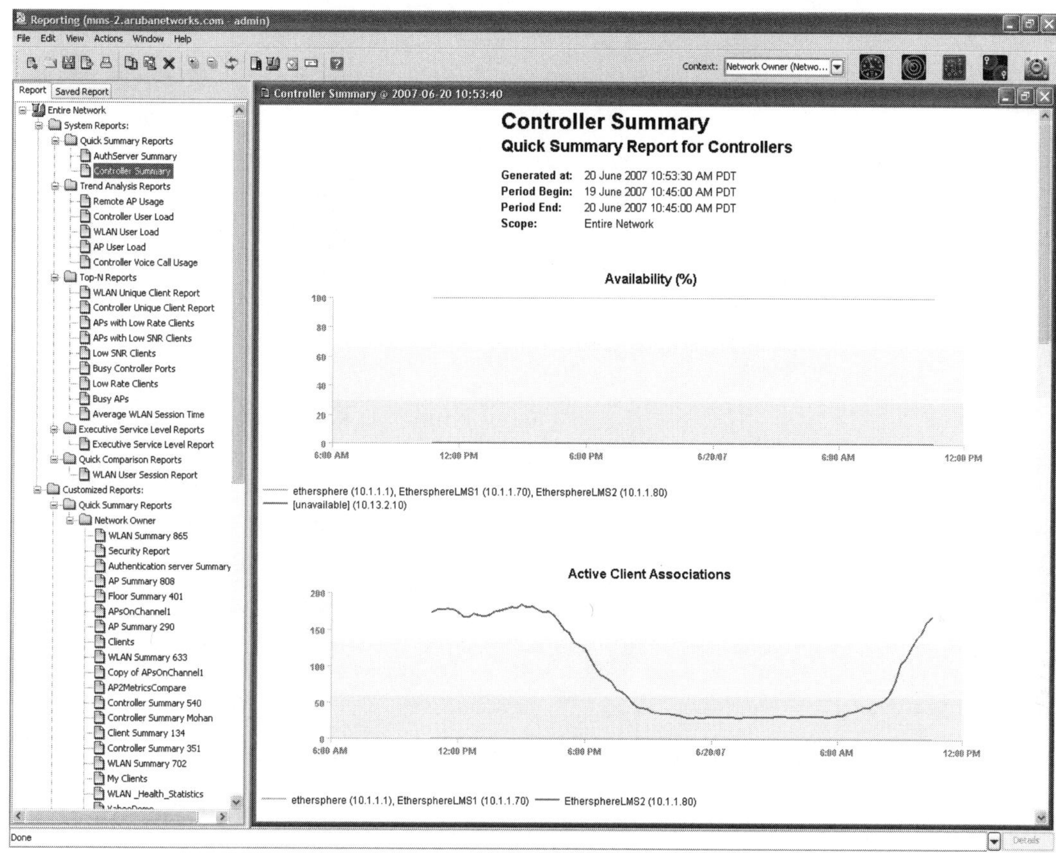

assisted site survey stage); once planning is complete, it is used to show live heat maps.

Another excellent feature of the MMS is client location. You can use this feature to show the approximate location of a client in your physical space. This is accomplished through triangulation, which reads the client's signal from different locations to approximate the client's actual location. Figure 6.31 shows this feature in action. The small triangle is the client's approximate location, and the larger triangle is shown to help the

FIGURE 6.29 MMS heat maps with separate channels

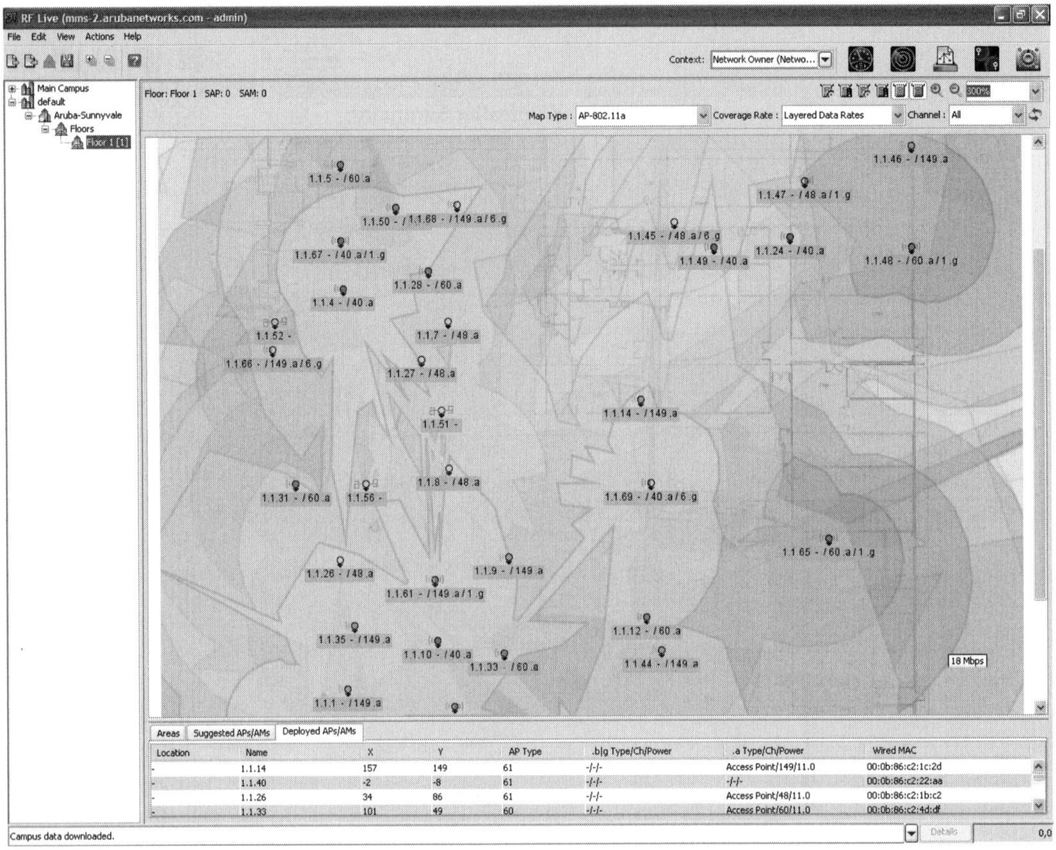

administrator see the method used to triangulate the client. This can be very useful when troubleshooting and when you need to locate a client that seems to be attacking your network.

Trapeze Networks RingMaster

The Trapeze Networks RingMaster application provides a planning component that can be used to perform site surveys and ongoing management of the WLAN. Figure 6.32 shows the planning tool with a floor plan loaded.

FIGURE 6.30 MMS heat maps with channels combined

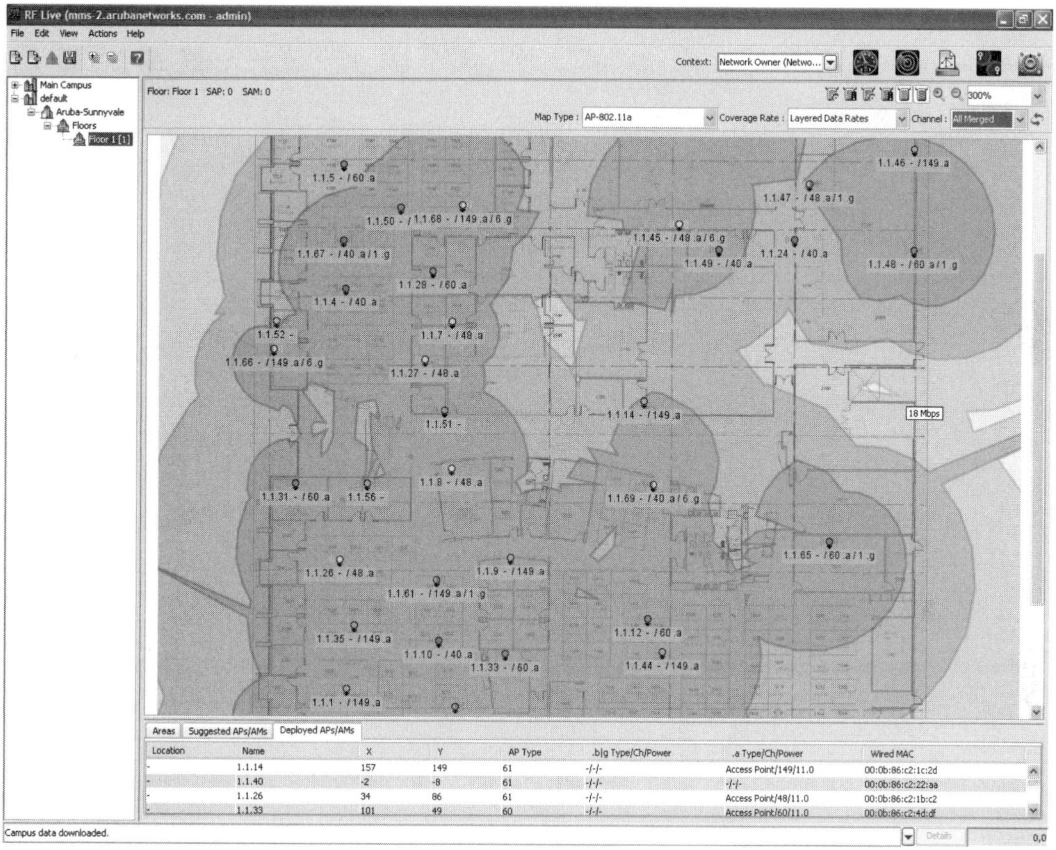

Once you have your floor plan loaded, you can begin defining the details of the building space. For example, you can specify the RF interference objects in the environment as seen in Figure 6.33. You can convert existing objects in the drawing into RF interference objects, and you can draw new interference objects that may not be in the drawing.

FIGURE 6.31 Client location

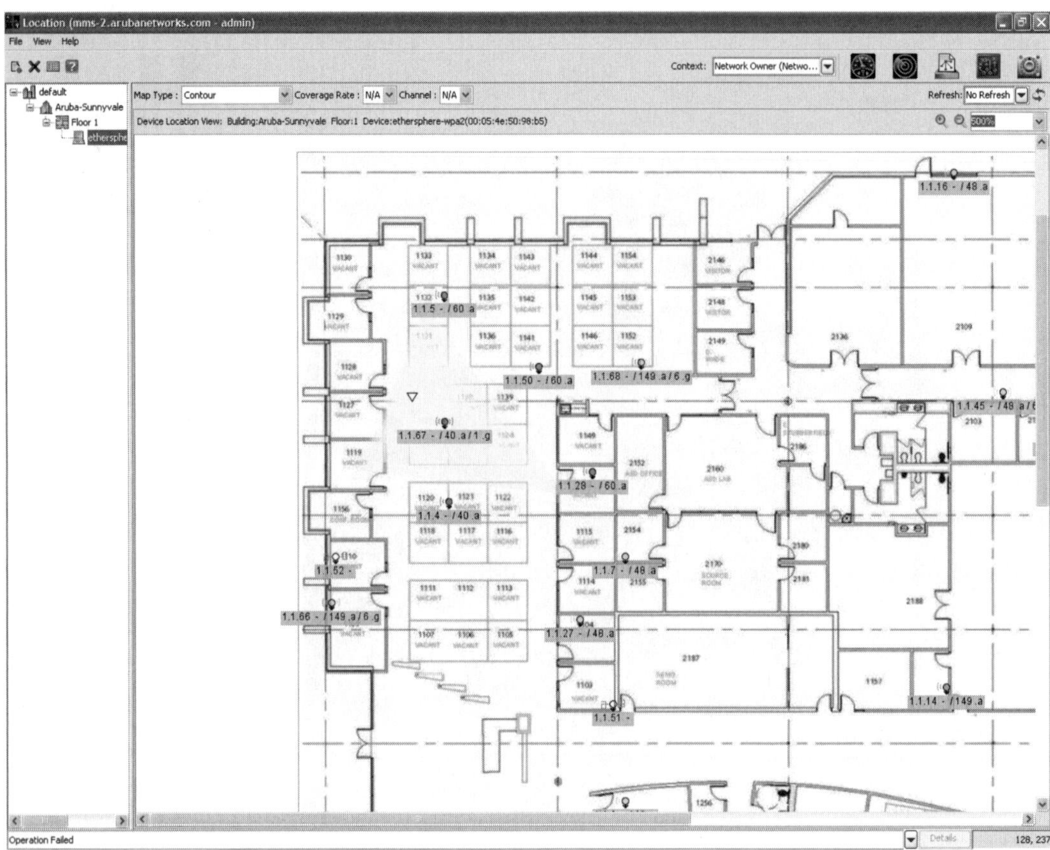

You can move on from here to specify the following for your WLAN:

- Wiring closets
- Coverage areas
- AP locations
- AP settings
- AP information for APs from other vendors (non-Trapeze)

FIGURE 6.32 RingMaster planning tool

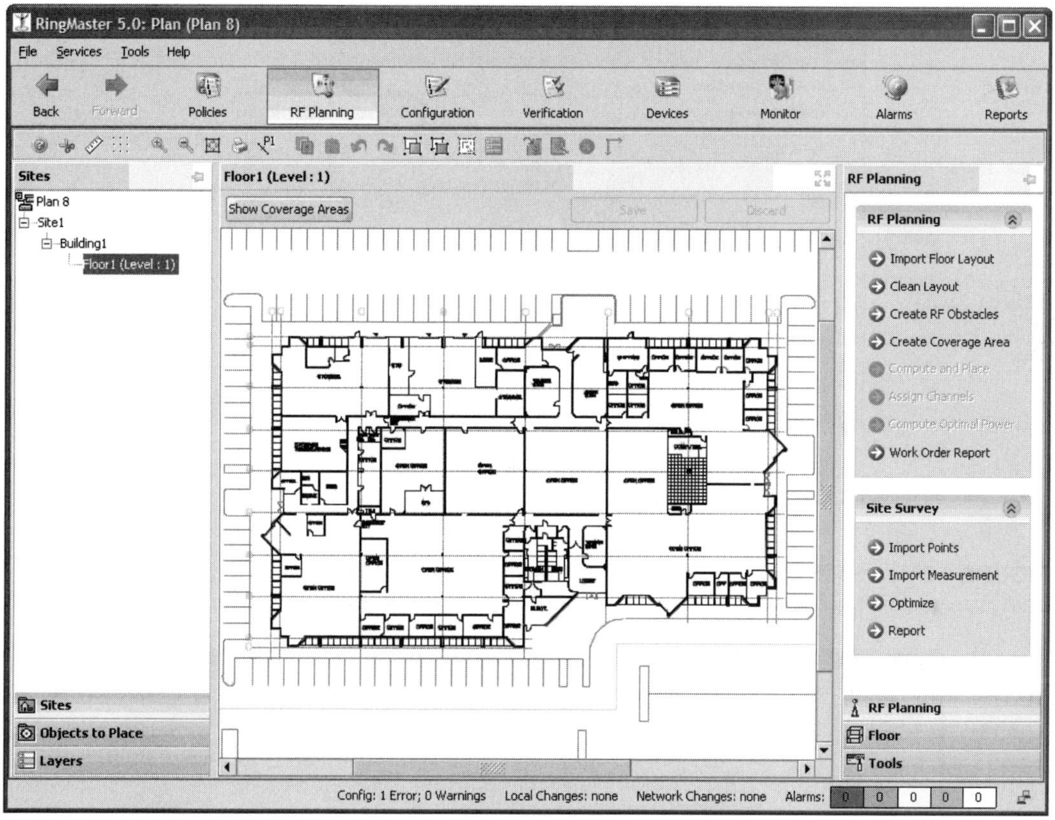

RingMaster shows the network coverage using the plan tool. Figure 6.34 shows this interface. This interface is used after you've imported RF measurements. In order to import these RF measurements, you must first use the Ekahau site survey software to gather them. RingMaster integrates with and has a dependency on the Ekahau software in order to take advantage of all its features.

FIGURE 6.33 Specifying RF obstacles such as exterior walls (Copyright 2007 Trapeze Networks – Screenshots are from RingMaster™ software, the network management suite from Trapeze Networks.)

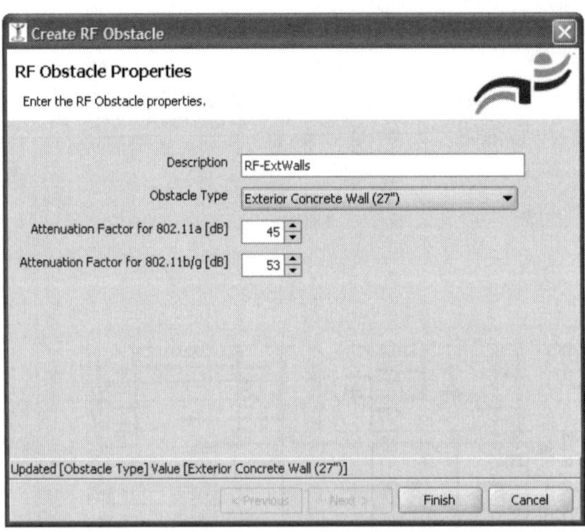

FIGURE 6.34 RF coverage in RingMaster (Copyright 2007 Trapeze Networks – Screenshots are from RingMaster™ software, the network management suite from Trapeze Networks.)

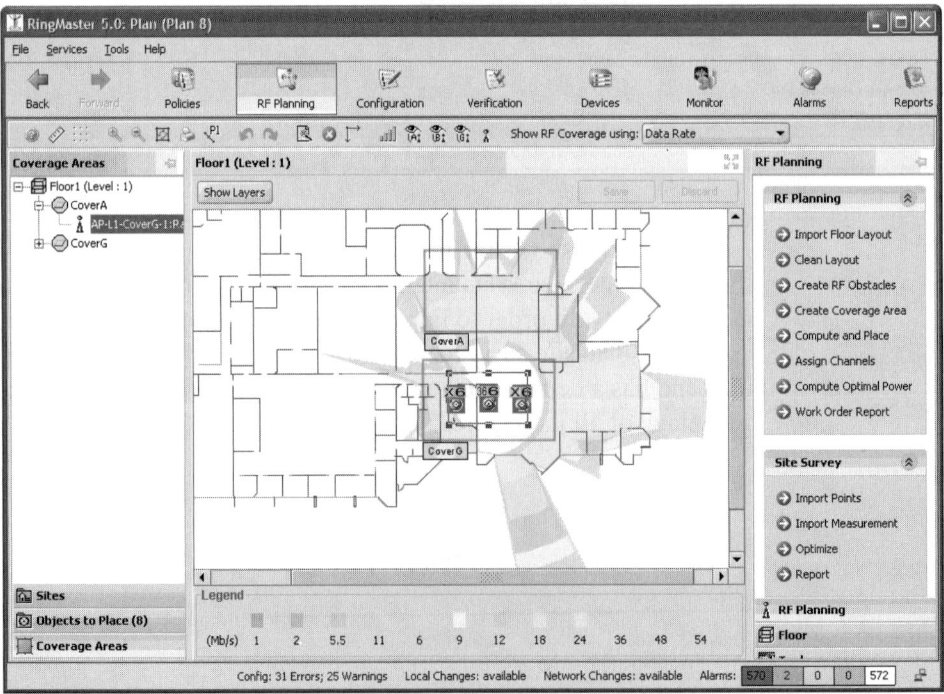

Once your network is implemented, like Aruba's MMS, RingMaster can detect and report on rogue APs. Figure 6.35 shows an example of this report.

Another valuable feature of the RingMaster application is its Compute and Place feature. This tool will allow you to compute the number of APs needed to provide the coverage you demand, and it will inform you of the suggested placement of these APs. Of course, this only works appropriately if you've done the work of defining the floor plan correctly and specifying interference objects accurately. In addition to computing the number of APs needed to achieve, for instance, a desired data rate and desired PHYs, RingMaster can calculate the number of APs needed for a desired capacity as seen in Figures 6.36 and 6.37.

FIGURE 6.35 Rogue AP report (Copyright 2007 Trapeze Networks – Screenshots are from RingMaster™ software, the network management suite from Trapeze Networks.)

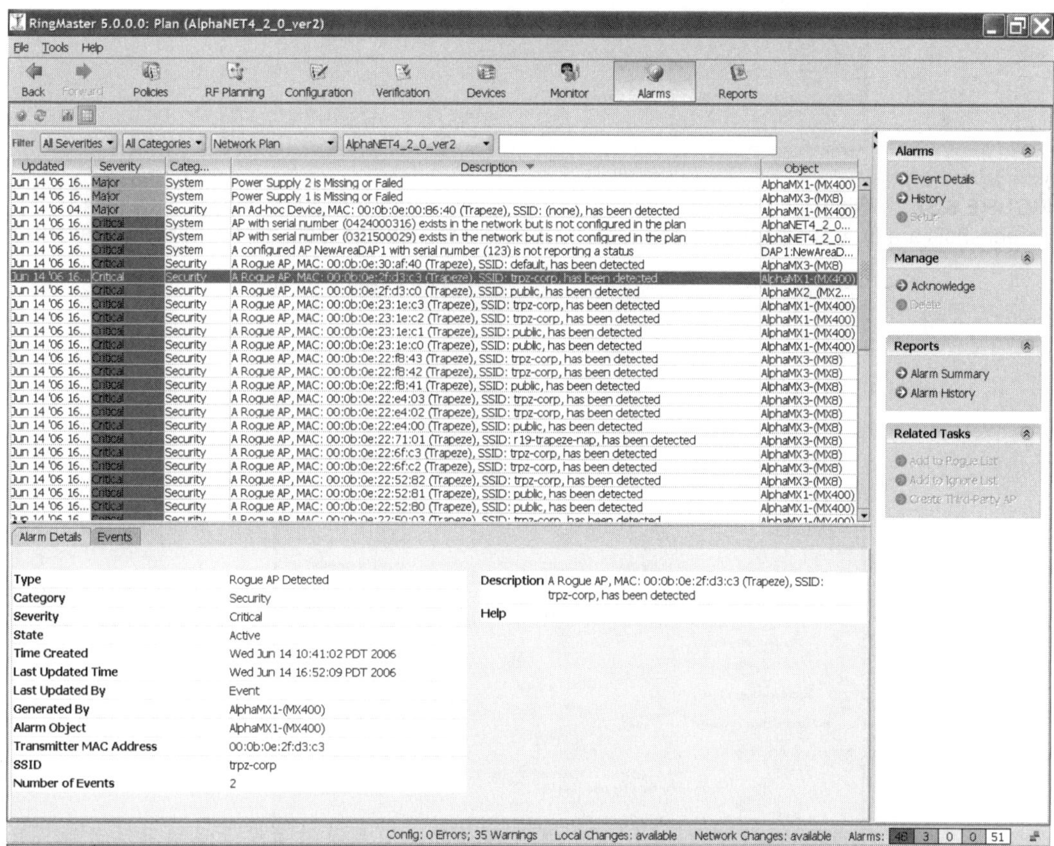

FIGURE 6.36 RingMaster's capacity planning tool (Copyright 2007 Trapeze Networks – Screenshots are from RingMaster™ software, the network management suite from Trapeze Networks.)

Create Coverage Area
Optional: Capacity Planning for Data
Select if you would like to use Capacity planning for data. If this is not selected, RF Planning will only be based on Coverage criteria.
CoverA
Use Capacity Calculation for Data
Per Station Throughput [Kb/s] 1,000
Expected Station Count 50
Station Oversubscription Ratio 5 : 1
Select the oversubscription ratio that best describes the average transmit behavior of the stations in your network
CoverG
Use Capacity Calculation for Data
Per Station Throughput [Kb/s] 1,000
Expected Station Count 50
Station Oversubscription Ratio 5 : 1
Select the oversubscription ratio that best describes the average transmit behavior of the stations in your network
Updated [Use Capacity Calculation for Data] Value [Yes]
< Previous
Next >
Finish
Cancel

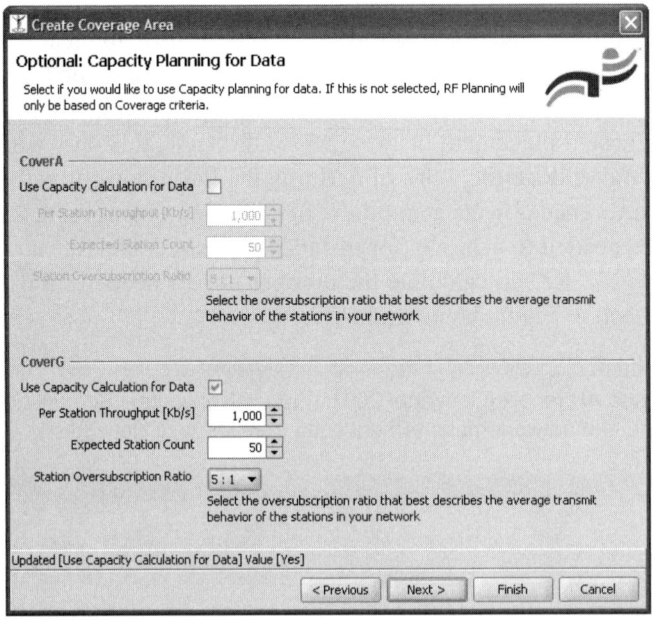

FIGURE 6.37 RingMaster's voice capacity planning tool (Copyright 2007 Trapeze Networks – Screenshots are from RingMaster™ software, the network management suite from Trapeze Networks.)

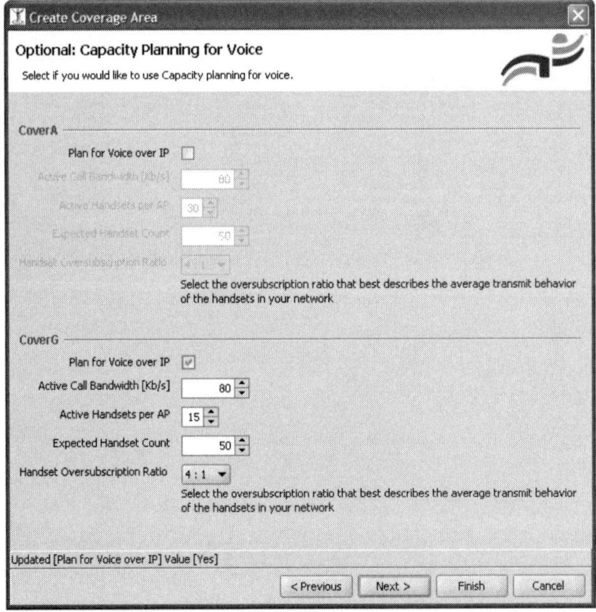

Like Aruba's MMS, RingMaster can also locate specific clients and triangulate rogue APs. Figure 6.38 shows an example of locating a rogue AP. You can also report on the number of clients associated with the WLAN, and you can sort by the switch (shown as MX in the image) as seen in Figure 6.39.

FIGURE 6.38 Locating a rogue AP (Copyright 2007 Trapeze Networks – Screenshots are from RingMaster™ software, the network management suite from Trapeze Networks.)

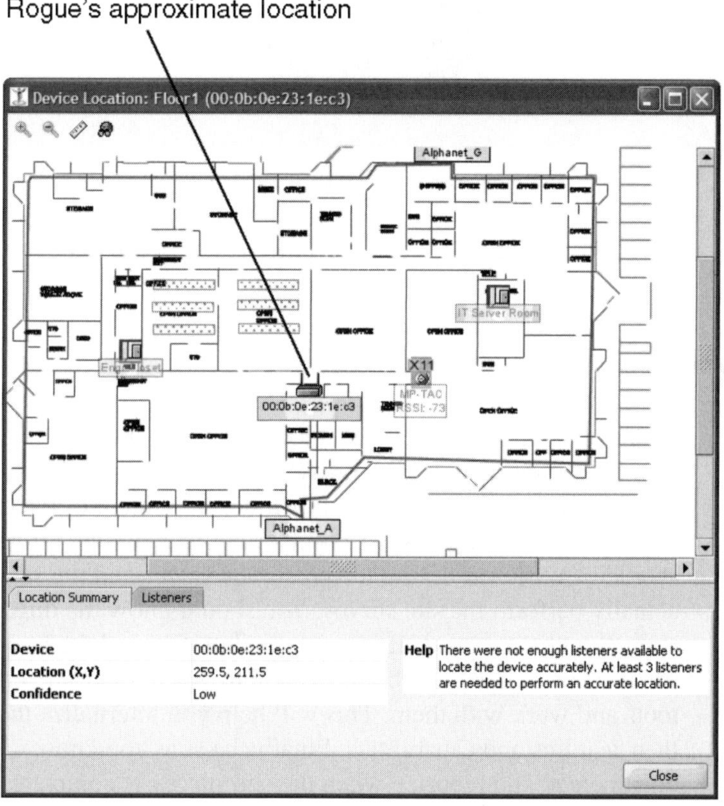

FIGURE 6.39 Showing client associations based on the MX to which they are connected (Copyright 2007 Trapeze Networks – Screenshots are from RingMaster™ software, the network management suite from Trapeze Networks.)

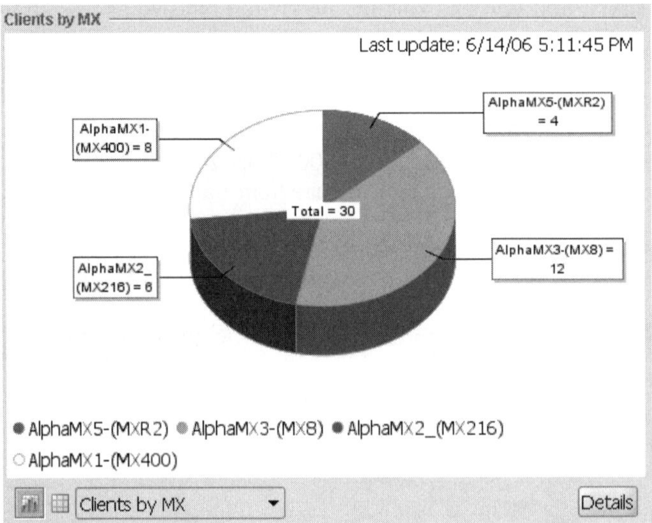

Summary

In this chapter, we've covered a lot of material, but this material is very important to your success as a CWNA candidate and a WLAN administrator and engineer. At this time, 16 percent of the exam covers WLAN site surveys. You will need to know about the information that should be retrieved during the presurvey stages and the steps needed to actually perform the site survey. You should know the differences between manual and automated site surveys and understand the basic features of the tools available to do both. Be sure to download trial versions of these tools and work with them. This will help you internalize the knowledge of their features and capabilities. Finally, be sure you know what should be documented and reported when the site survey is complete.

A site survey should include the following components:

- Propagation studies
  - Environmental effects on the RF signals
  - Coverage and capacity planning

    - Power output levels required
    - Antenna selection
- User, business, and functional requirements
- Channel selection
- Hardware and software identification

Ultimately, you are answering the following questions: How many access points are needed, where should they be placed, and what types should be selected and installed? The answers to these questions come through the many steps, tools, and documents discussed in this chapter.

Key Terms

- ☐ **capacity**
- ☐ **coverage**
- ☐ **manual site surveys**
- ☐ **predictive site surveys**
- ☐ **protocol analyzer**
- ☐ **requirements analysis**
- ☐ **RF site survey**
- ☐ **spectrum analyzer**
- ☐ **virtual site survey**
- ☐ **VoWLAN**

Review Questions

1. You've been asked to perform a site survey for a WLAN to be implemented in a hospital. The hospital has four floors and includes the traditional equipment found in most hospitals. Which of the following are common issues that you must consider?

   A. The use of existing equipment that generates RF energy

   B. The wall structures that include RF blocking designs

   C. The greater capacity of humans within the environment

   D. The impact of RF energy on medicines

2. Why should you perform an RF site survey? (Choose all answers that apply.)

   A. To verify that RF signals actually move throughout your environment

   B. To test the ways in which RF signals move throughout your environment

   C. To determine the number of needed APs

   D. To determine appropriate settings for APs

3. Why do VoWLAN implementations demand a different perspective from standard WLAN data networks?

   A. VoWLANs require the implementation of IEEE 802.11j devices.

   B. VoWLANs are more sensitive to delays and data loss.

   C. Data networks are more sensitive to delays and data loss.

   D. Data networks require the implementation of IEEE 802.11j.

4. What is the difference between a business objective and a technical objective?

   A. A business objective always saves money, whereas a technical objective always costs money.

   B. A business objective is a feature, and a technical objective is a benefit.

C. A business objective is stated from the business' perspective, and a technical objective is stated from a feature or technical perspective.

D. A business objective cannot be accomplished, but a technical objective can.

5. You have installed a centralized WLAN controller that supports autoconfiguration of the connected APs. You are walking through the environment with a client that is reporting back to the centralized controller. What kind of site survey are you performing?

A. Assisted

B. Automated

C. Manual

D. Virtual

6. You've just received a packet in the mail from a client who has requested that you perform a site survey in an environment that has never had a WLAN. The packet contains documents that you have requested. Which of the following documents are likely to be in this packet?

A. Floor plans

B. Network topology diagrams

C. WLAN hardware inventory

D. Current site survey documents

7. After installing the Aruba RF Plan software, you import a floor plan of the facility for which you desire to perform a virtual site survey. What other data are you likely to need to provide to the software package?

A. WLAN technology specifications

B. Local FCC regulations

C. Client operating systems in use

D. External RF interference sources

8. You work for a WLAN implementation company. You receive a call from a client requesting that you estimate the number of APs they will need to cover an outdoor WLAN. The WLAN will need to cover an area approximately 1200 meters by 1600 meters. There are no trees or buildings within the space, only picnic tables and a children's play area. They inform you that WLAN connectivity should be available in every square inch of this area and that it should perform well. What additional information will you need to estimate the number of APs needed other than that which has already been provided?

   A. Number of users connecting concurrently

   B. Needed throughput for each user

   C. Type of security required

   D. Kind of laptops being used

Review Answers

1. **A, B.** You must consider both the existing RF-generating equipment and the wall structures that are often designed to block RF energy in X-ray rooms. There is no known impact on medicines caused by the low-power RF energy generated by WLANs, and there are likely to be fewer people per square yard or meter in a hospital than in many other congested areas such as malls, amusement parks, or even offices, so this is certainly not a unique issue with hospitals.

2. **B, C, D.** You will perform a site survey to determine the appropriate number of APs, their settings, and the ways in which RF signals propagate through your facility, among other factors. RF signals will move throughout your facility; the only question is how.

3. **B.** VoWLAN implementations are more sensitive to delays and data loss than standard WLAN data networks. This is because of the human perception of poor quality in streaming video (video conference) or VoIP communications. The delays and data loss are still there in data networks, but we do not interact with these delays and data losses directly, so we are not aware of them at the same level.

4. **C.** Business objectives are usually stated from the business perspective in terms of better, faster, cheaper, and more features, and continuity. Technical objectives are usually stated from the technical perspective in terms of features and capabilities. For example, a business objective may be to protect sensitive business data from theft or interception as it travels the WLAN. The technical objective that links to this business objective may be to implement AES encryption for all data that traverses the WLAN.

5. **A.** You are most likely performing an assisted site survey. The centralized controller will automatically configure the APs on the basis of a scan of the APs and the information transmitted back to the controller from the client that you are carrying throughout the WLAN coverage area.

6. **A, B.** The packet most likely contains floor plans and network topology diagrams, among other documents. You are unlikely to find a WLAN hardware inventory document or any existing site survey documents, since the environment has never had a WLAN.

7. **A.** You will need to provide WLAN technology specifications such as whether you want to use ERP, HR/DSSS, OFDM, or all of these. You will not need to provide information about client OSs, local FCC regulations, or external interference sources. Most virtual site survey software packages will allow you to restrict the channels that can be used, but they have no real mechanism for virtualizing interference sources.

8. **A, B, C.** While you will not need to know the kind of laptops being used, you will need to know how many concurrent connections will exist, what the throughput demand is for each connection, and the type of security required. If the APs are performing the encryption and decryption, that will reduce the number of client connections each AP can handle. The number of concurrent users times the throughput demanded by each user must also be factored into the capacity plans.

CHAPTER

7

Infrastructure Hardware and Software

In This Chapter

CWNA Exam Objectives Covered:

- Identify the purpose of the following WLAN infrastructure devices and describe how to install, configure, and manage them
  - Autonomous and Lightweight Access Points
  - Enterprise and Remote Office WLAN Switches/Controllers
  - PoE Injectors and PoE-Enabled Ethernet Switches
  - WLAN Bridges and Residential WLAN Gateways
  - Enterprise Encryption Gateways
  - WLAN Mesh Routers
- Understand the different market types and appropriate gear for each market
- Explain forthcoming and newly introduced equipment types
- Be able to implement voice-capable WLANs
- Describe location appliances and real-time location tracking with 802.11 RFID tags

CWNA Exam Objectives Covered:

- ❖ Identify the use of the following WLAN accessories and explain how to select and install them for optimal performance and regulatory domain compliance
  - Amplifiers and Attenuators
  - Lightning Arrestors, Mounting Systems, and Grounding Solutions
  - Towers, Safety Equipment, and Concerns
  - RF Cables, Connectors, and Signal Splitters
- ❖ Describe the proper locations and methods for installing RF antennas
  - Pole/Mast, Ceiling, and Wall Mounts

In the preceding chapter, you learned how to discover the behavior of RF signals in a given area. This chapter helps you select the appropriate hardware for your needs. I will start the chapter by discussing the common WLAN hardware devices that are deployed in various WLANs without emphasis on the specific scenarios where the devices would be utilized. This first section will simply provide you with a reference of the features and configuration options for these common devices. The second section, "WLAN Markets and Appropriate Gear," will help you determine the appropriate hardware for specific scenarios. This will not only help you prepare for and pass the CWNA certification exam, but also help you make better decisions when you implement one or more WLANs in the real world.

After these first two sections, you will learn about some of the new equipment that is being offered in the WLAN market. This equipment includes the convergence of previously separate wireless technologies such as IEEE 802.11 and RFID. Next I will review VoWLAN hardware and implementation considerations. Finally, I will cover the WLAN accessories that tie it all together, such as cables, connectors, antennas, amplifiers, and more.

Installing, Configuring, and Managing WLAN Devices

There are WLAN hardware devices that are used in every WLAN, and there are devices that are only beneficial in larger implementations. This large section covers the following hardware devices that may be used in large and small WLANs, depending on the organization's needs:

- Access points
- Enterprise WLAN switches and controllers
- Remote office WLAN switches and controllers
- Power over Ethernet injectors and switches
- WLAN bridges
- Residential WLAN gateways
- Enterprise encryption gateways
- WLAN mesh routers

Access Points

Access points (APs) are the most frequently installed infrastructure (non-client) devices. They provide access to the WLAN and may bridge to a wired LAN. APs provide a point of access to the WLAN and derive their name from this functionality. As you learned in Chapter 5, each BSS has one and only one AP. When multiple APs work together to form a larger network throughout which clients may roam, they form an ESS.

In most cases, an AP will provide connectivity to a wired LAN or WAN for wireless client STAs; however, this does not have to be the case. APs are often used at construction sites to form controlled and secure networks that are entirely wireless (with the exception of the power cords connected to the APs) as just one example of the use of APs where access to wired networks is not the intent.

Autonomous access points are APs that contain the software for complete management of the WLAN processes within themselves. These were the only kind of APs in early WLANs until the lightweight AP was later developed. *Lightweight access points* are APs that contain limited software and depend on centralized WLAN switches or controllers to provide the remaining functionality. There is no standard for implementing lightweight versus autonomous APs, and the way in which they are implemented varies from vendor to vendor. Autonomous APs are sometimes called fat or thick APs, whereas lightweight APs are also called *access ports* (as opposed to APs) or thin APs. Figure 7.1 shows a network implementation using autonomous APs, and Figure 7.2 shows the use of lightweight APs.

Some APs can act as either an autonomous or lightweight AP, depending on the configuration determined by the WLAN administrator. When used as an autonomous AP, all the AP software features are enabled. When used as a lightweight AP (or access port), many of the AP software features are disabled or are simply controlled by the centralized WLAN switch or controller.

When lightweight APs are brought online (powered up and connected to the WLAN controller through their Ethernet port), they are automatically configured by the WLAN controller or switch. This may include the automatic installation or update of firmware (internal software used to run and manage the AP). Many vendors ship their lightweight APs with no firmware loaded; the firmware is installed when it first connects to the WLAN controller. Symbol (now owned by Motorola) does this with its 5100 series WLAN switches and access ports.

FIGURE 7.1 Autonomous AP implementation

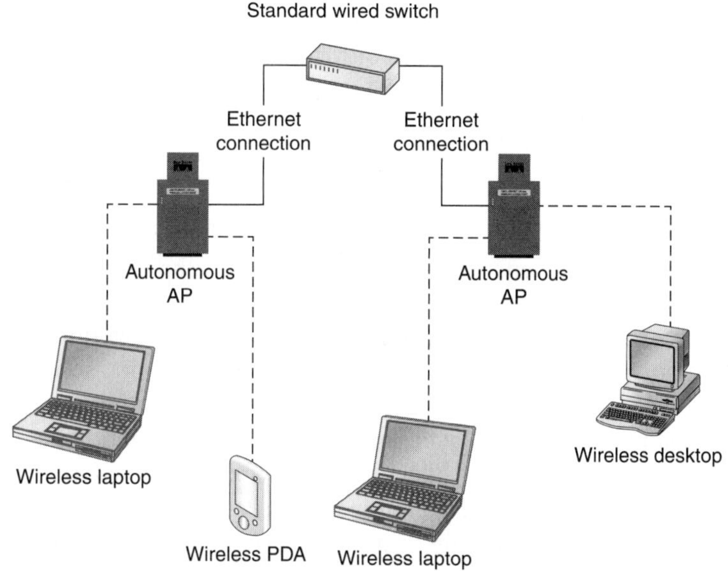

FIGURE 7.2 Lightweight AP implementation

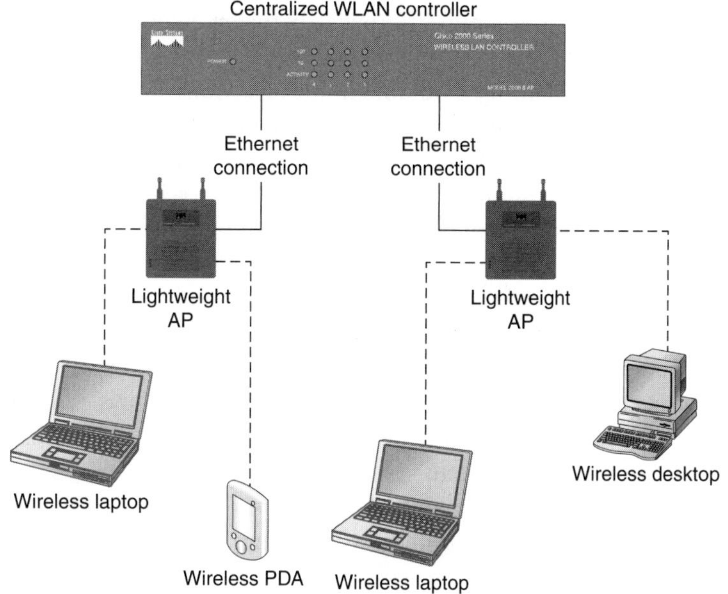

When an AP is converted to become an access port or lightweight AP, features may include

- Automatic updates of firmware files
- Support for multiple ESSs in a single AP
- Support for multiple VLANs
- Centralized management of all APs
- Automatic management of QoS features
- More encryption types than those supported by the AP internals

Autonomous APs that are converted to lightweight APs may also lose capabilities such as access through the serial port, support for wireless bridging and repeater operational modes, and other vendor-specific features. Generally speaking, you gain centralized management and you lose unique features of the autonomous AP; however, since conversion of autonomous APs to lightweight APs is usually only supported when APs are used from the same vendor as the WLAN controller being implemented, few features are available in the AP itself that are not in the WLAN controller's software.

An AP is basically a small computer that includes one or more radios and usually one Ethernet port. Inside the AP is a processor and memory. In fact, one of the big differences between enterprise-class APs and those designed for SOHO implementations is the processing power and the amount of memory available in the AP. Many WLAN administrators are surprised when they first learn that many APs either run a flavor of Linux or can run Linux through flash updates. It is important to remember that you may lose support from the device vendor if you flash the device with an operating system that is not supplied by the vendor. For example, firmware is floating around on the Internet that converts Linksys WRT54G WLAN routers into more enterprise-like devices with advanced features usually only provided in WLAN switch/AP combination installs. These features include VPN endpoint support for client connections, more powerful filtering, and centralized management and control. Again, if a WLAN administrator chooses to install such a firmware, she will likely lose all support from the hardware vendor.

APs, both autonomous and lightweight, come in many shapes and sizes. Some have antennas built in, and others use external antennas.

FIGURE 7.3 Symbol APs

They come in round, rectangular, and other shapes. Some are designed for mounting on walls or ceilings, and some are designed to be placed on desktops or shelves. Figure 7.3 shows multiple APs in the Symbol product line, and Figure 7.4 shows examples of Cisco APs. Figure 7.5 provides examples of SOHO-class APs from Linksys, and Figure 7.6 shows a sample Netgear AP.

APs come with common features and require various configuration processes. The following sections document each of these important factors. First, the common features will be covered, but it is important to note that, while these features are common, they are not available in all APs. Second, I will walk you through the basic installation and configuration of an AP.

FIGURE 7.4 Cisco APs

FIGURE 7.5 Linksys APs

Common Features

By common features, I mean features that are commonly seen in APs and not necessarily features that are common to all APs. Some APs will have all of the features listed here and more, while others may lack one or more of the listed features. Features that will be covered include

- Operational modes
- IEEE standards support
- Fixed or detachable antennas
- Filtering

FIGURE 7.6 Netgear APs

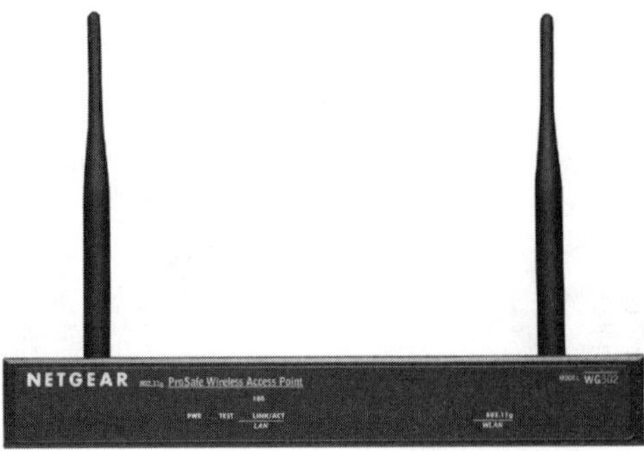

- Removable and replaceable radio cards
- Variable output power
- Ethernet and other wired connectivity
- Power over Ethernet support
- Security capabilities
- Management capabilities
- Mounting options

Operational Modes The IEEE 802.11 standard defines an AP only as a STA that provides access to the distribution services via the wireless medium for associated STAs. It does not define the three common operational modes that are found in APs. These modes (root, bridge, and repeater) are specific implementations of a WLAN STA for varied purposes; in some cases, they may be proprietary rather than matching an IEEE standard. For example, in bridge mode, an AP is implementing a network functionality that is not directly stipulated in the IEEE 802.11 standard. Root mode is the closest to the IEEE 802.11 standard, and many APs meet the IEEE 802.11 standard exactly when running in root mode.

The first mode offered by most APs is root mode. An AP operating in root mode is providing wireless clients with access to the WLAN and possibly a wired network. Root mode is the default mode of operation for all WLAN devices sold as APs. Some WLAN bridges are really APs that come with the operating mode set to bridge mode and are nothing more than a standard AP operating in bridge mode. Full-function WLAN bridges will implement a complete 802.1D bridging feature set; these devices are discussed later in this chapter, in the section "WLAN Bridges." When APs operate in root mode, they may still communicate with each other, but the communications are not related to bridging. In root mode, inter-AP communications are usually related to the coordination of STA roaming. Figure 7.7 shows a typical installation of an AP in root mode.

Bridge mode is used to create a link between two or more APs. When only two APs are used, a point-to-point link is created. When more than two APs are involved, a set of point-to-multipoint links are created. In a bridge mode implementation, the APs involved usually associate only with each other and do not accept client STA associations. Exceptions to this exist, but it is not the normal implementation, since it would reduce the throughput available for the bridge link connection. Figure 7.8 shows a typical installation of a set of APs in a point-to-point bridge mode implementation.

FIGURE 7.7 AP implemented in root mode

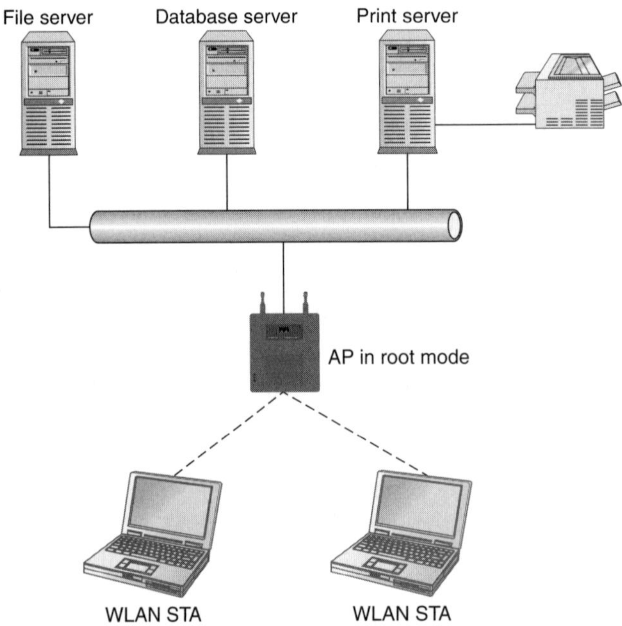

FIGURE 7.8 APs implemented in bridge mode

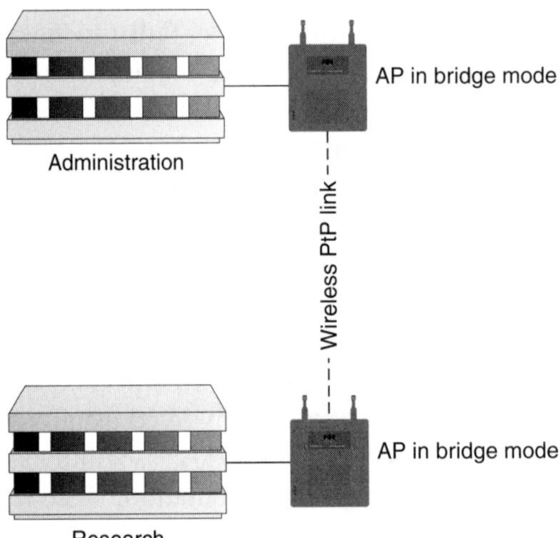

Figure 7.8 shows an implementation of bridge mode that reveals one possible scenario where it may be beneficial. The AP in the Administration building is associated with the AP in the Research building. The two otherwise disconnected LANs are merged into one via the WLAN bridge link created using bridge mode of the APs.

The final mode, repeater mode, is used to extend the range of a WLAN beyond its normal usable boundaries. The repeater AP acts as the AP for clients that would otherwise be out of range of the distant AP operating in root mode. Where a root AP is the connection point for many clients and is a client to no other APs, the AP in repeater mode is a client to the AP in root mode while also accepting connections from client stations itself.

Repeater mode in a WLAN AP should not be confused with the functionality of an Ethernet repeater. Ethernet repeaters regenerate the received signal in order to allow it to travel farther than it would otherwise travel. They do not decapsulate and encapsulate data as a WLAN repeater will. The AP running in repeater mode will decapsulate the data frames received from the clients and encapsulate them for transmission to the root-mode AP. In other words, the WLAN AP in repeater mode will receive data from the WLAN clients associated with it and then retransmit that data to the root-mode AP with which it is associated. Figure 7.9 shows an AP operating in repeater mode to provide access to remote clients.

Keep in mind that an AP operating in repeater mode must be able to communicate with the clients associated with it as well as the root-mode AP with which it is associated. Because of this, the repeater-mode AP will usually have to implement a basic service area (BSA) that overlaps with the BSA of the root-mode AP by at least 50 percent. This reduces the overall coverage area that may be provided if each AP were operating in root mode and forming an ESS; however, Ethernet connectivity is not always available to provide for the preferred implementation, and repeater mode may be used in these scenarios.

IEEE Standards Support APs on the market today support a wide range of IEEE 802.11 amendments, but it is difficult to find hardware that supports some of the older PHYs such as FHSS. Most equipment supports ERP, HR/DSSS, DSSS, or OFDM. The vendors usually report this support as 802.11g, 802.11b, 802.11, or 802.11a, respectively. Many devices are said to be 802.11b/g devices. This simply means that the devices implement the ERP PHY, which is capable of communicating with HR/DSSS PHY devices as well.

In addition to the PHYs that are supported, you should consider the standards-based security features that you may require. Some APs support IEEE 802.11i, and some do not. Some still support only WEP encryption, but thankfully these devices are becoming harder to locate.

FIGURE 7.9 AP in repeater mode

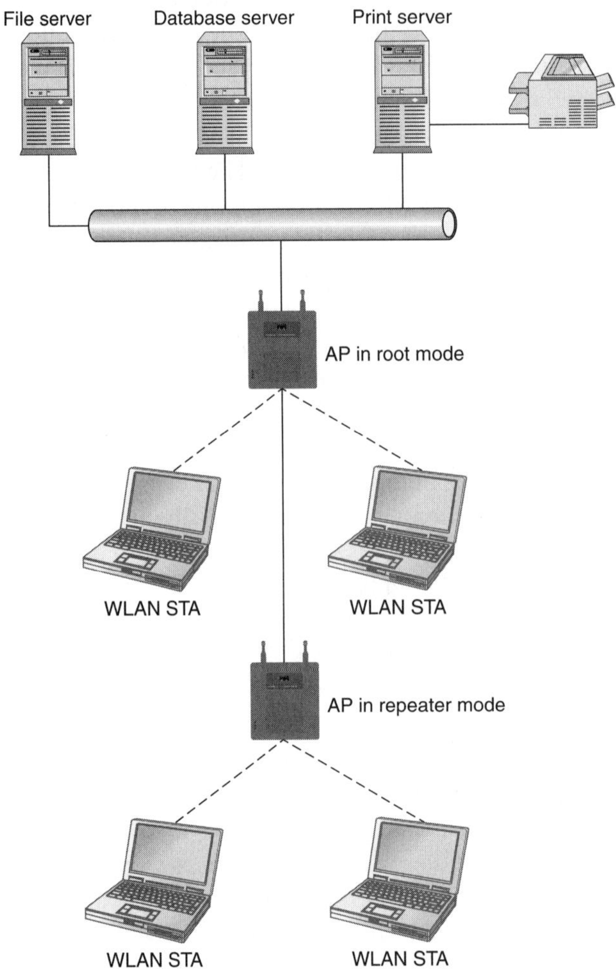

Most modern APs will support both WPA and WPA2 with preshared keys (PSK) at a minimum, and many will support WPA and WPA2 Enterprise, which utilizes a RADIUS authentication server.

Another standards-based feature to consider is Quality of Service (QoS). If you need support for QoS extensions, you should ensure that the AP has support for IEEE 802.11e or the Wireless Multimedia (WMM) certification by the Wi-Fi Alliance. These QoS features will be very important if you intend to support VoWLAN or video conferencing over the WLAN.

Newer APs tend to support the newer IEEE standards while also supporting older standards. One of the benefits of a newer ERP PHY–based device is that it can communicate at the 54 Mbps data rate with other ERP PHY devices and it can also communicate at the 11 Mbps data rate with older HR/DSSS PHY devices. Of course, the ERP protection mechanism kicks in whenever an HR/DSSS PHY device is associated with the ERP AP. This means that the AP will transmit a frame that can be understood by the HR/DSSS machine(s) before transmitting the frame that can only be understood by the ERP machine(s). This first frame is used to cause a backoff timer to kick in on the HR/DSSS machines so they will not interfere during the ERP frame transmission. This reduces overall throughput. The moral of the story is that one HR/DSSS device associated to your ERP AP will cause the entire BSS to slow down to some extent.

In addition to the benefit of backward compatibility with the HR/DSSS PHY, ERP PHY devices are able to support more data rates than HR/DSSS devices; so as the data rate changes, it does not necessarily drop by half at a single step as an HR/DSSS device does when it goes from 11 to 5.5 Mbps in one step.

Finally, APs may not support utilization in every regulatory domain. You should be sure to verify that the APs you are purchasing are authorized for use within your regulatory domain. IEEE 802.11h specifies support for European nations, and IEEE 802.11j specifies support for the regulatory domain of Japan. For more specific information regarding your regulatory domain, check with the regulation management organization in your country.

Fixed or Detachable Antennas Very few enterprise-class APs do not support detachable antennas. Some SOHO APs may have built-in antennas with no external antenna connectors, but this is rare and even these less-expensive devices usually support replacement antennas. Detachable antennas are beneficial from at least two perspectives: the physical location of the antenna and the selection of a different antenna type.

The ability to move the physical location of the antenna to a different location from that of the AP is a valuable one. You can use RF cabling to move the antenna to a location that is more practical for the transmission and reception of RF signals and locate the AP itself closer to power outlets. This can be advantageous when you do not have power outlets closer to the RF signal transmission and reception location.

The second benefit is that of replacing the antenna with a different antenna type. You may want to provide coverage down long, narrow corridors (patch or panel antennas), or you may want to provide coverage in an area horizontally with as little RF energy propagating upward and downward as possible (higher-gain omni antennas). Whatever the motivation, a detachable antenna provides you with the capability to better control how the RF energy is radiated from the antenna and therefore how the AP provides coverage in the BSA. Figure 7.10 shows an AP with a detachable antenna.

Filtering Most APs offer two kinds of filtering at a minimum. The first kind is MAC address filtering, and the second is protocol filtering. Filtering functionality provides the WLAN administrator with the capability to limit which STA frames can pass through the AP in terms of the hardware configuration of the STA (MAC address) or the protocol being used, such as HTTP.

MAC filtering has often been referred to as a security solution, but it should not be thought of as such. It may be useful from the perspective of making it harder to accidentally associate with the wrong AP, but MAC filtering should not be considered a security solution in WLANs. This is because MAC spoofing (stealing a MAC address from a valid STA) is easy to do and step-by-step instructions are readily available on the Internet. The only common value seen from MAC filtering today is its use in specific association limitation scenarios. For example, a training center near my home office uses laptop computers in the training rooms. They do not want the laptop computers to be moved from room to room, but instead want them to stay in designated rooms. The simple solution was to use MAC filtering in the AP in each room. Each room's AP contains the

FIGURE 7.10 D-Link AP with detachable antenna

MAC addresses of the laptops that are supposed to be in that room. The AP's output power is throttled back to reduce the coverage area provided. Now, if someone takes a laptop from the designated room to another room, the laptop will have to associate with an AP with a very weak signal in the remote room. Throughput suffers, and in most cases, the laptops cannot connect in such scenarios because the rooms are far enough apart. Again, if this were being done as a security solution, it would be a very bad idea. Any moderately skilled cracker can spoof a MAC address very quickly. So I cannot emphasize enough that MAC filtering should not be considered a security solution.

Protocol filtering can be used to disallow specific protocols or only allow specific protocols. This feature usually allows for filtering of both the frames arriving through the radio and the Ethernet port. You may also filter only the radio-side (wireless) frames or only the wired frames, depending on the AP and vendor. Some APs can filter out frames in terms of the actual file extensions the user or machine is trying to access on the Internet. For example, if the user attempts to access a WMV file and the WLAN administrator has chosen not to allow access to such streaming media for performance reasons, the AP can disallow such requests. Most APs can blindly block all HTTP requests or FTP requests and other such Internet protocols as well.

An additional kind of filtering, though less common, is that of wireless STA–to–wireless STA filtering. Some APs will allow you to create virtual APs (VAPs) within one physical AP. You can then determine if wireless STAs associated with one VAP can communicate with wireless STAs associated with another VAP (inter-VAP filtering). You can also determine if wireless STAs can communicate with other wireless STAs associated with the same AP (intra-VAP filtering). Finally, you can disallow all client-to-client communications and allow the STAs to use the AP only for access to the wired medium. This type of filtering can be useful when you want one physical AP to service public and private clients. The public clients may have limited access to the network and therefore to the private clients. The private clients may have normal access to the network. In this way, one AP effectively provides access to both internal users and public guests.

Removable and Replaceable Radio Cards Some APs are designed to support one PHY only, while others are designed to allow for multiple radios and therefore multiple PHYs. These multiple-radio APs are usually called dual-radio APs because one radio is needed for the OFDM PHY and another is needed for the HR/DSSS or ERP PHY. Whether the radio is HR/DSSS or ERP is dependent on whether the device is an 802.11b and 802.11a device or an 802.11g and 802.11a device. It is important to remember that all devices claiming to be IEEE 802.11g compatible must also allow associations with IEEE 802.11b devices. This is because the ERP PHY may provide for associations with devices that are using the HR/DSSS PHY. These devices may provide a feature for disabling HR/DSSS PHY associations, and this is often accomplished by allowing only associations that support data rates of more than 11 Mbps.

Many APs, like the Cisco 1200 series, provide for replaceable radio cards. This allows you to upgrade the device for future standards by upgrading the firmware or operating system and the radio cards. Figure 7.11 shows the 1200 series AP. The antennas shown include the OFDM PHY antenna (the square antenna) and the ERP or HR/DSSS antennas (the dipole or rubber ducky antennas). In the case of the 1200 series AP from Cisco, the 2.4 GHz PHYs (HR/DSSS and ERP) are supported by a built-in radio card and the 5 GHz PHY (OFDM) is supported by an add-on radio.

Many APs support replacement radios through the use of PCMCIA or CardBus WLAN NICs. In these cases, the replacement radio cards usually have to be purchased from the vendor that created the AP. This is due to the limited number of cards supported by the software running within the AP.

FIGURE 7.11 Cisco 1200 series AP with multiple radios and antennas

These APs that support replacement radio cards may support two modes of use. The first is to act as a single AP that is reached using multiple PHYs such as OFDM and ERP. The second is to have each radio card configured as if it were a separate AP. In this case, both cards will likely use the same PHYs and they will simply operate on different channels. For example, one card may operate on channel 1 and the other card may operate on channel 11. This allows the WLAN administrator to service twice as many clients in the coverage area while still using a single AP.

Variable Output Power Variable output power provides the WLAN administrator with the capability of sizing cells more accurately. Remember, this should not be considered a security solution by itself because a remote client with a powerful WLAN card and the right antenna can often still pick up the signal of the WLAN and also transmit data to the WLAN. However, as an RF management philosophy, cell sizing makes a lot of sense.

As an example, consider a facility with the need for four different WLANs (for security reasons or otherwise) that must coexist in a fairly small space. Throughput is not a paramount concern, since the users of the WLAN perform minimal data transfers though these data transfers happen several times per hour. Figure 7.12 shows a simplified floor plan of this facility. In order to implement the four distinct WLAN BSAs (cells), APs can be installed in areas A and D that use antennas that directs the majority of the RF energy inward. These antennas could be mounted on the walls near areas B and C and facing away from them. In areas B and C, APs could be installed centrally to the areas and using standard omnidirectional antennas. These APs could have their output power settings lowered to ensure that there is minimal overlap into areas that are not intended for coverage by these APs.

FIGURE 7.12 Simplified floor plan needing four distinct cells

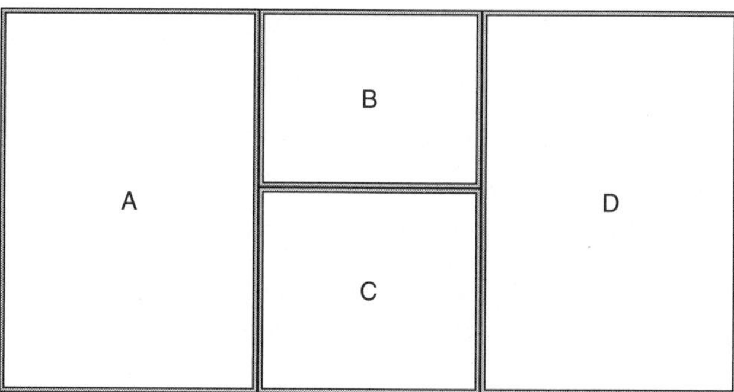

Of course, a scenario like this can be implemented to provide unique configuration parameters for each BSA; however, you must remember that this type of cell size reduction does not of itself equal security, but it would help in RF spectrum management in small areas that need different types of WLAN access such as that depicted here.

Some APs provide variable output power management based on percentages; others use actual output power levels. For example, an AP may allow you to specify that the output power be 25, 50, or 100 mW. Other APs may only allow you to state that the output power should be at 25, 50, or 100 percent. These are just examples, but it is important to know what you're looking for when you enter an AP's configuration interface. Figure 7.13 shows the variable–output power management (Transmission Power) interface for a 3COM 8760 AP. You can see that this device provides percentage-based management of the output power.

Ethernet and Other Wired Connectivity Unless an AP is providing WLAN services and access to a wireless-only LAN, the AP must have some interface through which it can connect to a wired LAN. In most APs, this will be an Ethernet connection. Depending on how old the AP is and the model of the AP, it may support only 10 Mbit Ethernet. Newer models

FIGURE 7.13 3COM 8760 Transmission Power management

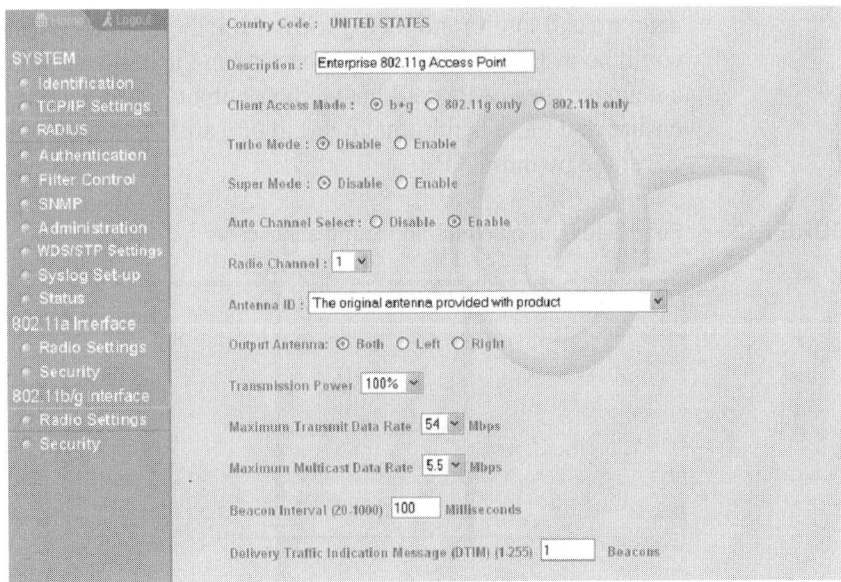

should support 100 Mbit and even Gigabit Ethernet. With an OFDM or ERP PHY, you should ensure that the AP provides at least a 100 Mbit Ethernet connection. This way the wired side can keep up with the wireless side. If the device supports a 54 Mbps PHY (which will likely give up to 26 Mbps data throughput) and a 10 Mbit Ethernet connection, the wired side will fail to keep up with the wireless side, giving the illusion of poor wireless performance. In multiradio devices with more than two radio cards, you will want to seek out a WLAN AP with a Gigabit Ethernet port. Of course, the switch to which the AP is connected must also support gigabit rates, and you may have to analyze other links in the chain from the AP to the common service providers users will be accessing. This is where data flow analysis can benefit you in your planning of the WLAN.

It is also important to remember management overhead that will be incurred on the wired side of the AP. Most centralized management systems, whether in a WLAN switch or controller or in a computer-based application, will perform their management through the Ethernet connection. This prevents the management activity from interfering with wireless activity; however, it may also utilize measurable portions of the Ethernet connection and this may be enough to warrant the use of 100 Mbit Ethernet ports as a minimum. I would certainly not buy a brand-new AP today that only has a 10 Mbit Ethernet port.

In addition to standard CAT5 or CAT6 cabling, some APs may support 100Base-FC fiber connections. Since fiber is rated for longer cable runs, it may provide a solution to a scenario where the AP needs to be located more than 100 meters (the limit of CAT5) from the switch port. Of course, this means the switch must support fiber as well as the AP.

Power over Ethernet Support It seems more enterprise-class APs support Power over Ethernet (PoE) than not. Support for PoE allows for the installation of APs in areas where no power outlets reside but where you can run network cables to carry the power. While PoE is very popular for WLAN devices, because it can provide extra features such as power cycling the device as well as powering the device in the first place, it is sometimes more cost effective to run the power to the area than to use PoE. This is usually the case when only one location needs the power outlet and the power run would only be a few feet.

Consider the implications of PoE carefully before deciding against it. You often hear that the primary benefit of PoE is the ability to install APs where there is no AC power outlet; however, it is certainly a major benefit to be able to power-cycle (stop and start) an AP that is installed in the ceiling and plugged into a power outlet there. Many PoE switches support the stopping and starting of power injection on the PoE ports using the graphical management tools the vendor provides. This means you can restart an AP from your desk even if you cannot get into the management interface of the AP and even if the AP has stopped responding to other management interfaces that communicate with the device through the network layers. To me, this is an equally valuable benefit to that of being able to place an AP where there is no power outlet.

PoE support is usually not found in SOHO APs like those from Linksys or Netgear. Most enterprise APs do support PoE, but check with your vendor to ensure you purchase a model that supports it if you need it. While more and more enterprise-class APs do support PoE, some still do not.

Mesh Networking Functions Modern APs often provide a mesh networking function. The function allows the AP (AP1) to act as a client to multiple other APs (AP2 and AP3 for example) and treat the individual associations with these other APs as ports across which it can bridge traffic for the STAs associated with it (AP1). When a client needs to reach a destination that is reachable through AP2 but that client is associated with AP1, AP1 will bridge the packets across the association with AP2 on behalf of the client.

There is a limit to the number of associations these APs can make. For example, the Symbol AP-5181 AP can create up to three mesh associations with other APs. The Symbol AP-5181 calls these connections client bridges or client bridge mode. At the same time, the device can act as a base bridge and accept incoming client bridge connections from other AP-5181 APs. With these capabilities, a somewhat dynamic mesh network can be built over time across which client traffic may be directed. All of the associations, in the Symbol APs, are based on the SSID (called the ESSID in Symbol's documentation, though this is not IEEE-standard terminology). In other words, the mesh network is built dynamically based on the SSID, and the other APs in client bridge mode, base bridge mode, or both are discovered through beacon scanning.

Figure 7.14 shows a network implementation using APs that support a mesh networking mode. In this case, MU1 is associated with AP1 and MU2 is associated with AP2. Since AP1 is a client bridge to AP2 and AP2 is a client bridge to AP3 while being a base bridge to AP1, both MU1 and MU2 can access the files on the file server. This is possible even though AP1 may not be connected to an Ethernet port. The association AP1 has with AP2 becomes the port across which it bridges network traffic destined for the file server.

FIGURE 7.14 Mesh networking mode implemented

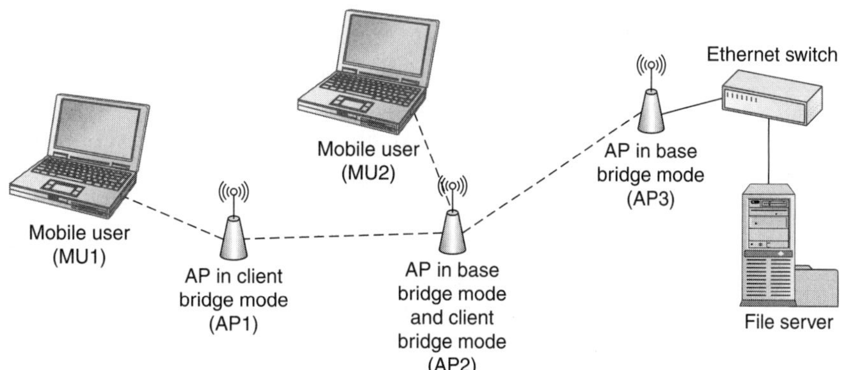

Hotspot Support More and more of the newer APs are coming equipped with hotspot support. This usually includes walled garden support and may also include connectivity to online payment processing services if you are providing a for-pay hotspot. Having this support built in is also useful when you simply want to provide a "guest" network for visitors to your organization's facilities.

Security Capabilities APs support a large pool of common security capabilities. These include

- MAC address filtering (a common item in vendors' lists of security features)
- IEEE 802.1X port-based authentication
- IEEE 802.11i
- SSH and SSH2 for management access
- HTTPS access to web-based management
- Legacy WEP (we shouldn't even call this a security capability, but vendors do)
- WPA/WPA2
- SNMP v3 for secure SNMP management
- Various EAP types (some are secure, some are not)
- Built-in firewalls
- Support for VPN tunnel endpoints and pass-through
- Content filtering

Most of these topics will be discussed in greater depth in Chapters 9 and 10, but your role as a WLAN administrator or engineer may include the selection of APs that support the security technologies required by your security policies. Today, these policies will likely specify that you cannot implement an AP that uses WEP for data encryption, and you must therefore select an AP that supports WPA-PSK at a minimum. More likely, in an enterprise implementation, you will be implementing full IEEE 802.11i support from this point forward—until a newer and better security technology comes along. This last statement is not meant to indicate that IEEE 802.11i is insecure, only that it will be some day. That day may be 10 years down the road, but it will come. By that time, the IEEE will likely have developed newer security recommendations and standards, and for that matter, IEEE 802.11 may not even be the common WLAN standard. Things change.

Management Capabilities APs will provide different methods for configuration and management of the devices. These methods will vary from vendor to vendor and from model to model within vendor's product lines. However, there are common methods utilized. These common methods include

- Console (serial)
- Telnet
- SSH
- SNMP
- Custom software applications
- Web-based interfaces

Console or serial interfaces are usually only provided on enterprise-class hardware. For example, Cisco, Proxim, Symbol, and 3COM devices are likely to come with console interfaces for configuring them. Linksys, Belkin, D-Link, and Netgear devices are less likely to come with such an interface. This should not be taken as a given; for example, the Netgear WG302 AP (see Figure 7.15) supports a console port as well as most of the other common management interfaces mentioned in this section. Many vendors that were once known solely as SOHO vendors are beginning to attempt to cross over into the enterprise market.

When using a console interface to configure an AP, you will usually connect a serial cable from your computer to the AP. You may also use

FIGURE 7.15 Netgear WG302 AP

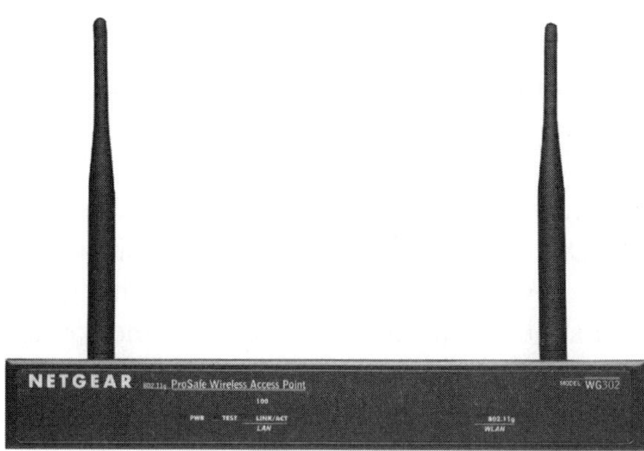

a USB-to-serial converter such as the one seen in Figure 7.16. Once connected, you will use a terminal program such as HyperTerminal, in Windows, to connect to the device. Once connected, you will use the CLI (command line interface) provided by the vendor. Each vendor's CLI will be somewhat different, and sometimes they will be wildly different. This is one of the major arguments for using consistent hardware throughout your organization: you only have to learn one set of CLI commands rather than a varied set. The good news is that the CLI is usually used at initial configuration or for device reload and the other graphical interfaces are usually used for ongoing maintenance and configuration support.

The telnet and SSH or SSH2 interfaces will be similar to the console management method in that the CLI will be utilized. The difference is that the CLI is being utilized across the network rather than through the console port and a serial cable. When using these management methods across the network, you should be careful to ensure that some form of encryption is in use. Otherwise, with telnet for example, the commands being transmitted from your machine to the AP are sent in clear text that is easily readable in any common Ethernet packet analyzer.

FIGURE 7.16 USB-to-serial converter

SNMP is widely supported among WLAN devices. Due to security vulnerabilities in earlier versions, you should choose only devices that support SNMP v3 and—eventually—higher. SNMP provides for centralized mass configuration management. SNMP is not a proprietary technology, so one centralized application can often manage multiple vendors' APs.

Custom software applications may come with the AP and are usually provided on a CD-ROM when they do. These applications are usually designed to run on Windows clients, since these clients are so popular in enterprises. The applications may provide first-time configuration only, or they may provide for ongoing configuration management. Due to the proprietary nature of these applications, they provide limited value to very large-scale installations.

Finally, web-based configuration interfaces take advantage of built-in web server software in APs to allow for remote configuration through the Ethernet interface. While you may be able to enable web-based management through the WLAN interfaces, I do not recommend it. This means that an attacker can try to guess the password and then manage the WLAN device across the WLAN. He or she will not even need to gain access to your physical network. For this reason, if you enable the web-based administration interface at all, it should only be enabled for the Ethernet port. Web-based management interfaces are provided on nearly all APs whether they are built for enterprise or SOHO use. Figure 7.13 showed a portion of the web-based interface on a 3COM AP.

In addition to the configuration features mentioned here, most WLAN APs also allow you to save the configuration to a file that can be downloaded from the device to a disk. This allows you to quickly and easily reload the configuration at a later point. It also provides for quick changes from one configuration to another. Some APs also provide onboard storage of multiple configurations among which you can switch.

Mounting Options APs may be placed on flat surfaces, or they may be mounted in many different ways. Mounting locations and methods include

- Wall mount
- Ceiling mount
- Pole mount

When an AP is mounted on the wall, screws are usually fastened into the wall and then the AP's mounting hardware is slipped over the screws. The screws may be tightened further and then the AP snapped into the mounting hardware, or the AP may have the mounting hardware already attached and the mounting is complete as soon as the AP is slipped onto the screws. With a ceiling mount, the AP is usually attached to similar mounting hardware, but the fasteners must be passed through the tile or other ceiling material. Finally, the pole mount method usually includes a wrapping brace that passes around the pole and then fastens to the AP's mounting hardware. Figures 7.17, 7.18, and 7.19 show examples of these three mounting methods. While these examples show screen shots of the mounting instructions for the Symbol 5131 and Symbol 5181 APs, most APs offer similar mounting instructions and capabilities.

Mounting an AP is more involved than just deciding among the wall, ceiling, pole, or flat surface mount options. You should actually determine

FIGURE 7.17 Wall mount slip-over holes and flat surface shock pads

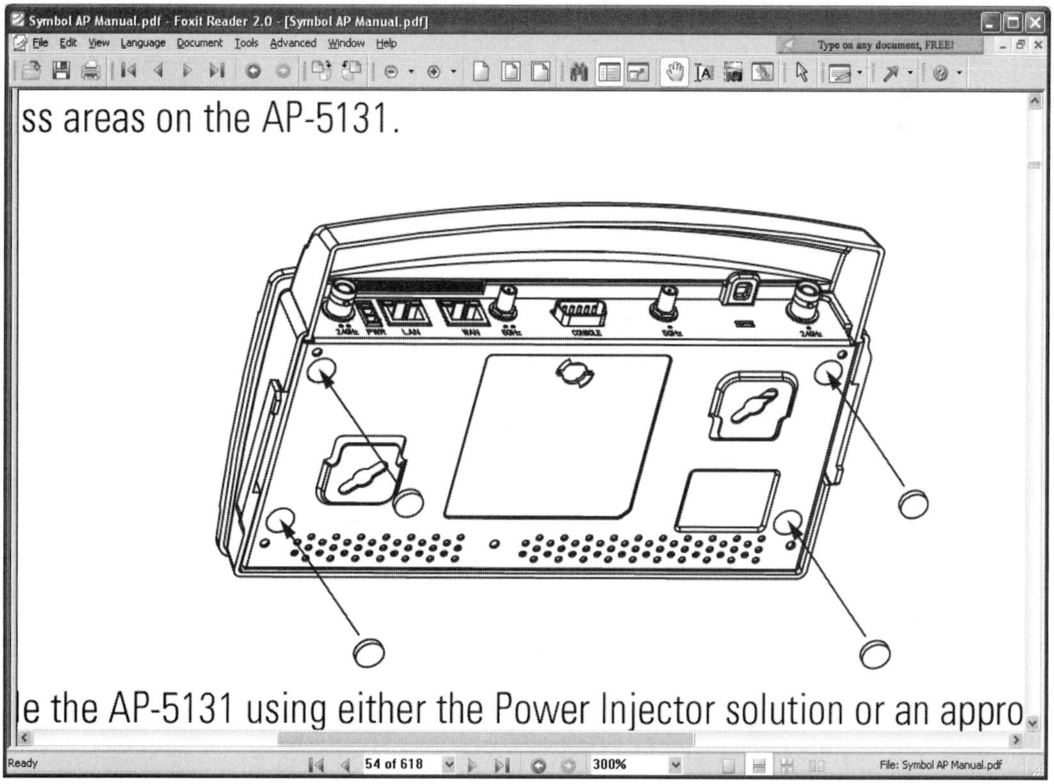

FIGURE 7.18 Ceiling mount pass-through fasteners for tiles

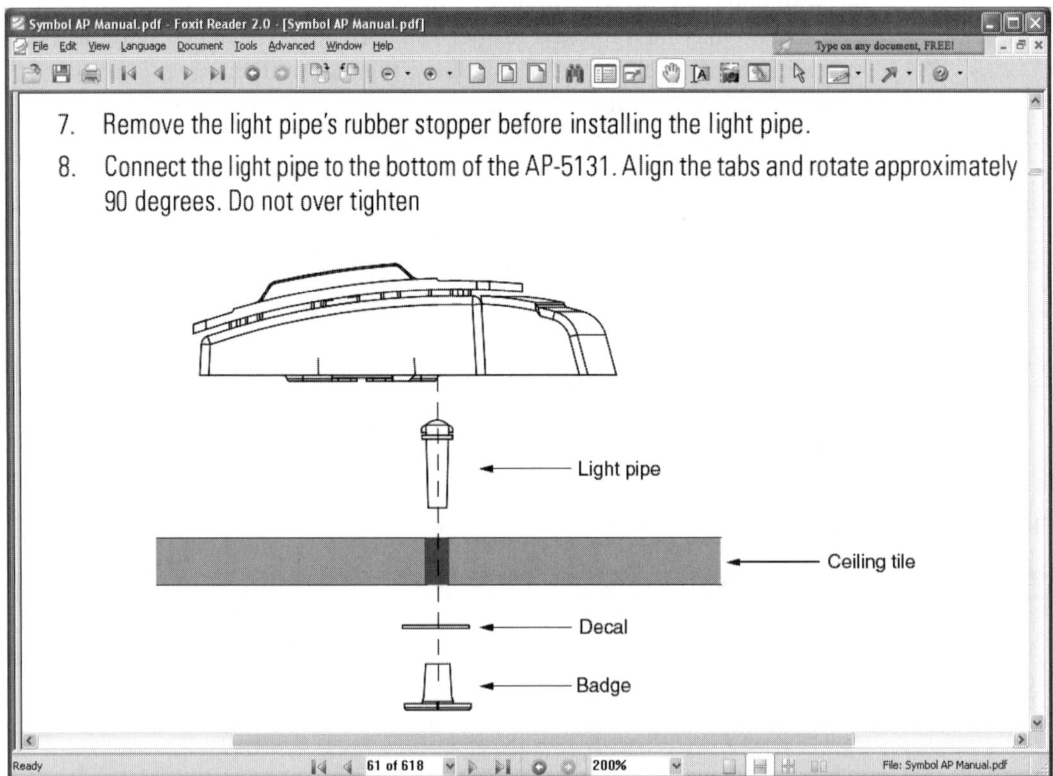

where the AP needs to be placed and then determine the mounting option available to you, given the location. In other words, the mounting method will usually be dictated by the location. The ultimate goal is to provide the proper coverage in the proper location, and this means that mounting methods are secondary.

Another factor to consider when choosing a mounting method is access. Will you be able to access the reset button on the device if needed? Will you be able to view the power and connectivity LEDs to determine operational status? These factors should be considered carefully. If you do not have access to the reset button or the power cord for power cycling, can you implement an AP that supports PoE for power cycling? While this will not provide easy access to configuration resets (as the configuration reset button would), it will allow you to power-cycle the device more easily.

FIGURE 7.19 Pole mount fastening option

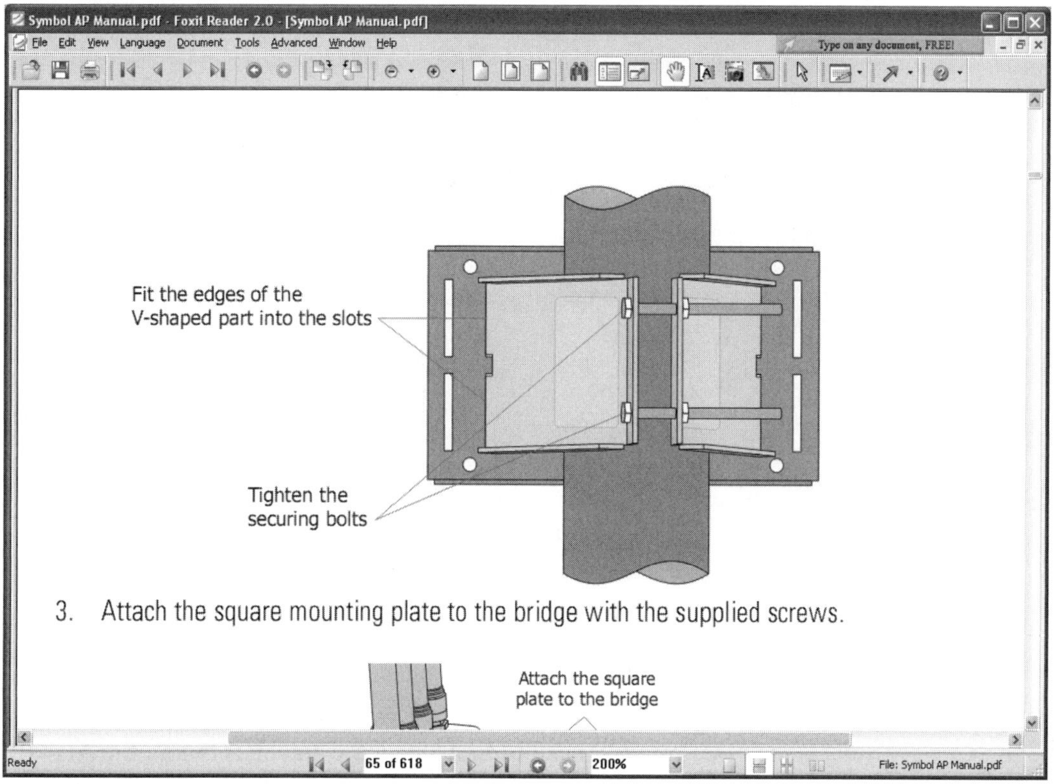

When mounting APs, and other WLAN devices, outdoors, you will need to consider weather issues. For example, will the AP be protected from rain and wind damage? The National Electrical Manufacturers Association (NEMA) has established a set of standards for electrical equipment enclosures. These NEMA enclosures are available for mounting APs and other WLAN devices outdoors. The NEMA Standards Publication 205 defines the various enclosure standards and is available at www.nema.org.

Figure 7.20 shows an example of a NEMA enclosure. In this case, a Symbol AP has been mounted in the enclosure. You can see that standard power connectors are supplied as well as an RF amplifier for connectivity to an external antenna. Consider that the enclosure itself may cause blockage of the RF signal from the antenna so you must mount the antenna in a way that the enclosure is not placed in the path of the RF signal between the antenna and the users.

FIGURE 7.20 NEMA enclosure with Symbol AP

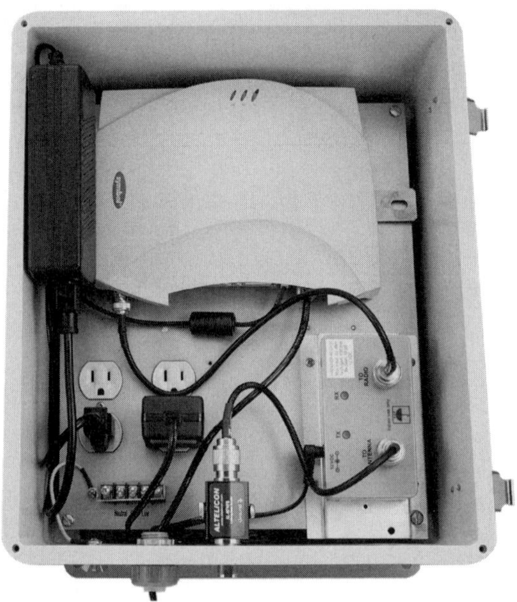

Configuration Process

Many new APs will come out of the box with the antennas detached. If this is the case, you will need to first attach the antennas before the AP will be able to radiate the RF signal. You may wish to wait, but this is really optional, since you will not be connecting the AP to the LAN until you have configured it properly.

As the last sentence suggested, you should configure the AP before connecting it to the actual wired LAN to which it will provide access. This helps to remove the potential for wired-side access before the AP is properly configured and reduces the likelihood that you will provide an entry way into your LAN—though only for a short time—during the configuration window. Most APs come from the factory with little or no security set, so they can certainly provide a point of vulnerability by default.

After the AP is properly configured according to your security policies and configuration standards, you will need to connect the AP to the wired LAN via the Ethernet port. You may also need to connect the antennas if you did not connect them before configuration or if you disconnected them during configuration for security reasons. Antennas should never be disconnected while the radio is enabled to avoid damage to your equipment.

Finally, you should test the AP to ensure that you can connect to it with a client configured with the appropriate security and configuration standards that match with the AP. If you are using an AP model for the first time, you may also want to perform some load testing to verify whether the AP works as advertised (in relation to throughput and concurrent connection) or not. You may need to adjust the number of installed APs according to real-world performance with some devices.

AP Summary

In the end, APs come in many different shapes and sizes, as seen in Figure 7.21. The devices in Figure 7.21 all come from one vendor, and yet they are very different in form factor and capabilities. APs usually support a common set of IEEE standards, security capabilities, and mounting options. Common management interfaces include console, telnet, and web-based interfaces, among others. Most APs that are used in enterprise installations today support SNMP for centralized management and may support custom software provided by the AP vendor. It is important that you as a WLAN administrator understand these options and be able to choose among them effectively.

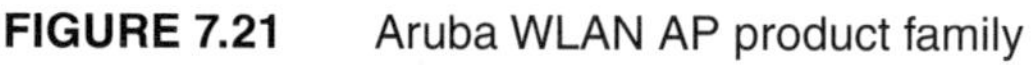

FIGURE 7.21 Aruba WLAN AP product family

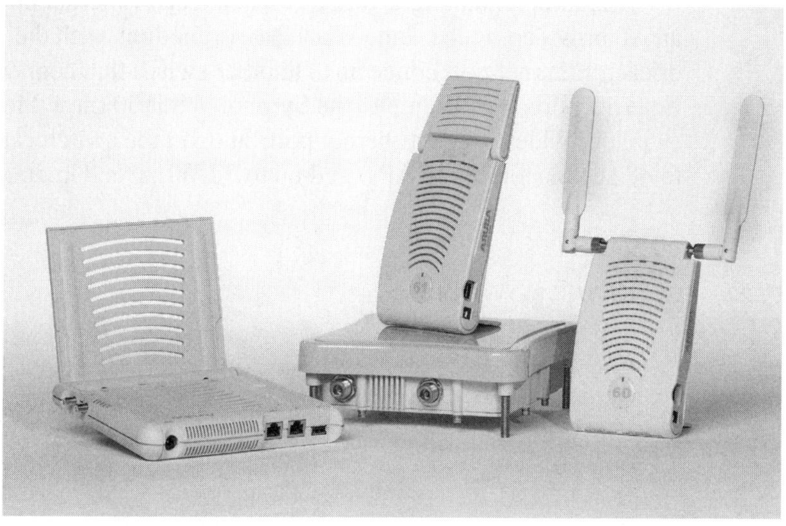

Enterprise WLAN Switches/Controllers

The edge architecture of WLAN APs placed at the edge and configured individually was fine for smaller networks; however, as larger and larger WLANs were implemented, it became apparent that configuring each AP at the edge was no longer feasible. Vendors rushed to create their own solutions to this enterprise-class dilemma. The result was the creation of WLAN switches or controllers. The only major difference between a WLAN switch and a WLAN controller is that the WLAN switch has the controller functionality built into it and the WLAN controller may be in a switch, a router, or some other device. For this reason, I'll use the term WLAN switch to refer to the features and capabilities that are commonly found in WLAN switches with WLAN controller capabilities built in as well as those found in WLAN controller components available as add-ons to routers and other devices.

A WLAN switch contains all or part of the functionality of one or more virtual APs. At first glance, a WLAN switch looks like any other switch when it is configured to have the capabilities of a regular LAN switch with additional support for WLAN control. Other WLAN switches, like the Symbol WS5100 pictured in Figure 7.22, have only a limited number of ports (usually two) and appear very different from standard switches. However, the Symbol WS2000, shown in Figure 7.23, is an example of a WLAN switch that appears to be a standard switch at first glance.

When implementing a WLAN switch, each Ethernet port connects to an AP provided by the same vendor that functions with the WLAN switch, or each Ethernet port connects to another switch that connects to multiple Ethernet ports. For example, the Symbol WS5100 (now Motorola) WLAN switch provides only 2 Ethernet ports and yet the switch can manage up to 48 access ports (thin APs) and up to 32 WLANs. Obviously, with one

FIGURE 7.22 Symbol WS5100 WLAN switch

FIGURE 7.23 Symbol WS2000 WLAN switch with access ports

Ethernet port for the access ports and the other for connectivity to the wired network, there must be a layered switching architecture. Indeed, you would connect 1 LAN switch to the access port Ethernet port and then connect access ports to this switch to provide the 48 access ports with connectivity to the WS5100 WLAN switch.

On the other hand, the WS2000 WLAN switch supports only the number of access ports equal to its Ethernet ports that are designated for access ports or wired devices. For this reason, it is limited to 1–6 access ports. The seventh port seen in Figure 7.23 is actually the WAN uplink port. Figure 7.24 shows the benefit of multiple integrated Ethernet ports in the WLAN switch. Here the WS2000 WLAN switch is handling both the three access ports and the single wired server without the need for extra switches. Imagine a small organization with only WLAN client computers and this single server running Windows Small Business Server or some such all-in-one server application. Further imagine that the WAN port is connected to an Internet router/gateway, and you have a full implementation for such a small organization.

Of course, every WLAN vendor says their WLAN switching solution is best. To be certain, each solution has its benefits and drawbacks. As a WLAN administrator, you must analyze the features offered and then choose the best solution for your implementation. This usually means looking through the vendor literature thoroughly and sometimes requesting test equipment to work with during the analysis phase of your WLAN implementation project. Some vendors will provide the test equipment

FIGURE 7.24 WS2000 switch serving both WLAN access ports and a wired server

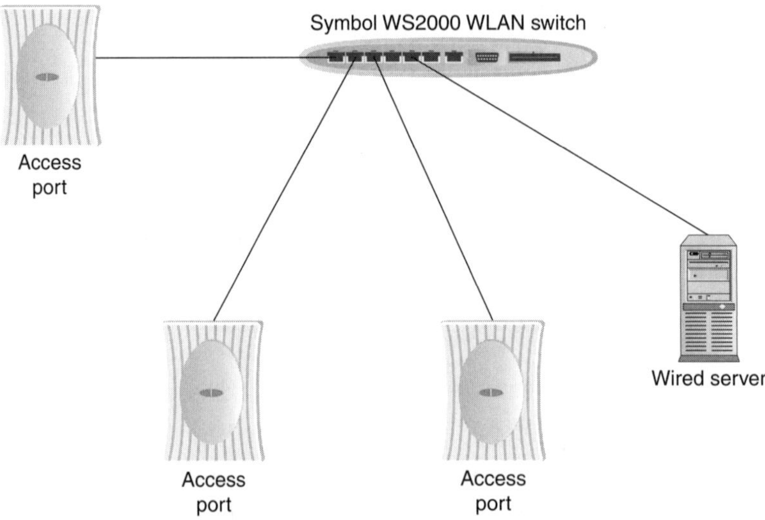

free of charge, and others will come in and perform a demonstration of the equipment for you. The reality is that smaller organizations are less likely to get free sample devices and larger organizations are more likely to get them. If you are in a smaller organization, the product manuals, which are usually available for free download from the vendor web sites, may suffice for your analysis.

When looking through the vendor literature, pay close attention to the IEEE standards that are supported as well as the proprietary ways in which the WLAN will be implemented. Larger vendors usually remain in business for long periods of time or are consumed by other vendors who continue to support their hardware. A perfect example of this is the Symbol hardware that is so common in WLANs. Symbol was acquired by Motorola, but Motorola has continued to support and sell the Symbol WS2000 and WS5100 series WLAN switches, among other devices. The point is this: if you go with a vendor who implements heavy proprietary technologies and their devices simply cannot operate in an IEEE-standard fashion (from a management perspective), you may be forced to replace all the equipment at a later date—possibly an earlier date than expected—if support is lost.

As was described in the Chapter 6, many WLAN switches include built-in site survey capabilities that are either assisted or automated in nature.

The assisted site surveys will require that you walk around within the facility, after a pool of access ports have been installed, with a compatible client that can send signal information back to the WLAN switch. The automated site surveys will simply configure the WLAN according to guidelines you can generally manage centrally at the WLAN switch. The latter method usually requires more overengineering (placing more APs than are absolutely needed), and the former usually requires less; however, many switches support both.

Common Features

Since many of the features of WLAN switches were already covered in the AP section, I will only list the common features here. Remember, a WLAN switch usually centralizes the "AP" processing into the switch and away from the AP. For this reason, WLAN switches often implement the features that are traditionally found in thick or autonomous APs. The following features are common:

- PoE injection into the Ethernet ports (may only be supported on a subset of the ports)
- Built-in firewall capabilities
- Port filtering and MAC address filtering
- Standards-based and proprietary WLAN security technologies such as WPA, WPA2, EAP, and IEEE 802.11i
- VPN tunneling
- Common management interfaces (web, telnet, CLI, SSH, console, etc.)
- Configuration file management
- Activity monitoring and logging
- Built-in RADIUS servers for EAP authentication types
- Redundant WLAN access ports for greater uptimes and easier maintenance
- Rate limiting for the various managed WLANs; this feature is very convenient for setting up two WLANs in the same area—one for VoWLAN (no rate limits) and the other for data (rate limited)
- Hotspot support, including IP redirect to map connections to a specific "starting" page

- RBAC (role-based access control) or identity-driven management (IDM) to provide different levels of access to different users, depending on RADIUS settings
- Voice prioritization for VoWLAN
- CAPWAP compatibility
- Wireless client roaming management and assistance
- QoS, including IEEE 802.1p and IEEE 802.11e
- Internal DHCP server
- Built-in Wireless Intrusion Detection System (WIDS)

For more information on any of the features listed here, or features not listed, be sure to visit the various vendor web sites listed next and download the product manuals for their WLAN switches. These manuals will go into the details of how each vendor implements the WLAN differently and help you understand the general use of WLAN switches in modern wireless networks. Consider visiting the following web sites at a minimum:

- Cisco: www.cisco.com
- Symbol (Motorola): www.symbol.com
- Aruba Networks: www.arubanetworks.com
- Meru Networks: www.merunetworks.com
- Trapeze Networks: www.trapezenetworks.com

Figures 7.25, 7.26, and 7.27 show examples of various WLAN switches. As you can see, some are in traditional rack-mountable encasements, and some use modern encasements that are designed to be positioned on a shelf. Either way, each vendor differentiates its product line by design, but more important, by features and capabilities.

FIGURE 7.25 Meru Networks MC500 WLAN switch, which is targeted at branch offices and SOHO organizations

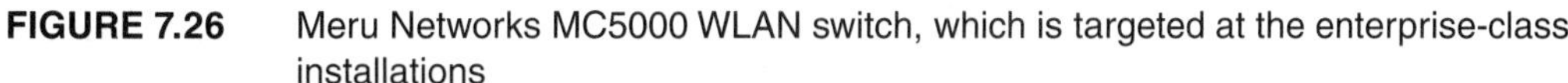

FIGURE 7.26 Meru Networks MC5000 WLAN switch, which is targeted at the enterprise-class installations

Configuration Process

The configuration process will vary depending on the switch vendor you choose; however, the process is generally similar when considered from a less-detailed level. The process usually looks something like this:

1. Perform the initial switch configuration.
2. Configure WLANs in the switch.
3. Connect access ports to the switch.
4. Ensure access ports are properly enabled and configured.

The first step is to perform the initial switch configuration. This usually entails specifying which port will be used for WLAN access port connectivity and which port will be used for WAN uplinks (may be a LAN link if it is used only locally and not for connecting to the Internet). If the WLAN switch contains multiple ports for connections to access ports or wired devices, you may configure the proper use of each port.

FIGURE 7.27 Aruba Networks WLAN switch, aimed at SOHO and branch office implementations

Next, you will need to determine if you are going to support one virtual WLAN or multiple virtual WLANs. Some switches will support multiple WLANs with one access port, and others will require multiple access ports to support multiple WLANs. You will need to determine the security settings and other configuration options for each WLAN or allow the switch to automatically select some or all of these features.

Now you are ready to connect the access ports and have them detected by the WLAN switch. Some systems will support autonomous APs as well, but they must be converted to behave as thin APs. This may be an automatic process of the WLAN switch, or you may have to perform some configuration changes manually.

Finally, ensure that the access ports are working properly and that you have the needed WLAN access in the needed locations. This will involve inspection through the WLAN switch management interface first. You will need to be sure everything "looks" right in the switch. Second, you will need to use a laptop or some other WLAN client device to connect to the WLAN or WLANs in the various locations to ensure that the WLAN is functioning as you need it to function.

Remember, each vendor's installation procedure will be different. Check with the vendors to see how their installation procedures fit into the generic installation process described here. You will usually find that they simply require specific and different steps within each of these four phases.

Remote Office WLAN Switches/Controllers

Switches like the Symbol WS2000 and the Meru MC500 are designed for branch offices and SOHO implementations. The key feature that usually qualifies these devices as *remote office* WLAN switches is the ability to implement a VPN tunnel. For example, consider the implementation in Figure 7.28. Here the VPN tunnel is created between the WAN port on the WS2000 switch at the remote office and the VPN server/concentrator at the Corporate HQ. This will be an IPsec-based tunnel and will provide authentication and encryption for the connection. This allows for one device—the WS2000 switch—to act as the VPN server/client, the WLAN switch/controller and the wired switch at the remote office.

FIGURE 7.28 Symbol WS2000 switch used to create a VPN tunnel

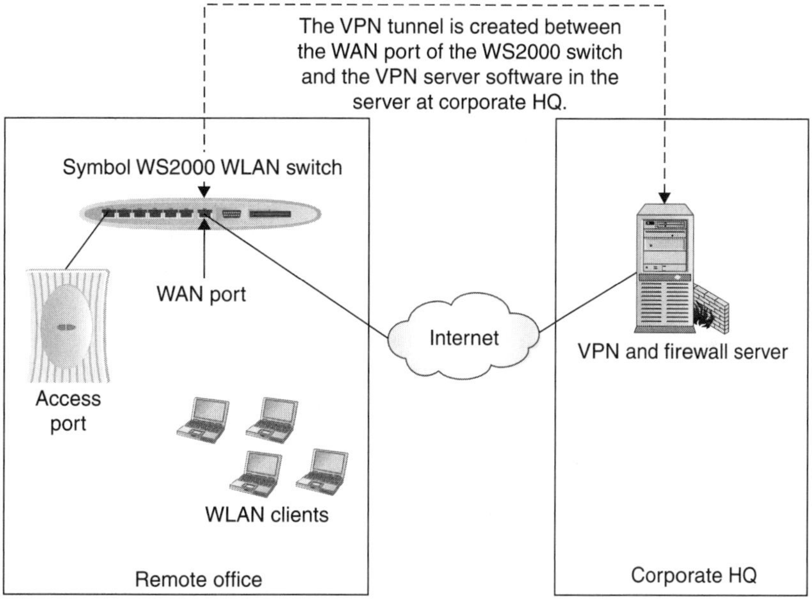

Because remote office WLAN switches are not intended to handle the workload of the enterprise-class WLAN switches, they are usually less powerful, less feature-rich, and less costly.

PoE Injectors and Switches

I have mentioned PoE multiple times already in this chapter. This is because the technology has proliferated in the WLAN market and many APs, switches, bridges, and other WLAN devices now support it. PoE is a method used to deliver DC voltage to a device over CAT5 cable. This DC voltage is used instead of a standard AC power outlet to power the device. (Most devices come with converters that convert AC power to DC power. PoE sends the power directly as DC power.)

CAT5 cables have four pairs of wires in them. Only two pairs are used to carry the data. This leaves the other two pairs for other purposes. In the case of PoE, the purpose is to carry power to the device being powered. In WLANs, these devices include APs, bridges, repeaters, and possibly other devices. Some implementations use the same pairs of wire that carry the data to carry the DC voltage, and some implementations use the extra pairs in the CAT5 cabling to carry the DC voltage separate from the data.

As I stated earlier in this chapter, one of the most common reasons for using PoE is to power a WLAN device where no AC power outlets are available. The other benefit of implementing PoE is the ability to cycle the device being powered from remote. This latter feature is usually available only when the PoE is being provided by a managed switch. The management interface of the switch will allow you to turn off the power on a given PoE-enabled port and then turn it back on. Power cycling is not supported by all PoE-enabled switches.

Yet another advantage of using PoE is that a licensed electrician is not usually required to install it. This is because the voltage that is running across the CAT5 cabling is so low. Most tech savvy individuals can run the cables and use PoE. There will likely be no building codes that will dictate specific guidelines for running the cabling and powering the end location. Figure 7.29 shows the way PoE would be utilized with an in-line PoE power injector, and Figure 7.30 shows the way PoE would be utilized with a PoE-enabled switch.

It is important that you know that PoE-enabled switches do not always provide power through all ports; in fact, they seldom do. Sometimes half of the available Ethernet ports are PoE enabled, and sometimes fewer than half can provide DC power to devices. Be sure to check the vendor's documentation to verify the number of PoE ports being provided by the WLAN switch or standard Ethernet switch you are implementing.

FIGURE 7.29 PoE with an in-line injector

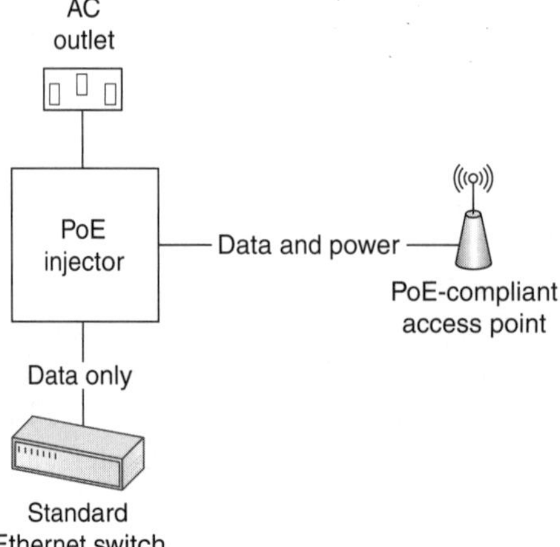

FIGURE 7.30 PoE with a PoE-enabled switch

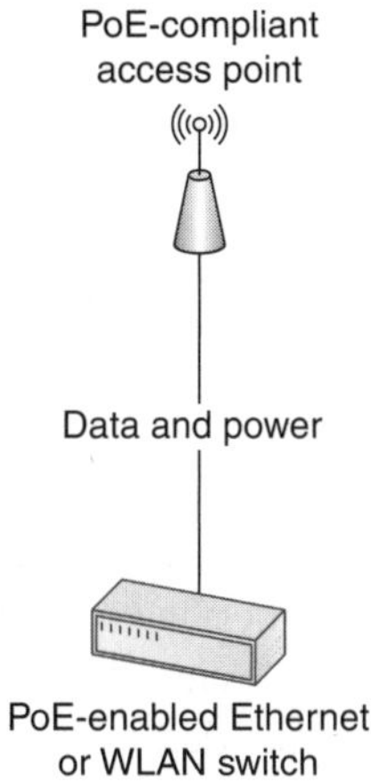

Common Features

There are different types of devices that can provide voltage through CAT5 cables, which power PoE-enabled devices. These types include single-port DC voltage injectors, multiport DC voltage injectors, and PoE-enabled switches.

The single-port PoE injectors will have a single input port and a single output port. The input port is where you connect the Ethernet cable that connects to the network's switch or hub, and the output port is where you connect the Ethernet cable that connects to the device to be powered. Figure 7.31 shows an example of a single-port PoE injector from ZyXEL Technologies (ZyXEL PoE-12). When using a single-port PoE power

FIGURE 7.31 Single-port PoE injector

injector like this, the power injector itself must be plugged into a standard power outlet. This means you will likely place the power injector in the closet (or location) with the switch or hub and not closer to the device being powered. Due to the number of power outlets required, single-port power injectors are recommended when only one or two devices need to be powered.

A multiport PoE power injector is really just a group of Ethernet input ports that pass through a power injection module and then pass on to a matching group of Ethernet output ports. These devices are usually also installed closer to the switch or hub and farther from the powered device. This is due to the likelihood of having a power outlet where the switch or hub is located, since the switch or hub will need power as well. Because multiport power injectors can power multiple devices but only require one power outlet connection, they are recommended in medium to large installations that require from 3 to 20 powered devices (though this is not an absolute cutoff point). When more devices require power, you will likely opt for a PoE-enabled switch.

Large enterprises and networks with more than 20 PoE-powered devices will likely choose to move up to PoE-enabled switches. These switches include power injection in the same unit that is the Ethernet switch. It means powering fewer devices through standard power outlets and reducing the number of components that can fail at any given moment. When you use a single-port power injector with an access point, you introduce multiple points of failure. Imagine there are 20 APs that you need to power in this way. You would need 40 CAT5 cables (20 from the switch to the power injectors and 20 from the power injectors to the APs), 20 power injectors, 20 power cords, 20 APs, and at least 1 switch. This means a total of 101 individual components that could fail and statistically increases the likelihood that you will have a failure at any given time. If you use a switch like the Cisco 3750-E switch that can provide PoE power injection on up to 48 ports, you reduce the components involved to only 41 components. You've eradicated the need for 20 CAT5 cables, 20 power cords, and 20 power injectors. The likelihood of a failure at any given moment has now been greatly reduced.

In addition to the failure probability reduction, you are gaining the benefit I discussed previously of being able to power-cycle the APs from a central location. With the single-port power injectors, you would still have to go to the physical location where the power injector is located and unplug it and then plug it back in (or flip an on/off switch if it is available). Figure 7.32 shows the Cisco 3750 line of switches with PoE capabilities.

FIGURE 7.32 Cisco 3750 switch with PoE capabilities

The 3750-E model is the one that provides power injection as a possibility for all 48 ports.

An additional benefit of PoE-enabled switches is that you do not usually have to enable PoE on all ports. For example, you can use some of the ports for wired devices or non-PoE APs and bridges while you use the other ports for PoE-enabled devices. This provides you with flexibility and is a valid argument for purchasing a switch that supports PoE from the factory or at least purchasing one that can have PoE support added at a later time.

Power over Ethernet (PoE) (IEEE 802.3-2005, Clause 33)

IEEE 802.3-2005 merged the older IEEE 802.3af PoE amendment into the core standard document. The old amendment is now known as Clause 33 in the IEEE 802.3-2005 document. Many, even most, vendors—at this time—are still referencing the standard as IEEE 802.3af, but you should know that it has been rolled into the primary standard now. If you download or access the IEEE 802.3-2005 standard in sections, Clause 33 is in the section 2 PDF file.

The standard defines a powered device (PD) and Power Sourcing Equipment (PSE). The APs we've discussed that support PoE would be examples of PDs. The power injectors and PoE-enabled switches would be examples of PSEs. The clause specifies five elements:

- A power source that adds power to the cabling system
- The characteristics of a powered device's load on the power source and cabling

- A protocol allowing the detection of a device that requires power
- An optional classification method for devices depending on power level requirements
- A method for scaling supplied power back to the detect level when power is no longer requested or needed

The standard then spends the next 57 pages providing the details of this system. You will not be required to understand the in-depth details of PoE for the CWNA exam (although this IEEE document can act as your source for more information); however, you should be familiar with the following two terms: midspan and endpoint power injectors.

The standard specifies that a PSE (power injector) located coincident with (inside) the switch (technically, the data terminal equipment or DTE in the standards) should be called an *endpoint PSE.* It also specifies that a PSE located between the switch and the powered device should be called a *midspan PSE.* WLAN switches and LAN switches with integrated PoE support would qualify as endpoint PSEs, assuming they are IEEE 802.3-2005 compliant. Multiport and single-port injectors would qualify as midspan PSEs, assuming they are IEEE 802.3-2005 compliant.

The IEEE 802.3-2005, Clause 33 specifications define five classes of powered devices. These classes are identified as Class 0 through Class 4. Class 0, which is the default for PoE implementations, uses a 15.4-watt minimum power level. Classes 1, 2, and 3 use minimum power levels of 4.0, 7.0, and 15.4 watts, respectively. Class 4 is reserved for future use. All PoE powered devices that pull a current of greater than 51 milliamps (mA) are classified as Class 0 devices. PoE devices with current levels less than 51 mA are classified as one of the five classes based on the mA range measured by the PSE. For more information, see the IEEE 802.3-2005 standard document.

Fault Protection

One final note about PoE: fault protection, is very important. Fault protection does the work of protecting the devices that are being powered by power injection or that are providing the power injection. A fault occurs when a short-circuit or some other surge in power occurs in the PoE chain. Faults can occur for the following reasons:

- A device does not support PoE but uses the extra two pins used by PoE or for some reason short-circuits the pins.
- An engineer connects an incorrectly wired CAT5 cable.

Due to the nature of things, the latter cause seems to be more common. I know I have inadvertently "miswired" a CAT5 cable or two in my time. It's fairly easy to do, since you're dealing with small wires using big fingers and crimpers that haven't been upgraded or improved for a few decades. When a fault occurs, the power injector should shut off DC injection onto the CAT5 cable in the path of the fault. Depending on the power injection device, you may need to manually reset the power injector or it may monitor the line and automatically reset when the fault is cleared.

WLAN Bridges

Early on, there was little difference between WLAN bridges and WLAN APs other than their intended use. Today, WLAN bridges often provide capabilities not provided by APs in bridge mode, and APs often provide capabilities beyond what a WLAN bridge placed in AP mode can provide. This is because there is a limited amount of RAM and processing power in these devices and features or capabilities must be sacrificed to provide the best support for the intended use.

It is important to note that the IEEE 802.11 standards do not specify a bridging mode or describe a WLAN bridge device. However, WLAN bridging usually employs some proprietary modifications to the WLAN MAC layer and also incorporates much of the IEEE 802.11 standard for the MAC layer. In some cases, the bridges will implement both a standard IEEE 802.11 MAC and the proprietary bridging capabilities at the exact same time. While it may be possible to create a bridge link with two WLAN bridges from two different vendors, it is not recommended. This is because they may be incompatible with each other and you'll only lose valuable installation time trying to get them to work together. Because of proprietary bridging methods that may be implemented, the devices may not work together.

In a wired network, a bridge is a device that connects two otherwise disconnected networks and quite often converts between one network type and another. WLAN bridges may perform this type of function where two WLAN bridges associate with each other and bridge two wired LANs across the IEEE 802.11 link. They may also work to bridge between a WLAN and a wired LAN, such as a wireless workgroup bridge.

There are two fundamental modes of operation for wireless bridges: root and non-root. There are multiple usage scenarios that include various mixtures and configurations of these two modes. Generally speaking, only one wireless bridge can be in root mode and any number of wireless bridges can be in non-root mode; however, modern bridge devices also allow for creative combinations of non-root-mode and standard AP functionality.

FIGURE 7.33 PtP link with bridges specified for root mode and non-root mode

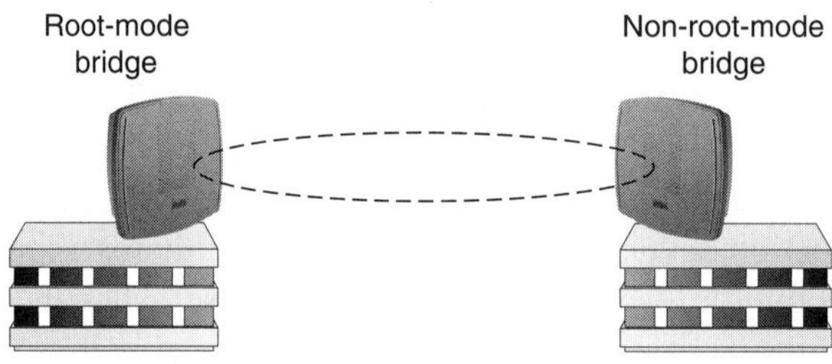

When one bridge is in root mode and only one other bridge is associated with it, that other bridge must be in non-root mode. This type of link is a point-to-point (PtP) link and is common between buildings. When one bridge is in root mode and multiple other bridges associate with it, those other bridges must be in non-root mode. This type of link configuration is a point-to-multipoint (PtMP) configuration. Figures 7.33 and 7.34 show PtP and PtMP links, respectively.

The Cisco Aironet 1310 Outdoor bridge is seen in Figures 7.33 and 7.34 and is shown in Figure 7.35 in large scale. This bridge can function as an AP

FIGURE 7.34 PtMP links with bridges specified for root mode and non-root mode

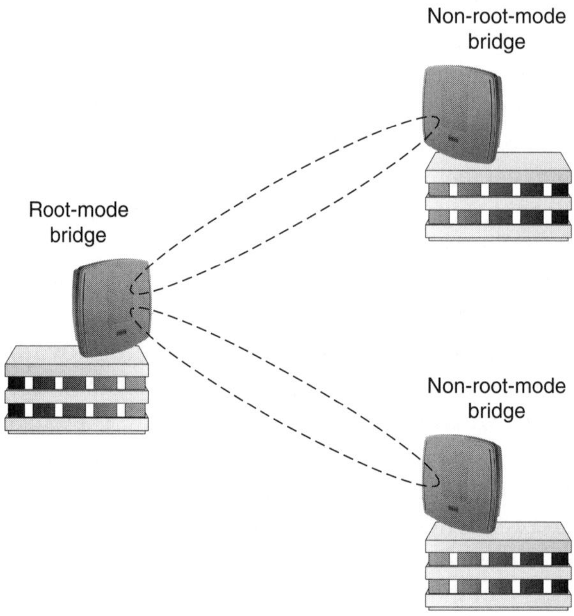

FIGURE 7.35 Cisco 1310 outdoor bridge

as well as a bridge. Additionally, many bridges from various vendors can perform in the following modes:

- Root bridge, which is the same as previously described
- Non-root bridge without clients, which is the same as previously described
- Non-root bridge with clients, which acts as an AP and a bridge at the same time (this is similar to a repeater, only it connects to a root bridge instead of a standard AP)

In addition to these modes of operation, many bridges can act as a root-mode AP (a standard AP), a repeater AP, and even a site survey client. Other bridges, like the 3COM WL-565B (outdoor) and WL-565 (indoor), can only operate in the root and non-root bridge modes.

It is absolutely essential that you remember the rules for root and non-root bridge modes. Only one bridge in a link or set of links can act as the root bridge at a time. In a PtP link, one unit is the root bridge and one is the non-root bridge. In a PtMP link set, one is the root and the others are non-root bridges.

Bridge Alignment

APs usually operate in an environment where the signal goes out from the AP's antenna in all directions or in a wide swath. This is because they are usually serving clients that are within a few feet or yards. Wireless bridges are different. They are used to create connections that span a few hundred feet to a few miles. For this reason, alignment is crucial. As an illustration of why alignment is more important at greater distances, consider Figure 7.36. Notice how the bottom set of circles shows that the line of sight misses the arrow in the left of the two circles completely from the farther distance. The top set of circles shows that, even though the alignment is off by the same angle, the line of sight still connects with the arrow in the left circle when the two circles are closer together.

In much the same way, two bridges that are farther apart are more sensitive to alignment issues. You can also demonstrate this sensitivity with a flashlight that can focus the light beam. Shine the beam on a wall near you and move it as slightly as you can. You will likely notice a small change in its location on the wall. Now shine it on a wall trace as far from you and move it in the same way. The movement will be much greater because of the distance between you and the wall.

You can align bridges using many methods, including

- Monitoring of RSSI or signal strength while slightly adjusting the bridges.
- Through LEDs that signify alignments. Cisco's Aironet 1400 series bridge has such a feature.

FIGURE 7.36 The importance of alignment at greater distances

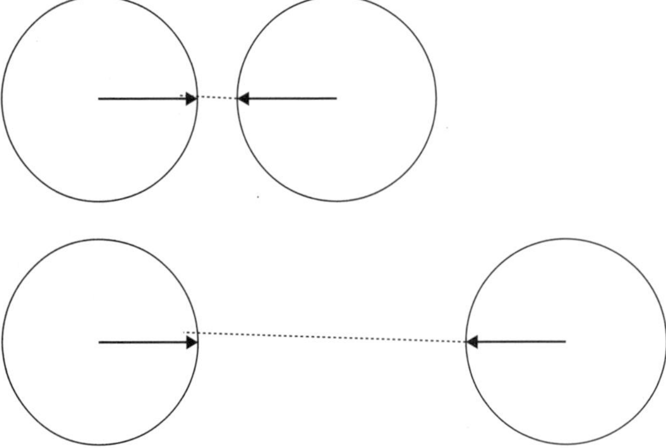

- Using a voltmeter that attaches to a connector on the bridge. The higher voltage reading indicates better alignment.
- For close bridge links, less than 200 or 300 yards within a campus, you may be able to perform data throughput tests to verify acceptable alignment. This may be helpful with less-expensive bridges or when using APs in bridge mode, since they are less likely to have alignment features.

When you are implementing very long-distance links (more than 2–5 kilometers), you may choose to use GPS equipment to assist in the location of your bridges. Due to terrain issues and other factors, such as weather, that have greater impact over longer distances, it is recommended that you attend training courses that focus specifically on building long-distance wireless links. The knowledge given here should be sufficient for a WLAN administrator, but you will need more in-depth knowledge if you plan to implement what could be called WAN links using standard IEEE 802.11 hardware.

Wireless Workgroup Bridge

A *wireless workgroup bridge (WGB)* is used to provide wireless access to a group of wired stations behind the bridge. You would typically install a WGB with the Ethernet port connected to a hub or switch that the local wired devices are also connected to. The WGB will then associate with an AP and bridge communications from the local wired devices to the wireless AP across the association link. Remember the repeater mode of an AP? This is very similar, only when an AP is in repeater mode, it is using its radio as both the AP to the distant clients and the client to the root-mode AP. When in WGB mode, a wireless bridge uses its Ethernet port to connect with distant wired clients and then it uses its radio to create a link to the AP that is in root mode.

Residential WLAN Gateways

Residential WLAN gateways are really just SOHO wireless routers such as the Linksys WRT54G or the D-Link DI-524 routers. Figure 7.37 shows the D-Link router.

Residential WLAN gateways share a common set of features, such as

- Support for standards (IEEE 802.11, HR/DSSS, ERP, OFDM, etc.)
- Security, including WPA/WPA2, IEEE 802.11i, 802.1X authentication
- VPN pass-through and sometimes VPN endpoints

FIGURE 7.37 D-Link DI-524 router

- Usually only web-based management, but sometimes telnet is included as well as custom applications
- Built-in firewall features
- Packet filtering and MAC filtering
- Ethernet ports as well as WLAN functionality
- Authentication when required by ISPs

While these WLAN routers are effective for home use and small offices, they cannot usually keep up with the workload in larger organizations. For this reason, enterprise installations seldom include WLAN routers, with the exception of meeting rooms or small departments. Even then, given the choice, most WLAN administrators would prefer to simply install an AP and manage it from the central network. SOHO implementations and home offices are still prime candidates for the utilization of wireless routers.

Enterprise Encryption Gateways

Enterprise encryption gateways (EEGs) sit between the WLAN (including the APs) and the wired LAN. EEGs like those pictured in Figure 7.38 require a secure client be installed on the wireless client STAs. This client software takes care of the encryption and authentication and manages the exchanges between the client and the EEG. Fortress Technologies also offers a secure client bridge, which is a hardware device that sits between a wired client (such as a printer or manufacturing device) that cannot run the secure client. The bridge connects wirelessly to an AP and then to the EEG to provide security to the wired client device. The wired client device is effectively turned into a secure wireless client through the use of the secure client bridge.

In enterprise implementations, EEGs like the AF7500 (shown in Figure 7.38) or the Fortress FC-X series (not shown) can be implemented and centrally controlled. Fortress Technologies, for example, provides MaPS (Management and Policy Server). MaPS can centrally configure multiple Fortress FC-X, AF7500, or AF 2100 EEGs.

It is important that you understand that the vendors seldom, if ever, call their devices enterprise encryption gateways. The vendors refer to these type of devices in different ways, and the CWNP Program has chosen to call a device that fits the description of an enterprise encryption gateway by this name. You might generically define an EEG as

> *A device that is installed upstream between the WLAN and the wired LAN that provides encryption and authentication management for the WLAN clients.*

To further clarify, an EEG encrypts the data between the WLAN clients and the EEG and sends decrypted data out the "upstream" side of the EEG. Consider the installation represented in Figure 7.39. You can see that multiple APs are linked to the EEG and that Windows CE–based VoWLAN phones, PDAs, and Windows laptop clients are all secured when connected with the WLAN and using the secure client. Note that, just as with encryption between an AP and a client, the wired side of the EEG that is upstream to the LAN is not encrypted.

WLAN Mesh Routers

WLAN *mesh routers* are devices that use proprietary Layer 2 protocols to form a mesh network. These networks are usually said to be self-forming,

FIGURE 7.38 Fortress Technologies security gateways

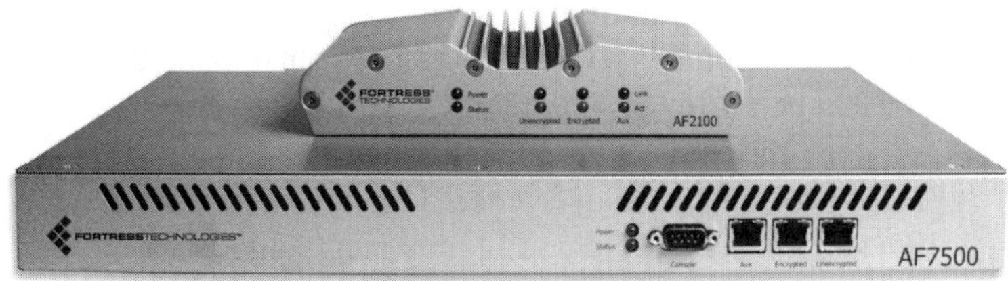

FIGURE 7.39 EEG installation in WLAN

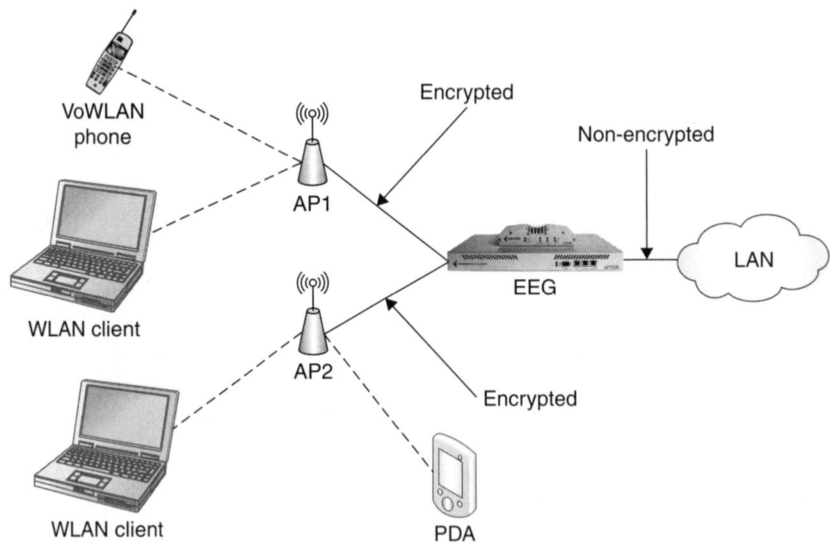

self-healing, and self-configuring. They are self-forming because they scan for other nearby mesh routers and form associations with them automatically. They are self-healing because they will automatically discover new routes to a destination as previously used routes become unavailable. They are self-configuring because they configure their routing tables and many other settings dynamically according to the discovered network topology.

The protocols that manage this self-forming, self-healing, and self-configuring process are the proprietary Layer 2 routing protocols. These proprietary protocols (meaning they are unique to each vendor) determine routing paths and other variables by inspecting signal strength and quality from neighboring mesh routers.

Don't let the term router confuse you here. WLAN mesh routers route through the radio interfaces. They may use one radio interface to both receive and retransmit frames, or they may have dual radio interfaces (or more) and have the ability to receive and transmit on all interfaces.

Some vendors do not call this feature mesh networking. Some simply specify that the distribution system (DS) does not have to be a wired network (assuming you are using a DS outside the built-in DS in the AP) but can be a wireless link to other APs. For example, the 3COM WL546 supports the use of a wireless distribution system (WDS), which can support PtP, PtMP, and multilayer links. The difference is that the 3COM WDS does not support self-forming. You must manually create all the links in each AP;

however, you can specify redundant links so that the network becomes self-healing after configuration. These types of networks are not usually called mesh networks, because they lack the self-forming characteristic.

WLAN Markets and Appropriate Gear

As a WLAN administrator, it is essential that you understand how to select the appropriate equipment for your network. You may find yourself implementing a WLAN that includes only a single AP and a handful of WLAN clients. You could also find yourself working with a WLAN with more than 1000 APs and tens of thousands of clients. Because of this, you must know how to select the appropriate gear.

There are three general categories of organizations that you may find yourself working in: SOHO, SMB, and Enterprise. The small office/home office (SOHO) usually includes fewer than 10 users and no more than 1 AP. A single AP can usually service this small number of users, and the need for a WLAN switch or centralized architecture is minimized, if not completely removed.

The small and medium-sized businesses (SMB) may find centralization beneficial, and WLAN vendors have developed hardware that is specifically designed for them. For example, the Meru MC500, Aruba 200, and Symbol WS2000 WLAN switches are perfect fits for organizations with up to roughly 30 APs. Since each AP may be servicing 10–20 users, these technologies can easily handle a few hundred users. The size of an SMB varies, depending on who is setting the number. I've seen vendors that say an SMB is any organization up to 1000 users, and I've seen vendors that stretch this number to 2500. Certainly hundreds of users can be supported by these entry-level WLAN switches. Figures 7.40 and 7.41 show examples of these SMB market WLAN switches.

FIGURE 7.40 Meru MC500 SMB WLAN switch

FIGURE 7.41 Aruba 200 SMB WLAN switch

Of course, enterprise-class WLANs require the more robust and powerful capabilities and features of enterprise WLAN switches, which also come with enterprise-class price tags. This is one reason vendors often create scaled-down versions of their WLAN switches for smaller organizations. The smaller organizations simply cannot justify the cost of the enterprise-class hardware. The Aruba 6000 switch shown in Figure 7.42 is an example of an enterprise-class WLAN switch, in addition to the Cisco and Symbol (WS5100) switches shown earlier in this chapter. This switch (actually called a mobility controller) can support hundreds of WLAN APs. In addition, it supports the standard features expected in a WLAN switch in the enterprise class.

FIGURE 7.42 Aruba 6000 enterprise WLAN switch

New WLAN Solutions

The WLAN market has been evolving at a very rapid pace for the last 6 or 7 years, and it doesn't show any signs of slowing yet. Because of this rapid growth, vendors are continually looking for ways to improve on WLAN technologies. Some vendors are doing this by improving traditional hardware like the example of the Cisco 3750g switch described in the next section. Other vendors are making improvements by providing wireless technology convergence capabilities; an example is the Symbol RFS7000 RF switch covered after that. Regardless of the approach taken, there are three trends already occurring and that will continue into the foreseeable future:

- Improving manageability
- Wireless technology convergence
- Increased data rates

While there are other trends and multiple devices coming to market that illustrate these trends, I'll focus only on these three. Additionally, I will feature only one product in each of the three areas, though I will feature a different product in each area. You should not assume these are the only products or vendors moving in these directions, as these are the typical trends seen with most WLAN vendors today.

Improving Manageability

Manageability becomes more important as WLANs grow larger. WLANs become larger as more users begin using the technology. As more users begin using the technology, more additional users begin to see its benefit and start using it too. I'm sure you can see how this cycle leads to rapid growth in WLANs and, therefore, an increased need for management simplification.

This trend is not new, as it started years ago with WLAN controllers, enterprise wireless gateways, and WLAN management software. As with any evolving market, one of these listed technologies (enterprise wireless gateways) has already been forgotten; however, this process of management simplification has not been forgotten and many vendors are revealing new technologies that make great improvements in these areas.

As an example of this, consider the Cisco 3750g switch, which includes an embedded Cisco 4400 WLAN controller. These switches can be stacked up to nine high and support a new technology known as Stackwise Technology. This technology makes the interconnected switches behave as one. This means there is one IP address and one management interface through which all of the switches are managed and configured. If you have one Cisco 3750g switch installed and configured and need to grow your network at a later time, you will simply need to add on another switch and connect it to the Stackwise Technology connector. The old switch (which will be acting as the master) will detect the new switch and update its software if necessary. It will then automatically configure the new switch with its own configuration parameters so that it is as if you've just added more ports to the existing switch. At this point, the new switch is brought online, and all of this happens without your intervention (aside from connecting the new switch).

Additionally, each switch in the stack can be uplinked through different routes to various destinations to provide fault tolerance in the connectivity to the different parts of your network. This automatic failover of uplinks means that you will have to intervene less often when links fail or ports go out. Figure 7.43 shows the Cisco 3750g switch. Cisco recommends the 3750g switch for customers with 250 users or more.

Wireless Technology Convergence

The Symbol RFS7000 (see Figure 7.44) switch contains everything you would expect in a modern WLAN switch and then some. The new feature that is most interesting to us here is the convergence of WLAN, RFID, and even WiMAX. Because of the inclusion of wireless technologies other than WLANs, Symbol has referenced the RFS7000 as an *RF switch* instead of a traditional WLAN switch. The key component here is that one device—the RFS7000—can manage your WLAN, RFID, VoWLAN, and WiMAX technologies. Instead of learning and using multiple management interfaces, one tool provides the

FIGURE 7.43 Cisco 3750g WLAN-enabled switch

FIGURE 7.44 Symbol RFS7000 RF switch

management of them all. We are likely to see other vendors moving in this direction as well, since so many organizations are implementing varied RF-based wireless technologies from Bluetooth to ZigBee to RFID.

Increased Data Rates

Finally, even though IEEE 802.11n is still incomplete and may not see ratification until 2008 or later, many vendors are already offering hardware based on the draft of the standard. These devices offer, at least, twice the data rate of the current ERP and OFDM PHY-based WLAN devices, and the final standard may actually provide for even greater data rates. Much as wired networks moved from 300-baud modem speeds to Gigabit Ethernet, WLAN technologies are moving rapidly closer to the gigabit speeds as well. Already, we've gone from 1–2 Mbps in the late 90s to 54 Mbps before we left the 90s (OFDM) and in the early part of this decade (ERP). Now we are looking at doubling the date rate—at a minimum—before this decade is out.

As WLAN data rates increase, it will become easier to implement eLearning solutions, video conferencing, VoWLAN, and other bandwidth-intensive or low-latency-dependent applications. Of course, if history is a teacher, we'll find other ways to use the bandwidth almost as quickly as it is created. We've only recently seen wide-scale installations of broadband Internet access for home users, and already thousands watch streaming videos at web sites from around the world.

Location Tracking with WLAN Solutions

Cisco offers a location appliance (Cisco Location Appliance 2700) that integrates APs and RFID tags for asset tracking and management. The system can map the location of assets based on RSSI information retrieved

FIGURE 7.45 Newbury Location Appliance

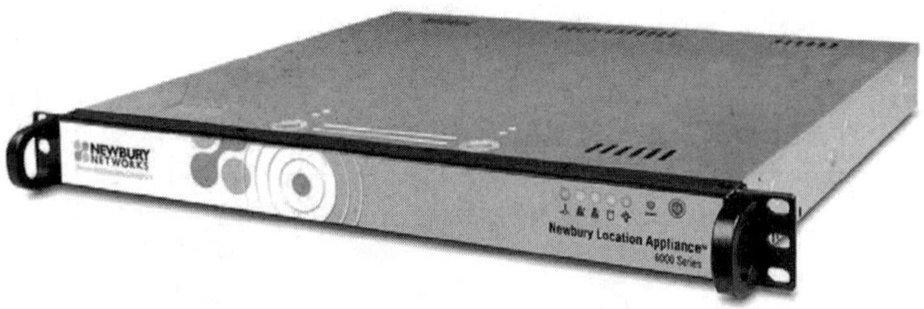

by the 2700 location appliance. The special tags used for asset tracking may require batteries, such as AAA batteries, depending on the tag vendor you select. Of course, this system does not directly protect you from the loss of battery power and then subsequent movement of the item. The system can, however, report the last location of the tracked item.

Cisco is not the only vendor to provide such a device. Newbury Networks released an asset tracking device in the last quarter of 2006. Called the Newbury Location Appliance, this device competes directly with the Cisco 2700 device and even supports some of the identical RFID vendor tags, such as those provided by PanGo. Figure 7.45 shows the Newbury Location Appliance.

The RFID tags used with these systems are called 802.11 RFID tags in that they use the 802.11 standard to communicate with standard APs. These APs pass their information back to the location appliance. Since the RFID tags are continually able to provide information about their location (either on request or at regular intervals), real-time location tracking is available.

Implementing Voice-Capable WLANs

The full scale of implementing VoWLAN is beyond the scope of this book and the CWNA certification; however, you will need to know the basic components involved in creating a VoWLAN implementation. This section defines these components.

VoWLAN Overview

Voice over IP (VoIP) has been implemented heavily in the wired LAN arena for a number of years. Early attempts at implementing VoWLAN encountered difficulties due to latency and the lack of QoS mechanisms in WLANs. However, modern WLAN switches and APs have come a long way in this area and implementing VoWLAN is more feasible than ever.

In order to implement VoWLAN, you will need the following components at a minimum:

- VoWLAN phone
- WLAN infrastructure
- Call management software

In addition to these, if you plan to allow VoWLAN clients to place calls to PSTN phones, you will need a voice gateway.

The VoWLAN phone or wireless IP phone is an appliance similar to a cell phone in appearance, but very different in functionality. These devices associate with IEEE 802.11 APs rather than cell towers, and they depend on a VoIP infrastructure to function. Wireless IP phones usually support the following features:

- IP address assignment
- VLAN support
- Security
- Firmware updates
- IEEE standards support
- Output power adjustments
- Support for specific APs

The last feature, support for specific APs, is very important. All wireless IP phones will not work with all APs. You should verify this with the vendor. It is also important to note that, at this point, most wireless IP phones only support HR/DSSS and not ERP. This means APs providing VoWLAN access will have to run in a protection mode that reduces overall throughput. This is one of the most common arguments for implementing a WLAN for VoWLAN and a separate WLAN for data. If your environment can support the RF activity, this is not a bad idea.

The second component is the WLAN infrastructure. This means you have WLAN APs and, hopefully, WLAN switches with specific support for VoWLAN. These switches usually allow you to configure specific QoS settings easily for the voice traffic on your WLAN.

Finally, you must have some kind of call management software running on the network. This is the server that the IP phones will connect to, in order to find and connect to other IP phones. Think of the call management software (or device) as being like the private branch exchange (PBX) for your IP phone network. An example of call management software is the Cisco Call Manager solution.

These three components—wireless IP phones, WLAN infrastructure, and call management software—will allow you to implement a local-only IP phone network. If you want the IP phone users to be able to place calls to traditional phones, you will also need to install a voice gateway. Voice gateways act like a sort of bridge between the IP phone network and the PSTN networks.

For more in-depth information on VoWLANs, I suggest Jim Geier's book *Deploying Voice over Wireless LANs* (Cisco Press, 2007).

WLAN Accessories

These various devices (APs, bridges, switches, etc.) must all be connected somehow. Particularly, the infrastructure must—at some point—connect to the antenna that radiates and receives the RF signals. This section discusses the components in-line between the AP or bridge and the antenna, including the following items:

- Amplifiers
- Attenuators
- Lightning arrestors
- Grounding rods/wires
- Towers, safety equipment, and concerns
- RF cables
- RF connectors
- RF signal splitters

Amplifiers

RF amplifiers are used to increase or amplify the RF signal strength. They are usually placed in-line between the AP or bridge and the antenna.

In most cases, amplifiers are used either to make up for the signal loss in long cable runs or to increase the amplification of the signal for longer bridge links. Amplifiers are not generally used for indoor installations of APs. Amplifiers may also be used when the link budget calculations reveal that the signal strength will be too weak otherwise.

As you learned in Chapter 2, there are two types of gain: active and passive. Amplifiers create active gain because they increase the "amount" of RF energy being transmitted. Antennas create gain by focusing the energy in a specific direction so that the amount of energy going in that direction is higher, though the overall amount of energy is not increased. Active gain extends the signal's range and quality in all supported directions, whereas a high-gain antenna will only increase the signal's range and quality in the intended direction.

Amplifiers require a power supply, since they are adding power to the RF signal. You will usually plug a DC converter into an AC outlet to power the amplifier, or you will have to install a DC injector in-line with or before the amplifier. In a similar fashion to PoE, the DC injector places power on the RF cable that runs to the amplifier, and the amplifier uses this power to amplify the signal. The power provided to the amplifier is sometimes called *phantom voltage* or *phantom power.*

There are two types of amplifiers: unidirectional and bidirectional. As the names imply, unidirectional amplifiers amplify the received or transmitted signal only, and bidirectional amplifiers amplify both the sent and received signals. A bidirectional amplifier may be used with a stationary WLAN client that needs to increase both the received signal strength and the transmitted signal strength. A unidirectional amplifier could be used on each end of a bridge link. Both bridges could be configured with a unidirectional amplifier in the transmit path. Since they are both transmitting with stronger power, they should be able to hear each other well enough.

Finally, two variations are also available in amplifiers: fixed-gain and fixed-output types. *Fixed-gain* amplifiers add a preconfigured amount of gain to the signal. For example, such an amplifier may increase the strength by 6 dB. With this setup, whatever be the input strength, it will be quadrupled by the amplifier—usually up to a certain maximum threshold. *Fixed-output* amplifiers are configured so that a certain range of input will always result in the same output power. For example, as long as the input power is in the range 5–50 mW, the output power will be 100 mW. This is an example of how one might function.

Choosing the Right Amplifier

When purchasing an amplifier, you must be sure to match frequency response. In other words, if you are using a 2.4 GHz AP, you will need to use a 2.4 GHz amplifier. If you are using a 5 GHz AP, you will need to use a 5 GHz amplifier, and so forth. It is important to match frequency, or the system will not work.

Second, you will need to ensure that the amplifier matches your system in ohms and VSWR. Otherwise, you will create an impedance mismatch and degrade the performance of the system or even damage the equipment.

You should know the input power and gain you need, given the link budget calculations that you've made. If you need 400 mW of output power, for example, and you have a 100 mW output power AP, you will need a 6 dB gain amplifier. This does not consider the potential losses from cables and connectors.

When mounting the amplifier, it is usually best to mount it as close to the antenna as possible. This will prevent losses due to long cable runs before received frames enter the amplifier. When transmitting—particularly with fixed-output amplifiers—there should be as little component loss incurred as possible between the amplifier and the antenna. This means, again, installing the amplifier as close to the antenna as possible.

It is also important to note that FCC CFR 15.204 specifies that every system used in the ISM and UNII bands must be certified as a complete system. The system is inclusive of everything from the transmitting device to the antenna and everything in between. This means that, in some cases, if you purchase and install an amplifier, you will be running an illegal system.

Some vendors sell complete systems, including amplifiers, that are certified, and other vendors take devices sold by many vendors and get them certified with their amplifiers to increase their potential market base. The FCC made allowance in July 2004 for sale of amplifiers that are designed to work with only specific systems with no requirement to certify them as separate systems. This action was taken in FCC Report & Order 04-165. More information about the various FCC regulations can be found by visiting www.fcc.gov.

Attenuators

Attenuators do the opposite of amplifiers. They decrease the strength of the RF signal. RF attenuators may be fixed-loss or variable-loss type. Fixed-loss attenuators reduce the signal by the same amount or to the same amount, regardless of the input signal—assuming the input signal is strong enough to be reduced to that amount. Variable-loss attenuators can be set to varied levels of loss.

Attenuators are usually used when a system exceeds the allowed output power specified by the FCC. Variable-loss attenuators are useful because you may need to add or remove cable lengths over time and these different lengths of cable will result in different loss needs.

Like amplifiers, attenuators must be designed to work on the same frequency as the system being attenuated. Attenuators, unlike amplifiers, can be placed practically anywhere in-line between the AP or bridge and the antenna because strength of signal is less important than weakness of signal in this case.

Lightning Arrestors

Lightning arrestors are installed in order to redirect or shunt electric currents caused by nearby lightning strikes. They are not meant to protect against direct lightning strikes. Sadly, if your antenna is struck directly by lightning, you will lose it and most likely the equipment to which it is attached.

Lightning arrestors are installed in series between the antenna and the AP or bridge (transceiver). Extra components installed between the lightning arrestor and the antenna, such as connectors or amplifiers, will not be protected by the lightning arrestor. For this reason, you should install the lightning arrestor closer to the antenna with nothing between it and the antenna—if possible. Lightning arrestors should be rated at <8 μs.

Among the features to look for in lightning arrestors are

- Meeting the IEEE standard of <8 μs
- Gas tube breakdown voltage
- Reusability
- Impedance
- Frequency response
- Connector types

The basic functionality of a lightning arrestor is as follows:

1. Lightning strikes near the wireless antenna.
2. Transient currents are induced into the antenna or RF transmission line.
3. The lightning arrestor senses these currents and immediately causes a short in order to direct the current to earth ground.

Grounding Rods/Wires

Grounding rods and wires make up a grounding system. The two main purposes of a grounding system are to provide a safe path for the current from lightning to travel to ground (or earth) and to ensure that all connected electrical systems share a common ground.

Lightning takes the path of least resistance when it strikes. If you intentionally create a path of least resistance, you can ensure that the power from the lightning does not damage your equipment (or at least reduce the likelihood that it will). In addition to the power of the lightning itself, the lightning traveling through high-impedance systems generates a tremendous amount of heat. This heat, known as ohmic heating, can get so hot that it starts fires and melts metal. Since lightning prefers the path of least resistance (low impedance), an effective grounding system will ensure that the lightning's effects are limited.

You can ground your WLAN system by driving a copper rod, known as a grounding rod, into the earth. Next, connect your equipment to that rod using low-impedance wires known as grounding wires. This grounding rod should be 8-feet deep in the earth for electrical installations, according to the National Electronics Council. Since this standard exists, it is usually used for grounding RF systems as well.

Since grounding can actually be a complicated issue and since it must be done right, I encourage you to hire a professional to ground your WLAN bridges and other devices (the entire system) when installing outdoors or on poles and cell towers.

Towers, Safety Equipment, and Concerns

Because OSHA standards and other requirements may prevent you from personally climbing a tower to install an antenna, you should consult a professional to have these antennas installed. In the rare case where the typical WLAN administrator can climb the tower, the proper safety equipment (harnesses, shoes, etc.) should be used in order to protect the climber. Check with your local enforcement agency and OSHA to determine the guidelines for your area.

RF Cables

RF cables are used to connect the transceiver to the antenna (and possibly other in-series devices). Cables have different levels of loss, and this should be considered when selecting the cabling for your system. Keep the following factors in mind when selecting RF cables for your implementation:

- Different cables have different levels of loss, so not all cables are the same.
- Make sure the impedance of the cable matches the rest of your system.
- Be sure to select a cable that is rated for the frequency you will be using.
- Check with the vendor to discover the loss incurred per foot or per 100 feet before selecting the cable.
- Higher frequencies mean greater loss in the same cable.
- Either master the art of building cables or hire a professional to cut the cables and install the connectors so that you do not unnecessarily introduce extra loss.

RF Connectors

RF connectors come in many shapes and sizes. The following types are common:

- N-type
- SMA
- BNC
- TNC

In addition, there are common variations of these types such as reverse polarity and reverse threading. These different types exist in an effort to comply with FCC regulations for components used in a wireless system. While dongles and pigtails exist, if they are used to convert from one type to another for the purpose of transmission, they constitute a breach of FCC regulations. However, if you are scanning only and not transmitting, you can indeed create your own cables, connectors, amplifiers, and more.

These connectors are found on the ends of cables, the backs of APs and bridges, and the ends of antennas (in the case of dipole or rubber ducky antennas).

RF Signal Splitters

RF splitters are installed in series between the transceiver and the antennas. The splitter receives a single input and has two or more outputs. They are not recommended for common use in WLANs but may be used with sectorized antennas. Other than these scenarios, RF splitters should be avoided in WLANs.

Antenna Installation

Much like the APs and bridges themselves, antennas can be mounted in various ways. These methods include pole or mast mount, ceiling mount, and wall mount.

Pole or mast mount installations are usually performed outdoors. In these cases, public coverage areas can be created very easily by mounting an antenna on a pole or mast—usually with some type of u-brace—and connecting it to an AP or WLAN router. If the antenna installation will be sensitive to alignment variations, be sure to fasten the pole in a solid concrete base. This will keep the pole from moving by large enough amounts to impact the alignment in a short period of time.

Ceiling mounts are useful for omnidirectional antennas. The antenna can be placed in such a way that it hangs down from the ceiling and provides coverage to the surrounding area. This is useful when you need to install an antenna in the center of a large open space and there are no poles or desks on which to place the antenna.

Wall mounts are used for both omnidirectional and semidirectional antennas. With omnidirectional antennas, the entire AP is usually mounted on the wall with the antennas attached directly to the AP. It is assumed that the RF signals will travel directly backward through the wall or will reflect and refract around it. Patch and panel antennas are also often mounted on walls. They will then propagate their RF energy inward to the inner building coverage area.

Sector antennas are often mounted on poles or masts. In addition to mounting the sector antennas, you must be sure to provide the proper amount of downtilt. This will allow the sector antennas to cover the appropriate area.

A Guided Tour of WLAN Components

The following sections will provide you with some exposure to core WLAN equipment and software. You should acquire some basic hardware in order to get hands-on experience with it before taking the CWNA exam; however, a valid alternative would be to attend the hands-on training provided by the CWNP Program or another provider so that you can experience this equipment. I will give you a brief tour of only one device in each of the following three categories:

- Access points
- WLAN switch/controller
- WLAN residential gateway

I've intentionally chosen a different vendor for each of the devices. You will see a Cisco access point, a Symbol WLAN switch, and a Buffalo residential gateway. The model numbers will be provided for reference, but these devices are only intended to expose you to the look and feel of the various web interfaces for WLAN devices. Any similar equipment would provide valuable hands-on experience as well.

In these sections, I will not be walking you through the step-by-step process for configuring any of these devices. The intention here is to expose you to the different capabilities that they provide.

Access Points

We will be looking at the web-based configuration interface for a Cisco Systems 1200 series AP in the following screenshots. I'll provide a screenshot of each configuration interface with a brief paragraph summarizing what you can do in each area. This should help familiarize you with the options available on this AP, which is a very common one in enterprise implementations that use autonomous APs.

Figure 7.46 shows the opening or first screen you see when connecting to a Cisco Systems 1200 series AP. As you can see, this launch page provides you with a dashboard-type report of the health of the AP from the perspective of the wired and wireless connection points. In this case, there are currently 0 clients associated with the AP and 0 repeaters. Both the FastEthernet and Radio0-802.11G radios are up and running smoothly.

FIGURE 7.46 1200 series AP

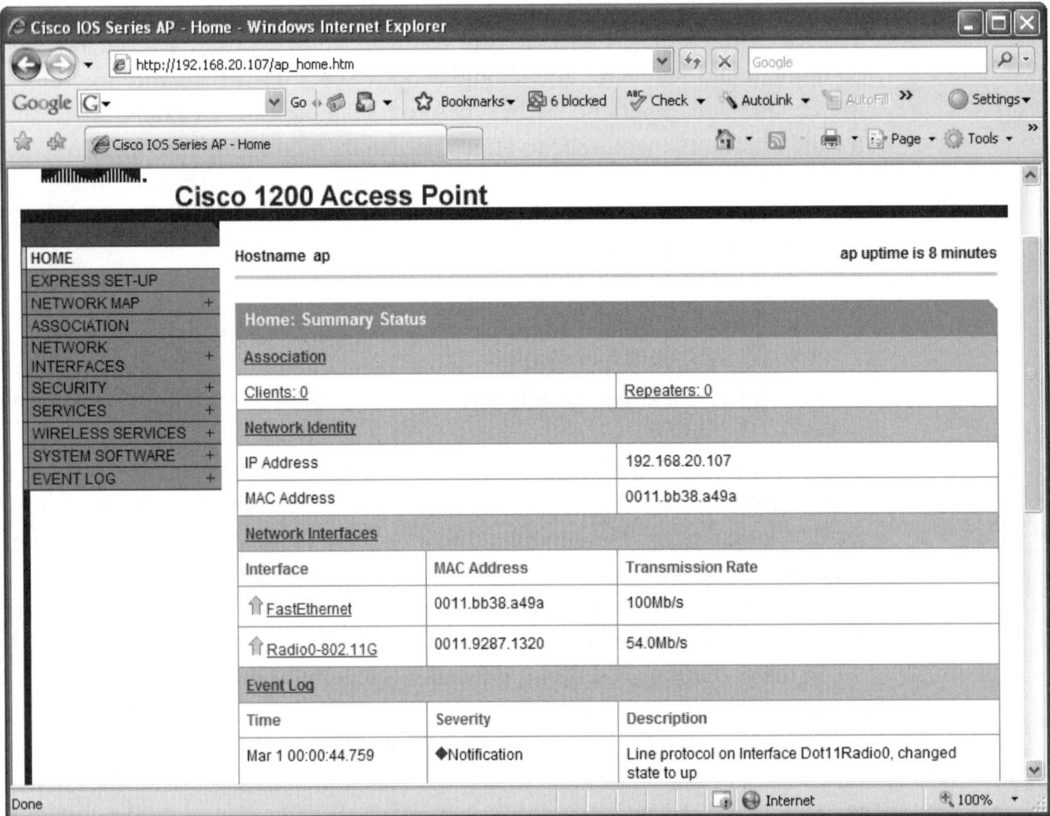

You can also see the Event Log section that makes up the lower portion of this home page. Much like a desktop or computer operating system, the operating system in the 1200 series AP is very powerful and can monitor the health of the hardware on which it is running and also log and report information about the devices' behavior over time. This is typical of enterprise-class autonomous APs and is one of the points of differentiation with SOHO-class hardware.

The Express Set-up page is similar to that found in SOHO equipment. Here you can configure the most basic settings related to the AP, such as the IP address, SNMP community strings, SSID, and other important settings. Note that you can disable the broadcast of the SSID in the Beacon frames and you can also optimize the radio network. Figure 7.47 shows this information. Optimizing the radio network automatically configures such settings as the fragmentation threshold, the data Beacon rate, the RTS

FIGURE 7.47 Express Setup page of the 1200 series AP

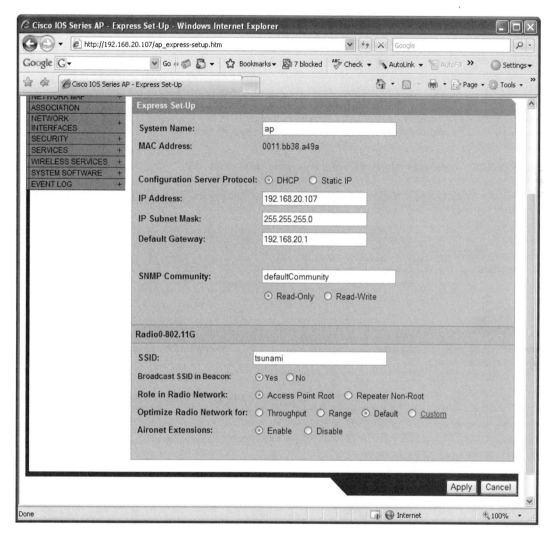

threshold, and more. By clicking Custom, you can manually set each of these settings. Cisco simply provides the Throughput, Range, and Default parameters to simplify your configuration process.

The Network Map and Association pages are used to view information about various network devices on your wired and wireless networks. The Association page is most often used to see the clients that are associated with the AP. Remember that you can see the number of associated clients immediately on the home page. On the Association page, you can filter to view only repeaters, only clients, or both. From here you can also see the individual activity of a specific client by clicking the MAC address of the client of interest. This is another feature that is not usually implemented in SOHO APs.

The Network Interfaces page provides summary information about each network interface installed in the AP. The 1200 series AP can support multiple radios and is usually configured with an ERP and OFDM radio when it is (or HR/DSSS and OFDM). Figure 7.48 shows the Network Interfaces page. You can also drill down to the individual radio interface and view its activity as well as change its settings.

FIGURE 7.48 Network Interfaces overview on the 1200 series AP

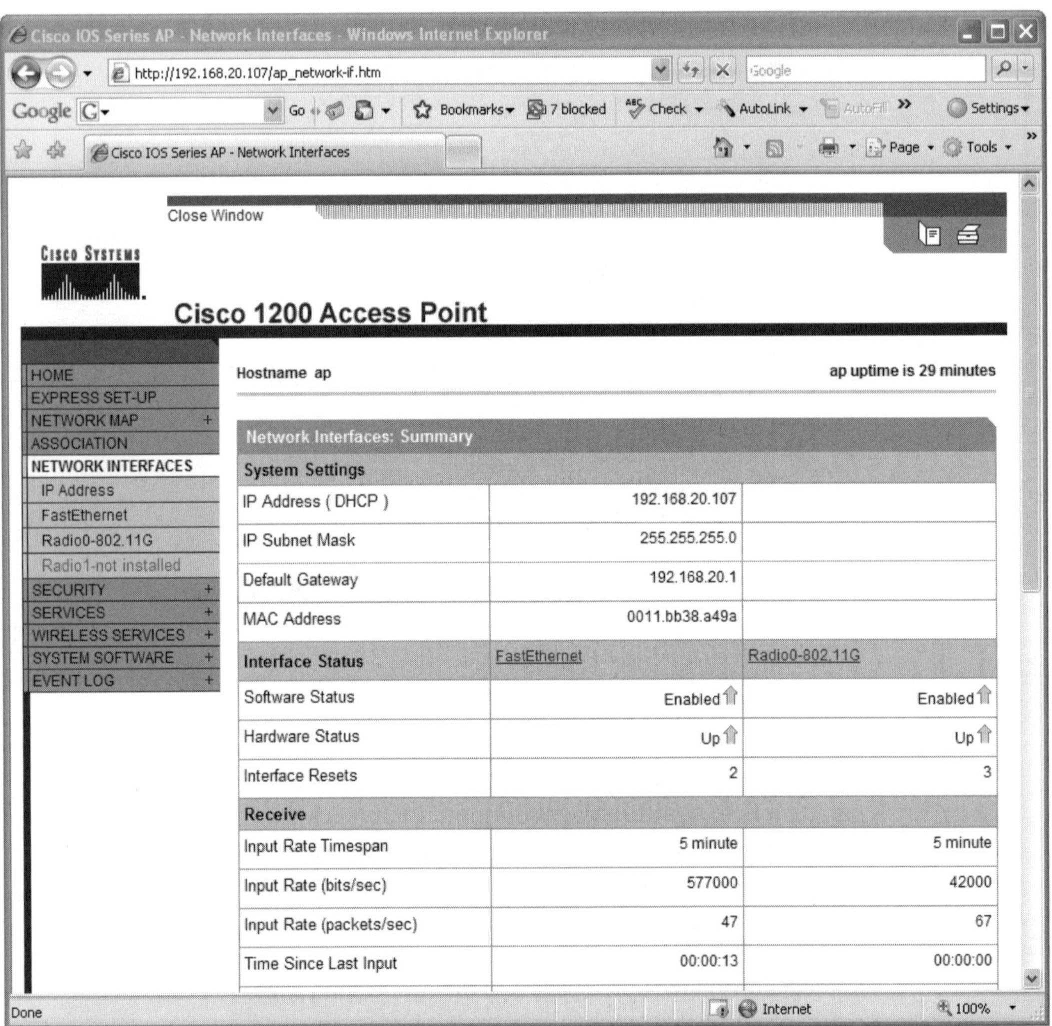

The Security page is used to configure security settings that are typical of most APs and a few that are unique to enterprise-class APs. For example, full RADIUS support is included in the local RADIUS server or local 802.1X authentication mechanisms.

The Services page is used to configure the various services that run on the Cisco Systems 1200 series AP. The service list can be seen in Figure 7.49 and includes

- Telnet
- CDP
- DNS
- Filters
- HTTP
- QoS
- SNMP
- NTP
- VLAN
- ARP caching

While the first page shows an overview of each service and lists the status of each service, you can click a service to see more information about it and to configure its parameters.

The remaining pages allow you to view and manage wireless services such as the AP service and the WDS service as well as manage firmware upgrades and configuration files. One of the earliest advantages of enterprise-class autonomous APs was the implementation of configuration management features that allow you to save different configurations and reload them as needed. This feature is also not common in SOHO-class APs.

WLAN Switch/Controller

The preceding section focused on an example of an autonomous AP. These APs are useful in large enterprises with small WLANs or small organizations with WLANs. In large organizations that implement WLANs inclusive of dozens or hundreds of APs, the need for centralized management and ease of reconfiguration becomes paramount. In these scenarios, a split-MAC model with a WLAN switch or controller and

FIGURE 7.49 Cisco Systems 1200 series Services page

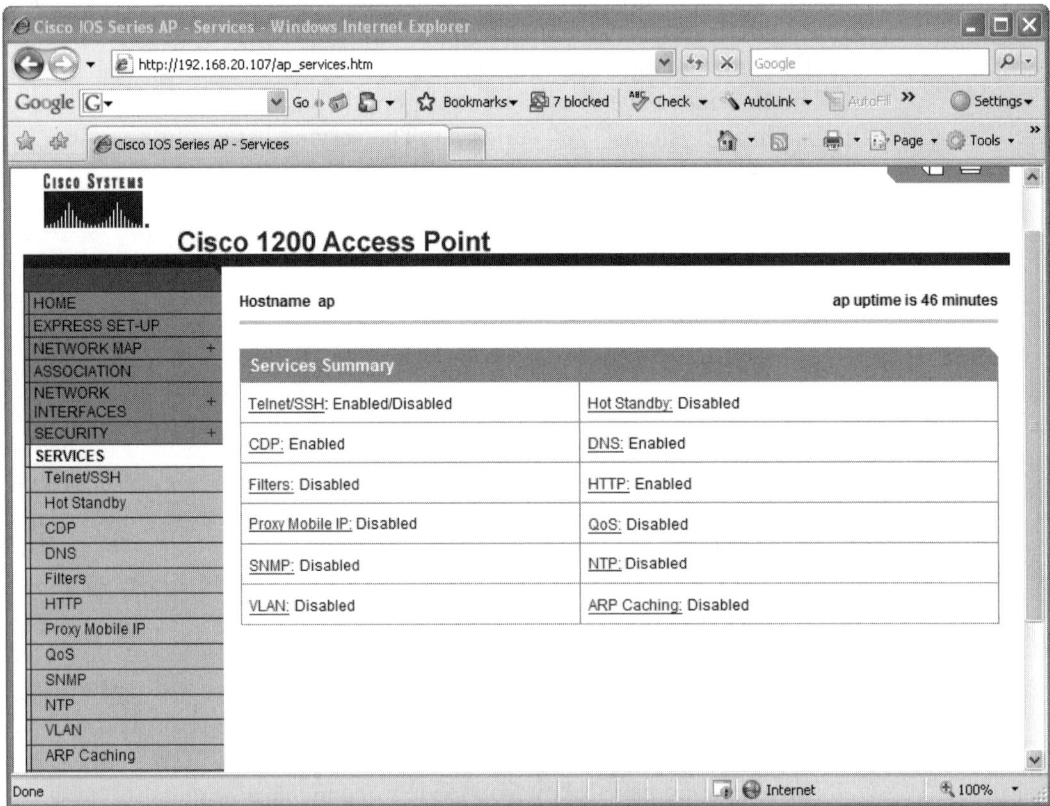

lightweight APs (also called access ports) is likely to bring increased value. In this section, I will take you on a brief tour of the management interface for the Symbol (now owned by Motorola) 5000-RS WLAN switch.

Like most infrastructure devices, the Symbol 5000-RS requires that initial configuration be performed through the console or serial interface to the device. To perform this initial configuration, you will connect a laptop or desktop computer to the switch with a serial cable. If your laptop does not have a serial port, as is the case for most modern laptops, you can purchase a USB-to-serial conversion cable that adds a standard COM port to your laptop for less than $50 in the United States.

Once the laptop or desktop is connected physically to the switch with a serial cable, you should set up a terminal emulation program according to the specifications of the WLAN device manufacturer. In this case, Symbol stipulates that the connection be made with the following parameters:

- 19,200 baud
- VT-100 terminal emulation
- 8 data bits
- 1 stop bit
- No parity
- No flow control

You can create such a connection using nearly any terminal emulation program, since these settings are very basic and common to most terminal applications. HyperTerminal, which ships with Windows clients, works fine.

Once you have connected through the serial interface and launched a terminal emulation application, you will be presented with a login prompt. Like switches from most vendors, Symbol devices have a default username and password. You would enter this information and then perform initial configuration tasks.

If you prefer to perform most of the configuration tasks in the GUI interface, you can get by configuring the network interfaces only at the command line. After you've configured these interfaces, you will need to configure the rest of the settings through a web browser. Remember that you can usually telnet into these enterprise-class devices as well. Figure 7.50 shows the HyperTerminal application connected to the Symbol 5000 switch and operating the command line interface (CLI).

With the initial configuration complete, you can connect to the web-based GUI interface to perform the remaining configuration steps that will prepare the switch for production. To connect to the graphical interface, you will connect to the switch using HTTPS and the IP address you configured in the CLI. Figure 7.51 shows the default interface presented to you after you enter your username and password. Here you can set up policies for both the wired network and the access ports (wireless network).

FIGURE 7.50 Setting up the switch from the CLI

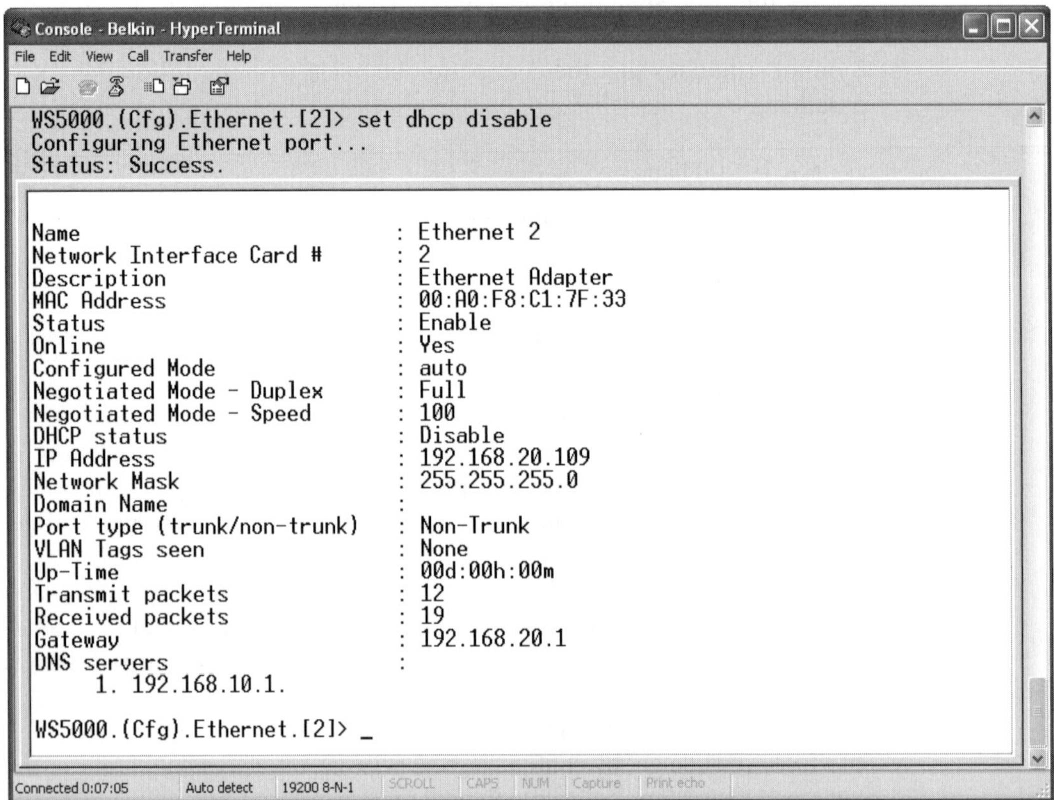

By switching to the Quick Start view, you can quickly configure the basic WLANs you want the switch to manage. You can control the amount of bandwidth consumed by a WLAN and the security features of that WLAN all from a central location. Note that you can change these settings at any time from a remote location as well. Figure 7.52 shows the Quick Start view.

WLAN controllers and switches, like the Symbol 5000, go through a process that is sometimes called adoption or mapping with the lightweight APs. This process usually involves the AP sending a packet to the switch so that the switch knows that the AP is available. The switch then applies any firmware settings, if necessary. Finally, the AP is configured by the switch to participate in the WLAN.

FIGURE 7.51 Symbol 5000 web-based management interface

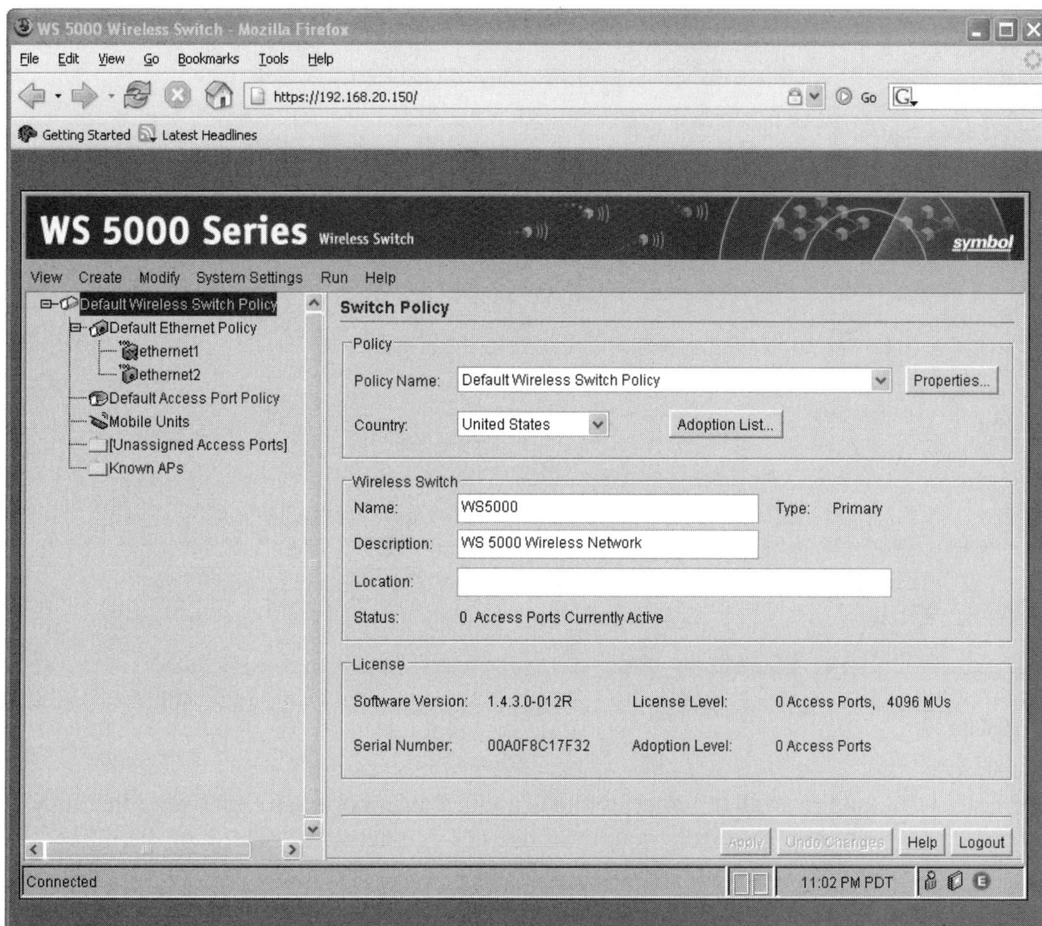

WLAN Residential Gateway

WLAN residential gateways are usually called wireless routers by the vendors that manufacture and distribute them. The example device you will see in this section is the Linksys WRT54G. While devices like this often provide features that seem to aggregate multiple enterprise-class devices together (for example, they combine an AP, router, VPN server,

FIGURE 7.52 Symbol 5000 Quick Start view

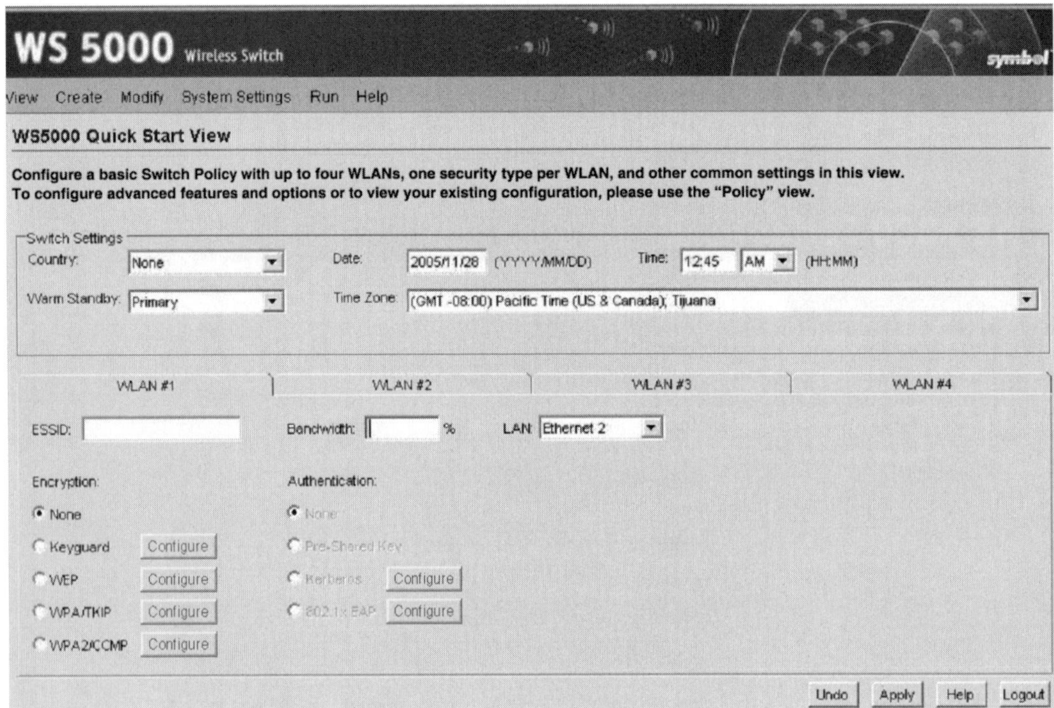

and firewall together in most cases), it is important to remember that they are not powerful enough for use in large networks. Think of them like a 486 SX computer running Windows 3.1, compared to a P4 3.6 GHz running Windows XP, and you have a good comparison between a Linksys WRT54G (like the 486) and the combination of an enterprise-class switch, router, AP, and firewall (like the P4). Of course, I'm not saying that the enterprise devices have P4s inside them, but I'm sure you can see the reality of this analogy.

Since the Linksys WRT54G is widely available on eBay and other sites for less than $50, I will not spend a tremendous amount of time on it here. I would encourage you to use it or a similar device to get some experience with residential gateways, if you have not already done so. Here, I will show you a few screens that demonstrate the differences between an AP and a WLAN router or residential gateway.

FIGURE 7.53 Routing table management on the WRT54G

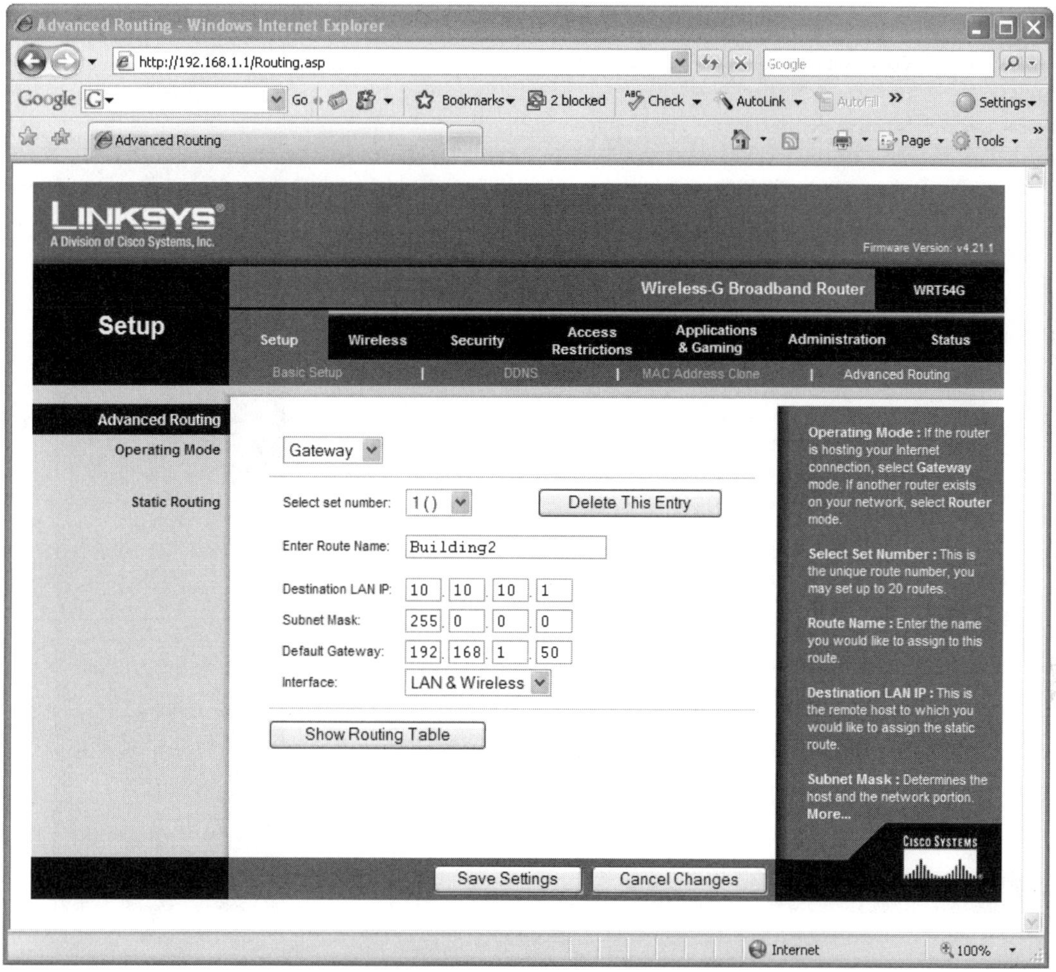

The most obvious feature that a WLAN residential gateway has that an AP does not is the ability to route data. APs simply bridge data from the WLAN to the wired LAN. Residential gateways can do more. Figure 7.53 shows a routing table management interface on the WRT54G broadband router.

The second major feature offered by a residential gateway is a DHCP server. Since most home networks do not have full servers

FIGURE 7.54 DHCP configuration

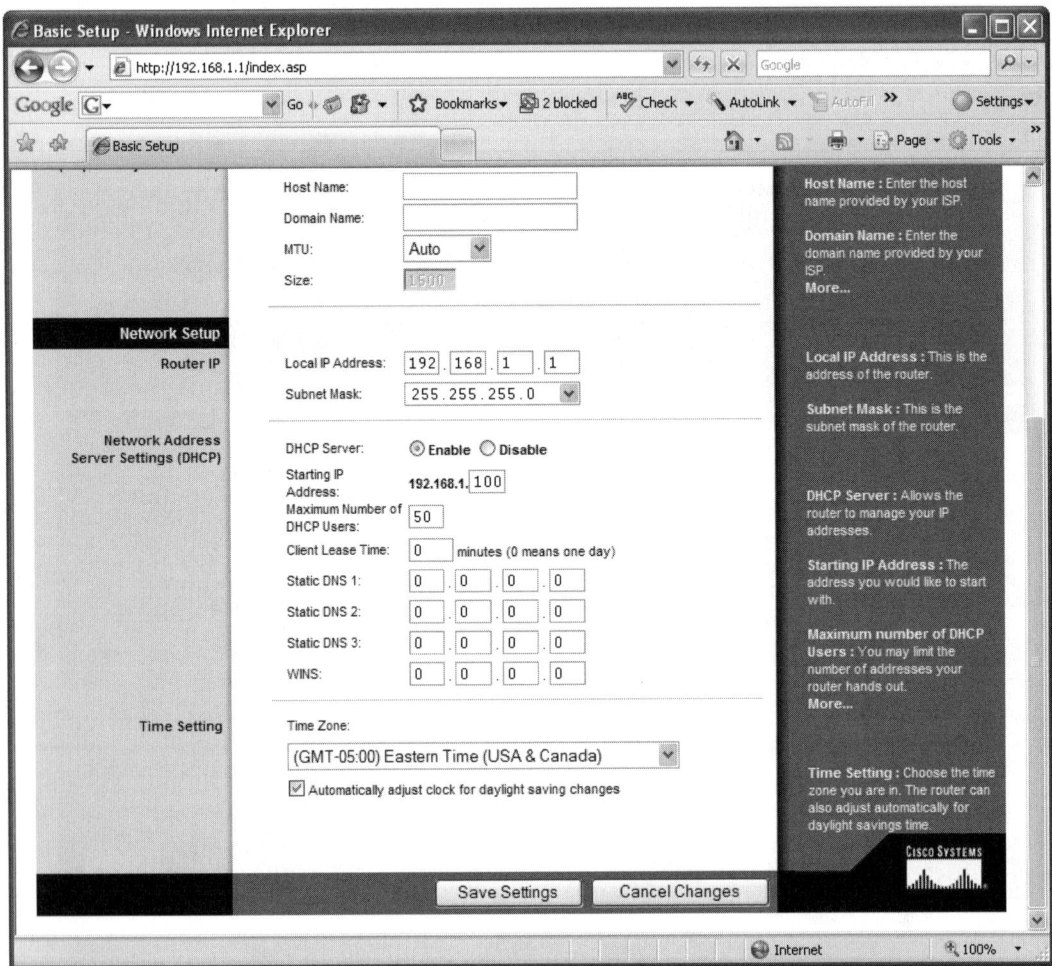

(though Microsoft is attempting to change this with Windows Home Server), the provision of DHCP to the network is an added benefit of a residential gateway. Figure 7.54 shows a DHCP configuration screen on the Linksys WRT54G.

Another feature of residential gateways is the built-in firewall capabilities. The firewalls in residential gateways are certainly not enterprise class, but they can provide some level of protection for a home or SOHO implementation.

FIGURE 7.55 Firewall setup

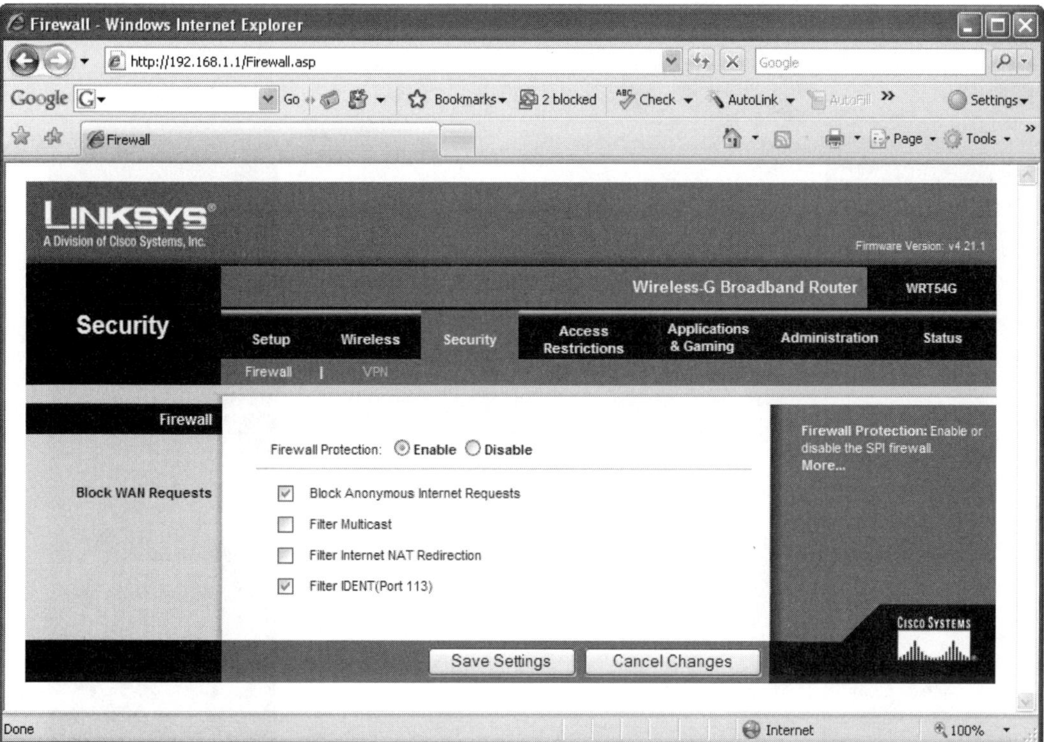

Figure 7.55 shows this capability. As you can see, there are basic functions such as blocking incoming requests so that all communications must start or originate from inside your network, IDENT 113 stealthing, and filtering of multicast messages from your ISP. These firewall features are very basic to say the least.

Finally, among the most advanced features of residential gateways is that of Internet access filtering and policies. For example, the Linksys WRT54G can allow or deny PCs access to the Internet, based on the time of day or the day of the week, and it can also block specific services based on TCP ports (port-based firewalling). Figure 7.56 shows this final interface that I will present to you in this chapter.

FIGURE 7.56 Internet filtering

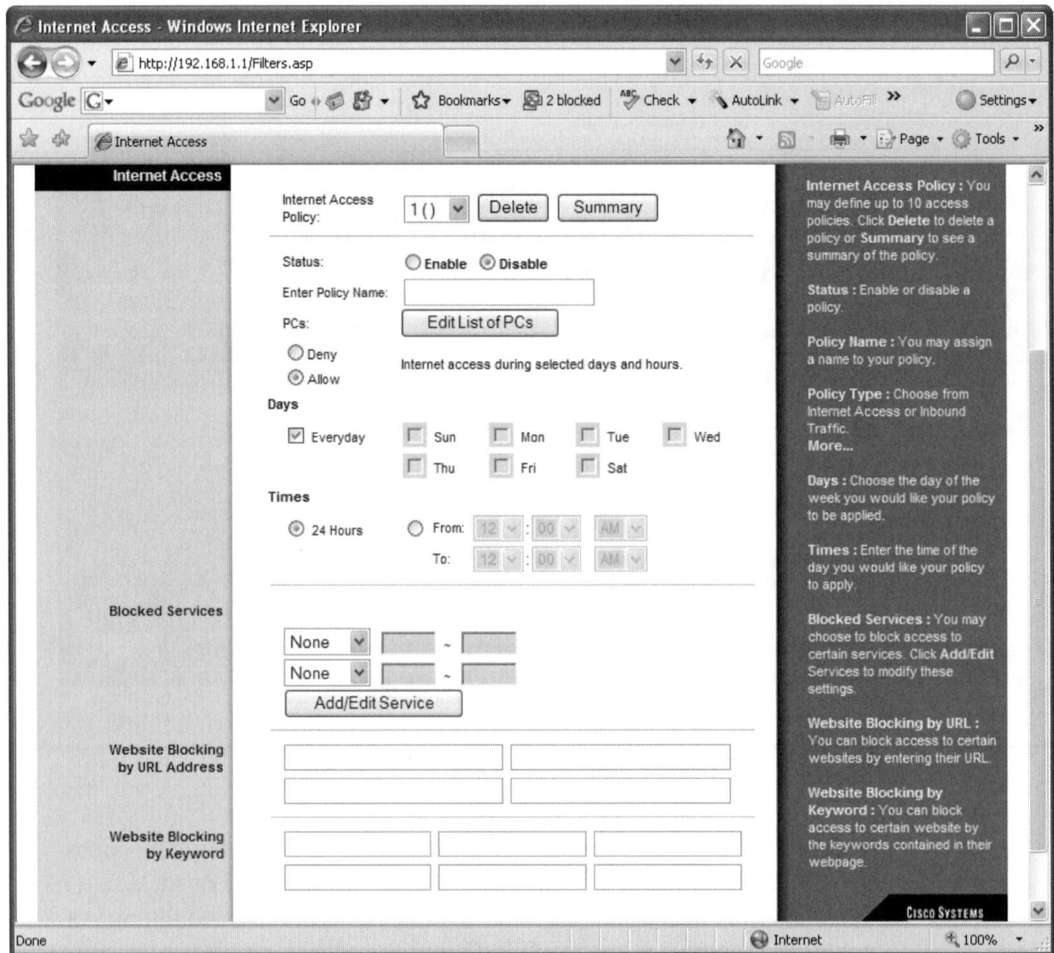

Summary

This chapter introduced you to the major components used in WLAN infrastructures. You learned first about the access point (AP), which is the most common WLAN component installed in enterprise network. You learned about the common features of APs and the various configuration options available.

Next you learned about WLAN switches or controllers. These devices provide for centralized management of the WLAN edge. Instead of having to configure each AP individually, you can configure them massively from a central location. After this, you learned about Power over Ethernet (PoE) and WLAN bridges. You learned how PoE can solve power supply problems as well as provide ongoing support from the perspective of power cycling. You also learned how WLAN bridges can be used to connect disconnected wired networks or to create a secondary connection for fault tolerance.

Finally, you learned how to determine which components to use in SOHO, SMB, and enterprise installations, and you learned about the many components used in a WLAN system. The components included cables, connectors, amplifiers, attenuators, and lightning arrestors.

Key Terms

- ☐ **access points**
- ☐ **access ports**
- ☐ **amplifiers**
- ☐ **attenuators**
- ☐ **autonomous access points**
- ☐ **enterprise encryption gateway**
- ☐ **grounding rods**
- ☐ **lightning arrestors**
- ☐ **lightweight access points**
- ☐ **mesh routers**
- ☐ **PoE**
- ☐ **remote office WLAN switch**
- ☐ **residential WLAN gateway**
- ☐ **RF cables**
- ☐ **RF connectors**
- ☐ **RF signal splitters**
- ☐ **VoWLAN**
- ☐ **wireless workgroup bridge**
- ☐ **WLAN bridge**
- ☐ **WLAN switch**

Review Questions

1. You are a WLAN administrator, and you have been asked to relocate an antenna approximately 200 feet away from the transceiving AP. You are concerned that a cable run of this distance will reduce the signal strength to a point where the output power at the antenna is not sufficient. What kind of device could potentially be installed in order to make up for the loss incurred from the 200 feet of cable?

   A. Attenuator

   B. Amplifier

   C. Lightning arrestor

   D. Grounding rod

2. You are installing a WLAN that will consist of more than 900 APs. Because of this, you are certain that individual configuration of each AP would be far too time consuming. Which of the following devices may help you by providing centralized configuration of the APs? (Choose all that apply.)

   A. Enterprise encryption gateway

   B. WLAN controller

   C. WLAN bridge

   D. WLAN switch

3. You have a WLAN with 13 APs from a specific vendor that support the HR/DSSS PHY. You are in a situation where you need to add five more APs to the network, but the model of AP you have installed is no longer available. Since you are installing the 5 new APs anyway, you are considering the benefits of upgrading the 13 existing APs at the same time. Which of the following are valid benefits of the newer ERP PHY devices over the older HR/DSSS devices? (Choose all that apply.)

   A. More supported data rates for the dynamic rate changes

   B. Support for the HT PHY in IEEE 802.11n

C. Support for the HR/DSSS PHY devices for backward compatibility

D. Support for up to 108 Mbps

4. Which of the following devices could be used to implement a PtP link with the proper configuration? (Choose all that apply.)

A. WLAN bridge

B. WLAN switch

C. WLAN AP

D. Residential wireless gateway

5. An AP that includes full intelligence within itself and does not depend on any other device to function is called by a particular name. What is that name?

A. Lightweight AP

B. Access port

C. Thin AP

D. Autonomous AP

6. You've installed an enterprise-class WLAN. You have provided outdoor access by placing an omnidirectional antenna in the center of a picnic area located on the corporate property. When you installed the outdoor antenna, you also installed a lightning arrestor to protect your WLAN equipment. The antenna took a direct hit of lightning yesterday. What should you expect the result to be, since you've installed the lightning arrestor?

A. The arrestor should have diverted the energy away from your AP.

B. The arrester should have melted and cut off the energy at that point.

C. The antenna is likely destroyed and other equipment in-line may also be destroyed.

D. The antenna is likely destroyed from the energy passing through it, but the rest should be just fine.

7. A remote office WLAN switch has been installed in your organization's Columbus, OH office. Fewer than 20 employees work in the Columbus office. You want to allow these employees to access the corporate office network in Arlington, VA, and you want to do this with an existing high-speed Internet connection. The Internet connection has a 6 Mbit down speed and a 2 Mbit up speed at the remote office. The corporate office has a dedicated 5 Mbit bidirectional link to the Internet. The remote office users will mostly need to check e-mail on the corporate office network across the Internet-based link, but they will sometimes need to transfer files and access intranet web pages. What single solution might you employ, since you have the Internet connection and a remote office WLAN switch already installed?

   A. Just let them check their e-mail across the Internet.

   B. Create a VPN tunnel between the remote office WLAN switch and a VPN server at the corporate office.

   C. Create a VPN tunnel between each computer at the remote office and a VPN server at the corporate office.

   D. Use SSL for browsing the corporate office intranet web pages.

8. Which of the following are valid modes in which APs may operate? (Choose all that apply.)

   A. Root

   B. Repeater

   C. Bridge

   D. Switch

9. You are configuring an AP for the first time. It is being installed in an environment that implements an intelligent edge design with no WLAN switches or controllers. Since the AP is autonomous, you must configure all the settings manually or using some other vendor-specific tool. You want to configure it using the HyperTerminal program in Windows. What kind of management connection will you make?

   A. Web-based

   B. Telnet

C. Console

D. SSH

10. You have an EEG installed to provide security for your WLAN clients. There are three APs connected to a switch (switch A) that is uplinked to the EEG. The EEG is then linked to the wired LAN through another switch (switch B). Fifteen WLAN clients are using the three APs for network connectivity. At what points is the data being encrypted, assuming a standard installation of an EEG and that no application-layer encryption is being performed? (Choose all that apply.)

A. Between the APs and the WLAN clients

B. Between the APs and switch A

C. Between switch A and the EEG

D. Between the EEG and switch B

11. You have installed an endpoint PSE. What have you likely installed?

A. WLAN switch

B. WLAN bridge

C. WLAN AP

D. Ethernet repeater

12. As the WLAN administrator of an enterprise network, you have been asked to implement VoWLAN. Which of the following components are likely to be a part of your installation? (Choose all that apply.)

A. A call manager

B. Wireless IP phones

C. Voice gateway

D. WLAN infrastructure

13. A local school district has asked for your assistance in connecting a remote school room to the main school building with a wireless link. There is already a WLAN in the main school building, and the signal is still very strong at the remote school room. The computers in the remote school room are all wired together with a switch, but they do not have WLAN client devices installed. There are eight computers and a printer in the remote school room. What single device could be added, in this scenario, to create the wireless link from the remote school room to the main building's AP? This device must allow the computers in the remote school room to communicate with computers in the main building, and vice versa.

A. Wireless workgroup bridge

B. Ethernet hub

C. Wireless bridge

D. Ethernet router

Review Answers

1. **B.** An amplifier can be used to make up for losses incurred from cables and connectors in the path from the transceiver to the antenna, and vice versa. Amplifiers can also be used to strengthen the signal in other situations. Attenuators cause loss or weaken the signal strength. Lightning arrestors and grounding rods do not intentionally impact signal strength.

2. **B, D.** WLAN controllers and switches can provide centralized configuration management of APs, bridges, and other RF devices. An EEG provides centralized configuration of authentication and encryption only and is oblivious to other WLAN configuration settings such as the WLAN channel and transmitter output power. A WLAN bridge is a device that may need centralized configuration, but they are usually configured directly, since there are fewer in deployment. They certainly cannot provide centralized configuration for APs.

3. **A, D.** Newer ERP PHY devices offer more data rates than HR/DSSS PHY devices while still offering backward compatibility with HR/DSSS PHY devices. If a device supports the data rate of 108 Mbps, it is operating in a nonstandard mode at this time. Only the release of the IEEE 802.11n amendment (or some other such standards-based amendment) will change this. ERP PHY devices will be forwardly compatible with IEEE 802.11n devices (HT PHY), but not because of what the ERP devices do. The compatibility will come from what the HT PHY devices do that provides the backward compatibility.

4. **A, C.** Either a WLAN bridge or a WLAN AP can be used to implement a PtP link. Devices that are sold as WLAN bridges usually come with more rugged cases (when designed for outdoor use) than APs, but the bridging functionality is relatively the same. Some WLAN bridges perform better than APs placed in bridge mode because they have no extraneous software and are designed specifically for bridging.

5. **D.** An AP that is self-reliant is an autonomous AP. Lightweight and thin APs are two terms that are often used to refer to APs that rely on external intelligence such as a switch/AP configuration. Access ports are also lightweight APs.

6. **C.** The antenna, as well as other items in the path from antenna to the AP, is probably destroyed. The lightning arrestor is only intended to handle the energy that results from a lightning strike in close proximity, not that from a direct hit. A direct hit is too powerful for most solutions and will likely damage the equipment.

7. **B.** By implementing a VPN tunnel between the remote office WLAN switch's WAN port and the VPN server at the corporate offices, you secure the e-mail, file transfers, and intranet pages all at once. If each user has to create a VPN tunnel, this introduces much more overhead in management and bandwidth. The SSL and "just check e-mail" solutions do not solve all the problems as a single solution.

8. **A, B, C.** APs may operate in Root, Bridge, or Repeater mode, but they may not operate in Switch mode. Many WLAN devices come with switches built into them, but if they are APs, the AP is not the switch itself. The device simply happens to have a switch in it for wired ports, and the AP provides an additional wireless port.

9. **C.** You will make a console connection. You will use a serial connection from your PC to the AP and then connect through the HyperTerminal program. The telnet, web-based, and SSH connections would all occur through the Ethernet port.

10. **A, B, C.** When an enterprise encryption gateway (EEG) is used, the data is encrypted during the entire journey from the WLAN client to the EEG, but it is not usually encrypted from the EEG to the rest of the wired LAN. For this reason, the data is encrypted between the WLAN clients and the APs, between the APs and switch A, and between switch A and the EEG. However, it is not likely to be encrypted between the EEG and switch B.

11. **A.** An endpoint PSE is a power injector at an endpoint or at one end of an MDI connection. Therefore, you've probably installed a WLAN switch with built-in Power over Ethernet (PoE) support. Had you installed a midspan PSE, you would likely have installed a single-port or multiport power injector that is inserted between the switch/hub and the AP or bridge being powered.

12. **A, B, C, D.** You will need all four items in most cases. The voice gateway may not be needed in scenarios where you only require that internal users can call internal users; however, if you must route calls through standard phone networks (like PSTN), you will need to install a voice gateway. The wireless IP phones are the client devices that will be used to place calls. The WLAN infrastructure will provide, at least, the first part of the path from the device placing the call to the device being called. The call manager (either software or a device) will be responsible for "finding" a called device when a calling device places a call.

13. A. A wireless workgroup bridge is a device that can act as a client to an AP and a bridge to a group of wired devices. Ultimately, a wireless workgroup bridge treats the wireless link to the AP as one port and the local Ethernet port as the other "end" of the bridge. This allows it to move data from the local Ethernet across to the remote wireless AP so that the distant wired network can be wirelessly linked to the AP.

CHAPTER

8

Client Devices and Software

CWNA Exam Objectives Covered:

- ❖ Describe the purpose of the following WLAN client devices and explain how to install, configure, and manage them
  - PC Cards (ExpressCard, CardBus, and PCMCIA)
  - USB, CF, and SD Devices
  - PCI and Mini-PCI Cards

In This Chapter

Installing, Configuring, and Managing WLAN Client Devices

WLAN client devices play an extremely important role in your WLAN and come in many different form factors with many different features and capabilities. Choosing the right network interface card (NIC) involves understanding the requirements of the user and the capabilities of the WLAN client. It also involves understanding the requirements of the WLAN client device such as operating system requirements and form factor specifications. You will learn how to make these decisions in this chapter. While this is a short chapter, it contains essential knowledge to help you prepare for the CWNA exam and your career as a WLAN administrator.

WLAN Client Device Internals

Every WLAN client device is composed of a similar set of hardware components and software elements. The hardware components include chipsets for radio control and management, antennas for RF transmission and reception, and interfaces for connectivity to the device intended to communicate on the WLAN. The form factor, whether it be PCI, Compact Flash, or Mini-PCI, determines the interface to the communicating device. The chipset and antenna are points of differentiation. Chipsets provide the actual implementation of the IEEE 802.11 PHYs that are supported by the client device. For example, a chipset may support only the transmission of 2.4 GHz ISM signals and support the DSSS, HR/DSSS, and ERP PHYs, or a chipset may support the 2.4 GHz ISM signals and the 5 GHz UNII signals as well, which allows for support for the OFDM PHY. A device that supports both the ERP and OFDM PHYs is often called an IEEE 802.11a/b/g adapter. The CWNP Program refers to such a device as an ERP/OFDM device because it actually implements the ERP and OFDM PHYs. Most of these devices cannot operate both PHYs at the same time but must switch between them or operate on only one of them.

Client devices usually have built-in antennas, but many devices do also support the use of external antennas. By supporting external antennas, the vendor allows for the device to be used in very unique ways for testing and site surveying purposes. For example, the device can be set up with an external semidirectional antenna to compare communications quality as opposed to a dipole antenna.

Installing, Configuring, and Managing WLAN Client Devices

The methods used to install a WLAN client device vary depending on the form factor of the device and the software needed to provide functionality within the supported operating systems. The following client devices are discussed in this chapter:

- PC Cards
- USB, Compact Flash, and SD devices
- PCI and Mini-PCI cards
- Wireless presentation gateways

In the preceding chapter, I covered some of the newer devices available in the WLAN infrastructure market. In this chapter, I will provide you with information related to a newer WLAN device called a Wireless presentation gateway. While these devices do not function as traditional client network interface cards, they do act as a WLAN STA on an ad hoc or infrastructure network and provide services to the other WLAN STAs. With unique WLAN devices such as this, it is difficult to categorize them as being either infrastructure or client devices. I have chosen to discuss them in this chapter because they do not play a traditional routing, switching, or bridging function as infrastructure devices do.

Each WLAN network interface card specification is discussed from three perspectives: features, installation routines, and PHY compatibilities. With these three pieces of information, you will be able to choose the right WLAN client device for your situation.

PC Cards (ExpressCard, CardBus, and PCMCIA)

PC Cards are the most common type of add-on WLAN NICs used in laptop computers. They may also be used in desktop computers, though this practice is becoming less common. PC Cards provide the benefit of easy removal and replacement as new standards are developed and new security capabilities are implemented. The PC Cards come in three major types: PCMCIA, CardBus, and ExpressCard.

The earliest standardized laptop or notebook computer add-on card was the PCMCIA (Personal Computer Memory Card International Association) card.

These cards come in three form factors: Type I, Type II, and Type III. The length and width are the same for all three form factors (being 85.6 mm long and 54.0 mm wide), but the thickness varies according to card type. The Type I, Type II, and Type III cards have thicknesses of 3.3, 5.0, and 10.5 mm, respectively. Because they differ only in thickness, many laptops are built that support one Type III card or two Type II cards. Most WLAN NICs that use the PCMCIA standard are Type II or Type III cards. This is due to the chipsets needed to run the IEEE 802.11 processes and the power requirements. Figure 8.1 shows a WLAN card that is a PCMCIA Type II card compatible with Type II or Type III slots.

Over the years, the PCMCIA standard has evolved to include newer capabilities. In fact, from June 1990, when the first PCMCIA standard was completed, to April 2001, there were eight releases (complete new standard) and seven updates (minor modifications or changes not warranting a new release). The newer CardBus standard is actually PCMCIA release 5.0–8.0. In other words, it is the newest version of the PCMCIA standard. The biggest difference between a pre-5.0 PCMCIA card and a CardBus (post-5.0 PCMCIA) card is that the newer cards support a 32-bit bus, while the older cards support only a 16-bit bus. Figure 8.2 shows an example of a CardBus WLAN card. You might say that CardBus is high-performance (50 Mbits per second) PCMCIA, where PC Cards are low-performance (10 Mbits per second) PCMCIA. As you might guess, PC Cards are fine for HR/DSSS devices, but they cannot keep up with the speeds of ERP or OFDM devices.

The newest add-on card standard is the ExpressCard. ExpressCards can be roughly half the size of PCMCIA cards and are also lighter. Rather than

FIGURE 8.1 Linksys WPC11 PCMCIA WLAN Type II card

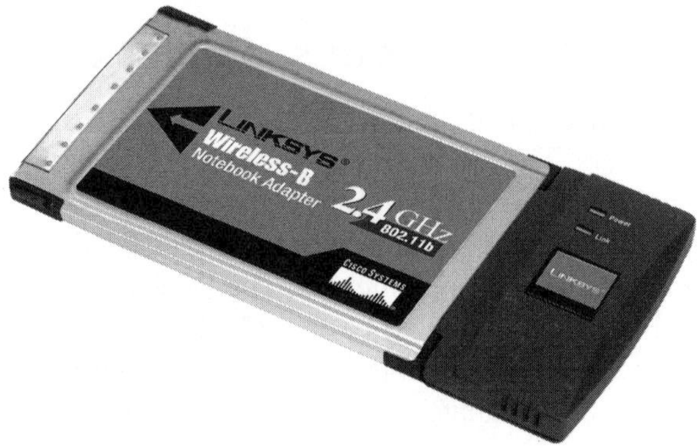

FIGURE 8.2 Linksys WPC54g CardBus (PCMCIA 5.0 and above) WLAN card

just supporting PCI applications like the PCMCIA cards, the ExpressCards support PCI Express applications. The ExpressCards connect directly to PCI Express and USB ports in the host computer rather than connecting to the CardBus port. Figure 8.3 shows an ExpressCard/34 from Belkin that is a pre-N device, which also supports ERP and HR/DSSS connectivity. These pre-N devices may or may not be compatible with the final IEEE 802.11n standard, once it is ratified, as they are based on the current draft of the standard. WLAN administrators should keep this in mind when making purchasing choices at this time.

The ExpressCards come in one of two form factors: ExpressCard/54 and ExpressCard/34. The ExpressCard/54 is 54 mm wide, and the ExpressCard/34 is 34 mm wide. Both cards used a 34-mm-wide connector, and ExpressCard/34 cards will work in ExpressCard/54 connector slots. The same is not true in reverse. An ExpressCard/54 card will not work in a slot that is designed only for ExpressCard/34 and is only 34 mm wide; however, most laptops with ExpressCard slots contain a universal slot that can support both form factors. At the time of this writing, no

FIGURE 8.3 Belkin ExpressCard/34 form factor WLAN card

ExpressCard/54 form factor WLAN devices could be located. It seems that most vendors are choosing to implement the ExpressCard/34 form factor. This is a logical decision, since the ExpressCard/34 devices will work in any computer with an ExpressCard slot—either 34 or 54.

Ultimately, there are only two kinds of WLAN NICs that use the form factor discussed in this section: PCMCIA and ExpressCard. This is because the CardBus cards are actually just PCMCIA cards that use a later version of the PCMCIA standard supporting 32-bit bus architectures. The ExpressCard, while based on the PCMCIA standards, uses a different form factor and does not work in a Type I, II, or III PCMCIA slot. Generally, the phrase PC Card is used to reference devices that comply with the pre-5.0 PCMCIA standard, and the term CardBus is used to reference devices that comply with the PCMCIA 5.0 or higher standard.

PHY Compatibilities

These PCMCIA and ExpressCards are capable of supporting all the PHYs implemented in IEEE 802.11 as amended. There are PC Cards for HR/DSSS, ERP, and OFDM PHYs, and there are CardBus cards for all of these as well. Remember also that an ERP card is going to be compatible with HR/DSSS. For this reason, an ExpressCard that states it is IEEE 802.11g compatible will also be IEEE 802.11b compatible. Many ExpressCards being sold today are pre-N devices that support the IEEE 802.11n draft document. These cards are also compatible with the older ERP and HR/DSSS standards.

Features

WLAN client devices based on the PCMCIA and ExpressCard standards offer the same basic features of WLAN devices in differing form factors. Common features include

- Support for IEEE 802.11 standards
- Support for security technologies such as WPA and WPA2
- Client software for discovering and connecting to WLANs
- Device drivers for supported operating systems
- May support external antennas, though this is the exception and not the rule
- May support 2.4 GHz and 5 GHz WLAN standards (i.e., both ERP and OFDM)

Installation

Many modern operating systems support plug-and-play detection of added hardware. This feature makes the installation of PCMCIA and ExpressCard devices easier when the drivers are available. It is still the responsibility of the install technician or user to understand how to provide device drivers to the operating system's plug-and-play process. Vendors will usually provide the drivers for their WLAN NICs on a CD-ROM that ships with the device; however, newer drivers are almost always available from the vendor's web site and should be evaluated. Sometimes a newer driver removes features or detracts from the quality of the driver, and sometimes it adds features and improve the quality of the driver (and client software). As a WLAN network administrator, you cannot assume that a newer driver is better, but you must test the drivers to ensure continued stability and capability.

Since PCMCIA and ExpressCard devices are removable, the installation process involves inserting the card into the appropriate slot on the laptop or desktop computer. After the card is inserted, the operating system will detect that card and configure it with the proper device drivers, assuming they are already on the system. In most cases, the device vendor recommends installing the drivers and/or client software first and then inserting the device. This provides the drivers to the operating system so that the device can be automatically configured when inserted.

You can learn all the technical details about the PCMCIA cards and the ExpressCard cards, which are beyond the scope of the CWNA exam, by visiting www.PCMCIA.org or www.ExpressCard.org.

USB, CF, and SD Devices

USB adapters have become very common for both laptop and desktop computers. They come in two primary implementation models. The first is a dongle-type adapter that plugs directly into the USB port, and the second is a device that connects to the USB port through a connector cable. Figure 8.4 shows both types of devices.

The greatest advantage of USB devices is that they are fairly universal (after all, the term USB stands for Universal Serial Bus). Saying that the USB device is universal is a reference to the fact that USB devices can be used with desktops, laptops, tablet PCs, and any other device that supports the USB interface and provides proper drivers for the WLAN NIC.

FIGURE 8.4 Linksys USB dongle-type adapter and Netgear cable-connected adapter

Compact Flash cards are frequently called CF cards. They are small form factor WLAN devices and are most frequently used in handheld computers such as PocketPCs and Palm OS devices and look similar to the one seen in Figure 8.5. CF cards can be connected directly to the supporting device, such as a PocketPC device, or they can be connected through a PCMCIA adapter card when used in laptop or desktop computers. The CF cards do have a tendency to drain the battery power of PDAs very quickly. This is particularly true of the IEEE 802.11g devices.

The Secure Digital IO, or SD, cards are very similar to the CF cards. They are a small form factor WLAN client device that can be used in portable and desktop computers. Devices can be purchased that support

FIGURE 8.5 Linksys IEEE 802.11g CF card

both flash storage and Wi-Fi connectivity in one unit. This multifunction capability can make them attractive to users of portable devices, so organizations should be careful to specify the appropriate use of such devices in the acceptable use policies. Figure 8.6 shows an SD WLAN client device.

PHY Compatibilities

Early versions of the CF and SD WLAN devices only supported the HR/DSSS PHY due to power constraints. Newer implementations also support the ERP PHY. Support for the OFDM PHY is much more difficult to find. There are USB devices that support all of the PHYs currently implemented in IEEE 802.11 as well as the draft for IEEE 802.11n.

Features

Support for similar features to those found in PC Cards can be found in USB, CF, and SD devices. It is more difficult to find support for advanced technologies in the CF and SD form factors than in the USB form factor. For example, the Linksys WCF54g pictured in Figure 8.5 only supports WEP encryption and does not support WPA or WPA2 for enhanced security. USB devices are capable of supporting all modern security standards and capabilities, but it is important that you ensure the specific device you are selecting does support the security specifications that you demand.

FIGURE 8.6 SD WLAN NIC

Installation

Installation of a USB WLAN NIC is very similar to that of PC Cards. Install the drivers and/or software and then connect the USB device or cable to an available USB port. In rare situations, you may be required to connect the USB device before you perform the driver installation.

The CF and SD cards will require the installation of appropriate driver software on the PocketPC or PDA phone in which they are being installed. This may require synchronization with a laptop or desktop computer before or after the insertion of the WLAN device. Check your vendor's installation manuals to be certain.

PCI and Mini-PCI Cards

The WLAN NICs covered up to this point are all devices that are connected through external connectors to laptops, desktops, and PDAs. PCI and Mini-PCI adapters differ in that they are installed internally. If you choose not to use a USB device for a desktop computer, you will most likely select an internal WLAN card. This means you will be using a PCI or PCI Express (PCIe) device. Figure 8.7 shows a PCI adapter, and Figure 8.8 shows a PCIe adapter. You must ensure that your desktop computer supports the interface specification of the WLAN NIC (either PCI or PCIe).

Mini-PCI cards are used in laptop computers as well as some WLAN infrastructure devices. Those used in WLAN infrastructure devices are used to provide supports for differing PHYs while sharing consistent software and logic processing. Many newer laptops support the Mini-PCI specification;

FIGURE 8.7 PCI adapter from D-Link

FIGURE 8.8 PCIe adapter from D-Link

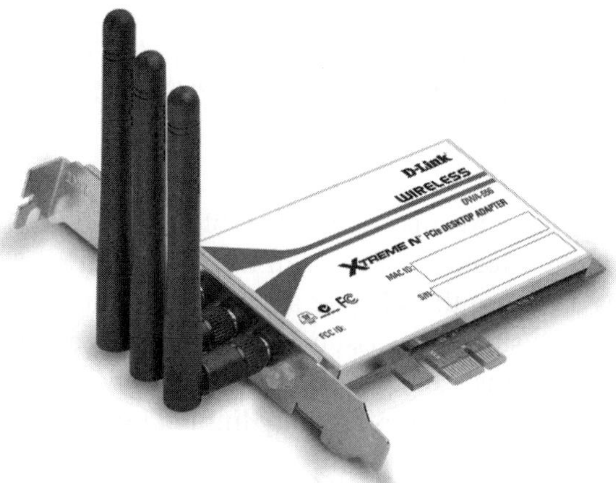

however, not all laptops provide easy access to the Mini-PCI port. For this reason, some WLAN network administrators choose to use PC Cards, ExpressCards, or USB devices when upgrading the WLAN support in these laptops. The internal Mini-PCI card is usually just disabled in such situations. Figure 8.9 shows a PCIe Mini-PCI card.

FIGURE 8.9 Mini-PCI card from Intel

PHY Compatibilities

WLAN NICs in the PCI and Mini-PCI form factors are available for every PHY specified in the IEEE 802.11 standards as amended as well as implementations of the draft 802.11n PHY (HT).

Features

PCI and Mini-PCI cards may support all of the IEEE 802.11 standards as well as proprietary features. They will likely support all the features listed for PC Cards earlier in this chapter and will have the capabilities to support all newer security standards, assuming the device is a newer device. Because of the internal connection to the system bus, power is usually not a problem and the capabilities are only limited by the chipset used.

Installation

The difference between PCI/Mini-PCI cards and the other devices mentioned in this chapter is that the PCI/Mini-PCI cards will require screwdrivers and other tools as you remove cases and covers to access the device. Desktops will require the removal of the computer case cover in order to access the PCI or PCIe card, and laptops will require the removal of one or more covers to access the Mini-PCI card. In extreme situations, with poorly designed laptop cases, you may even be required to remove the keyboard in order to access the area where the Mini-PCI card is installed.

Wireless Presentation Gateways

Wireless presentation gateways allow multiple computers equipped with WLAN cards to share a centralized display device. In most cases, this centralized display device will be a projector used to display the computer screen in a large format; however, they will also connect to standard CRT and LCD monitors. Figure 8.10 shows a typical installation and use of a wireless presentation gateway.

PHY Compatibilities

Wireless presentation gateways are standard IEEE 802.11 STAs and, therefore, may support HR/DSSS, OFDM, and ERP PHYs. While a wireless presentation gateway may implement OFDM, I have not seen any such devices. The devices on the market support HR/DSSS and ERP PHYs only. Additionally, many LCD projectors are beginning to support wireless connectivity out of the box without the need for any external devices.

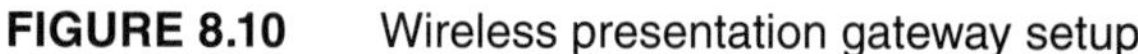

FIGURE 8.10 Wireless presentation gateway setup

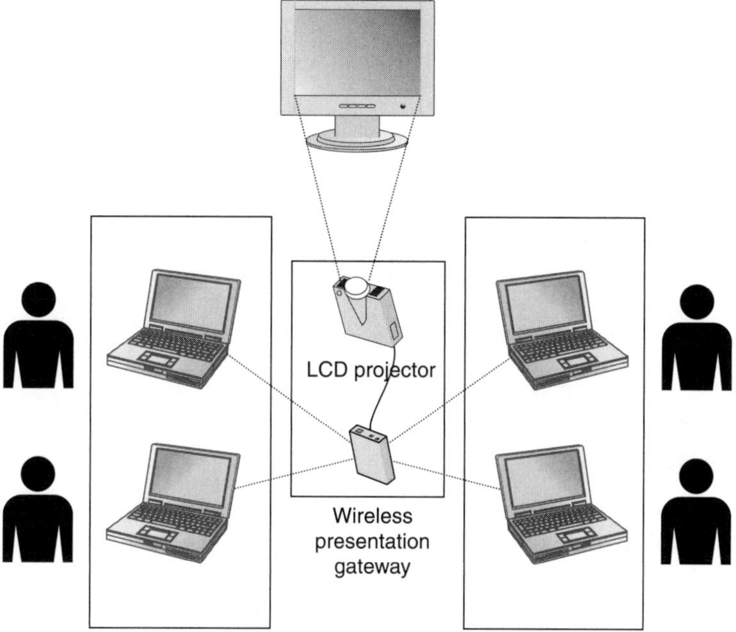

Features

Wireless presentation gateways, such as the D-Link DPG-2100 shown in Figures 8.11 (the device) and 8.12 (the configuration interface), usually include the following features:

- Support for multiple presenters
- IEEE 802.11 standard WLAN implementation
- VGA or DVI connectivity
- Possible RCA or S-Video connectivity
- Transfer of computer screen as well as audio streams
- Ethernet connectivity for Internet bridging and immediate ESS WLAN implementation (the device acts as an access point as well as a wireless presentation gateway)
- Presentation client software installable from the wireless presentation gateway to the connecting devices. No CD-ROM required

FIGURE 8.11 D-Link wireless presentation gateway

Installation

Installing a wireless presentation gateway usually involves the following steps:

1. Connect the wireless presentation gateway to the projector or monitor that will act as the shared display.
2. If an Ethernet connection is provided for Internet bridging and you desire to use it, connect the Ethernet port on the wireless presentation gateway to a live Ethernet connection.

FIGURE 8.12 D-Link wireless presentation gateway configuration interface

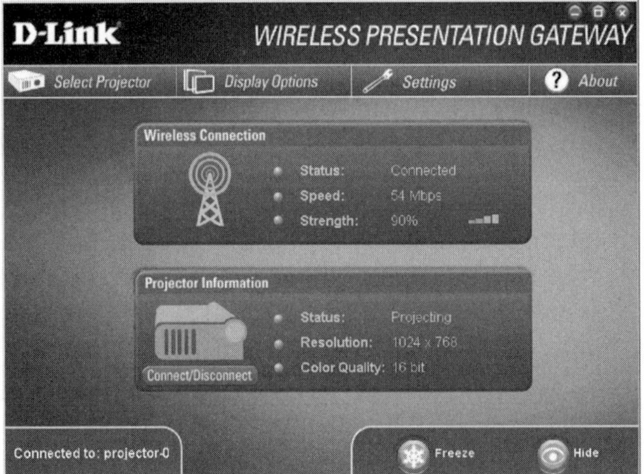

3. Connect the wireless presentation gateway to an AC outlet and power it on.
4. From one of the client computers that will connect to and utilize the wireless presentation gateway, connect to the SSID of the wireless presentation gateway. This SSID will vary by vendor.
5. Install any necessary client utilities for connecting with and managing the wireless presentation gateway.
6. Use these utilities to control which client devices may access and control the wireless presentation gateway.
7. Set up your display to be routed through the wireless presentation gateway client software as well as your local display output.

Installing a WLAN Client Device

This section provides a walk-through of a sample WLAN client device installation. While I will be demonstrating the installation of a specific WLAN NIC, the basic process holds true for most WLAN client devices. I will begin by discussing the option of using built-in WLAN support features of your operating system as compared to using the client software that comes with the WLAN NIC. Next, I will cover device driver and client software installation, and finally, I will show you the process of connecting to a WLAN with both the built-in Windows wireless client and the NIC vendor's client software.

Operating System Clients Versus NIC Vendor Clients

Some operating systems include wireless client software that supports various security technologies and WLAN hardware. For example, Windows XP supports the Wireless Zero Configuration (WZC) client that can be used to connect to a WLAN with IEEE 802.11 standard hardware (pictured in Figure 8.13). Many organizations select the WZC client that is built into Windows XP for the simple reasons that it is there and that the users are often familiar with it from personal laptop and desktop experience. However, not all WLAN NICs fully support WZC, and the configuration methods can become complex in these situations. When this is the case, it is often better to use the NIC vendor's client software instead.

FIGURE 8.13 Wireless Zero Configuration in Windows XP

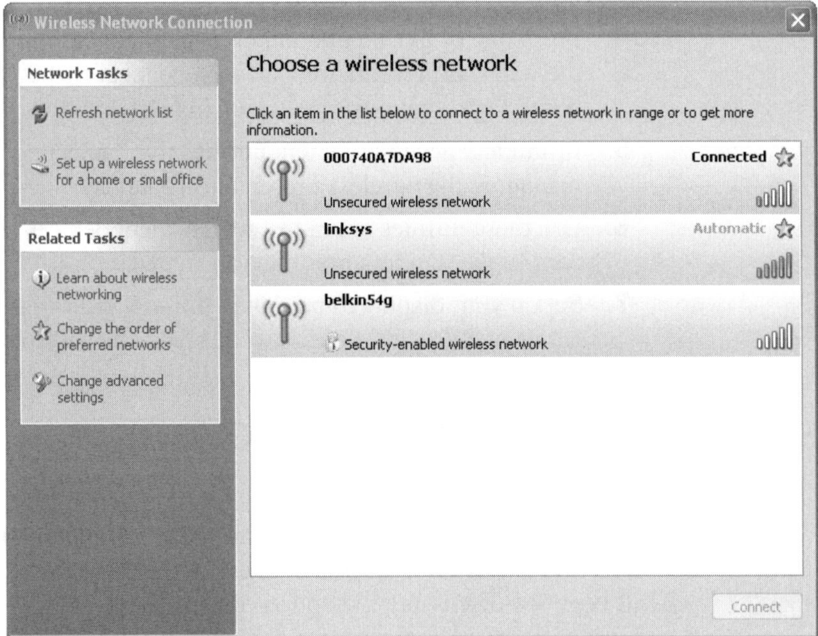

NIC vendor client software also often provides unique features that are not available in the WZC interface. Mac clients can connect using the Network dialog when using an AirPort wireless card or a compatible PC Card. The Mac Network dialog is shown in Figure 8.14.

Installing WLAN Client Drivers and Software

Most WLAN clients come with a CD-ROM containing the drivers for the device. Many laptops already have WLAN clients installed when they come from the factory. In the following pages, I will demonstrate the installation of a WLAN CardBus card from Ubiquiti Networks. This card, shown in Figure 8.15, is the SuperRance CardBus card. It is a 300 mW output CardBus card that supports IEEE 802.11a (OFDM) and IEEE 802.11g (ERP). Of course, since the card supports ERP, it also supports HR/DSSS for backward compatibility.

FIGURE 8.14 Configuring WLAN connectivity on a Mac

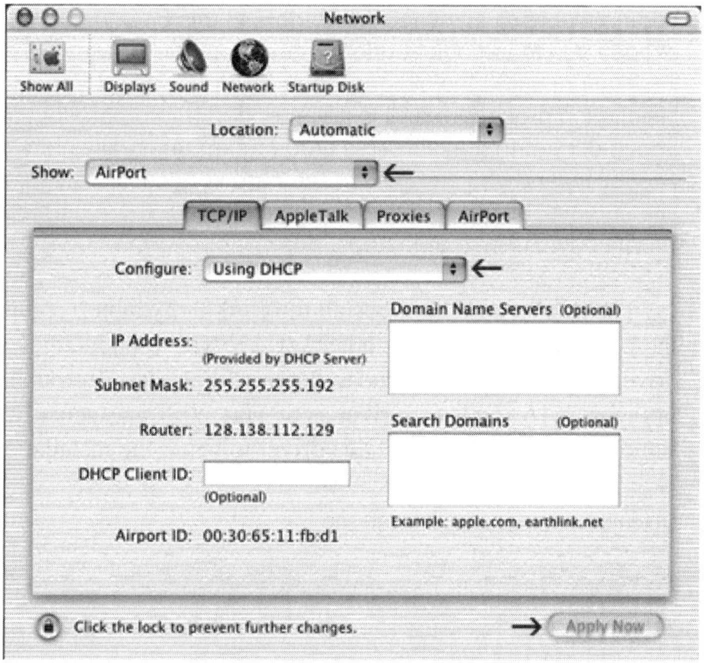

FIGURE 8.15 Ubiquiti Networks SuperRange CardBus card

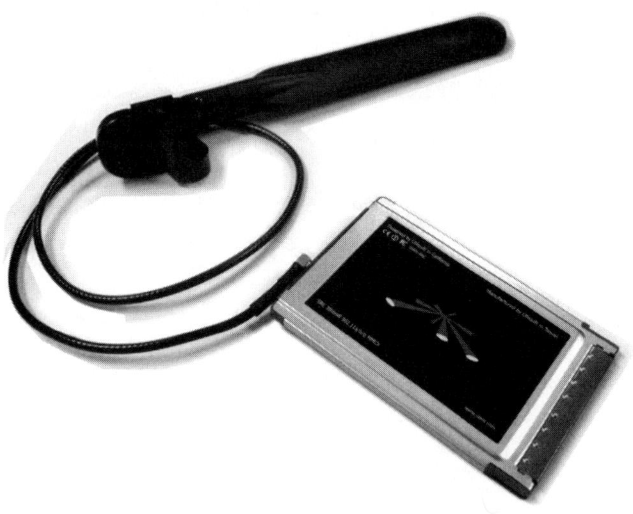

> The CWNA program is a vendor-neutral program. For this reason, I do not sponsor any specific vendors in this book. It is my intention to expose you to various vendors throughout the chapters. This example installation, using the Ubiquiti card, is intended to demonstrate a common installation procedure and is not intended to promote this particular card above others. In addition, this card has an unusually high–output power capability, and you should use the card very cautiously for testing and/or site surveys, as it will not likely behave as the more common cards or WLAN devices in your laptops, desktops, and PDAs.

The first step I took to install the card in my laptop computer was to visit the Ubiquiti web site. Like other WLAN NIC vendors, they often provide driver updates, and I decided to begin with the latest version. As you can see in Figure 8.16, the latest driver as of May 2007 was actually released that same month. I downloaded this driver to begin the installation process.

FIGURE 8.16 Ubiquiti Networks support web site

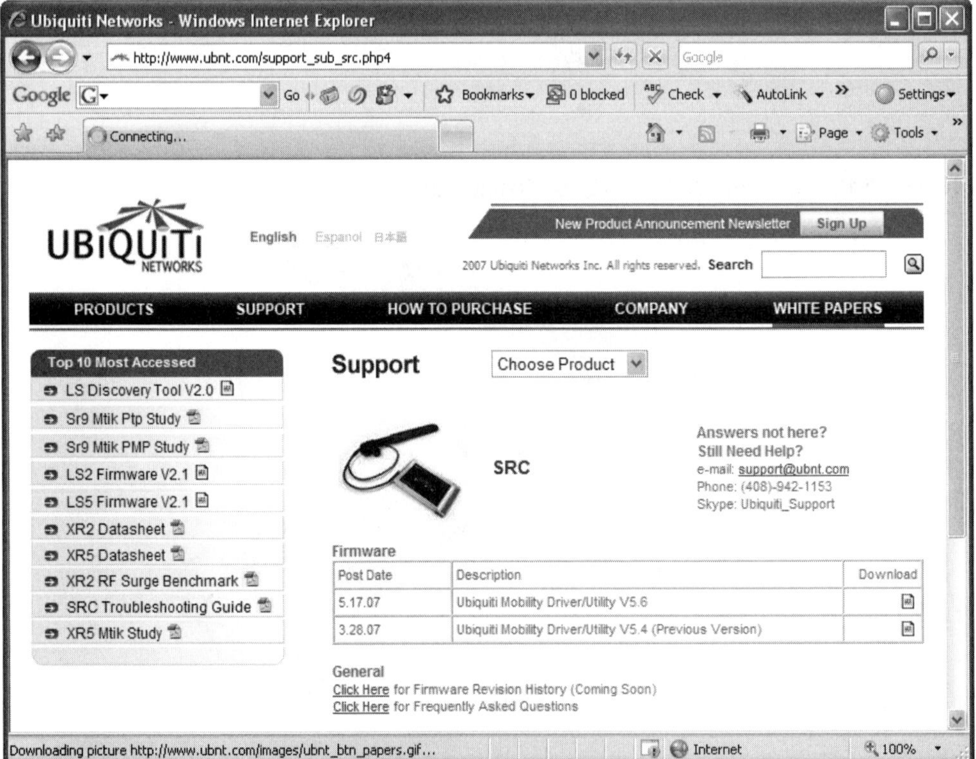

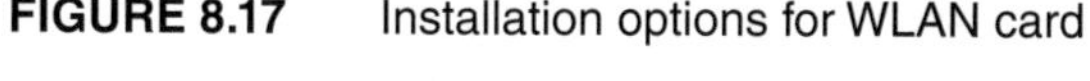

FIGURE 8.17 Installation options for WLAN card

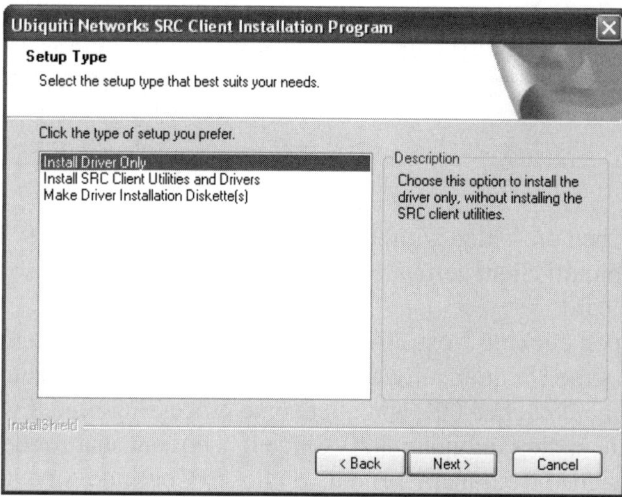

After downloading the most recent drivers and client utilities, I executed the installation program that was downloaded. As is typical with installation routines, a Welcome screen was displayed. I clicked Next, indicated my agreement with the license document, and clicked Next again. This resulted in the screen shown in Figure 8.17. Since this is a downloaded driver installation, it provides me with the option to make driver installation diskettes. The other options provided allow me to install the driver only for my wireless card or to also install the client software.

This is a very important decision. If I choose to install the driver only, I will have to configure my WLAN client with the WZC interface or a third-party WLAN client. If I install the client software that comes with the Ubiquiti card, I may be provided with extra features. In this case, I chose to install the SuperRange Card Client Utilities and Drivers and then clicked Next.

At this point, I receive the warning message shown in Figure 8.18. This card requires that it be inserted before the installation process can continue. I inserted the card and clicked OK. Next I chose to install the software to the default location and clicked Next.

After this, I chose to install the default program group on the Start menu, and I read a notification message that informed me I could configure the SuperRange card either with the Ubiquiti software or with WZC.

FIGURE 8.18 Warning message requiring card insertion

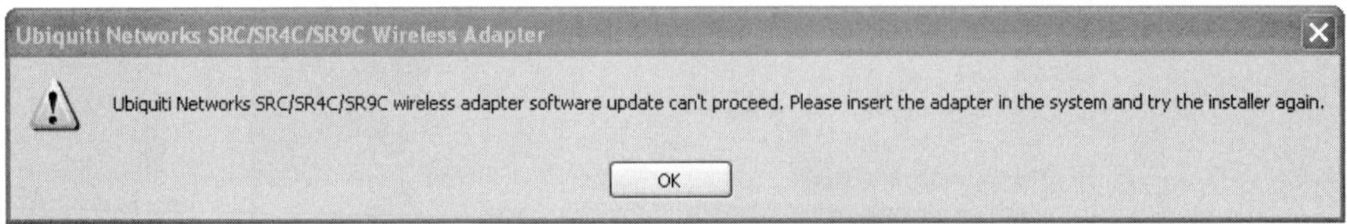

I was then presented with the dialog shown in Figure 8.19. I chose to use the Ubiquiti client software to ensure that I was able to use all the features of the card.

Upon clicking Next, I was presented with a notification dialog telling me that the Ubiquiti software would configure the card automatically at this time. I clicked OK, and after some processing time, I was presented with the dialog in Figure 8.20. Since it is not unusual for device drivers to be unsigned from many vendors, I clicked Continue Anyway to complete the installation.

After more processing and installation of files, the installation was completed and I clicked Finish. At this point, I right-clicked the Ubiquiti client software icon in the Windows XP task tray and selected Open Ubiquiti Client Utility (Figure 8.21), which results in the display of the dialog seen in Figure 8.22.

FIGURE 8.19 Selecting the WLAN supplicant

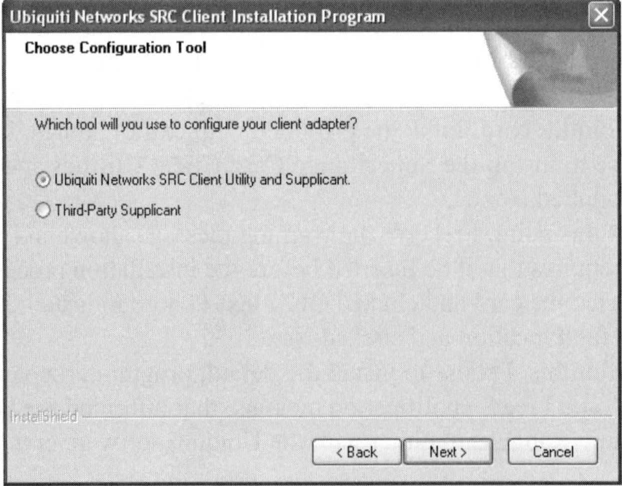

FIGURE 8.20 Verifying unsigned software and drivers

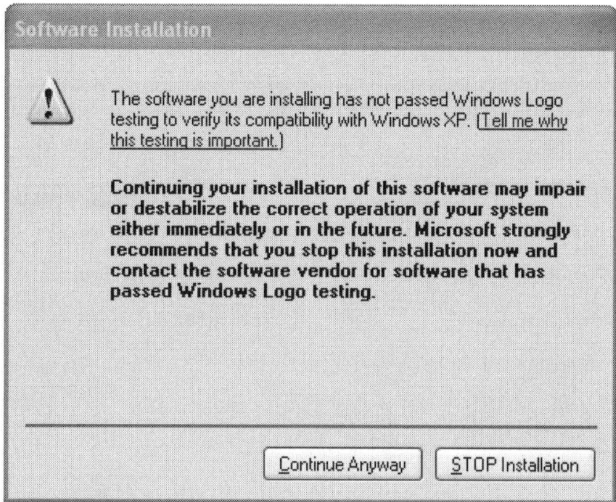
Software Installation
The software you are installing has not passed Windows Logo testing to verify its compatibility with Windows XP. (Tell me why this testing is important.)
Continuing your installation of this software may impair or destabilize the correct operation of your system either immediately or in the future. Microsoft strongly recommends that you stop this installation now and contact the software vendor for software that has passed Windows Logo testing.
Continue Anyway
STOP Installation

Connecting to a WLAN

Since I had a wireless connection previously configured using the built-in wireless client on my laptop, the Ubiquiti software picked up this profile automatically and configured the card to connect to that same network. You can see the connection status in Figure 8.22.

This client software provides advanced status information like that seen in Figure 8.23 as well as channel scanning tools for location of WLANs. It is also interesting to note that, from the exact same location, the Ubiquiti card is able to maintain a 24 Mbps data rate and the built-in WLAN card in my laptop can only maintain an 11 Mbps data rate. This holds consistent while I am transferring data as well.

FIGURE 8.21 Opening the Ubiquiti client software

Help
Exit
Open Ubiquiti Client Utility...
Preferences...
Disable Radio
Manual Login
Reauthenticate
Select Profile
Show Connection Status

FIGURE 8.22 Ubiquiti client software showing connectivity status

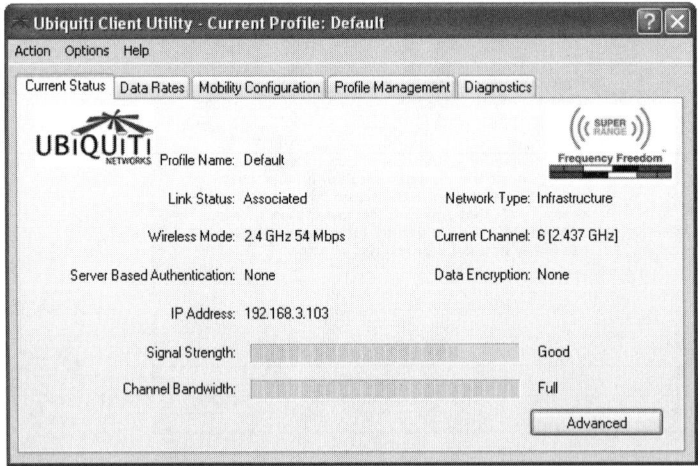

One of the more advanced features of this client card is the ability to manually control roaming selectivity. As you can see in Figure 8.24, you can leave the settings at the default and let the card's drivers manage them, or you can optimize the settings for bandwidth or distance. You can also customize the setting for your specific needs. When set to Optimize Bandwidth, the client software will attempt to find a new AP and roam to it any time the data rate falls below 54 Mbps for 802.11a or below 11 Mbps for 802.11g and 802.11b. When set to Optimize Distance, the client software

FIGURE 8.23 Advanced Status page

Advanced Status

Network Name (SSID):	000740A7DA98	Current Signal Strength:	-82 dBm
Server Based Authentication:	None	Current Noise Level:	-95 dBm
Data Encryption:	None	Up Time:	00:15:05
Authentication Type:	None	802.11b Preamble:	Short & Long
Message Integrity Check:	None	Current Receive Rate:	24.0 Mbps
QoS:	None	Current Transmit Rate:	18.0 Mbps
Associated AP Name:	Unavailable	Channel:	11
Associated AP IP Address:	Unavailable	Frequency:	2.462 GHz
Associated AP MAC Address:	00-07-40-9F-7C-03	Channel Set:	United States
Power Save Mode:	Normal		
Current Power Level:	300 mW		
Available Power Levels (802.11a):	120,95,60,48,30,24 mW		
Available Power Levels (802.11b/g):	300,238,189,119,75,38 mW		

OK

FIGURE 8.24 Mobility configuration settings

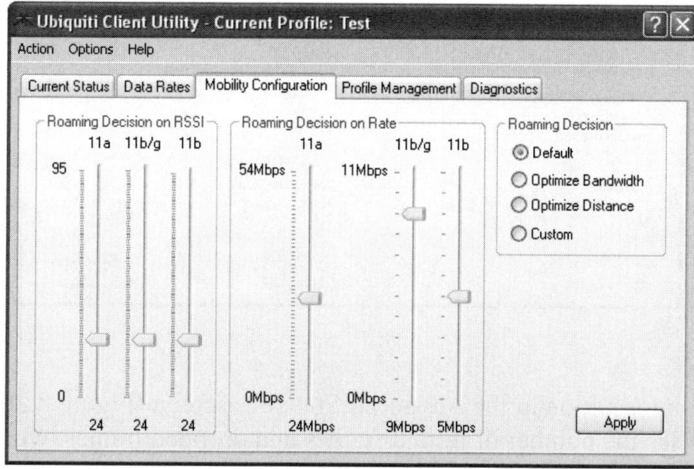

will attempt to roam to a stronger signal AP when the 802.11a data rate is below 24 Mbps, the 802.11g data rate is below 9 Mbps, or the 802.11b data rate is below 5 Mbps. This feature is one that would certainly not be available if you chose to use the built-in WZC client in Windows XP.

Finally, the Ubiquiti client software can be used to track statistics related to your WLAN connection. Figures 8.25 and 8.26 show the statistics and advanced statistics dialogs. While the statistics screen is useful (Figure 8.25), you can see the tremendous benefit of the

FIGURE 8.25 Ubiquiti client software statistics dialog

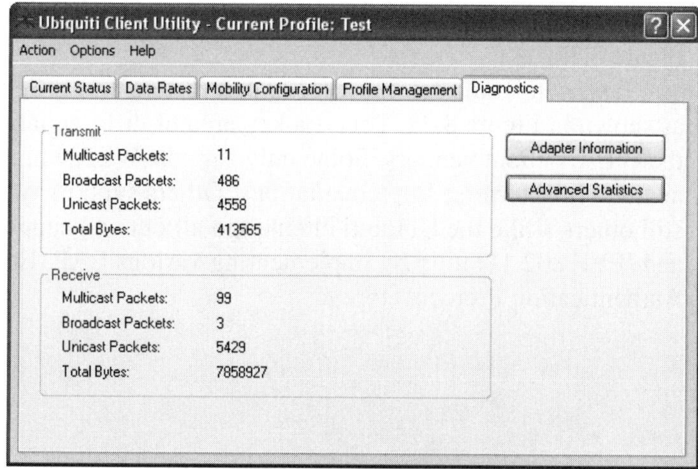

FIGURE 8.26 Ubiquiti client software Advanced Statistics dialog

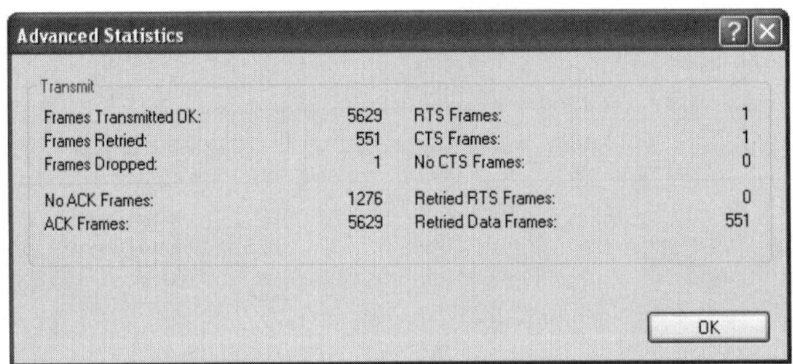

information in the Advanced Statistics screen (Figure 8.26). Here you can see the number of retried frames and dropped frames, which can be an indicator of the overall health of your connection.

Creating Connection Profiles

Most WLAN client software utilities provide a method for creating connection profiles. These profiles make it easier to reconnect to WLANs again in the future, and they may provide automatic connectivity when the WLAN comes in range. Automatic connectivity should be used with great caution, as many client utilities will connect to any WLAN as long as it is configured to use the same SSID. This can lead to unwanted connections when traveling with the wireless client.

The Ubiquiti client software provides connection profiles on the Profile Management tab of the application. Here you can configure a profile name and the valid SSIDs that can be used to connect to this profile as seen in Figure 8.27.

Next, you would set the security parameters on the Security tab as shown in Figure 8.28. This is a key area of differentiation among the WLAN client vendors. Some only support WEP, which should be avoided in enterprise implementations. Others support WPA only, while still others—like the Ubiquiti client—go all out and support WPA/WPA2 and IEEE 802.11i fully by implementing various EAP (Encapsulated Authentication Protocol) types.

FIGURE 8.27 Creating a profile

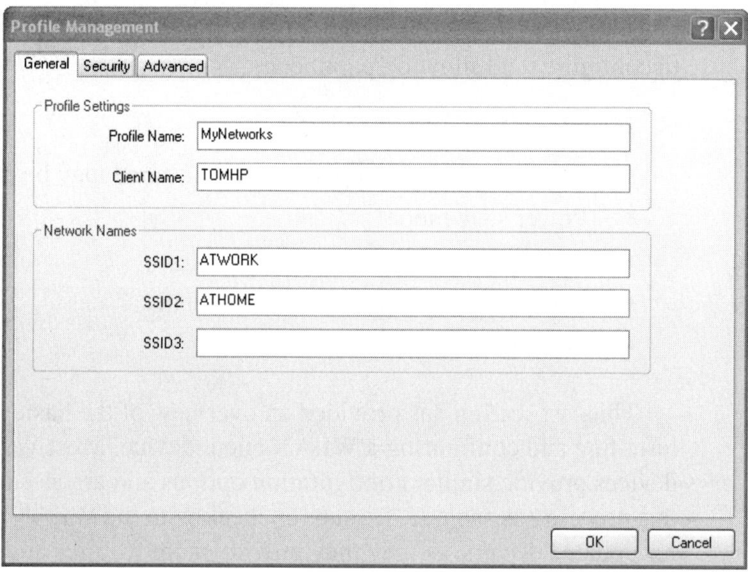

FIGURE 8.28 Configuring security for the profile

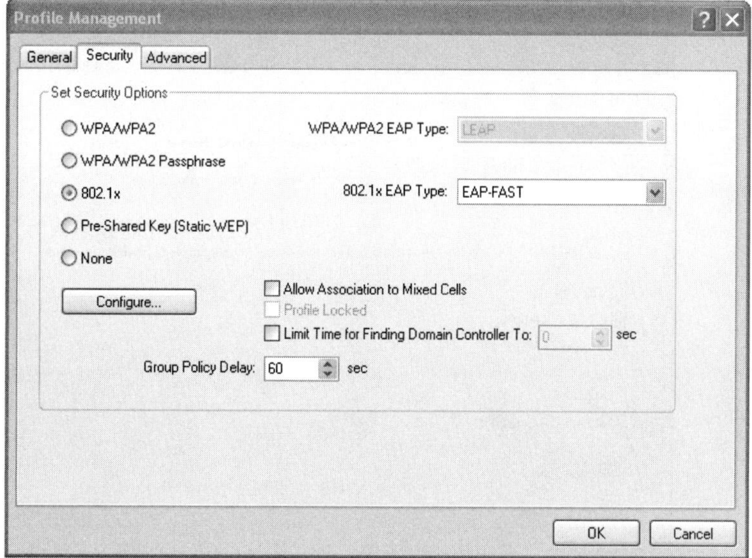

Finally, you can configure settings such as the PHY types you want to connect to if the card supports multiple PHYs and you can configure other unique parameters. As shown in Figure 8.29, the Ubiquiti client allows you to configure the following parameters:

- Transmit power levels
- Wireless modes (supported PHYs—some may be proprietary)
- Power save mode
- Network types (BSS or IBSS)
- IEEE 802.11 preambles to implement
- Authentication mode

This last section has provided an overview of the basic process of installing and configuring a WLAN client device. Most WLAN client devices provide similar configuration options and are as easy to use as this process has seemed. Be sure to check with the WLAN NIC vendor for updated drivers, as they may provide more features and, often more important, security enhancements.

FIGURE 8.29 Configuring advanced profile parameters

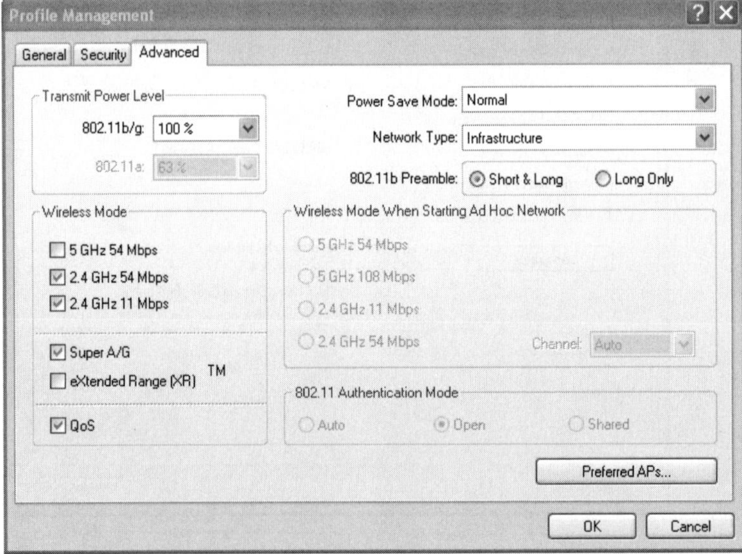

Summary

In this chapter, you learned about the various WLAN client types that are available. The PC Cards were introduced, including the older PCMCIA-type cards that are 16-bit and the newer, 32-bit PCMCIA cards known as CardBus cards. The new ExpressBus card type was also introduced. Next, you learned about the USB, Compact Flash, and Secure Digital IO WLAN clients. The last standard WLAN client type was the PCI and Mini-PCI card. You also learned about wireless presentation gateways, which are technically infrastructure devices, since they implement an AP, but they were covered in this chapter because they are not usually used in an infrastructure implementation from the perspective of providing ongoing network access.

Finally, you walked through an installation of a typical WLAN client device from driver and software installation through to configuration and connection. You learned about the common differences between the built-in Windows XP WZC client and vendor-specific wireless NIC client software.

Key Terms

- ☐ **CardBus**
- ☐ **ExpressCard**
- ☐ **Mini-PCI**
- ☐ **PC Card**
- ☐ **PCI**
- ☐ **PCIe**
- ☐ **PCMCIA**
- ☐ **Secure Digital**

Review Questions

1. You have a PocketPC PDA on which you wish to provide Internet connectivity through your company's WLAN. The device has no built-in WLAN functionality. What are the WLAN client device types that may work with this unit, assuming the vendors support your particular PocketPC implementation?

   A. PCMCIA

   B. SD

   C. CF

   D. PCIe

2. You want to track advanced statistics related to your WLAN connection. Which WLAN client software should you use and why?

   A. WZC, because it supports viewing advanced statistics when running Windows XP Service Pack 2

   B. WZC, because it supports viewing advanced statistics out of the box

   C. The NIC's client software, because it is more likely to support viewing of advanced statistics

   D. The NIC's client software, because it will always support viewing of advanced statistics

3. You want to configure your desktop computer to connect to the WLAN. It does not currently have a WLAN NIC installed. Which of the following form factors will work in your desktop computer without additional converters?

   A. PCI

   B. PCMCIA

   C. CardBus

   D. USB

Review Answers

1. **B, C.** The Secure Digital IO and Compact Flash form factors are likely to work with the PocketPC unit. You must verify compatibility with the hardware vendor, but devices are readily available for newer versions of the PocketPC OS.

2. **C.** The NIC's client software is more likely to support viewing of advanced statistics. There are third-party tools that may work in conjunction with WZC to enable viewing advanced statistics, but Microsoft has not provided the ability out of the box or with Service Pack 2. It is not certain that the NIC's client software will support viewing of advanced statistics. You should check with the hardware vendor or simply install the client software to determine if such features are supported.

3. **A, D.** Most desktops will not support PCMCIA or CardBus cards. These cards are more likely to work in laptops, notebooks, or tablet computers. There are converters available to allow the connection of a PCMCIA card to a desktop, but the question disallowed such technologies. The only remaining valid answers are PCI and USB adapters, which would both work with desktop computers.

PART

Securing Wireless LANs

In This Part

CHAPTER

9

Wireless Vulnerabilities and Attack Methods

CWNA Exam Objectives Covered:

- Describe the following types of WLAN security attacks, and explain how to identify and prevent them where possible
    - Eavesdropping, Man-in-the-Middle, and Hijacking Attacks
    - Denial of Service (Physical and Data Link Attacks)
    - Management Interface Exploits
    - Encryption and Authentication Cracking

In This Chapter

WLANs have vulnerabilities that are common to all computer networks, and they have vulnerabilities that are specific to IEEE 802.11 networks. When something is implemented in the same way over and over again, it becomes more likely that someone will eventually discover the weaknesses in that thing if weaknesses exist. This is seen in the most popular operating systems and software applications, and in the most popular WLAN networks, which are IEEE 802.11 based.

IEEE 802.11 networks showed their biggest security vulnerability when the one real security feature was hacked in the first few years of its existence. This security feature was WEP (discussed later in this chapter and the next). Other optional configuration parameters have been touted as security features over the years, but either they were never intended as such or vulnerabilities were known from their inception. These features include things like MAC filtering and disabling the broadcast of SSIDs from access points. As you will see, in these next two chapters, neither of these features provide any real security.

This chapter will present the inherent weaknesses in standards-based IEEE 802.11 networks that do not implement the newest version of Clause 8 in a secure fashion based on the solutions first introduced in the IEEE 802.11 amendment.

Identifying and Preventing WLAN Security Attacks

Clause 8 was included in the original IEEE 802.11-1997 standard; however, it only offered the use of authentication mechanisms and WEP encryption that were shown to be very weak very quickly. With the ratification of the IEEE 802.11i amendment, Clause 8 has been heavily updated to include support for better security technologies that can eradicate (at least for now) the majority of the security vulnerabilities discussed in this chapter. A robust security network as specified in the new version of Clause 8 that is implemented with a strong EAP type is very difficult, if not impossible to hack into at this time. The original Clause 8 only spanned about 11 pages, whereas the new clause is almost 100 pages long. There is obviously more information included, and so far, it has proved to provide a security framework that is very strong.

In fairness to the IEEE, since I have not seen it clearly documented elsewhere outside the standards, the original specification stated that WEP was intended to protect "authorized users of a wireless LAN from *casual* eavesdropping" (emphasis added). It was never intended as a robust security technology in the first place. I would argue that it still protects authorized users from casual eavesdropping, depending on how you define casual. The question is: Do you want to casually protect your enterprise data from casual attacks? You'll read more on this in Chapter 10.

In this section, I will provide an overview of the common attack methods used against WLANs. These methods include

- Eavesdropping
- Hijacking
- Man-in-the-middle
- Denial of service (DoS)
- Management interface exploits
- *Encryption cracking*
- *Authentication cracking*
- MAC spoofing
- Peer-to-peer attacks
- Social engineering

Eavesdropping

Because a WLAN sends data through the open air, an antenna placed in the right location and connected to a WLAN NIC can read this data. It is impractical to prevent an attacker from "reading the frames" out of the air, if the attacker can get close enough to your WLAN to pick up the signal. He will not have to associate with the WLAN to view the frames that are being transmitted, and this is very important to remember.

If you just read that last paragraph and begin to think, "Wait. I thought you could encrypt the data," you are absolutely correct. You can encrypt the data, but I can still read the frames using a WLAN analyzer application. I may not be able to decipher the meaningful data that is in the frames, but I can read the frames, and that cannot be stopped. Since you cannot stop an attacker from reading the frames, you must ensure that you are using an encryption method that is solid enough to protect against a fast attack. In other words, if an attacker can hack your encryption in just a few minutes, it's not strong enough. As you may know, WEP encryption can indeed be hacked in just a few minutes and should not be used in any production WLAN when newer encryption schemes are available. You will learn more about the weaknesses of WEP in Chapter 10.

Some people refer to wardriving as casual eavesdropping. *Wardriving* is the process of locating WLANs that have not been configured for your access. In recent years, it has evolved to act as an umbrella term for nearly any method used to find a WLAN. Some wardriving may be innocent in intent, but this does not make it any more legal. You should avoid accessing or penetrating WLANs that were not set up for your use or on which you were not granted permission to perform testing. There may be legal ramifications of such behavior.

If you are accessing a public hotspot, you are not wardriving. You are accessing a hotspot that has been set up for your use. For example, at the time of this writing, the Panera Bread store down the street from me provides free WLAN Internet access. If I access the Internet through their network, I am not wardriving. I am simply accessing the network that has been set up for my use. The same is true when I access a hotel's free Wi-Fi service when I am staying there as a customer.

On the other hand, if I drive down the street in my neighborhood and find and use an open WLAN—either intentionally left open or unintentionally—I may actually be committing a crime, depending on local regulations. This is a very serious issue and will likely grow to become more serious as time passes. When you access a network, be sure you've been given the right to do so—even if you are performing a penetration test. In the situation where you've been asked to perform a penetration test, I suggest you acquire a written contract that stipulates what and how you will be allowed to access the network.

Others suggest that wardriving does not even fit into the category of eavesdropping, since you are not actually "listening" to meaningful conversations. For our purpose here, we can categorize wardriving as eavesdropping because the wardriver is listening for frames that are not intended for his or her use. That is the fundamental definition of *eavesdropping*: the intercepting and reading of messages and information by unintended recipients.

The following tools may all be used for casual eavesdropping or WLAN network location:

- MacStumbler
- KisMac
- NetStumbler
- KisMet
- Easy Wi-Fi Radar

Figure 9.1 shows the Easy Wi-Fi Radar application, which is a relatively new entry to the WLAN locator or stumbler application pool.

There is a more sinister type of eavesdropping, however. This malicious type of eavesdropping involves the capture of data packets that are traversing the wireless medium (WM). In order to do this, the attacker will need to utilize a WLAN protocol analyzer. This is a software application that is designed for or also supports the capturing of IEEE 802.11 frames through a WLAN NIC.

Many regulatory domains have finalized laws making it a crime to listen in telephone conversations without previous authorization.

FIGURE 9.1 Easy Wi-Fi Radar

The recording of telephone conversations, even those initiated voluntarily by the customer, is illegal in the United States. This is why you hear the message, "This call may be recorded," when you call so many customer service support centers. A number of these regulatory domains have extended these laws, or written new ones, that cover all electromagnetic communications. Since WLANs use electromagnetic waves for communications, their frames would be covered under such regulations. Don't take these laws lightly. Though there have not been many reported cases of prosecutions up to this point, this should not be taken as a sign that governments will not enforce these laws. In the United States, we've seen local governments become more aware of WLAN security issues and take steps to help their citizens and local organizations protect themselves from computer crimes.

There are both commercial and freeware applications that can be used for malicious eavesdropping. Applications are available for the Windows, MAC, and Linux platforms. The following list includes some of the more common WLAN protocol analyzers available today:

- OmniPeek Personal (free)
- AiroPeek (commercial)
- Network Instruments Observer (commercial)
- AirMagnet Laptop Analyzer (commercial)
- Javvin CAPSA (commercial)
- Ethereal (open source), now WireShark
- CommView for Wi-Fi PC (commercial)
- CommView for Wi-Fi PocketPC (commercial)

Figure 9.2 shows the CommView for Wi-Fi application running on a PocketPC. This tool is mostly used for wardriving, since it is limited in the data it can retrieve. Figure 9.3 shows the full CommView for Wi-Fi application running on a PC as an evaluation version.

Eavesdropping is a common precursor to the attack methods covered in the remainder of this section. For example, you may need to acquire a MAC address, in order to spoof that MAC address for connectivity, if you are attempting to hack into a WLAN that uses MAC filtering.

FIGURE 9.2 CommView for Wi-Fi PocketPC

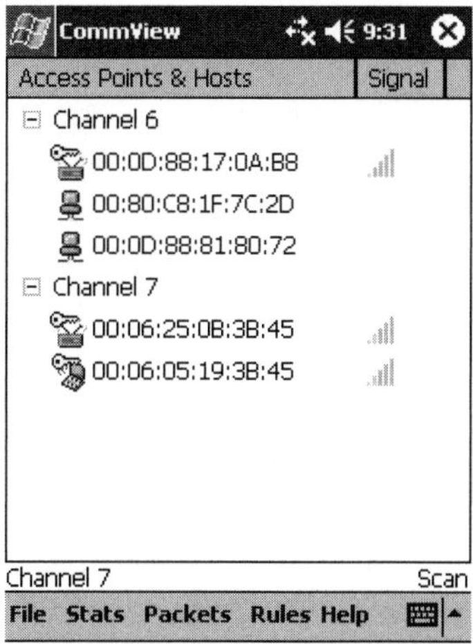

FIGURE 9.3 CommView for Wi-Fi PC

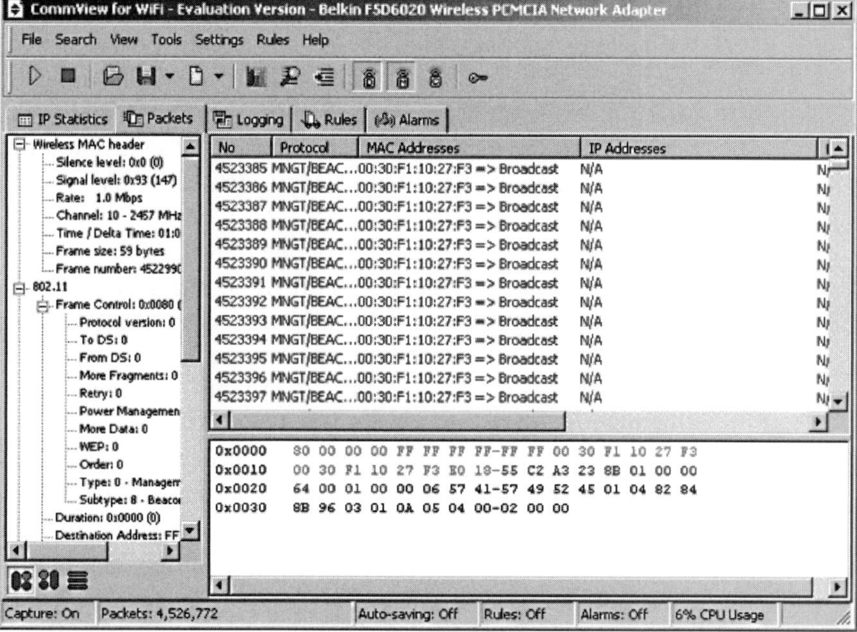

Hijacking

Hijacking is a situation in which an unauthorized user takes control of an authorized user's wireless LAN connection. In a WLAN, hijacking is done at Layer 2 for DoS and at Layer 3 for attacking purposes, although you could perform certain DoS attacks with a hijack of Layer 3 as well. The process of hijacking Layer 2 (the MAC layer) is outlined here:

1. The attacker starts his own AP, usually through software running on his computer.
2. The attacker configures his AP to use the same SSID as the WLAN to which the victim is currently associated.
3. The attacker sends a deauthentication frame (or turns on a high-powered RF signal generator, causing interference that results in the victim needing to reassociate), forcing the victim to look for a new AP with which to associate.
4. Since the attacker's AP is closer and provides a stronger signal, the victim associates with the attacker's AP and the user of the machine doesn't realize he is no longer associated with the valid AP.

If we stop at this stage, the result is a DoS scenario. Because the victim is no longer connected to the AP that actually provides access to needed services, services have been denied. However, the attacker can run a DHCP server on his machine that provides an IP address to the victim's STA. After the victim STA has a working IP configuration, the attacker can then attempt to access the victim station to steal data or plant viruses, worms, and more.

The attack can be taken to another level. At this level, the attacker uses two WLAN NICs. One acts as the AP to hijack Layer 2, as outlined in the four preceding steps, and the other acts as a standard WLAN client of the valid AP to which the victim was originally associated. The attacker then allows bridging across the two WLAN NICs, which is supported by a number of operating systems like Windows XP.

With this latter configuration, a *man-in-the-middle* attack is successfully accomplished. The victim can continue to browse the Internet or use other services provided by the valid AP. At the same time, the attacker can launch various attacks against the victim STA or simply monitor the traffic that is

FIGURE 9.4 WLAN hijacking attack and man-in-the-middle

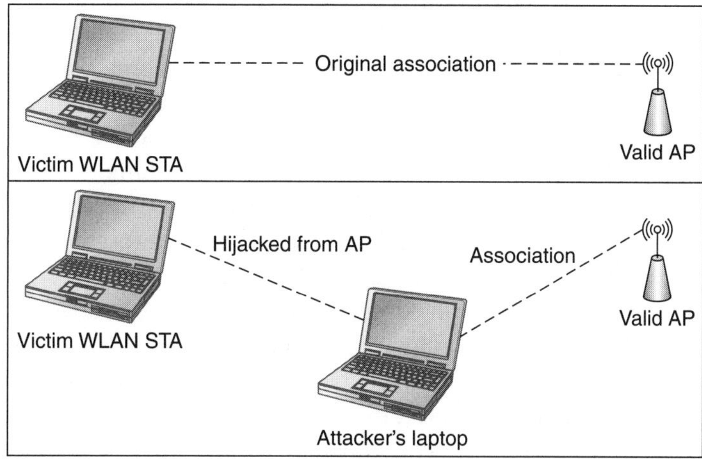

passing through the newly arranged bridge path through his computer. When you configure such a man-in-the-middle attack, you have hijacked Layers 1, 2, and 3 and have the ability to continue attacking the victim STA, without the user realizing that anyone is even accessing his computer. Figure 9.4 shows a graphical representation of the architecture of such an attack.

Windows Client Vulnerabilities

In addition to the hijacking concept presented here, Windows clients introduce an interesting vulnerability. By default, many Windows clients send out probe requests looking for "preferred networks." These are networks that you've connected to in the past; they can be seen in the Wireless Networks tab of the Properties dialog for your wireless connection in the Network Connections container. The order in which they appear is the order in which Windows attempts to connect to these networks. If the client cannot find a preferred network from this list, it will not simply stop scanning. Instead the client will scan for a randomly chosen network based on a randomly generated SSID. While this behavior may seem odd, it was implemented with good intentions. If there were no preferred networks available, the client would need to power off the WLAN device and then power it back on in order to scan for preferred networks again at some interval. Rather than having the user notified of a device being turned on and off, the developer chose to leave it on and probe for an assumed unavailable network with a random SSID.

It didn't take long for security crackers and hackers to realize the vulnerability exposed. While standard APs are configured with a specific SSID that they listen for in probe requests and transmit in Beacon frames (by default), new software-based APs can respond to any probe request and say, "Yeah, that's me. I'm the SSID you are probing for." In other words, cracking tools are out there that allow you to set up a rogue AP that responds to any SSID for which a client is probing. Now, when a Windows client probes for the randomly generated SSID, the rogue AP can even respond to this. An example of such a cracking tool is the software-based AP named Karma on the Linux platform.

The only real protection you have against such attacks (when using the Windows default client) is to keep your WLAN card powered off when you're not using it and be sure to remove any unsecured wireless networks from your preferred network list immediately after using them. If any unsecured wireless networks exist in your preferred network list, your computer will associate with an unsecured software-based AP running Karma (or some other tool) automatically. This remote attack machine can provide your computer with an IP address, and then the attacker can begin launching an attack against your machine. Another prevention technique would be to use a different WLAN client from the built-in Windows client. Many people are still unaware that you can disable the built-in Windows client and use a third-party WLAN client application that provides much greater security.

Denial of Service

Denial of service attacks are launched specifically against WLAN networks at Layer 1 (Physical) and Layer 2 (Data Link). A *denial of service* attack is a category of attacks that includes any actions resulting in the inability of users or systems to access needed resources. DoS attacks can be simple to implement or very complex. For this reason, they can be launched by attackers with little skill as well as attackers with in-depth knowledge of IEEE 802.11 networks.

The Layer 1, or Physical layer, attacks are also known as *RF jamming* attacks. This is done using devices that output RF energy, usually across the entire 2.4 GHz spectrum used by IEEE 802.11 devices. When these intentional radiators put out the RF energy at the power levels they support, it drowns out the RF energy being transmitted by valid STAs on your WLAN. Since the device (called a signal generator) puts out a signal that drowns out the signals of the WLAN, it effectively causes a DoS scenario. The interference can also be narrowband and still cause problems on your WLAN if the band fits nicely in the center of your configured IEEE 802.11 channel. Since the AP will not likely be configured to automatically adjust its channel in the face of interference (though some APs do have this capability), a DoS scenario can even be caused by narrowband signal generators.

Unintentional DoS scenarios can also exist due to the interference caused by microwave ovens, cordless phones, and other devices that share the frequency bandwidth with the WLAN. These unintentional DoS scenarios can wreak havoc on your WLAN even though they are not malicious. In general, they can be detected through the reports that come in from your users of degraded performance on the network. If these complaints begin to surface suddenly, it could be an indicator that something has changed in your environment. Look for new microwaves, new cordless phones, or even new WLANs installed by employees or nearby organizations.

Because signal generators are somewhat expensive, Layer 1 DoS attacks are not usually as common as Layer 2 DoS attacks on WLANs. A Layer 2 attack is launched by exploiting the processes used for frame management and network communications in a WLAN. For example, an attacker may spoof a deauthentication frame. This means that the attacker generates a frame on the WM that uses (spoofs) the MAC address of the AP, and the frame generated is a deauthentication or disassociation frame. These frames are management frames and, more specifically, notification frames. They cannot be ignored by the client STAs, so the client stations will be denied access to the WLAN as long as the attacker continues to transmit the spoofed disassociation or deauthentication frames.

There are additional Layer 2 DoS attacks that can be executed against a WLAN. You do not need to understand the details of their functionality for the CWNA exam, but it is helpful to know they exist. These additional methods include

- PS-Pool floods
- Association floods
- Authentication floods
- Empty data floods

The last one, empty data floods, is possible because you can use many different tools to generate data packets. If you install two or three WLAN adapters in a laptop computer and then enter any WLAN area, you can generate data frames of the maximum frame size on a continual basis. Since you are doing this with three different adapters at the same time, chances are good that you will tie up most of the available throughput in the service area. The closer you are to the AP and the more powerful the output of your WLAN adapters, the more likely you are to consume a large portion of the network's throughput. This is often said to be a data flood attack instead of a Layer 2 attack because the frames are intended to be used to carry upper-layer data and, in fact, they are generated by applications residing at the upper layer of the OSI model. For this reason, this is usually called a data flood attack, but a data flood attack is at least a partial DoS attack as well.

Eventually, the IEEE 802.11 standard will include protected management frames, and this will help prevent the true Layer 2 DoS attack methods. The IEEE P802.11w draft is in version 1.0 at the time of this writing. Much like the IEEE 802.11i amendment, the IEEE 802.11w amendment defines more robust methods to be used in WLANs. Where 802.11i specifies a robust security network, P802.11w defines robust management frames. In fact, P802.11w is written in such a way that it depends on 802.11i as an existing entity in the standard. For this reason, the draft document for P802.11w states that it is based on the draft for the rollup assumed to be released sometime in 2007 as IEEE 802.11-2007.

As a reference note, draft standards are prepended with a P while in draft stage to indicate that they are preliminary standards. Once a standard is ratified, the document name is appended with a dash and the year of the ratification. For example, IEEE 802.11n would currently be IEEE P802.11n in proper notation. If the standard is ratified in 2008, it would become IEEE 802.11n-2008 at that time.

For now, the use of a spectrum analyzer will help you track down the location of the interfering device. You may find an individual in the parking lot with a signal generator, or you may find that one of your users has installed a rogue AP in the corner of his office and configured it to use the same channel as your WLAN. Since he is sitting so close to the AP, he hasn't really noticed much of an interference problem, particularly since he is the only one using it. This is actually more common than finding the attacker with the signal generator—at least in my experience.

Management Interface Exploits

Most APs support a web-based management interface. When an attacker connects to an open WLAN, one of the first things she will usually do is attempt to connect to *x.x.x.*1, where the *x* represents the portion of the IP address in that octet. In other words, she will look at the IP address assigned to her machine. Imagine it is 10.10.10.18. She will attempt to connect to 10.10.10.1 with her web browser. This is because a WLAN residential gateway and many wireless routers use this IP addressing scheme for their default configuration. Some APs default to an IP address of 10.0.0.2, and others default to 192.168.1.245. However, most enterprise APs will have IP addresses assigned by the WLAN administrator. As an attacker, however, all she has to do is attempt to connect to each IP address in her subnet (determined by inspecting the IP address and subnet mask in her received configuration) or use a scanning tool that will attempt to connect to port 80 on each IP address. In short order, she will likely find the web-based interface of the AP or WLAN router if it is enabled.

One of the simplest solutions to this problem is to disable the web-based administration interface for WLAN connections. Figure 9.5 shows one WLAN router's screen for doing this. You must also consider the other configuration methods such as telnet and SSH. Be sure they are either disabled or secured with passwords that are very difficult to guess.

It is not uncommon for an attacker to turn a *management interface exploit* into a type of DoS attack. I've seen multiple scenarios where the attacker gained access to the AP or WLAN router and then configured the MAC filters to only allow his or her client access. This gave the attacker full access to the provided throughput for some period of time until the exploit was discovered. In all of these cases that I've encountered, the WLANs were wide open and had not implemented any effective security solutions. WPA-PSK or WPA2-PSK with a sufficiently long and cryptic preshared key would have prevented the attack in every one of these scenarios. Two of the organizations were large enough to justify implementing WPA2-Enterprise and use very strong levels of encryption and authentication.

FIGURE 9.5 Linksys WRT-54g web management configuration

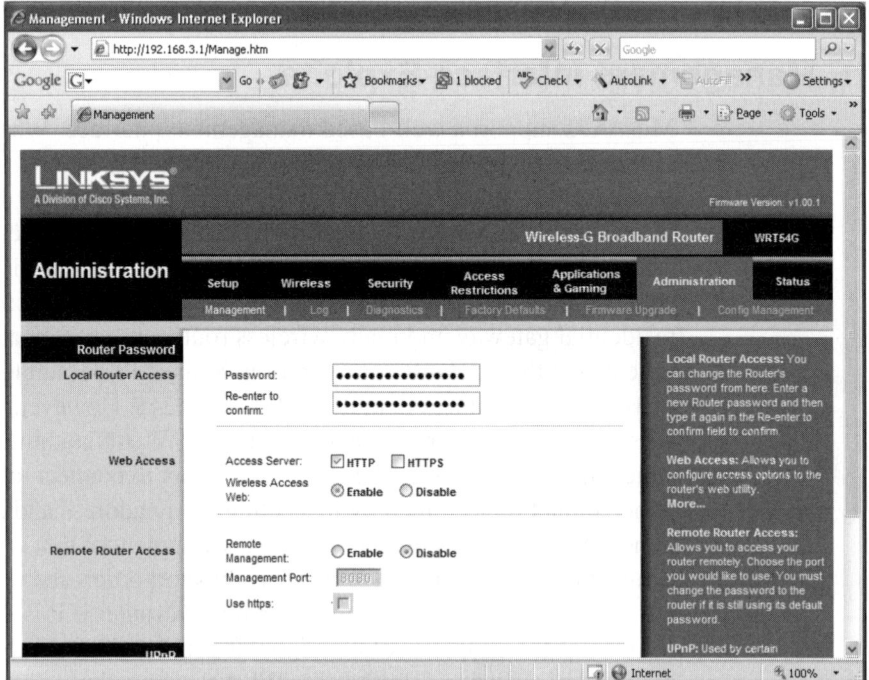

Encryption Cracking

I was speaking at a government technology conference in California in May 2006. The topic was that of WLAN security, and they had asked me to demonstrate *WEP cracking*. The event planner had asked me if 30 minutes would be enough time to demonstrate the WEP crack. I said that we would have time left over. In order to make the demonstration more impacting, I asked an attendee to enter a WEP key while I was not looking and I asked the attendee to make it a complex key with uppercase, lowercase, and numeric characters. Then I had the attendee use his laptop to connect to the WLAN router that we were using for the demonstration and transfer a large file from an FTP server. While he was transferring the data, I performed a data capture still not knowing the WEP key. After about 4 minutes, I had just over 300MB of data and was ready to crack the WEP key.

I quickly converted the data to a format that could be used by the WEP cracking tool I was using and then ran the cracking tool against the data. In about 3 seconds, the entire group was looking at the WEP key. I asked the attendee who had entered it if it was the right one, and he replied, "Wow! Yeah."

This was not news to people who work in WLANs every day. This group, however, had not been exposed to the speed at which WEP could be cracked. The total time, including the time spent by the attendee entering the WEP key and then my capture of the data during transfer, was just over 6 minutes. Normally an attacker does not need to take time to enter a WEP key, so if there is sufficient traffic on the WLAN, the attacker can usually capture enough data to get the WEP key in 3–5 minutes and then crack it in 3–5 seconds. Even if there is not sufficient traffic, methods are available to force the generation of enough traffic so that the attacker can gather the needed data. You will learn more about these weaknesses in WEP in Chapter 10.

Some newer WLAN devices intentionally avoid weak Initialization Vectors and make it much more difficult to crack the WEP key. In fact, they make it impossible to crack the WEP key in 3–5 minutes at this time.

Authentication Cracking

With the weaknesses found in the WEP implementation, the IEEE began development of a more secure authentication and encryption algorithm. While they were developing what eventually became an amendment to IEEE 802.11 as 802.11i, the Wi-Fi Alliance created a certification known as WPA. Their WPA2 certification is based on the ratified IEEE 802.11i document, and WPA was based on part of the 802.11i draft document available at an earlier time. Today, documents often refer to WPA and WPA2 as if they are the same thing, but there are differences. For example, WPA does not implement the Advanced Encryption Standard (AES) but WPA2 does. However, both can be implemented using passphrases or authentication servers. When implemented with an authentication server, they are more secure, assuming a strong EAP type is used (EAP types are covered in Chapter 10). One particular EAP type that was thought to be secure, but turned out to be very weak, was LEAP from Cisco. I cover its weaknesses and the ASLEAP utility in Chapter 10. WPA2 is a mandatory feature for all new equipment that receives the Wi-Fi Certification from the Wi-Fi Alliance.

Devin Akin has posted an excellent demo video of the cracking process used to crack LEAP authentication at www.Vestivus.com. If you want to see a demonstration of this process, be sure to watch his video. When you visit the site, search for "Cracking Cisco LEAP with ASLEAP for WIN32."

When using a passphrase and preshared key (PSK), to authenticate client STAs using WPA or WPA2, there is a known vulnerability. An attacker can listen for the four-way handshake that is involved in the WPA authentication process and use the CoWPAtty tool, as one example, to discover the passphrase. If the attacker does not capture a four-way handshake quickly, she can transmit a disassociation frame to the STA to force it to process the four-way handshake again. With the handshake frames, knowledge of the SSID, and a dictionary of possible passwords or passphrases, the attacker can eventually retrieve the passphrase and PSK. This type of attack is often called *WPA cracking.*

The primary protection against this attack, at this time, is to use enterprise-class security instead of the PSK. In other words, implement an EAP type that is secure, such as PEAP or EAP-TTLS, instead of using passphrases. You are likely to find yourself in an organization, if you install many WLANs, that cannot or will not support a full authentication infrastructure. This usually happens in SOHO installations or SMBs. There are solutions to this like TinyPEAP, but in most cases, you can use a longer passphrase that is not a word at all (something like gu7YjhU67BbrYYZ89klop09) and gain enough security for these installations. According to some researchers, it could take years to brute-force a passphrase like the one represented here even with a P4 3.8 GHz processor.

Even a longer passphrase can be very weak. For example, my company's name is SYSEDCO. I could set the PSK passphrase to SYSEDCO43040, which is my company's name and my ZIP code. However, even though it's long, it could be easily guessed and should be avoided.

MAC Spoofing

One of the earliest attempts at securing WLANs was to implement MAC address filtering. This simple technology involved including the list of MAC addresses that are allowed to authenticate with the AP of including the list of MAC addresses that are not allowed to authenticate. Figure 9.6 shows a typical configuration interface for this feature.

FIGURE 9.6 Configuring MAC filtering in a Linksys device

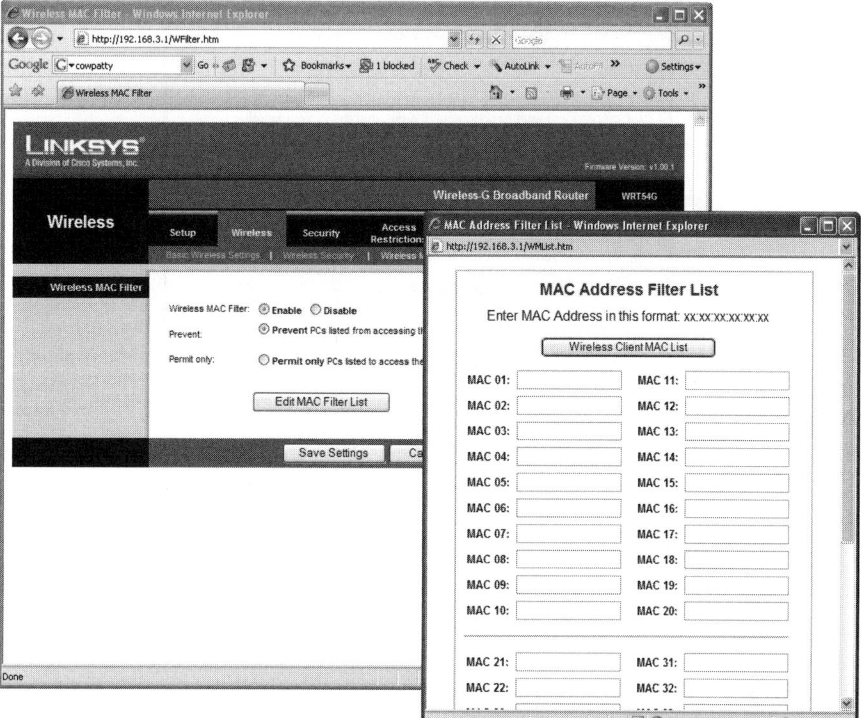

The feature is based on the fact that all IEEE 802.11 WLAN NICs have a physical address known as the MAC address. This address is either encoded into a NIC or is stored as a configuration parameter. The MAC address is normally read from hardware by the NIC device driver, but the device driver can be instructed to ignore what was read from the NIC hardware and to use a different address. The problem is that, since many devices have a MAC that is specified as a configuration parameter, MAC addresses can be spoofed (faked or stolen). If an attacker can discover a valid MAC address, he can easily change the MAC address of his NIC to match. Figure 9.7 shows the Device Manager interface for changing a MAC address, which is available for many different WLAN devices.

In addition to the built-in interface of many WLAN NICs, you can utilize applications like SMAC (shown in Figure 9.8) to change the MAC address of your WLAN card. SMAC works with almost any NIC, wired or wireless.

FIGURE 9.7 Device Manager MAC modification interface

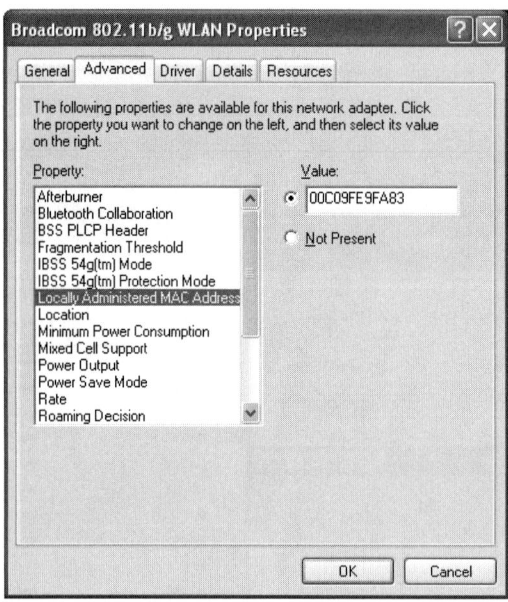

FIGURE 9.8 SMAC 2.0 MAC spoofing tool

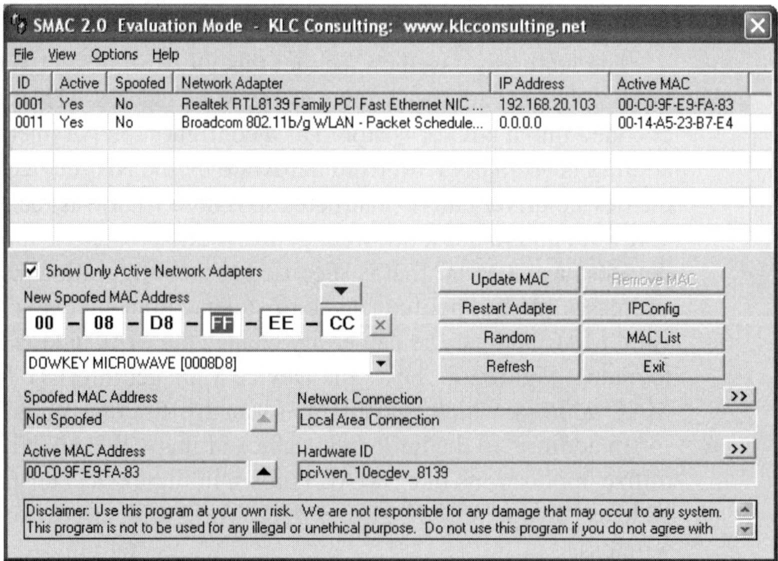

Using simple eavesdropping tools like CommView for Wi-Fi or OmniPeek Personal, an attacker can quickly determine the MAC address of users that are currently associated with your AP. If they are associated, their MAC addresses must be in the allowed list. All that the attacker has to do now is configure her MAC address and then authenticate and associate with the AP. This is why MAC filtering should not be considered a security solution at all. It may be considered a configuration enforcement solution of sorts, such as those described in Chapter 7, but it should not be considered a security solution.

A common response to the reality of scenarios like this is "The attacker would have to have the right WLAN card to work with these eavesdropping tools, wouldn't he?" The answer is an affirmative one, but remember that attackers can pick up equipment at eBay now for very little cost.

Peer-to-Peer Attacks

A *peer-to-peer attack* occurs anytime one WLAN STA attacks another WLAN station that is associated with the same AP. Hijacking attacks are sometimes referred to as peer-to-peer attacks as well.

These types of attacks must be protected against, as they are usually malicious. There is no real reason for an attacker to gain access to another peer computer other than theft or damage. Attackers may desire to penetrate your network in order to use it to gain access to the Internet. That is often their single intent. When an attacker tries to gain access to a client STA on your network, they are not likely to be doing it for Internet access. Instead, they are likely to be performing a data theft or destruction attack. They may be attempting to install back doors into your network or other malicious software. Whatever their intention, it is seldom going to be benign.

To understand the potential severity of a peer-to-peer attack, consider the data that is often held on a user's laptop. Many users have personal information on their laptops as well as information belonging to the organization. The personal information may include account names and passwords for online banking and other sensitive systems that the users access. The organization's information can include anything the users have read to access on the network. Users will often copy this information to the hard drive of their laptops so that they can view the information while traveling. Many times, the users are traveling through airports, which is just such a place where peer-to-peer attacks are likely to occur.

You can protect against these types of attacks using two common methods: endpoint security solutions or Public Secure Packet Forwarding (PSPF). Endpoint security involves the installation of an application on your WLAN STAs that monitors and reports on any attempts made by other STAs to access the monitored STA. This kind of software may be bundled in with anti-spyware or antivirus software. PSPF is a Cisco technology that allows you to disable access to WLAN client STAs by other STAs associated with the same AP or even the same ESS. Other vendors offer similar functionality, though they may call it by a different name. Figure 9.9 illustrates the concept of a peer-to-peer attack. Notice that the malicious file is passing through the AP. This is normally the only way one STA can communicate with another in an infrastructure BSS. If STA-to-STA communications are disallowed, the attacker would have to perform a more complex hijacking hack to get the same malicious file onto the victim's STA.

An additional concern in peer-to-peer scenarios is the attacks that can occur in an ad hoc or IBSS network. In an ad hoc network, the users typically intend to share files with each other. For this reason and the fact that most computers today run Microsoft Windows, Windows file sharing is often enabled. This opens the door for attacks. In these types of ad hoc

FIGURE 9.9 Peer-to-peer WLAN attack

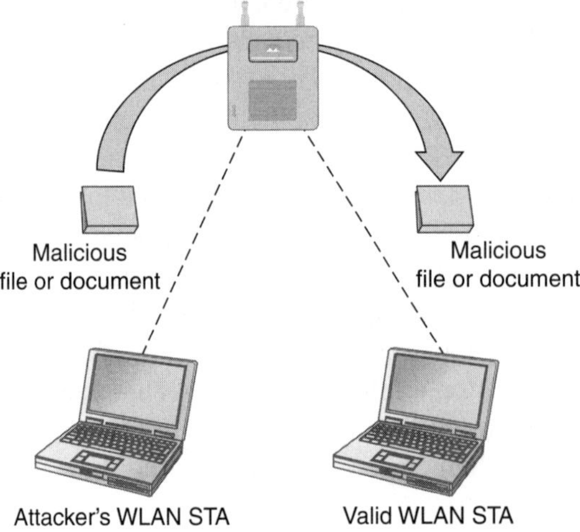

networks, the users should have firewall software installed (or more robust WLAN endpoint software, if it's available) and be trained in how to use it to limit the machines that can connect to their file shares and computer.

Another concern from the perspective of ad hoc networks is the common situation you find at airports and other public spaces. It is not at all uncommon to turn on your Windows-based laptop and select to "View Available Wireless Networks," only to find that there are dozens of ad hoc networks in existence. Many of these, no doubt, are innocently configured machines with no ill intentions; but there can be no question that many of the ad hoc networks configured to have the identical SSID as that of the local airport or hotspot is there waiting for the unsuspecting user to connect so that the attacker can infiltrate the victim's machine.

In one recent encounter, I noticed an ad hoc network with the same name as the airport's network, so I decided to find this network source. I used software to monitor the strength of the signal coming from that network and moved around slowly until the signal became stronger and stronger. I eventually found myself seated next to a man about my age, with his laptop open and running. I asked if he was having fun running his own little network and allowing people to associate with it. Without saying a word, he quickly closed his laptop, placed it in his bag, and walked away. Yes, the malicious hacker is out there. Your users must be educated, and you will need to know how to protect against them as well.

It is my sincere hope that every person who acquires his or her CWNA will go on to acquire the CWSP certification. It goes into more depth on the security-related topics, and as this book's brief introduction has hopefully shown you, you need that depth to thoroughly secure a WLAN. I will take you a little deeper still in Chapter 10, but this certification gives you the knowledge you need to administer the security in a WLAN. CWSP will provide you with the knowledge needed to implement, analyze, test, and administer the security in your WLAN. Don't stop your journey half way.

These kinds of peer-to-peer attacks shed light on the importance of data classification procedures. *Data classification* can be defined as the process of labeling or organizing data in order to indicate the level of protection required for that data. For example, you may define data classification levels of private, sensitive, and public. Private data would be data that should only be seen by the organization's employees and may only be seen by a select group of the organization's employees. Sensitive data would be data that should only be seen by the organization's employees and approved external individuals. Public data would be data that can be viewed by anyone.

For example, the information on the organization's Internet web site should fall in the classification of public data. The contracts that exist between the organization and service providers or customers should fall in the classification of sensitive data. Finally, trade secrets or internal competitive processes should be classified as private data. This is just one example of data classification, but it help, you to determine which data users should be allowed to store off-line and which data should only be accessed while authenticated to the network. By keeping private data off of laptops, you help reduce the severity of a peer-to-peer attack that is launched solely to steal information.

Social Engineering

Social engineering is a technique used for persuading people to give you something that they should not give you. Successful social engineering attacks occur because the target might be ignorant of the organization's information security policies or intimidated by an intruder's knowledge, expertise, or attitude. Social engineering is one of the most dangerous and successful methods of hacking into any IT infrastructure—wired or wireless.

Even in networks using more secure technologies like WPA-PSK as opposed to WEP, an attacker may be able to persuade an employee to reveal the passphrase that is being used. Once the attacker has the passphrase, he will plug it into his own computer and wireless packet analyzers to view sensitive data in real time, just as though there were no security. For this reason, social engineering has the potential of rendering even the most sophisticated security solution useless.

Hackers (used in the negative sense of the term here) do not always fit the common profile of a technical recluse who is non-sociable and unable to communicate well. Many times, the most successful and damaging network intrusion is accomplished in broad daylight through clever efforts of someone who walks into a business like he owns it. In the very same manner, a hired professional security auditor should openly attempt intrusion as one tactic of testing security policy adherence.

There are some well-known targets for this type of attack:

- The Help Desk
- On-site contractors
- Employees (end users)

The Help Desk

Because the Help Desk exists to provide help, it may become an easy target for a social engineering attack. The Help Desk employees are probably used to assisting internal employees with network configuration issues and WLAN access problems. For this reason, they are probably well armed with information about how to configure a client computer to access the organization's WLAN. These professionals should be trained on what to give out and what not to give out over the phone. There should also be some form of identity verification mechanism in place any time they do assist someone in gaining access to the WLAN. Items that might be marked as private and needing such identity verification are

- Hidden SSIDs of access points
- PSK passphrases, if used
- Physical locations of access points and bridges
- Usernames and passwords for network access and services (i.e., e-mail)

The auditor should (and the hacker *will*) use three particular tactics when dealing with Help Desk personnel:

- Forceful, yet professional language
- Playing dumb, afraid, or stressed (people like to help relieve other people's stress)
- Speaking the language of the organization (for example, if the technology group has a special name like *CompanyName* Information Services, be sure to use that terminology or, even better, the acronym for that term)

All of these approaches have the same effect: getting the requested information. Help Desk personnel understand that their job is to help people with their problems. They also understand that their manager will not be happy with them if their customers are not happy with the service they are receiving. Many times, a threat to speak with, or write a letter to, the manager can help the social engineer to get the Help Desk person to give over the requested information just to appease and settle down the social engineer.

Playing dumb is a favorite of many social engineers. The Help Desk person is usually disarmed and stops paying attention when they figure out that the person to whom they are speaking knows very little. This situation is exacerbated when the "dumb" customer (the social engineer) is overly polite and thankful for the help. It's important that a Help Desk person be alert to this tactic at all times. A social engineer is likely to call over and over, hoping to speak with different representatives, and taking different approaches with each.

When you speak the language of the organization, you fit in. If you do not, there is an almost subconscious awareness that something is wrong, and this may cause the victim to be on higher alert, which is exactly the opposite of what a social engineer wants. For example, if the company Teddy Bears and Rocking Chairs, Inc., has a technology group called TBIS (Teddy Bears Information Systems), you want to be aware of this as a social engineer. You may be able to get information by saying something like, "I've been talking to people from TBIS all day and it hasn't resolved my problem. Are you the one person in that group who actually knows what you're doing?" This appeals to the vanity of the listener and makes them feel better about trusting you. How would you know the group is called TBIS? Of course, you got this information from a company report that was intended for internal distribution but was published on the company's web site.

Contractors

A second group that the social engineer may target is that of temporary contractors. Contractors usually have no loyalty to the company in the first place, and this can lead to a more liberal handling of private company information. Sometimes, contractors are actually the individuals performing the network attack. This was the case with Kevin Mitnick in many of his attacks in the 1990s. He was employed as a contractor and proceeded to attack the organization and steal proprietary knowledge, costing companies millions of dollars by some estimates. In many of these cases, he used social engineering methods to acquire the information. The fastest solution to the contractor dilemma is to be sure to give contractors only the level of access they need to get their jobs done and then train employees well in identifying social engineering or in protecting company interests. However, because advanced social engineers are very skilled at their craft, you must consider that it is very likely that a user will give up valuable information to these individuals. Storage-level encryption and intrusion prevention or monitoring systems may help in these scenarios.

Employees

It is not uncommon to walk down the hallway of an organization and hear one employee loudly calling out his username and password to another employee in a different cubicle or work area. We tend to develop trust for people we work with on a regular basis, and this often causes us to take actions we really shouldn't take. High trust is a very good thing for productive work, but it can also lead to the sharing of sensitive information that should not be shared.

Many users—and IT professionals—do not understand that the motivation behind individual user accounts and passwords (or any other individual authentication mechanism) is not just to give them the right access to the right things. That's certainly part of it, but another part is that of auditing. When a user gives his or her account and password to another user, the ability to link actions to individuals is lost. Better training programs are needed in many organizations to resolve this issue.

In the end, social engineering is a very powerful attack method that cannot be protected against by technologies alone. This attack method takes advantage of the ever-present human factor, and to protect against it, we must improve our humans and not just our technologies. Better training is required, and refresher training classes may also be needed. The good news is that you can usually provide the needed awareness training class in a 45- to 90-minute window once or twice a year. It can even be incorporated into annual employee meetings, but it must not be forgotten.

Know Your Enemy

Over the years, there has been a fair amount of research on why crackers crack and the kinds of personalities that tend to become crackers. The reality is that the pool includes introverts and extraverts. It includes people who are in it for the money, the fame, and even the cause (whatever it might be). Because of this, I've chosen to look at the technical proficiency of the attacker rather than the emotional, social, or financial motivations of the attacker. By considering the technical proficiency, I can better organize my protection mechanisms to deal with the threats that I am most likely to face. The three categories I look at are the following:

- Wannabees
- Gonnabees
- Killerbees

Of course, these are my terms and not part of the CWNA program's tested material. However, these categories serve as an excellent thinking tool when you look at different technologies. For example, I can say that a WPA-PSK implementation with a six-character alphanumeric nonword passphrase will protect against most Wannabees, but it will not protect against Gonnabees or Killerbees. However, my home network is more likely to be attacked by a Wannabee than the other two categories.

The Wannabees are often called Script Kiddiez by the security community. This name has been associated with them because they cannot really crack a system; however, if they have step-by-step instructions, they can penetrate a system that has a known vulnerability. In the preceding paragraph, I said that the Wannabees wouldn't likely breach my six-character passphrase for WPA-PSK. The reason is simple. They are parked at the Stop sign in front of my house, and as soon as they see my network would require some effort, they go on to my neighbor's network that is wide open. These attackers are usually not malicious toward the specific network they are attacking. They will attack any network that has a known vulnerability. There are cases where Wannabees perform intentional attacks against networks that represent philosophies or ideas to which they are opposed, but these attacks are the exception and not the rule.

Those that I categorize as Gonnabees are the crackers and hackers with a moderate to high level of skill. They may use a mix of instructions and existing knowledge, but they are much more dangerous than the Wannabees if they choose to use their skills for bad rather than good. I would like to think that there are more Gonnabees on the side of obedience to the law than there are law breakers, but this is only wishful thinking, since there is no real way to track how these skilled crackers and hackers use their abilities. To protect against this skill level, I will need to implement strong authentication and confidentiality.

The final level, the Killerbees, is the category of attackers who combine the technical proficiency of the Gonnabees with deep knowledge of human engineering. This allows them to become masters of social engineering as well as technical cracking. There is no more skillful foe. End-user training and strong authentication and confidentiality will be needed, but greater measures will also need to be taken. Continual awareness of changes in the environment will be necessary as well as frequent re-education of the user community. This is more important in larger organizations that receive more media coverage and are therefore more likely to be targets of attacks at this level. Smaller organizations that are involved in markets that see strong resistance from various social groups must also be on the lookout.

Of course, regardless of the level of technical skills possessed by the attackers who threaten you, there are minimum security measures you should always employ. For example, intrusion monitoring and activity logging should always take place at some level. Regular updates to software and firmware is also a given.

Every organization should take measures to protect against the Wannabees. These individuals with little technical skill but a desire to penetrate networks and possibly cause damage abound. You can protect your network from these attackers using standard security precautions, which include

- Using modern secure encryption technologies
- Patching computers and devices with updates to software and firmware
- Providing periodic awareness training to your end users
- Implementing effective authentication, authorization, and accounting procedures

To protect against the Gonnabees and Killerbees, you have to go a step further. Standard security practices will thwart many attack attempts by these advanced crackers, but you must implement stronger security mechanisms when applicable. You will determine applicability by balancing the value of your assets against the risk of attack. For example, a small company that sells nuts and bolts has a much lower risk level than a small organization that exists in order to promote a social agenda. The former organization is involved in work that most people would consider trivial or non-divisive. The latter organization is more likely to be considered divisive and nontrivial. For this reason, the latter organization is more likely to be attacked by both skilled and unskilled crackers. Most small organizations do not implement advanced intrusion prevention systems, but the latter organization—in this case—may need to implement just such a solution.

General Security Principles

This chapter has introduced you to the wireless vulnerabilities and attack methods that are commonly executed against IEEE 802.11 networks. The next chapter will introduce you to the protection mechanisms that are available and will also expose a few more vulnerabilities. I will end this chapter with a brief overview of two security concepts that are often referenced when dealing with computer security, network security, or internetwork security, which I will refer to as *information security* to encompass all three of these traditional terms. This will prepare you for the chapter that follows. The two concepts are

- CIA
- AAA

CIA

CIA stands for *confidentiality, integrity,* and *availability.* This acronym is often used to reference these three extremely important concepts in information security. They are sometimes called the *CIA security triad* or just the *CIA triad.* Figure 9.10 represents this concept.

FIGURE 9.10 CIA security triad

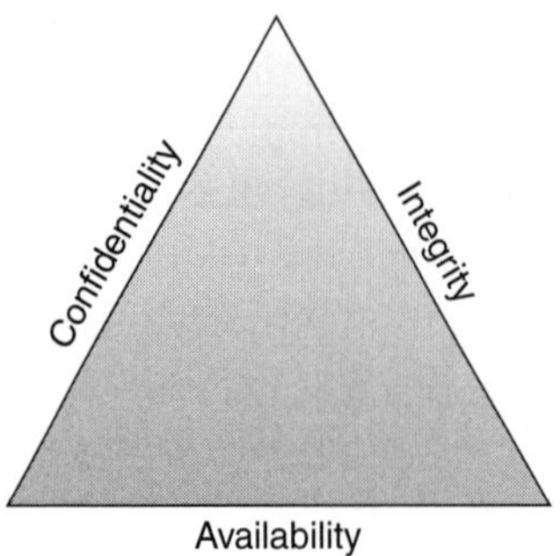

Confidentiality is the concept of keeping private information private. It is accomplished by restricting access to the information when it is stored, transferred, or utilized in any other way. During storage it is achieved by encrypting the data in some cases and restricting access to it in all cases. During transfer, it is achieved through the use of encryption. During utilization, it is achieved by means of physical security, which controls access to the area where the information is being used on screen or in print format. An example of weak confidentiality is the WEP encryption in IEEE 802.11.

Integrity is the concept of data consistency. In other words, the data is what it should be. This must be true when the data is transferred from one place to another. For example, a man-in-the-middle attack may involve receiving data from an unsuspecting client and changing it in some way before it is sent to the destination. When this occurs, the data integrity has been violated. This is usually protected against, through the utilization of hashing algorithms and CRC methods. A hijacking attack that evolves into a man-in-the-middle attack, then, is an example of an integrity violation.

Availability simply states that the right data is available to the right people at the right time in the right place. This is a factor of data throughput as much as it is of data security. However, if you've provided sufficient throughput and then an attacker performs a DoS attack, availability suffers. A DoS attack, then, is an example of a security breach that would violate the principle of availability.

These three concepts must be considered when implementing your WLAN. Not only must you consider how you will provide confidentiality, integrity, and availability, but you must also consider which is most important. For example, stronger encryption may require more overhead that in turn reduces availability (throughput). The same is true for various integrity algorithms. If availability is highly important, you will have to either sacrifice the level of confidentiality and/or integrity or implement hardware that is powerful enough to overcome the overhead. This means that your WLAN will cost more, but it is often worth the cost.

AAA

The second fundamental concept of information security is *authentication*, *authorization*, and *accounting (or auditing)*, which is called the *AAA* (pronounced triple-A) in many references. Think of these three factors like this:

- *Authentication* Who are you?
- *Authorization* What do you want?
- *Accounting* What have you done?

If you remember these three simple questions, you'll always be able to remember these three important factors. As you can already see, without all three, I cannot really have accountability on my network. As a definition of accountability, consider the following:

Accountability is the concept that says all network users are responsible for the actions taken by their individual network accounts.

In other words, the users are responsible for protecting their accounts as well as the actions they take while connected to the network with those accounts. This is an important concept. Without this concept of accountability, you have users sharing their authentication information with other users and you lose all accountability on the network. Of course, enforcement is another story completely different. I've seen many environments with security policies that stipulate that users shall not share their credentials with other users; however, I've seen very few environments that successfully enforce this with a measurable penalty that demands compliance.

When you consider the three factors of AAA, authentication simply must come first. You must first verify the identity of an individual before you can grant him access to resources as an individual. Authorization is the granting of access to resources. Since this is the case, strong authentication is essential to solid information security. If your authentication is weak, the trickle effect will be weak or irrelevant authorization and accounting. If you authenticate users but do not utilize effective authorization (for example, you allow everyone to access everything), then your accounting will serve a much diminished purpose. The point of accounting or auditing is to track who does what and when they do it on your network. If everyone can do everything, users will be very slack in protecting their credentials, and therefore, the entire AAA concept is weakened. As you can see, you need all three to have strong information security.

Chapter 10 will reveal the various technologies that are available to implement both CIA and AAA in WLANs. You will learn about encryption technologies, data integrity algorithms, and protection mechanisms to find and eradicate DoS attacks. You'll also learn to authenticate, authorize, and account for what your WLAN users do on the network.

Summary

In this chapter, you learned about the different WLAN attack methods that are common. You discovered some of the inherent weaknesses of WLANS, which is the first part of the journey to learning to secure them. In the process, you discovered how attackers can view the frames on your network, decrypt the traffic on your network, and hack the preshared keys used to authenticate to your network. You also learned how attackers can take over a user's computer and attack it or monitor the traffic going in and out of it. Now that you know how attackers attack you, you're ready to move on to Chapter 10, where you'll learn how to protect against their attacks.

Keywords

- ☐ **AAA**
- ☐ **authentication cracking**
- ☐ **CIA**
- ☐ **denial of service (DoS)**
- ☐ **eavesdropping**
- ☐ **encryption cracking**
- ☐ **hijacking**
- ☐ **management interface exploits**
- ☐ **man-in-the-middle**
- ☐ **peer-to-peer attack**
- ☐ **social engineering**
- ☐ **WEP cracking**
- ☐ **PSK cracking**

Review Questions

1. You are the network administrator for an SMB located in West Virginia. The single AP your organization uses is configured with WPA-PSK, and the preshared key is set to your company name followed by the number 7. Is this a secure implementation and why?

   A. Yes. It is secure because WPA-PSK resolved the problems with WEP.

   B. Yes. It is secure because the preshared key is at least five characters long.

   C. No. Because it only includes the company name plus one digit, it could be easily guessed.

   D. No. Because WPA-PSK is just as insecure as WEP, it should never be used.

2. While performing a penetration test on a WLAN, you attempt to connect to the IP address of the AP in a web browser. Your connection is denied when connecting through the WLAN. What attack method is being protected against in this scenario?

   A. Denial of service

   B. Authentication cracking

   C. Encryption cracking

   D. Management interface exploits

3. An attacker starts a software-based AP on his laptop. He then scans for the SSID of the AP at the coffee shop hotspot where he is located. He sets his software-based AP to use the same SSID. What type of attack is he likely beginning? (Choose all that apply.)

   A. Hijacking

   B. Encryption cracking

   C. Man-in-the-middle

   D. Authentication cracking

4. You receive calls from five different users in a 10-minute window of time. Each of them tells you that the WLAN is no longer available. You connect to the IP address of the AP across the wired network and can connect with no problem. This reveals that the AP is still running fine. What kind of attack is likely to be occurring?

   A. Hijacking

   B. Encryption cracking

   C. Denial of service

   D. Management interface exploit

5. An attacker is preparing to perform an eavesdropping attack at a hotspot. Like most hotspots, this one uses no encryption, so the attacker knows she can view the data frames easily. She runs NetStumbler and determines that there are two APs providing coverage in her area. One is on channel 1, and the other is on channel 11. To which AP will she need to associate in order to launch the eavesdropping attack?

   A. Both

   B. The one on channel 1

   C. The one on channel 11

   D. Neither

Review Answers

1. **C.** When the passphrase includes the company name or some other easily guessed word or phrase and one digit, the entire phrase is easy to guess and does not provide adequate security.

2. **D.** This scenario demonstrates the protection against management interface exploits. Attackers often attempt to connect to the IP address of the AP using a web browser in order to guess passwords to the web-based interface. If they can get in, they can take over the device.

3. **A, C.** He is most likely beginning a hijacking or a man-in-the-middle attack because both of these attack methods usually begin by setting up a software-based AP.

4. **C.** The most likely attack is a denial of service (DoS) attack. Since you can access the AP, it is not likely to be a Layer 2 management frame flooding attack. It is most likely an attack where a signal generator is in use at Layer 1.

5. **D.** She will not need to associate with an AP in order to eavesdrop on the network. She can simply start her WLAN protocol analyzer and capture frames on channel 1 or 11.

CHAPTER

10

Designing and Implementing Security for Wireless LANs

CWNA Exam Objectives Covered:

- ❖ Identify and describe the strengths, weaknesses, appropriate uses, and appropriate implementation of IEEE 802.11 security-related items
  - Pre-RSNA and RSNA Security
  - AAA Security Components
- ❖ Describe, explain, and illustrate the appropriate applications for the following client-related wireless security solutions
  - Client Devices
  - Role-Based Access Control
  - IPsec VPN
  - Profile-Based Firewalls
  - Captive Portals/Web Authentication
  - Network Access Control (NAC)
- ❖ Describe, explain, and illustrate the appropriate applications for the following WLAN system security and management features
  - Rogue AP and Client Detection and/or Containment
  - SNMPv3/HTTPS/SSH2
- ❖ Describe the following general security policy elements
  - IEEE 802.11 Network Security Policy Basics
- ❖ Describe the following functional security policy elements
  - Advanced WLAN Security Topics

In This Chapter

In the preceding chapter, you learned about the common attacks executed against WLANs. This chapter will provide you with the knowledge needed to protect against these attacks and more. You will first learn about the early WLAN security technologies and their vulnerabilities, and you will then learn about the newer security solutions that overcome these vulnerabilities. After this, various security solutions are covered, such as VPNs, role-based access control, endpoint security, and profile-based firewalls. Next, you will learn about some specific and important security systems that are used to detect *rogue access points* and manage infrastructure devices. Finally, you will discover the basics of WLAN security policies and of some advanced security technologies.

Implementing IEEE 802.11 Security

In the beginning, there was the wired equivalent privacy (WEP) protocol. There were unforeseen weaknesses in this protocol, and it was filled with darkness. Then the IEEE said, "Let there be a new Clause 8," and there was a new Clause 8 and darkness fled from the face of the WLAN.

So begins the story of modern WLAN security. Older technologies have been deprecated, as they should be, and newer technologies are being implemented. It is beneficial to understand the early technologies and their weaknesses so that you can understand the modern technologies and their strengths. For this reason, I'll start this section with a brief review of pre-RSNA security and then move on to document the modern technology, RSNA security. This section will conclude with an overview of the components of AAA security.

Pre-RSNA Security

The IEEE standard refers to the original security specifications provided by Clause 8 as *pre-RSNA* security. The standard also indicates that all pre-RSNA security solutions have been deprecated, with the exception of Open System authentication. Since this is true, you might be tempted to ignore these older WLAN security technologies as a WLAN administrator; however, I suggest that you learn the basic reasons that these technologies proved insecure. This will help you justify newer technology expenditures and determine the best way to secure your modern network. It may also help you understand what needs to occur before you can remove legacy equipment that doesn't support RSNA-capable standards. Additionally, the CWNA exam specifications state that you must be able to identify and describe the strengths and weaknesses of pre-RSNA equipment and standards.

In order to fully understand the pre-RSNA security standards, the following topics will be addressed:

- Open system authentication
- Shared Key authentication
- Wired equivalent privacy

Open System Authentication

Open System authentication has not been deprecated, since it is still used as the starting point for modern authentication and encryption implementations such as WPA and WPA2. Open System authentication is essentially a null authentication in that any client requesting authentication is approved for authentication as long as the AP (or recipient STA in an IBSS) is configured for Open System authentication (the dot11AuthenticationType is set to Open System). There is no actual verification of identity, but it moves the IEEE 802.11 state machine forward in the association process.

Open System authentication includes the transfer of only two frames. Both frames are management frames and are of the subtype *authentication.* The first frame is transmitted from the authentication initiation STA to the authenticating STA (an AP in an infrastructure BSS). This frame includes an authentication transaction sequence number equal to 1. The second frame is transmitted from the authenticating STA to the authentication initiation STA and includes an authentication transaction sequence number equal to 2. This second frame will include a status code field that indicates the success or failure of the authentication. A value of 0, in the status code field, indicates that the authentication was successful. Figure 10.1 depicts the authentication process used with Open System authentication.

The IEEE 802.11 standard does specify that an "STA may decline to authenticate with another requesting STA," but it does not specify when it would be appropriate to do so. The declining of an authentication request, when using Open System authentication, is left up to the vendors implementing the IEEE 802.11 standard.

FIGURE 10.1 Open System authentication process

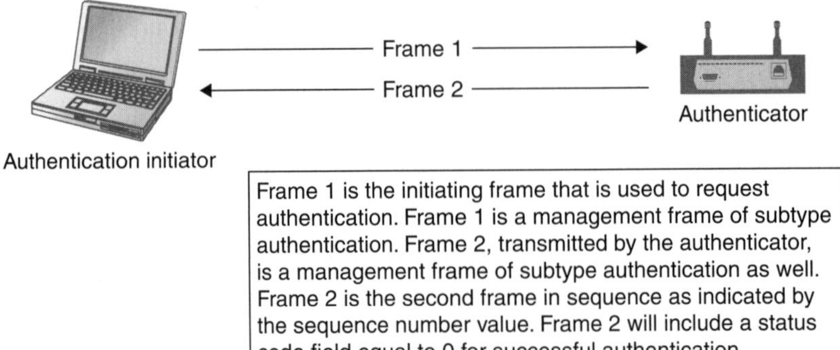

Frame 1
Frame 2
Authenticator
Authentication initiator
Frame 1 is the initiating frame that is used to request authentication. Frame 1 is a management frame of subtype authentication. Frame 2, transmitted by the authenticator, is a management frame of subtype authentication as well. Frame 2 is the second frame in sequence as indicated by the sequence number value. Frame 2 will include a status code field equal to 0 for successful authentication.

Shared Key Authentication

Shared Key authentication was thought to be more secure than Open System authentication at the time of their joint specification in the IEEE 802.11-1997 standard. This was due to the fact that Shared Key authentication verified the requestor using a real authentication method, whereas Open System authentication simply authenticated the requestor, regardless of identity. However, Open System authentication leaves the door open for the use of advanced and evolving security technologies that run across the association created using null authentication. Shared Key authentication relies on a specific set of security technologies, namely, WEP and *RC4*, which have proven to be insecure in their IEEE 802.11 implementation. As stated by the standard, Shared Key authentication "is only available if the WEP option is implemented."

Shared Key authentication uses a secret key that is shared by the requestor (the STA desiring to be authenticated) and the responder (the STA performing the authentication). The method of communicating this secret key into the two STAs in the first place is not specified by the IEEE 802.11 standard, but it is most usually implemented by manually typing the key into the client's network card configuration software interface. The standard specifies that this secret key shall not be transmitted across the WLAN and assumes that a secure channel was used for installation of the secret key on the requestors as well as the responders.

In the traditional Shared Key system, the requestor is a WLAN client STA and the responder is a WLAN AP. The responder may also be another WLAN client STA or any other IEEE 802.11–compliant device. Figure 10.2 shows the

FIGURE 10.2 Shared Key authentication process

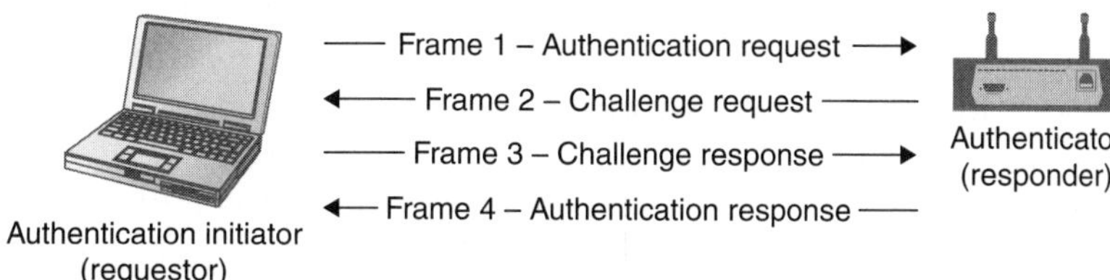

Frame 1 is the initiating frame from the requestor to the responder. Frame 2 is a management frame that includes challenge text from the responder. Frame 3 is a management frame that includes the encrypted challenge text received in Frame 2 and is submitted to the responder for varification. If the responder can successfully decrypt the challenge response with the secret key, the requestor is assumed to also have the secret key and Frame 4 is sent as a successful authentication response.

frame exchange sequence in a Shared Key authentication implementation. As you can see, unlike Open System authentication, the Shared Key authentication process involved more than just requesting authentication and then blindly approving it. There are four frames involved in the Shared Key authentication system. The first frame is the initial authentication request frame. Assuming the responder is configured for Shared Key authentication, the responder will respond to the request frame with challenge text that will be used to authenticate the client's possession of the secret key. The requesting client will then encrypt the challenge text with the secret key and send the challenge text back to the responder in the encrypted state. The responder decrypts the challenge text using the secret key. If the result matches the challenge text, then the requestor has been authenticated and a successful authentication response frame is sent to the client.

While this authentication process (Shared Key) appears to be much more secure than Open System authentication (and indeed it was for a short time), its dependence on WEP for the encryption of the authentication challenge response and the ongoing communications was its greatest weakness. As you will see, WEP was an insecure implementation of encryption that was quickly cracked and can be cracked today in less than 5 minutes on most older hardware. Newer equipment often implements algorithms that attempt to avoid using weak initialization vectors (IVs), but the encryption is still too vulnerable to recommend for anything but the most casual wireless environment.

Wired Equivalent Privacy

The original IEEE 802.11 standard specified the *Wired Equivalent Privacy (WEP)* protocol for the purpose of providing security that was comparable to that of wired networks. Specifically, the goal was to prevent casual eavesdropping on a WLAN. In all honesty, I don't know anyone who would define *casual eavesdropping* as capturing a few million WLAN frames in order to find the few thousand interesting ones and then using a cracking tool to discover the WEP key so that you can read the captured frames and also decrypt live frames off of the WLAN. However, the IEEE must have intended for casual eavesdropping to mean protection against such behavior because they state, in the draft for IEEE 802.11-2007, that "they (pre-RSNA security standards) fail to meet their security goals." Indeed, WEP has failed as a security solution and should not be implemented in any WLAN by choice. The weaknesses of WEP will be discussed in the later subsection "WEP Weaknesses."

WEP and RC4 WEP-40 uses a 40-bit key for encryption. The encryption algorithm used is RC4. WEP-104 not only uses a 104-bit key for encryption but also uses RC4 as its encryption algorithm. 40-bit keys are certainly considered small by today's security standards, but exportability of the encryption technologies implemented based on the standard was the most likely reason for limiting the key size to 40 bits initially. Vendors implemented 104-bit keys quickly, and the IEEE acknowledges them in the more recent updates to Clause 8 of IEEE 802.11.

If you see a configuration interface that refers to a 64-bit or 128-bit WEP key, this is because the WEP implementation uses an IV that is 24 bits long for both 40- and 104-bit WEP. Of course, 40 plus 24 is 64 and 104 plus 24 is 128. The *IV* is a non-static 24-bit number that is generated for each frame. However, a 24-bit pool results in only 16,777,216 possible unique IVs. This limited pool requires the reuse of IV values at some eventual time. The 24-bit IV is transmitted in cleartext. For this reason, the encryption is said to be 40-bit or 104-bit type and not 64-bit or 128-bit type, although it is quite common to see vendors intermingle the nomenclature. Some vendors have even expanded WEP by allowing a 128-bit encryption key for a total 152-bit WEP key when the 24-bit IV is added. This is nonstandard and, if implemented, requires the use of a specialized *supplicant* (client) that can handle the nonstandard encryption key size.

WEP is only intended to protect the data payload in a frame. For this reason, the header portion of the frame is not encrypted. The header includes the source and destination MAC addresses and can easily be read using a protocol analyzer that supports the capture of 802.11 frames. One major problem with WEP, as I'll discuss in detail next, is that once you have a valid WEP key, you can decrypt all the packets that use that WEP key. This works with all captured data packets from the capture session and can be replayed later when a valid WEP key is used in the protocol analyzer. A hacker can use this method to capture encrypted packets, and later, after successfully performing a brute force or dictionary attack, all the packets can be viewed in their unencrypted form.

The WEP Process An understanding of the basic WEP process will help you to understand the weaknesses that are covered next. The WEP process starts with the inputs to the process. These inputs include the data that should be encrypted (usually called plaintext), the secret key (40 bits or 104 bits), and the IV (24 bits). These inputs are passed through the WEP algorithms to generate the output (the ciphertext or encrypted data).

Since WEP is a Layer 2 security implementation, it doesn't matter what type of data is being transmitted as long as it originates above Layer 2 in the OSI model. In order to encrypt the data, the RC4 algorithm is used to create a pseudorandom string of bits called a keystream. The WEP static key and the IV are used to seed the pseudorandom number generator used by the RC4 algorithm. The resulting keystream is XORed against the plaintext to generate the ciphertext. The ciphertext alone is transferred without the keystream; however, the IV is sent to the receiver. The receiver uses the IV that was transmitted and the stored static WEP key to feed the same pseudorandom number generator to regenerate the same keystream. The XOR is reversed at the receiver to recover the original plaintext from the ciphertext.

While the full details of WEP's functionality are beyond the scope of this book and the CWNA exam, it is important to note that the plaintext that is actually encrypted includes the upper-layer payload plus an integrity check value (ICV) that is used to verify that the frame was not modified between the sender and the receiver. The ICV is encrypted with the data payload and becomes part of the ciphertext.

WEP Weaknesses WEP was never intended to provide impenetrable security but was only intended to protect against casual eavesdropping. With the rapid increase in processor speeds, cracking WEP has become a very short task, and it can no longer be considered for protection against any organized attack. The weaknesses in WEP include the following:

- Brute force attacks
- Dictionary attacks
- Weak IV attacks
- Reinjection attacks
- Storage attacks

In late 2000 and early 2001, the security weaknesses of WEP became clear. Since then many attack methods have been developed and tools have been created that make these attack methods simple to implement for entry-level technical individuals.

The *brute force* attack method is a key-guessing method that attempts every possible key in order to crack the encryption. With 104-bit WEP, this is really not a feasible attack method; however, 40-bit WEP can usually be cracked in 1 or 2 days with brute force attacks using more than 20 distributed computers. The short time frame is accomplished using a distributed cracking tool like jc-wepcrack. jc-wepcrack is actually two tools: the client and the server. You would first start the tool on the server, configure it for the WEP key size you think the WLAN uses that you are cracking, and provide it with a pcap file (a capture of encrypted frames) from that network. Next, you launch the client program and configure it to connect to the server. The client program will request a portion of the keys to be guessed and will attempt to access the encrypted frames with those keys. With the modern addition of field-programmable gate arrays (FPGAs), which are add-on boards for hardware acceleration, the time to crack can be reduced by more than 30 times. In fairness, the 20 computers would have to be P4 3.6 GHz machines or better. If you chose to go the FPGA route, you would be spending a lot of money to crack that WEP key. Since smart enterprises will no longer be using WEP, you are not likely getting access to any information that is as valuable as your hacking network.

The *dictionary attack* method relies on the fact that humans often use words as passwords. The key then is to use a dictionary cracking tool that understands the conversion algorithm used by a hardware vendor to convert the typed password into the WEP key. This algorithm is not part of IEEE 802.11 and is implemented differently by the different vendors. Many vendors allow the user to type a passphrase that is then converted to the WEP key using the Neesus Datacom or MD5 WEP key generation algorithms. The Neesus Datacom algorithm is notoriously insecure and has resulted in what is sometimes called the Newsham 21-bit attack because it reduces the usable WEP key pool to 21 bits instead of 40 when using a 40-bit WEP key. This smaller pool can be exhausted in about 6–7 seconds on a P4 3.6 GHz single machine, using modern cracking tools against a pcap file. Even MD5-based conversion algorithms are far too weak and should not be considered secure because they are still used to implement WEP, which is insecure due to weak IVs as well.

The *weak IV attacks* are based on the faulty implementation of RC4 in the WEP protocols. The IV is prepended to the static WEP key to form the full WEP encryption key used by the RC4 algorithm. This means that an attacker already knows the first 24 bits of the encryption key, since the IV is sent in cleartext as part of the frame header. Additionaly, Fluhrer, Mantin, and Shamir identified "weak" IVs in a paper released in 2001. These weak IVs result in certain values becoming more statistically probable than others and make it easier to crack the static WEP key. The 802.11 frames that use these weak IVs have come to be known as *interesting frames*. With enough interesting frames collected, you can crack the WEP key in a matter of seconds. This reduces the total attack time to less than 5–6 minutes on a busy WLAN.

The weak IVs discovered by Fluhrer, Mantin, and Shamir are now among a larger pool of known weak IVs. Since 2001, another 16 classes of weak IVs have been discovered by David Hulton (h1kari) and KoreK.

What if the WEP-enabled network being attacked is not busy and you cannot capture enough interesting frames in a short window of time? The answer is a *reinjection attack*. This kind of attack usually reinjects ARP packets onto the WLAN. The program aireplay can detect ARP packets by their unique size and does not need to decrypt the packet. By reinjecting the ARP packets back onto the WLAN, it will force the other clients to reply and cause the creation of large amounts of WLAN traffic very quickly. For 40-bit WEP cracking, you usually want around 300,000 total frames to get enough interesting frames, and for 104-bit WEP cracking you may want about 1,000,000 frames.

Storage attacks are those methods used to recover WEP or WPA keys from their storage locations. On Windows computers, for example, WEP keys have often been stored in the registry in an encrypted form. An older version of this attack method was the Lucent Registry Crack; however, it appears that the problem has not been fully removed from our modern networks. An application named *wzcook* can retrieve the stored WEP keys used by Windows' Wireless Zero Configuration. This application recovers WEP or WPA-PSK keys (since they are effectively the same—WPA just improves the way the key is managed and implemented) and comes with the Aircrack-ng tools used for cracking these keys. The application only works if you have administrator access to the local machine, but in an environment with poor physical security and poor user training, it's not difficult to find a machine that is logged on and using the WLAN for this attack.

WEP makes up the core of pre-RSNA security in IEEE 802.11 networks. I hope the reality that WEP can be cracked in less than 5 minutes is enough to make you realize that you shouldn't be using it on your networks. The only exception would be an installation where you are required to install a WLAN using older hardware and you have no other option. I've encountered this scenario in a few churches where I've assisted in their network implementation. The problem was not with the infrastructure equipment in any of the scenarios. The problem was with the client devices that the church members wanted to use to connect to the WLAN. These devices did not support WPA or WPA2, and we were forced to use either WEP or no security at all. While WEP can certainly be cracked quickly, at least it has to be cracked. Open System authentication with no WEP, WPA, or WPA2 security is just that: open.

In the end, business and organizations that have sensitive data to protect must take a stand for security and against older technologies. This means that you should not be implementing WEP anywhere in your organization. When you have the authority of a corporation, the government, or even a non-profit oversight board, you can usually sell them on the need for better security with a short (5-minute or less) demonstration of just how weak WEP is.

RSNA Security

Since pre-RSNA security is unable to protect modern WLANs, another solution is needed. Of course, you wouldn't have pre-RSNA security if you didn't have RSNA security. *Robust security network association (RSNA)* security implements better security technologies than pre-RSNA, and it implements them in such a way that allows them to evolve as security needs change. This is accomplished through support for the Extensible Authentication Protocol. This section will introduce you to the concepts of RSNA security. For more in-depth information on RSNA security, you should consult the IEEE standards and the CWSP Certification Official Study Guide, Second Edition or higher. The concepts covered here include:

- IEEE 802.11, Clause 8 (previously IEEE 802.11i)
- TKIP and RC4
- CCMP and AES
- IEEE 802.1X
- Preshared Keys
- Certificates and PACs
- The four-way handshake
- Key Hierarchies
- Transition Security Network

IEEE 802.11, Clause 8

The IEEE 802.11i amendment (ratified in 2004) is being rolled into the IEEE standard as an updated version of Clause 8. Additional modifications were made to Clauses 5, 6, 7, 10, and 11; however, the greatest amount of change was seen within Clause 8. Clause 8 of the IEEE 802.11 standard is simply titled *Security*. The concepts covered in this clause include both authentication and confidentiality. Entity authentication is provided by either Open System authentication (RSNA) or Shared Key authentication (pre-RSNA). Confidentiality is provided through the use of WEP (pre-RSNA), TKIP (RSNA), or CCMP (RSNA).

RSNA equipment is said to be capable of creating an RSNA, and pre-RSNA equipment is not capable of such. It is also interesting to note that the standard specifies that an *robust security network (RSN)* can only truly be established if mutual authentication occurs. The standard does not control the type of authentication, but it does specify that EAP-MD5 would not be considered a valid solution, since it does not perform mutual authentication.

As you can see from the preceding two paragraphs, there are many terms that need to be understood in order to comprehend the full functionality of the new IEEE 802.11 security standards specified in Clause 8. The following definitions will act as a foundation for our further discussion:

Robust security network association (RSNA) An authentication or association between two stations that includes the four-way handshake.

Robust security network (RSN) A WLAN that allows for the creation of RSNAs only. To qualify as an RSN, there can be no support for associations not based on the four-way handshake. The Beacon frame will indicate that the group cipher suite being used is not WEP.

Four-way handshake An IEEE 802.11 pairwise key management protocol that confirms mutual possession of a pairwise master key (PMK) between two parties and distributes a group temporal key (GTK).

Pairwise master key (PMK) A key derived from an extensible authentication protocol (EAP) method or obtained directly from a pre-shared key (PSK), the highest level key in the IEEE 802.11 standard.

Group temporal key (GTK) A key used to protect multicast and broadcast traffic in WLANs.

To summarize these definitions, an RSN is a WLAN that will only allow for RSNAs. These RSNAs are established through a four-way handshake that results in the generation of the PMK and the provision of the GTK to the authenticating STA. Once this RSNA is set up, the STA may communicate on the WLAN with confidentiality and integrity.

TKIP and RC4

The *temporal key integrity protocol (TKIP)* is an optional encryption method defined in IEEE 802.11 as amended. TKIP uses RC4 encryption like WEP; however, the weaknesses of WEP are addressed by enlarging the IV pool (it is 48 bits instead of 24 bits) and using true 128-bit static keys. TKIP also implements a stronger integrity checking algorithm in the message integrity check (MIC) algorithm instead of the ICV used with WEP.

TKIP is not as processor intensive as CCMP, as you are about to learn. For this reason, many older devices were able to be upgraded through firmware patches to support TKIP. If you are using an older device that only shows WEP support in the configuration interface, consider consulting the vendor for a firmware upgrade. While the device will not likely be upgradable to CCMP and AES, it may be able to implement TKIP. The Wi-Fi Alliance released a certification known as Wi-Fi Protected Access (WPA) before the IEEE 802.11i amendment was ratified in 2004. WPA is essentially the TKIP/RC4 implementation documented in Clause 8 of IEEE 802.11 as amended.

CCMP and AES

Clause 8 stipulates a default encryption method called *counter mode with cipher block chaining-message authentication code (CCMP).* CCMP uses the *Advanced Encryption Standard (AES)* instead of RC4, which is based on the Rijndael algorithm. CCMP/AES utilizes a 128-bit encryption key and actually encrypts in 128-bit blocks. The protocol uses an 8-byte MIC for integrity checks that is stronger than that used in the TKIP implementation.

The AES cipher is very processor intensive because it works with larger numbers and is a more complex algorithm than RC4. For this reason, many older devices cannot be upgraded to support CCMP and AES. These old devices cannot participate in an RSN unless they can be upgraded to support TKIP as a minimum.

A device that claims to be IEEE 802.11i compliant or, soon, IEEE 802.11-2007 compliant in the area of security may support CCMP/AES or TKIP/RC4 or both. Most vendors will likely implement both, but it is important that you verify TKIP support is included if you need it for backward compatibility with older hardware. This is because the IEEE standard specifies the encryption and security technologies as optional even though CCMP is said to be the "default." Both CCMP and TKIP are optional (as is WEP) to the standard; therefore, a device that is IEEE 802.11 compliant may implement no security at all. If you purchase a device that was manufactured after the year 2003 and it is Wi-Fi Certified, it must support WPA at a minimum, which means it will support TKIP at a minimum.

IEEE 802.1X Authentication and Key Management (AKM)

The *IEEE 802.1X* standard specifies port-based authentication. In order for a port to be used for normal network operations, the device connected to the port must be authenticated. While IEEE 802.11 STAs do not have physical ports to which they are connected, the IEEE standard specifies that an STA shall have a port access entity (PAE). The PAEs control the forwarding of data to and from the MAC. An AP always implements an authenticator PAE role, and an associating STA always implements a supplicant PAE role. These roles play a part in the IEEE 802.1X framework.

The IEEE 802.1X framework is said to be generic because it does not specify a specific authentication type for use across its framework. Both wired and wireless 802 LANs can use IEEE 802.1X, and they both include the following concepts:

- Authentication roles
- Controlled and uncontrolled ports
- IEEE 802.1X generic authentication flow framework

Authentication Roles The three authentication roles specified in IEEE 802.1X are the *supplicant*, *the authenticator*, and *the authentication server (AS)*. In a WLAN, the supplicant is the STA desiring to be authenticated to the WLAN. The authenticator is usually an AP, but it may be another device with AP functionality such as a network-attached storage device with built-in AP support or a computer running a software-based AP. The AS is most frequently a RADIUS server installed on a network server or included in a network appliance. In addition to an AP acting as the authenticator, a combination of an AP and a WLAN switch or controller can act together as the conduit to the wired network where the AS exists.

Controlled and Uncontrolled Ports Two ports are defined by the IEEE 802.1X standard for the purpose of authenticating connected systems. They are the controlled and uncontrolled ports. These ports are best thought of as virtual ports. Consider the following text from the IEEE 802.11 standard as amended:

> A single IEEE 802.1X Port maps to one association, and each association maps to an IEEE 802.1X Port. An IEEE 802.1X Port consists of an IEEE 802.1X Controlled Port and an IEEE 802.1X Uncontrolled Port. The IEEE 802.1X Controlled Port is blocked from passing general data traffic between two STAs until an IEEE 802.1X authentication procedure completed successfully over the IEEE 802.1X Uncontrolled Port.

You can see from this small excerpt that the controlled and uncontrolled ports are not really some physical implementation, but they are a logical implementation that results in the logical (WLAN association) or physical (wired LAN) implementation of an IEEE 802.1X Port. The core takeaway is that an STA cannot perform general network communications until it has authenticated. Authentication happens across the uncontrolled port and general network communications usually occur across the controlled port. The controlled port is enabled for use once the authentication and key management exchange has occurred successfully.

In 802.1X-2001, only the authenticator ever had a controlled port. In 802.1X-2004, both supplicant and authenticator may have a controlled port and will where mutual authentication is supported.

IEEE 802.1X Generic Authentication Flow Framework The generic authentication flow specified by the IEEE 802.1X standard allows for the use of many different authentication types to be used. These authentication types are known as *extensible authentication protocol (EAP)* types and will be discussed in more detail later. Figure 10.3 shows the generic IEEE 802.1X authentication flow.

When port-based authentication is enabled in an AP, it will request the identity of the supplicant when Open System authentication has completed. The supplicant provides the requested identity in a format useful to the AS based on the EAP type implemented. The authenticator (AP) forwards this to the AS. The AS responds with a request for more information needed for authentication, and this is forwarded to the supplicant from the authenticator. The supplicant responds appropriately, and the authenticator forwards this response to the AS. The AS responds with authentication validation or invalidation, depending on whether the client was able to provide the proper credentials.

FIGURE 10.3 Generic IEEE 802.1X authentication flow process

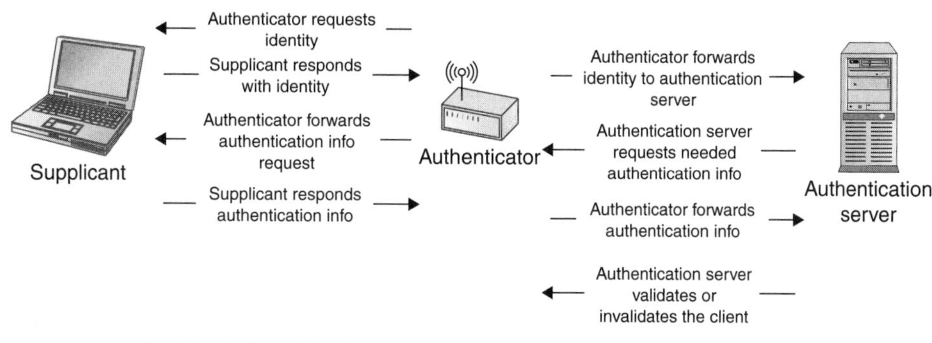

Preshared Key (PSK) / Passphrase Authentication

When a preshared key (PSK) is used instead of an AS external to the AP, the IEEE standard specifies the following operations be carried out:

- STAs discover the AP's security policies through passive monitoring of the Beacon frames or through active probing. The pairwise master key (PMK) is set to the value of the PSK.
- The four-way handshake is performed (see the later section "The four-way Handshake").
- The authenticator sends the GTK to the supplicant for use in decryption of multicast and broadcast frames.

PSK authentication is sometimes also called passphrase authentication. This is because the standard configuration interfaces allow you to type a passphrase that is converted to the PSK. Proprietary interfaces may allow direct entry of the PSK. This implementation of the IEEE 802.11, Clause 8 security is synonymous with WPA-Personal or WPA2-Personal, depending on whether you are implementing RC4 or AES for encryption. WPA certifies equipment that uses TKIP as being interoperable with other equipment that also uses TKIP. WPA2 certifies equipment that uses CCMP as being interoperable with other equipment that also uses CCMP. All new equipment that receives the Wi-Fi Certification supports WPA2. No new equipment is being certified as only WPA.

Remember that WPA and WPA2 are both vulnerable to brute-force attacks if you use weak PSKs. If you choose to implement WPA- or WPA2-Personal, you should be sure to use a passphrase that is long and not a word or combination of words. What is long? This varies depending on whom you ask, but generally speaking, a passphrase of 20 characters or longer that is alphanumeric and case sensitive is considered to be very difficult (time consuming) to crack with brute force. In enterprise installations, it is better to use a RADIUS server and a strong EAP type.

The four-Way Handshake

The four-way handshake occurs after the determination of the PMK. Remember that the PMK is the PSK in preshared key implementations and it is derived using the EAP type in implementations that use RADIUS.

Either way, the four-way handshake is used to establish the temporary or transient keys with the AP. Figure 10.4 shows the four-way handshake as a graphical representation. Notice that the handshake occurred between the authenticator and the supplicant and not between the AS and the supplicant, which is a common misconception.

FIGURE 10.4 The four-way handshake

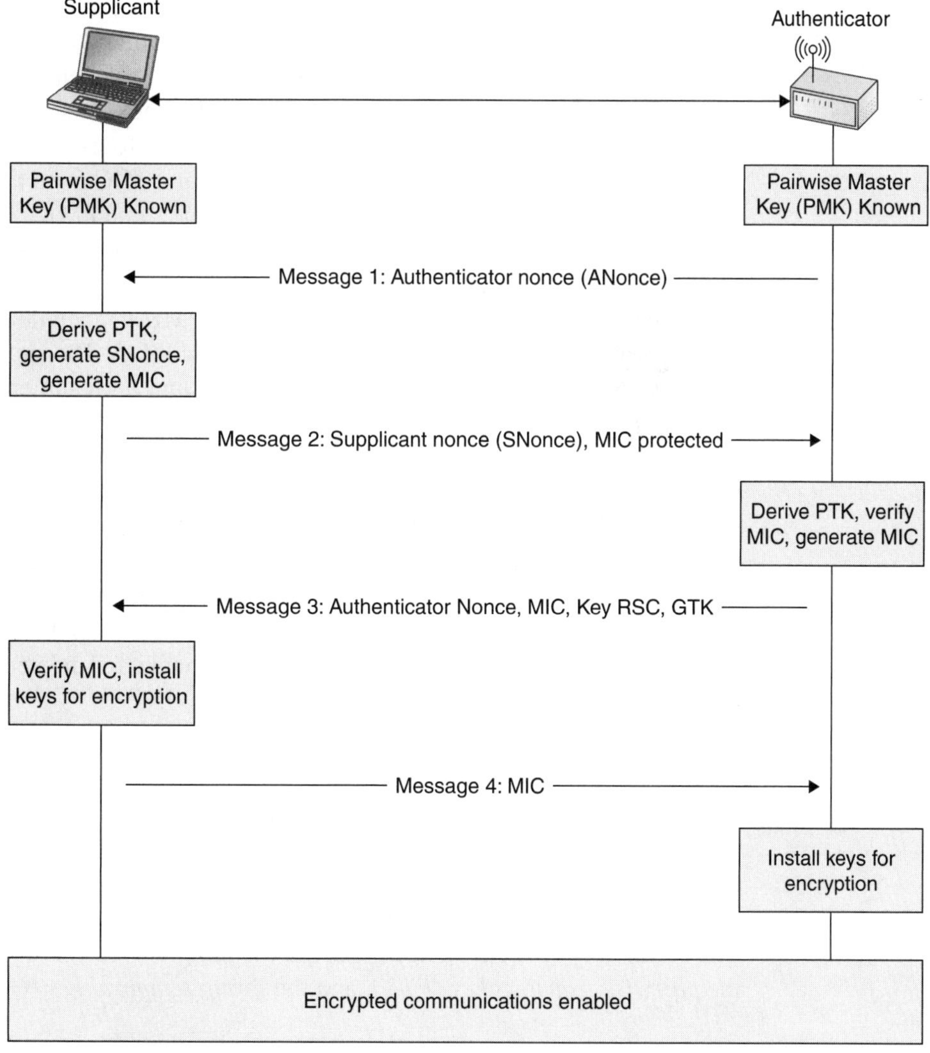

The four-way handshake is really a four-packet exchange between the authenticator and the supplicant. The first exchange is a number used once (nonce) that is generated at the authenticator and sent to the supplicant. This number is known as the authenticator nonce or the ANonce. The supplicant generates the pairwise transient key (PTK) from the PMK that it has stored as the PSK or that it received during the EAP authentication process. This PTK is used to generate a MIC. This results in the second exchange, which is the supplicant sending the MIC and its SNonce (supplicant nonce) to the authenticator. Notice that the supplicant also generated its own number used once. The authenticator then uses the SNonce to generate a MIC based on the PTK that it has generated from its PMK. The authenticator will either get the PMK from the stored PSK or as information received from the AS previous to the four-way handshake.

Once the authenticator receives the SNonce and MIC from the supplicant, it can verify that the supplicant has the same PMK. This is done by using the PTK generated at the authenticator from the PMK to generate a MIC against the SNonce. If the MICs match, this means that the authenticator and supplicant have the same PMK. If they do not match, there is a problem and the four-way handshake will fail. The supplicant may have to go through the initial Open System and EAP authentication processes again.

After the authenticator verifies the MIC sent from the supplicant, the authenticator sends a packet to the supplicant indicating that the verification was successful. This third exchange also includes a MIC that the supplicant can regenerate using its PTK to verify the authenticator really has the same PMK. Once the supplicant receives this third exchange and verifies the authenticator, the supplicant responds with the fourth exchange. The fourth exchange simply says, "Thanks for the verification process. I've installed the keys and you should too."

Key Hierarchies

The preceding section introduced a number of keys, and because the CWNA exam does not go into the depth of this information that the CWSP exam does, the section didn't cover some key types. Those that were not mentioned have been mentioned in other sections of this chapter already. The commonly referenced key types are the *pairwise master key (PMK),* the *pairwise transient key (PTK),* and the *group temporal key (GTK).*

The PMK is the highest key in the IEEE 802.11 hierarchy. This key is used to generate the other keys known as transient or temporal keys. The PMK is used to generate the PTK keys that are actually used to encrypt the data traveling across your network. Additionally, the GTK is used to secure multicast and broadcast frames and may be derived randomly or from a *GMK*, if such a master key is implemented.

Certificates and PACs

Depending on the EAP type you choose to implement, certificates may be required. A *certificate* can be defined as a digitally signed statement that contains information about an entity and the entity's public key (*Dictionary of Information Security,* Syngress Publishing, 2006). Certificates may be generated internally if the generating organization has implemented a public key infrastructure (PKI) or they may be acquired externally through third-party organizations. Networks that choose to implement certificate-based EAP types that require certificates for both the AS and the supplicants will usually choose to implement an internal certificate authority or PKI. Networks that choose to implement EAP types that only require certificates at the AS may choose to implement an internal PKI or to acquire the certificate externally.

One particular EAP type, EAP-FAST, uses a shared secret known as the *protected access credential (PAC).* The PAC is the combination of the PAC-Key (shared secret), an opaque element, and other PAC data. The PAC is used to create a tunnel that is then used to perform the actual authentication. EAP-FAST is defined in RFC 4851. For more information about the PAC and EAP-FAST, consult the RFC document.

Transition Security Network (TSN)

If a WLAN allows the creation of pre-RSNA and RSNA security associations at the same time, it is said to be a *transition security network (TSN).* In other words, it supports both the older WEP technologies and the newer TKIP and CCMP solutions at the same time. Because of this, TSN networks are not considered secure. WEP attack methods work against a TSN as if it did not support RSNA security associations. The unicast data being transferred between the authenticator and the supplicant using an RSNA, however, is still protected. Access to your WLAN is the weak point.

AAA Security Components

The AAA model of authentication, authorization, and accounting was introduced in Chapter 9. This section covers the following AAA security components:

- EAP types
- Remote authentication dial-in user service (RADIUS)
- LDAP databases
- Local authentication databases

EAP Types

The previous sections of this chapter allude to the concept of EAP types many times. The IEEE 802.11 standard as amended does not dictate the EAP type that should be used, but it does suggest that an EAP type supporting mutual authentication should be used in order to implement an RSNA. EAP stands for extensible authentication protocol. The different EAP types are all used for authentication, and the fundamental concept of EAP is extensible in that the authentication can be handled in many ways. While the full details of each EAP type is beyond the scope of the CWNA certification and this study guide, Table 10.1 does provide a comparison of the different EAP types, their capabilities, and a recommendation as to whether they should be used in production networks or not.

Some of the key factors to consider when selecting an EAP type are the need for certificates, whether mutual authentication is provided, and if the protection of authentication credentials is strong. Table 10.1 quickly reveals that EAP-MD5 and LEAP (Cisco's Lightweight EAP) should not be used due to the weakness of credential protection. LEAP, when weak client passwords are used, can be cracked with ASLEAP. It should be noted that most companies do not enforce strong password usage. EAP-MD5 is not intended for production use; EAP-MD5 is only intended for testing and configuration analysis.

RADIUS

The remote authentication dial-in user service (RADIUS) is documented in RFC 2865. In an IEEE 802.11 RSN, RADIUS is most commonly implemented as the AS protocol. RADIUS servers are provided by many vendors and come in the form of services that run on network operating

TABLE 10.1 EAP Types

	EAP-MD5	LEAP	EAP-TLS	EAP-TTLS	PEAP	EAP-FAST
Certificates – client	No	No	Yes	No	No (MSCHAP v2), Yes (TLS)	No
Certificates – server	No	No	Yes	Yes	Yes (all)	No
Password authentication for clients	No	Yes	No	Yes	Yes (MSCHAP v2), No (TLS)	Yes
PACs used	No	No	No	No	No	Yes
Credential protection	Weak	Weak	Strong	Strong	Strong	Strong
Encryption key management	No	Yes	Yes	Yes	Yes	Yes
Mutual authentication	No	Yes	Yes	Yes	Yes	Yes
Recommended for production	No	No	Yes	Yes	Yes	Yes

systems as well as self-contained network appliances, which are usually nothing more than a bundling of the Linux OS and the provided services these days. Figure 10.5 shows an example of a network that might be implemented using Microsoft's Internet Authentication Service (IAS) as the RADIUS server and Active Directory as the authentication database. Note the Certification Services running on the RADIUS server to provide certificate management for the network. Additionally, the RADIUS server must support the EAP method you plan to use for authentication.

The example network implemented in Figure 10.5 may be using the PEAP EAP protocol with a certificate provided for the server and the clients, or it may be implemented with server certificates only. The server certificate can be used to set up the tunnel through which MSCHAP v2 authentication can be processed on the basis of accounts stored in Active Directory. This is just one example implementation, and in this case, the IAS service on the Windows Server is acting as the RADIUS server.

FIGURE 10.5 RADIUS and other services on a Microsoft network

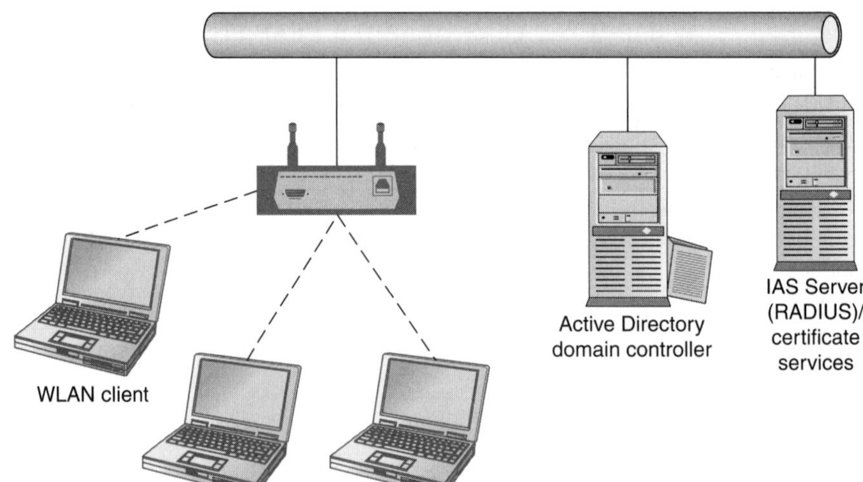

LDAP-Compliant/Compatible and Local Databases

Many RADIUS servers support connectivity with an LDAP-compatible database for user authentication. Novell eDirectory and Microsoft Active Directory are both LDAP-compliant databases. Additionally, it is common to support a limited number of users in the internal database of the RADIUS server. Many can only support a few hundred users, and some can support thousands. Few RADIUS servers scale as well as a dedicated directory service, which can handle hundreds of thousands of users.

Common Terms

The technologies covered so far in this chapter, with the exception of WEP, work together to provide security to your network. Authentication and confidentiality are provided through the various levels of RSNA implementations. Table 10.2 helps to bring these technologies together and explain some common terms that are used to reference them. Those noted as "legacy certifications" will only apply to existing hardware or hardware purchased used, since new hardware is no longer being certified as WPA-Personal or WPA-Enterprise.

TABLE 10.2 Wi-Fi Security Terminology

Wi-Fi Alliance Certification/ Alternate Term	Authentication Method	Cipher Suite	Encryption Algorithm
WPA-Personal/ WPA-PSK (legacy certification)	Passphrase/ Preshared Key	TKIP	RC4
WPA-Enterprise (legacy certification)	802.1X/EAP	TKIP	RC4
WPA2-Personal/ WPA2-PSK	Passphrase/ Preshared Key	CCMP (default but optional) TKIP (optional)	AES (default but optional) RC4 (optional)
WPA2-Enterprise	802.1X/EAP	CCMP (default but optional) TKIP (optional)	AES (default but optional) RC4 (optional)

WLAN Client Security Solutions

In addition to the standard infrastructure security solutions that have been addressed so far in this chapter, you should take specific measures to secure your WLAN clients. There are also WLAN security tools and techniques that you should be aware of beyond the scope of the IEEE 802.11, Clause 8 standard. These include role-based access control, profile-based firewalls, network access control, *IPsec VPNs*, and *captive portals*.

Client Devices

The security of client devices should be considered from at least three perspectives. The first is the security features of the client software. Next is the need for endpoint security solutions that protect the client from direct attack. Finally, the users must be educated about the proper use of their wireless clients.

Security Features of Client Software

Some WLAN client software applications provide full internal support for IEEE 802.11 RSNA connections. Some WLAN adapters do not provide for this feature at all or require that you use a third-party application as the

FIGURE 10.6 Odyssey Access Client for 802.1X authentication

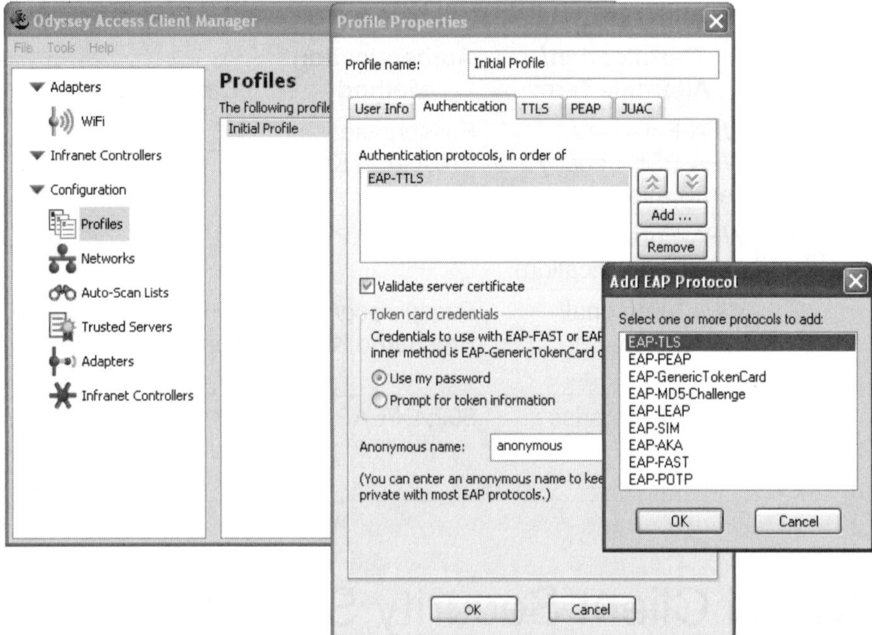

EAP supplicant. An example of a third-party 802.1X supplicant (also called a client) is the Juniper Networks Odyssey Access Client (formerly of Funk Software). This client supports TKIP and CCMP configuration and nearly all the different EAP types. The hardware (WLAN NIC) must also support AES in order to use the Odyssey Access Client to use CCMP. Figure 10.6 shows the Odyssey client with the EAP types dialog displayed.

Endpoint Security

Endpoint security can simply be defined as security that is enforced at the endpoint. The problem is that there are many vendors pouring different meanings into the phrase endpoint security today. For this reason, it is difficult to find a single solution that provides the complete package you need for endpoint security. At a minimum, your clients will need antivirus and antispyware solutions. Additionally, some products offer WLAN connection monitoring and can report when another WLAN STA attempts to connect to your station. These packages may also be able to detect when your machine roams to a different AP and alert you of this. Other solutions protect from WiPhishing attacks as well. Ultimately, you must consider the use of your clients and find the solution or combination of solutions that meets your needs.

Phishing is a recent term hat is used to refer to attacks that are aimed at gaining information. They seem to have gotten their start in e-mail messages, but now we also have the concept of *WiPhishing,* or phishing across Wi-Fi. In this case, phishing takes on a slightly different meaning. The reference is to the process of setting up an AP that is sometimes called an *evil twin* on the same SSID as a valid network. When the clients connect to the WiPhishing AP, the attacker can harvest information from the client by setting up a log-on page that looks just like the normal log-on page. This is a threat at hotspots and other public networks and can be a threat in some private networks as well.

User Training

The last element of client device security, though certainly not the least, is user training. The users in your organization should be educated on the proper use of WLAN clients so that they can help protect your client devices and your organization's sensitive data. This training should include any configuration settings they will be required to manage as well as education about social engineering and other attack methods that they may be able to detect.

Many organizations are opting to provide their users with access to cell provider Internet services in order to avoid allowing their users to connect to wireless hotspots. Free wireless hotspots are seldom secure, as they have to be open for users to connect and use them. The acceptable use agreements that are displayed and to which the user must agree protect the network provider, but they do nothing to protect the client station that is connecting to the hotspot. You may choose to implement a VPN solution to help alleviate this problem, but it is up to the user to initiate the VPN connection once he or she is connected to the hotspot. Providing a cellular-based high-speed Internet connection can resolve many of these security issues.

Role-Based Access Control

Role-based access control (RBAC) is a feature provided by most WLAN switches. It provides the ability to restrict network access to authorized users, but more specifically, it can granularly limit access to portions of the network or specific services on the network. RBAC involves users, roles, and permissions. Think of roles as resembling groups in traditional network account management and the users as resembling the traditional network user accounts. You can create users and assign them a role and then grant permissions to the role rather than the individual users. Permissions include firewall-type filters, Layer 2 permissions, Layer 3 permissions, and even bandwidth-limiting permissions.

As an example, imagine you want to allow guests to log on to your network. You may authenticate these guests via a captive portal. The captive portal page will clearly tell the user to enter the user name of "guest" and a password of "guest"; however, the guest user may be assigned the role that limits the connection to a maximum of 128 kbps bandwidth and allows only ports 80, 100, and 25 (HTTP, POP3, and SMTP, respectively). The guest users will never know that there are other services on your network because they cannot access them.

Profile-Based firewalls

Profile-based firewalls are firewalls that can enforce differing filtering rules based on profiles built from user names, group names, or other identifying characteristics of the connecting client. WLAN switches may support the concept of a profile-based firewall, and the rules for the firewall may complement those enforced by RBAC. If the user logs on as a member of a filtered group, the user may not be able to pass specified types of traffic (usually based on TCP ports). When logged on as a member of another group, the user may have no limitations imposed by the profile-based firewall.

As with every technology, it seems the term *profile-based firewalls* has been used in many different ways. For example, Windows Server 2008 refers to profile-based firewalls, but it is not referring to filtering the client according to the client's profile. It is referring to filtering the inbound and outbound allowances according to the profile of the network to which the computer is attached. This is also true in Windows Vista.

Network Access Control (NAC)

Network access control (NAC) builds on the concepts of RBAC and profile-based firewalls and takes these concepts one step further. With a NAC system in place, your WLAN switch vendor can integrate with the NAC

FIGURE 10.7 Identity Engines 3000E NAC appliance

service provider (such as Microsoft IAS and ISA server, Cisco Systems, CAYMAS Systems, or Identity Engines) in order to quarantine WLAN clients that do not meet the security requirements to connect to your network. If a client is quarantined, the client can be automatically patched to meet your requirements (the usual behavior for organizationally owned assets), or it can be redirected to a captive portal-type web page where the user can optionally install the patches or security software. Once the client has been patched or modified to meet the requirements of your NAC policies, the client can be authenticated onto the production network. Figure 10.7 shows a network appliance implementation of a NAC server from Identity Engines. Additionally, solutions are available from Cisco Systems (NAC Appliance), Microsoft (Network Access Protection), or the Trusted Computing Group (Trusted Network Connection).

Captive Portals/Web Authentication

A captive portal is implemented when all the traffic coming through an AP is initially directed to an access control device on the wired LAN. The access control device is used to authenticate the user and provide access to resources on the wired LAN, which may include Internet access. If you've connected to a WLAN at a hotel or hotspot that first routed you to a log-on screen that required you to agree with the terms of use, you've likely experienced the concept of a captive portal. When you connected, though your home page may have been Google.com, you were redirected to the captive portal page before you could navigate to your normal home page. After authenticating (which can be as simple as click a button that reads, "I agree," or as complicated as providing a code and your contact information), you can communicate with other web sites as you normally would.

A captive portal is usually implemented using a WLAN switch or controller. These captive portals may support more than just logging you on to the network. They may be able to provide VPN tunnel endpoints or other security mechanisms that protect the data transfers that occur after the authentication as well as the initial authentication itself.

It is important to note that all captive portals are not created equal. Many devices or services only reroute HTTP (TCP port 80) to the web server used for authentication and authorization. If the client computer uses some other protocol (most commonly ICMP or DNS is used), the device or service that normally reroutes the client to the authentication server will allow the packets through to the Internet. All an attacker (in this case a freeloader or someone who wants to use the Internet access for free) has to do is set up a service on an Internet-connected machine to which he can connect using ICMP or DNS. This concept is sometimes called ICMP tunneling or DNS tunneling. Basically, the normal HTTP information is tunneled through the ICMP or DNS connection to the attacker's Internet-connected machine (you can call this the tunnel server). From there, the Internet-connected machine routes the HTTP information back out to the Internet and then tunnels responses from the Internet back to the attacker through the ICMP or DNS tunnel. There are video and text tutorials floating around the Internet that teach attackers how to perform this penetration.

IPsec VPN

In addition to the methods covered so far, you can still secure WLAN client communications using VPN protocols. While the PPTP protocol still abounds and is widely supported, it has fallen out of common use in the enterprise context because of the security vulnerabilities discovered in the protocol. At the same time, IPsec has been on the rise as a solution for VPN tunnels that use the L2TP or Layer 2 Tunneling Protocol.

IPsec (the term is short for IP security) is actually a security solution that involves three potential provisions: confidentiality, integrity, and non-repudiation. Confidentiality is provided by encrypting the payload or data that is transmitted. Integrity is ensured through hashing algorithms such as MD5 or the more secure SHA-1. Non-repudiation is ensured in that the message digest (the result of the hashing algorithm) is encrypted with the secret key or some credential that only the sender would know but the receiver can access. This may be a public/private key pair where the sender encrypts the data with her private key and the receiver decrypts it with the public key. If the message digest can be successfully decrypted, the sender cannot deny sending the initial packet and therefore cannot repudiate the data.

IPsec has often been said to be an unnecessarily complex VPN protocol, but in reality, it doesn't have to be that complex. You simply have to ensure that you enable the same encryption and hashing settings on both ends of the VPN connection. You will usually want to use the strongest form that is supported by both devices. The reality is that some vendor's implementation of IPsec will simply not connect to other vendor's implementations. For this reason, some have chosen to purchase dedicated VPN devices (sometimes called VPN concentrators or routers) to place on either side of the connection being secured.

Many SOHO WLAN routers support VPN capabilities right out of the box. This can be an excellent feature for connecting remote offices. For example, I assisted one company that has five computers at one location and three computers at another. Both locations had high-speed Internet connection, and they wanted to create a virtual WAN across the Internet links. We set up the WLAN router at each end to use dynamic DNS for name–to–IP address resolution and then configured the VPN tunnel between the two routers. Since the two locations were less than a mile apart, the configuration was done and the WAN link in place in less than an hour.

Be sure to check with your ISP to verify that you will not be in breach of your usage agreement by setting up such a VPN connection.

Here's another example: While working on a large municipal wireless backbone project where the customer was deploying a point-to-multipoint bridge solution using U-NII-3 5.8 GHz Cisco bridges, there was one multipoint location that provided connectivity for five remote bridges. The multipoint location was two-thirds of the way up a 500-foot tower on top of a 2500-foot mountain in the middle of metropolitan area. Once the wireless backbone connections were established, verified, and optimized, VPN connections were established over the top of the already highly secure wireless connection at the request of the customer. While this slightly impacted throughput and performance, the peace of mind it provided was well worth it in the customer's eyes.

Another common use of VPN technology is that of protecting WLAN clients that connect to unprotected and open hotspots. By requiring these clients to first create a VPN tunnel with a device on your corporate network and then routing them back out to the Internet through that VPN connection, you ensure that the communications between the WLAN client and the local hotspot AP are completely encrypted and secure.

FIGURE 10.8 WLAN client connecting with a VPN at an unsecured hotspot

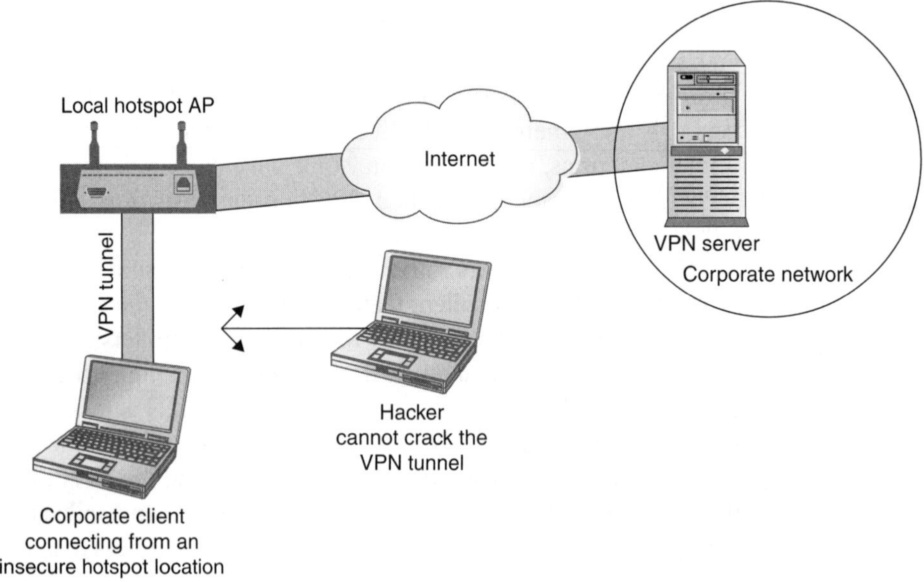

Figure 10.8 depicts this setup. Now those hungry hackers hanging around the hotspot cannot easily steal user accounts and other sensitive data that may be traversing the local hotspot WLAN.

You can also implement such VPN solutions for local WLANs within your company. In other words, you could implement a VPN server and require that the WLAN clients connecting locally create a VPN tunnel before beginning other communications. This is often suggested as a solution for older WLAN clients that do not support any security mechanism beyond WEP; however, clients that old may find that the overhead of managing the VPN tunnel brings their network connection to a snail's pace as well. It's probably still best to upgrade these older WLAN clients.

WLAN System Security and Management

It is not only the users' connections that must be secured, but the management connections must be secure as well. In this section, I will focus on two key elements of WLAN security: secure management and rogue AP detection.

SNMPv3/HTTPS/SSH2

If you manage the APs in your WLAN independently (meaning they are not lightweight APs or access ports), you should be sure to use a secure method of management. While you can connect to many APs using standard HTTP by default, this is not a practice you want to follow. All HTTP traffic is transmitted as clear text. Figure 10.9 demonstrates this. In this case, I've blocked out the identifying information to protect the site owners, but you can clearly see the log-on is "swettmarden" and the password is "drow1ssap1." This is because the web server does not use *HTTPS* for the log-on process and the credentials are passed in the clear. Of course, this scenario was created completely for the purpose of this document, but this scenario occurs every day thousands (if not millions) of times around the world.

FIGURE 10.9 Screen capture of a log-on captured in WireShark

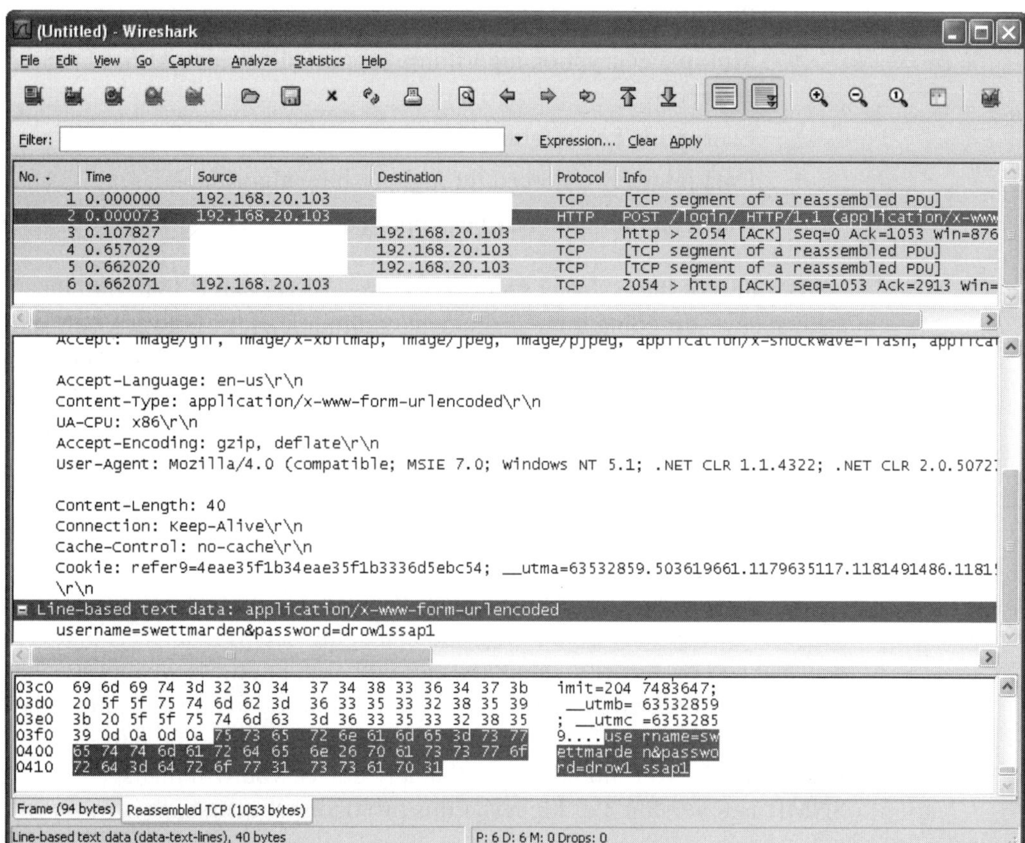

For this reason, HTTPS should always be used when a web-based interface is used to manage your APs. If the AP does not support HTTPS, it is best not to use HTTP to manage the device. HTTPS actually uses SSL and requires that a certificate be made available to the server. APs that support HTTPS have a certificate installed in the AP already. SSL is a Layer 7 encryption technology.

Another Layer 7 encryption solution is SSH. The first version of SSH has known vulnerabilities and should be avoided, but *SSH2* is considered secure at this time. SSH2 is usually used to provide command-line interface (CLI) access to the managed device. SSH2 provides the following benefits in a secure networking application:

- Public and private key authentication or username and password authentication
- Data signing through the use of public and private key pairs
- Private key passphrase association
- Multiple encryption algorithms supported, such as AES, 3DES, and DES
- Encryption key rotation
- Data integrity enforced through hashing algorithms
- Data compression may be supported

Because of these strong security features, SSH2 can help to mitigate against eavesdropping on management communications between you and the managed device. It can also help prevent man-in-the-middle attacks and replay attacks. The most common use of SSH2 is to implement a secure command shell or CLI across the network instead of having to connect to the console (serial port) of the managed device. Remember that telnet is just as insecure as HTTP by default because they both send their data packets as clear text that is easily readable by network protocol analyzers like WireShark.

The *Simple Network Management Protocol (SNMP)* is a standard solution for centrally monitoring and managing network devices. SNMP was plagued by security vulnerabilities early on, but these weaknesses have been addressed in SNMPv3. Version 3 has added authentication and privacy controls to help protect the management information passed on your network. You should ensure that any device you will manage with SNMP uses version 3 or higher of this protocol. Of course, as is true with any technology, you must be proactive and continually be on the lookout for new vulnerabilities that would impact your network. That which is secure today may be vulnerable tomorrow.

Rogue AP and Client Detection and/or Containment

Much emphasis has been placed on rogue APs throughout the years since WLANs first began to be implemented, and they still pose a threat to our networks today. A *rogue AP* can be defined as any AP that is operating in your "owned" space but that has not been authorized by you. The rogue AP may have been placed by an intruder seeking to gain access to your wired network, or it may have been placed by a well-meaning user hoping to make his or her life easier and more mobile while at work. Either way, the rogue AP is a threat to your security.

There are two primary reasons that motivate an attacker to install a rogue AP in your environment. The first is to gain access to your wired or wireless network. The second is to attack your valid wireless client STAs.

In the first case, the attacker will usually find an out-of-the-way spot where a live Ethernet port provides connectivity to the wired LAN. He will connect the Ethernet port to the AP using a standard cable and then power the AP with a nearby power outlet. Some APs may even be powered by battery if the attacker only needs access for a short time. Once the attacker has the AP in place, he can begin attacking your wired LAN or other WLANs that may be connected to the wired LAN. Of course, the attacker has to be willing to lose his AP in a scenario like this because he risks not being able to retrieve it after the attack. With the physical security being as lax as it is in many organizations, however, the retrieval may not be too difficult.

Many rogue APs are placed by intruders for the sole purpose of gaining high-speed Internet connectivity. They often know that companies have very fast connections to the Internet, and since they will be the only user connected to the AP, they can download a tremendous amount of illegal software, movies, music, and more in a short window of time. This malicious use of your network can be protected against by using an Internet proxy server that requires authentication.

Protecting against the placement of such APs is important. The first thing you consider is the disabling of all Ethernet ports that are not assigned a permanent usage. When those ports are needed, they can be enabled through software or by simply plugging in the Ethernet cable at the switch. In addition to this, you should have good physical security in place that deters such behavior. Even fake surveillance cameras can go a long way here. Install a fake surveillance camera in areas where you think an attacker may attempt to install a rogue AP. The presence of this device—as long as it looks real—will frequently deter the attacker.

The second motivation for placement by an attacker is that of direct attack against your WLAN clients. In this case, the attacker may be using the AP to perform a hijacking attack in an attempt to gain access to the data on the WLAN computers. She may also be attempting to install backdoors on these WLAN clients that will allow her access to the network in the future. In these scenarios, rogue AP detection can be more difficult. The attacker may be a temporary employee who has valid access to the premises and has been granted permission to use her laptop at work. She may be running a software-based rogue AP, or she may be using a USB-power pocket AP like the one shown in Figure 10.10.

Protecting against this type of rogue AP can be more difficult. The attacker is not connecting to an Ethernet port and does not likely desire to. Therefore, disabling unused ports will not be helpful. The best protection against this type of rogue AP attack is to implement a secure IEEE 802.1X/EAP authentication type that uses mutual authentication. This will also help protect your clients from other rogue AP–type attacks.

Detecting Rogue APs

There are really two primary ways to detect rogue APs: through the wired interface and through the wireless interface. Remember that a rogue AP is still a rogue AP, and it will therefore transmit Beacon frames at a regular interval. If you use a site survey tool to map the RF coverage in your

FIGURE 10.10 D-Link Pocket AP (DWL-G730AP)

area and then perform a pass-through with this tool again periodically—comparing the two RF coverage maps—you can detect the existence of new APs. This would be one method of rogue AP detection through the wireless interface.

Another method of detection through the wireless interface would be to keep up-to-date documentation of the number of APs you have installed that can be detected at a given location. Then you can go to that location—and other locations as well—and use a tool like NetStumbler to see if more APs are now present. When you see a new AP, note its MAC address and you can then monitor the signal strength of the Beacons from that MAC address while moving throughout the area. You should notice the strength weakening and strengthening as you move around. Using this process, you should eventually be able to find the approximate location of the AP and then the AP itself.

You can also detect rogue APs through the wired port. Many APs are installed by users who want the flexibility provided by a WLAN. These users will seldom know how to prevent you from detecting the AP through the wired port. Most APs installed by attackers are not configured in such a way to prevent you from detecting them through the wired port either. The secret is in the fact that these rogue APs are usually cheap SOHO APs or routers and either they do not support the disabling of the HTTP management interface on the Ethernet port or, again, the installer doesn't know how to do so.

Since you know that an HTTP server is running on most APs and it is not running on most desktop PCs or even many network servers, you can perform a port scan subnet by subnet looking for IP addresses with port 80 open. When you discover an IP address with port 80 open that wasn't there before, it's possible that you've discovered a rogue AP. A trick you can use is to do the following:

1. When you've finished installing your WLAN and you know there are no rogues at this point, do a port scan of every segment and save the output to a text file.
2. Now, every week or so, you can run the same port scan during off-peak hours (if you have them) and save the new scan to a different file.
3. Finally, use any of dozens of file comparison tools to look for differences. Or, even better, write your own script that compares the two files and only tells you of new references to ports 80 (HTTP) and 23 (telnet).

With this process, you can build your own rogue detection system very easily. It will not be foolproof, but it certainly is better than no detection system at all. If your network supports this, you could even write your script in such as way so that it disables the Ethernet ports where the new TCP ports 80 or 23 were found and e-mails you a report. You can take action as soon as you receive the e-mail, but the script has disabled the device in the meantime, just in case it is a rogue AP. This provides you with a form of automatic containment. It works well in SOHO implementations and smaller SMBs.

In larger enterprises and larger SMBs, you will need to install more powerful centralized management solutions. For example, Cisco System's Unified Wireless Network solution takes advantage of the fact that all Cisco controllers include a method to automatically detect rogue APs on and off the network. This allows you to spend your time doing more than running scripts and setting up manual solutions.

Preventing Rogue APs

The old saying reminds us that an ounce of prevention is worth a pound of cure. This is certainly true for rogue APs. There are a number of methods you can use to prevent individuals from connecting unauthorized APs to your wired network. These include

- *Disabling unused Ethernet ports.* This was covered earlier and is a simple solution, but it should not be relied on by itself because people do make mistakes and leave ports open.
- *Using port security on switches.* Many switches support port-based filtering by MAC addresses and other parameters. You can specify that the only MAC addresses that can connect to your switch are those in the specified list. This is not a wireless MAC address in this case, so the attacker would have to guess a valid MAC address rather than sniffing for one on the WLAN.
- *State clearly in your acceptable use policy that users cannot install APs.* This will most certainly not prevent the installation of all rogue APs, but it will deter many from installing them.
- *Implement network access control technology.* This will cause the attacker's computer to go straight to the quarantine area when he or she accesses the network. The NAC device/server would be installed between the switch that provides connectivity to your

Ethernet ports and the rest of the network. Any device that connects will now have to be authenticated and validated, which will make many attackers run away quickly for fear of being caught by the IT professionals who knew enough to protect that port.

- *Implement enterprise-capable WLAN solutions that automatically detect and report rogue APs and graphically show their locations.* Cisco's Unified Wireless Network solutions detect and report rogue APs automatically and can display their location through the Wireless Control System management solution. Aruba's Mobile Management System provides similar functionality.

As you can see, there are multiple methods that you can use to prevent the connection of rogue APs to your wired LAN. Some of these methods are psychological and others are technological, but a combination of both types usually works best.

IEEE 802.11 Network Security Policy Basics

Security policies for WLANs are covered in depth in the *CWSP Certifies Wireless Security Professional Official Study Guide, Second Edition.* The CWNA exam requires that you understand the basic components of a security policy so that you can implement a WLAN that is in compliance with that policy. While the CWSP certification requires that you understand security policies enough to create them, here you only have to use them.

A security policy will define the measures taken to secure the network, the audit methods used to ensure network security according to policy, and the penalties that will occur, should an individual breach that policy. For example, the SANS Security Policy Project (available at www.sans.org/resources/policies) provides templates for many types of security policies. The Wireless Communications Policy document for SYSEDCO opens with these remarks:

> This policy prohibits access to SYSEDCO networks via unsecured wireless communication mechanisms. Only wireless systems that meet the criteria of this policy or have been granted an exclusive waiver by InfoSec are approved for connectivity to SYSEDCO's networks.

I took the liberty of inserting my company name into the policy where the template simply says <*Company Name*>. You can see, from the opening of this policy, how it sets the stage for prohibiting access to the network using improperly secured devices and even prohibits the use of rogues APs. The policy also includes the following enforcement statement:

> Any employee found to have violated this policy may be subject to disciplinary action, up to and including termination of employment.

The policies at the SANS Security Policy Project are a good place to start, but you will need to customize them for use in your organization. For example, this WLAN policy from which I've quoted requires the use of VPN tunnels, but you may decide that this is not necessary for your organization.

Security policies may be divided into two segments: general and functional. General security policies will describe the overall view of the network. Functional security policies will describe specific technology procedures that must or should be implemented in the environment.

Describe the Following General Security Policy Elements

General security policies usually give a high-level overview of the way the network security should be implemented and managed. They may include the following sections of information:

- *Statement of Authority*
- *Target Audience*
- *Violation Reporting and Enforcement*
- *Risk Assessment*
- *Impact Analysis*
- *Security Auditing*

The statement of authority will identify the individual, group, or organization that has the authority to enforce the policies. The target audience will identify the individuals that must comply with the policy, and violation reporting and enforcement statements will determine how a violation incident will be handled.

The risk assessment will begin with the identification of assets and the threats posed against those assets. Once these assets are identified and the threats determined, an impact analysis will help to discover the loss to the organization, should the risk occur. Finally, security auditing procedures and frequencies should be defined so that the administrative staff knows what is expected of them and how to meet those expectations.

Describe the Following Functional Security Policy Elements

Functional security policies specify how specific security-related technologies should be utilized. There will often be a separate document for each technology or concept. The functional policy will provide specific methods that result in the mitigation of threats identified and described in the general policy.

An example of a functional policy may be that all Ethernet ports utilize IEEE 802.1X port-based access control in all conference rooms and public areas. This can help prevent the installation of rogue APs. The general policy may have defined rogue APs as a threat, but the functional policy defined the protection mechanism to be enforced. Functional policies may include the following sections, or each of these may be individual policy documents:

- Password policies
- Training requirements
- Acceptable use
- WLAN access requirements
- Encryption standards
- E-mail usage
- Internet usage
- Asset management

Security Policy Recommendations

The following sections document recommended practices that should be included in your security policies. Remember that you must actually perform these acts in order for them to be effective. Many security policies make good doorstops because they are created but never fully implemented.

Baseline Practices

The following are intended to be general baseline guidelines for WLANs in three markets: small office/home office (SOHO), small and medium businesses (SMB), and enterprise-class installations.

SOHO SOHO implementations seldom require enterprise-class security that includes RADIUS servers and IEEE 802.1X/EAP authentication. However, the following should serve as a minimum baseline at this time:

- Upgrade all APs and clients to the latest firmware and software revisions.
- Use all WPA2 hardware if possible.
- Change the manufacturer settings for SSIDs, log-on accounts, etc.
- Enable Open System authentication and use WPA- or WPA2-Personal.
- Use a strong passphrase that is long enough to resist brute force and dictionary cracks.

SMB Small and medium businesses will usually not have the budgets of large enterprises, but they should insist on upgrading the baseline recommended for SOHO installations in the following ways:

- Use all newer hardware that supports WPA2-Personal at a minimum as much as possible.
- For legacy devices that cannot use WPA-level security (such as barcode readers and older wireless IP phones), implement separate VLANs that prevent anything on the unsecure VLAN from getting to the corporate network.
- Preferably use WPA2-Enterprise with a RADIUS server.

Enterprise Enterprises with hundreds and even thousands of users cannot accept the lower security baselines of the SOHO and SMB. This is mostly a matter of asset value, and the large enterprises have more to lose, so they should be willing to spend more to protect it. The baseline should now be upgraded to include the following:

- If they do not exist, a full set of documented security policies for the wired and wireless LANs should be developed.
- Perform periodic security audits to verify that the network is still operating according to policy and is secure.
- Use only WPA2-Enterprise and fall back to WPA-Enterprise if need be.
- Do not implement preshared keys anywhere. They are too difficult to manage in a large implementation and are not as secure.

- Use VLANs to isolate users from one another and from services as needed.
- Implement a Wireless Intrusion Prevention System.
- Consider implementing network access control.

Implementation Practices

Ensure that your devices are configured while detached from the network. Attaching a default configured device to the network opens you up to temporary attack while the device is still insecure. Configure the device using the console port of a direct Ethernet cable if you choose to configure the device with the web-based interface. Once the device is configured to meet your security standard, bring it online.

Physical Security

If you cannot provide guarded entrance to your facility, consider installing wireless IP cameras that can monitor your facility 24 × 7. As noted earlier, you can also install fake cameras to deter attackers that would otherwise readily install rogue APs without fear. Additional physical security concerns include:

- End-user training
- Disabling unused physical ports
- Installing APs central to the facility or with antennas that propagate the RF energy inward toward the facility instead of outward toward your parking area

It is very important that you realize this last item will not guarantee that an attacker cannot "see" or "read" the information traversing your WLAN. This will only make it more difficult and should not be considered an actual security solution. The main purpose of proper antenna selection is gaining the coverage you need, not gaining a security advantage.

Advanced WLAN Security Topics

There are many WLAN security topics that can impact your WLAN, and you should be aware of them, though you do not have to become a master of these topics to pass the CWNA exam or implement an effective and secure WLAN. VLANs, the first technology I will cover in this section, differ somewhat from vendor to vendor, even though standards do exist for much of their operation. The second and final topic covered, layered security, is really a culmination of everything we've discussed in this chapter.

VLANs

A virtual LAN (VLAN) is used to define the logical separation of a physical LAN into multiple networks or broadcast domains. Two VLANs act much like two physical LANs in that they cannot communicate with each other unless they are configured with routers between them.

In most WLAN equipment that supports VLANs, the SSID is used to determine the VLAN that a WLAN STA should participate in. Different VLANs will have different features such as authentication methods and encryption methods. This can provide you with a simple solution for providing a public network and a private network through the logical segmentation provided by VLANs. The settings that can be configured separately for each VLAN often include:

- Authentication type
- Encryption method
- Number of allowed clients
- QoS settings

Since VLANs only allow nodes to communicate with other nodes in the same VLAN—unless a bridging or routing device is used—you can implement solutions like that represented in Figure 10.11. Note the VLAN trunks between the LAN switch A and switch B and between the APs and the switches. The VLAN trunk uses IEEE 802.1Q encapsulation to allow for this magic to work. The two WLAN clients on VLAN A can communicate with each other even though they are in separate physical networks, and the VLAN A and VLAN B clients on the left cannot communicate with each other even though they are on the same physical network. This capability is provided by VLAN technology.

Layered Security

Our final topic is really an aggregation of all that we've learned. Taking the topics of IEEE 802.1X/EAP authentication and encryption key management, VLANs, network access control, and others and bringing them all together helps us arrive at the final security solution: layered security.

FIGURE 10.11 VLAN configuration for WLANs

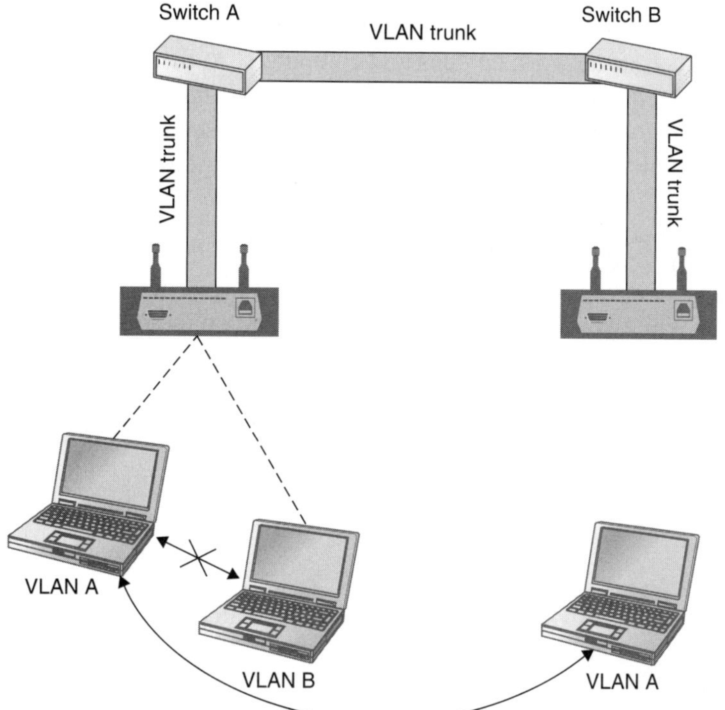

Think of layered security as building a brick wall outside your home and then putting insulation inside the walls as well. The internal insulation protects you from the seeping cold that the bricks miss. Now put up foam panel board before you put on the drywall and you have even more protection from the cold (or heat, depending on where you live). The point is that different materials work together to provide you with better protection than any one material could. Network security can be strengthened through similar means.

Think of it like this: If an attacker is able to install a rogue AP on your wired LAN, do you have measures in place to prevent the AP from receiving a valid IP address? If the AP does receive a valid IP address, do you have authentication and authorization measures in place on your network to keep the attacker away from sensitive data? If the attacker does bypass your authentication and authorization, do you have your most sensitive data encrypted so that it will be difficult for the attacker to utilize?

Another way to conceive of layered security is to think of the different security measures you can use at the different layers of the OSI model. For example, at the Physical layer, you can provide physical security to prevent theft of network devices and computers. At the Data Link or MAC layer, you can provide encryption and Wireless Intrusion Prevention Systems. As you can see, either perspective of layered security helps you to deepen your thinking and improve the security of your network.

Common Security Myths

While you will not necessarily be tested on the following knowledge, it is important that I emphasize the myths related to WLAN security. Many recommendations either provide no added security or minimal added security. Some recommendations actually open your client computers up for attack. The myths that I will address include:

- MAC filtering
- SSID hiding
- All modern equipment uses "better WEP"
- WLANs can't be secured

The first myths focus on recommendations that provide either minimal or no security and the last one reverses the perspective to focus on the false conception that WLANs simply cannot be implemented in a secure manner.

MAC Filtering

Vendors of wireless devices and books on wireless networking often provide a list of the "Top 5" or "Top 10" things you should do to secure your WLAN. This list usually includes MAC filtering and SSID hiding or cloaking. The reality is that neither of these provides a high level of security. MAC addresses can easily be spoofed, and valid MAC addresses can be identified in just a few moments. For example, an attacker can weed out the AP in an infrastructure BSS by looking for the MAC address that sends out Beacon frames. This will always be the AP in the BSS. With this filtered out of the attacker's protocol analyzer, he has only to find other MAC addresses that are transmitting with a destination MAC address equal to that of the AP. Assuming the captured frames are data frames, the attacker now knows a valid IP address.

There is no question that MAC filtering will make it more difficult for an attacker to access your network. The attacker will have to go through the process I've just outlined (or a similar process) in order to obtain a valid MAC address to spoof. However, you are adding to your workload by implementing such MAC filtering and you have to ask, "Am I getting a good return on investment for my time?" The answer is usually no. Assuming you are using TKIP or CCMP with a strong EAP type for authentication (or even preshared keys), this will be so much more secure than MAC filtering could ever hope to be that it makes the extra effort of MAC filtering of minimal value. I recommend that you not concern yourself with MAC filtering in an enterprise or SMB implementation. It may be useful in a SOHO implementation, but I question its value even then.

SSID Hiding

Hiding or cloaking the SSID of your WLAN falls into a similar category as MAC filtering. Both provide very little in the way of security enhancement. Changing the name of your SSID from the vendor defaults can be very helpful, as it will make dictionary attacks against PSK implementations more difficult. This is because the SSID is used in the process of creating the pairwise master key. Hiding the SSID only makes it difficult for casual eavesdroppers to find your network. Hiding the SSID also forces your valid clients to send out probe requests in order to connect to your WLAN, whether using the Windows Wireless Zero Configuration utility or your vendor's client software. This means that, when the user turns on his or her laptop in a public place, the laptop is broadcasting your SSID out to the world. This could be considered a potential security threat, since a rogue AP of any type can be configured to the SSID that is being sent out in the probe requests. Of course, as was previously mentioned, modern software-based APs can respond to random SSIDs generated by WZC, but hiding your SSID effectively makes every WLAN client in existence vulnerable to such attacks, since they will all have to send probe requests with the SSID now.

I always recommend changing the SSID from the default, but I never recommend hiding the SSID for security purposes. Some people will hide the SSID for usability purposes. Turning of the SSID broadcast in all AP's Beacon frames will prevent client computers from "seeing" the other networks to which they are not supposed to connect. This may reduce confusion, but SSID hiding should not be considered a security solution.

An argument can be made such as the following: "MAC filtering and SSID hiding are not strong security techniques, but they are security techniques because they make it more difficult to penetrate the network." Let's compare this to our physical world. For example, closing your door at night is not a strong security technique, but it is a security technique because the intruder now has to turn the door knob and push the door open to enter your house. Does that sound right to you? Me neither.

All Modern Equipment Uses "Better WEP"

When the initial scare hit, many vendors looked for solutions to the weak IVs used in the current (at the time) WEP implementations. Eventually many vendors began implementing newer WEP solutions that attempted to avoid the weak IVs. As early as 2003, I noticed people posting on the Internet and saying that the newer hardware didn't have this problem. In fact, I have a network-attached storage device that was purchased in 2005 that includes a built-in AP. This device is running the most recent firmware from the vendor (D-Link, in this case), and I can connect a brand new Intel Centrino chipset laptop to the device using WEP. While monitoring from another computer, I am able to capture weak IVs and crack the WEP key in a matter of minutes. You simply cannot trust that a vendor has actually implemented algorithms that protect you against WEP weaknesses just because it is newer hardware. Instead, you would need to monitor the communications with the device in order to determine if weak IVs are being used. It's easier to implement WPA or WPA2, so I recommend that.

WLANs Can't Be Secured

Don't allow these last few false security methods to keep you from implementing a WLAN. WLANs can be implemented in a secure fashion using IEEE 802.11i (Clause 9 of IEEE 802.11-2007) and strong EAP types. In fact, they can be made far more secure than most wired LANs, since most wired LANs do not implement any real authentication mechanisms at the node level. If you buy into the concept that WLANs cannot be secured and you decide not to implement a WLAN for this reason, you will likely open your network up to more frequent rogue AP installations from users that desire to have wireless access to the network. The simplest way to avoid or at least diminish the occurrence of user-installed rogue APs is to implement a secure WLAN for the users.

Summary

This chapter provided an overview of the security mechanisms available in WLANs. You learned about the weaknesses of earlier solutions such as WEP and Shared Key authentication, and then you learned about the solutions found in IEEE 802.11, Clause 8 as amended (formerly known as IEEE 802.11i). You then moved on to learn about rogue access points and advanced security technologies that help you provide greater security and peace of mind for your WLAN and you.

Key Terms

- ☐ **Advanced Encryption Standard (AES)**
- ☐ **authentication server**
- ☐ **authenticator**
- ☐ **captive portals**
- ☐ **CCMP**
- ☐ **extensible authentication protocol (EAP)**
- ☐ **HTTPS**
- ☐ **IEEE 802.1X**
- ☐ **IPsec VPNs**
- ☐ **network access control (NAC)**
- ☐ **profile-based firewalls**
- ☐ **RC4**
- ☐ **robust security network (RSN)**
- ☐ **robust security network association (RSNA)**
- ☐ **rogue access points**
- ☐ **role-based access control (RBAC)**
- ☐ **SSH2**
- ☐ **supplicant**
- ☐ **temporal key integrity protocol (TKIP)**
- ☐ **Wired Equivalent Privacy (WEP)**

Review Questions

1. You are implementing an IEEE 802.11, Clause 8 security solution based on the amendment made in IEEE 802.11i. You have implemented a RADIUS server and have clients that are capable of using multiple EAP types, including the one configured for use on the RADIUS server. You want to implement what would be classified as WPA2-Enterprise. Since you have the RADIUS server and the clients, what piece of the network are you missing?

   A. Authentication server

   B. Authenticator

   C. Supplicant

   D. Network access control

2. You want to scan a subnet on your network that includes Ethernet ports easily accessible to would-be attackers. Which ports are you likely to scan for, in order to locate possible rogue APs? (Choose all that apply.)

   A. 389

   B. 80

   C. 12

   D. 23

3. The manager of the factory where you work as a network technician has asked you to implement a secure WLAN. In your research, you determine that your organization should implement AES encryption and the 802.1X-EAP authentication and key management protocol. You've also determined that you will be installing too many APs and clients to configure each one with a preshared key passphrase. Which Wi-Fi Alliance certification will meet your needs?

   A. WPA-Personal

   B. WPA2-Personal

C. WPA-Enterprise

D. WPA2-Enterprise

4. Which of the following factors indicate that a pre-RSNA connection is being used?

   A. WPA-Personal is enabled.

   B. VLANs are not supported.

   C. RBAC features have been turned off.

   D. WEP is being used as the group cipher suite.

5. You are installing a network for a small company named Instant Art that is run out of the owner's home. Only two computers will use the WLAN, and you are installing a Linksys WLAN residential gateway between the WLAN clients and the DSL Internet connection. Given this scenario, which of the following would be a good choice for the WPA-PSK passphrase?

   A. HomeBusiness

   B. InstantArt

   C. B7YbLoO977gH67jUyUftr

   D. None of the above: No WPA-PSK passphrase is a good choice

Review Answers

1. **B.** You are missing the authenticator or, in this case, the access point. The clients will act as the supplicants and the RADIUS server will act as the authentication server. Network access control, through a valid security solution, is not required to implement a WPA2-Enterprise solution.

2. **B, D.** Port 80 is used by the HTTP configuration interfaces of most APs, particularly the less-expensive ones often used as rogue APs. Port 23 would be used by the telnet service if the AP supports it. Ports 389 and 12 are not likely to benefit you in your search for rogue APs.

Port 12 is unassigned at this time, and port 389 is usually used for LDAP communications.

3. **D.** Only WPA2-Enterprise will meet all your needs. It will provide CCMP/AES and will not require (or support) the use of a preshared key. WPA-Enterprise, while not requiring the use of a preshared key, will require the use of TKIP/RC4, which does not meet your encryption, authentication, and key management requirements. In addition, WPA equipment can no longer be purchased as new equipment, since the Wi-Fi Alliance is no longer certifying equipment as WPA. Both WPA- and WPA2-Personal are excluded by their use of preshared keys, regardless of the other features that may or may not be supported.
4. **D.** If WEP is being used by the connection, it is a pre-RSNA connection. WPA-Personal qualifies as an RSNA connection, and VLANs and RBAC features are not directly related to RSNAs.
5. **C.** The correct answer would be B7YbLoO977gH67jUyUftr. This passphrase is sufficiently long and is not a dictionary word or phrase. Brute force would have to be used against it. InstantArt and HomeBusiness sound like passphrases that would be easy to guess. It is not true that "no WPA-PSK passphrase is a good choice."

PART IV

Installation and Analysis Tools

In This Part

CHAPTER

11

Wireless Problem Discovery and Solutions

CWNA Exam Objectives Covered:

- Identify the purpose and features of the following wireless analysis systems and explain how to install, configure, integrate, and manage them as applicable
  - Handheld and Laptop Protocol Analyzers
  - Basic Protocol Analysis
  - RF Spectrum Analyzers
  - WIPSs with Integrated Spectrum Analysis
  - Distributed Wireless Intrusion Prevention Systems (WIPSs)
  - Distributed RF Spectrum Analyzers

In This Chapter

This chapter begins the process of aggregating all the knowledge presented in the preceding chapters of this book. In this chapter and the next, you will learn how to use the knowledge you have of RF signals, RF behavior, WLAN standards, and WLAN hardware in order to troubleshoot and optimize WLANs. This chapter provides the foundation for the next. You will learn to differentiate between *protocol analyzers* and *spectrum analyzers* and when to use each one. You will also learn about various automated monitoring solutions such as wireless intrusion detection systems (WIDSs) and wireless intrusion prevention systems (WIPSs). These technologies are designed to help secure your WLAN, but they can also be beneficial from an analysis perspective. Finally, you'll learn about a new kind of spectrum analyzer known as a distributed RF spectrum analyzer.

Installing, Configuring, Integrating, and Managing WLAN Analysis Systems

WLAN analysis systems help you design, secure, troubleshoot, and optimize your WLAN. These analysis systems include individual devices that are used manually and collections of monitoring devices that are used automatically or centrally. I will cover the following WLAN analysis tools in this chapter:

- Handheld and laptop protocol analyzers
- Basic protocol analysis
- RF spectrum analyzers
- Wireless intrusion prevention systems
- Distributed RF spectrum analyzers

Handheld and Laptop Protocol Analyzers

A WLAN protocol analyzer is used to capture data packets as well as IEEE 802.11 MAC layer frames and decode their contents. The information is usually presented in a very readable format that is easier to understand than simply looking at a series of 1s and 0s. For example, many protocol analyzers break the frame headers down in such a way that each bit is explained in real-world terms and concepts. This process is often called frame or packet decoding.

Handheld and computer-based (usually used on laptops) protocol analyzers have existed for many years. Most of these applications are designed for wired protocol analysis. Because WLAN devices are so different (depending on the chipsets used for the wireless communications), even protocol analyzers that are designed for WLANs or support WLAN analysis as well as wired are often incompatible with many of WLAN network cards. For example, many early WLAN protocol analyzers supported one chipset alone. You were required to purchase that specific chipset (a network card that was based on it) if you wanted to use the protocol analyzer. Today, the situation has improved, but there are still no protocol analyzers that work with every WLAN network card. In fairness to the software vendors who create the protocol analyzers, this is—at least in part—due to the way that different operating systems (OSs) interact with WLAN devices.

Figure 11.1 shows the OmniPeek Personal web page, where you can learn about the different chipsets supported by this WLAN protocol analyzer. As you can see, at the time of this writing, USB drivers were not supported; however, a large pool of Atheros chipsets and drivers are supported, as well as some Intel Centrino–based WLAN adapters.

When evaluating protocol analyzers, it is very important that you determine whether the software supports your chosen hardware. Many WLAN administrators find it is easier to build a custom laptop for WLAN protocol analysis than to try to find an analyzer that supports their laptop. By purchasing a laptop with CardBus support and then purchasing the recommended card (or cards) for the protocol analyzer you've chosen, you remove the guesswork from the scenario. Keep in mind that you may have to install different drivers for different protocol analyzers, even though they support the same card. This can be very time consuming, and some administrators have chosen to actually install the OS on their computer multiple times—in a multiboot configuration—so that they can boot into the OS installation that is preconfigured for the device and analyzer they desire to use at that time.

Newer laptop computers are now coming with ExpressCard slots. Where you used to get two PCMCIA card slots (commonly called PC Card slots), you now may have one PC Card slot and one ExpressCard slot. You may not even know this until you try to slide a PC Card into the ExpressCard slot—it won't fit! Why is this significant? With two PC Card

FIGURE 11.1 OmniPeek Personal–supported drivers page

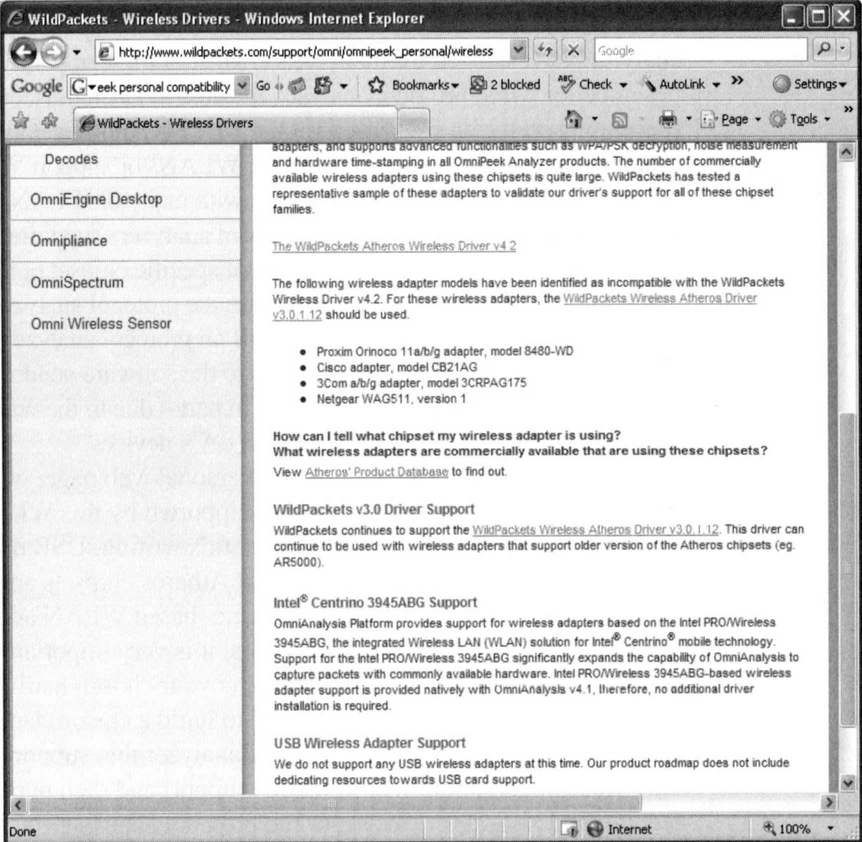

slots, you could have one in use with your Cognio or AirMagnet Spectrum Analyzer card with external antenna and use the other one for your favorite wireless protocol analysis card with or without an external antenna. Now, you'll have to either use the embedded Wi-Fi radio on the laptop or find an ExpressCard that has a supported chipset for either protocol analysis or spectrum analysis. Vendors have been slow to accept the ExpressCard format, but by the time you read this, there should be several supported ExpressCard devices on the market.

This is one area where the Linux OS is arguably easier to use. Windows often requires much more effort to perform WLAN analysis (from a device driver perspective only) than Linux. However, Windows is more likely to provide a graphical interface for its tools than Linux (though the newer versions of the Mac OS are certainly changing this). Ultimately, you must choose the OS that supports the tools you want and need to use. I personally find that I can perform more than 95 percent of what I need to do in Windows, and since I support Windows networks for a living, it just makes sense for me to keep learning more about the Windows environment. When I can't get it done in Windows, I boot into Linux and get it done there; however, if I can stay in Windows, I will be much more productive in the environments I manage.

I know other administrators who use Linux very heavily, and they do this even though they manage a Windows environment. The good news is that WLAN analysis and troubleshooting has evolved so that it can be performed from the Mac, Windows, Linux, and other platforms. Since the CWNA certification is vendor neutral, you will not be tested on your knowledge of Mac WLANs versus Windows WLANs and so on. Use what works for you, but be sure you understand how the technology is actually working and not just how to click the right buttons. This will make you a more effective WLAN administrator and troubleshooter.

In addition to the protocol analyzers used on computers, handheld protocol analyzers are available. These devices are often based on the PocketPC OS and are available through a variety of vendors. Most are very simplistic (primarily due to the limited screen size and processing power) in comparison to the laptop/desktop protocol analyzer packages in that they usually only report the available WLANs, the configuration settings for these WLANs, and possible information related to signal strength and quality. Though some may suggest that these tools are not true protocol analyzers, the reality is that they do indeed analyze the WLAN protocols at the MAC layer and report their findings to you. What they do not usually do is allow you to view the low-level WLAN frames directly. There are exceptions, such as CommView for Wi-Fi PPC.

You can purchase and download applications that will help you perform WLAN protocol analysis on PocketPC devices from vendors like TamoSoft (CommView for Wi-Fi PPC) and freeware applications like MiniStumbler. Figures 11.2 through 11.4 show various screens in the CommView for Wi-Fi PPC handheld protocol analyzer.

FIGURE 11.2 CommView for Wi-Fi showing available networks

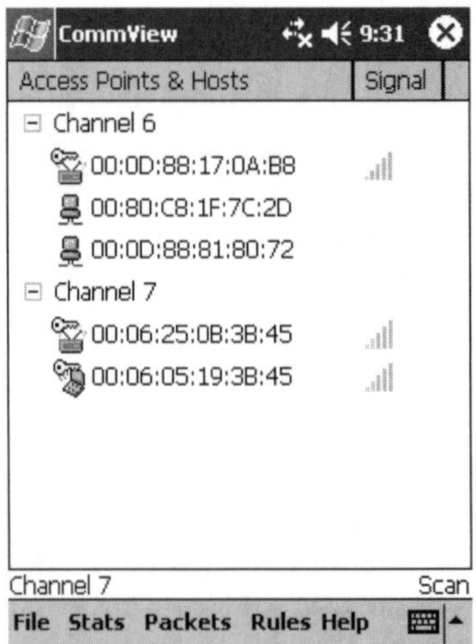

Basic Protocol Analysis

In this section, I will introduce you to the basics of protocol analysis. I will demonstrate the concept using OmniPeek Personal. OmniPeek Personal is a free Windows-based protocol analyzer that supports a number of network cards with Atheros chipsets as well as others. This product is comparable

FIGURE 11.3 CommView for Wi-Fi showing packets

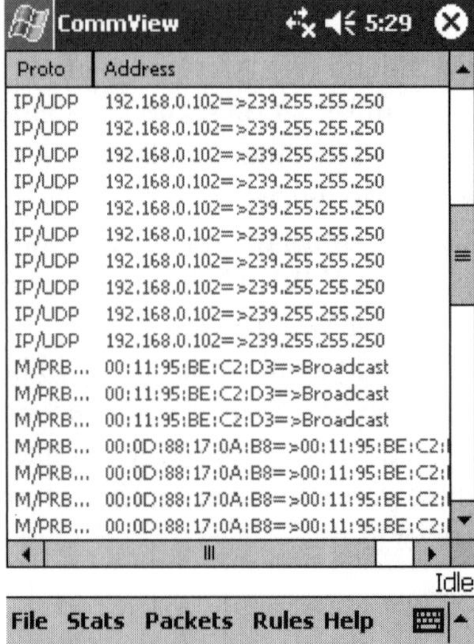

FIGURE 11.4 CommView for Wi-Fi showing capture settings and WEP decoding

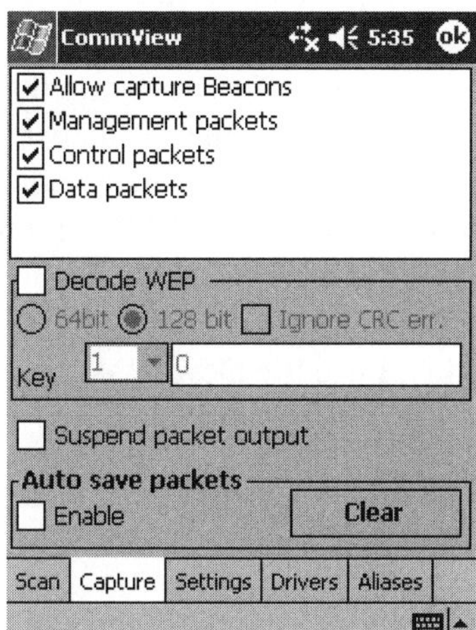

to commercial applications such as AiroPeek NX and CommView for Wi-Fi in its capturing and filtering capabilities. It is limited in the number of network devices that can be used within the application, but most administrators will find that they use one or two WLAN cards at most. You can download OmniPeek Personal after filling out a registration form at www.wildpackets.com.

In this section, I will walk you through the installation of OmniPeek Personal on a typical computer and then demonstrate the use of this tool as a WLAN analyzer. First I'll cover the installation process, which can be slightly more complex than your average business application. Then I'll show you how to capture the flow through the IEEE 802.11 state machine as we move a WLAN client from unauthenticated and unassociated to authenticated and associated. Finally, we'll see how to apply filters to a captured set of WLAN packets and frames or to a live capture process.

Installing OmniPeek Personal

After you've registered for and downloaded the OmniPeek Personal installation package, you can begin the installation process. There are really two ways to go about the installation. First, you could try installing the application and keep your fingers crossed in hopes that it will work with your currently installed WLAN drivers. Second (and this is my preferred method), you can download the appropriate drivers for your card and install them before installing OmniPeek Personal. We'll do the latter in this case.

This means the first step is to visit the WildPackets web site and determine the appropriate drivers for your card. The URL used for this purpose was www.wildpackets.com/support/omni/omnipeek_personal/wireless at the time of this writing. This page is shown in Figure 11.1 earlier in this chapter. The good news is that once you install the driver, you will likely be able to use it for both OmniPeek Personal and your normal network operations.

I am using a Proxim Orinoco 11 a/b/g card (8480-WD) for this example, so I needed to download the Atheros driver version 3.0.1.12. The driver is downloaded as a Zip file, so I need to decompress it to a folder on my hard drive. After doing this, I use the Device Manager to update the driver. The following steps get it done (in Windows XP):

1. Right-click My Computer and select Manage.
2. Select Device Manager in System Tools.
3. Expand the Network Adapters container in the Device Manager.
4. Right-click the Orinoco 802.11abg device and select Update Driver (see Figure 11.5).

FIGURE 11.5 Selecting the WLAN adapter in Device Manager

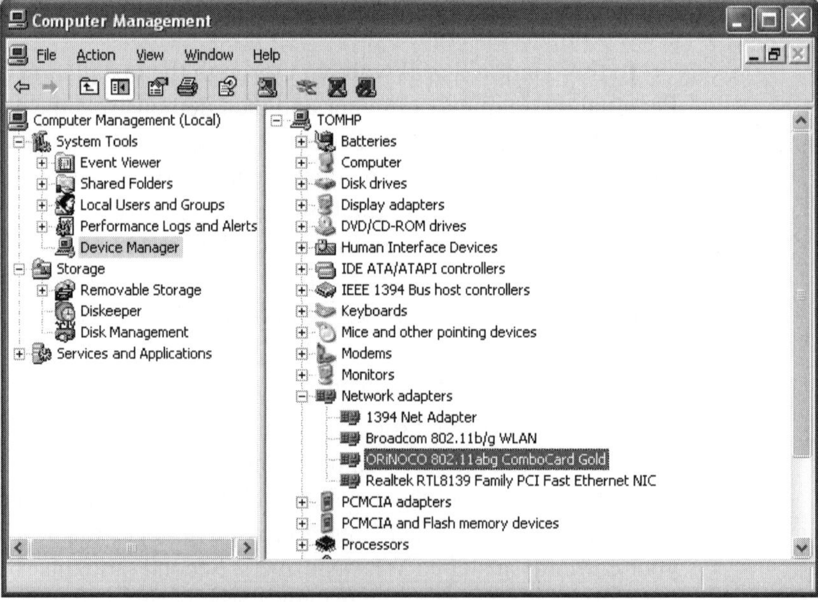

FIGURE 11.6 Specifying that you do not want to search the Internet

5. The Hardware Update Wizard is launched.
6. You do not want to look online for drivers. Check No, Not This Time, if prompted, and click Next (see Figure 11.6).
7. On the next screen, select Install From A List Or Specific Location and click Next.
8. On the next screen, select Don't Search, I Will Choose The Driver To Install and click Next (see Figure 11.7).
9. Click the Have Disk button.
10. Click the Browse button.
11. Browse to the folder where you extracted the driver files downloaded from WildPackets and select the inf file contained there.
12. Click Open and then click OK.
13. Select the driver for your card from the list and click Next.
14. If prompted, click Continue Anyway on the Windows logo test dialog (see Figure 11.8).
15. Click Finish to complete the process.

FIGURE 11.7 Indicating that you do not want to search the local computer

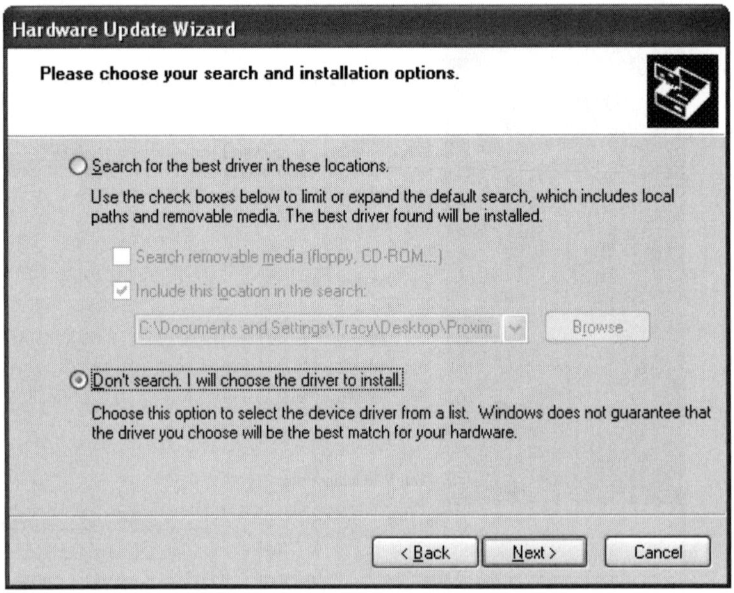

Hardware Update Wizard
Please choose your search and installation options.
Search for the best driver in these locations.
Use the check boxes below to limit or expand the default search, which includes local paths and removable media. The best driver found will be installed.
Search removable media (floppy, CD-ROM...)
Include this location in the search:
C:\Documents and Settings\Tracy\Desktop\Proxim
Browse
Don't search. I will choose the driver to install.
Choose this option to select the device driver from a list. Windows does not guarantee that the driver you choose will be the best match for your hardware.
< Back
Next >
Cancel

FIGURE 11.8 Accepting the driver in spite of the Windows logo program

Hardware Installation
The software you are installing for this hardware:
ORiNOCO 802.11abg ComboCard Gold
has not passed Windows Logo testing to verify its compatibility with Windows XP. (Tell me why this testing is important.)
Continuing your installation of this software may impair or destabilize the correct operation of your system either immediately or in the future. Microsoft strongly recommends that you stop this installation now and contact the hardware vendor for software that has passed Windows Logo testing.
Continue Anyway
STOP Installation

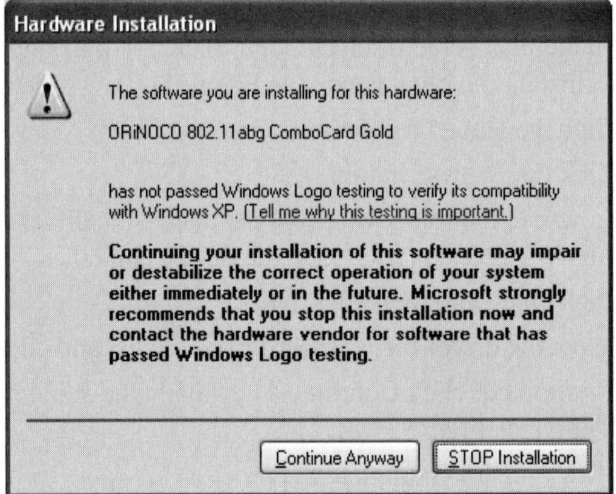

At this point you have installed a device driver that is compatible with OmniPeek Personal. I should also point out that you may be asked to overwrite a newer drive with an older one during this process. This is because the newer driver provided by the NIC vendor may not work with OmniPeek Personal.

The next step is to actually install OmniPeek Personal. The installation process is very simple and requires no complicated decisions, so I will not include that process here. Once OmniPeek Personal is installed, you are ready to begin capturing WLAN packets and frames.

One of the most difficult steps involved in getting a WLAN protocol analyzer to work on your computer is selecting the right driver. For this reason, it is often easiest to select the protocol analyzer first and then buy the WLAN adapter that works well with it. An example of an inexpensive WLAN adapter that works well with OmniPeek Personal is the TrendNet TEW-501PC.

Creating Your First Capture

Now that we have OmniPeek Personal installed, we can begin using it to capture WLAN packets and frames. There are really two modes in which you can capture information through a WLAN adapter. The first is Ethernet mode, and the second is like an RF monitor mode. The first mode will only track upper-layer data packets as if you were monitoring on a wired network. The second mode will capture IEEE 802.11 management frames, control frames, and so on. When I say you can capture packets and frames, I mean you can capture information about the TCP/IP protocol communications (packets) and information about the WLAN communications (frames).

In the following example, I will demonstrate the capture of the initial Open System authentication to a WLAN. You will see the authentication request and response first and then the association request and response. Remember that this Open System authentication sequence will occur in any secure WLAN. This is because the newer security technologies do not use Shared Key authentication, so Open System authentication precedes the association with the AP and then the authentication to the network can be negotiated using an 802.1X/EAP solution or another authentication mechanism.

When you launch the OmniPeek Personal protocol analyzer, you are presented with a screen similar to that in Figure 11.9. If you look closely at the dialog, you will notice that it is asking you to configure the settings for the Monitor. You can either select an adapter to use with the Monitor or you can select None. I will click None and click OK so that the Monitor mode is not associated with a WLAN device, since I am not interested in all of the activity taking place on the WLAN at this time. Note that you can use the Monitor and perform a capture at the same time using the same

FIGURE 11.9 OmniPeek Personal opening screen

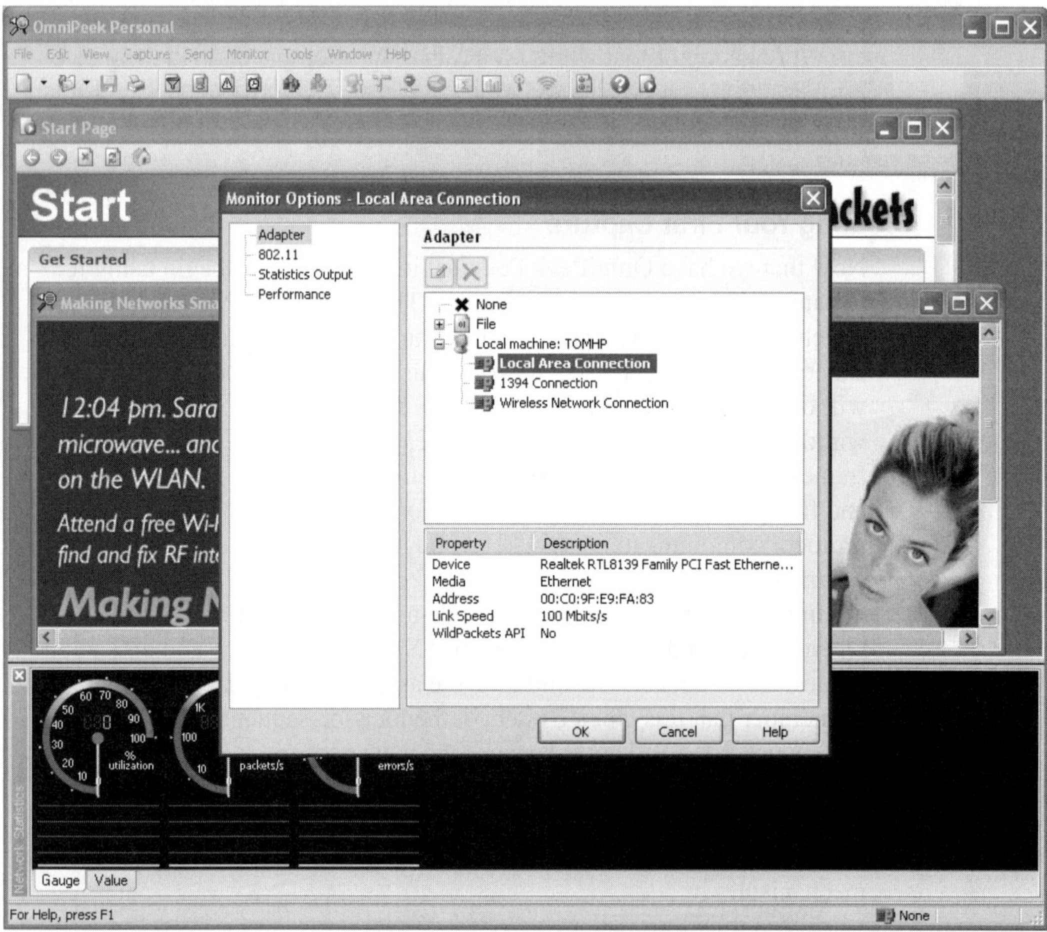

WLAN interface. I will also close the log window and network statistics window at the bottom of the screen. Finally, I will close the news window that shows updated information from WildPackets and I will maximize the Start window. In the end, my OmniPeek screen looks like Figure 11.10.

Since we are going to be capturing the Open System authentication process and association process, which together includes four management frames and four control frames, I have an AP and client setup just waiting to go through the process. The AP is configured to use channel 1, so we will want to configure our capture to capture packets from channel 1. For now, we'll set up OmniPeek Personal to capture everything on the WLAN and we'll configure it to capture this information only on channel 1.

FIGURE 11.10 OmniPeek Personal after windows have been rearranged

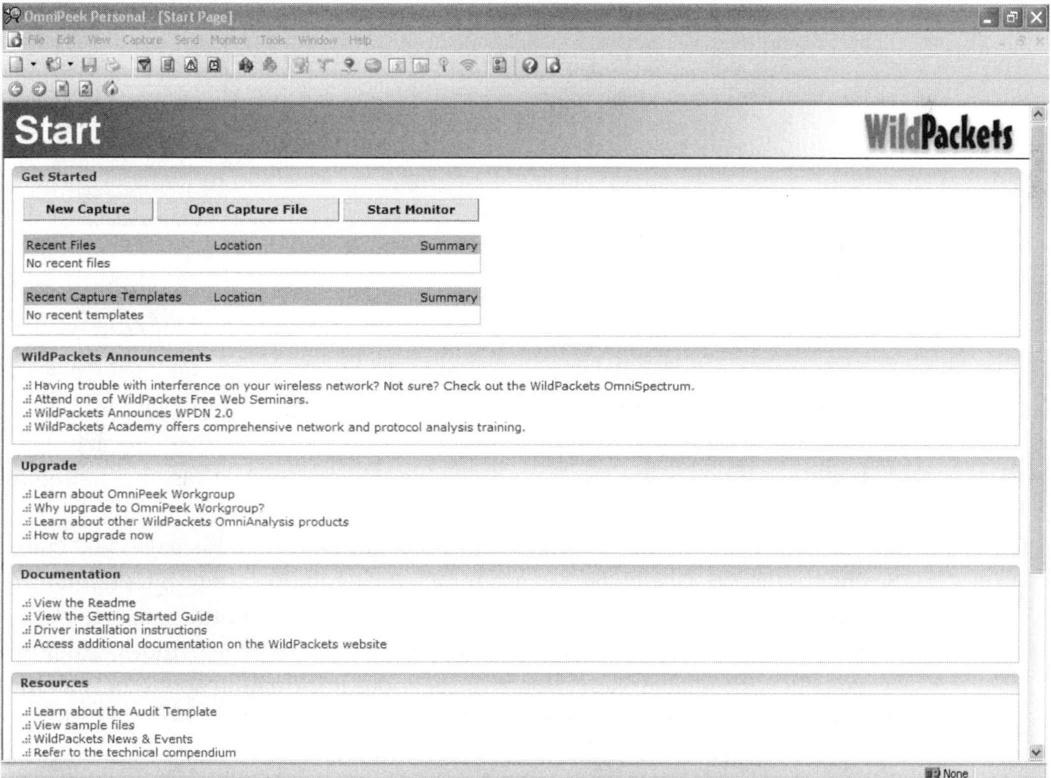

FIGURE 11.11 Configuring general capture settings

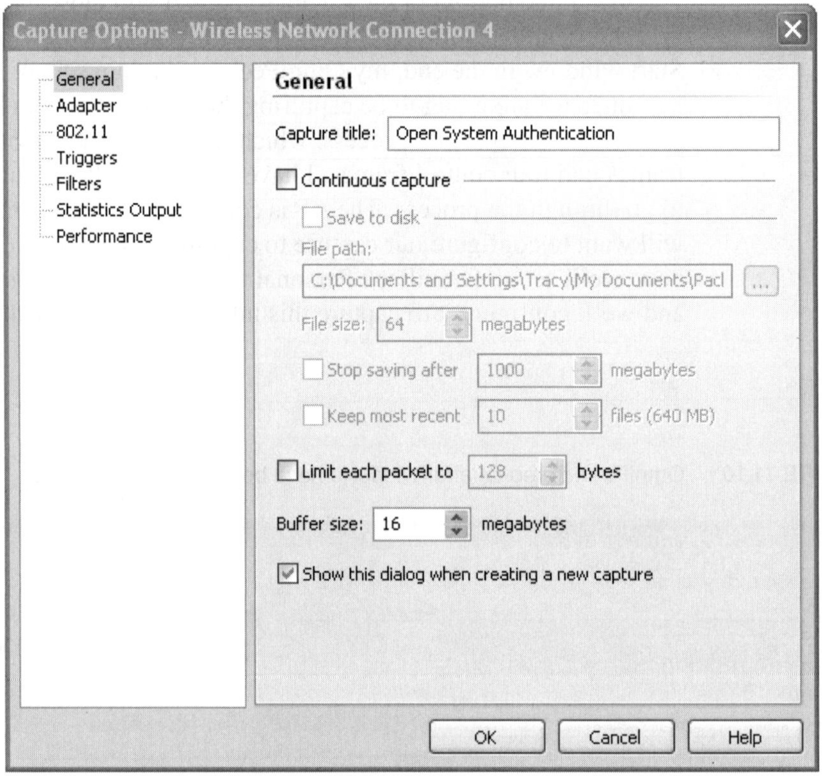

To do this, I will click the New Capture button in the Start window. This presents me with the dialog seen in Figure 11.11. On the General page, you can configure a name for the capture file. We've named ours Open System Authentication. Notice you can set up a continuous capture with file size limits and limits on the total number of files to be used. You can also configure the size of the buffer that is used to keep data in memory for analysis.

The next page we'll look at is the Adapter page. On this page, you can choose the WLAN adapter to use for capturing the data. The adapter names are not always meaningful because Windows assigns arbitrary names like Wireless Network Connection 4. You can rename these in Windows, but if you click the adapter here, you will see more information about the specific device in the lower pane (see Figure 11.12).

This is also the location where you would choose to read capture information from a file if you've previously created a capture. This is

FIGURE 11.12 Selecting an adapter

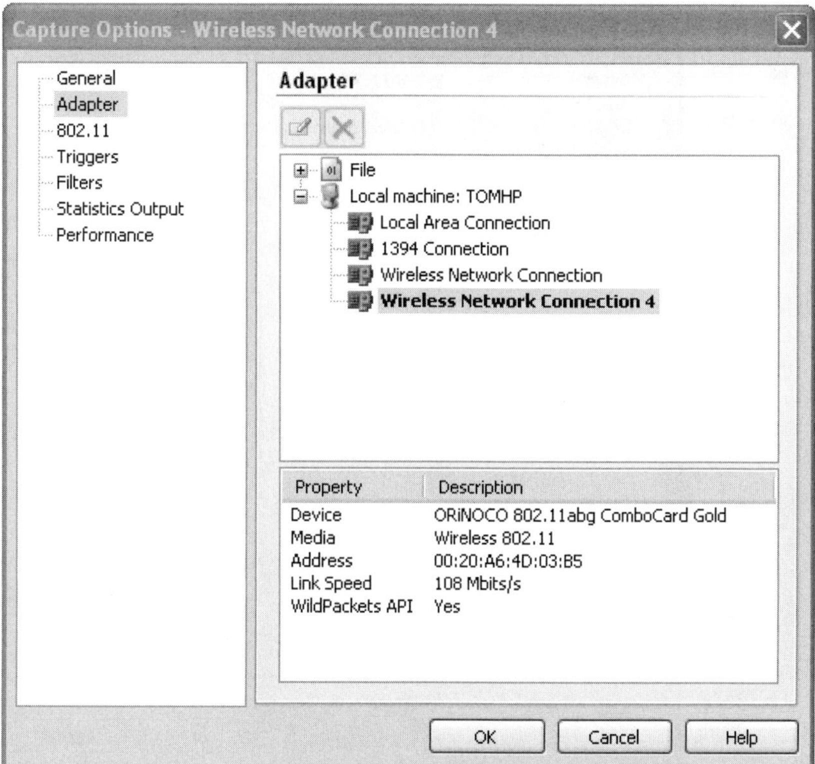

useful for analyzing logged captures that are built over long periods of time. They can be useful for performance analysis as well as usage analysis. You can determine behavior trends such as busy times during the workday and so on.

I've selected my Orinoco WLAN adapter, and so I'm now ready to move on to the 802.11 page, where I can select the channel from which to capture information. In this case, I only have to select channel 1 and provide no encryption key, since there is no encryption in use on this network. Figure 11.13 shows this selection.

At this point, I will click OK to get to the point where I can begin capturing WLAN traffic. I am presented with the screen shown in Figure 11.14. Here I can click the Start Capture button in order to begin capturing WLAN traffic. However, since I am planning to capture the Open System authentication flow, I will not click the Start Capture button immediately.

FIGURE 11.13 Selecting the WLAN channel

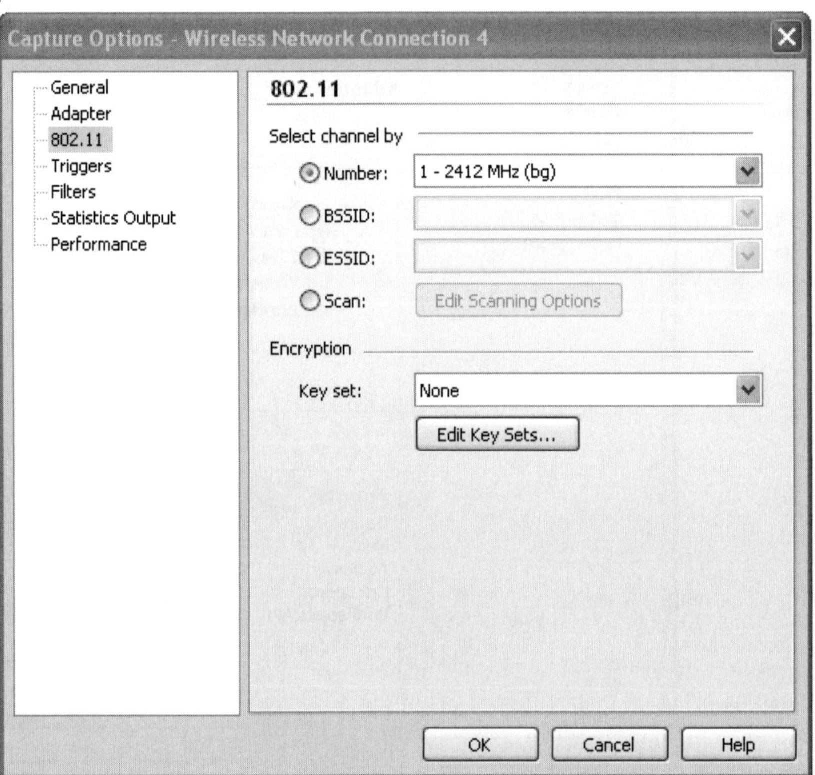

If you do not see the window exactly as Figure 11.14 shows it, click the Show Decode View button. Hover over each button at the top of the capture window until you see a pop-up that says Show Decode View. You will now be able to click a single captured frame and immediately see it in the lower pane of the window.

First, I need to be sure my client computer is ready to being the connection process with the AP. It is ready, so I will click the Start Capture button and immediately direct my WLAN client to connect to the AP on channel 1. After the client finishes the connection process, I click the Stop Capture button. Now, keep in mind that I am running OmniPeek Personal on one computer and I am connecting to the AP with a different computer. The computer running OmniPeek Personal is capturing the communications between the other client and AP without being

FIGURE 11.14 Capture window without a capture running

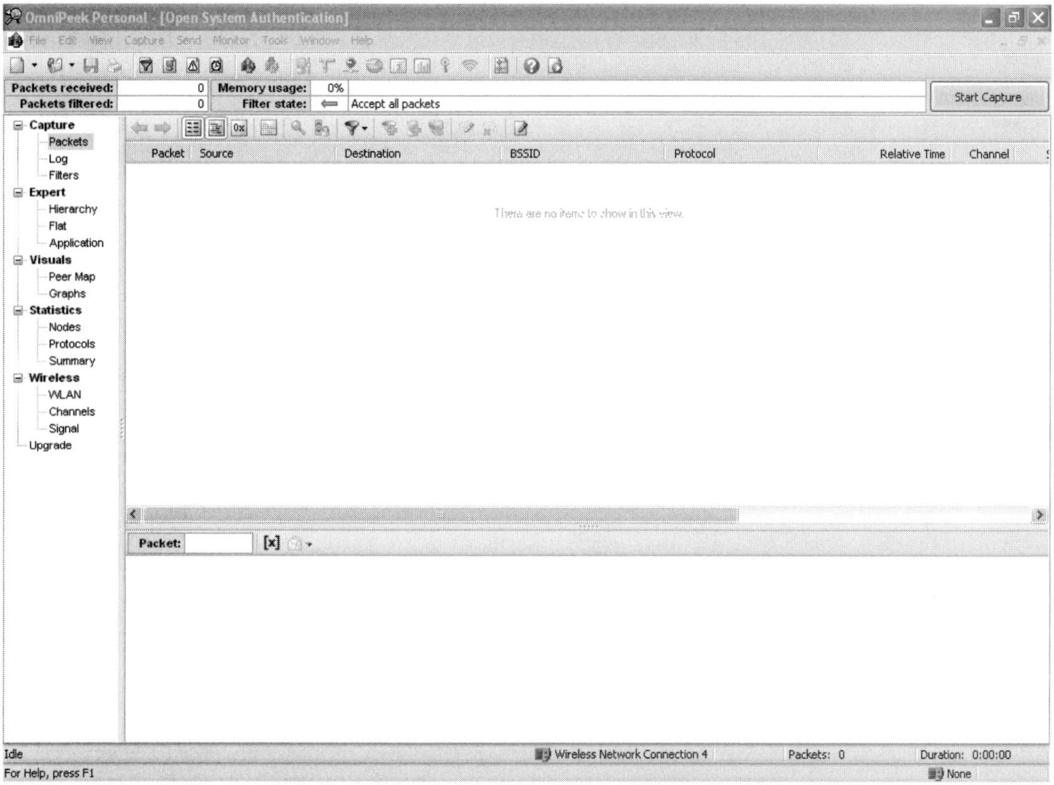

associated with the AP itself. Figure 11.15 shows the capture file after the authentication and association process has completed and displays the four management and four control frames accordingly.

You will notice in Figure 11.15 that the first authentication frame is selected. In the lower pane, you can see that it is a management frame of subtype authentication. In the top pane, you will notice that there is an authentication frame and then an ACK (acknowledgment) frame. Next there is another authentication frame and then another ACK frame. The first authentication frame was an authentication request from the client to the AP. The first ACK frame was an acknowledgment from the AP to the client that the AP had received the authentication frame. The second authentication frame was an authentication response frame from the AP to the client, and the second ACK frame was an acknowledgment frame from the client to the AP. At this point, the first two management frames (authentication) and the

FIGURE 11.15 Open System authentication process captured

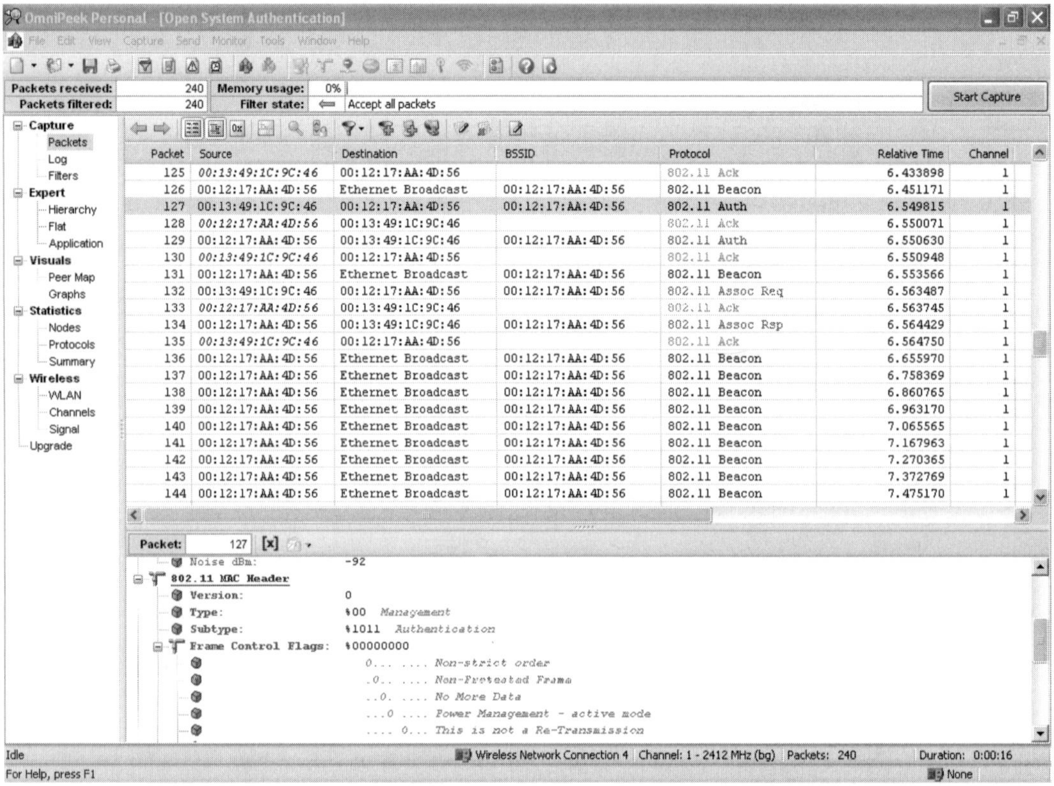

first two control frames (ACK) have been transmitted. Since Open System authentication is used, the authentication response frame is a formality that is almost always successful, as seen in Figure 11.16. This information can be seen by clicking the second "Auth" frame in the top pane and then scrolling down until you see the information in the bottom decode pane.

FIGURE 11.16 Successful authentication

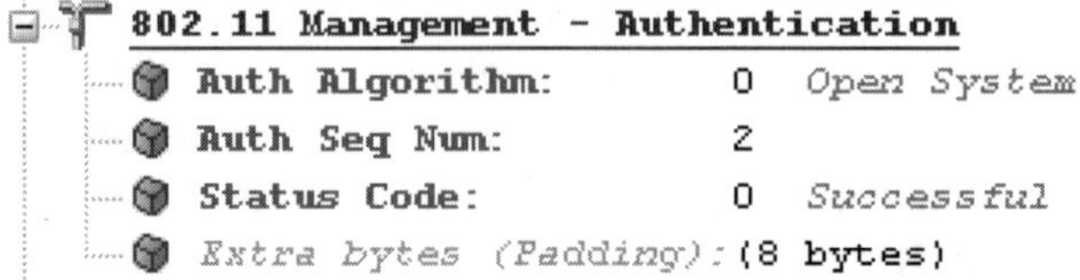

At this point, the IEEE 802.11 state machine for this client has gone from unauthenticated/unassociated to authenticated/unassociated. The next step is to associate with the AP. As you can see in Figure 11.15, there is a Beacon frame between the four frames used to authenticate to the AP and the four frames used to associate with the AP. I'll show you how to filter out the Beacon frames in a moment. For now, consider the next four frames after the Beacon frame that is packet number 131. Packet 132 starts the association process with an association request frame. This is followed by an ACK frame from the AP. The AP sees that the client STA is already authenticated and responds with an association response frame with a status of successful. In addition, information such as supported data rates is included in the association response frame.

By double-clicking the association response frame (packet 134 in my capture), I can zoom in on the details of that frame. Figure 11.17 shows

FIGURE 11.17 Association response frame details

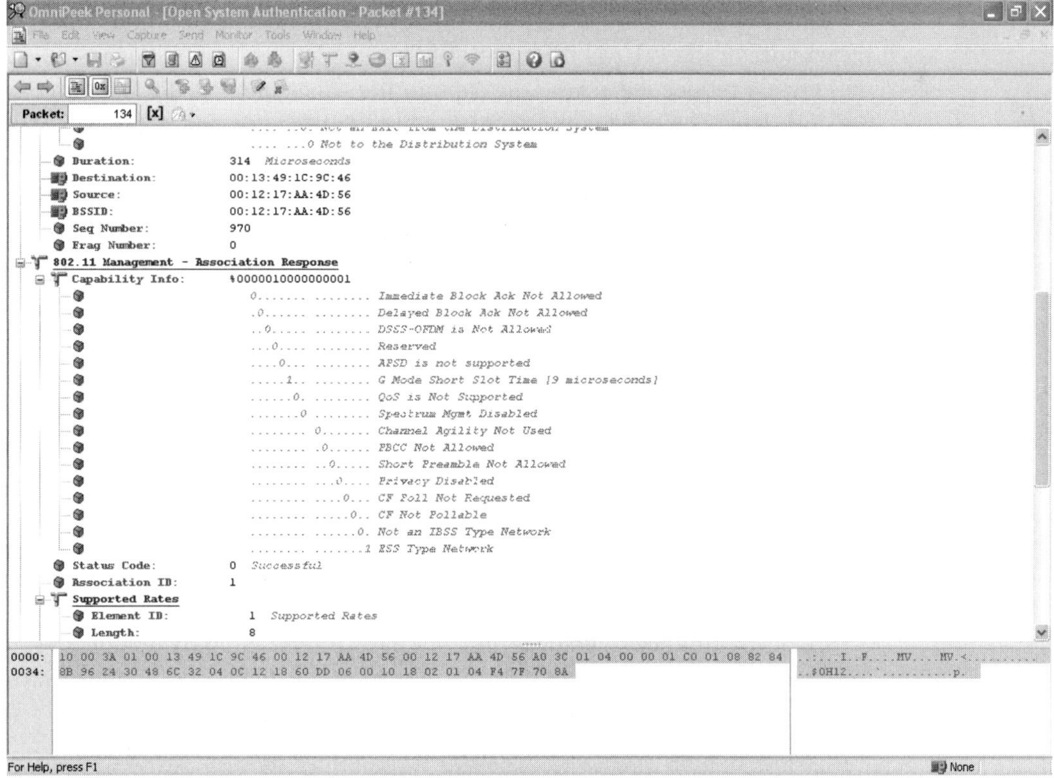

the details provided. You can see the compatibility information element and the values that are configured for it. For example, this network is an ESS-type network and not an IBSS (bit 16 is set to 1 and bit 15 is set to 0 in the compatibility information element). You can also see that QoS is not supported, as well as other settings. Of course, the status is successful, indicating that our client has reached the needed state for network communications: authenticated/association.

Filtering Captures

In the capture file we've built, the Beacon frames clutter the collection frames so that it is more difficult to find the other frames you may be looking for. If you are not seeking to analyze Beacon frames, you can filter them out of the view. To do this, click the button at the top of the capture window that looks like a funnel and shows Display Filter in a pop-up window when you hover over it. In the drop-down list, select 802.11 No Beacons to filter out Beacon frames. After doing this, you can see that the collection of packets is greatly reduced, as indicated in Figure 11.18.

Filtering the display is very useful, but you can also apply filters during the capture of the WLAN information. This can be very useful because it will greatly reduce the size of the capture file, since unneeded frames are not collected. The most common example of this is choosing not to capture Beacon frames. To see this, close the current capture window if you're following along and simply choose not to save the capture when prompted. Next, click the New Capture button in the Start window. Configure the appropriate settings on the General, Adapter, and 802.11 pages. Select the Filters page to configure a filter as seen in Figure 11.19. Notice I have selected to accept only packets not matching the filter and that the filter specifies 802.11 Beacon frames.

If you apply the filter shown in Figure 11.19 and then click OK and Start Capture, you will immediately notice that OmniPeek Personal is filtering out many of the packets that it detects on the wireless medium. In fact, Figure 11.20 shows that during a short window of capturing, 113 packets were filtered out. The total number of packets detected was 259. This means I've reduced the packets I have to look through by nearly half. This is accomplished by simply filtering out Beacon frames.

Finally, OmniPeek Personal may not have filters set up by default to accomplish the filtering you desire. For example, the Probe Request and Probe Response frames are plentiful in a default capture, but there is no filter configured by default to remove them specifically. There is

FIGURE 11.18 Beacon frames removed from the capture display

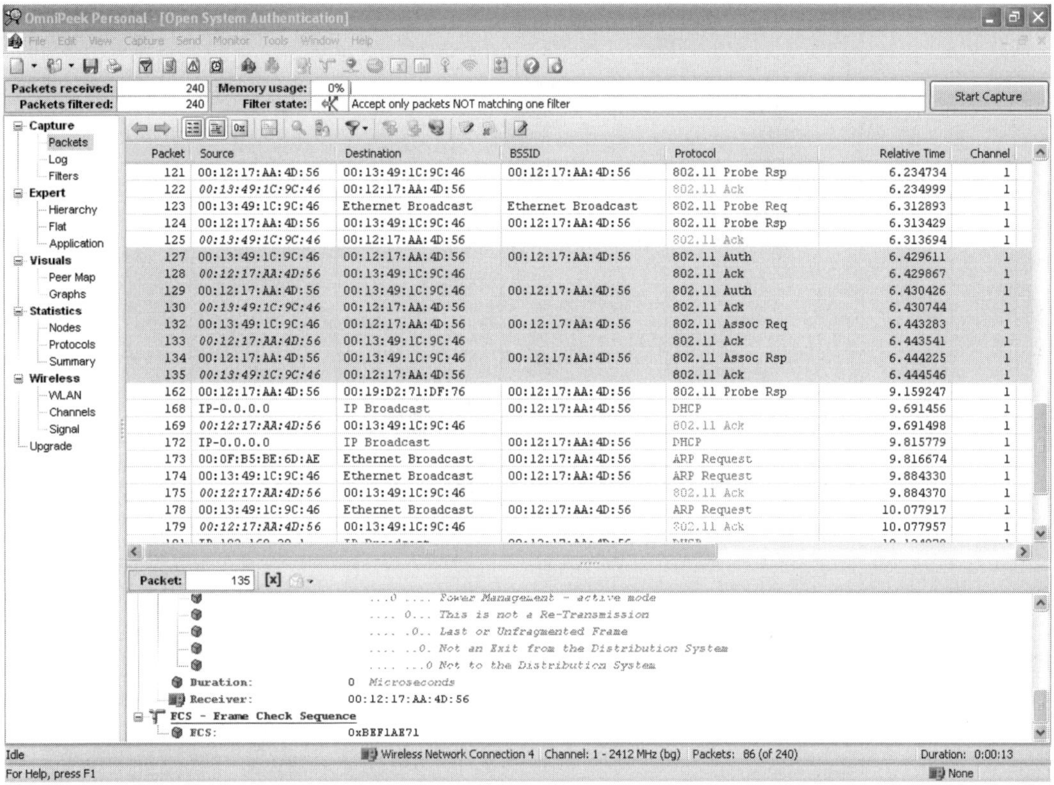

a management frame filter, but that will also remove authentication and association frames. I can create filters for filtering out Probe Request and Probe Response frames. However, another solution would be to create filters that look specifically for authentication and association frames. This is the approach I will take.

I will start by closing any open captures. Next, I will select the View menu and choose Filters. This view is shown in Figure 11.21. Notice I've already created the Probe Req and Probe Res filters. Now, I'll create the authentication frame and association frame filters so that you can see how it is accomplished.

The first thing I will do is click the button with the big green plus sign. This is the Insert Filter button. To continue with the naming convention

FIGURE 11.19 Configuring filters to be used during a capture

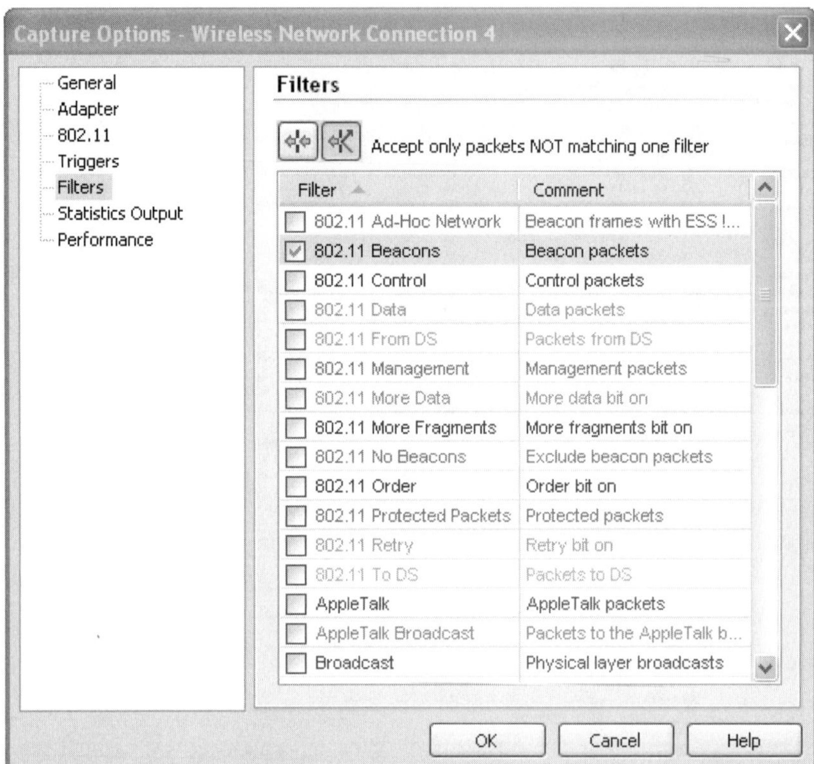

used in OmniPeek Personal by default, I will name the new filter 802.11 Authentication Frames. In this case, the type can remain set as Simple and I will not create a comment, since the name is self-describing. The next step is to check the Protocol Filter check box and then click the Protocol button. You'll be presented with a screen similar to that in Figure 11.22. Select Generic ProtoSpec from the drop-down list at the top of the dialog and then click 802.11 Auth in the bottom list. Click OK.

When you've completed this process, the Insert Filter dialog will look similar to that seen in Figure 11.23. Click OK to insert the filter. You would perform a similar process to insert a filter for association frames, but since there are two frame types, you will need to create a filter for each (association request and association response).

After you've created all three new filters, you can create a new capture and configure it to only capture frames matching these new filters.

FIGURE 11.20 Capturing the authentication/association process with Beacons filtered out

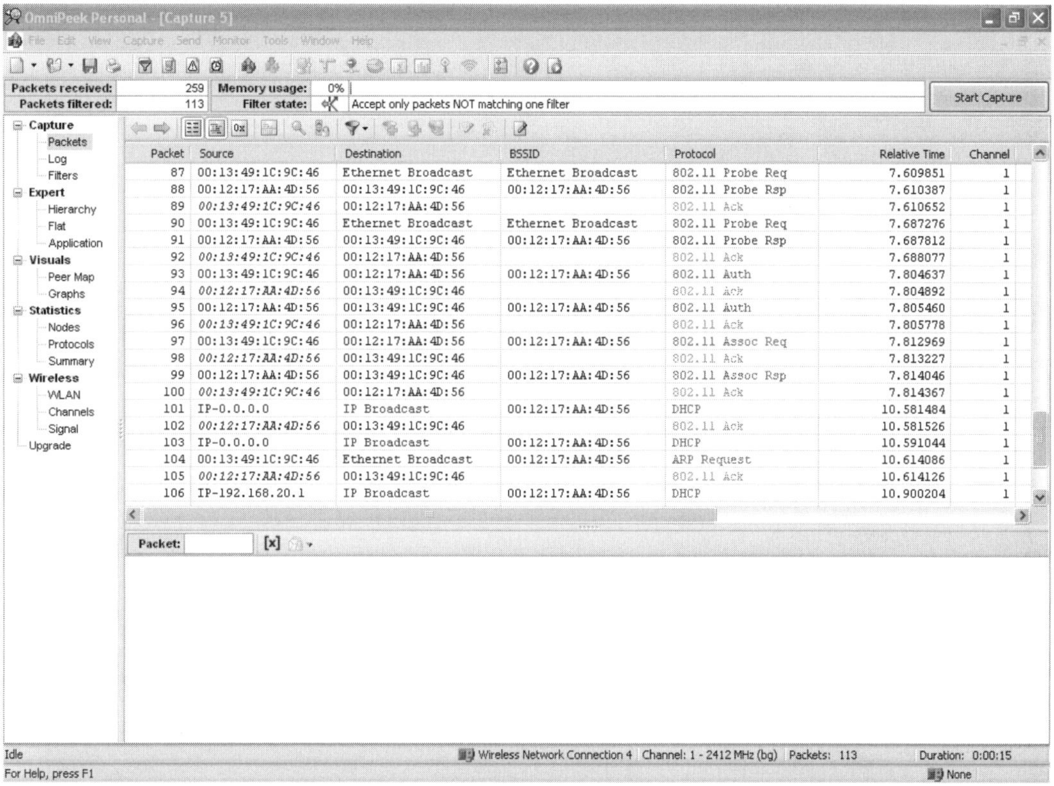

OmniPeek Personal - [Capture 5]

Packets received: 259 Memory usage: 0%
Packets filtered: 113 Filter state: Accept only packets NOT matching one filter

Start Capture

Packet	Source	Destination	BSSID	Protocol	Relative Time	Channel
87	00:13:49:1C:9C:46	Ethernet Broadcast	Ethernet Broadcast	802.11 Probe Req	7.609851	1
88	00:12:17:AA:4D:56	00:13:49:1C:9C:46	00:12:17:AA:4D:56	802.11 Probe Rsp	7.610387	1
89	00:13:49:1C:9C:46	00:12:17:AA:4D:56		802.11 Ack	7.610652	1
90	00:13:49:1C:9C:46	Ethernet Broadcast	Ethernet Broadcast	802.11 Probe Req	7.687276	1
91	00:12:17:AA:4D:56	00:13:49:1C:9C:46	00:12:17:AA:4D:56	802.11 Probe Rsp	7.687812	1
92	00:13:49:1C:9C:46	00:12:17:AA:4D:56		802.11 Ack	7.688077	1
93	00:13:49:1C:9C:46	00:12:17:AA:4D:56	00:12:17:AA:4D:56	802.11 Auth	7.804637	1
94	00:12:17:AA:4D:56	00:13:49:1C:9C:46		802.11 Ack	7.804892	1
95	00:12:17:AA:4D:56	00:13:49:1C:9C:46	00:12:17:AA:4D:56	802.11 Auth	7.805460	1
96	00:13:49:1C:9C:46	00:12:17:AA:4D:56		802.11 Ack	7.805778	1
97	00:13:49:1C:9C:46	00:12:17:AA:4D:56	00:12:17:AA:4D:56	802.11 Assoc Req	7.812969	1
98	00:12:17:AA:4D:56	00:13:49:1C:9C:46		802.11 Ack	7.813227	1
99	00:12:17:AA:4D:56	00:13:49:1C:9C:46	00:12:17:AA:4D:56	802.11 Assoc Rsp	7.814046	1
100	00:13:49:1C:9C:46	00:12:17:AA:4D:56		802.11 Ack	7.814367	1
101	IP-0.0.0.0	IP Broadcast	00:12:17:AA:4D:56	DHCP	10.581484	1
102	00:12:17:AA:4D:56	00:13:49:1C:9C:46		802.11 Ack	10.581526	1
103	IP-0.0.0.0	IP Broadcast	00:12:17:AA:4D:56	DHCP	10.591044	1
104	00:13:49:1C:9C:46	Ethernet Broadcast	00:12:17:AA:4D:56	ARP Request	10.614086	1
105	00:12:17:AA:4D:56	00:13:49:1C:9C:46		802.11 Ack	10.614126	1
106	IP-192.168.20.1	IP Broadcast	00:12:17:AA:4D:56	DHCP	10.900204	1

Idle — Wireless Network Connection 4 Channel: 1 - 2412 MHz (bg) Packets: 113 Duration: 0:00:15
For Help, press F1

Now you will not see Beacon frames, Probe Request frames, or ACK frames. You'll only see the authentication and association frames. Figure 11.24 shows a capture window with only authentication and association frames captured. Notice the total number of frames versus the filtered frames in the upper-left corner.

This section was not intended as an endorsement for OmniPeek Personal; however, this is an excellent free protocol analyzer that can be used during your preparations for the CWNA, CWSP, or CWNE certification. It is very useful to monitor the behavior of your WLAN in order to truly understand how it functions, especially since it can display captured frames in real time, unlike many analyzers. There are other WLAN protocol analyzers as well, and you should evaluate all of the available tools when making a selection for your organization.

FIGURE 11.21 Filters view in OmniPeek Personal

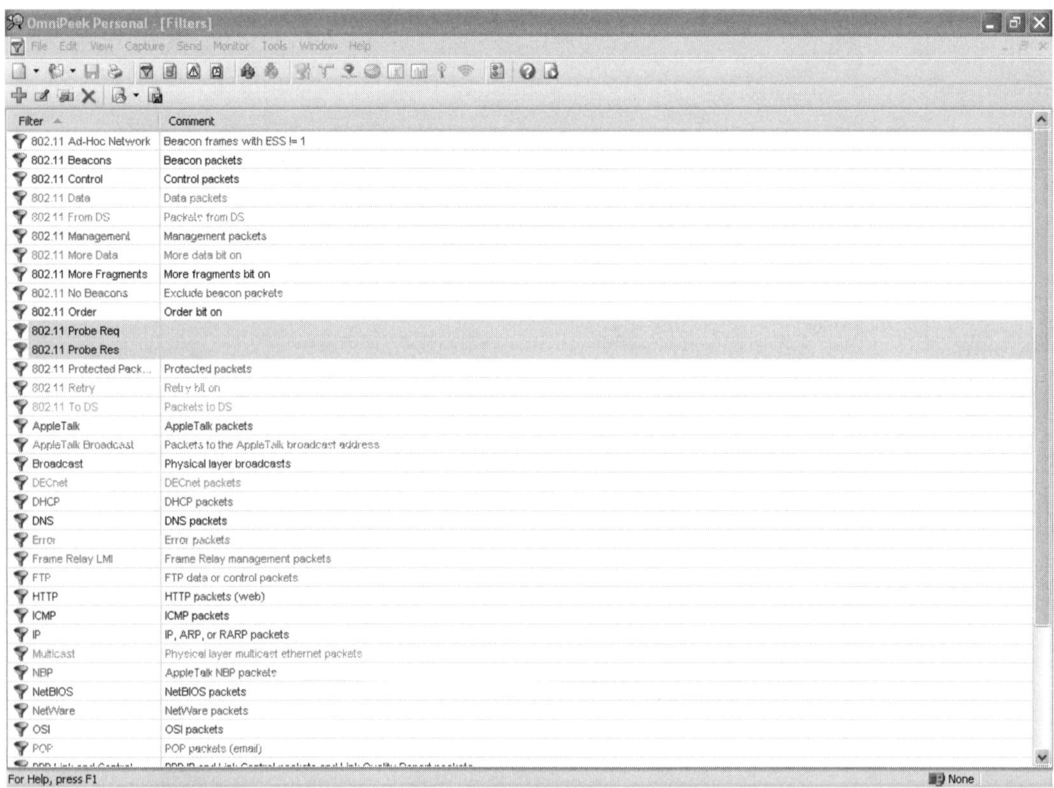

Common Uses of Protocol Analyzers

Protocol analyzers are commonly used to discover WLAN problems like frame retransmissions, heavy fragmentation, and frame corruption. They can also serve as an excellent learning tool as you discover how WLANs operate at the MAC and PHY layers. Of course, they are also used by attackers to capture WLAN frames for encryption cracking and authentication cracking. This is reason enough to become familiar with the tools yourself. This way, you know what you are protecting yourself from.

FIGURE 11.22 Protocol Filter dialog

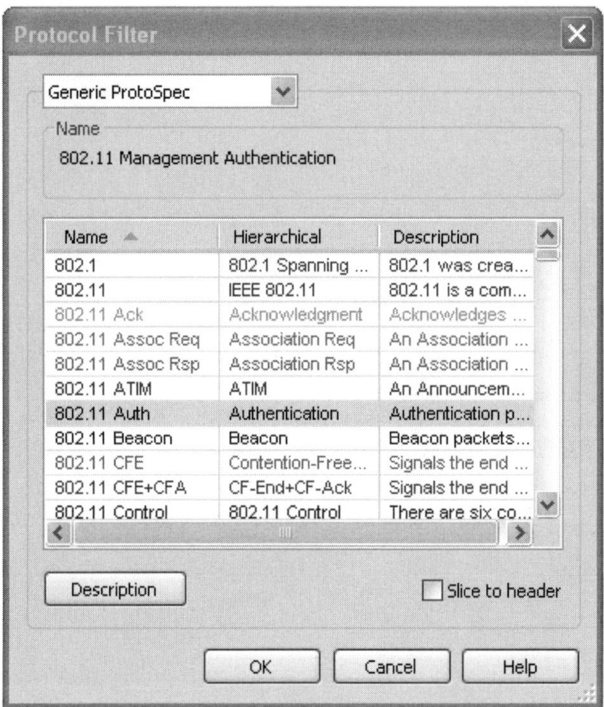

RF Spectrum Analyzers

Tools like CommView for Wi-Fi, AiroPeek NX, OmniPeek Personal, and others are useful when you want to actually view the data that is traversing your WLAN. But what if your only desire is to learn about the RF activity in your areas for site survey purposes or possibly rogue AP detection or interference elimination? In this case, you may prefer to use a spectrum analyzer.

FIGURE 11.23 Insert Filter dialog completed

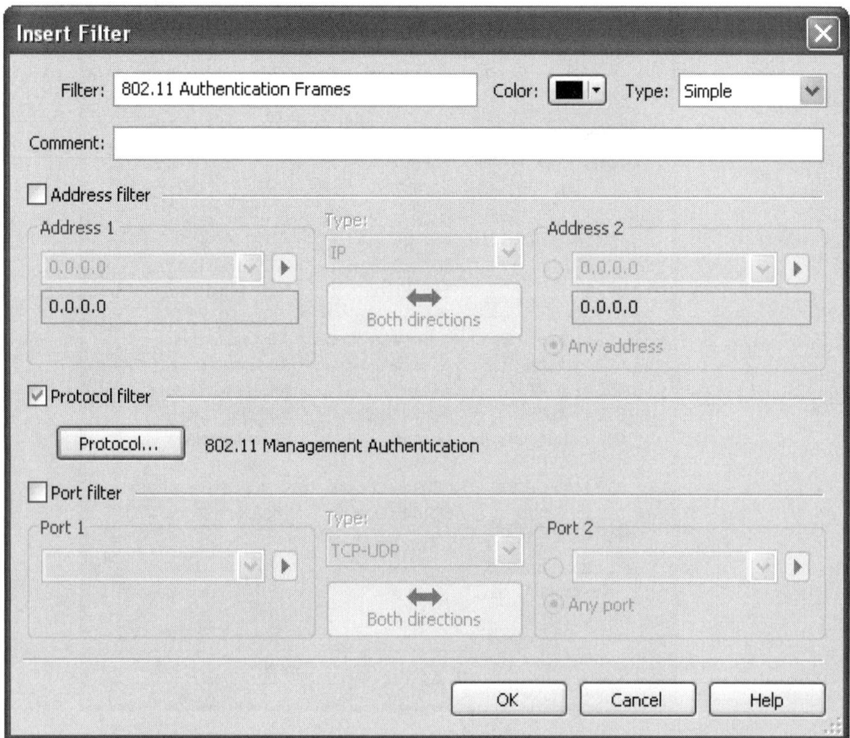

A spectrum analyzer gives you a graphical and statistical view of the RF energy being generated within a certain portion of the RF spectrum. Spectrum analyzers may be portable handheld devices like the one shown in Figure 11.25, or they may run on laptop computers like the one shown in Figure 11.26.

The handheld spectrum analyzers usually support a much wider bandwidth than is used by WLANs, but they can be configured to monitor just the frequency ranges used by the WLAN. For example, the Willtek 9101 spectrum analyzer shown in Figure 11.25 can report information from 100 kHz to 4 GHz. Therefore a device like this could easily be used to monitor the 900 MHz frequency band used by older equipment and newer phones and the 2.4 GHz frequency band used by FHSS, DSSS, HR/DSSS, and ERP, but it could not be used to monitor OFDM activity in the 5 GHz frequency band.

FIGURE 11.24 Filtering to only authentication and association frames

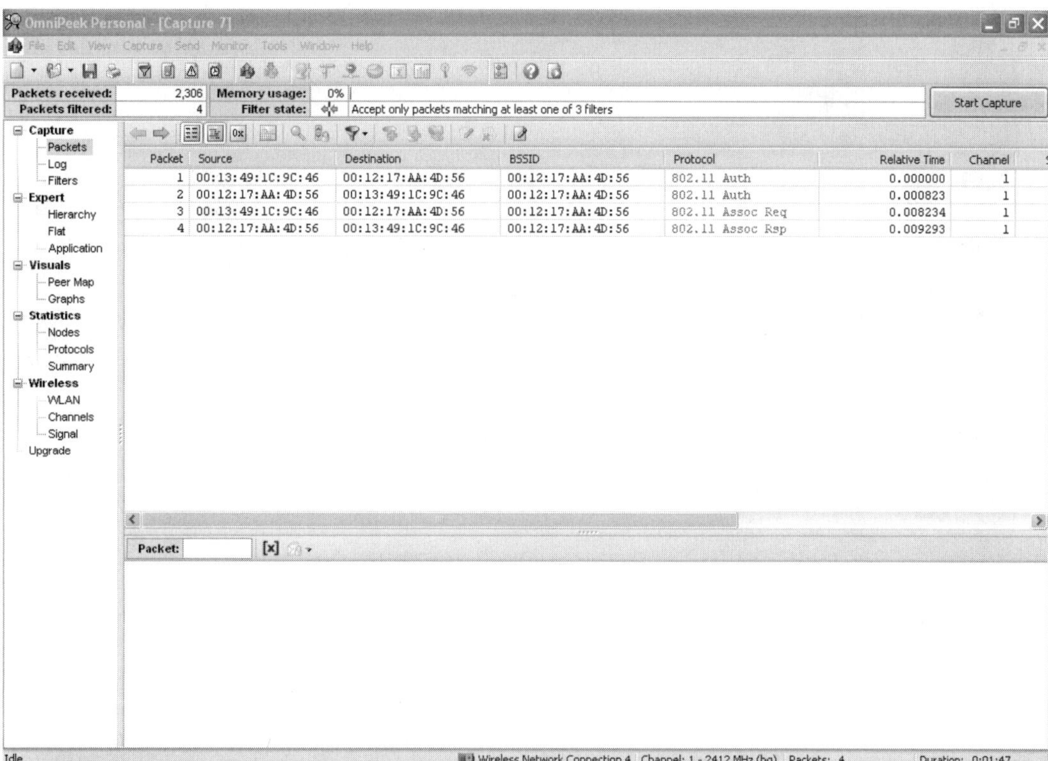

Another benefit of using a spectrum analyzer to detect rogue APs, as opposed to a tool like NetStumbler, is that the spectrum analyzer will even see activity being generated by older FHSS systems. It is very unlikely that you will see a rogue FHSS AP, but if one was installed, you could not detect it with most modern WLAN stumbler applications. Figure 11.27 shows the Willtek 9101 spectrum analyzer monitoring WLAN channel 11.

MetaGeek makes the Wi-Spy spectrum analyzer that is shown in Figure 11.26. The version shown is a USB dongle-type adapter. MetaGeek is about to release a new version at the time of this writing that will support an external antenna for greater receptivity. One of the awareness moments for new administrators in the WLAN specialty is when they first see WLAN activity on a spectrum analyzer. It is at this moment that

FIGURE 11.25 Willtek 9101 spectrum analyzer

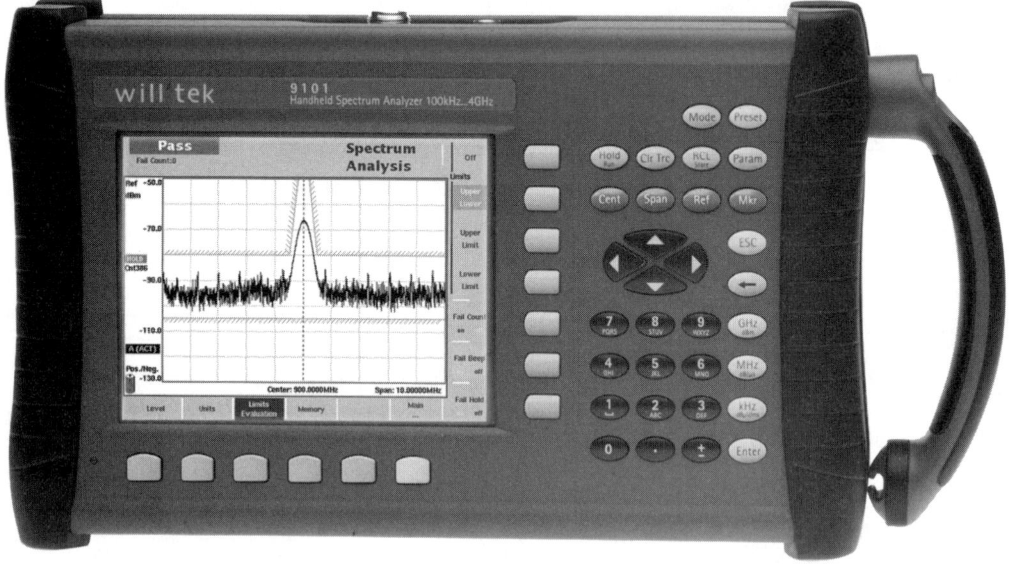

you can see—not in a diagram, but in reality—the real width of a WLAN channel. For example, Figure 11.28 shows a screen capture of the Wi-Spy Chanalyzer software running. I've clicked on channel 1 to highlight it, as it is the most active channel in the area where I am currently located. Notice how wide the bandwidth usage really is. You can clearly see why overlapping channels is a problem in WLANs. In this case, the activity in channel 1 is bleeding over into channel 5 and even into channel 6 at low levels.

FIGURE 11.26 Wi-Spy 2.4 GHz USB-based spectrum analyzer

FIGURE 11.27 Monitoring channel 11 with a handheld analyzer

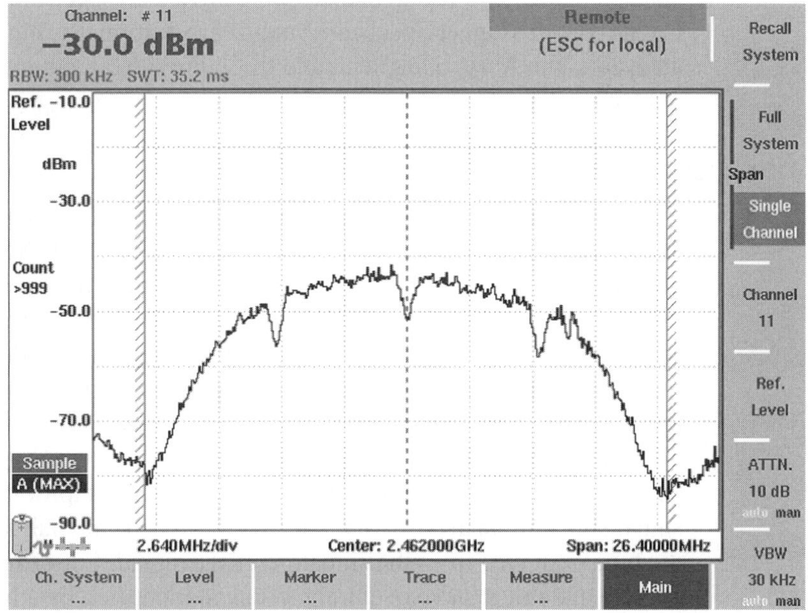

FIGURE 11.28 Viewing WLAN channel activity in a spectrum analyzer on a laptop

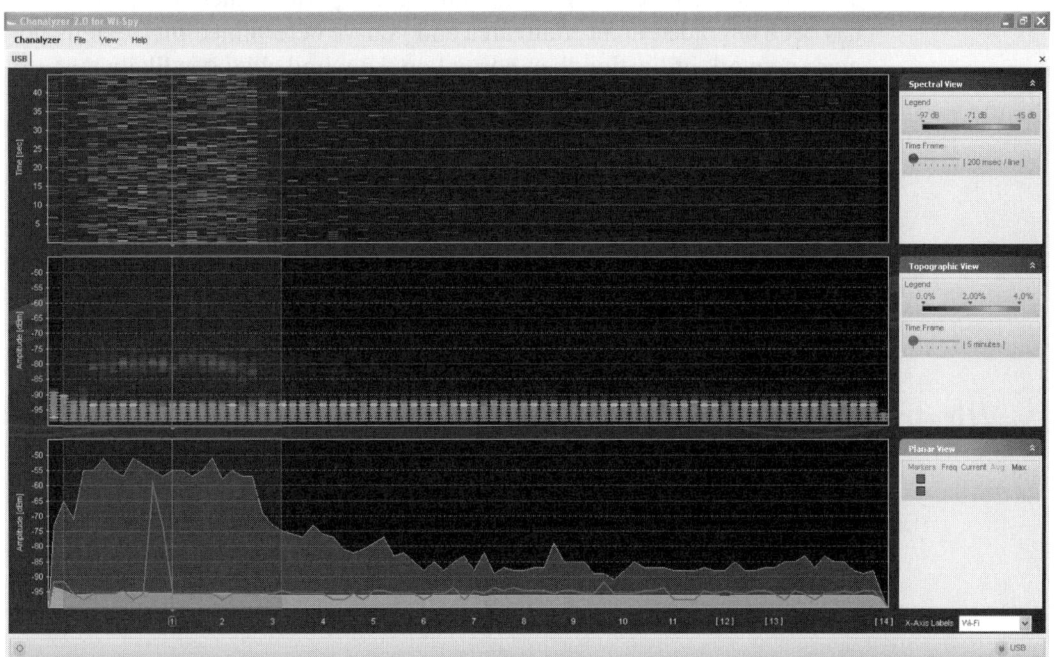

Most enterprise-class environments and independent WLAN consultants will choose to use the more advanced spectrum analyzers like Cognio or AirMagnet Spectrum Analyzer. Additionally, high-end spectrum analyzers like Anritsu, Agilent, and those provided by companies like HP may also be used.

Common Uses of Spectrum Analyzers

Spectrum analyzers are used for troubleshooting WLANs, performing site surveys, and even security auditing and analysis. Dedicated spectrum analyzers, such as the Willtek 9101 profiled earlier, are usually used more in large environments with the large budgets available to acquire them. Inexpensive solutions like the Wi-Spy spectrum analyzer do not offer the features of advanced tools, but they can give you a good idea of the activity occurring in your environment.

When used in site surveys, spectrum analyzers are mostly used to detect existing sources of interference. They can be very helpful if they support signal signature analysis, which allows the spectrum analyzer to identify the type of device from the signature of the signal. For example, Bluetooth devices and microwave ovens can often be identified by advanced spectrum analyzers.

As a troubleshooting tool, spectrum analyzers are often used in a "walk around" mode. When users complain that the performance of the WLAN has been degraded in a certain area and you've determined that there is no more network utilization than normal on the wired side, it is likely that a new source of interference has been introduced in the users' area. It may be a rogue AP or something as simple as a microwave oven. You can walk through the area while monitoring signal activity to see if you can find the interference source.

Finally, detecting a denial of service (DoS) attack at the Physical layer is very difficult through automated wireless intrusion detection systems. For this reason, you may find yourself looking for an RF signal generator in the hands of an attacker who has launched a DoS attack against your WLAN.

Wireless Intrusion Prevention Systems

Wireless intrusion detection systems (WIDSs) and *wireless intrusion prevention systems (WIPSs)* are newer entrants to the WLAN market, but they have evolved very quickly. A WIDS or WIPS is usually used to detect unauthorized WLANs. The only practical difference between a WIDS and a WIPS is that the detection system only detects the intrusion on your network but the prevention system actually prevents that intrusion. More specifically, a WIDS will usually detect the intrusion and notify you of it, but the WIDS will not automatically take action on the network. The WIPS will detect the intrusion, notify you, and usually do one of the following when a rogue AP or device is detected:

- Tarpitting the device (client rogues)
- Containing the device (rogue client)
- Containing the rogue AP
- Disabling the Ethernet port in the switch (rogue AP)

Tarpitting the device is usually done when a rogue client is detected. This is accomplished by causing the rogue client to associate with a sensor. The sensor then keeps the client busy enough that the rogue client doesn't associate elsewhere. Basically, the sensor ties up the client until a more permanent intervention can be executed.

Rogue client containment is accomplished by preventing the client from associating to anything that is considered unauthorized in the WLAN environment. Containment is usually accomplished by sending continuous deauth frames to the client device.

Rogue AP containment can also be used. APs in the surrounding area, participating in the rogue AP containment process, constantly transmit deauth frames as if they were coming from the rogue AP, thus preventing any clients from associating to that AP. Obviously, this creates interference to other valid devices and should be remedied as quickly as possible.

The best way to prevent rogue APs is, once it is determined they are on the corporate wired network, to disable the Ethernet port to which they are connected. This is usually accomplished through SNMP or some other method. The WIPS system will detect that the rogue AP is on the wired network and then find that AP's Ethernet port in the appropriate switch's content addressable memory table. Once the port has been identified, the WIPS system will disable the port.

WIPSs with Integrated Spectrum Analysis

Newer WIPS technology includes the integration of spectrum analysis information. For example, the AirMagnet Enterprise suite is a centralized WLAN management solution that includes a WIPS and spectrum analysis internally. The spectrum analysis feature was incorporated into AirMagnet Enterprise with the release of version 7.5. The solution is implemented by installing the central software and installing spectral sensors throughout your facility. Using spectrum analysis fingerprinting or signature analysis, the solution can even define the exact kind of interference being generated, whether from microwave ovens, Bluetooth, or some other RF-emitting device.

Distributed Wireless Intrusion Prevention Systems (WIPSs)

Distributed WIPSs use sensors similar to the spectrum sensors mentioned previously. Some vendors provide sensors that perform localized processing, and others send raw data back to the centralized controller software. Those that perform localized processing reduce the bandwidth consumed by the communications from the sensors to the centralized software across the wired LAN. This bandwidth consumption is minimal (often 100 times less than that coming from actual data being generated by clients). You will have to decide between the two, although this decision is quickly being made irrelevant as more and more of the vendors include this logic at the sensor.

Distributed RF Spectrum Analyzers

While most spectrum analyzers are single, stand-alone solutions like those profiled previously in this chapter, vendors are now releasing distributed spectrum analyzers that use a sensor model with centralized monitoring software. One company that offers such a solution is Cognio. The solution provided by Cognio includes a centralized server and remote spectrum sensors. The sensors send the RF statistics back to the centralized server, which can use this data to detect and report interference issues at the Physical layer. These distributed RF spectrum analyzers are basically used as a Physical layer WIDS.

Protocol and Spectrum Analysis Case Studies

Devin Akin, the CTO of Planet3 Wireless, originally authored these case studies and graciously allowed me to modify and present them here. They illustrate common scenarios where the use of protocol analyzers and spectrum analyzers would be beneficial, and they are an excellent addition to this chapter.

Case Study 1: Security

Westcott Telecom's management team has decided that it is time to implement wireless LAN technology in order to improve productivity in their Field Services division. Before haphazardly deploying wireless LAN technology, the team asks the organization's best engineer, Mr. Jones, to oversee security solution testing in the research and development lab. Mr. Jones makes a list of items that he wants to have in his security solution, and another list of items that he wants to avoid having in his security solution. As Mr. Jones tests each security solution, he compares them to the lists he has prepared. One of the items on his list of things to avoid is transmission of the wireless client's user name in clear text across the RF medium. He is aware that this may lead to dictionary attacks, and he desires to prevent them.

After configuring his protocol analyzer to look for a string called user in all captured frames, Mr. Jones begins building and testing security solutions. Mr. Jones is using a test user called *user1* in his sample configurations. He analyzes each authentication process and reviews the analyzer's findings. Figures 11.29 and 11.30 illustrate configuration of a filter and a notification when the filter is matched.

FIGURE 11.29 Filter configuration in CommView for Wi-Fi

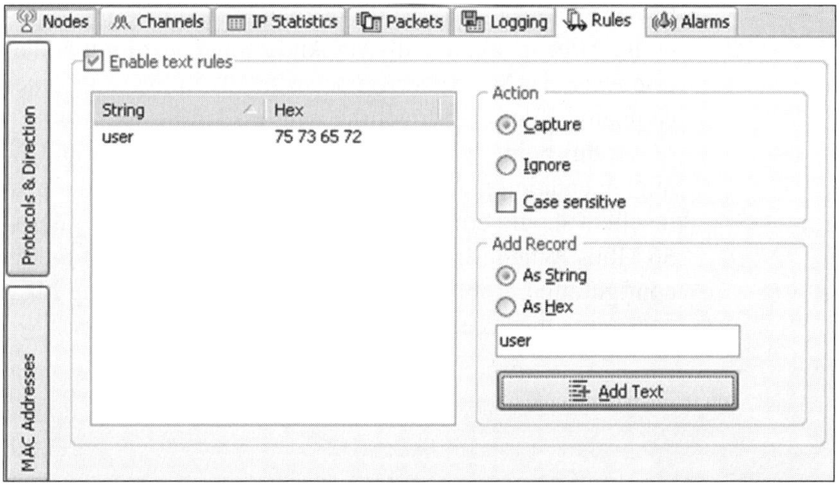

As the images show, several frames reveal the user name *user1* as plain text. Since this is unacceptable, Mr. Jones flags the applications that sent the frames in question. He can now investigate these applications to determine whether a secure mode is available or not. If not, he can choose different applications that meet his security criteria.

Case Study 2: Performance

Coleman Research Ltd. has implemented an OFDM (IEEE 802.11a) solution, and the access points were all left configured for the default supported rates when they were deployed. The engineering department often uses the wireless network to transfer large CAD drawings to the company's file server. These file transfers often take a few minutes to complete. The engineering staff has noticed that while the files always transfer at 54 Mbps data rates due to the short distance between stations and the access point, the speed at which the file transfers complete varies greatly. This has caused a tremendous drop in productivity, and Mr. Coleman has asked for help from the company's wireless analyst, Mr. Fisher.

Mr. Fisher captures frames during one of the file transfers and notices the frames shown in Figure 11.31.

Mr. Fisher notices that along with the 54 Mbps data frames captured from the engineer's file transfer, data frames transmitted through the same access point at 6 Mbps and 9 Mbps are coming from another computer outside the engineering department. After some investigation, Mr. Fisher finds that the shipping manager's computer is connecting at data rates as low as 6 Mbps due to the distance to the engineering department's access point. After speaking with Mr. Anderson, the shipping manager, Mr. Fisher discovers that Mr. Anderson occasionally uploads documentation to the company's file server over the wireless LAN.

At this point, Mr. Fisher consults the site survey and WLAN implementation plans. The site survey implementation plan shows that no client should connect to the access points at data rates slower than 36 Mbps. When Mr. Fisher sees this, he realizes that there must be a configuration problem at the network center allowing Mr. Anderson to connect to the access point at unauthorized data rates.

FIGURE 11.30 Filtered capture in CommView for Wi-Fi

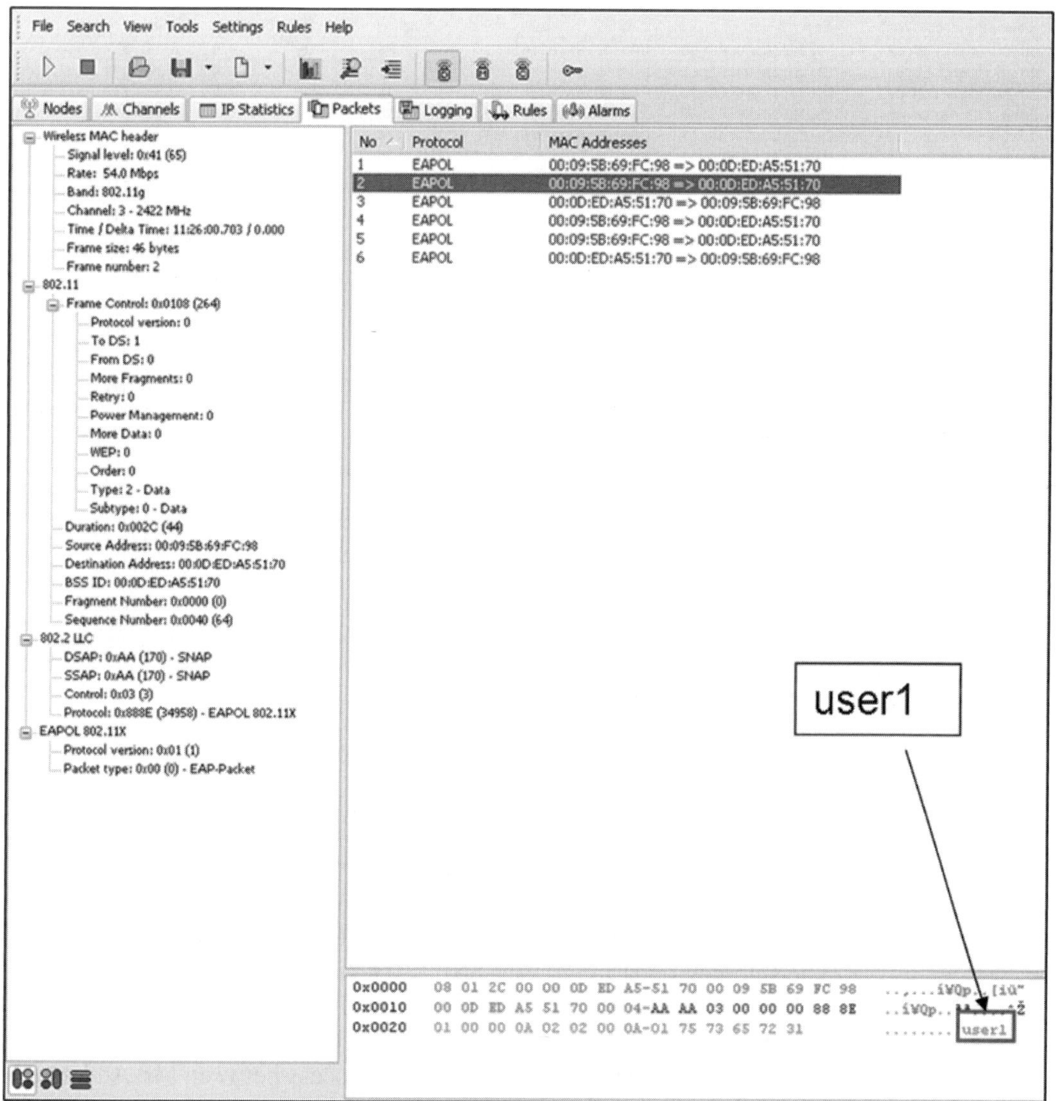

FIGURE 11.31 Two file transfers at different data rates

Source Physical	Dest. Physical	BSSID	Channel	Signal	Data Rate	Size	Protocol
00:E0:B8:5C:5B:CF	00:09:5B:66:E6:80	00:0D:65:B8:61:63	36	70%	9.0	1336	FTP Data
00:09:5B:66:E6:80	00:0D:65:B8:61:63		36	27%	6.0	14	802.11 Ack
00:E0:B8:5C:5B:CF	00:09:5B:66:E6:80	00:0D:65:B8:61:63	36	70%	9.0	864	FTP Data
00:09:5B:66:E6:80	00:0D:65:B8:61:63		36	30%	6.0	14	802.11 Ack
00:09:5B:66:E6:80	00:E0:B8:5C:5B:CF	00:0D:65:B8:61:63	36	20%	6.0	76	FTP Data
00:0D:65:B8:61:63	00:09:5B:66:E6:80		36	68%	6.0	14	802.11 Ack
00:E0:B8:5C:5B:CF	00:09:5B:69:FC:98	00:0D:65:B8:61:63	36	52%	54.0	1100	FTP Data
00:09:5B:69:FC:98	00:0D:65:B8:61:63		36	75%	24.0	14	802.11 Ack
00:E0:B8:5C:5B:CF	00:09:5B:69:FC:98	00:0D:65:B8:61:63	36	54%	54.0	864	FTP Data
00:09:5B:69:FC:98	00:0D:65:B8:61:63		36	74%	24.0	14	802.11 Ack
00:09:5B:69:FC:98	00:E0:B8:5C:5B:CF	00:0D:65:B8:61:63	36	80%	48.0	76	FTP Data
00:0D:65:B8:61:63	00:09:5B:69:FC:98		36	54%	24.0	14	802.11 Ack
00:E0:B8:5C:5B:CF	00:09:5B:69:FC:98	00:0D:65:B8:61:63	36	55%	54.0	1100	FTP Data
00:09:5B:69:FC:98	00:0D:65:B8:61:63		36	78%	24.0	14	802.11 Ack
00:E0:B8:5C:5B:CF	00:09:5B:69:FC:98	00:0D:65:B8:61:63	36	55%	54.0	1336	FTP Data
00:09:5B:69:FC:98	00:0D:65:B8:61:63		36	78%	24.0	14	802.11 Ack
00:09:5B:69:FC:98	00:E0:B8:5C:5B:CF	00:0D:65:B8:61:63	36	78%	48.0	76	FTP Data
00:0D:65:B8:61:63	00:09:5B:69:FC:98		36	70%	24.0	14	802.11 Ack
00:09:5B:66:E6:80	00:E0:B8:5C:5B:CF	00:0D:65:B8:61:63	36	27%	6.0	76	FTP Data
00:0D:65:B8:61:63	00:09:5B:66:E6:80		36	70%	6.0	14	802.11 Ack
00:09:5B:66:E6:80	00:E0:B8:5C:5B:CF	00:0D:65:B8:61:63	36	25%	6.0	76	FTP Data
00:0D:65:B8:61:63	00:09:5B:66:E6:80		36	70%	6.0	14	802.11 Ack
00:E0:B8:5C:5B:CF	00:09:5B:69:FC:98	00:0D:65:B8:61:63	36	70%	54.0	864	FTP Data
00:09:5B:69:FC:98	00:0D:65:B8:61:63		36	70%	24.0	14	802.11 Ack
00:09:5B:69:FC:98	00:E0:B8:5C:5B:CF	00:0D:65:B8:61:63	36	78%	48.0	76	FTP Data
00:0D:65:B8:61:63	00:09:5B:69:FC:98		36	70%	24.0	14	802.11 Ack
00:E0:B8:5C:5B:CF	00:09:5B:69:FC:98	00:0D:65:B8:61:63	36	70%	54.0	864	FTP Data
00:09:5B:69:FC:98	00:0D:65:B8:61:63		36	75%	24.0	14	802.11 Ack

Since Mr. Fisher determined that Mr. Anderson's computer should not be connecting to the engineering department's access point at all, another investigation ensues. Each access point at Coleman Research is configured for an individual VLAN ID that corresponds to the department that uses it. The shipping department uses SSID 103, which is mapped to VLAN 103. The engineering department uses SSID 101, which is mapped to VLAN 101. Mr. Anderson's computer is configured with SSID 103, but after analyzing the wireless authentication process between Mr. Anderson's computer and the shipping department's access point, Mr. Fisher notices that Mr. Anderson's computer is being disassociated after a successful authentication. Figure 11.32 shows the captured frames. Notice the disassociation and deauthentication frames at the end of the authentication/association frame exchanges.

FIGURE 11.32 Captured frames from the shipping department's access point

Packet	Address 1	Address 2	Address 3	Flags	Channel	Data Rate	Size	Protocol
30	00:0D:ED:A5:51:70	00:09:5B:66:E6:80	00:0D:ED:A5:51:70	*	1	1.0	34	802.11 Auth
31	00:09:5B:66:E6:80			#	1	1.0	14	802.11 Ack
32	00:09:5B:66:E6:80	00:0D:ED:A5:51:70	00:0D:ED:A5:51:70	*	1	11.0	34	802.11 Auth
33	00:0D:ED:A5:51:70			#	1	11.0	14	802.11 Ack
34	00:0D:ED:A5:51:70	00:09:5B:66:E6:80	00:0D:ED:A5:51:70	*	1	1.0	83	802.11 Assoc Req
35	00:09:5B:66:E6:80			#	1	1.0	14	802.11 Ack
36	00:09:5B:66:E6:80	00:0D:ED:A5:51:70	00:0D:ED:A5:51:70	*	1	54.0	94	802.11 Assoc Rsp
37	00:0D:ED:A5:51:70			#	1	24.0	14	802.11 Ack
38	00:0D:ED:A5:51:70	00:09:5B:66:E6:80	00:0D:ED:A5:51:70		1	54.0	40	EAPOL-Start
39	00:09:5B:66:E6:80	00:0D:ED:A5:51:70	00:0D:ED:A5:51:70		1	54.0	82	EAP Request
40	00:0D:ED:A5:51:70			#	1	24.0	14	802.11 Ack
41	00:0D:ED:A5:51:70	00:09:5B:66:E6:80	00:0D:ED:A5:51:70		1	54.0	40	EAPOL-Start
42	00:09:5B:66:E6:80			#	1	24.0	14	802.11 Ack
43	00:09:5B:66:E6:80	00:0D:ED:A5:51:70	00:0D:ED:A5:51:70		1	54.0	82	EAP Request
44	00:0D:ED:A5:51:70			#	1	24.0	14	802.11 Ack
45	00:0D:ED:A5:51:70	00:09:5B:66:E6:80	00:0D:ED:A5:51:70		1	54.0	53	EAP Response
46	00:09:5B:66:E6:80			#	1	24.0	14	802.11 Ack
47	00:0D:ED:A5:51:70	00:09:5B:66:E6:80	00:0D:ED:A5:51:70		1	54.0	53	EAP Response
48	00:09:5B:66:E6:80			#	1	24.0	14	802.11 Ack
49	00:09:5B:66:E6:80	00:0D:ED:A5:51:70	00:0D:ED:A5:51:70		1	54.0	82	EAP Request
50	00:0D:ED:A5:51:70			#	1	24.0	14	802.11 Ack
51	00:0D:ED:A5:51:70	00:09:5B:66:E6:80	00:0D:ED:A5:51:70		1	54.0	80	EAP Response
52	00:09:5B:66:E6:80			#	1	24.0	14	802.11 Ack
53	00:09:5B:66:E6:80	00:0D:ED:A5:51:70	00:0D:ED:A5:51:70		1	54.0	82	EAP Success
54	00:0D:ED:A5:51:70			#	1	24.0	14	802.11 Ack
55	00:0D:ED:A5:51:70	00:09:5B:66:E6:80	00:0D:ED:A5:51:70		1	54.0	64	EAP Request
56	00:09:5B:66:E6:80			#	1	24.0	14	802.11 Ack
57	00:09:5B:66:E6:80	00:0D:ED:A5:51:70	00:0D:ED:A5:51:70		1	54.0	82	EAP Response
58	00:0D:ED:A5:51:70			#	1	24.0	14	802.11 Ack
59	00:09:5B:66:E6:80	00:0D:ED:A5:51:70	00:0D:ED:A5:51:70		1	54.0	84	EAPOL-Key
60	00:0D:ED:A5:51:70			#	1	24.0	14	802.11 Ack
61	00:09:5B:66:E6:80	00:0D:ED:A5:51:70	00:0D:ED:A5:51:70	*	1	54.0	30	802.11 Disassoc
62	00:0D:ED:A5:51:70			#	1	24.0	14	802.11 Ack
63	00:0D:ED:A5:51:70	00:09:5B:66:E6:80	00:0D:ED:A5:51:70	*	1	1.0	30	802.11 Deauth
64	00:09:5B:66:E6:80			#	1	1.0	14	802.11 Ack

Instead, Mr. Anderson's computer is being successfully authenticated and associated through the engineering access point, since the engineering and shipping departments are located adjacent to each other. Mr. Fisher checks the group assignment for Mr. Anderson's user in the RADIUS server and finds that his user is misconfigured to be part of the engineering group, which is assigned to VLAN 101. This mistake is verified by a wired capture between the engineering access point and the RADIUS server as shown in Figure 11.33.

A simple change to the RADIUS server configuration alleviated a performance problem caused by a security misconfiguration.

FIGURE 11.33 Captured wired frames between the engineering access point and the RADIUS server

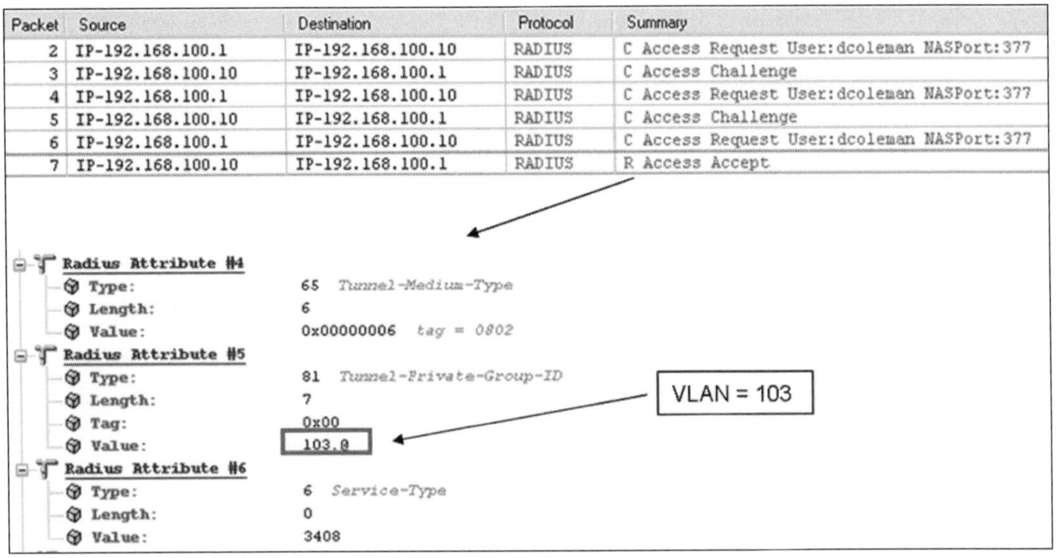

Packet	Source	Destination	Protocol	Summary
2	IP-192.168.100.1	IP-192.168.100.10	RADIUS	C Access Request User:dcoleman NASPort:377
3	IP-192.168.100.10	IP-192.168.100.1	RADIUS	C Access Challenge
4	IP-192.168.100.1	IP-192.168.100.10	RADIUS	C Access Request User:dcoleman NASPort:377
5	IP-192.168.100.10	IP-192.168.100.1	RADIUS	C Access Challenge
6	IP-192.168.100.1	IP-192.168.100.10	RADIUS	C Access Request User:dcoleman NASPort:377
7	IP-192.168.100.10	IP-192.168.100.1	RADIUS	R Access Accept

Radius Attribute #4
- Type: 65 Tunnel-Medium-Type
- Length: 6
- Value: 0x00000006 tag = 0802

Radius Attribute #5
- Type: 81 Tunnel-Private-Group-ID
- Length: 7
- Tag: 0x00
- Value: 103.8

VLAN = 103

Radius Attribute #6
- Type: 6 Service-Type
- Length: 0
- Value: 3408

Case Study 3: General Fault Finding

Donohue's Aircraft Repair Depot recently upgraded their single–access point wireless LAN from HR/DSSS to ERP so that more technicians working in the hangar could simultaneously communicate with the file server located in the parts department. While using the HR/DSSS network that was previously installed, they were unhappy with the performance and thought that HR/DSSS technology was simply slow and that the chosen PHY was the problem. After upgrading, performance did not improve as expected, so they contacted an analyst, Mr. Parsons, to determine the root cause of the problem(s).

Mr. Parsons begins by placing an analyzer close to the access point. He notices that Donohue's access point is using channel 11, the RF medium is not very busy, and a relatively small number of frames are being transmitted even during the busiest part of the work day. Figure 11.34 illustrates the low RF medium usage.

FIGURE 11.34 Protocol analyzer showing the low RF medium usage

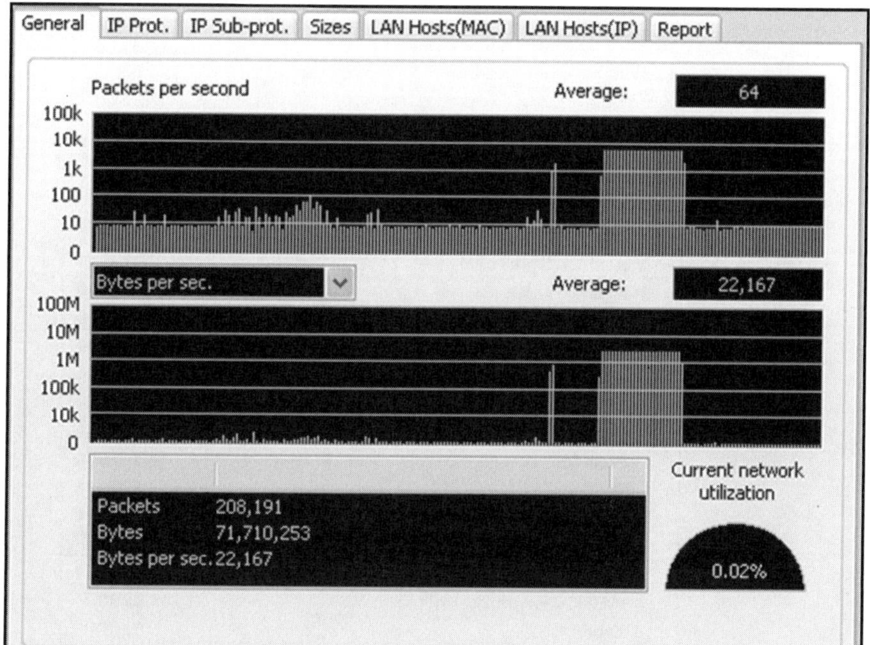

Next, Mr. Parsons notices that the number of retransmissions is abnormally high, considering that "normal" is less than 3 percent and "high" is around 10 percent on average. The reason for the retransmissions is that many frames are being corrupted. Figure 11.35 illustrates an analyzer displaying retransmission percentages.

Mr. Parsons has now established that there is a relatively low amount of traffic on the RF medium, but retransmissions are high. Since the CSMA/CA protocol typically leads to retransmissions under a heavy load, the retransmissions are likely due to RF interference or severe multipath. To test this theory, Mr. Parsons uses a spectrum analyzer and sees the display shown in Figure 11.36.

FIGURE 11.35 Abnormally high retransmission count

Statistic	Current
⊞ General	
⊞ Errors	
⊞ Counts	
⊞ Size Distribution	
⊞ Wireless	
⊟ 802.11 Analysis	
Average Signal Strength	73.726
Average Signal dBm	-0.149
Average Noise	0.000
Average Noise dBm	0.000
802.11 Data	30.655%
802.11 Management	22.024%
802.11 Control	43.750%
Local	65.774%
From DS	17.560%
To DS	13.095%
DS-DS	0.000%
Retry	21.131%
WEP	30.655%
WEP ICV Errors	0.000%
Order	0.000%

After finding that channel 1 has a significant source of narrowband RF interference with harmonics that fall into the channel 11 series of frequencies, Mr. Parsons tries to find the source. He finds that the source of this RF interference is a power tool that is used repeatedly throughout the day to repair aircraft engines. Since this tool must be used, the alternative to discontinued use is to move the access point to channel 6. This change gives the client devices and access point the best chance of receiving uncorrupted frames. After moving the access point to channel 6, performance improves dramatically, and the problem is resolved in the best possible way, given the constraints of the scenario.

FIGURE 11.36 Spectrum analyzer showing narrowband RF interference

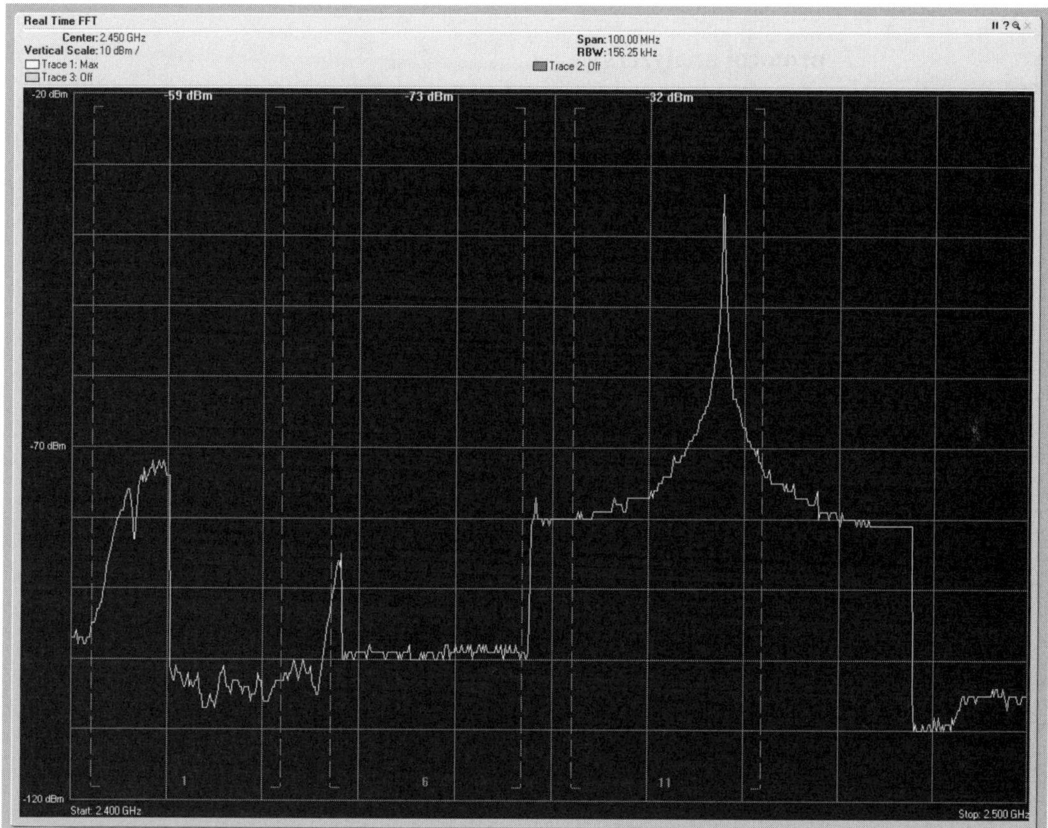

Summary

In this chapter, I introduced you to protocol and spectrum analyzers. You learned the basics about distributed analyzers and discovered how to use the OmniPeek Personal protocol analyzer. This knowledge will become very valuable to you as we move into Chapter 12. This knowledge will also benefit you as a WLAN administrator when you begin troubleshooting common WLAN problems and scenarios.

Key Terms

- ☐ **protocol analyzers**
- ☐ **spectrum analyzers**
- ☐ **wireless intrusion detection systems (WIDSs)**
- ☐ **wireless intrusion prevention systems (WIPSs)**

Review Questions

1. You are experiencing poor connectivity in a BSA in the accounting department of your organization. You want to view the RF activity in that area from a Physical layer perspective, and you are not interested in the actual data traversing the network. Your goal is simply to see the RF activity in the area. Which of the following tools are you likely to use once you arrive in the accounting department?

   A. Distributed RF spectrum analyzer

   B. Handheld spectrum analyzer

   C. Wireless intrusion prevention system

   D. Protocol analyzer

2. You want to prevent attackers from attaching rogue APs to your wired network. Which of the following solutions will allow you to prevent these rogue APs from functioning on your wired LAN?

   A. WIDS

   B. WIPS

   C. Spectrum analyzer

   D. Protocol analyzer

3. A vendor tells you that her system can remotely monitor the RF spectrum and report the spectral information back to central headquarters. She tells you that you must install at least one device at reach remote location. What is this device called?

   A. Access point

   B. WLAN router

   C. Spectrum sensor

   D. Spectrum analyzer

4. You want to evaluate the kind of information that is traveling on your WLAN. You plan to capture the WLAN data for a 24-hour period and then use an automated analysis tool to report on the different kinds of traffic such as TCP, FTP, etc. What tool will you use to capture the traffic?

   A. Spectrum analyzer

   B. Protocol analyzer

   C. Traffic filter

   D. Handheld spectrum analyzer

Review Answers

1. **B.** You will most likely use the handheld protocol analyzer. The distributed RF spectrum analyzer and the wireless intrusion prevention system are ruled out by your arriving in the accounting department. You would more likely use these two tools from a centralized location. The protocol analyzer tells you about the data and management information traversing the WLAN, and this is irrelevant to you in this scenario.

2. **B.** The WIPS (wireless intrusion protection system) is more likely to "prevent" the rogue from functioning on your wired LAN. The WIDS (wireless intrusion detection system) will most likely only warn you of the rogue AP. The spectrum and protocol analyzers may help you manually locate the rogue AP, but by the time you've located it, the device has probably been functioning on the wired LAN for some time.

3. **C.** The device is most likely a spectrum sensor. The sensor transmits the spectral information back to the centralized application that is actually used to analyze the data. This remove device would not be called a spectrum analyzer, although a spectrum analyzer may be used to evaluate the data that the sensor collects. APs and WLAN routers are not used as remote sensors.

4. **B.** The protocol analyzer can capture the actual data and management frames traversing your WLAN. The spectrum analyzers will not help in this case, and traffic filters are used within some protocol analyzers.

CHAPTER

12

Troubleshooting and Testing Tools

CWNA Exam Objectives Covered:

- Identify and explain how to solve the following WLAN implementation challenges using features available in enterprise-class WLAN equipment
  - System Throughput
  - Co-Channel and Adjacent-Channel Interference
  - RF Noise and Noise Floor
  - Narrowband and Wideband RF Interference
  - Multipath
  - Hidden Nodes
  - Near-Far Problem
  - Weather
  - Troubleshooting VoWLAN Issues

Troubleshooting WLANs is an important part of the administrator's job. Many times, WLANs do not function as expected once they are implemented, and it is up to the administrator or installation engineer to find out why and resolve the issues. This means having a good plan for troubleshooting the problem and understanding common problems that occur in WLANs so that you can recognize and eradicate or minimize them. The first section of this chapter will help you develop a plan for troubleshooting, which is not something you will be tested on when you take the CWNA exam. The second section, "WLAN Implementation Challenges," covers the common problems experienced in WLANs on which you will be tested. A cursory reading of the first section will suffice; however, its value should not be minimized. An in-depth understanding of the second section is more crucial to your success as a CWNA candidate and a WLAN administrator.

Troubleshooting Methodologies

A methodology can be defined as a standard way to do something; therefore, a troubleshooting methodology is a standard way to troubleshoot. The benefit of methodologies is multifaceted. First, they help to ensure that you do all the things you need to do to complete a task or set of tasks. Second, they provide you with collective knowledge when developed over time. By collective knowledge, I mean that knowledge that you do not possess yourself and yet benefit from it. For example, most of us have never researched the statistics to know if wearing a seat belt is safer than not wearing a seat belt when we drive; however, we trust the research done by others, and therefore, we wear our seat belts (it also helps to motivate us when the law requires it). A good troubleshooting methodology will cause you to take steps for which you may not fully understand the purpose, but you will still get the benefit.

I'll share four different methodologies with you in this section as well as one concept that will help you in the troubleshooting process. The four methodologies are

- REACT
- OSI model
- Hardware/software model
- Symptom, diagnosis, and solution

You will not be tested on the troubleshooting methodologies documented in this section, "Troubleshooting Methodologies." They are provided for your reference and to help you become an even better troubleshooter. You will be tested on the common WLAN problems documented in the later section of this chapter "WLAN Implementation Challenges."

REACT

Early in my information technology career, I worked as a help desk analyst and a telephone troubleshooter. I found that I would frequently forget to do an important thing in the troubleshooting process that would cost me minutes or even hours of time—not to mention the added stress. For this reason, I developed an acronym to remind me of the stages I should go through when troubleshooting a problem. This way, I can work through the acronym until I reach a solution. I always reach a solution by the end of the acronym. The reality is that sometimes the solution is a complete reload of a device's firmware and settings and sometimes it is a complete reload of a client computer's operating system; however, more often than not, a simpler solution is found.

The REACT acronym stands for the five stages of troubleshooting:

- Research
- Engage
- Adjust
- Configure
- Take Note

I'll cover each stage briefly in the following sections so that you can understand how they fit together and why I go through these stages.

Research

I remember, it was probably in 1997, that I was trying to resolve a problem with a Microsoft Access 95 database. Every time the user tried to open the database, she received an error that read "A device attached to the system is not functioning." Now, I don't know about you, but when I see an error about a device, the first thing I think of is hardware. I spent more than 2 hours trying to verify that all the hardware was functioning properly, and of course, it was. By this time, the end of the day had arrived and I went home tormented by my failure to resolve the problem (hopefully I'm the only one who suffers like this when I can't fix a computer problem).

The next day, I decided to do some research, so I opened the MSDN CD (that's right, it used to fit on one CD and have plenty of space left over). I searched for the error message and found that the error could be generated if VBRUN300.DLL was corrupt. If you haven't been around long, VBRUN300.DLL was used by all Visual Basic 3.0 applications. The only problem was that Microsoft Access and this database did not rely on Visual Basic 3.0's runtime for anything; however, my mind was racing. The jungle of my mind was suddenly clear and I realized the implications: If the corruption of VBRUN300.DLL could cause the error, maybe any corrupt DLL could cause the error. I reinstalled Microsoft Access and the error went away.

You are probably wondering what the moral of this intriguing story is. The moral is that I could have saved the first two hours of work with a few minutes of research. My new standard became Research at least 15 minutes before moving to the adjust stage with any new problem that requires troubleshooting. Not all problems require troubleshooting, and the confusion that usually comes into play is the result of a misunderstanding of what troubleshooting really is. Here is my favorite definition:

Troubleshooting is the process of discovering the unknown cause and solution for a known problem.

You see, if I know the solution to a problem, I am repairing and not troubleshooting. In other words, I will only start with research when it is a real troubleshooting scenario according to this definition. In the end, by researching for just 15 minutes, I find that the cause and solution are often learned without spending any time adjusting various settings and parameters to resolve the issue. For example, if my client cannot connect to the WLAN and is receiving a specific error message when the client software first loads, I will search for this error message at Google.com to see what I can discover. I may also search the vendor's web site. If I don't find the cause or solution, I will usually get direction so that I can focus on the right area as I move to the engage or adjust stages.

Engage

While you may be eager to move from research to adjust, you should engage the user if he or she is involved in the problem. Ask a question like "Do you know if anything has changed about your system in the past few days?" Notice I didn't say, "Did you change anything?" The latter question will usually cause people to become defensive and fail to get you any valuable information. The users do not usually have any knowledge of what caused the problem, but when they do, it can save you hours or even days of trouble. Always engage the user. Other questions that might be beneficial include:

- Have you seen any strange activity in the area lately? (Rogue APs.)
- Has the problem only recently begun, or has it been happening for some length of time?
- Are you aware of any others experiencing similar difficulties?
- When was the last time it worked?
- Is it turned on? (Seriously.)

Adjust

Interestingly, we've just now arrived where I see many techs, WLAN administrators, or network administrators beginning. Don't feel bad—I've done it many times myself. This is the stage where you begin trying different things to see if you can track down the cause of your problem. You might try updating the firmware on an AP or installing new device drivers for a client adapter. You could also change settings or disable features to see if the problem goes away. The point is that this is where you begin the "technical" side of troubleshooting.

Once you've completed these first three stages, you've always come to a solution. Again, this solution is sometimes reinstalling the application or operating system, but things are working again. You may have your solution after the research stage, or you may have it after the engage stage. Whether you make it all the way to the adjust stage or you solve the problem earlier in the process, you are now ready to move to what I call the ongoing stability stages: configure and Take note.

Configure

This is the first of the two ongoing stability stages. In the configure stage, you ensure that the systems and devices are configured and are operating according to your standards before leaving the physical area (or remote management tool). This allows you to maintain a standardized environment, and a standardized environment is usually more stable. Of course, with a reinstallation, you will need to reinstall according to the original specifications for the installation and then apply any configuration changes that have been approved or processed since that time.

Take Note

This final stage completes the process and ensures that you get the greatest benefit out of this methodology going forward—this is the second ongoing stability stage. By documenting your findings, what I call *take note,* you provide a searchable resource for future troubleshooting. For example, the situation I shared earlier where the device error was generated should be documented, and I suggest documenting the following at a minimum:

- The problem with any error messages if they existed
- The cause concisely explained
- The solution with any necessary step-by-step approach
- Any learned principles, such as a DLL being referenced as a device by the operating system

If your organization does not provide a centralized trouble ticket tracking system or help desk solution, I encourage you to consider creating your own database. You can use any desktop database application like Microsoft Access or FileMaker. Just be sure you can document the needed information and query it easily.

OSI Model

The OSI model can also be used for troubleshooting purposes. The concept here is to walk up or down the OSI model analyzing the system at each layer. This allows you to break the problem into logical sections and then verify that the system is operating properly in each of these sections (OSI layers). You may choose only to analyze Layers 1 through 3, or you may choose to evaluate all seven layers (or even eight layers if you're considering the user layer, which is sometimes called Layer 8).

Layer 1

Layer 1 is the Physical layer, and this would mean evaluation of the WLAN client devices or infrastructure devices to ensure that they are working properly at the hardware level. For example, is the radio still functioning appropriately or not? With client devices, this can be tested quickly by removing the WLAN client device (assuming it's a USB, a CardBus, or another kind of removable device) and installing it in another computer that is using the exact same model device and is working. If the new computer stops working too, the WLAN device is most likely at fault at the hardware level or the software level (firmware). If it is an AP and you have a spare, you could load the identical configuration on the spare and place it in the same exact location to see if the problem persists. If it does not, again, the radio—or some other hardware/firmware issue—may be failing.

An additional key is to evaluate the hardware used by Layer 1 (sometimes called Layer 0). Once you get to the wired network, you may also evaluate patch panels, connectors, and cabling at this point. Another area where failure may occur in relation to Layer 1 is the Ethernet connection between the AP and the wired LAN. If your clients are authenticating and associating with the AP, but they cannot obtain an IP address from your DHCP server (assuming you're using one), the Ethernet connection may not be working. Go to a wired client and try to connect to the AP via the Ethernet connection. Can you? If not, verify that the Ethernet cable is good, that the port on the switch is working, and that the Ethernet port in the AP is still functioning (by connecting directly to the AP and trying to connect).

Layer 2

The second layer you will usually evaluate is Layer 2. This is where the bridges and switches live. Make sure the switch ports are still working properly, that VLANs are configured appropriately, and that port security settings are set accurately on your switches. Check the configuration in your bridge or bridges to ensure that they are configured correctly. Be sure the wireless link on each wireless bridge is still working and that the signal strength is still acceptable for operations. Since bridges evaluate incoming frames and forward them according to information in the frame, be sure that your bridging rules or filters are set up appropriately. Of course, with both bridges and switches, the problem can be at the cable and connector level, but you will have checked that already at Layer 1.

Layer 3

If you've evaluated the radios, cabling, and connectors at Layer 1 and you've checked the bridges and switches at Layer 2 and you've still not found a solution, you might have to move on to Layer 3. Here you'll need to check the routing tables to ensure proper configuration. Make sure any filters applied are accurate. Using common desktop operating system tools like *ipconfig, ping,* and *arp,* you can ensure that you can route data from one location on the network to another.

Upper Layers

Finally, if you've tested the first three layers and can't find a problem there, the network infrastructure is probably working fine. It's time to move to the upper layers. Look at the configuration settings in your applications and client software for WLAN utilization. Be sure that the authentication mechanisms are installed and configured correctly. Try using different tools and software that provide the same basic functionality. Do they work? If so, there may be a compatibility problem with the specific application you're using and the hardware on which it is operating. As noted in Chapter 11, many WLAN administration tools (protocol analyzers, for example) work with only a limited number of devices.

As you can see, the OSI model of troubleshooting can help you both focus and move through a sequence of testing procedures until you find the true source of the problem. I've only touched on the concept here, but you can take it farther by learning more about what happens at each layer and the tools that can be used to test at that layer. For example, you can use a spectrum analyzer to test and troubleshoot the Physical layer and a protocol analyzer to inspect the Data Link layer of WLANs.

Hardware/Software Model

The hardware/software model is a troubleshooting methodology that is used in an attempt to narrow the problem to either hardware or software. There are certain problems that are commonly hardware problems, and there are others that tend to be software problems. Many administrators will attempt to troubleshoot software first and then hardware. Others will do the opposite. In most cases, the situation will help you to determine which should be your first point of attack. If everything is working in a system except one application, that is often a good sign that the software is the problem. If multiple applications that use the same hardware are experiencing the same problem, that is often a good sign that the hardware is the problem. These are not absolute rules, but they are good general guidelines.

TABLE 12.1 Hardware Problems and Symptoms

Problem	Symptoms
Client adapter failed	Device driver will not load, client cannot connect, OS reports errors loading the device
Firmware outdated	No support for newer security features, poor performance, reduced stability
Improper antenna installed or antenna disconnected	RF coverage in the wrong place, signal too weak at a distance
Bad cables	Could cause improper power for PoE devices or low SNR for antennas

Hardware Problem

In WLANs, there are hardware problems that present certain symptoms. While I cannot provide you with an exact list of symptoms mapped to problems, the list in Table 12.1 is a good place to start.

Software Problems

Table 12.2 lists common software problems and their symptoms.

TABLE 12.2 Software Problems and Symptoms

Problem	Symptoms
Client software misconfigured	Client cannot connect, cannot receive an IP address, unable to browse the network
Improper passphrase entered	Client associated with the AP but cannot log on to the network
DHCP server down	Client associates with the AP but cannot acquire an IP address
RADIUS server down	Client associates with the AP but cannot log on to the network

Symptom, Diagnosis, and Solution

Because certain symptoms usually surface with specific problems, many issues can be resolved in a similar way to human health issues. Look at the symptom, identify the most likely cause (diagnosis), and then treat it (solution). Repeat this process until the problem is resolved.

Symptom

Defining the symptoms means gathering information about the problem. What is happening? Where is it happening? What technology is involved? Which users, if any, are involved? Has it always been this way? Answering questions like these will help you determine the various details about the problem. Good questions are at the core of effective problem definition.

Diagnosis

Given the information gathered from your symptoms analysis, what is the most likely cause or what are the most likely causes? You can treat one or all, but you will most likely learn more by treating one cause at a time. In other words, try one solution based on your diagnosis first and evaluate the results. This gives you expert knowledge over time or what some call "intuition."

Solution

The solution is the potential fix for the problem. You may try replacing a CardBus PC card because you determine that, given the symptoms, the most likely cause is a failed card. After replacing the card, you note that you are experiencing the exact same problem. Next you may decide to try both cards in another machine that is currently using the same card model and is working. When you do this, both cards work in the other computer. Next you may attempt to reload the drivers in the malfunctioning computer, but this doesn't help either. In the end, you discover that the CardBus port is experiencing intermittent failures in the malfunctioning laptop. You send it to the vendor for repairs.

This example demonstrates how the diagnosis and solution look, in what I call the adjust phase in my REACT methodology. You make changes and try different tactics until something solves the problem. You document the solution for future reference, but you also mentally document it. This is called experience, and as you get more and more of it, you eventually approach the level of expertise that helps you solve problems more quickly. For this reason, I look at problems as stepping stones to a better future, because solving this network or computer problem today will only make me more able to solve similar and different problems tomorrow.

Systems Thinking

Systems thinking is the process of analyzing all interdependent components that compose a system. In other words, it is the opposite of being narrow-minded in the troubleshooting process. I've seen administrators blame everything from network connectivity to application errors on an operating system or a particular brand of PC instead of looking for the actual problem. While some operating systems and some PC brands may seem more prone to problems than others, the reality is that there are probably thousands of individuals out there who have had the opposite experience as you. In other words, if you like the computers from company A because they are very stable and you don't like the computers from company B because of your experience with them, there is likely someone (or thousands) out there who feels exactly the opposite because of his or her experience.

The point is simple: Rather than focusing on a vendor that I do not like, I must focus on the actual problem and seek a solution. When I do this, I'm less likely to just reinstall every time a problem comes up. I want to ask questions like these:

- What are the systems or devices between this device and the network or device with which it is attempting to communicate?
- What other devices are attempting to communicate with the same system at this time?
- What has changed in the environment within which the system operates?
- Has the system been physically moved recently?

Asking these kinds of questions causes you to evaluate factors that are more related to the actual system you have in place and less related to the vendors that have provided the components. Indeed, if a vendor has provided you with bad components over a period of time, you will likely discontinue partnering with that vendor; however, blaming the problem on a single vendor every time does not help me solve the problems I am facing right now. For that, I need systems thinking and a good methodology.

Whether you adopt one or more of these methodologies, pursue another methodology, or create one of your own, you should consider how you troubleshoot problems and then be sure it is an efficient and effective process.

WLAN Implementation Challenges

Believe it or not, wireless communications that use RF waves have now been taking place for more than 100 years. From radio to WLANs, similar problems have been encountered. However, WLANs introduce some new dilemmas that are not faced at the same level in radio communications such as CB and ham radio. For example, data throughput is not an issue for these hobbyists, who love to chat with people around the globe. For them, you can just turn up the power (within legal limits) and extend the range. There might be a little "fuzz" on the link, but the human ear and mind are amazingly adept at filtering out the "fuzz" and retrieving the human speech.

WLAN radios are not nearly as tolerant of *interference* and free space path loss–imposed attenuation. For this reason, throughput management is an important part of the WLAN administrator's regular job. Additionally, there are scenarios where the administrator must determine the cause of weakened signals and find a solution. Should more APs be installed on different channels? Can the administrator move an AP or antenna a few feet and greatly impact the coverage area? Is the weather causing problems for the outdoor links? These questions and more will be answered in this section as we investigate the following common issues in WLANs:

- System throughput
- Co-channel and adjacent-channel interference
- RF noise and noise floor
- Narrowband and wideband RF interference
- Multipath
- Hidden nodes
- Near-far problem
- Weather
- Troubleshooting VoWLAN issues

System Throughput

Installing a WLAN that provides access to users is only a partial solution. The access provided must be sufficient for the users' needs. This usually means providing sufficient throughput for the users to use the applications they require. There are many issues that affect the available throughput in a WLAN, including the chosen PHY, wired-side limitations, and more. This section will introduce you to the topics you'll need to understand to provide your users with the throughput they need to get their jobs done efficiently.

PHY Limitations

The first choice that will impact the available throughput is the PHY or PHYs you decide to implement. There are obvious issues like the data rate supported by OFDM and ERP as compared to HR/DSSS, but there are also not-so-obvious issues like ERP protection mechanisms.

When an AP implements the ERP PHY and an HR/DSSS STA associates with that AP, the AP will usually implement a protection mechanism that reduces the overall throughput of the WLAN. This is because transfers that use the OFDM modulation included in the ERP PHY must first set the NAV in all non-ERP STAs that are associated with the AP. This is done by transmitting RTS and/or CTS frames with a duration that is greater than or equal to the time needed to transmit the actual OFDM-modulated frame and responses. The extra overhead reduces the throughput of an ERP BSS drastically and should be considered when implementing your WLAN. You can often increase more than double the total throughput in a BSS by ensuring that only ERP-based clients are allowed to connect to any WLAN in the vicinity and overlapping channels. Furthermore, you can force the AP to reject associations below a particular data rate so that even visiting client STAs (those that are out of your control) will not impact your BSS on an ongoing basis. As an example, in tests performed by CNET Labs (reviewed April 17, 2003, by Brian Nadel), a Buffalo AirStation WLAN router provided 19.6 Mbps of throughput in an ERP-only configuration, but this dropped to 7.9 Mbps in a mixed-mode implementation with both ERP- and HR/DSSS PHY-based clients (see reviews.cnet.com for more information.).

You must also consider the range of the PHY you select. Generally speaking, an ERP PHY-based BSS will have a greater range with higher data rates at a greater distance than OFDM PHY-based BSSs. The HT PHY (IEEE 802.11n) should provide an even greater range than that provided by ERP devices today.

Wired-Side Limitations

As I mentioned in Chapter 6, you must ensure that the wired ports on your APs and WLAN routers are fast enough to keep up with the WLAN. This includes not only the Ethernet port that is in the AP or router, but also the Ethernet port that the AP or router connects to. If the port is a 10 Mbps port, it will not be able to keep up with the demands of the WLAN, assuming the users communicate more with devices and services on the wired LAN than they do with each other.

In most cases, you will want a minimum of a 100 Mbps port for connections to the APs and a 1000 Mbps port for the uplink connection from the switch to the rest of the network. For example, you may choose to connect 5 APs to a switch and have an average of 15 users associate with each AP. If the switch provides only a 100 Mbps uplink to a 1000 Mbps infrastructure, the uplink port in the switch will act as a bottleneck that downgrades the average maximum throughput for your five APs. Having a 1000 Mbps (gigabit) uplink can resolve this issue.

While this book and the CWNA exam are focused on WLANs, it is important to remember that the experience of your WLAN users will be greatly impacted by the performance of your wired LAN as well. Some administrators make the mistake of assuming that the WLAN will be so much slower than the wired LAN that they will not have to focus on the wired side at all. This is a dangerous assumption.

Another fact to consider is that many wired switches, particularly those aimed at the SOHO and SMB market, are labeled as gigabit switches, but they function in 100 Mbps mode much, if not all, of the time. Look closely at the documentation to see if the switch operates at the rate of the slowest connected device or if it operates each port independently and at the highest rate that the connected device and switch support. The vast majority of devices use wire speed non-blocking ASICs, which means that each connection can function at the highest speed supported by both the port and the connecting device.

Testing Tools

There are many tools that can report the throughput ratings for a network connection (whether wireless or wired). One example of such a tool is the free bandwidth monitor included in the Axence NetTools suite available at

FIGURE 12.1 Axence NetTools bandwidth monitoring

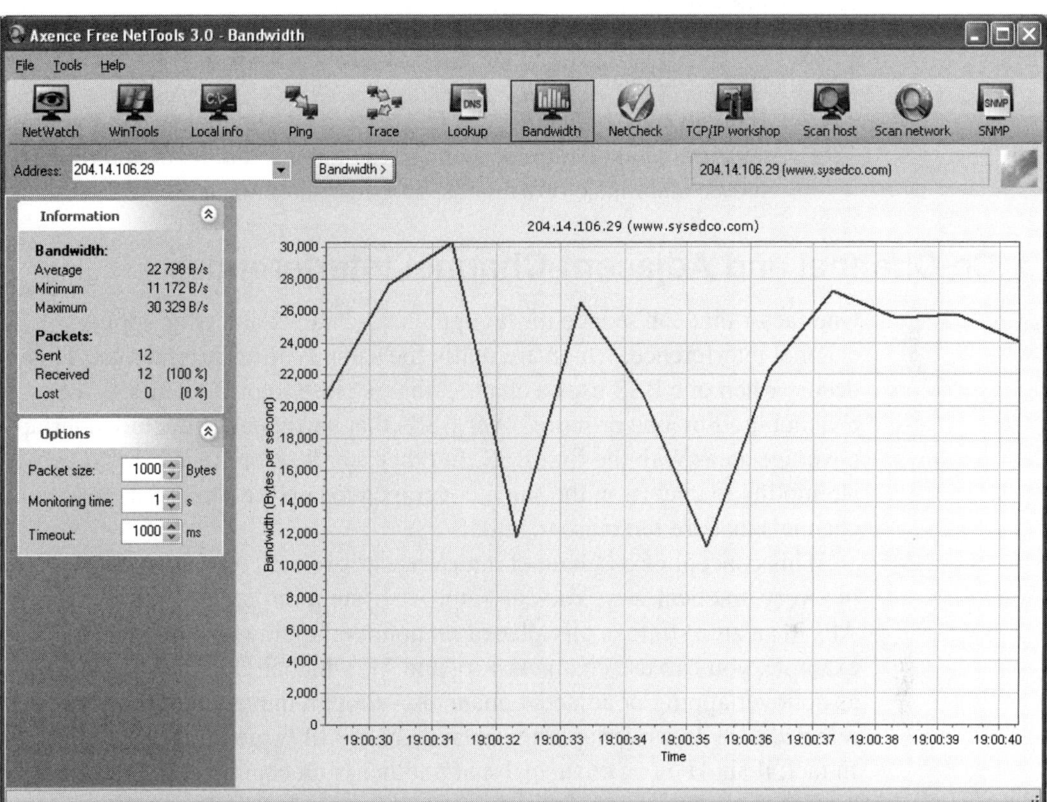

www.AxenceSoftware.com. This software can report on network bandwidth, ping histories, traceroutes, and DNS lookups—all of which can be very beneficial in any network troubleshooting scenario, not just WLANs. Figure 12.1 shows the bandwidth-monitoring component of this suite.

Possible Solutions

The solutions to throughput problems include the following:

- Install more APs in the coverage area using different channels and possibly lower–output power settings.
- Install OFDM-based APs and clients that use nonoverlapping channels and can accommodate many more APs in a coverage area.

- Install faster switches between the APs and the wired network infrastructure.
- Remove all HR/DSSS client devices from your WLAN coverage space and channel.
- Ban, through both enforced and documented policies, bandwidth-consuming applications such as streaming radio, legal and illegal movie and music downloads, and other large data downloads.

Co-Channel and Adjacent-Channel Interference

One factor that can reduce throughput is co-channel and overlapping-channel interference, which are really the same type of interference. This occurs when one BSS uses a channel that is close to or the same as the channel used by one or more other BSSs that partly or completely overlaps coverage areas with the first BSS. In other words, more than one WLAN is attempting to coexist in the same coverage area on the same channel or on channels that are too close together.

This concept of co-channel interference is related to *system throughput* in a very practical way. You can improve system throughput by colocating APs in an area strategically placed on nonoverlapping channels. For example, you can use channels 1, 6, and 11, which are often referred to as nonoverlapping or adjacent channels—though they would be better referred to as less overlapping, since there is still some level of overlap. In fact, if an AP is on channel 1 and another is on channel 6 in the same area and they both use very high output power settings, they can have a detrimental effect on each other. This would be known as adjacent-channel interference. When channels specified as adjacent (HR/DSSS and ERP specify channels 1, 6, and 11) interfere with each other because they are too close to each other or are using output power levels that are too high, it is called adjacent-channel interference.

To resolve this issue, when overlapping coverage areas with colocated devices, make sure the output power is not higher than is needed. This will reduce adjacent interference. Co-channel interference, for example, using channels 1 and 2, cannot really be overcome by using lower–output power settings—assuming the two APs are in the same coverage area. To resolve this type of interference, you will need to remove one of the APs or change the channel so that there is more separation. If only two APs need to be placed in a coverage area to provide the needed throughput and there are no other nearby WLAN cells, you can usually get the best results by simply setting the APs to channels 1 and 11.

Co-channel or adjacent-channel interference may be identified by large numbers of frame retransmissions. Additionally, throughput is often reduced because the STAs in a BSS will accept and process duration values of received transmissions from other nearby BSSs that are on the same channel. This results in a reduction in throughput, since the STAs think the network is busy and do not try to transmit their waiting frames.

To determine if you are transmitting with too much power from an AP, use a protocol analyzer to capture frames on a channel that is 3–4 channels off from the AP and see how many frames you capture. For example, if the AP is transmitting on channel 11, capture on channels 6, 7, or 8 and see how many, if any, frames you pick up from the AP (Beacon frames do just fine). Figure 12.2 shows a capture using OmniPeek Personal on channel 7 that picked up the Beacon frame from the AP on channel 11.

RF Noise and Noise Floor

RF noise may be defined as RF energy or signals generated by RF systems other than those with which the detecting system intends to communicate. For example, a WLAN STA configured to listen to an AP on channel 11 would consider RF signals transmitted from an AP on channel 9 at high power levels to be RF noise. This RF noise may cause corruption of frames. Interestingly, what is RF noise to one device may be the RF signal to another.

The *noise floor* is defined as the background level of RF noise, and the *signal-to-noise ratio* is the difference between the strength of the signal for which a device is monitoring and the strength of the noise floor.

FIGURE 12.2 High output power resulting in co-channel interference

```
Status:              0x00000000
Packet Length:       92
Timestamp:           19:28:47.460132000 06/13/2007
Data Rate:           2   1.0 Mbps
Channel:             7   2442MHz  802.11bg
Signal Level:        67
Signal dBm:          -48
Noise Level:         18%
Noise dBm:           -82
802.11 MAC Header Version=0 Type=%00 Management Subtype=%1000 Beacon Duration=0 Microseconds Destination=Ethernet Broadcast Source=00:0F:B5:19:9D:C6 BSSID=00:0F:B5:19:9D:C6 Seq Numb
802.11 Management - Beacon
  Timestamp:           152985983  Microseconds
  Beacon Interval:     100
  Capability Info=%0000010000100001
  SSID ID=0 SSID Len=14 SSID=NETGEAR-TRAVEL
  Rates= ID=1 Rates: Len=4 Rate=1.0 Mbps Rate=2.0 Mbps Rate=5.5 Mbps Rate=11.0 Mbps
  Direct Sequence Parameter Set
    Element ID:          3  Direct Sequence Parameter Set
    Length:              1
    Channel:             11
  CFPS= ID=4 CFPS: Len=6 CFP Count=0 CFP Period=2 CFP Max Dur=0 CFP Dur Remaining=0
  TIM= ID=5 TIM: Len=4 DTIM Count=0 DTIM Period=1 Bitmap Offset=0 xxxx xxx. Traffic Ind.=0 .... ...0 Part Virt Bmap=0x00
  ERP= ID=42 ERP: Len=1
```

Narrowband and Wideband RF Interference

Narrowband and wideband interference can cause corruption of data in WLANs. You can often detect that interference exists by looking at the frames in a WLAN analyzer, which can report CRC errors or corruption. When CRC errors are reported, it indicates that the signal strength was great enough to receive the RF signal, but that noise joined with the signal and corrupted the data as the signal traveled from the transmitter to the receiver. This results in retransmissions and, therefore, reduced throughput.

WLANs deal with this in different ways. One way is to reduce the data rate, which provides for more fault tolerance in the data transfer and can handle more interference without losing data. Another way is documented in Chapter 4: By fragmenting the frames, smaller frames are transmitted and fewer of the frames will become corrupted. The fragmentation threshold can be used to control the point at which fragmentation is utilized.

Multipath

Since WLANs have RF LOS instead of just visual LOS, the RF receivers can receive signals that travel directly from the transmitter to the receiver as well as signals that reflect and diffract off or around other objects and then travel to the receiver. *Multipath* is the term for signals traveling multiple paths and still arriving at the receiver. Multipath can be good for the communication link and can be bad for the communication. Some newer wireless technologies take advantage of multipath in order to increase the data rate and throughput of wireless communications. An example of this is the MIMO technology on which the HT PHY is based in the IEEE 802.11n draft document.

Results of Multipath

As I stated, multipath can provide good and bad results. In most cases, the results are negative unless specific technologies are implemented to deal with them. The results include:

- Increased signal amplitude at the receiver
- Decreased signal amplitude at the receiver
- Data corruption
- Signal nullification

Increased signal amplitude at the receiver can result from multiple signal paths arriving at the receiving antenna in phase. This is known as *upfade.* Of course, the signal is not stronger than when it was transmitted and, in fact, will always be weaker than the originally transmitted signal; however, the signal may be stronger than it would have been at the point of reception, had the upfading not occurred.

As you learned in preceding chapters, free space path loss ensures that the received signal will be weaker than the transmitted signal. As the wave travels, the wave front broadens and the signal strength at a given point will therefore be less.

Multipath may also cause signal reduction or a decrease in the signal amplitude. When this occurs, it is known as *downfade* and should be considered during the selection of antennas at the time of the site survey. Downfade occurs when two copies of the same signal arrive at the receiver out of phase.

In addition, out-of-phase signals may also cause corruption of the main signal. This is because the amplitude of the received signal is reduced to such a point that the receiver can only understand part of the frame being transmitted and not the complete frame. This usually happens when the signal-to-noise ratio is very low. In other words, the RF signal is very close to the noise floor. This result of multipath usually causes a retransmission of the corrupted frame from the transmitter, and there may need to be multiple retransmissions before the frame actually makes it through.

The final result of multipath, *nulling,* occurs when one or more reflected waves arrive at the receiver out of phase with the main wave. In this case, instead of weakening the signal, the main wave's amplitude is canceled and the signal cannot be received by the receiver. In these cases, retransmission of the frame will not likely resolve the problem unless the multipath occurred because of a moving vehicle in the area, which is not the likely case. You will most likely have to reposition one or both of the ends of the link.

Detecting Multipath

Since you cannot actually see waves as being in phase or out of phase, you can only detect multipath by looking for its symptoms. These symptoms include links that should work, based on standard link budget calculations, and that are experiencing problems and dead spots in the RF coverage during a site survey or during the implementation of the WLAN. High retransmissions in links that should be working—based on link budgets and analysis of the RF noise floor when your transceivers are off—may also be an indication that multipath exists.

Solutions for Multipath

There are really two main solutions to multipath. The first is to reposition objects, such as the receiving or transmitting antenna—or both—in order to remove the multipath. The second is to use diversity antennas. APs and WLAN routers that have two antennas but are only ERP or OFDM PHYs (not HT PHYs) are usually diversity configured. This simply means that the radio will listen to one antenna and then the other at the beginning of a frame transmission and will then receive the frame using the antenna with the best signal. Since multiple clients are being served, the AP may switch from one antenna to the other for nearly every frame, or it may use one antenna most of the time. There is usually no way to tell which antenna receives the most traffic.

Hidden Nodes

Hidden nodes are STAs that can be seen by the AP and can see the AP but cannot see one or more other STAs, and one or more other STAs cannot see the hidden nodes. Because of this scenario, the hidden nodes cannot hear the other clients or at least one of the other clients communicating and may attempt to communicate while the other nodes or nodes are active. Hidden nodes usually occur because of some large obstacle like a solid wall between the STAs or because of insufficient transmit power. For example, the AP may be placed on top of a thick block or brick wall, and clients that are lower and on either side of the wall can see the AP, but they cannot see each other.

The result will be collisions that cannot be avoided without the implementation of some function to clear the channel. This might include RTS/CTS.

A signature of the hidden node problem is increased corruption near the AP and increased retransmissions from the clients even though there is no increased corruption near the client. Using a protocol analyzer near the AP, you will notice frame corruptions. Using a protocol analyzer near the client STA, you will notice retransmissions approximately equal in percentage to the frame corruptions near the AP. The frames are being corrupted near the AP because that is where the signals from the one hidden node and the other hidden node "run into" each other. (Notice that both STAs are hidden nodes because they cannot see each other.)

It is important that you realize that there will almost always be hidden nodes in a WLAN (assuming it uses an omnidirectional antenna and has client STAs on all sides) and that the existence of hidden nodes is not a problem in and of itself. When the hidden nodes begin to cause too many retransmissions, it may become a performance issue on your WLAN. Use a protocol analyzer as mentioned in the preceding paragraphs to determine if 10–20 percent of the frames (from a particular client STA) are being retransmitted. If they are, you will likely need to perform one of the following steps to solve the problem:

- Use RTS/CTS.
- Increase power output at the client STAs.
- Remove obstacles.
- Move the client STAs.
- Ensure the APs and STAs transmit at the same power using IEEE 802.11h and Transmit Power Control (TPC).

Using RTS/CTS can help alleviate the overhead incurred from a bad hidden node scenario, but it should not be used as the automatic solution to a hidden node problem. Consider trying the other options first to see if they resolve your problem. If they do, they will not likely impact the WLAN's throughput as much as RTS/CTS would and they may actually improve the throughput instead.

Increasing the output power at the nodes increases the likelihood that all or most nodes will be able to hear all or most other nodes. There are client adapters now that use power output levels as high as 300 mW, and this is higher than most indoor APs. Theoretically, if the AP is transmitting at 100 mW with a 7 dBi antenna and your clients are transmitting at 300 mW with a similar or higher-gain antenna, there should never be a situation where a client can hear the AP but not other clients. In the real world, it is not practical to think that you will use 300 mW of output power on every client or that you will be able to use external antennas on every client. Additionally, due to absorption, reflection, refraction, diffraction, and scattering that occurs in WLANs, even with high output power, the scenario can certainly exist where two nodes cannot hear each other.

In these latter scenarios, you may be able to move the nodes just a few feet or remove obstacles to resolve the hidden node problem. However, the reality is that regardless of what you do, in a WLAN with many nodes, there will most likely be hidden nodes. Your goal is to reduce the negative impact these hidden nodes have on the overall throughput of your WLAN.

Near-Far Problem

The *near-far problem* is a result of a high-powered STA closer to the AP drowning out a similarly powered or low-powered STA farther from the AP. The farther station simply cannot get enough "talk time" over the activity created by the closer STA. Near-far problem can appear as if a card has failed in the client computer. You can configure the card and be certain that the software is configured correctly and still not be able to authenticate and associate with the AP. Sometimes looking at the WLAN implementation plans can help, but due to the nature of WLANs (users are mobile and that means STAs are also), the plan may not reflect the actual location of devices.

The way to identify near-far problem is usually to evaluate whether the inability to connect with and communicate with the AP is an intermittent problem or a consistent problem. If it is intermittent, it may be a near-far problem. To determine this, monitor the clients closer to the AP when the distant client cannot connect. Are there more clients closer to the AP each time the distant client cannot connect? If there are, near-far problem is the likely culprit. You can also look for retransmissions from the client and corruption of frames coming from the client close to the AP in a way similar to the hidden node problem.

In most cases, the CSMA/CA coordination functions take care of near-far problem with no administrative intervention. In situations where it does not, the following possible solutions should be attempted:

- Increase the output power at the distant node.
- Decrease the output power of the closer nodes.
- Move the remote node closer to the AP.
- Move the AP closer to the distant node.
- Install another AP closer to the distant node or a wireless between the AP and the distant node repeater.

The easiest of these would be increasing the power at the distant node or moving the distant node. The next best option is to decrease the power at the closer nodes, and installing a new AP or repeater would be next. Moving the existing AP may cause more problems than you are currently experiencing. You should always evaluate the original site survey to determine why the AP was placed in its current location before moving it to another.

Transmit Power Control (TPC), first introduced in the IEEE 802.11h amendment, also helps diminish the occurrence of near-far scenarios. TPC was introduced in order to comply with regulatory requirements in some domains, but it provides benefits in the areas of interference and range control for WLANs.

Weather

Many of the situations I've covered so far in this chapter are related to indoor WLANs, with little impact on outdoor bridge links or outdoor WLANs. Multipath is the biggest exception to this statement. Weather is probably the biggest consideration that adds great variability to outdoor links and WLANs. Severe weather, such as major thunderstorms and ice storms with very heavy wind and hail, can diminish the quality of your outdoor WLAN links and even reduce the coverage area of an outdoor hotspot or standard WLAN (although I don't think I'll be outside browsing the Internet during a thunderstorm or ice storm). The two biggest factors are likely to be snow buildup on trees and wind.

When snow accumulates on trees or hilltops, it can encroach on the first Fresnel zone. This may cause reduced quality in your links or make the links impossible to maintain. Additionally, in outdoor hotspot-type WLANs that are in wooded areas such as parks, the extra snow (frozen water) can cause increased attenuation of the RF signals. Additionally, snow and ice buildup on outdoor antennas can push them out of alignment.

While wind does not impact RF waves, it can certainly misalign antennas that are not well mounted. This is why grid antennas are often better than dish antennas, as they can handle more wind loading. The simple explanation is that the wind can pass through the grid instead of having to move the antenna.

Troubleshooting VoWLAN Issues

In VoWLAN, system capacity, throughput, and latency become a really big issue. If your VoWLAN calls are continually or even frequently dropped, users will eventually stop using them, even though you may spend thousands of dollars to provide them with the capabilities. Because of the overhead introduced by WLANs and the handoff times involved in roaming, VoWLAN implementations must be considered very carefully. When selecting equipment, it is usually best to select equipment from the same vendor for the APs and the wireless IP phones and the infrastructure so that you can be sure that they will all work together to support the same roaming capabilities, QoS features, and IEEE standard.

Common problems in VoWLAN implementations include

- Dropped calls during roaming
- Dropped calls when staying within a BSS
- Calls not going through to the target

Dropped calls during roaming is usually a problem with the roaming procedure and not really a general problem with WLAN capacity. For an effective VoWLAN implementation, you will practically be required to use a WLAN implementation that uses APs controlled by a centralized switch or WLAN controller that can maintain the connection as the wireless IP phone roams from one BSS to another or from one ESS to another. In the future, the IEEE standard will ratify fast-roaming procedures that can be implemented in various vendors' equipment, and this may provide for the ability to implement a mixture of APs, controllers, call managers, and wireless IP phones from different vendors, but we are not likely to see this for a few years, since it makes more sense for the vendors to ensure their equipment works with only their equipment at this time.

Dropped calls when staying in a BSS are usually a problem with WLAN capacity or RF interference and jamming. You may have to install APs for VoWLAN and other APs for data use or at least install APs that are QoS aware and can give priority to VoWLAN packets.

Calls not going through to the target is usually the result of the target phone being out of the coverage area. The call will most likely fall back to voice mail in such scenarios. However, the problem is that the intended target may have been in the facility, but he or she was in an area that simply lacked coverage. The solution, in this scenario, is to reevaluate your site survey and repair it so that the WLAN provides adequate coverage where it is needed.

VoWLAN and Roaming

The basic roaming procedures accorded by the IEEE 802.11 standard, at this time, are based on authentication and reassociation. When an STA determines that it should roam—usually based on RSSI values—it will authenticate with the new AP and reassociate with it. It will disassociate with the previous AP, if it is playing nice. This roaming can take a little time, and if the APs are set up in virtual LANs so that they use the same DHCP servers and/or IP subnets, the STA may even be able to keep its IP address. Since most laptop applications use TCP for data transport, there is retransmission and fault tolerance built in to keep a connection and/or transfer going. VoWLAN, on the other hand, uses UDP for data transfer, and this is connectionless and without delivery confirmation. This means that data sent (or that would have been sent) during roaming is simply lost.

The standard roaming time of the IEEE 802.11 authenticate, reassociate, and deassociate process has been tested and estimated to be between 200 and 500 ms. VoWLAN needs an end-to-end delay of no more than 150 ms. This means the WLAN delay component needs to be far less than it normally is. In fact, many implementers aim for a delay of less than 50 ms. By designing wireless IP phones to scan for APs "in the background" and preauthenticate to likely roaming targets, VoWLAN vendors have been able to accomplish this reduction. This, in addition to proprietary management of sessions using call managers and WLAN controllers, has allowed many organizations to implement effective VoWLAN systems.

Summary

You may have noticed that much of the focus of this chapter was on ensuring your users have the throughput they need to use the WLAN effectively. It's about reducing retransmissions, keeping the data rate as high as possible, and eradicating as much interference as you can. If you keep this focus in mind, you'll generally have a well-performing WLAN that meets your users' needs.

Key Terms

- ☐ **hidden node**
- ☐ **interference**
- ☐ **multipath**
- ☐ **near-far problem**
- ☐ **noise floor**
- ☐ **RF noise**
- ☐ **system throughput**

Review Questions

1. You are using a WLAN protocol analyzer and notice that a large number of frames are being corrupted near the AP. You move away from the AP and notice fewer corrupted frames but an approximately equally percentage of retransmissions. You have client STAs located at equal distances all around the AP and the STA that is retransmitting the frames is approximately 100 feet from the AP. Which of the following problems is most likely occurring?

   A. Hidden node

   B. Multipath

   C. DoS attack

   D. Rogue AP

2. You've installed a VoWLAN system that includes 35 wireless IP phones and 10 APs spread throughout your factory. Users have been complaining about dropped calls, but they say the dropped calls only seem to occur when they walk from one end of the factory to the other. What is the likely problem?

   A. Roaming is taking too long.

   B. There is not enough capacity in the BSS.

   C. The call manager is too slow.

   D. You are using proprietary technology.

3. The WLAN in the engineering department is not performing as you expected. You have two APs. One is on channel 1, and the other is on channel 6. In order to make sure you got your money's worth, you set the output power of both APs as high as they could go. There are only 15 computers that use the 2 APs, but the performance seems to be less than a 1 or 2 Mbps DSL connection at times. Which of the following may be valid solutions? (Choose all that apply.)

A. Turn down the output power of the APs.

B. Move the AP on channel 6 to channel 11.

C. Ensure that the 15 computers are spread fairly evenly across the APs.

D. Use a protocol analyzer to see if there is co-channel interference.

4. Which of the following are valid potential solutions to the near-far problem? (Choose all that apply.)

A. Increase the output power of the AP.

B. Increase the output power of the "far" STA.

C. Reduce the output power of the AP.

D. Move the thick wall.

5. Twelve months ago, you implemented a WLAN and you purchased all equipment that is marketed as IEEE 802.11g compliant. Generally your WLAN performs very well, but occasionally the performance is degraded during meetings. During these meetings, employees from another location bring their laptops and connect to the WLAN, but there are always fewer than three additional nodes. However, the throughput of the WLAN seems to drop in half. What is the most likely source of this problem?

A. Hidden node

B. Near-far

C. Multipath

D. Normal ERP behavior

6. Which of the following are real-world results of multipath? (Choose all that apply.)

   A. Upfade

   B. Downfade

   C. Nulling

   D. Hijacking

7. How can co-channel or adjacent-channel interference be identified in a protocol analyzer?

   A. By looking at the network utilization

   B. By capturing frames on one channel and seeing frames from another channel

   C. By turning on "co-channel analysis"

   D. By enabling interference analysis

Review Answers

1. **A.** Since the corruption is occurring near the AP and retransmissions occurring near the node, it is most likely hidden node.

2. **A.** Most likely the problem is that roaming (or more specifically the reassociation that takes place during roaming) is taking too long. When the roaming takes too long, the VoWLAN call will be dropped. It is most likely roaming and not a capacity issue because it only occurs when the users walk from one end of the factory to the other and not when they stay in a general area.

3. **A, B, C, D.** By reducing the output power of the APs so that they only provide the coverage needed, you reduce the likelihood of co-channel interference. By moving the AP on channel 6 to channel 11, you all, but, remove the possibility of co-channel interference. By spreading the client STAs as evenly as possible among the APs, you ensure that one

AP is not overloaded. You could indeed use a protocol analyzer to see if there is bleeding from one channel into another.

4. **B.** By increasing the output power at the far node, you help that node overcome the powerful signals of the near node(s). Increasing the output power of the AP will not help in this scenario. Moving the thick wall may help in a specific hidden node problem, but it is not usually the issue in a near-far situation. Reducing the output power of the AP is no more beneficial to increasing the output power of the AP. The output power of the far node is the issue, not the power of the AP.

5. **D.** Normal ERP PHY behavior is to implement protection procedures anytime an HR/DSSS machine connects to the BSS. The employees from the other location are most likely introducing HR/DSSS devices to your ERP BSS. When the protection mechanism is in place, throughput is more than halved. Hidden node, near-far, and multipath problems are not likely to suddenly cause this kind of problem and do so only when these other employees attend meetings.

6. **A, B, C.** Upfade, downfade, and nulling are all possible results of multipath. Hijacking is a WLAN attack method and is not the result of multipath. Upfade occurs when two copies of the same original signal arrive at the receiver at the same time such that they increase the received amplitude of the signal. Downfade occurs when two copies of the same signal arrive at the receiver out of phase, and the result is a decrease in amplitude. Nulling occurs when two copies of the same signal arrive at the receiver out of phase and cancel each other so that the signal is nullified.

7. **B.** You can discover co-channel and adjacent-channel interference by configuring the protocol analyzer to capture frames on one channel (for example, channel 6) and then seeing that it captures frames transmitted from another channel (for example, channel 9).

APPENDIX

The CWNP Rosetta Stone

The IEEE standards have evolved over time, and this has resulted in many amendments and new terms and technologies being introduced to the standard. At first, these new capabilities were referenced by their amendment document name. For example, the ERP PHY was referenced as 802.11g, and the HR/DSSS PHY was referenced as 802.11b. The problem with this method has now surfaced. Since the IEEE eventually rolls amendments into the standard, the amendment documents go away and the standard becomes larger. For this reason, the CWNP program has moved away from referencing the various PHYs supported by IEEE 802.11 based on their amendment document and has decided to reference them by their given name in the standards.

This issue, and others, has motivated the CWNP program to release a document they call the Rosetta Stone. This document maps the names used on the CWNP examinations to their intended meanings. For example, the Rosetta Stone document explains what *IEEE 802.11 standard (as amended)* means and it explains that *Dynamic Rate Switching (DRS)* is the standards-based way to reference what some vendors call Automatic Rate Switching or Dynamic Rate Selection. These are just two examples of the valuable information in the Rosetta Stone document.

With the permission of the CWNP program, the Rosetta Stone document is reprinted here as version 1.08. This was the most recent version as of June 2007. You will want to check the www.CWNP.com web site for periodic updates that may occur. The following information is ©Copyright 2007, CWNP Program and is reprinted here by permission.

CWNP Exam Terms

IEEE 802.11 standard (as amended) This name refers to the most current 802.11 standard (currently 802.11-1999 (R2003)), including all ratified amendments, supplements, and corrigenda. Many definitions in this document refer to clauses of the 802.11 standard. For example, DSSS is specified in IEEE 802.11-1999 (R2003) Clause 15 but is often simplified as "Clause 15." Amendments are updates (changes) to the standard. Standards bodies like the IEEE often create several amendments to a standard before "rolling up" the ratified amendments (finalized or approved versions) into a new standard. All ratified amendments to the 802.11-1999 (R2003) standard (e.g. 802.11a, 802.11b, 802.11g, etc.) have been rolled into the new IEEE 802.11-2007 standard.

IEEE 802.3-2005, Clause 33 PoE This name refers to the Power-over-Ethernet (PoE) standard formerly known as IEEE 802.3af. The IEEE 802.3af is an amendment to the IEEE 802.3-2002 standard. Occasionally, this may be referred to in a shortened form as "Clause 33 PoE", or just "PoE". Clause 33 of the IEEE 802.3-2005 standard refers to the ability to deliver DC power over Category 5 (or greater) data cable for the purpose of powering network infrastructure (or other) devices. For example, access points are typically powered via PoE.

Dynamic Rate Switching (DRS) This name is used in 802.11g, Clause 9.6 referring to multirate support whereby stations may change their data rate (and hence coding and modulation types in use) as they move toward or away from an access point in order to maintain a high quality connection. This was previously referred to as either "Automatic Rate Switching (ARS)" or "Dynamic Rate Selection (DRS)," both of which were vendor-specific names for this functionality.

Power Save (PS) mode Power management of a non-AP station (STA) operates in either active mode or power save mode. An STA in power save mode is either in an awake or doze state. Power-save mode conserves battery life while the STA dozes, but complicates frame delivery with additional queuing, frame types, and frame exchange sequences. Vendors have called this "Power Save Poll (PSP)" mode or sleep mode. Wireless STAs that are always powered by an AC outlet should never be configured for power save mode.

Active Mode Power management of a non-AP station (STA) operates in either active mode or power save mode. An STA in active mode is always in an awake state. Vendors have called this "Continually Aware mode (CAM)" and other similar variations. Wireless STAs that are always powered by an AC outlet should always be configured for active mode to realize better performance.

Wi-Fi Multimedia (WMM) A certification created by the Wi-Fi Alliance for support of multimedia applications with Quality of Service (QoS) in Wi-Fi networks. The Wi-Fi Alliance started interoperability certification for WMM (Wi-Fi Multimedia) as a profile of the IEEE 802.11e QoS extensions for 802.11 networks. WMM prioritizes traffic demands from different applications and extends Wi-Fi's high quality end-user experience from data connectivity to voice, music, and video applications under a wide variety of environment and traffic conditions. WMM defines four access categories (voice, video, best effort, and background) that are used to prioritize traffic so that these applications have access to the necessary network resources. Additionally, WMM-enabled Wi-Fi networks concurrently support legacy devices that lack WMM functionality. The WMM best effort access category and legacy devices transmit with the same priority.

WMM-PS or U-APSD The IEEE 802.11e amendment introduced Automatic Power Save Delivery (APSD) functionality in two flavors: Scheduled and Unscheduled. The acronyms used by the standard for these are S-APSD and U-APSD. The Wi-Fi Alliance adopted U-APSD in their Wi-Fi Multimedia Power Save (WMM-PS) certification. Both U-APSD and WMM-PS refer to the same power saving functionality introduced by the IEEE 802.11e amendment.

Wi-Fi Alliance Formerly known as the Wireless Ethernet Compatibility Alliance (WECA), the Wi-Fi Alliance is a nonprofit international association formed in 1999 to certify interoperability of Wireless Local Area Network products based on the IEEE 802.11 standard and amendments. Wi-Fi Alliance certification programs address Wi-Fi products based on IEEE radio standards (e.g. 802.11a, 802.11b, 802.11g), wireless network security (WPA, WPA2, and WPS for personal and enterprise deployments), authentication mechanisms used to validate the identity of network devices (EAP), and support for multimedia content over Wi-Fi networks (WMM and WMM-PS).

DSSS Direct-sequence spread spectrum (Clause 15). This transmission technology is specified in the 802.11-1999 standard and uses 1 and 2 Mbps data rates. 802.11b and 802.11g amendments specify support for DSSS for backwards compatibility with 802.11 networks. The 802.11a amendment does not offer support for DSSS.

HR/DSSS High-rate direct sequence spread spectrum (Clause 18). New modulation types were introduced to enhance data rates to 5.5 and 11 Mbps. HR/DSSS is backward compatible with DSSS, meaning an HR/DSSS station can also understand DSSS transmissions at 1 and 2 Mbps. 802.11b was the first 802.11 amendment to support HR/DSSS. The 802.11g amendment specifies support for HR/DSSS for backward compatibility with the 802.11b amendment. The 802.11a amendment does not offer support for HR/DSSS.

OFDM Orthogonal Frequency Division Multiplexing (Clause 17). This transmission technology was introduced in the IEEE 802.11a amendment and is used in the 5 GHz UNII bands. It allows data rates of 6, 9, 12, 18, 24, 36, 48, and 54 Mbps, with mandatory support of 6, 12, and 24 Mbps. OFDM is not backward compatible with HR/DSSS or DSSS because it is used in a different frequency band and it uses a different modulation technique. The acronym OFDM is also used to describe the modulation technique it pioneered, which was then used as one of the several modulations supported by the ERP. The IEEE 802.11a amendment introduced use of OFDM, which was then also used in the 802.11g amendment at a later time.

ERP Extended Rate Physical (Clause 19). This clause specifies further rate extension of the PHY (physical layer specification) for the direct-sequence spread spectrum (DSSS) system of Clause 15 and the extensions of Clause 18 (HR/DSSS). This PHY operates in the 2.4 GHz ISM band and builds on the payload data rates of 1 and 2 Mbps, as described in Clause 15, that use DSSS modulation and builds on the payload data rates of 1, 2, 5.5, and 11 Mbps, as described in Clause 18, that use DSSS, CCK, and optional PBCC modulations. ERP-OFDM draws from Clause 17 (OFDM) to provide additional payload data rates of 6, 9, 12, 18, 24, 36, 48, and 54 Mbps. Of these rates, transmission and reception capability for 1, 2, 5.5, 11, 6, 12, and 24 Mbps data rates is mandatory.

Non-ERP Non-Extended Rate Physical (Clauses 15 and 18). This term describes STAs that are not ERP STAs but that can interoperate with ERP STAs, specifically DSSS and HR/DSSS.

ERP-OFDM A required ERP modulation specified by the 802.11g amendment that uses the capabilities of Clause 17 (OFDM) with the following exceptions:

1. The frequency plan is in accordance with 18.4.6.1 and 18.4.6.2 instead of 17.3.8.3.
2. CCA has a mechanism that will detect all mandatory Clause 19 sync symbols.
3. The frequency accuracy (see 17.3.9.4 and 17.3.9.5) is ±25 PPM.
4. The maximum input signal level (see 17.3.10.4) is –20 dBm.

5. The slot time is 20 μs in accordance with 18.3.3, except that an optional 9 μs slot time may be used when the BSS consists of only ERP STAs.
6. SIFS time is 10 μs in accordance with 18.3.3. See 19.3.2.3 for more detail.

ERP-PBCC An optional ERP modulation specified by the 802.11g amendment. This is a single-carrier modulation scheme that encodes the payload using a 256-state packet binary convolutional code. These are extensions to the PBCC modulation in Clause 18. ERP-PBCC modes with payload data rates of 22 and 33 Mbps are defined in 19.6.

DSSS-OFDM An optional ERP modulation specified by the 802.11g amendment. This is a hybrid modulation combining a DSSS preamble and header with an OFDM payload transmission. DSSS-OFDM implements payload data rates of 6, 9, 12, 18, 24, 36, 48, and 54 Mbps that are defined in 19.7. The supported rates are the same as the ERP-OFDM supported rates.

ERP-DSSS A required ERP modulation specified by the 802.11g amendment that uses the capabilities of Clause 18 (HR/DSSS) with the following exceptions:

1. Support of the short PLCP PPDU header format capability of 18.2.2.2 is mandatory.
2. CCA (see 18.4.8.4) has a mechanism that will detect all mandatory Clause 19 sync symbols.
3. The maximum input signal level (see 18.4.8.2) is –20 dBm.
4. Locking the transmit center frequency and the symbol clock frequency to the same reference oscillator is mandatory.

ERP/OFDM This is our way of saying 802.11a/g. This name represents two PHYs; ERP (Clause 19) and OFDM (Clause 17). Since the 802.11a and 802.11g amendments have been made obsolete with the release of the 802.11-2007 standard, using the term "802.11a/g" is now meaningless in keeping with the 802.11 standard terminology.

WPA-Personal and WPA2-Personal Wi-Fi Protected Access Personal Mode (versions 1 and 2) are designed for home and small office/ home office (SOHO) users who do not have authentication servers available.

It operates in an unmanaged mode that uses a preshared key (PSK) for authentication instead of IEEE 802.1X/EAP. This mode uses applied authentication in which a passphrase is manually entered on the access point to generate an encryption key (called the PSK). Consequently, it does not scale well in the enterprise. The PSK is typically shared among users. A PSK of sufficient strength—one that uses a mix of letters, numbers, and non-alphanumeric characters—is recommended. Personal Mode uses the same encryption methods as Enterprise Mode. It supports per-user, per-session, per-packet encryption via TKIP/RC4 with WPA or CCMP/AES with WPA2. Home and SOHO users should consult a vendor to learn more about deploying WPA-Personal or WPA2-Personal and PSK for their environments. WPA2 also supports TKIP v2, which is not compatible with the TKIP v1 used by WPA. WPA and WPA2 were developed by the Wi-Fi Alliance based upon the IEEE 802.11i amendment.

WPA-Enterprise and WPA2-Enterprise Enterprise Mode operates in a managed mode to meet the rigorous requirements of enterprise security. It leverages the IEEE 802.1X authentication framework that uses an Extensible Authentication Protocol (EAP) method with an authentication server to provide strong mutual authentication between the client and authentication server via the access point or WLAN controller. In this mode, each user is assigned a unique key mechanism for access to the WLAN. This affords a high level of individual privacy. For WPA, TKIP/RC4 encryption is used. TKIP employs an encryption cipher that issues encryption keys for each data packet communicated in each session of each user, making the encryption code extremely difficult to break. For WPA2, CCMP/AES encryption is used. CCMP/AES is stronger than TKIP/RC4, thus providing additional network protection; however, CCMP/AES requires more processing power than many legacy WLAN devices provide. A hardware upgrade to more modern equipment is usually required for CCMP/AES support. TKIP uses the RC4 encryption cipher originally used in WEP, typically requiring only a firmware upgrade to most legacy equipment. WPA2 also supports TKIP v2, which is not compatible with the TKIP v1 used by WPA. WPA and WPA2 were developed by the Wi-Fi Alliance based upon the IEEE 802.11i amendment.

MSDU Medium Access Control (MAC) Service Data Unit. This is the data presented at the MAC service access point (the entry point into the MAC sublayer) by upper layer protocols. An MSDU can be comprised of data from the LLC sublayer and/or any number of layers above the Data Link layer.

MPDU Medium Access Control (MAC) Protocol Data Unit. The unit of data exchanged between two peer MAC entities using the services of the physical layer (PHY). It is comprised of an MSDU (data payload), an MAC header, and a trailer.

MMPDU Medium Access Control (MAC) Management Protocol Data Unit. The unit of data exchanged between two peer MAC entities to implement the MAC management protocol. MMPDUs are sourced and sunk at layer 2 of the OSI model (between immediate transmitters and receivers). They are never forwarded across an access point like an MSDU.

Enterprise Encryption Gateway (EEG) An EEG is an L2 encryption device (similar to VPN) that allows for strong authentication and encryption of data across a wireless medium. The client devices have client-side authentication/encryption software, and the EEGs are the encryption termination point in the network. Autonomous access points are placed downstream from the EEGs and may act as an 802.1X authenticator.

WLAN Controller Also known as a "WLAN switch." WLAN controllers communicate with lightweight (also called "thin") access points (APs). The architecture that uses WLAN controllers and lightweight APs is often called a "Split MAC" architecture. Lightweight APs typically have less intelligence or processing capabilities than autonomous (also called "thick" or "fat") APs. A WLAN controller houses most of the intelligence in this architecture and is used to centrally control (thus the name) and manage the access points. The predominant reason for the industry migration to this architecture is the simplified, centralized management and control of large groups of access points from a single controller.

Robust Security Network (RSN) A security network that allows only the creation of robust security network associations (RSNAs). An RSN can be identified by the indication in the RSN Information Element (IE) of Beacon frames that the group cipher suite specified is not Wired Equivalent Privacy (WEP). This means that the group cipher suite will be either CCMP or TKIP.

wVoIP/VoWLAN/VoWiFi/VoFi These terms refer to the transmitting of Voice over Internet Protocol (VoIP) over an 802.11 data link. These terms are considered interchangeable, though the CWNP Program has standardized on wVoIP.

Fast/Secure Roaming (FSR) This is a generic term for describing fast, secure handoffs between access points within an ESS. Using Robust Security Network (RSN) features such as CCMP with fast authentication methods such as preauthentication (with autonomous APs) and opportunistic PMK caching (with WLAN controllers with lightweight APs), client stations can roam from BSS to BSS performing only a 4-Way Handshake instead of a full 802.1X/EAP authentication. FSR is necessary for high-quality VoIP over 802.11 WLANs (wVoIP).

Information Element Information Elements are flexible data structures within 802.11 management frames defined to have a common general format consisting of a 1 octet Element ID field, a 1 octet length field, and a variable-length element-specific information field. Each element is assigned a unique Element ID as defined in the 802.11 standard. The Length field specifies the number of octets in the Information field. Information elements occur in the frame body in order of increasing IDs. This arrangement allows for the flexible extension of the management frames to include new functionality without affecting older implementations.

Information Field A fixed-length, mandatory component within 802.11 management frames. These are sometimes called "fixed fields" due to the terminology used by the 802.11-1999 (R2003) standard. In the 802.11-2007 standard, these fields have been renamed to "Information Field."

Octet A term used to describe 8 bits of data. Interchangeable with the term "byte." The term "octet" is used more often in standards such as IEEE 802.11 because it is considered more accurate than "byte."

Adjacent Channel/Nonadjacent Channel/Overlapping Channel The CWNP Program complies with the IEEE 802.11 standard's definitions of these terms.

	DSSS	HR/DSSS	ERP	OFDM
Adjacent	≥ 30 MHz	≥ 25 MHz	= 25 MHz	= 20 MHz
Nonadjacent	N/A	N/A	> 25 MHz	> 20 MHz
Overlapping	< 30 MHz	< 25 MHz	< 25 MHz	N/A

The 802.11 standard loosely defines adjacent channels as any channel with nonoverlapping frequencies for the DSSS and HR/DSSS PHYs.

With ERP and OFDM PHYs, the standard loosely defines an adjacent channel as the first channel with a nonoverlapping frequency space.

This contradicts how the term "adjacent channel interference" is typically used in the marketplace. Most Wi-Fi vendors use this term to loosely mean both (1) interference resulting from overlapping cells, and (2) interference resulting from the use of overlapping frequency space. For example, vendors typically use this terminology in a case where AP-1 (channel 1) is located near AP-2 (channel 2).

WLAN Profile A group of settings within an 802.11 WLAN controller that characterizes the parameters needed for a client station to connect to the network infrastructure wirelessly. For example, authentication type, cipher suite, QoS, VLAN, RADIUS parameters, ESSID, and protocol filters can be configured as a group of WLAN Profile parameters, and a WLAN controller may have many such profiles configured simultaneously. The purpose of WLAN Profiles is to simulate many independent wireless LANs within a single WLAN infrastructure.

Wireless Network Management System (WNMS) A network device management system that is used for monitoring, configuring, and updating autonomous access points or WLAN controllers with lightweight access points. Some vendors make only WNMS systems to manage other vendors' equipment and some vendors make WNMS to manage only their own WLAN controllers and access points. Sample features include device configuration and management, user monitoring, government and industry compliance reporting, and automating of routine tasks.

Unlicensed National Information Infrastructure (UNII) bands These bands are located between 5 GHz and 6 GHz and are defined by the FCC for use by unlicensed RF transmitters. They consist of the following frequency bands.

Band	CWNP name:	Often called:
5.15–5.25 GHz	UNII-1	Lower UNII
5.25–5.35 GHz	UNII-2	Middle UNII
5.470–5.725 GHz	UNII-2E	UNII-2 Extended
5.725–5.825 GHz	UNII-3	Upper UNII

Glossary

absorption The process that occurs when an RF signal is lost into an object. This means that the object has converted the RF signal into heat.

access control The prevention of access to unauthorized resources by users and systems.

access device A common term for a networking device through which client devices connect to a network, for example a typical access point device.

access point A wireless local area network (WLAN) device through which an associated WLAN device uses the WLAN. Specifically, an entity with station functionality that provides access to the distribution services over the wireless medium.

access port A term some vendors use for an access point that depends on a central controller for some of its functions. See lightweight access point.

active mode The mode a station is in when it is not using power management.

active scanning The process used by a station (STA) to find an access point where the STA sends out probe requests and listens for probe responses instead of just listening for beacon frames.

ad hoc network An alternate term often used to reference an independent basic service set (IBSS).

adjacent channel A channel that meets the IEEE specifications for adjacency. ERP channels are adjacent if there is 25 MHz of separation between the center channels of the two channels' frequencies. OFDM channels are adjacent if there is 20 MHz of separation between the center channels of the two channels' frequencies. DSSS and HR/DSSS channels are adjacent if there is at least 30 MHz (DSSS) and 25 MHz (HR/DSSS) of separation between the center channels of the two channels' frequencies. Note that DSSS and HR/DSSS require the specified amount of separation or more and ERP and OFDM require exactly the specified amount of separation.

Advanced Encryption Standard (AES) The encryption standard that replaced the Digital Encryption Standard (DES) in order to improve encryption strength. It is based on the Rijndael algorithm.

amplification The process of creating gain in an RF signal. It is the opposite of attenuation.

amplifiers Devices that can amplify or create gain in an RF signal.

amplitude The strength of an RF signal.

antenna The element used in a wireless device or system to transmit and receive radio signals. Antennas come in many forms and sizes and can be omnidirectional, semidirectional, or highly directional.

association The service that maps a station to its access point.

ATIM An ad hoc traffic indication message is the frame used by an IBSS station to convey its transmit buffer status when the receiving IBSS station is in power management mode.

attenuation The weakening of an RF signal. It is the opposite of amplification.

attenuator A device that weakens an RF signal.

authentication A service used to identify a system as authorized to associate, or as authorized for 802.1X port access.

authentication server A device that provides 802.1X authentication service to an authenticator.

authenticator A device at one end of a point-to-point LAN segment that facilitates the 802.1X authentication of the device at the other end.

autonomous access point An access point that operates without a vendor-specific central controller. Also known as a thick access point.

bandwidth Either the difference between the upper and lower frequencies used by a channel, or the sheer number of bits per second that may be communicated through the channel, including all frame protocol overhead, or else sometimes the number of payload bits that can be communicated through the channel in a second. In the latter senses, it is more properly called throughput.

basic service area (BSA) The area that contains members of a basic service set (BSS). This are may also contain members of other BSSs.

basic service set (BSS) A group of STAs that have synchronized using the JOIN primitive and one station that has used the START primitive.

bit An individual information element that can be equal to a 1 or a 0. A single bit can represent any two values to an application.

BSSID The 48-bit globally unique identifier for a BSS.

byte A collection of bits. Usually 8 bits in computer systems.

capacity Simply defined as the amount that can be contained or managed. System capacity is usually a measurement of storage space or data space. In communications systems, capacity is a reference to the amount of data that can be transferred through the system in a given window of time.

captive portal A public hotspot vendor solution that redirects unauthorized web browser requests to an authorization page.

channel An instance of a communications medium (radio frequency bandwidth) used to pass information between two communicating STAs.

channel separation/channel spacing The difference between the center frequencies of two nonoverlapping channels that are adjacent. Adjacent channels are defined differently in the IEEE 802.11 standard (as amended) for the 2.4-GHz PHYs and the 5-GHz PHYs.

colocation A combination of distance, signal strength, and channel that places two stations within radio range of one another and requires them to contend for access to the common RF medium. If the two stations are members of different BSSs, then the BSSs are said to be colocated.

contention window A range of integers from which one is chosen at random to become the backoff timer in a DCF implementation.

coordination function The function that is used within a basic service set (BSS) to determine when an STA may communicate on the wireless medium (WM).

core device A common term for a networking device that neither connects to client devices nor provides services to the network other than packet forwarding.

coverage A term used to refer to the physical space covered by an access point. An administrator might say that she needs to provide coverage in the Accounting department, and she means that she needs to be sure the RF signal from the access point is of acceptable quality in that physical area that contains the Accounting department.

data rate The instantaneous rate at which bits are communicated in a WLAN during a single frame transmission.

dBd Decibels to dipole (dBd) is a measurement of RF signal strength compared to a practical dipole antenna. dBd is 2.14 dB stronger than dBi.

dBi Decibels to isotropic (dBi) is a measurement of RF signal strength compared to an ideal isotropic radiator.

dBm Decibels milliwatts (dBm) is an absolute measurement of power where 0 decibels is equal to 1 milliwatt.

decibel (dB) A numerical unit designed to avoid the direct use of exponential numbers. Zero decibels is ten to the power of zero tenths, or one. Three decibels is ten to the power of three tenths or about two. Ten decibels is ten to the power of ten tenths or ten. Decibel is a convenient unit for expressing exponential power gain and loss of an RF signal.

delay spread The difference in time between the arrival of two copies of the same transmission when multipath occurs.

Denial of Service (DoS) An attack that is used to prevent valid users from accessing a network or system.

diffraction The bending of an RF signal around an obstacle that often results in a redirection of the signal's main path and may result in RF shadow.

distributed coordination function (DCF) A coordination function where the same logic exists on all STAs in a BSS when the network is in operation.

distribution device A common term for a networking device that does not connect to client devices but provides services to the network such as packet filtering and forwarding, sometimes used to describe access point-to-access point bridging.

distribution service The service that delivers MAC service data units (MSDUs) within the distribution system (DS).

distribution system The system used to interconnect a collection of local area networks (LANs) and basic service sets (BSSs) to form an extended service set (ESS).

direct sequence spread spectrum (DSSS) One of the original Physical layer technologies specified in the IEEE 802.11 standard that provides instantaneous data rates of 1 or 2 Mbps and operates in the 2.4-GHz frequency band.

DTIM Delivery traffic indication message is a TIM that announces broadcast or multicast frames in the access point transmit buffer. See TIM.

dynamic rate switching The process used by WLAN clients to change their data rate in order to maintain optimal throughput and communications on the WLAN link for a given signal strength.

encryption The process of obfuscating data so that it cannot be viewed by non-intended systems or individuals.

enterprise encryption gateway (EEG) An industry term for a device that provides encryption services to a wired or wireless network or both.

equivalent isotropically radiated power (EIRP) The hypothetical power that is delivered evenly in all directions by an imaginary isotropic radiator. The product of the transmitter plus any losses incurred by cables and connectors plus any antenna gain. There will always be some antenna gain.

ERP The extended rate PHY added to the IEEE 802.11 standard by the IEEE 802.11g amendment.

extended service set (ESS) A collection of one or more basic service sets that appear as one MAC sublayer to the LLC sublayer.

extensible authentication protocol (EAP) A standards-based model used to implement various authentication types such as certificates and preshared keys or passphrases.

fade margin A fudge factor of the link budget to ensure that the signal will be strong enough come what may.

FCC The Federal Communications Commission (FCC) is responsible for defining limitations and allowances for radio frequency communications—among other things—in the United States and its territories. They define the regulations that are then implemented in IEEE and other standards.

fragmentation The process of converting a single frame into multiple smaller frames in order to reduce retransmission overhead when occasional interference corrupts one part of the overall transmission.

free space path loss The weakening that occurs naturally in an RF signal as it travels and the wave front broadens, plus the effective size of a receiving dipole antenna matched to the frequency of the transmission.

frequency The rate at which an RF wave, or any wave, repeats itself, commonly measured in hertz, MHz, or GHz.

frequency hopping spread spectrum (FHSS) One of the three Physical layer technologies specified in the original IEEE 802.11-1997 standard that allowed for 1 and 2 Mbps data rates in the 2.4-GHz spectrum, now obsolete.

Fresnel zones Ellipsoidal volumes around the line of site that carry the RF energy from transmitter to receiver. The first Fresnel zone must be at least 60 percent clear of major intrusions to maintain a healthy RF link.

gain The increase of a signal's strength.

grounding rods Elements used to provide electric current with a path of least resistance to ground. They cannot protect against direct lightning strikes but can help redirect lower levels of electrical energy that may result from nearby lightning strikes or other electrical surges.

hidden node A problem that occurs in WLANs when two transmitting stations cannot hear each other but can both be heard by one of the intended receivers. This problem was addressed in the original 802.11-1997 standard by RTS/CTS and given the name "hidden node" by the IEEE 802.11 Handbook.

HR/DSSS Originally specified in the IEEE 802.11b amendment, the high-rate/direct-sequence spread spectrum Physical layer specifies data rates up to 11 Mbps.

IEEE The Institute of Electrical and Electronics Engineers specifies standards based on regulations defined by regulatory bodies.

IEEE 802.11 The standard that defines the use of radio frequency signals to implement WLANs.

IEEE 802.11a See OFDM.

IEEE 802.11b See HR/DSSS.

IEEE 802.11e An amendment to the IEEE 802.11-2003 standard that specifies Quality of Service (QoS) features for WLANs. Ratified in 2005, this amendment makes changes to Clauses 5 through 11 of the IEEE 802.11 standard.

IEEE 802.11g See ERP.

IEEE 802.1X A standard, independent of the IEEE 802.11 standard, that defines port-based authentication. This standard is referenced by IEEE 802.11 as being used to implement a robust security network (RSN).

independent basic service set (IBSS) A BSS that does not include an access point. The STAs communicate directly with each other.

infrastructure basic service set (BSS) A BSS that does include an access point. The STAs communicate with each other through the access point.

intentional radiator The point in an RF system where power is delivered to an antenna.

interference That which occurs when RF energy in the same frequency corrupts RF communications.

isotropic radiator A theoretical antenna that can radiate RF energy equally in all directions.

lightweight access point Industry term for an access point that depends on a centralized controller to provide services to WLAN clients and only includes partial distribution service functionality internally.

link budget The signal strength needed to provide stable and consistent wireless communications.

LOS Line of sight can be either visual or radio frequency line of site (LOS). Visual LOS represents the ability for a human to see a remote object, which sometimes involves reflections and/or refractions. RF LOS represents the ability for two RF devices to see or communicate with each other, which sometimes involves reflections and/or refractions.

loss That which occurs when an RF signal's strength is weakened.

milliwatt The measurement most frequently used when referencing output power of WLAN devices.

multipath That which occurs when multiple copies of the original signal arrive at the receiver at the same time after reflection, diffraction, scattering, and other RF behaviors.

nonadjacent channels Channels with a separation between their center frequencies of more than the IEEE standard specifications for adjacent channels. Only ERP and OFDM specify nonadjacent channels as of IEEE 802.11-2007. DSSS and HR/DSSS consider channel separations greater than the IEEE standard-specified minimums for adjacent channels as adjacent channels.

octet A term that describes 8 bits of data. A byte is generally thought to be 8 bits, but a byte can be fewer than 8 bits, and it can be more than 8 bits. An octet is specifically an 8-bit byte.

OFDM Orthogonal Frequency Division Multiplexing (OFDM) is a PHY specified originally in the IEEE 802.11a amendment to the IEEE 802.11 standard. Data rates up to 54 Mbps are provided in the 5-GHz frequency band. OFDM techniques are also used by ERP and HT PHYs.

overlapping channels DSSS, HR/DSSS, or ERP channels with center frequencies separated by less than that which is specified as the minimum separation for adjacent channels in the IEEE 802.11-2007 standard.

passive scanning The process used by a WLAN STA when it listens for Beacon frames in order to find an AP with which to associate.

protocol analyzer A tool used to decode packets on a network.

reflection That which occurs when an RF signal bounces off of an object and travels in a new direction.

refraction That which occurs when an RF signal changes direction as it passes from one medium into another.

scattering That which occurs when an RF signal encounters objects smaller in diameter than its own wavelength. The signal is reflected in many different directions, greatly weakening the signal.

site survey The process of evaluating RF behavior in an environment and determining the best way to implement a WLAN based on this information.

spectrum analyzer A tool used to view the RF energy in a range of frequencies.

throughput The rate at which payload data can be transferred through a system.

TIM The traffic indication message is the information element carried in beacon frames used by an access point station to convey its transmit buffer status when the receiving associated station is in power management mode.

VoWLAN IP telephony over the WLAN is the use of a WLAN to transport IP voice communications.

Wi-Fi Alliance An organization that certifies equipment to be interoperable with other equipment in the WLAN industry based on their certification standards.

wireless medium (WM) The medium—or intervening substance or electromagnetic waves through or on which signals may travel—that is used to transfer data between two Physical layer (PHY) entities in a WLAN.

Index

B

D

E

G

H

I

J

K

L

S

T

U

V

W

Y

Z